second edition

AMERICA'S TROUBLES

a casebook

edited by
HOWARD E. FREEMAN
Brandeis University and Russell Sage Foundation

NORMAN R. KURTZ
Brandeis University

Prentice-Hall, Inc., Englewood Cliffs, New Jersey

Library of Congress Cataloging in Publication Data

FREEMAN, HOWARD E. COMP.
America's troubles.

1. United States—Social conditions—1960–
—Addresses, essays, lectures. I. Kurtz, Norman R.,
joint comp. II. Title.
HN59.F7 1973   309.1'73'092   72-7300
ISBN 0-13-032615-1

HN
59
, F7
1973

© 1973, 1969 by Prentice-Hall, Inc., Englewood Cliffs, New Jersey

10   9   8   7   6   5   4   3   2   1

PRINTED IN THE UNITED STATES OF AMERICA

PRENTICE-HALL INTERNATIONAL, INC., *London*
PRENTICE-HALL OF AUSTRALIA, PTY. LTD., *Sydney*
PRENTICE-HALL OF CANADA, LTD., *Toronto*
PRENTICE-HALL OF INDIA PRIVATE LIMITED, *New Delhi*
PRENTICE-HALL OF JAPAN, INC., *Tokyo*

about the editors

HOWARD E. FREEMAN

Howard E. Freeman is Morse Professor of Urban Studies at the Florence Heller Graduate School for Advanced Studies in Social Welfare of Brandeis University. He also holds an appointment with the Russell Sage Foundation of New York City.

Professor Freeman is editor of the *Journal of Health and Social Behavior* and is an advisory editor of the *Community Mental Health Journal*. In the past he was associate editor of *Social Problems* and of the *American Sociological Review*. He is a past chairman of the Medical Sociology Section of the American Sociological Association. In 1963, Dr. Freeman was co-winner of the Hofheimer Prize of the American Psychiatric Association for his book, *The Mental Patient Comes Home*. He is also co-author of *The Clinic Habit, Social Problems: Causes and Controls,* and *Social Research and Social Policy,* and co-editor of *The Handbook of Medical Sociology,* and *Man and the Social Scene*. His articles on deviant behavior, medical care, and mental health have appeared in a number of sociological, psychological, and health journals and handbooks. During 1972 and 1973 he is The Ford Foundation's Social Science Advisor for Mexico, Central America, and the Caribbean.

NORMAN R. KURTZ

Norman R. Kurtz is Associate Professor of Social Research at the Florence Heller Graduate School for Advanced Studies in Social Welfare, Brandeis University. He received his Ph.D from the University of Colorado in 1966. Professor Kurtz is Associate Editor of the *Journal of Health and Human Behavior*. His publications concern social processes and the problems of urbanization among minority groups and medical care delivery. He is currently doing research in areas of medical care.

CONTENTS

PREFACE

This book was developed originally because we believed that there were insufficient case study materials available for instructors and students to use in undergraduate courses in sociology. Naturally, we are most pleased that the first edition has been used extensively in social problems and deviant behavior courses as well as in introductory sociology and various specialized offerings in social science departments. Perhaps most gratifying is the wide use of the book in courses in such fields as English and Speech, where a consideration of socially relevant material now is the mandate.

This edition follows the same format as the first edition; we have selected case materials that are as dramatic as possible without being distorted and that illustrate the conflicts of individual with institution, interorganizational struggles, and adversary situations that involve individuals and organizations. Cases are selected which portray individuals and organizations both as provocateurs and victims of conflict. Each section provides four cases for analysis.

They are arranged consistently so that for each problem focus material is presented on a social conflict where 1) an individual victimizes another individual; 2) an individual provokes an organization; 3) an organization is the protagonist and an individual the victim; and 4) the conflict is between two organizations.

Only one-half of the forty original cases from the earlier edition have been retained. Some twenty new cases were selected because of their timeliness and their relevance. Students will find that often they are already familiar with events surrounding the cases presented and can bring their knowledge as well as their opinions to bear in analyzing the material. The timeliness also is reflected in the reconceptualization of the sections. One reason to modify the sections structure was to allow for the introduction of two entirely new sections —on the consequences of war and on pollution.

We are extremely grateful to the professors and students who have informed us of deficiencies in the first edition and who have encouraged us to revise the volume. We hope the reader will find this volume academically useful and stimulating.

H. E. F.
N. R. K.

INTRODUCTION

One of the most penetrating critics of community life in the United States, the late C. Wright Mills, characterized the decade of the fifties as an era of indifference and social restraint.[1] In contrast, the sixties were characterized by overt conflict and intense activity. This was a period of protest, of open hostility, and of explicit questioning of our basic social values. The seventies promise to continue the protests, hostile behavior, and cynical questioning of the sixties, albeit in a somewhat more reserved manner. It is unlikely that the pendulum will swing back to indifference and restraint. It is simply impossible for the young, the poor, the blacks, and other minority group members, victims of crime, and others injured by the workings of the social system to sit back and "take it." Moreover, political and social leaders who are intensely dedicated to doing something about America's troubles, despite the risks to themselves, their families, and their personal standing in the community, continue to emerge.

Of course, some community members remain complacent about the current scheme of things. Self-interests cause others to resist any imaginative efforts at social change. Still others are dissatisfied with community conditions but fail to exercise their privilege to advocate modifications in the existing social order. Policy makers, moral leaders, and social commentators quite properly are distressed by the large number of citizens who fail to participate in remedying the social problems confronting us. Nevertheless, the explicit expressions of concern among political leaders, clergymen, business executives, educators, and representatives of other major social institutions, as well as the challenging activities of university students, black Americans, and other minorities, testify to the widespread and intense interest that exists in the social problems of today. Many persons in the community are outspoken and insist that the time has come to correct the injustices and inequities that pervade our society and the social problems that afflict its members.

Whether or not current concern with the problems of the social order is related to a worsening of social conditions is a matter of debate; perhaps the question can be answered only in the future, in historical perspective. But

---

[1] C. Wright Mills, *The Sociological Imagination* (New York: Oxford University Press, 1959), pp. 8–13.

the existence of widespread dissatisfaction is certainly evident in the violence, the riots, and the strikes that have occurred and that apparently will continue to erupt. It is indeed an era of open social conflict and a time testing the values held inviolable by past generations and only openly challenged in the last decade or so.

The stance of sociologists also has changed markedly. Debates about so-called "objectivity" in the work of the social scientist have almost ceased.[2] Most sociologists have concluded that while it is possible to operate as scientists and to present social happenings objectively, what is studied and the actions taken in the face of research findings represent a commitment that cannot be value-free. Today the controversial question is: How far can the social scientist go in his efforts as an advocate of policies and programs and still remain identified with "the scientific community" and "intellectualism"; how much of his time and energy can he devote to his involvement in policy-making and practitioner roles and still continue to produce the theoretical and analytical work of his scientific discipline?

Some social scientists exercise considerable restraint about participating in policy and program development directed at modification of the social order and amelioration of social problems. They do so on the grounds that such activity will minimize their opportunities to make long-range scientific contributions. But it is increasingly difficult for the social scientist to adhere to admonitions that he should not overextend himself by taking on too many immediate-action oriented assignments.[3] Day-to-day engagements with individuals who occupy political and practitioner roles, and the major social conflicts that the social scientist sees everywhere in sharp focus demand his attention. In research and writing he deals increasingly with the immediate social concerns of the community. In these times, programs of restoration and rehabilitation are derived in a number of cases from his theories and from findings of investigations of the determinants of social ills. Increasingly, the orientation of some practitioners and policy-makers today are rooted directly in the conceptual views and empirical research of the discipline of sociology.[4] While the cogency of the conceptual ideas and the craftsmanship of empirical studies in sociology are open to serious criticism and limitations as far as scientific endeavors go, the recent era of open social conflict has markedly influenced and hastened the application and use of whatever sociologists have available. The general acceptance of the sociologist and his tools and theories by persons searching for answers to community problems has further implicated the sociologist in the practical concerns of current social issues.

[2] See, for example, such recent discussions as Alvin W. Gouldner, "The Sociologist as Partisan: Sociology and the Welfare State," *The American Sociologist*, Vol. 3, No. 2 (May 1968), 103–17.
[3] Melvin M. Tumin, "In Dispraise of Loyalty," *Social Problems*, XV (Winter 1968), 267–79.
[4] Howard E. Freeman and Wyatt C. Jones, *Social Problems: Causes and Controls* (Chicago: Rand McNally & Company, 1970), pp. 7–9.

It remains to be seen whether the ideological and operational commitments necessary for such close involvement in the practical aspects of community problems are detrimental or beneficial to the development of a body of scientific knowledge about the community and its activities. Indeed, the moral and ethical concerns of the sociologist about problems of community life are not necessarily relevant to objective scientific inquiry and endeavor. The commitment to one side or another of the issue that often accompanies involvement in problem areas may complicate the process of developing systematic accounts of the social arena. However, many sociologists today feel, and perhaps justly so, that ethical and moral issues are imperative and that cold scientific concerns must take second place. It is felt by numerous sociologists that involvement in social action will not fatally hamper the progress of science.

Regardless of the position taken, it is clear that the function of a sociologist is to look at the social order, describe what is going on, and, if possible, offer some explanation of what is observed. Part of his responsibility as a student of social life is to provide a better understanding and to give a clear meaning to particular events in society. The sociologists' intense concern with contemporary issues has resulted in a wide variety of books, monographs, and journal articles expounding new or increasingly sophisticated explanations, providing more precise or additional empirical information, and offering innovative or new-sounding suggestions for social amelioration. Not only do colleagues direct documents specifying ways to achieve progressive social change to one another and at policy-makers and practitioners, there is also an increased emphasis on communicating the knowledge of sociology to students in universities and to concerned community members.[5] A vast library of scholarly and technical works and a number of textbooks are concerned with current social problems, and there is a growing emphasis on popular reports and sociological explanations in the mass media.

Despite interest in the sociological enterprise among the general public, despite the closer contact of sociologists with the community, and despite an awareness of the need to put forth their knowledge, an examination of the problems of social conflict remains incomplete for most people. There is insufficient descriptive material available in an organized fashion about the social issues that are of major concern. It is simply not possible in the existing sociological literature to easily locate adequate descriptive accounts that permit an appreciation of the social problems confronting us.

The purpose of presenting this collection of cases on contemporary social conflict is modest. It is an attempt to provide a description of what is going on, an effort to provide a feeling for the social conflicts that currently occupy the attention of sociologists and community members alike. The notion that it is important to be in touch with the phenomena that one wishes to study is not a novel one. For instance, survey investigators almost invariably counsel each

---

[5] *Trans-Action*, for example, provides reports of social research in a manner easily digested by a broad audience.

other to engage, at least in passing, in the collection of data themselves, and rarely do community researchers recommend analyzing information about a place they have never been.

Many investigators seek to become a part of the environment in which they are interested. For instance, one sociologist interested in mental illness became a "patient" in order to understand some of the problems of hospitalization.[6] Another sociologist, interested in gambling, felt it important to spend some time as a dealer in a Nevada casino. Of course, one can develop the principle of participation into an absurdity. The researcher cannot, or should not, always engage firsthand in the sociological events he is interested in studying. Students of marital conflict cannot marry every informant, and investigators of organized crime ordinarily do not join the underworld. Participating actively in everything studied is unusual, but many serious students of social phenomena attempt to understand "the action" by taking a semi-participant role and spending considerable time and energy in the hospitals, the slums, and the prisons they are studying, and by affiliating themselves with the delinquents, minority groups, and other "problem persons" that they are concerned about. Others seek to accomplish the same purposes by use of informants or experts who have been close to phenomena in which they are interested. Ideally, perhaps, all students of social conflict and of problems of deviance and disorganization in contemporary American society should be required to have an array of firsthand experience. But this sort of educational program is impractical because of the demands of time on the student, the difficulty of gaining access to many groups and situations, and the problems of supervision during such experiences. An alternative is to provide, via the written word, accounts of various arenas of social conflict in contemporary society with as much as the tone, the emotion, and the feeling of the social events and processes as possible. The cases provided here, although secondhand accounts of what is going on, were selected to do just this, to provide a general background for understanding the nature and content of conflict in our society.

THE SELECTION OF CASES

In seeking to organize a series of cases which might serve as a means for appreciating contemporary social conditions and processes, it soon became clear that such cases were not likely to appear in scholarly sociological literature. Engaging descriptions of social conflicts by sociologists are scarce, suggesting, perhaps, how distant many in the discipline really are from their subject matter. Even more, this scarcity is a commentary on the style of sociologists, who rarely provide the data. Instead, they devote most of the pages they publish to interpretations of data that are stored in their files. It seemed useful, then, to have a set of descriptive reports. In presenting these cases, the

---

[6] William Caudill, *The Mental Hospital as a Small Society* (Cambridge, Mass: Harvard University Press, 1958).

concern is not to interpret the events; this task is the enterprise of the student and the professor.

Popular magazines, much more frequently than the sociological journals, have been the source of cases contained in this volume. Many of the accounts represent the work of newspaper and magazine reporters, some are autobiographical in nature. No pretense is made that the cases contained here represent unbiased and entirely objective reports. Working members of the communication media seek to interpret events according to their particular social and political orientations, and even when they are consciously attempting to provide an objective account, their social blinders remain at least partly intact. Sometimes in reading the various cases, it becomes obvious that the writers have sympathy or contempt for one or more of the parties involved. Moreover, the selection of the particular material included here naturally reflects the social and political concerns of the editors of this volume.

Although the goal of organizing this volume is simply that of providing an appreciation of contemporary social conflicts, an amount of conceptual development was required. Without it, the end result would have been a chaotic hodgepodge of more or less interesting tales. One of the issues confronted was the choice of the areas of social conflict to be represented in the volume.

The sociological literature presents a number of discussions of the characteristics of social problems and areas the student should concern himself with from an educational and research standpoint.[7] In seeking to identify social problems, analysts of social conditions and social relations emphasized different criteria in making their judgments. Some pay more attention than others to the extent to which behavior and conditions contradict traditions of our Judeo-Christian value system; some more than others are concerned with the degree to which behavior or conditions vary from the ways the majority of community members behave or from the conditions under which they live; still others use as criteria the actions and situations which provoke responses from social control agents, police, health and welfare agents, and so on.

In estimating the importance of one area of concern over another, the sociologist almost always, implicitly or explicitly, includes an evaluation of the extent to which the problem either challenges the stability of the social order, or minimizes the realization of the full potential for social development of community members, or results in rigidities in social life which stifle communal and personal opportunities for innovation and orderly social change.[8] A trend in sociology today is the explicit acknowledgment of the legitimacy of such

---

[7] Robert A. Nisbet, "The Study of Social Problems," in Robert K. Merton and Robert Nisbet, eds., *Contemporary Social Problems* (3rd ed.), (New York: Harcourt Brace Jovanovich, Inc., 1971), pp. 1–25. Also, Howard S. Becker, ed., "Introduction," in *Social Problems: A Modern Approach* (New York: John Wiley & Sons, Inc., 1966), pp. 1–35.

[8] Robert K. Merton, "Social Problems and Sociological Theory," in Robert K. Merton and Robert Nisbet, *Contemporary Social Problems*, pp. 793–845; Freeman and Jones, *Social Problems*, pp. 16–20.

value assessments by the sociologist. While there is hardly complete consensus among mature students of social problems on the conditions and behavior that are of most concern and that merit the most intensive scrutiny, there is a remarkable degree of congruence on what areas are included from one orderly analysis to the next.

Naturally, knowledge of the problems of social disorganization and deviance commonly considered in various textbooks has influenced the contents of this volume. But within the confines which come with a commitment to a discipline, the selection of cases in the volume also represents an empirical process. Once aware that it would be necessary to move out from the sociological literature in order to find the needed material, a relatively systematic review of a large body of popular literature was undertaken. It was possible to take into account, in selecting topics, the frequency that various behaviors and social conditions manifest themselves in magazines and other media widely circulated in the community.

Undoubtedly some readers will feel that problems of serious concern to the community and to social scientists have been omitted; we make no claim of comprehensiveness. The selections contained in this volume, however, are on topics that repeatedly occupy current concern, as reflected their appearance in periodicals responsive to the interests of persons in the general community. We do not want to be put in the position of arguing that what appears on the newsstand should be allowed to channel the activities of persons interested in social conflict, or of maintaining that the convergence between popular interests and topics typically covered in systematic reviews of social problems represents a definitive means of identifying the most relevant areas of social conflict. Nevertheless, the repeated discussions of these topics in the popular media and in the social problem texts provide some support for the notion that they are among today's most important issues.

THE CHARACTER OF SOCIAL CONFLICT

Sociologists and other social scientists who devote themselves to studying social processes and interpersonal relationships are constantly frustrated by the complex and often seemingly illusive causes of deviance and disorganization in contemporary America. Moreover, easy solutions to current social troubles in the United States are readily apparent only to those who stand back and avoid serious confrontations with the society's problems. Although efforts to unravel the determinants of conflicts in the social order have resulted in relatively sophisticated statements of possible domains of factors involved, their relative influence as causes of specific problems are not understood very well and can rarely be specified with precision. It is also difficult to identify those determinants of America's problems that are most vulnerable to modifications which might lead to the amelioration of social stresses.

Analysts of social life who undertake detailed empirical investigations and scholars who develop theories of social behavior have presented a large body of writings on the determinants or causes of social troubles. A continuing task of sociologists, and a major one, of course, is the development of theories of causation which take into account the total range of factors impinging upon the behavior of individuals and groups of individuals. Nevertheless, it should be emphasized that only limited inroads have been made in developing explanations for the various social problems in contemporary communities.

It is generally assumed that social conflicts stem from the interaction of what may be referred to as qualities of individuals and qualities of the social structure. The actions of community members, either in the various social roles they occupy or as represented by the collective behavior of organized groups, come into conflict with the behavior of other persons or organizations when there is a lack of congruence in the objectives of the parties or when one individual or organization regards certain acts or potential acts as detrimental to its place in the social order.

Although genetic, biological, and temperamental characteristics of single individuals are important, potential conflict stemming from these individual characteristics are mediated by the ways in which social life is structured. Most areas of social conflict represent interactions in which an individual's social characteristics, such as economic status, ethnic affiliation, or social prestige, are directly involved. Similar characteristics, while usually more ambiguously defined, also are involved in conflicts between organizations or between individual and organization. Interpersonal and interorganizational relationships are guided and sustained by a series of norms and values that reflect the commitments of individuals and groups; in the continuity of social life they become pervasive determinants of the behavior of community members. An individual internalizes them; they determine his actions as a member of the community. Groups in the community and the community in general regard these norms and values as being important to the maintenance of society and often do not question them. Consequently, both individuals in social roles and organized groups in collective behavior are deeply involved in safeguarding the norms and values that have endured and are held critical to the meaning and conducted of social life. Norms and values can be seen as the frameworks within which social realities are defined for individuals and organizations.

Social conflict is rooted in acts which violate norms and values regarded as important, often sacred, by individuals or organizations. Conflict may be provoked by individual or organizational actions which violate the informally expressed norms of aggregates of individuals or the formally stated ones of organization. Violations, whether perceived or real, are usually met with resistance. For example, an individual may risk life and limb to save his home from the threats of an organizational decision to renew the neighborhood in which he lives. An organization may invest great energy in fighting discrimination practiced by a powerful individual, even if that discrimination is only a potential threat. Often organizations devote their time to counteracting the influence of other organizations, such as the effort of dental groups interested in fluoridation and political groups ideologically opposed to such a measure. An individual may perceive that his welfare is threatened by another individual, as in the case of the victim of an aggressively deranged person. Conflict between such parties may arise not only when violations of norms and values actually occur, but also when they appear as a threat or when they occur to others in similar circumstances.

Our interest is not in what might be described as idiosyncratic social events, but in events which occur with some regularity and which are publicly defined as problematic for society. Thus, the focus on individuals in relation to a social problem may be in terms of the qualities they have in common, or the way they perform social roles, or the particular behavior roles they adopt, or the association they engage in which identifies them with the particular problem. Individuals may be a party to a social conflict because of the behavior they display in their day-to-day social roles as workers, students, parents, children, and the like. Others are identified with a problem because of ideas which community members hold about qualities they possess, qualities which may or may not be relevant to their place in the community, as in the case of being black, an adolescent, old, lower class, or physically handicapped. Still other individuals are regarded as parties to conflicts because of particularly unusual or abhorrent behavior they exhibit, such as homosexuality, mental illness, or prostitution.

It is possible, then, to focus on individuals, or more precisely, on individuals with identifiable qualities, behaviors, or roles. But it is also possible to look at organizational structures—the large number of communal groups in the community—and their involvement in social conflicts. All of us are familiar with the vast number of voluntary groups, fraternal societies, and corporate bodies that exist in the United States. Some of these structures represent aggregates of individuals who have organized themselves for a particular task or are interested in a common goal or set of goals. Another type of organizational structure exists at a more abstract level, a structure that sociologists refer to as the major institution or system in the community. The concept of social institutions or social systems represents efforts to delineate the various social aggregates which are generally acknowledged to be engaged in a set of common communal activities. The economic, political, educational, religious, and familial arrangements in the contemporary community, for example, may be thought of as organizations. Maintenance of social life and stability of the social order is predicted on a reasonable degree of implicit recognition of the legitimacy of the functions of such organizations. While all sociologists do not agree on the extent to which different communal tasks are the assignments of particular institutions, there is widespread acceptance of the idea that, as diffuse as such systems often appear, they constitute an essential part of the workings of the social order.

The community itself may also be conceptualized in the same structural terms. The community, as an organization, may refer to individuals living within a common political boundary who have loyalties and responsibilities to a particular political and social life. When the notion of the community as an organization is used here, however, it refers to more than the town we live or work in, or the state we pay our taxes in, or even the country as a whole. The concept of the community as an organization here refers to collectivities of persons who have a common place of residence, certain formal or defined sets of relationships with one another, and a psychological identification which is reinforced by adherence to such common elements as tradition, language, and the like.

It is perhaps obvious that, as in the use of the concept *individual,* the concept of an *organizational entity* defies a definition precise enough so that it is accessible across conceptual frameworks which rise out of different special interests. The concept can be defined only in terms of empirical observation that is relevant to specific concerns. Thus, some cases in this volume describe social conflict resulting from encounters individuals have with various voluntary, fraternal, or political groups, while others portray conflict between individuals and traditional societal institutions, and still others deal with their relations to community as a whole. Our interest is not with a particular organization, be it the American Rifle Association, Harvard University, or the city of Boise, Idaho. In a sociological sense, it is not important to concern oneself with organizations when they represent interesting social units; they are important because social conflict often stems from ways in which individuals engage with different types or organizations, and because social conflict can result from the discrepancies in means and goals between one organizational entity and another. Just as individuals are related to social conflicts because of certain qualities, their performance in social roles, and their unusual conduct, so too do aggregates of individuals—organizations—also become involved.

In many instances of social conflict the nature of the interaction is such that it is unclear who is the villain and who the victim or injured party, at least from the perspective of the pervasive norms of the American community. The paid killer of a crime syndicate who takes the life of a respectable businessman is an instance of social conflict in which most analysts would agree on the labels to be given to the parties involved. More often, however, conflicting norms are present, and the identification of the parties becomes much more shaky and dependent, to a considerable degree, on the perspectives of the analysts involved. How does one decide who is the scoundrel and who the abused in the case of students who destroy university property while demonstrating against their educational conditions? Then too, there are instances in which protagonist and victim shift roles during the course of an event of social conflict, such as cases of ghetto residents who begin demonstrating in an orderly manner, are impeded by overzealous police, and end up looting and destroying the dwellings and businesses of apparently uninvolved parties. Nevertheless, looking at social conflicts as interactions in which one of the parties is more or less the initiator, the provocateur, the protagonist, while another is seen as the respondent, the party struck out against, the victim, makes it possible to organize case material in a way that insures some range of systematically selective material.

Thus, in each of the social problem areas considered in this volume, an effort is made to present four cases: a conflict in which an individual is the protagonist and another individual is the victim; a conflict in which the individual is protagonist and the organization the victim; a conflict in which the organization is the protagonist and the individual the victim; a conflict in which an organization is the protagonist and another organization is the victim.

A brief discussion will precede each social problem and will seek to identify the protagonists and victims in each case. It should be emphasized, however, that not all analysts of social conflict may agree with the identification of the particular party in each case as protagonist and the other as victim. Indeed, the reader sometimes simply must judge the matter for himself.

THE
IMPOVERISHED

The lack of economic wherewithal plays a critical role in a host of social problems, particularly in this age in which man's livelihood is no longer primarily dependent on his ability to produce the food and fiber necessary for existence, but on his ability to compete for the rewards of a technologically-oriented society. The concept of poverty refers to more than being at the bottom rung of the economic ladder; it includes other handicaps such as the lack of skills and know-how for survival in modern society. The reward system has produced sharp discrepancies between those who are "in" and enjoy the benefits of an affluent society, and the poor who are "out" and are often completely cut off from any opportunities to participate in activities which lead to needed goods and services.

Efforts either to ameliorate poverty or to intervene in the processes which produce new generations of the poor seem restricted, perhaps because the most obvious solutions threaten the very structures and societal arrangements which promote the well-being of those members of society who are successful. Poverty is a structural and institutional problem, and it can be affected only by establishing new means by which many more members of society can qualify and compete for available rewards. In order to accomplish marked modifications, resources and wealth must be redistributed and allocation of rewards changed, and this, at the very least, will inconvenience those who have geared their industry and habits to traditional methods for success. But the increase of persons in nonproductive roles, the rising costs of supporting them, and the spread of active dissatisfaction among the poor themselves presses for radical changes. The steps which society takes or fails to take are crucial. The decisions which are made will be a reflection of the willingness or the reluctance of affluent members of society to disrupt their lives with new ideas and personal sacrifices.

| INDIVIDUAL vs. INDIVIDUAL | INDIVIDUAL vs. ORGANIZATION |

MAKING IT: THE BRUTAL BARGAIN

Although the view that it is possible for anyone in the United States to succeed is exaggerated, channels of upward mobility do exist. But the struggling aspirant often experiences a wide variety of frustration, shame, and discomfort in the course of making it. In this case, the author reports on his experience of socialization for success and the nature of a relationship with an individual whose interest in helping him may have been genuine, but could well be regarded as thoughtless and cruel. The experience, with its stress and strain, describes the often torturous personal relationships which are part of the process of moving out of poverty and lower-class status. How frequently must the poor who succeed stand ready to be victims of the thoughtless criticism of those who would help them?

EVEN THE SAINTS CRY

The lives of the poor are often subjected to radical shifts in physical and social environments by well-meaning agencies. The young Puerto Rican mother that Oscar Lewis writes about was moved from a disreputable slum to a much better housing project. The step upward, however, brought her into contact with a community which had norms and expectations strange and unfamiliar to her. The consequences of her engagement with the new community were, at the very least, unpleasant. Social skills acceptable and used in the slum antagonized persons in the new community. Her failure to fit in the new social milieu greatly deprived her in terms of social relationships; she was aware, however, of the material benefits of the new environ if she modified her behavior to conform with the community.

ORGANIZATION
vs.
INDIVIDUAL

ORGANIZATION
vs.
ORGANIZATION

LET US
NOW PRAISE DR. GATCH

While the lack of occupational skills and opportunities for employment are characteristic problems of the poor, they suffer other inequities as well. Medical and social services are often denied the poor, including individuals who are too young, too old, or too handicapped to participate in the economic life of their community. Particularly hurt by such denials are black people and other minority group members who fail to receive adequate services and treatment because of both ethnicity and poverty. This article describes how the powerful members of a South Carolina county join forces to suppress the efforts of a heroic physician who tries to help the unfortunate, and how they try to minimize the visibility of this shameful situation. The article does not end on a very optimistic note; Dr. Gatch may be a somewhat tragic figure in that his antagonists are strong and unbending. While the article focuses on a physician and his opponents in a semi-rural southern community, the same situation exists in many core city areas in the North and the West, as well as in the South.

LET THEM EAT PROMISES

The Poor People's Campaign, headed by Dr. Martin Luther King's successor, David Abernathy, is a dim memory despite the extensive news coverage of the large band of persons who traveled to Washington and camped there in order to effect social change. Not just a memory is the fact that hundreds of thousands (and probably millions), of Americans go to bed hungry, wake up hungry, and remain hungry. One demand was for marked increases in Federal funds for food for the poor—not an unreasonable demand in the face of other types of financial commitments of the Federal government, and the practice of subsidizing farmers to restrict production. But the Abernathy organization, in its dealings with the White House including Mr. Johnson himself, came up against the hard walls of bureaucracy and political reality that seem to prevail more often than the cries of such dedicated groups as the supporters of the Poor People's March. In the end the effort was minimally successful; somehow neither the approach, the specific program, or the time was right to provide food for the many hungry Americans.

Making It: The Brutal Bargain

NORMAN PODHORETZ

One of the longest journeys in the world is the journey from Brooklyn to Manhattan—or at least from certain neighborhoods in Brooklyn to certain parts of Manhattan. I have made that journey, but it is not from the experience of having made it that I know how very great the distance is, for I started on the road many years before I realized what I was doing, and by the time I did realize it I was for all practical purposes already there. At so imperceptible a pace did I travel, and with so little awareness, that I never felt footsore or out of breath or weary at the thought of how far I still had to go. Yet whenever anyone who has remained back there where I started— remained not physically but socially and culturally, for the neighborhood is now a Negro ghetto and the Jews who have "remained" in it mostly reside in the less affluent areas of Long Island—whenever anyone like that happens into the world in which I now live with such perfect ease, I can see that in his eyes I have become a fully acculturated citizen of a country as foreign to him as China and infinitely more frightening.

That country is sometimes called the upper middle class; and indeed I

Reprinted by permission of the publisher from Norman Podhoretz, *Making It* (New York: Random House, Inc., 1967). Copyright © 1967 by Norman Podhoretz.

am a member of that class, less by virtue of my income than by virtue of the way my speech is accented, the way I dress, the way I furnish my home, the way I entertain and am entertained, the way I educate my children—the way, quite simply, I look and I live. It appalls me to think what an immense transformation I had to work on myself in order to become what I have become: If I had known what I was doing I would surely not have been able to do it, I would surely not have wanted to. No wonder the choice had to be blind; there was a kind of treason in it—treason toward my family, treason toward my friends. In choosing the road I chose, I was pronouncing a judgment upon them, and the fact that they themselves concurred in the judgment makes the whole thing sadder but no less cruel.

When I say that the choice was blind, I mean that I was never aware —obviously not as a small child, certainly not as an adolescent, and not even as a young man already writing for publication and working on the staff of an important intellectual magazine in New York—how inextricably my "noblest" ambitions were tied to the vulgar desire to rise above the class into which I was born; nor did I understand to what an astonishing extent these ambitions were shaped and defined by the standards and values and tastes of the class into which I did not know I wanted to move. It is not that I was or am a social climber as that term is commonly used. High society interests me, if at all, only as a curiosity; I do not wish to be a member of it; and in any case, it is not, as I have learned from a small experience of contact with the very rich and fashionable, my "scene." Yet precisely because social climbing is not one of my vices (unless what might be called celebrity climbing, which very definitely *is* one of my vices, can be considered the contemporary variant of social climbing), I think there may be more than a merely personal significance in the fact that class has played so large a part both in my life and in my career.

But whether or not the significance is there, I feel certain that my long-time blindness to the part class was playing in my life was not altogether idiosyncratic. "Privilege," Robert L. Heilbroner has shrewdly observed in *The Limits of American Capitalism*, "is not an attribute we are accustomed to stress when we consider the construction of *our* social order." For a variety of reasons, says Heilbroner, "privilege under capitalism is much less 'visible,' especially to the favored groups, than privilege under other systems" like feudalism. This "invisibility" extends in America to class as well.

No one, of course, is so naïve as to believe that America is a classless society or that the force of egalitarianism—powerful as it has been in some respects—has ever been powerful enough to wipe out class distinctions altogether. There was a moment during the 1950s, to be sure, when social thought hovered on the brink of saying that the country had to all intents and purposes become a wholly middle-class society. But the emergence of the civil-rights movement in the 1960s and the concomitant discovery of the poor—to whom, in helping to discover them, Michael Harrington interestingly enough applied, in *The Other America*, the very word ("invisible") that Heilbroner later used with reference to the rich —has put at least a temporary end to that kind of talk. And yet if class has become visible again, it is only in its grossest outlines—mainly, that is, in terms of income levels—and to the degree that manners and style of life are perceived as relevant at all, it is generally in the crudest of terms. There is something in us, it would seem, which resists the idea of class. Even our novelists, working in a genre for which class has traditionally been a supreme reality, are largely indifferent to it—which is to say, blind to its importance as a factor in the life of the individual.

In my own case, the blindness to class always expressed itself in an outright and very often belligerent refusal to believe that it had anything to do with me at all. I no longer remember when or in what form I first discovered that there was such a thing as class, but whenever it was and whatever form the discovery took, it could only have coincided with the recognition that criteria existed by which I and everyone I knew were stamped as inferior: we were in the *lower* class. This was not a proposition I was willing to accept, and my way of not accepting it was to dismiss the whole idea of class as a prissy triviality.

Given the fact that I had literary ambitions even as a small boy, it was inevitable that the issue of class would sooner or later arise for me with a sharpness it would never acquire for most of my friends. But given the fact also that I was on the whole very happy to be growing up where I was, that I was fiercely patriotic about Brownsville (the spawning ground of so many famous athletes and gangsters), and that I felt genuinely patronizing toward other neighborhoods (especially the "better" ones like Crown Heights and East Flatbush which seemed by comparison colorless and unexciting)—given the fact, in other words, that I was not, for all that I wrote poetry and read books, an "alienated" boy dreaming of escape, my confrontation with the issue of class would probably have come later rather than sooner if not for an English teacher in high school who decided that I was a gem in the rough and took it upon herself to polish me to as high a sheen as she could manage and I would permit.

I resisted—far less effectively, I can see now, than I then thought, though even then I knew that she was wearing me down far more than I would ever give her the satisfaction of admitting. Famous throughout the school for her altogether outspoken snobbery, which stopped short by only a hair (and sometimes did not stop short at all) of an old-fashioned kind of patrician anti-Semitism, Mrs. K. was also famous for being an extremely good teacher; indeed, I am sure that she saw no distinction between the hopeless task of teaching the proper use of English to the young Jewish barbarians whom fate had so unkindly deposited into her charge and the equally hopeless task of teaching them the proper "manners." (There were as many young Negro barbarians in her charge as Jewish ones, but I doubt that she could ever bring herself to pay very much attention to them. As she never hesitated to make clear, it was punishment enough for a woman of her background—her family was old-Brooklyn and, she would have us understand, extremely distinguished—to have fallen among the sons of East European immigrant Jews.)

For three years, from the age of thirteen to the age of sixteen, I was her special pet, though that word is scarcely adequate to suggest the intensity of the relationship which developed between us. It was a relationship right out of *The Corn Is Green*, which may, for all I know, have served as her model; at any rate, her objective was much the same as the Welsh teacher's in that play: she was determined that I should win a scholarship to Harvard. But whereas (an irony much to the point here) the problem the teacher had in *The Corn Is Green* with her coal-miner pupil in the traditional class society of Edwardian England was strictly academic, Mrs. K.'s problem with me in the putatively egalitarian society of New Deal America was strictly social. My grades were very high and would obviously remain so, but what would they avail me if I continued to go about looking and sounding like a "filthy little slum child" (the epithet she would invariably hurl at me whenever we had an argument about "manners")?

Childless herself, she worked on me like a dementedly ambitious mother with a somewhat recalcitrant son; married to a solemn and elderly man (she was then in her early forties or thereabouts), she treated me like a cruelly ungrateful adolescent lover on whom she had humiliatingly bestowed her favors. She flirted with me and flattered me, she scolded me and

insulted me. Slum child, filthy little slum child, so beautiful a mind and so vulgar a personality, so exquisite in sensibility and so coarse in manner. What would she do with me, what would become of me if I persisted out of stubbornness and perversity in the disgusting ways they had taught me at home and on the streets?

To her the most offensive of these ways was the style in which I dressed: a T-shirt, tightly pegged pants and a red satin jacket with the legend "Cherokees, S.A.C." (social-athletic club) stitched in large white letters across the back. This was bad enough, but when on certain days I would appear in school wearing, as a particular ceremonial occasion required, a suit and tie, the sight of those immense padded shoulders and my white-on-white shirt would drive her to even greater heights of contempt and even lower depths of loving despair than usual. *Slum child, filthy little slum child.* I was beyond saving; I deserved no better than to wind up with all the other horrible little Jewboys in the gutter (by which she meant Brooklyn College). If only I would listen to her, the whole world could be mine: I could win a scholarship to Harvard, I could get to know the best people, I could grow up into a life of elegance and refinement and taste. Why was I so stupid as not to understand?

II

In those days it was very unusual, and possibly even against the rules, for teachers in public high schools to associate with their students after hours. Nevertheless, Mrs. K. sometimes invited me to her home, a beautiful old brownstone located in what was perhaps the only section in the whole of Brooklyn fashionable enough to be intimidating. I would read her my poems and she would tell me about her family, about the schools she had gone to, about Vassar, about writers she had met, while her husband, of whom I was frightened to death and who to my utter astonishment turned out to be Jewish (but not, as Mrs. K. quite unnecessarily hastened to inform me, *my* kind of Jewish), sat stiffly and silent in an armchair across the room squinting at his newspaper through the first pince-nez I had ever seen outside the movies. He spoke to me but once, and that was after I had read Mrs. K. my tearful editorial for the school newspaper on the death of Roosevelt—an effusion which provoked into a full five-minute harangue whose blasphemous contents would certainly have shocked me into insensibility if I had not been even more shocked to discover that he actually had a voice.

But Mrs. K. not only had me to her house; she also—what was even more unusual—took me out a few times, to the Frick Gallery and the Metropolitan Museum, and once to the theater, where we saw a dramatization of *The Late George Apley*, a play I imagine she deliberately chose with the not wholly mistaken idea that it would impress upon me the glories of aristocratic Boston.

One of our excursions into Manhattan I remember with particular vividness because she used it to bring the struggle between us to rather a dramatic head. The familiar argument began this time on the subway. Why, knowing that we would be spending the afternoon together "in public," had I come to school that morning improperly dressed? (I was, as usual, wearing my red satin club jacket over a white T-shirt.) She realized, of course, that I owned only one suit (this said not in compassion but in derision) and that my poor parents had, God only knew where, picked up the idea that it was too precious to be worn except at one of those bar mitzvahs I was always going to. Though why, if my parents were so worried about clothes, they had permitted me to buy a suit which made me look like a young hoodlum, she found it very difficult to imagine. Still, much as she would have been embarrassed to be seen in public with a boy whose parents allowed him to wear a zoot suit, she would have been somewhat less embarrassed than she was now by the ridiculous costume I had on. Had I no consideration for her? Had I no consideration for myself? Did I want everyone who laid eyes on me to think that I was nothing but an ill-bred little slum child?

My standard ploy in these arguments was to take the position that such things were of no concern to me: I was a poet and I had more important matters to think about than clothes. Besides, I would feel silly coming to school on an ordinary day dressed in a suit. Did Mrs. K. want me to look like one of those "creeps" from Crown Heights who were all going to become doctors? This was usually an effective counter, since Mrs. K. despised her middle-class Jewish students even more than she did the "slum children," but probably because she was growing desperate at the thought of how I would strike a Harvard interviewer (it was my senior year), she did not respond according to form on that particular occasion.

"At least," she snapped, "they reflect well on their parents."

I was accustomed to her bantering gibes at my parents, and sensing, probably, that they arose out of jealousy, I was rarely troubled by them. But this one bothered me; it went beyond banter and I did not know how to deal with it. I remember flushing but I cannot remember what if anything I said in protest. It was the beginning of a very bad afternoon for both of us.

We had been heading for the Museum of Modern Art, but as we got off the subway, Mrs. K. announced that she had changed her mind about the museum. She was going to show me something else instead, just down the street on Fifth Avenue. This mysterious "something else" to which we proceeded in silence turned out to be the college department of an expensive clothing store, De Pinna. I do not exaggerate when I say that an actual physical dread seized me as I followed her into the store. I had never been inside such a store; it was not a store, it was enemy territory, every inch of it mined with humiliations. "I am," Mrs. K. declared in the coldest human voice I hope I shall ever hear, "going to buy you a suit that you will be able to wear at your Harvard interview." I had guessed, of course, that this was what she had in mind, and even at fifteen I understood what a fantastic act of aggression she was planning to commit against my parents and asking me to participate in. Oh no, I said in a panic (suddenly realizing that I *wanted* her to buy me that suit), I can't, my mother wouldn't like it. "You can tell her it's a birthday present. Or else I will tell her. If I tell her, I'm sure she won't object." The idea of Mrs. K. meeting my mother was more than I could bear: my mother, who spoke with a Yiddish accent and whom, until that sickening moment, I had never known I was so ready to betray.

To my immense relief and my equally immense disappointment, we left the store, finally, without buying a suit, but it was not to be the end of clothing or "manners" for me that day—not yet. There was still the ordeal of a restaurant to go through. Where I came from, people rarely ate in restaurants, not so much because most of them were too poor to afford such a luxury—although most of them certainly were—as because eating in restaurants was not regarded as a luxury at all; it was, rather, a necessity to which bachelors were pitiably condemned. A home-cooked meal was assumed to be better than anything one could possibly get in a restaurant, and considering the class of restaurants in question (they were really diners or luncheonettes), the assumption was probably correct. In the case of my own family, myself included until my late teens, the business of going to restaurants was complicated by the fact that we observed the Jewish dietary laws, and except in certain neighborhoods, few places could be found which served kosher food; in midtown Manhattan in the 1940s, I believe there were only two and both were relatively expensive. All this is by way of explaining why I had had so little experience of restaurants up to the age of fifteen and why I grew apprehensive once more when Mrs. K. decided after we left De Pinna that we should have something to eat.

The restaurant she chose was not at all an elegant one—I have, like a criminal, revisited it since—but it seemed very elegant indeed to me: enemy territory again, and this time a mine exploded in my face the minute I set foot through the door. The hostess was very sorry, but she could not seat the young gentleman without a coat and tie. If the lady wished, however, something could be arranged. The lady (visibly pleased by this unexpected—or was it expected?—object lesson) did wish, and the so recently defiant but by now utterly docile young gentleman was forthwith divested of his so recently beloved but by now thoroughly loathsome red satin jacket and provided with a much oversized white waiter's coat and a tie—which, there being no collar to a T-shirt, had to be worn around his bare neck. Thus attired, and with his face supplying the touch of red which had moments earlier been supplied by his jacket, he was led into the dining room, there to be taught the importance of proper table manners through the same pedagogic instrumentality that had worked so well in impressing him with the importance of proper dress.

Like any other pedagogic technique, however, humiliation has its limits, and Mrs. K. was to make no further progress with it that day. For I had had enough, and I was not about to risk stepping on another mine. Knowing she would subject me to still more ridicule if I made a point of my revulsion at the prospect of eating non-kosher food, I resolved to let her order for me and then to feign lack of appetite or possibly even illness when the meal was served. She did order—duck for both of us, undoubtedly because it would be a hard dish for me to manage without using my fingers.

The two portions came in deep oval-shaped dishes, swimming in a brown sauce and each with a sprig of parsley sitting on top. I had not the faintest idea of what to do—

should the food be eaten directly from the oval dish or not?—nor which of the many implements on the table to do it with. But remembering that Mrs. K. herself had once advised me to watch my hostess in such a situation and then to do exactly as she did, I sat perfectly still and waited for her to make the first move. Unfortunately, Mrs. K. also remembered having taught me that trick, and determined as she was that I should be given a lesson that would force me to mend my ways, she waited too. And so we both waited, chatting amiably, pretending not to notice the food while it sat there getting colder and colder by the minute. Thanks partly to the fact that I would probably have gagged on the duck if I had tried to eat it—dietary taboos are very powerful if one has been conditioned to them—I was prepared to wait forever. And, indeed, it was Mrs. K. who broke first.

"Why aren't you eating?" she suddenly said after something like fifteen minutes had passed. "Aren't you hungry?" Not very, I answered. "Well," she said, "I think we'd better eat. The food is getting cold." Whereupon, as I watched with great fascination, she deftly captured the sprig of parsley between the prongs of her serving fork, set it aside, took up her serving spoon and delicately used those two esoteric implements to transfer a piece of duck from the oval dish to her plate. I imitated the whole operation as best as I could, but not well enough to avoid splattering some partly congealed sauce onto my borrowed coat in the process. Still, things could have been worse, and having more or less successfully negotiated my way around that particular mine, I now had to cope with the problem

of how to get out of eating the duck. But I need not have worried. Mrs. K. took one bite, pronounced it inedible (it must have been frozen by then), and called in quiet fury for the check.

Several months later, wearing an altered but respectably conservative suit which had been handed down to me in good condition by a bachelor uncle, I presented myself on two different occasions before interviewers from Harvard and from the Pulitzer Scholarship Committee. Some months after that, Mrs. K. had her.triumph: I won the Harvard scholarship on which her heart had been so passionately set. It was not, however, large enough to cover all expenses, and since my parents could not afford to make up the difference, I was unable to accept it. My parents felt wretched but not, I think, quite as wretched as Mrs. K. For a while it looked as though I would wind up in the "gutter" of Brooklyn College after all, but then the news arrived that I had also won a Pulitzer Scholarship which paid full tuition if used at Columbia, and a small stipend besides. Everyone was consoled, even Mrs. K. Columbia was at least in the Ivy League.

The last time I saw her was shortly before my graduation from Columbia and just after a story had appeared in the *Times* announcing that I had been awarded a fellowship which was to send me to Cambridge University. Mrs. K. had passionately wanted to see me in Cambridge, Massachusetts, but Cambridge, England, was even better. We met somewhere near Columbia for a drink, and her happiness over my fellowship, it seemed to me, was if anything exceeded by her delight at discovering that I now knew enough to know that the right thing to order in a cocktail lounge was a very dry martini with lemon peel, please.

III

Looking back now at the story of my relationship with Mrs. K. strictly in the context of the issue of class, what strikes me most sharply is the astonishing rudeness of this woman to whom "manners" were of such over-riding concern. (This, as I have since had some occasion to notice is a fairly common characteristic among members of the class to which she belonged.) Though she would not have admitted it, good manners to Mrs. K. meant only one thing: conformity to a highly stylized set of surface habits and fashions which she took, quite as a matter of course, to be superior to all other styles of social behavior. But in what did their superiority consist? Were her "good" manners derived from or conducive to a greater moral sensitivity than the "bad" manners I had learned at home and on the streets of Brownsville? I rather doubt it. The "crude" behavior of my own parents, for example, was then and is still marked by a tactfulness and a delicacy that Mrs. K. simply could not have approached. It is not that she was incapable of tact and delicacy; in certain moods she was (and manners apart, she was an extraordinarily loving and generous woman). But such qualities were neither built into nor expressed by the system of manners under which she lived. She was fond of quoting Cardinal Newman's definition of a gentleman as a person who could be at ease in any company, yet if anything was clear about the manners she was trying to teach me, it was that they operated—not inadvertently but by deliberate design—

to set one at ease *only* with others similarly trained and to cut off altogether from those who were not.

While I would have been unable to formulate it in those terms at the time, I think I must have understood perfectly well what Mrs. K. was attempting to communicate with all her talk about manners; if I had not understood it so well, I would not have resisted so fiercely. She was saying that because I was a talented boy, a better class of people stood ready to admit me into their ranks. But only on one condition: I had to signify by my general deportment that I acknowledged them as *superior* to the class of people among whom I happened to have been born. That was the bargain—take it or leave it. In resisting Mrs. K. where "manners" were concerned—just as I was later to resist many others—I was expressing my refusal to have any part of so brutal a bargain.

But the joke was on me, for what I did not understand—not in the least then and not for a long time afterward—was that in matters having to do with "art" and "culture" (the "life of the mind," as I learned to call it at Columbia), I was being offered the very same brutal bargain and accepting it with the wildest enthusiasm.

I have said that I did not, for all my bookishness, feel alienated as a boy, and this is certainly true. Far from dreaming of escape from Brownsville, I dreaded the thought of living anywhere else, and whenever my older sister, who hated the neighborhood, began begging my parents to move, it was invariably my howls of protest that kept them from giving in. For by the age of thirteen I had made it into the neighborhood big time, otherwise known as the Cherokees, S.A.C. It had by no means been easy for me, as a mediocre athlete and a notoriously good student, to win acceptance from a gang which prided itself mainly on its masculinity and its contempt for authority, but once this had been accomplished, down the drain went any reason I might earlier have had for thinking that life could be better in any other place. Not for nothing, then, did I wear that red satin jacket to school every day. It was my proudest possession, a badge of manly status, proving that I was not to be classified with the Crown Heights "creeps," even though my grades, like theirs, were high.

And yet, despite the Cherokees, it cannot be that I felt quite so securely at home in Brownsville as I remember thinking. The reason is that something extremely significant in this connection had happened to me by the time I first met Mrs. K.: without any conscious effort on my part, my speech had largely lost the characteristic neighborhood accent and was well on its way to becoming as neutrally American as I gather it now is.

Now whatever else may be involved in a nondeliberate change of accent, one thing is clear: it bespeaks a very high degree of detachment from the ethos of one's immediate surroundings. It is not a good ear alone, and perhaps not even a good ear at all, which enables a child to hear the difference between the way he and everyone else around him sound when they talk, and the way teachers and radio announcers— as it must have been in my case— sound. Most people, and especially most children, are entirely insensitive to such differences; which is why anyone who pays attention to these matters can, on the basis of a man's accent alone, often draw a reasonably accurate picture of his regional, social, and ethnic background. People who feel that they belong in their familiar surroundings—whether it be a place, a class, or a group—will invariably speak in the accent of those surroundings; in all likelihood, indeed, they will never have imagined any other possibility for themselves. Conversely, it is safe to assume that a person whose accent has undergone a radical change from childhood is a person who once had fantasies of escaping to some other world, whether or not they were ever realized.

But accent in America has more than a psychological or spiritual significance. "Her kerbstone English," said Henry Higgins of Eliza Doolittle, "will keep her in the gutter to the end of her days." Most Americans probably respond with a sense of amused democratic superiority to the idea of a society in which so trivial a thing as accent can keep a man down, and it is a good measure of our blindness to the pervasive operations of class that there has been so little consciousness of the fact that America itself is such a society. While the broadly regional accents—New England, Midwestern, Southern—enjoy more or less equal status and will not affect the economic or social chances of those who speak in them, the opposite is still surely true of any accent identifiably influenced by Yiddish, Italian, Polish, Spanish—that is, the languages of the major post-Civil War immigrant groups (among which may be included American-Irish). A man with such an accent will no longer be confined, as once he would almost automatically have been, to the working class, but unless his life, both occupational and social, is lived strictly within the milieu in whose tone of voice he speaks, his accent will at the least operate as an obstacle to be overcome (if, for example, he is a school-teacher aspiring to be a principal), and at the most as an effective barrier to advancement (if, say, he is an engineer), let alone to entry into the governing elite of the country. (For better or worse, incidentally, these accents are not a temporary phenomenon destined to disappear with the passage of the generations, no more than ethnic consciousness itself is. I have heard third-generation American Jews of East European stock speaking with thicker accents than their parents.)

Clearly, then, while fancying myself altogether at home in the world into which I was born, I was not only more detached from it than I realized; I was also taking action—and of very fundamental kind—which would eventually make it possible for me to move into some other world. Yet I still did not recognize what I was doing—not in any such terms. My ambition was to be a great and famous poet, not to live in a different community, a different class, a different "world." If I had a concrete image of what greatness would mean socially, it was probably based on the famous professional boxer from our block who had moved to a more prosperous neighborhood but still spent his leisure time hanging around the corner candy store and the local poolroom with his old friends (among whom he could, of course, experience his fame far more sharply than he could have done among his newly acquired peers).

But to each career its own sociology. Boxers, unlike poets, do not undergo a cultural change in the process of becoming boxers, and if I was not brave enough or clever enough as a boy to see the distinction, others who knew me then were. "Ten years from now, you won't even want to talk to me, you won't even recognize me if you pass on the street," was the kind of comment I frequently heard in my teens from women in the neighborhood, friends of my mother who were fond of me and nearly as proud as she was of the high grades I was getting in school and the prizes I was always winning. "That's crazy, you must be kidding," I would answer. They were not crazy and they were not kidding. They were simply better sociologists than I.

As, indeed, my mother herself was, for often in later years—after I had become a writer and an editor and was living only a subway ride away but in a style that was foreign to her and among people by whom she was intimidated—she would gaze wistfully at this strange creature, her son, and murmur, "I should have made him for a dentist," registering thereby her perception that whereas Jewish sons who grow up to be successes in certain occupations usually remain fixed in an accessible cultural ethos, sons, who grow up into literary success are transformed almost beyond recognition and distanced almost beyond a mother's reach. My mother wanted nothing so much as for me to be a success, to be respected and admired. But she did not imagine, I think, that she would only purchase the realization of her ambition at the price of my progressive estrangement from her and her ways. Perhaps it was my guilt at the first glimmerings of this knowledge which accounted for my repression of it and for the obstinacy of the struggle I waged over "manners" with Mrs. K.

For what seemed most of all to puzzle Mrs. K., who saw no distinction between taste in poetry and taste in clothes, was that I could see no connection between the two. Mrs. K. knew that a boy from Brownsville with a taste for Keats was not long for Brownsville, and moreover would in all probability end up in the social class to which she herself belonged. How could I have explained to her that I would only be able to leave Brownsville if I could maintain the illusion that my destination was a place in some mystical country of the spirit and not a place in the upper reaches of the American class structure?

Saint Paul, who was a Jew, conceived of salvation as a world in which there would be neither Jew nor Greek, and though he may well have been the first, he was very far from the last Jew to dream such a dream of transcendence—transcendence of the actual alternative categories with which reality so stingily presents us. Not to be Jewish, but not to be Christian either; not to be a worker, but not to be a boss either; not—if I may be forgiven for injecting this banality out of my own soul into so formidable a series of fantasies—to be a slum child but not to be a snob either. How could I have explained to Mrs. K. that wearing a suit from De Pinna would for me have been something like the social equivalent of a conversion to Christianity? And how could she have explained to me that there was no socially neutral ground to be found in the United States of America, and that a distaste for the surroundings in which I was bred, and ultimately (God forgive me) even for many of the people I loved—and so a new taste for other kinds of people—how could she have explained that all this was inexorably entailed in the logic of a taste for the poetry of Keats and the painting of Cézanne and the music of Mozart?

Even The Saints Cry

OSCAR LEWIS

This article describes the experiences of a young Puerto Rican mother, Cruz Rios, who moved from La Esmeralda—one of the oldest

Reprinted by permission of Random House, Inc., from Oscar Lewis, *La Vida* (New York: Random House, Inc.). Copyright © 1965, 1966 by Oscar Lewis.

slums in San Juan only a short distance from the governor's palace— about four miles east to Villa Hermosa, a new government housing project in a middle-class section of Rio Piedras. Cruz' story illustrates the difficult problems of adjustment in her new environment and helps us understand why, in spite of the efforts of well-intentioned governments and the spending of huge sums of money on public housing, the positive effects hoped for by social planners are not always forthcoming.

When I began my study of Cruz in 1963, she was just 17 and living alone on relief with her two children. She lived in a small, dark, one-room apartment for which she paid a rental of eight dollars a month. Her kitchen was a tiny corner alcove equipped with a three-burner kerosene stove and a water faucet jutting out from the wall. She shared a run-down hall toilet with two other families and paid a neighbor $1.50 a month for the privilege of an extension cord which supplied her with electricity.

Cruz, a crippled, mulatto girl with reddish brown kinky hair and a pretty face, was lame since early childhood. She left school after the fifth grade, set up house with her sweetheart at 14 and gave birth to her first child at 15. Two years later, before the birth of her second child, she separated from her husband, Emilio, who refused to recognize the baby as his own.

Part I gives the reader a glimpse of living conditions in the slum; part II, recorded five months after Cruz had moved, gives her reactions to the housing projects. (Names of all places and people in this tape-recorded narrative have been changed to guarantee the anonymity of the narrator.)

I

Here in La Esmeralda, the only thing that disturbs me are the rats. Lice, bedbugs, and rats have always been a problem in my room. When I moved in here a year ago, the first thing I found were little baby rats. "Kill them!" my friend Gloria said. "Ay Bendito! I can't do it. Poor little things—they look like children," I said, and I left them there in a hole. The next day they were gone. I didn't kill them, they just disappeared. I cleaned up the house and about a month later they were going back and forth through the room from one hole to another, with me just looking at them.

When Alejandro was living with me, more rats came because there was a hen with eggs under the house. A rat had given birth and had eaten some of the chicks. The owner took the hen and 29 chicks out of there because there were baby rats underneath the hen too. The man threw them out but a week later they came back and were all over the place, even getting into the pan with the baby's milk and eating up whatever I left around.

One Sunday my *mamá* said, "Let's buy a rat trap and see if we can't get rid of some of them." Well, we tried it and that day between us and the next-door neighbor we caught 29 little rats. After a while, more came. Anita used to chase them across the room to see if she could catch them, and the boys who came to the house would say "Look, a rat."

I would tell them, "Let it be, it's one of the family. They keep me company, now that I'm all by myself. I'm raising them for soup."

So I left them alone, but before I knew it, there were great big rats here. One Sunday I said to Catin, who had just eaten a bread cutlet, "Catin, you'd better go bathe or the rats will eat you up." Then I forgot about it and she lay down. Later I took a bath and went to bed. About midnight, Catin screamed, *Ay, ay, ay,* it bit me!" The first thing that came to my mind was that it was a snake or a scorpion. "What bit you?" I asked and when I turned on the light, she said, "Look, look!" and I could see a rat running away.

She had been bitten on the arm and I could see the little teeth marks. I squeezed out the blood and smeared urine and bay rum on it.

Then I said, "Catin, you'd better come into my bed with me. God knows whether it was because the crib is dirty or you are dirty." I was wearing only panties, Chuito and Anita were naked, but Catin was wearing a jacket and pants. Well, later that same rat came and bit her again on the other arm. I sprinkled bay rum all over the bed where she was sleeping and rubbed it on her and nothing else happened that night.

The next day I went to the church and told the Sister that the girl had been bitten by a rat. She told me that if Catin didn't start running a fever, to leave her alone, and if she did, to take her to the hospital. Then I said to Catin, "You see? That's what happens when you don't bathe." She took a bath every day after that.

At the end of the year, Anita got a rat bite on the lip. I squeezed it out for her and it dried up and she didn't get a fever or anything. A few days after that, I was sitting in a chair with my arm hanging down when a rat came and *pra!* it tried to take off my finger. It wanted human flesh. I lifted my hand, and the rat ran to a hole and disappeared.

Then I said to myself, "These rats have to be finished off. I can't live like this with so many blessed rats. There are more rats than people."

And I bought a trap from the man next door. I fixed the bacon myself and put it in the trap. First I caught a real big rat, then another, and another. Three in all that same night. But there were still more left.

The next morning, I heard screams coming from Rosa Maria's room up above. I said, "Rosa, what's wrong?" Her little boy was crying and shaking his hand, with a rat hanging from it. "Kill it," I said, but he answered, "I can't. Its teeth are stuck in my finger." Finally he got if off by dragging it along the floor. Rosa Maria attended him but the next day the child had a fever which kept going up. The doctor said that the boy was getting tetanus and had to go to the hospital.

The people upstairs leave a lot of rotting clothes piled there, and cans of food and rice. If they don't get rid of that filth, the rats won't leave. I asked the landlord to cover the holes because the rats keep coming in and out as if they were in a bus terminal. He said he didn't live here and I should do it myself.

There are lots of cockroaches in my room too. And new fleas have come in, I don't know from where, except probably from the rats themselves. There are also crickets and lizards. These houses are hollow underneath, and below the floor there's a lot of old boards and filth and all kinds of garbage that has accumulated, and at night the animals come crawling up.

I've noticed that it's on Thursday nights that the rats give us the most trouble. Every other Thursday, before the social worker comes, I clean my house from top to bottom so there are no crumbs on the floor for the rats to eat and no dirty dishes for them to clean. I've learned that unless I leave something for them, the rats come closer and closer to us. When the house is clean, we are in more danger of getting bitten.

II

The social worker told me it would be a good idea to get the children out of La Esmeralda because there's so much delinquency there. My moving to the housing project was practically her idea; she insisted and insisted. Finally one day she came to me and said, "Tomorrow you have to move to the *caserio* in Villa Hermosa." I didn't want to upset her because she's been good to me, so I said okay.

You should have seen this place when I moved in. It was bursting with garbage and smelling of shit, pure shit. Imagine, when the social worker opened the door that first day, a breeze happened to blow her way. She stepped back and said, "Wait, I can't go in. This is barbarous." I had to go outside with her. I tell you, the people who lived here before me were dirtier than the dirtiest pig. When I moved out of my little room in La Esmeralda, I scrubbed it so clean you could have eaten off the floor. Whoever moved in could see that a decent person had lived there. And then I came here and found this pig-sty, and the place looked so big I felt too little and weak to get it clean. So, fool that I am, instead of sending out for a mop and getting right down to work, I just stood in a corner and cried. I locked the door and stayed in all day, weeping. I cried floods.

And this place isn't like La Esmeralda, you know, where there's so much liveliness and noise and something is always going on. Here you never see any movement on the street, not one little domino or card game or anything. The place is dead. People act as if they're angry or in mourning. Either they don't know how to live or they're afraid to. And yet it's full of shameless good-for-nothings. It's true what the proverb says, "May God deliver me from quiet places; I can defend myself in the wild ones."

Everything was so strange to me when I first moved here that I was scared to death. I hated to go out because it's hard to find your way back to this place even if you know the address. The first couple of times I got lost, and I didn't dare ask anybody the way for fear they would fall on me and beat me. If anyone knocked on my door I thought four times before deciding to open it. Then when I did, I took a knife along. But I'm not like that any more. I've made my decision: if someone wants to kill me, let him. I can't live shut in like that. And if anybody interferes with me it will be the worse for them. I have a couple of tricks up my sleeve and can really fuck things up for anybody when I want to.

After a few days, I finally started cleaning up the place. I scrubbed the floors and put everything in order. I even painted the whole apartment, although I had to fight tooth and nail with the man in charge of the buildings in order to get the paint. That old man wanted to get something from me in return, but I wouldn't give it to him. I never have been attracted to old men.

The apartment is a good one. I have a living room, bedroom, kitchen, porch and my own private bathroom. That's something I never had in La Esmeralda. I clean it every morning and when the children use it I go and pull the chain right away.

I never had a kitchen sink in La Esmeralda either, and here I have a brand new one. It's easy to wash the dishes in these double sinks because they're so wide and comfortable. The only trouble is the water, because sometimes it goes off and the electricity, too—three times since I've been here.

I still don't have an ice-box or refrigerator but the stove here is the first electric one I've ever had in my life. I didn't know how to light it the day I moved in. I tried everything I could think of, backward and forward. Luckily, the social worker came and she lit it for me, but even so I didn't learn and Nanda had to show me again that afternoon. She has worked for rich people so long that she knows all those things. I really miss my own little kerosene stove, but Nanda wanted it, so what could I do? She's my *mamá* and if she hankered after a star I would climb up to heaven to get it for her if I could.

The main advantage of the electric stove is that when I have a lot of work to do and it gets to be ten or eleven o'clock, I just connect the stove and have lunch ready in no time. In La Esmeralda I had to wait for the kerosene to light up well before I could even start to cook. And this stove doesn't smoke and leave soot all over the place, either. Still, if the power fails again or is cut off because I don't pay my bill, the kids will just have to go hungry. I won't even be able to heat a cup of milk for them. In La Esmeralda, whenever I didn't have a quarter to buy a full

gallon of kerosene, I got ten cents worth. But who's going to sell you five or ten cents worth of electricity?

I haven't seen any rats here, just one tiny little mouse. It doesn't bother me much because it lives down below, in a hole at the bottom of the stairs. There's no lack of company anywhere, I guess—rats in La Esmeralda and lots of little cockroaches here.

This apartment is so big that I don't have to knock myself out keeping it in order. There's plenty of room for my junk. I even have closets here, and lots of shelves. I have so many shelves and so few dishes that I have to put a dish here and a dish there just to keep each shelf from being completely empty. All the counters and things are no use at all to me, because I just cook a bit of oatmeal for the children and let them sit anywhere to eat it since I have no dishes with which to set a table. Half of my plates broke on the way from La Esmeralda. I guess they wanted to stay back there where they weren't so lonely.

Here even my saints cry! They look so sad. They think I am punishing them. This house is so big I had to separate the saints and hang them up in different places just to cover the empty walls. In La Esmeralda I kept them all together to form a little altar, and I lit candles for them. In La Esmeralda they helped me, but here I ask until I'm tired of asking and they don't help me at all. They are punishing me.

In La Esmeralda I never seemed to need as many things as here. I think it is because we all had about the same, so we didn't need any more. But here, when you go to other people's apartments and see all their things . . . It's not that I'm jealous.

God forbid! I don't want anyone to have less than they have. It's only that I would like to have things of my own too.

What does bother me is the way people here come into my apartment and furnish the place with their mouths. They start saying, "Oh, here's where the set of furniture should go; you need a TV set in that corner and this one is just right for a record-player." And so on. I bite my tongue to keep from swearing at them because, damn it, I have good taste too. I know a TV set would look fine in that corner, but if I don't have the money to buy one, how can I put it there? That's what I like about La Esmeralda—if people there could help someone, they did; if not, they kept their mouths shut.

I really would like a TV though, because they don't have public sets here, the way they do in La Esmeralda. I filled in some blanks for that program, Queen for a Day, to see if I can get one as a gift. It was Nanda's idea and she's so lucky that maybe I will get it. If I do, then at least I could spend the holidays looking at TV. And the children might stay home instead of wandering around the neighborhood so much.

The traffic here really scares me. That's the main reason I don't like this place. Cars scud by like clouds in a high wind and, I'm telling you, I'm always afraid a car will hit the children. If something should happen to my little penguins, I'd go mad, I swear I would. My kids are little devils, and when I bring them in through the front door, they slip out again by climbing over the porch railing. Back in La Esmeralda, where our house was so small, they had to play out in the street whenever people came over, but here there is plenty of room to run around indoors.

Maybe I was better off in La Esmeralda. You certainly have to pay for the comforts you have here! Listen, I'm jittery, really nervous, because if you fail to pay the rent even once here, the following month you're thrown out. I hardly ever got behind on my payments in La Esmeralda, but if I did, I knew that they wouldn't put me out on the street. It's true that my rent is only $6.50 a month here while I paid $11.50 in La Esmeralda, but there I didn't have a water bill and I paid only $1.50 a month for electricty. Here I have already had to pay $3.50 for electricity and if I use more than the minimum they allow in water, I'll have to pay for that too. And I do so much washing!

It's a fact that as long as I lived in La Esmeralda I could always scare up some money, but here I'm always broke. I've gone as much as two days without eating. I don't play the races at El Comandante any more. I can't afford to. And I can't sell *bolita* numbers here because several cops live in this *caserio* and the place is full of detectives. Only the other day I almost sold a number to one of them, but luckily I was warned in time. I don't want to be arrested for anything in the world, not because I'm scared of being in jail but because of the children.

Since I can't sell numbers here, I sell Avon cosmetics, I like the pretty sets of china they give away, and I'm trying to sell a lot so that they'll give me one. But there's hardly any profit in it for me.

In La Esmeralda I could get an old man now and then to give me five dollars for sleeping with him. But here I haven't found anything like that at all. The truth is, if a man comes here and tries to strike up a conversation I usually slam the door in his face. So, well, I have this beautiful, clean apartment, but what good does it do me? Where am I to get money? I can't dig for it.

In La Esmeralda we used to buy things cheap from thieves. They stole from people who lived far away and then they came to La Esmeralda through one of the side entrances to sell. And who the hell is going to go looking for his things down there? Not a chance! You hardly ever saw a rich person in La Esmeralda. We didn't like them, and we scared them off. But so far as I can tell, these dopes around here always steal from the *blanquitos*, the rich people, nearby. Suppose one of them took it into his head to come here to look for the missing stuff? What then?

Since I've moved I'm worse off than I have ever been before, because now I realize all the things I lack and, besides, the rich people around here are always wanting everything for themselves. In La Esmeralda you can bum a nickel from anyone. But with these people, the more they have, the more they want. It's everything for themselves. If you ask them for work, they'll find something for you to do fast enough, but when it's time to pay you'd think it hurt them to pull a dollar out of their pocket.

Listen, to get a few beans from some people who live in a house near here I had to help pick and shell them. People here are real hard and stingy. What's worse, they take advantage of you. The other day I ironed all day long for a woman and all I got for it was two dollars and my dinner. I felt like throwing the money in her face but I just calmly took it. I would have been paid six dollars at the very least for a whole day's ironing in La Esmeralda. At another lady's house near here I cooked, washed the dishes, even scrubbed the floor, and for all that she just gave me one of her old dresses, which I can't even wear because it's too big for me.

Right now, I don't have a cent. The lady next door lets me charge the food for breakfast at her husband's *kiosko*. She's become so fond of me, you can't imagine. Her husband won't sell on credit to anybody, but there's nothing impossible for the person who is really interested in helping you out. She trusts me, so she lets me write down what I take and keep the account myself.

I buy most of my food at the Villa Hermosa grocery. It's a long way from here and I have to walk it on foot every time I need something, like rice or tomato sauce. It's a supermarket, so they don't give credit, but everything is cheaper there, much cheaper. A can of tomato sauce costs seven cents there and 10 cents in La Esmeralda. Ten pounds of rice costs $1.25 in La Esmeralda and 99 cents here. The small bottles of King Pine that cost 15 cents each in La Esmeralda are two for a quarter here.

Sometimes Public Welfare gives me food, but not always, and I don't like most of the things they give. That long-grained rice doesn't taste like anything. It's like eating hay. The meat they give has fat on top and it comes in a can and it's real dark. They say it's corned beef but I don't know. The same goes for that powdered milk. Who could drink the stuff? In La Esmeralda I saved it until I was really hard up and then I sold it to anybody who was willing to shell out a quarter for it to feed it to their animals or something. But I don't dare do that here because it's federal government food, and it's against the law to sell it. I could get into trouble that way in a place like this, where I don't know anybody. I might try to sell that stuff to a detective without realizing who he was and I'd land in jail.

I haven't been to La Esmeralda often since I moved here, because I can't afford it. Every trip costs 40 cents, 20 cents each way. I want to pay off all my debts in La Esmeralda so that I can hold my head high and proud when I go there. I want people to think I've bettered myself because one can't be screwed all one's life. Even now when I visit, still owing money as I do, I put on my best clothes and always try to carry a little cash. I do this so Minerva, Emilio's aunt, won't get the idea I'm starving or anything like that. She really suffers when she sees me in La Esmeralda, and I do all that just to bother her. I dress up the kids real nice and take them to call on everybody except her.

When I first moved out of La Esmeralda, nobody knew that I was leaving, in the first place because it made me sad and in the second place because that old Minerva had gone around telling everybody she hoped I'd clear out. She even said it to my face. I'd yell back at her, "What right do you have to say that? Did you buy La Esmeralda or something?"

Another reason why I hardly ever go to La Esmeralda is because Emilio spies on me. He has come after me in the *caserio* just the way he did in La Esmeralda, though not as often. He likes to use the shower in my new

apartment when he comes. When I start home after visiting La Esmeralda, he gets into his car and drives along behind me, offering to give me a lift. But, listen, I wouldn't get into that car even if I had to walk all the way from San Juan to Villa Hermosa. I put a curse on that car, such a tremendous curse that I'm just waiting to see it strike. I did it one day when Anita had asthma and I had no money to take her to the hospital. I happened to glance out of the window and I saw Emilio stretched out in his car, relaxed as could be, as if he deserved nothing but the best. I let go and yelled with all the breath in my chest, "I hope to God someday you'll wear that car as a hat. I hope it turns to dust with you all fucked up inside it." Now I can't ride in the car, because I'm afraid the curse will come true some time when both of us are in it.

You can't imagine how lonely I feel here. I have friends, but they're sort of artificial, pasted-on friends. I couldn't confide in them at all. For example, I got pregnant a little while ago, and I had to have an abortion. I nearly went crazy thinking about it. Having a baby is nothing, it's the burden you have to take on afterwards, especially with a cowardly husband like mine who takes the easiest way out, denying that the child is his. So there I was, pregnant and, you know, I was ashamed. I was already out of La Esmeralda, see? Well, I know that my womb is weak, so I took two doses of Epsom salts with quinine and out came the kid. You can't imagine how unpleasant that is. In La Esmeralda you can tell everybody about it, and that sort of eases your heart. But here I didn't tell anybody. These girls I know here are *señoritas,* mere children, and something like that . . . *ay, bendito!*

But, to tell you the truth, I don't know what they call a *señorita* here in Villa Hermosa. The way it is in La Esmeralda, a girl and boy fall in love. For a few months they control themselves. Then they can't any more, and the boy does what he has to do to the girl. The hole is bigger than the full moon and that's that. They tell everybody and become husband and wife in the eyes of all the world. There's no trying to hide it. But here you see girls, who by rights should already have had a couple of kids, trying to keep from being found out. They'll go to a hotel with their sweethearts and let them stick their pricks into every hole in their body except the right one. And then they're so brazen as to come out of that hotel claiming they're still *señoritas.* It's plain shameless.

There are some policemen here who make love like this to some girls I know. Well, the policeman who did it to my friend Mimi came and told me that if I loaned him my bed for a little while he would give me three pesos. As that money wouldn't be bad at all and as he wasn't going to do it to me, I rented him the bed and grabbed the three pesos. Let them go screw! They locked themselves in the bedroom for a little while and then they went away. It was none of my business. If they didn't do it here, they would go do it somewhere else. And she didn't lose her virginity or anything here. So my hands are clean.

Sometimes I want to go back to La Esmeralda to live and other times I don't. It's not that I miss my family so much. On the contrary, relatives can be very bothersome. But you do need them in case you get sick because then you can dump the children on them. Sometimes I cry for loneliness here. Sometimes I'm bored to death. There's more neighborliness in La Esmeralda. I was used to having good friends stop by my house all the time. I haven't seen much of this neighborhood because I never go out. There's a Catholic church nearby but I've never been there. And I haven't been to the movies once since I've been living here. In La Esmeralda I used to go now and then. And in La Esmeralda, when nothing else was going on, you could at least hear the sea.

In La Esmeralda nobody ever made fun of my lameness. On the contrary, it was an advantage because everyone went out of his way to help me: "Let me help the lame girl. Let me buy *bolita* numbers from Lame Crucita, because cripples bring luck." But it isn't like that here, where people just laugh. That's why I'd like to live in La Esmeralda again or have Nanda move in here with me.

The social worker told me that I could go to the hospital and have an operation to fix my back. But who could I leave my little baby crows with? And suppose what they do is take my guts out in order to make me look right? Still, now that I live in a place like Villa Hermosa, I would like to have an operation to make me straight.

Let Us Now Praise Dr. Gatch

BYNUM SHAW

Almost ten years ago the telephone rang in the office of a young doctor who had just set up practice in the small coastal community of Bluffton (pop. 356), near Beaufort, South Carolina. The call was a plea for help: on Daufuskie Island, a remote Gullah settlement accessible only by boat, an old woman lay in unconscious limbo. Her family could not tell whether she was dead or alive.

Dr. Donald E. Gatch, then not yet thirty, slipped a flashlight into his medical bag and set out on his errand without a second thought. There was no money on Daufuskie, but there was need. He paid $20 for the thirty-mile round-trip ride, and from a public landing he hiked to a sea-weathered shanty where the old Negress lay on a rude bed. There was no light in the house, and when Gatch called the patient's name there was no response. Automatically, he took up her wrist to check for pulse. As he lifted her arm the skin came away in his hand.

"I knew she was not dead," he recalls. "The skin felt alive in my fingers." He reached in his bag, took out the flashlight and played its beam on the bed. As a general practitioner he was already hardened to the sight

Reprinted by permission of the author and the author's agents, Scott Meredith Literary Agency, from *Esquire* (June 1968), pp. 108–11, 152–56.

of the many forms of disease, but in this case, as his eyes adjusted to the spray of light, he could not repress a shocked gasp. "Her arms, her legs— her entire body was full of maggots. Medical books don't cover that condition, not the complete infestation of the body. How do you treat maggots?"

The patient died, and Dr. Gatch believed then and he believes now that although the immediate cause of death might have been listed as some "acceptable" disease like pneumonia, the real cause of death was plain hunger. That pathetic case made a profound impression on the young doctor, and in the intervening decade he has been seeking out and doing battle with the hunger and parasites of Beaufort County. In the war thus far, the worms have been winning.

It has been, of course, a war in which there have been few allies, for it has been waged on the level of the dirt-poor outcasts of the Great Society. Beaufort County, ideally located and wonderfully warmed, has been striving with considerable success to build a tourist trade. It has a rich patina of history and is mightily endowed with the mossy legacy of the plantation South. Talk of intestinal parasites tends to blight the charm of live oaks, cypress knees, wisteria and sailing regattas. But the *Ascaris lumbricoides* (roundworm) and *Trichuris trichiura* (whipworm) are there, along with the *Tillandsia usneoides* (Spanish moss).

Dr. Gatch established that, beyond doubt, six years ago. With a team of doctors from the Public Health Service's National Institute of Allergy and Infectious Diseases at Columbia, S.C., he conducted stool tests of two hundred twelve residents mainly along Goethe (pronounced goatie) Lane in Bluffton. The findings, subsequently published in the January, 1963, *Public Health Reports,* showed that 7.8 percent had one or more species of worms. More than eighty percent of children under five were infected. Those figures, comparable to rates found in Columbia, Egypt, South Africa and the Cook Islands, suggested to the researchers that tidewater South Carolina might "represent one of the areas of highest endemicity for the continental United States." Health authorities in Beaufort County accepted the study as valid, deplored the condition aloud and for the most part went on about their business.

Only Gatch kept talking and agitating and relating worms to malnutrition. Gatch is not the ordinary member of the medical profession; he abhors the fraternal society; not a Southerner, he regards even the poor or illegitimate Negro as a human being; he reads books and listens to music of every beat; and gradually he came to be regarded as a medical troublemaker, tolerable only as long as his voice echoed meaninglessly across the forsaken rice paddies that encircle Bluffton.

But last November Gatch committed what can only be regarded in Beaufort County as the unpardonable sin. He went up to Columbia, the state capital and, before a citizens' inquiry investigating hunger and poverty, engaged in what The Beaufort *Gazette* sadly described as "running his mouth." What Gatch did was to say that in Beaufort County people were dying of starvation, that they were allowed to start starving before they were born, and that he personally had presided at eight deaths which he could honestly attribute only to hunger.

Of those dead, three in one family, all were Negroes whose strength had been sapped by worms, and Gatch's conclusion rocked South Carolina: "If eight people, white children in Beaufort County, had died of parasites, something would have been done aeons ago."

He told about rickets, which everybody had heard about, and kwashiorkor, which nobody had heard about. The latter is a disease common to West Africa; it results from protein deficiency, and Gatch said he encountered a "fairly large number" of preschool children with a disease suspiciously resembling kwashiorkor.

He told about "Goatie" Lane, and roundworm counts averaging 45,074 eggs per gram of feces. In a kind of earnestness eloquent for its unstudied simplicity, he said, "The parasite problem is bad, but there just ain't no damn sense in this country having hungry people, and we got a bunch of them. I just can't understand why we can't make food available."

The board of inquiry, representing the Washington-based Citizens Crusade Against Poverty, asked Gatch to comment on a study published in the June, 1966, issue of the *American Journal of Clinical Nutrition* which found that in Greenville County, South Carolina, the Negro infant mortality rate was fifty per thousand —twice that of South Carolina whites.

Gatch said the deaths resulted from a combination of factors. "In our area we have no obstetricians: we have mostly midwives. And it starts prenatally in the fact that the doctors and the hospitals push welfare patients going to midwives rather than being delivered in the hospitals. So only a very small number of Negro patients are delivered in the hospital. They get a poor start to begin with, and there is a tremendous nutritional problem. There is a lot of hunger and a lot of absolute caloric deficiency. Then there is a real problem with different kinds of deficiencies—proteins and vitamins and so on."

He said he was aware that "big" institutional doctors never see the kinds of cases he deals with. "These patients don't get to large medical centers. They die before they get there."

Health, he added, is not an isolated condition. "It's a sanitation problem ('almost none of these people have outside privies; they have no privies'), it's a food problem, it's a treatment problem. And without a massive education program and a coordinated effort you are just putting money down the drain." The whole complex "is such a monumental problem," he said, that if the health authorities "really faced it squarely they wouldn't have the time or the money to deal with anything else."

Because the victims are indigent Negroes, in large part illiterate and in many cases illegitimate, "this isn't on anybody's priority list," he said.

The board, which had invited Gatch to testify, thanked him and he went back to his practice in Bluffton and at the county seat in Beaufort

(pop. 6,298), where he opened a second office about a year ago. He discovered immediately that he had become the most unpopular man in Beaufort County. This time his parasites and starving children had appeared not in the pages of a little-read technical journal but in the Yankee papers, on Yankee network television and even in the Communist press—which in South Carolina is part of the same parcel. In customary Southern tradition, white Beaufort closed ranks.

The opening salvo, fired by Dr. H. Parker Jones, Beaufort County Health Officer, all but branded Gatch a liar. "I have been in public health for more than fifteen years," Jones said, "and I have never seen a case of starvation or extreme malnutrition." No death recorded in the county for the preceding year, he declared, could be attributed to either malnutrition or intestinal parasites.

The second round was joined by every other member of the medical fraternity of Beaufort County. In a statement issued by Dr. Richard G. Price, chief of staff of the Beaufort County Memorial Hospital, the fourteen physicians said the "rare cases of infant malnutrition" they encountered were invariably the result of "parental inexperience, indifference or gross neglect."

The unflappable Gatch, refusing to lose his aplomb, clucked privately, "Whose indifference? Whose neglect?"

His colleagues also accused the ingrate Gatch of maligning "one of the best-organized and most closely supervised midwife programs in the entire U.S.A."

"Hell," snorted Gatch, "there's no such thing as a good midwife program. What's good about going into a dirty shanty and delivering a baby on newspapers spread out on the floor? That's medicine?"

"In summary," the opposition said, "an objective analysis of the various allegations made reveals no factual substantiation."

There had, in fact, been no attempt to check with Gatch on the authenticity of his findings, and the establishment *Gazette*, joining in the cry for Gatch's goat, did not demand an inquiry of any kind. Instead it mourned editorially that the country doctor had done the county "a great disservice" in Columbia and had made poor "public relations" for Beaufort. "What goes with Dr. Gatch?" the newspaper asked.

What was going with Gatch right at that moment, in late November, was a series of abusive (and anonymous) telephone calls, public ridicule and the contempt of his fellow physicians. The establishment went too far, however, when at a hospital staff meeting there was a hissed demand for Gatch's resignation.

Overnight the beleagured physician won a ground swell of excited support from a Negro community which for years had been relatively unmilitant. The assault on their favorite medical counselor gave the Negroes a uniting cause, and their energy crystalized in the formation of a "new breed" Grassroots Rehabilitation Involvement Program (G.R.I.P.). To a demand that Gatch be retained on Beaufort County Memorial Hospital's staff they added a long list of grievances involving employment, health, education and welfare. The package was handed to the powers of Beaufort in early December, and in a display of muscle G.R.I.P. threw an economic

boycott on the city. Negroes were urged to do their Christmas buying in one store away from the center of town or if possible to do it outside the county seat. Participation was not total, but it was effective enough to scare the power structure. Talks were initiated, and the direct heat was taken off the offending physician.

The whole thing had taken a turn which Donald Gatch had never envisioned when he embarked on his war on worms. Chance had brought him to South Carolina, and chance had caught him up in a medical whirlwind which touched on nearly every area of the much larger civil-rights rebellion sweeping the nation. Gatch does not consider himself a racial activist. "I'm a doctor," he said. "My sole interest is in human life." At thirty-eight he is a slight (five-foot seven), mild man with an unruly thatch of brown hair and red-mottled skin which often shows the signs of razor abrasion. In caricature, his face would be drawn as a fox. He is seldom rattled and is given rarely to anger. But passion rings in his voice when he speaks of medical mission.

He almost missed the medical profession. A native of McGrew, Nebraska (in his day a settlement just about half the size of Bluffton), he spent his youth on a small ranch. "It was really a farm. My folks bought the place in 1929, and they had a hard time during the Depression. I know what poverty is." As the family's situation improved, however, he was able to attend Nebraska Wesleyan University at Lincoln, and he seriously considered a career as a professor of philosophy. During a "completely undistinguished" hitch as an Army private at Ford Ord, California, however, his ambition changed, and after his discharge he got his degree and went on to medical school at the University of Nebraska. He chose an internship at the Memorial Hospital in Savannah, Georgia, for two reasons: "For one thing, I had never been South, and I wanted to see that part of the country. And for another, the financial arrangements at Savannah were the best I was offered." His establishment of a practice at Bluffton, equidistant from Savannah and Beaufort, was a natural outgrowth of several pleasant years at the Georgia line. "I looked around for a small town without a doctor, where the pace would be fairly slow and easy." Bluffton seemed the ideal answer: "I thought I could lead a nice life there."

At the start he made a serious error—by Southern standards. Without inbred prejudice, he is color-blind as a doctor, and on the day he set up shop he had a single waiting room with a partition, but without segregation for blacks and whites. "It never occurred to me to segregate the sick," he said. "The white folks around here never forgot it. The Negroes didn't, either." By professional, get-ahead, make-a-million standards he also had made another error: he deliberately chose a poverty pocket which could not sustain a rich practice. "My first year in Bluffton I grossed maybe $3,000. In the ten years the bad debts have climbed to $150,000. It's there on the books. Just a figure. Meaningless. Lots of doctors could tell the same story. Some of these people can't pay. They never will. So what do you do? Refuse them treatment?" Last year, after the opening of his second office in Beaufort (also with a single waiting room), his billings for the twelve months would have run to "about $100,000, and I could have expected to collect around $75,000. But that was before the white patients started boycotting *me*." The sum appears handsome, but it does not represent net income. From it must be taken the salaries of his staff of five, rental for the two offices and payments on his equipment.

All of Gatch's expenses must be met out of income. "For some reason," he said, tongue large in his cheek, "the banks around here won't lend me money. Bad risk, I guess."

Although Gatch now lives in Beaufort ("I needed to be closer to the hospital"), the Bluffton practice remains his pride. During office hours there are more cars parked under the trees around the converted ranch house than anywhere else in town. The former dwelling is as well equipped as many a more ambitious clinic. It has a modern X-ray room, a spirometer for lung studies, ultrasound devices for treating muscle strain, a positive-pressure machine, an electrocardiograph installation and a full-time medical technician with all the resources necessary for performing the standard tests in blood chemistry and urinalysis. The equipment alone represents an investment of $25,000. "I'll always be in debt for this stuff," Gatch said. He also has in his office the only complete drug supply for miles around. Bluffton has no pharmacy, and when Gatch prescribes, the prescription comes out of his drug chest, whether the patient has the money or not. "With that kind of arrangement," Gatch said, "the drug cupboard operates at a continuing loss. But these people need medicine: if they have no money for drugs, they have no money for transportation; this is the only place they can go. So do you deny them medicine because they can't pay for it?" He shrugged.

Talk of money reminded him of one of his favorite theses: "You can make money in medicine. All you have to do is set up a production line. Charge $3 a call, including drugs. Run them through. But that's veterinary stuff, that's not practicing medicine! If you're going to do an honest job in a place like this you've got to have good equipment."

Occasionally Gatch packs his office in a bag and travels the sixty miles to a Georgia settlement known as Tiger Ridge, where he calls on about two hundred whites scattered through the hills. They are a withdrawn, suspicious people, so deeply inbred that some of the children have one blue eye and one brown. Boys start chewing tobacco at five. "Man. I'd like to do a clinical study there," Gatch said. "No telling what kind of strange bugs we'd find."

The Bluffton practice yielded one permanent, unexpected dividend. Rich Yankees have taken over the old plantations in the area as summer retreats, and Gatch occasionally is called in, sometimes professionally, sometimes socially. Three seasons ago, at the plantation home of Lady Jean Campbell, one of Norman Mailer's former wives, Gatch met a British girl who was in the United States on a brief vacation. A whirlwind, three-week romance was climaxed by marriage, and the unlikeliest resident of Beaufort County—and one of the most uncomplaining—is twenty-one-year-old Anita Gatch. A dark-maned beauty with classic Mediterranean features, she has a placid face which bears traces of her Polish, Russian, Italian and Spanish ancestry. Mrs.

Gatch, a devotee of pop and psychedelic art, with years of training for the stage in ballet and piano behind her, is adroit at giving unsettling answers.

Asked how she has adjusted to Beaufort after a life in London, she said, "Is it so important where one lives? Don is here. I paint. My children [Rex, two, and Eric, one] keep me busy. We went to England last year, and I was glad to get back here. I had never noticed the contrast before, the Americans are—more open. They are easier."

Anita runs a tidy household, filled with good books, records by the stack and in which pictures beam their comfort from the walls. It is a pleasant retreat Gatch needs, because his working hours take him into almost unimaginable depths of squalor.

On a day after a rare January freeze he stopped on a dismal lane near Bluffton and pointed to a backlot shanty shivering in the wind. "Woman lives there with five children," he said. "All illegitimate. All got worms." He walked through the field to the shack. Two boys, three or four years old, sat listlessly on the decaying log step. He patted them on the head and a spindle-legged woman came to the open door. Behind her, wood burned in a rusting, thin-gauge stove that was used for both heating and cooking. Gatch pointed to her legs, so bent that she was pygmied. "Rickets," he said. He turned to the woman and asked, "What'd you give these kids for breakfast?"

"I give 'em grits."

"What you gonna give 'em for lunch?"

"I doan know."

"For supper?"

"I doan know."

"You got anything to eat in the house?"

"No, suh."

In an alcove a month-old baby lay under a tattered blanket on a broken bed. The walls were papered with the sports section of the Savannah *Morning News*, and torn cardboard sagged over the broken panes of the only window. The baby pulled at a soiled bottle filled with blue milk. "Where'd that milk come from?" Gatch asked.

"Dat baby's daddy, he take care a him."

"Who takes care of the others?"

"Doan nobody."

"You get any welfare?"

"No, suh."

Gatch turned to leave. "Dammit, dammit, dammit," he said. "You see, they are punishing illegitimacy. This woman has illegitimate children, so she is denied help. You see who they're punishing? Those boys." He stopped over one of the children and pulled up a torn shirt to expose a bloated belly. "That's worms," he said. "These boys ever pass worms?"

The woman nodded dejectedly. "Dey did when you give 'em dat medicine."

"You got a privy?"

"No."

"Where you go?"

"Nex' doah."

"All the time?"

"No."

"You go to the woods, don't you?"

The woman nodded.

Gatch started back to the car. "That's one of the problems," he said. "Sanitation. To get the worms is easy, but the kids get reinfected immediately. It takes two years, with treatment every three months. That way the eggs die in the soil. People say to me, 'Your patients got worms? Why don't you treat them?' Well, I'm one man. What we need in here is a whole task force, with time and equipment and money. And people say, 'Worms? What's so bad about that? Everybody has worms, one time or another.' Sure they do. Treated, worms are no problem. White kids, kids in families with just a little money, get treatment. The kids I'm talking about don't get treated. Or the adults. And nobody knows how many there are, and nobody's trying to find out."

He got in the car and started the motor. His horn-rimmed glasses had slipped down on his nose, and he reached to straighten them. The earpiece was gone. "I got to get over to Savannah some day and get that fixed," he said. "Let me tell you about that woman there. One Monday she brought her nine-year-old daughter to my office. Same legs like that. A dwarf. The kid's appendix had been ruptured for two days. We took her over to Beaufort Memorial, and when we were doing the appendectomy we found some roundworms. The surgeon said, 'Of course, in these colored children the closer we get to the ilium in the stomach the more worms we'll find, because these kids don't have much to eat.' And that's where they head. *The worms get the food before the kids do.*"

On the way to another stop Gatch told about a woman who had brought her baby to his office with symptoms of asthma. "It *was* a kind of asthma, an allergy. It was caused by worms migrating through the lungs. When the worms were eliminated the asthma cleared up. It's related to all kinds of things: pneumonia, anemia. I get kids in my office with a hemoglobin count of six to eight. Normal's twelve to sixteen. Most places you'd put a kid like that in the hospital. I just give 'em some iron. I haven't lost one of 'em yet."

Asked whether he had ever attempted to get a foundation grant for research, Gatch replied, "I've tried them all. National institutes of health. Big foundations. Most of them think giving money to a small country doctor is throwing it away. They either want to work it through a university, or they want you to be in Africa. If I were in Africa, I could get plenty of money. But this isn't Africa."

He stopped the car again in front of a shack which had broken in the middle. The center was resting on the ground. Over the window crude wooden shutters had been nailed to keep out the cold. An old woman answered Gatch's knock and set the door aside. It had not known hinges for a long time. Inside, the house was dark. Light of any kind was too expensive. Except daylight, which was too cold. The floor on both sides of the house rolled uphill on an angle, and in the close air there was a sickening smell of urine and feces. In one dark room an old woman lay bedridden, completely crippled by arthritis.

"How are you?" Gatch asked.

"Can't complain," she groaned.

"What'd you have for breakfast?"

"Liddle bit a grits 'n' peas."

"What you gonna have for lunch?"

"Grits 'n' peas."

"You get welfare?"

"Yes, suh!"

"How much?"

"I doan know."

"She really doesn't know," Gatch explained. "Somebody else has to cash her check for her. That's another one of the problems down here. Illiteracy. People don't know how to get help, whether they're entitled to it, how to apply for it. If we could just start something for the bottom one percent." Beaufort County has a population approaching 58,000, of which around 22,000 are Negroes. At most, Gatch thus is projecting a total rehabilitation program which would involve no more than six hundred people. "Just for a change, let's start at the bottom and work up," he said. "If we could start something here, some pilot endeavor, we might by extension assist the entire South. And not just the South. These are not isolated conditions. In some degree, they exist all over the country."

The old arthritic woman turned his thoughts to drugs. "We're doing ourselves a great disservice in this country in our attitude toward some of the psychedelic drugs. LSD. Marijuana. I'm not talking about kicks, now. I mean ethical medicine. No telling what we might be able to accomplish in psychiatry or cancer with some of these things. Even aphrodisiacs are important medically. There's one drug—it's psychedelic—which can be bought for about a dollar a gallon. It's a great pain-killer, and it's ingested through the skin. With a gallon of that stuff that old woman back there could swab herself every day. She'd be a lot more comfortable and a lot happier. But it would be against the law for her to have it. The medicine she can have costs her $15 a month, and she can't afford it. That's crazy."

At another stop at a rotting, drafty

hovel like so many others around Bluffton, a teen-aged girl had stayed home from school to care for eight younger brothers and sisters. "Some of these kids should be in school," Gatch said, "but they don't have proper clothing. At night they pile four or five of 'em in a bed. Or sleep them on the floor." He stamped on the floor, and the dust flew.

"Where's your mother?" Gatch asked the girl.

"She at wuk."

"Where she work?"

"At the factory."

Gatch explained. "The woman is an oyster shucker. In a good week, in season, she'll make $15. Not much to take care of all these kids."

Asked how the family would survive, the doctor said, "Some of these kids won't. They'll die. Of pneumonia. Something like that. If they had decent food and decent shelter they wouldn't get pneumonia. And that's what I mean when I say people down here are starving to death. Only the hardiest survive. The statistics call me a liar. 'Not a single case of starvation.' I call the statistics a liar."

He spoke to the girl again. "You got an inside bathroom?"

"No."

"A privy?"

"No."

"Running water?"

"No."

"Electricity?"

"No."

Gatch spoke another aside. "They don't all have two cars and a television set, but that's the popular belief."

On one such excursion through the wormlands, Gatch picked up an unexpected convert. Wilton Graves, a fifty-two-year-old Hilton Head Island motel operator who has represented Beaufort County in the State Legislature for fourteen years, was one of the few members of the power structure willing to be shown. A tough businessman who came up through the ranks of poverty himself, Graves was a skeptic. But he had one priceless asset: an open mind. After a trip through the Gatch nightmare, he was visibly shaken.

"I thought I knew what poverty was," he said, "but I never saw anything like this. I honestly did not know conditions like these existed in Beaufort County."

Graves asked school officials to develop information on the bedrock poor. Mrs. Vallie Connor, who works with the federal school-aid program, came up with some shocking findings. She talked to principals whose food resources were so meager that they could provide free lunches only on alternate days. On one day half the hungry ate; the next day the other half had their turn.

Further evidence of hunger was supplied by John Gadson, a bright young Negro educator who testified that on many occasions he had had to take Negro high-school students home because their stomachs ached from lack of food. (The Negro school dropout rate is eighty percent.)

Graves persuaded Senator James M. Waddell Jr., and Representative W. Brantley Harvey Jr., the other members of the Beaufort legislative delegation, to provide the leadership needed for a study of county poverty. "There are no votes in this," Graves said, "but somebody has to take a stand."

"Well, I've been in the Legislature long enough," Waddell said.

Graves's team then offered to do what no white authority in Beaufort County had yet dared to undertake:

to meet with the leaders of G.R.I.P., the Negro organization, and to look at anything the Negroes wanted to show.

The tour, although covering a wider area than Gatch's beat, confirmed his allegations. An old woman on Wassau Island lived in a hut, without income of any kind. She knew nothing of welfare or Social Security benefits. In the Burton section a family of eight subsisted on $44 a month; in a tumbling shack nearby a family of fifteen fought a constant battle with starvation. In the Dale community there were fifteen children in one house, representing several generations; the family's total income: $40 a week.

After the inspection, Senator Waddell said publicly that "there is no doubt that there are cases of dire poverty, bad housing, lack of proper sanitary facilities and good water supplies in the county." Gatch had broken through the wall of complacency, because no other official agency in Beaufort County had been willing to go quite that far.

In a concurrent development, the Penn Community Services, a highly respected century-old private social agency at Frogmore, near Beaufort, presented to the County Health Department a parasite study which substantially confirmed Gatch's assertions regarding infection. With the help of Lieutenant Mack Bonner, a Marine Corps doctor at Parris Island, Penn ran stool tests on fifty-five preschool children in Big Estate and Pritchardville, at opposite ends of Beaufort County. Of the children tested, thirty, or 54.5 percent, showed "a high intensity" of roundworm and whipworms.

Penn said that because its study was conducted in haste, it had found no conclusive evidence of gross malnutrition, but in a warning note it set words to Gatch's ten-year-old refrain:

"The seriousness of worm infection," Penn said, "is not always realized. Members of the County Board of Health without medical training should understand what takes place in the process of becoming infected with worms. The eggs are taken into the body through the mouth. They go to the stomach, where they enter the circulatory system as if they were food. Eventually the eggs end up in the lungs, where they are incubated. While these eggs are developing in the lungs there is a danger of pneumonia. As the developing worms grow, they cause irritation and are usually coughed up and are then swallowed to return to the stomach. There they grow and thrive on the food which would otherwise be used by the body. This causes nutritional problems, loss of weight, listlessness and even bowel restriction. If left to thrive in a person's body, worms can cause death."

The Penn report, which placed highest priority on eradication of parasite infection, did not receive enthusiastic endorsement at the Health Department. On the day it was issued, the department asserted stubbornly that "illegitimacy and poor housing are our greatest health problems." Without question, they are serious problems in Beaufort, and neither Gatch nor G.R.I.P. denies it. In January the Health Department had sixteen Negro mothers under prenatal care. Of the sixteen, ten were unwed. One of the married mothers was having her fifteenth child; the concept of birth control is almost impossible to spread, because illiteracy (forty-six percent of Beaufort's Negroes over 25 are "functionally illiterate") and superstition combine to prevent its acceptance. The uneducated poor suspect that birth-control pills cause cancer, and that intrauterine rings are dangerous.

It is hinted that Gatch opposes birth control. "It's a damned lie," he retorted. "I was the first doctor in Beaufort County to insert intrauterine rings, and some of my colleagues removed them under the mistaken supposition that the rings cause changes that might lead to cancer."

Although the case for Gatch is building up, the effort to destroy him not only as a doctor but also as a man persists. When his charges began to appear supportable, a cruelly scurrilous whisper campaign began. It was suggested behind the hand that Gatch was a moral degenerate who has no right to speak for ethical medicine. The smirking reference is to an incident of three years ago when Dr. Gatch was arrested and lodged in jail on a charge of sodomy. It made a big splash in the Beaufort area papers. It made no splash at all, however, when Gatch insisted on a speedy trial and when the complaining witness, a teen-aged boy, could give no coherent evidence on the witness stand. The charge against Gatch was thrown out of court, and the doctor has in his possession an affidavit from the complainant admitting that the charge was fabricated.

The real case against Gatch is that he is a loner who speaks his mind.

He does not radiate the accepted image of the doctor. To the company of his colleagues he prefers the company of Savannah nonprofessionals, and in Beaufort his social life has been constricted to a circle of Negro friends. That relationship, however, has given him a keen insight into black thought and, as a philosophical question, race relations concern him.

"The white people here—and for that matter all over the country—do not realize how deeply resentful the Negroes are. The young ones leave home and go North. They may prosper, but they can't forget how underprivileged and oppressed their people back home are. Their resentment is expressed in contempt for all whites, and there is enough of that resentment to breed revolution. The whites just don't understand that."

Over a beer one evening when the strain in Beaufort was at its worst, Gatch tried to summarize what his thirty-eight years had taught him. When the words came he spoke not as a man of medicine but as a student of philosophy, for what he said concerned eternal verity. "I used to think truth was like a flash of lightning. You couldn't mistake it." He took a sip of beer and packed his pipe with his favorite tobacco, H. Sutliff's Mixture No. 79. "I don't believe that anymore. Truth is like a hippopotamus. You've got to keep prodding it, or it won't move."

Gatch is still prodding the hippopotamus. And he won't shut up.

Let Them Eat Promises

NICK KOTZ

When Dr. King planned the Poor People's Campaign, he stated its objectives only in the broadest terms— massive new programs for jobs and housing, and a guaranteed annual income. When his successor as head of the Southern Christian Leadership Conference, the Reverend Ralph David Abernathy, arrived in Washington on April 28 with an advance delegation of 100 poor people, he had few specific objectives in mind. On this preliminary visit, Abernathy, planned only "to present the leadership of this country with a moral manifesto that talks in terms of needs" —needs for jobs, housing, income, land, food, and self-determination. In his view, details of the program would follow naturally, suggested by the dynamics of the protest movement as it developed. This had been the pattern of several of Dr. King's successful campaigns in the South.

A number of campaign aides, however, tried to convince Abernathy that he must be considerably more specific when he began to visit various government departments the next morning. Washington simply does not react, they said, to broad moral manifestoes. If the poor people were to function effectively as Washington lobbyists, they must have definite pro-

Reprinted from *Let Them Eat Promises: The Politics of Hunger in America*. Englewood Cliffs: Prentice-Hall, © 1969 by Nick Kotz. pp. 154–61, 164–91.

grams for both legislative and executive action. For specifics, Abernathy then turned to Marian Wright, who had inspired Kennedy and Clark in Mississippi a year earlier and who now served as the Poor People's Campaign chief liaison officer with the government. Assisted by Kennedy aide Peter Edelman, Poverty Subcommittee Counsel Bill Smith, and black officials in the Johnson Administration, Miss Wright drew up a practical program to fulfill the high promises of new social legislation. Aside from a call for major new housing and job programs, the emphasis was on reform of existing programs and institutions. It was a radical program, but only in the sense that it called on cynical Washington to practice fully the spirit and intent of laws already on the books.

The Justice Department was asked to begin enforcing civil rights laws which had been passed in dramatic, filibuster-breaking debate, and then given only minimal enforcement attention. The Department of Health, Education, and Welfare was told to reform its welfare program rules, so that they provided elementary justice to welfare recipients. The Office of Economic Opportunity was asked to make "maximum feasible participation of the poor" in its programs a reality rather than a motto. When the Poor People's issues list turned to the Agriculture Department, Miss

Wright applied her special knowledge and interest in food programs. The Poor People's Campaign demanded that the Agriculture Department carry out the reforms recommended the previous week by the Citizens' Board of Inquiry and the Committee on School Lunch Participation: free and reduced-price food stamps, more and better commodities, free lunches for the nation's poor children, emergency action in the Board of Inquiry's "256 hunger counties," and fulfillment of the Administration's 1967 pledge to place a food program in each of the nation's 1,000 poorest counties.

The next morning, April 29, 1968, with neatly typed proposals in hand, Reverend Abernathy launched the Poor People's Campaign in Washington.

As the 100-member delegation made its way about the capital, Washington's sedate business-suit-and-briefcase world raised its eyebrows. Perhaps official Washington was startled because it had expected to greet another well-organized delegation of businessmen, farmers, or doctors—each delegate wearing a neat identification tag and conscientiously carrying out his assignment to knock at the door of his congressman. Instead the capital found itself confronted by a noisy, emotional group of people whose principal common bond was a shared experience of misery.

Wherever it went, the group was disorganized and late. This in itself was enough to cause shock waves—who ever heard of poor supplicants keeping a busy Cabinet officer waiting for two hours? There was a tendency for everyone to talk at once, and there was confusion about where the next appointment would be. But there was also—if Washington could find the sensitivity to filter out the unaccustomed distractions—an intense, honest presentation of critical human issues which no $100,000-a-year corporate lobbyist-lawyer could have framed as effectively.

Abernathy met with both Republican and Democratic congressional leaders who affirmed his right to petition the Congress for redress of grievances. He assured them his demonstration would be peaceful. It was all very polite. And, as he left each Cabinet office, Abernathy spelled out the timetable for the campaign. The government would be given *ten days* to study the demands of the Poor People's Campaign. "At the end of that time," Abernathy said, "we will be back—not with 150 as today but 3,000 to 5,000 strong and we will demand answers. We are going to back up our words with the most militant, nonviolent direct action in this country's history."

As best he could, President Johnson was preparing for an extremely delicate task. While he bargained with arch-conservatives in Congress over billions of dollars in spending cuts as the price of a tax bill, he also was searching for positive responses to defuse the potentially incendiary Poor People's Campaign; the thousands of poor people were pouring into Washington, less than three weeks after the worst of the King assassination riots.

From his White House office, Joe Califano dialed the Secretary of Agriculture. "The President wants you to work up two sets of responses to the Poor People's Campaign," Califano told Orville Freeman. "He wants a list of things we can do *without* congressional action, and another list of the responses which will require legislation. This whole thing is absolutely top secret. I want to emphasize that. We've got to maintain the highest security."

The plan was so secret that Califano, unwilling to risk memos that might be seen by many eyes, delivered the President's instruction verbally to each member of the Cabinet.

At an April 30 Cabinet meeting, the President emphasized the need for speed in developing answers to Abernathy. Careful timing was needed, the President said, in order to coordinate the intricate tax maneuverings in Congress with the effort to satisfy the poor people, so that solving one problem did not adversely affect the other. To expedite and coordinate the operation, Califano assigned a White House staff member to work with each department of government.

DeVier Pierson, a young Oklahoman, drew the Agriculture Department assignment. Moving swiftly, Pierson called a White House meeting on May 2 to discuss responses to Abernathy's demands for better food programs. At last, the Agriculture Department appeared eager for reform. Moreover, Pierson found an influential White House enthusiast in Presidential assistant Charles Murphy, a longtime friend of the President and an old hand Washingtonian whose career had included service both as Undersecretary of Agriculture and as a lawyer-lobbyist. He had the special experience to know that Abernathy's charges against the Agriculture Department were well founded.

Murphy's plan called for immediate spending of $170 million to improve the commodity and food stamp programs and to provide more free school meals for poor youngsters. Furthermore, he proposed a $25 billion program to guarantee "that by 1970 or 1971 every American will be given a reasonable opportunity to avoid hunger or malnutrition which affects him through no fault of his own." A $2 billion food stamp program would be operated like a negative income tax, with stamps to be distributed by the Internal Revenue Service. Stamps would cost less and the poor would receive more of them.

The Murphy proposal brought immediate and eager support from Agriculture Secretary Freeman, who for more than a year had taken the brunt of food program criticism.

At the next White House meeting on May 6, Agriculture Undersecretary John Schnittker was given two days to work up final details on a legislative package which, it was expected, the President then would deliver to legislative leaders. The proposal called for spending $100 million of Section 32 funds to add more nutritious foods to the commodity program, and also requested an additional $200 million from Congress to begin expansion and reform of the food stamp program.

As the massive march on Washington approached, enthusiastic officials at both the Agriculture Department and in those White House offices closest to the President expected a "go" signal from Lyndon Johnson at any moment. The green light never came on, and one reason was clearly stated when the President sent Charlie Murphy's proposal back to him.

"That's something to consider," the President said, "but *nothing* must be permitted to interrupt the negotiations with Congress to get that tax bill!" The President turned down the proposal on the grounds it would endanger his maneuvers to win the needed $10 billion of new revenue.

As the Agriculture Department and the White House staff hurriedly worked up food reform programs and pushed them toward the President's desk, Lyndon Johnson was undergoing the single most trying period of his year-long effort to pass the tax bill. At a secret White House meeting on April 30 (the same day he urged his Cabinet to plan responses for Abernathy), the President thought he had reached a compromise with Ways and Means Chairman Mills and Appropriations Chairman Mahon for a 10 percent surcharge tax increase, purchased from them with promises for a $4 billion spending cut in 1969, a $10 billion reduction in obligational authority, and an $8 billion reduction of spending authorized in earlier years but not yet spent. But within 48 hours Arkansas conservative Mills denied he had agreed to a deal. Angered by Mills in particular and Congress in general, the President publicly accused the Congress of virtual blackmail on the tax issue as he delivered an angry, 1,200-word off-the-cuff response at a press conference. By May 8, when he received the food aid proposal from Schnittker, the tax bill was back on track again with Mills, but problems were coming from a different direction. House and Senate conferees had approved the tax package provisional to a $6 billion spending cut. Liberals were infuriated and Johnson was worried that deep cuts in basic Great Society legislation would be required.

A food aid law might be desperately needed by the hungry poor, but Lyndon Johnson was concerned at that point only with the mentality of men who could defeat a tax bill—

men like Congressman O. C. Fisher, of Texas, who said of the approaching Poor People's Campaign, "The invading hordes headed this way will leave crime, immorality, bloodshed, arson, and looting in their wake." The Poor People were being reviled daily on the House and Senate floors, the House Public Works Committee voted to keep the campaigners from camping on government property, and Senator John McClellan of Arkansas warned the White House about possible subversive motives.

Publicly, the President tried to maintain equilibrium and hold the middle ground. "We do expect the poor will be better served after that viewpoint is presented," he said, "though every person in the Capital should be aware of the possibilities of serious consequences, flowing from assemblage of large numbers over any protracted period of time in the seat of government where there is much work to be done and very little time to do it."

Poor people from all over America marched to camp in the plywood tents in the center of Washington and to tell their stories to the nation—a thousand stories that the country needed desperately to hear and learn from. But they came at the wrong time, they did the wrong things, and the country was not listening. Washington was enveloped in chaos.

It rained in Washington from the middle of May until the middle of June, almost one solid month of downpour in the muggy, soggy heat —an agonizing combination to the 3,200 poor people camping on the parkland between the Washington Monument and the Lincoln Memorial. It turned Resurrection City into a stinking quagmire of deep, oozing mud. The mud, always an intimate part of the lives of the rural poor, became important here because the story of the Poor People's Campaign was measured in inches of muck.

After the first few days, most of the Washington reporters stopped writing about the people and why they were there, and concentrated on the mud and the bad tempers of the poor people who were trying to live in it.

In the orderly process of government, success of an issue often depends on the skill of its advocates in understanding who holds the key to power on that issue, and how to approach that person in a friendly or persuasive manner. Despite liaison groups organized by sympathetic congressmen, the most powerful committees of Congress were not friendly and were not persuaded. Robert Kennedy, the hunger issue's most popular advocate, was far away, campaigning for the Presidency in the Middle and Far West, and what he had to say about the forgotten poor most often was lost as the press concentrated on the frantic power battle for the Democratic nomination.

The unfriendly Congress evidently gave little thought to the fact that if the poor people had the means to do things the "right way"—to hire a full-time lobbyist to touch the vital pressure points, to provide position papers, inserts for the Congressional Record, steaks and wine for the congressmen —they wouldn't be poor. They were lobbying in the only way they knew how. In the *New Yorker* magazine, Calvin Trillin accurately characterized the overall political and press performance:

"The poor in Resurrection City have come to Washington to show that the poor in America are sick, dirty, disorganized, and powerless— and they are criticized daily for being sick, dirty, disorganized and powerless."

Despite the squabbles, the disorder, the sermonizing, and the fact that the specific needs and desires of the Negro poor, the Mexican-American poor, and the Indian poor do not necessarily coincide, the various factions were locked into agreement on one issue: Poor people need food, and the food programs do not work.

Reverend Abernathy began to aim his campaign directly at the Department of Agriculture, ordering a round-the-clock demonstration for the sprawling, ugly building that houses the vast bureaucracy, and attempting, time after time, to voice his demands to Freeman.

Finally, Orville Freeman and Ralph David Abernathy faced each other in a sweltering Department of Agriculture conference room, packed with every rain-soaked poor people's campaigner and reporter who could manage to squeeze through the door. Both men mopped at their sweaty faces—Freeman with a white handkerchief, Abernathy with a bright red bandana. Outside, the continuing rain poured in sheets against the windows and added further gloom to an already dismal afternoon.

Abernathy had come to get answers to his demands for improved food programs, and even though two weeks had passed since his "10 days" were up, it was still too soon for Orville Freeman. Both men wanted desperately for this late May meeting to be a success, yet both knew that it would not be. Freeman had sent his written response the previous evening, and they were now going through the ritual tumultuous public discussion which had become a hallmark of the campaign.

For three weeks, Freeman had waited for a White House answer to the proposed food package, and no answer had come from a President who was as preoccupied with war, inflation, and taxes as he was infuriated at the poor people's street drama.

Annoyed by a bombardment of liberal criticism, which now included the hard-hitting CBS news documentary on hunger (shown May 21), Secretary Freeman wanted to get off the spot but could not move. Finally, he decided on two actions— expanding the limited commodity distribution program by adding fruit juices, scrambled egg mix, canned milk, instant mashed potatoes, canned chicken, and instant hot cereal; and providing food supplements for babies and nursing and expectant mothers. Fearing that President Johnson would veto even this action, the Secretary got *implicit* agreement from White House assistant Joe Califano and Budget Director Zwick, and then went ahead with the $100 million program.

Freeman knew this spare response would not satisfy the demands of the poor, for he belatedly had come to realize that the basic malfunction of the food program was stamps, which cost too much money and provided too little food. He knew also that even beginning this kind of reform would cost at least several hundred million dollars, and that a full reform would cost more than a billion. But above all, he knew that Lyndon Johnson did not seem prepared to spend anything.

In the steamy, crowded conference room, the Secretary of Agriculture was plainly uncomfortable. As questions came popping from every corner, Freeman tried to tell the poor people they might be visiting the wrong man. "I've done about all I can do," he said. "I'm human enough; you might be advised to spend some time with my colleagues."

"Are you telling people they are just waiting, wasting their time?" he was asked.

"I'm next door," he replied. "I'm convenient."

Pressed about the food stamp formula and expansion of the program, the Secretary came closest to telling what he wanted to say, but could not: "The President has this and other matters under consideration." Like most of Washington, Orville Freeman was not attuned to the issue of moral imperative that was being raised by the poor people, but on the other hand, he was misunderstood by them. They saw only his stubborn defense of past progress, and did not know that he secretly was trying to make a political adjustment to their needs. As troubled and pressured as Orville Freeman felt, he could not end the meeting, which droned on and on with a decreasing semblance of order. Ralph David Abernathy also suffered, for he could see by now that—barring some kind of miracle—the tactics of nonviolent militant protest would produce no poverty victories in Washington. The southern minister fell silent, his head bowed, as the poor people screamed at Freeman. Miss Wright and Jesse Jackson, who were better informed on the issue than Abernathy was, continued their futile debate—futile because Freeman was powerless to act, and because the campaign itself did not contain the dynamics for success in Washington.

As he sat slumped in a wooden chair in the Agriculture Department, Abernathy reflected how different had been the results in Selma and Birmingham, where the civil rights movement was bloodied and brutalized, but produced great legislative victories. He was now using the same confrontation tactics that just three years before had brought waves of sympathy from the North, but this time he sought to evoke the national conscience about national conditions which result in poverty all across America—not merely about decaying southern social and political structures. He was calling on the nation to reorder its economic priorities, and no brutal southern sheriff was going to get the job done for him.

Abernathy had just realized that when a Negro was bloodied by dogs in Birmingham for the right to sit in a restaurant, the white northerner was a sympathetic ally. When the same Negro, who never had been able to afford that hard-won southern right, tried to dramatize his hunger in Washington, the same white northerner disapproved. It was easy enough to blame a southerner for barring his restaurant door, and it cost nothing to suggest remedies; but who was the northern white man to blame for nationwide hunger, except himself, and who would have to pay for its cure?

In the early evening, the inconclusive meeting came to an end. It was the last time Freeman and Abernathy would meet during the campaign. Little of this drama was reported except what the shortsighted press was able to make out of mud, misery, and squabbling. The public tired of hearing about the noisy shouting matches. They were being asked to think why some citizens were hungry, dirty, ill-fed, and ill-housed, and to look at them in all their poorness walking through the nation's capital.

Public annoyance at these confrontation tactics was now reflected in the Harris poll, which showed 61 percent of white America disapproving of the campaign. And if the Poor People's Campaign did not stir the nation's conscience at the beginning it certainly was doomed after the first rock was thrown at the Supreme Court.

During a May 29 demonstration at the Supreme Court building, several rocks crashed through basement windows. It was possible but not proven that the rocks had been thrown by persons from Resurrection City. On the positive side that same day, the Senate produced one of the few legislative victories of the campaign, and a dramatic hearing about human need stirred a Senate committee. Press treatment of these three events tells much about the inability of the Poor People's Campaign to reach the American people.

The rock-throwing incident produced banner headlines in newspapers across the country. The facts were unclear about responsibility for the broken windows as campaign marshals helped restore order, and the turmoil at the court was brief. Few stories devoted more than a sentence to the reason for the protest demonstration—a Court decision upholding Washington state regulations barring Indians from net fishing in their traditional fishing grounds. But the news for the day focused on the visual drama in the Capital, not on the plight of America's first citizens trying desperately to cling to their age-old means of nutrition and survival.

Little or no attention was paid to the hard-won fight across the street at the United States Senate, where Senator Jacob Javits' amendment to release $227 million of Section 32 funds for use to feed the hungry was passed in a breathtaking 31–30 vote.[1]

But the most meaningful event of the day for poor, hungry Americans was virtually a non-event, because most of the nation's press ignored it. Attorney Marian Wright, seeking out individual poor people in Resurrection City, had structured a presentation to reveal every conceivable viewpoint about hunger, and about the operation of governmental food programs. She brought 15 people to the huge hearing room in the basement of the New Senate Office Building, and they all spoke from the heart, with no prepared words, no coaching from advisers.

Many of the most important human facts about the politics of hunger were laid bare at that Senate hearing, but the country was not listening.

On June 6 Senator Robert F. Kennedy was murdered in Los Angeles and the faint flicker of hopeful light went out in Resurrection City. The press descended in mass to test the emotions of the poor at the death of their only white hero. The reporters expected anguished wailing, wondered why it wasn't there, and were resented by the poor for wondering. For the poor, the murder was barely surprising. From their viewpoint, it was almost a certainty now that all the leaders who tried to help them would be murdered. One more good

man was dead, and many of the poor were too drained of emotion even to cry. They would neither perform nor riot—to the relief of Washington officialdom who expected a repeat of the rioting following Dr. King's death. Abernathy quietly led a delegation to the funeral at Arlington cemetery and then they walked back across Memorial Bridge to the mud of Resurrection City, the dream that had become just one more nightmare.

As things went from bad to worse, Abernathy and his lieutenants started looking for a way out. Working desperately to salvage some tangible gain for poor Americans before the encampment was torn down by an angry, harassed government, the campaign's friends tried to achieve at least some meaningful reforms by Solidarity Day, June 19. The "June 'teenth," anniversary of the Emanicipation Proclamation, might stimulate a spark of national conscience, as thousands of Americans from all over the country planned to join the Resurrection City residents in a one-day demonstration of support. Hopefully, Solidarity Day would repeat the successful 1963 March on Washington, when Martin Luther King's impassioned oratory had stirred the nation. Several high Johnson Administration officials shared that hope and they frantically worked to produce a miracle for Solidarity Day.

While 75 demonstrators shouted beneath his second-floor window, "We want food . . . We want freedom . . . We want Freeman!" Agriculture Undersecretary John Schnittker launched a new effort to develop a legislative package for the President. Together with Budget Bureau official Bernard Gladieux, Undersecretary Schnittker (a Robert Kennedy intimate who had

---

[1] The Javits proposal died from inaction in the House of Representatives.

privately sought to help throughout the Poor People's Campaign) designed a new program to provide the poor with more food stamps at less cost. But when Schnittker contacted the White House with the new plan, word came back "Nothing doing while the tax bill is pending!"

Seeking out old friends who had helped before, legislative adviser Marian Wright and the Reverend Jesse Jackson, leader of the Southern Christian Leadership Conference's highly successful Chicago program, met with aides of Vice President Hubert Humphrey. They explained to sympathetic John Stewart and William Welsh that the poor people would end the encampment if the President would only make reforms in the food aid programs. They asked that the reforms be announced on Solidarity Day.

After a briefing by Stewart, Humphrey telephoned President Johnson that night (June 11) to tell him the campaign could be terminated on very reasonable terms. Following up with a memorandum to the President the next day, Humphrey emphasized: "The key is a package dealing with hunger and food. . . . A major breakthrough here—one which could be defended publicly on the sound humanitarian basis of feeding hungry people—would be interpreted by the SCLC leadership as an honorable basis of ending the Campaign." The only other requirements were that the Administration seek repeal of the congressionally imposed welfare freeze, announce support for the concept of a public service employment bill, and support the concept of greater participation by the poor in the planning and implementation of programs affecting them. Humphrey

urged that such a program "could be the device for bringing the Poor People's Campaign to a constructive and honorable end with Resurrection City dismantled by June 23."

"From the Administration's point of view," Humphrey wrote, "the settlement could be cast in a totally affirmative fashion. 'We are acting to see that no American goes to bed hungry; we are acting to insure that every American who wants to work and is able to work has a job.' This posture largely avoids the charge that we were responding to intimidation and undue pressure."

Humphrey concluded that such a settlement "would strengthen the hand of responsible Negro leaders, meet the most urgent needs of hunger and jobs, and add to the Administration's already considerable accomplishments in these areas." Abernathy, attempting to carry out his end of a negotiated settlement, scaled down his demands to match this list. His food program now was identical to the one Johnson's own aides had recommended to the President weeks earlier.

Although Vice President Humphrey offered his services as mediator, and was supported in his plan by Attorney General Ramsey Clark (to whom President Johnson had assigned responsibility for the Poor People's Campaign), it is doubtful that the President ever read Humphrey's message. The memo was stopped en route by White House aide Harry McPherson, who believed that President Johnson would react unfavorably. The President already had been pressured too hard on food aid and on the Poor People's Campaign, he said. Judging from the President's outburst at Orville Freeman the same day as the Humphrey memo, McPherson had correctly sensed Johnson's mood.

Freeman, again acting without Presidential clearance but with the knowledge of White House aide Califano, decided to support 108 liberal congressmen[2] who by this time had asked for an unlimited authorization for the food stamp program. Testifying before the House Agriculture Committee on defense of the food stamp program, Freeman asked for the unlimited authorization. The Secretary reasoned that he would thus satisfy the liberals without actually committing the President to more spending, since an appropriations bill still would be needed to implement an increase in actual food stamp funds. Within seconds after Freeman uttered the word "unlimited," Poage and ranking Republican Page Belcher of Oklahoma snarled that this didn't sound like the same administration that had just promised to cut $6 billion in spending. One Agriculture Committee member promptly telephoned these sentiments to the White House and a furious Lyndon Johnson told Freeman his completely unauthorized statement had endangered the tax bill.

The tax increase was scheduled for a final vote in the House the afternoon following Solidarity Day, and Lyndon Johnson was not about to risk last-minute defeat by unveiling a new spending plan or by giving anything to the unruly demonstrators.

[2] Representative Leonor Sullivan, Agriculture Department officials and traditional Democratic leaders worked up the petition which became part of another trade with southerners, permitting the food stamp expansion in return for an extension of the farm subsidy program.

Despite protests from the District of Columbia Appropriations Subcommittee, the campers' permit was extended for one week, to allow for Solidarity Day, and on June 19, more than a hundred thousand middle-class Americans joined Resurrection City residents and marched from the Capitol to the Lincoln Memorial. The throng stood united in front of Abraham Lincoln's statue, remembering a happier occasion there five years earlier, when Dr. Martin Luther King, Jr., had told of his dream for a better America. This time they received no word of support from the White House.

The next day Congress finally passed the tax increase with its $6 billion dollar spending slash, and Washington police used tear gas to rout 300 demonstrators from an attempted sit-in in the street beside the Department of Agriculture.

Four days later, a thousand heavily armed policemen captured a nearly deserted Resurrection City, while its few hundred remaining inhabitants purposely violated the off-limits grounds of the United States Capitol. They concluded their unsuccessful campaign with their own arrests. Ralph David Abernathy attempted to make one last plea to Freeman, met briefly with his executive assistant, then went to the Capitol to be arrested with his followers.

If the Poor People's Campaign had begun with hopes that the nation's conscience could be aroused, it ended as a disaster, with even its leaders agreeing that the encampment on the Mall had been a mistake. A few substantial reforms in the administration of federal programs had been won, but the poor people had failed to touch the soul of the country, and they knew it. Most of those remaining finished their jail terms and started home, convinced that the nation did not care.

By that time, however, a host of Washington officials *did* care strongly about food program reform. Some had actually been moved by the Poor People's Campaign. Only hours after the tax bill cleared conference, the men who cared started back toward the President with their new proposals. With the tax bill finally out of the way they thought President Johnson would be sure to favor their plans.

Drafted by Agriculture Undersecretary Schnittker, the new hunger program was shaped into a memorandum from Secretary Freeman to President Johnson, beginning: "To meet the highest priority food needs in the next 12 months will require adding $300—400 million to the food program in the 1969 budget. *This will not end hunger in the U.S., but it will make a big down payment on a program to end hunger shortly.*"

Freeman went on to explain that legislative actions to carry out such a program were well along in Congress, but he also offered the President an alternate $145 million program, merely to pay for the commitments Agriculture already had made to the Poor People's Campaign. The main point of the memo, however, was a strong recommendation for a $410 million program reforming the food stamp formula and improving food assistance to poor school children.

Enthusiastic White House aides, including the President's close adviser Charles Murphy, grabbed the memo and escalated Freeman's proposal into a $465-million program for 1969, and a three-year, $2-billion commitment

which would "guarantee every American freedom from starvation and serious malnutrition." Because Murphy, Vice President Humphrey, and others close to him had been urging him to take another look at the food program, President Johnson consented to listen to the proposal, and told Joe Califano to call a meeting.

At 5:30 p.m. on June 28, 1968, Agriculture Secretary Freeman, Budget Director Zwick, and White House assistants Murphy, Califano, Pierson, and James Gaither filed into the President's oval office, confident that Johnson would now act positively on food for the hungry poor. Earlier in the day, the Chief Executive had signed the tax bill; now, finally, he could devote his attention to other domestic matters. So, while his staff waited expectantly, President Johnson glanced for the first time at a simply outlined four-page memo in which Califano had described the proposal.

Halfway down the second page, the Presidential eyes focused on the heading "Actions by Freeman" and the explanation: "Merely to carry out the commitments recently made by Secretary Freeman to improve the commodity distribution and food stamp programs in fiscal 1969 would require $145 million over the 1969 budget." Lyndon B. Johnson looked up at Orville Freeman, frowned, and exploded.

"A hundred and forty-five million dollars—I never authorized you to do that!" the President raged. "Don't you realize that I have just signed a tax bill promising to cut spending by *six billion dollars?*"

Freeman was totally taken aback by Johnson's latest tirade. The Secretary had announced the improvements in the commodity program more than a month earlier and had made repeated references to them without repercussions from the Chief Executive. Orville Freeman turned toward Califano and said, "Joe cleared it."

When Califano nodded his head in agreement, the President turned his anger toward Budget Director Zwick, whose chief function is to safeguard the Presidential budget.

"I didn't clear it but I was aware of it," Zwick said nervously. "Joe cleared it and we thought he was speaking for you."

Johnson fumed that he now was compelled to reduce spending and wasn't going to start that exercise by adding almost half a billion dollars to the budget.

Freeman attempted to explain that food aid no longer was an isolated legislative program but now was tied together politically with a four-year extension of the farm program. "Liberal and southern Democrats already are working together as they did in 1964 to trade support on measures for an expanded food stamp program and for continued farm price supports," he said. But President Johnson ended the meeting abruptly, ordering Califano to revise the plan downward to meet only minimum requirements, and gruffly told Freeman to send him a memorandum clarifying the political situation on Capitol Hill.

An agitated Orville Freeman returned to his office. For more than a year he had lived with intense conflicting pressures on the food issue. When he had first accepted the Cabinet job, his principal political assignment from President Kennedy, and later from President Johnson, had been to cajole Southern conservatives like Ellender, Poage, and Whitten to

win necessary agricultural programs and to keep "the farm problem" off the President's back. Secretary Freeman had carried out his assignment well, with hundreds of hours spent carefully catering to the super-conservative personalities of men like Ellender and Whitten. Civil rights and poverty had been given low priorities for him in those early years, making it difficult to switch gears when these issues finally focused on his department in the late 1960s. He had taken excessive criticism from liberals for 16 months, even though he now, at last, favored reform and the criticism belonged at the doorstep of the White House.

When he reached his own office Orville Freeman called in his secretary and hastily dictated for the President an emotion-charged memorandum which revealed a great deal about the Agriculture Secretary and his views on both the politics of hunger and Lyndon Johnson.

"The current attack on the Administration alleging callousness and incompetence in the face of widespread hunger and malnutrition is the most difficult problem to handle for me since the Billie Sol Estes case,"[3] Freeman began. "In the Billie Sol Estes case the effort was solely to destroy the Administration. This is part of the current pattern, but also the present attacks hope to capture public attention and support so that other objectives they have in the war on poverty can be accomplished."

Although he alleged that the issue had been raised from such conspir-

---

[3] Estes used Texas Democratic and Washington Agriculture Department connections to further moneymaking schemes for which he was indicted and convicted in federal court.

atorial motives, Freeman told the President that hunger was a very real problem, one he had seen with his own eyes. Further, he dictated, it was now getting a strong, emotional dose of public attention because of the Citizens' Board of Inquiry and the school lunch reports, the CBS television program, and "the tactics and efforts of the so-called poor people."

Although he was still receiving thousands of critical letters as a result of the "shockingly irresponsible CBS program," Freeman said "my counterattack [against the program] had been important."[4]

"The counterattack has given us at least a sounding board, for my charges have captured attention and some of the real facts are coming to public attention," Freeman wrote. "In the process, I believe people will become aware of all the things we have done and are doing to meet the food requirements of the needy."

In his attempt to justify the actions which brought on the Presidential tongue-lashing, Freeman wrote a small essay on the politics of hunger. "Where I have felt it necessary," he said, "I have yielded a bit and liberalized the program. Otherwise, in my best judgment, we would have been painted into a very tight corner and made to look callous and indifferent. . . . I can assure you in making some

[4] Freeman publicly condemned the CBS program for its very minor factual inaccuracies and its failure to praise what he considered to be improvements in the food programs. Freeman failed to see or to admit that the primary purpose of this powerful program was to show that hunger existed in America, despite federal food programs. Columnist Carl Rowan said Freeman could have better used his anger in public criticism of the Jamie Whittens of Congress.

concessions where the use of Section 32 funds are concerned, I was not acting counter to the President's intentions as I understood them at that time.

"At the same time I have made some concessions in the programs where we were most vulnerable if we stood hard and yielded not at all, I have stood fast on other points. I won't relate them all. Free food stamps for the lowest income group is an example. There are many others where I have simply said no. This firmness has come through to the public.

"At least, I find many people who write or come to me and say thank goodness you are standing firm and not letting this ragtail, bobtailed group of so-called 'Poor People' push you around. What I have tried to do is hold to the middle ground so that people around the nation sensitive to the hunger and malnutrition problem will not feel that the Administration has been completely callous, cold, and heartless. At the same time I have tried hard to avoid an image of being intimidated or weak-kneed.

"I hopefully recommend that you decide on a generous food package and send a special message to the Congress soon. . . ."

With this message, the food issue headed back on one of its many trips to President Johnson's desk.

White House aides Califano, Gaither, and Murphy, along with officials at the Budget Bureau and Agriculture Department worked over the week-end of June 29—30, revising the food program so they could get it back to the President on Monday.

At 6 p.m. Monday, July 1, 1968, Califano sent into the President a two-and-a-half page memorandum concisely outlining a scaled-down $285 million food program he said had been agreed to by Freeman, Zwick, Gaither, Pierson, Murphy, and himself. About one-half the money would be used to meet commitments made by Freeman to the poor people and to counties which had been promised the food program. But the new food package's most important ingredient was a $95 million plan to begin liberalizing the food stamp program for families with between $30 and $170 monthly income.

If another meeting were necessary, Califano suggested, it should be held the next day because "it would be important to move quickly after the [congressional] recess to get the necessary legislative action."

Knowing that Lyndon Johnson always liked "to keep his options open," Califano—after strongly urging action —offered three options for the President's personal check mark. These were "Set up meeting with Zwick, Murphy, and Gaither tomorrow. Proceed with drafting of the message [to Congress]. See me."

The President read Califano's memo and scrawled a big check mark by the option, "See me."

"Give me some reasons why I should approve this program," President Johnson told Califano. The assistant argued that the Administration had made commitments and would look bad in not keeping them.

"You say I've made a commitment," the President said. "Get me the words of that commitment."

Califano pointed out that in signing the Food Stamp Act in 1967 the President had pledged that he would place a food program in each of the nation's 1,000 poorest counties which lacked one. That had led to "Project

331,"[5] and now some of the extra food stamp money was needed to start programs in about 50 of these counties.

"I didn't know that commitment was going to cost money," Johnson snapped. "The next time you send me a commitment, let me know how much it is going to cost." (President Johnson made no decision on the food program but he did give Joe Califano a new "extra duty" assignment: whenever a speech draft was prepared for the President, Califano had to examine it carefully and note on it whether it committed the President to any spending. This punishment lasted for about a week, until President Johnson's mind turned to other matters.)

After the new proposal lay dormant for several days, Vice President Humphrey personally appealed for approval of the food plan, now that the tax increase bill was safely enacted.

"I've given my word to Congress [on the spending cut]," Johnson replied in turning down Humphrey's entreaty. "If you can get Congress to do something, fine. But we've made a commitment. We've talked to Ellender, Poage, and Whitten. I'm not going to be the one to break that agreement. That's what they're waiting for up there. If I break the agreement, we'll never get anything else through Congress."

No one close to the President is quite certain what agreement he

[5] President Johnson vowed to place a food program in each of the 331 poorest counties (out of the 1,000 lowest in per capita income) that did not already have a food program. This approach did not touch the poor in counties where poverty was masked statistically by the affluence of many other residents.

made with whom, or whether he actually promised southern reactionaries that he would not propose broad changes in food programs. The hard-won combination tax increase and appropriation reduction bill certainly made no such commitment. Its only promise was to reduce spending somewhere, and the President had all the options of deciding where. The matter is not clarified by the fact that, about this same time, President Johnson went before the weekly meeting of the government's congressional liaison officers and told them not to be concerned about emasculation of domestic programs.

"Now, don't any of you bleeding hearts worry," he told them. "Lady Bird and Luci and Lynda have already got on to me about not cutting education and health. I'm not going to get them mad. We'll make the reductions in the SST, the space program, and some military construction spending, and then you watch Congress. They'll put the money right back in."

Although Humphrey was now frantically involved in his bid for the Presidential nomination, the Vice President tried one last device to persuade the President. Both his wife Muriel and Mrs. Arthur Krim, wife of the film magnate and chief Presidential fund raiser, were active members of the President's Commission on Mental Retardation and both were concerned about studies showing the possible effects of malnutrition on infant mental development. He knew the President was fond of Mathilda Krim, and thought that perhaps she could get through to him. Unable to reach her on the telephone, Humphrey did something he usually carefully avoided—he put into written

form a criticism of President Lyndon Johnson.

"It is just intolerable to me that there is such a problem of malnutrition and undernourishment in the United States, with our great agricultural production. It hurts the children the most, and they are the least able to bear it," he wrote to Mathilda Krim.

"Through it all, there are ways the President could have helped—in approving some of Orville Freeman's budget requests, in supporting legislation on the Hill, and suggesting administrative change—but he has not. The thought came that you might be the person who could say a word or two to encourage him to move more conclusively to solve this hunger problem.

"Someone associated with the health field could bring to him a new point of view. So many people have talked about hunger from the poverty and racial perspective that it has tended to blur the sheer physical impact of hunger.... We need to put the hunger issue aside from special interests and see it as the human interest it is."

Mathilda Krim telephoned the President in Texas to ask his help in fighting hunger, but Johnson still refused to act.

During the last months of the Johnson Administration, Orville Freeman, White House aides, and even the normally conservative Budget Bureau doggedly continued bringing the President plans to make a national commitment against hunger.

When a final supplemental appropriations bill was being prepared in the last days of the 90th Congress, Califano and Budget Director Zwick urged the President to seek the full

$90 million of increased food stamp appropriations which Congress had authorized, even without backing from the White House.

"How can I single food out, when education and all these other programs also need money?"

"Because Congress has authorized it," the President was told.

"Well, they won't fund it. They'll leave me holding the bag," the President said. "It's out of the question. Forget it."

. Then, two days later, at a meeting with the various congressional appropriations chairmen, the President apparently had a sudden change of heart, and in a move which surprised everyone concerned, asked them for the money. But it was late in the day. Congress did approve $55 million for the food stamp program, but this amount barely covered the commitments Agriculture had made to counties almost a year before.

When it came time for him to sign the Food Stamp Extension Bill, Budget Bureau and White House aides tried to get President Johnson to establish a Food and Nutrition Council and to make at least a verbal commitment to end hunger. The proposal text would have clearly stated the problem and what needed to be done. The text was discarded by the President.

Although the President had said "no" about as many times and in as many ways as a man could, Administration insiders persisted in the belief that he would face this problem before he left office. "Wait for Lyndon Johnson's last budget and State of the Union message," they kept saying.

With such thoughts in mind Agriculture Secretary Freeman went to the White House after the election in November for one last try at the food issue.

"Mr. President," he argued. "This is our last chance. You've had all these terrible restrictions and pressures. Why not now, for once in eight years, fund a budget that makes up the Great Society. I'd like you to put in a budget that I believe in and you believe in. Let Nixon cut it."

Using yet another line of reasoning, Johnson now told Freeman, "I just don't know about these programs. Food comes and food goes. You don't get anything for it. Education and job training get more for the money."

Because the President appeared so completely negative on the issue, Freeman sent him a final memorandum, saying he would be misunderstood if he did not at least request the full $340 million food stamp authorization. In the end, Freeman was authorized to commit a program, including quite minor food stamp reform, that would cost the Nixon Administration $340 million in fiscal 1970 unless Nixon tried to change signals. President Johnson's final argument, and perhaps the best of many he used during the year, was that he should not make decisions for the new administration.

On at least 12 specific occasions his aides and Cabinet officers had recommended food aid reform and Lyndon Johnson had said "no." None of those closest to his thinking and decision-making are certain what really stopped the President on the issue of hunger and malnutrition in America. They know only that the President's motives were often complex, even conflicting. When he turned down the Task Force reports in 1966 and 1967, the President was skeptical about the existence of a little-publicized problem, and perhaps he was in this no different from most Americans. But this was the particular type of problem that usually appealed personally to Lyndon Johnson. He liked tackling and quickly solving basic problems involving human beings—and hunger certainly met this criterion.

He had legitimate concern about moving on the hunger issue while the tax bill was hanging in the balance with conservative Wilbur Mills. On these grounds, any criticism of the President must go right to the issue of the Vietnam war itself and to the government's sense of national priorities. As the war expanded and became increasingly more expensive, Johnson felt strongly that fund-raising and anti-inflationary measures had top priority. Once the tax bill passed, however, other reasons must be found to explain the President's inaction. He had selected many other issues from congressional proponents and made them his own, but perhaps in this case, he, like Jamie Whitten, saw a Kennedy maneuver. He disliked Robert Kennedy intensely and this had been a Kennedy issue from the outset.

There is no doubt that Lyndon Johnson believed he was being pushed and, if there was one thing he resented, it was having other people make up his mind for him. His fury at Freeman for making overtures to the poor people and asking Congress for an unlimited food stamp authorization convinced his advisers that Johnson felt others were trying to commit him. He fumed repeatedly about Freeman's actions in increasing the cost of the commodity program and recommending a larger food stamp program. He suspected that Freeman, Murphy, Zwick, Califano, and others on his own staff were making decisions behind his back. And in several instances they almost were—out of a sense of desperate frustration to get a decision from him.

"What can we do to get the President to act?" a Humphrey aide asked Presidential assistant Harry McPherson.

"You might stop pushing him," McPherson replied. "He doesn't like it."

The tactics of the Poor People's Campaign were opposed by public opinion, and poll-watcher Johnson perhaps didn't want to appear pushed into action by what even Orville Freeman called a "ragtailed, bobtailed group."

Did Lyndon Johnson disapprove of food programs because "you don't get anything for it?" According to a close White House aide, this comment indicated Johnson's strong dislike of food aid as "welfare," while the President's own populist thinking supported programs which provided opportunity. If this were the key to the President's negative behavior, it ignored the fact that an infant crippled by malnutrition could never be helped by any amount of education or job training.

At one point, Johnson deferred action by contending that Congress would not approve food stamp reform. If he truly believed this, the master congressional politician had not studied 1968 congressional action on the issue. Majorities in both the House and the Senate had approved major food program expenditures and reforms, but the efforts could not be coordinated without full Presidential backing. There is little doubt that

Congress would have taken major steps forward on the hunger issue in 1968 if Lyndon Johnson had only lent his support.

Perhaps in the end, President Lyndon Johnson, like many of us in America, consciously and unconsciously practiced the politics of ignorance. His pride was great and it was difficult for him to admit, after five years of trying hard to build a Great Society, that a most basic problem of poverty had not even been examined, much less solved.

If President Johnson failed completely to confront the *full* hunger and malnutrition issue during his term in office, at least he contributed toward progress in improving the government's food aid programs. Specific programs aimed at providing food for the poor rose from $173 million in the last year of the Eisenhower administration to $403 million in fiscal 1968 and $655 million in fiscal 1969. Beginning with President Kennedy's first executive order, the two successive Democratic administrations did start slowly converting surplus disposal programs into human food programs.

Major strides were taken in 1968, principally because liberals in Congress finally followed the early leaders and fought to get programs through. The initial efforts of Senators Kennedy, Clark, Mondale, Javits, and McGovern and Congressmen Foley, Goodell, and Quie eventually involved most liberal-to-moderate members of both political parties. These men attempted with some success to roll over the opposition of the Poages and Whittens, even though the President would not. The results were an improved commodity distribution program, a $43 million appropriation to provide free or reduced priced meals to needy children, the bare beginnings of a reformed food stamp program that really serves the poor, and the creation of the Senate Select Committee which would probe the politics of hunger in 1969. The hunger effort of 1968 really ended, though, with the breakup of Resurrection City and the few congressional breakthroughs for better food programs.

part two

THE
OTHER AMERICANS

Racial and ethnic discrimination is not a new phenomenon in American society. Each successive wave of immigrants has encountered various negative reactions from the dominant white Anglo-Saxon Protestant group, or as sociologists refer to them, WASPS. Immigrants found in their new habitats, that such differentiating characteristics as language, religion and customs were used to identify them and to limit their participation and opportunities in society in both obvious and subtle ways. Nevertheless, most minority groups in the United States experience overwhelming discrimination only temporarily.

The case of the Negro, or black man (as he seems to prefer to identify himself today), is held by some to be qualitatively different from the discrimination suffered by non-black groups. The persistence and pervasiveness of discrimination against black people is unique. No other group of any size in the United States has been subjected to inequities so comprehensive and intense as those faced by the black man. Moreover, no other group has either challenged the existing social order or provoked the animosity and hostility of the larger community to so marked a degree. Many aspects of social life, such as movement away from the core city, *de facto* segregation in education, and the rise of new groups of extreme political reactionaries, are in part expressions of the race issue. Furthermore, contrary to other immigrant groups, the black man cannot fade into the dominant society without radical changes in the values of the white community member and in the structural arrangements of the social order, which implicitly discriminate against non-white people. Today the plight of the black man and the consequences of his efforts and the efforts of sympathetic whites to remedy the pervasive discrimination represent perhaps the most pressing problem confronting the United States.

INDIVIDUAL	INDIVIDUAL
vs.	vs.
INDIVIDUAL	ORGANIZATION

PORTRAIT OF A KLANSMAN

No single set of social or psychological characteristics can be drawn up to identify the bigot. Alsop's article provides a portrait of a man who appears as a unique example of the racial discriminator. Raymond Cranford's determination to keep the black man in his place is rooted in his emotional makeup, his life experiences, and the gratification he receives as leader of a ruthless organization. It is not possible to separate the activities of the Klan from the individual behavior of Raymond Cranford. As an individual, he rallies the energies and talents of others to persecute black people. The Klan simply provides a convenient structure in which such nefarious individual ambitions can be realized.

ORGANIZER

While blacks represent the largest group of "other Americans" who suffer the consequences of mass and pervasive discrimination, other minorities in the United States are treated at least as harshly. Many immigrant groups go through periods of poverty and suffering, able to obtain only the lowest level of jobs, segregated into ghetto communities, with few opportunities for upward social and economic mobility. Mexican Americans, who constitute a major part of the migratory farm labor force in the United States, are among the severely exploited and live under the most awesome conditions. Only in recent years have they been able to fight back. This fight is due, to a large extent, to the efforts of a single individual, César Chávez. This article, by Peter Matthiessen, describes Chávez as a man battling to win decent working conditions and a fair wage for the thousands of Spanish-speaking farm workers who toil long hours and move about the country from one exploitative situation to another.

ORGANIZATION
vs.
INDIVIDUAL

ORGANIZATION
vs.
ORGANIZATION

NIGHTMARE JOURNEY

Reactions of the larger community to the riots and violence of the ghetto have been bizarre and extreme. Bob Clark, a Negro news photographer, describes what happened to him in the Detroit riots. Although Clark was injured while legitimately photographing the racial disturbance, the police dealt with him only in terms of his color. Few individuals would argue against police intervention efforts in the face of arson and looting, no matter how sympathetic they are to the cause of the black man. Yet Clark's account reveals how inappropriately an organization may respond to crises. It is likely that such unsympathetic and cruel conduct by agents of social control in the community will have an irrevocable impact on the black man and will serve to exasperate a commitment to violence.

THE PANTHERS
AND THE POLICE

There is continual dispute about the extent of organization of the Black Panthers. Some characterize the group as a close-knit national organization, others as a loose confederacy, and still others as a series of independent bodies that sometimes informally work together. There is also wide divergence of opinion on the extent to which this group initiates violent activities and actually uses physical force. That they are not afraid to challenge established order openly, unlike black men of thirty or forty years ago, is indisputable. That they are concerned with protecting their black brothers and promoting the well-being of their people is also indisputable. Whether justified or not, police have organized (some claim with direction from a national level) and moved to encounter physically different Black Panther groups. As a result, police departments have been accused of needlessly wounding and killing key leaders of the Black Panthers and of using every unscrupulous means imaginable to diminish their power and influence. Epstein describes a series of cases in which the police, as an organization, have victimized Black Panther groups in different parts of the country.

Portrait of a Klansman

STEWART ALSOP

Raymond Cranford, an Exalted Cyclops of the Ku Klux Klan in North Carolina, is a bullet-headed man with expressionless, black-rimmed eyes, who wears his hair close cropped, military fashion. Cranford fully expects to be framed by the Federal Bureau of Investigation, or killed by Negroes or Communists, and he always has a rifle or pistol within easy reach. He talks a good deal about the last war, in which he was wounded, and about the Communists, who are, he believes, getting ready to assume power, and about guns, which he loves. But wherever a conversation with Cranford starts, it always comes back to the same subject—what Cranford calls "niggers."

"The word Negro," he explained, within five minutes of our meeting, "that's not in my vocabulary. There's colored folks and there's niggers, there ain't no Negroes."

I first met Raymond Cranford at the airport in Raleigh N. C., where we had lunch. That lunch was my first exposure to his way of talking, which is a kind of brutal monologue. The Raleigh airport restaurant is desegregated, and I pointed to a Negro who was eating next to a white man at one end of the lunch counter. I asked Cranford if the Negro's presence bothered him.

Reprinted with permission of the author from *Saturday Evening Post*, April 9, 1966, pp. 23–27.

"If that man sitting next to him wants to eat like a nigger," said Cranford, "that's his business. But if that nigger was to come to this table, I'd know how to handle him. I'd say I'd got some alligators I'd like to feed." He looked around the table with a small, closed-mouth grin—he does not show his teeth when he smiles, and he hardly ever laughs. Then the monologue started. A few excerpts will suggest its flavor.

"A white nigger, that's worse than a nigger. A white nigger's a man's got a white skin, and a heart that's pumpin' nigger blood through his veins. If it comes to a fight, the white nigger's gonna get killed before the nigger."

"You come from Washington? I call Washington Hersheytown—ninety percent chocolate and ten percent nuts."

"We believe a white man's got his civil rights too. I'll lay down my life for those rights, if I have to. These nigger civil rights, they're gonna end in the white man's bedroom."

"We don't believe in burning crosses on a man's lawn. If I'm gonna burn a cross, I ram it through the man and burn it." This with a small grin.

"When the Communists take over, they're gonna kill me quick. Well, you only got one time to die."

"I got a daughter, she's nineteen years old. I love my daughter, but if I find her with a nigger, I'll take my gun and I'll blow her brains right out of her head."

These observations are not very pretty or enlightening, and in the time I spent with Raymond Cranford, I heard them repeated almost literally *ad nauseam*. And yet it is worth trying to understand Raymond Cranford, for he is one of a very large number of Americans who are wholly alienated from the comfortable American society that most of us know. In the Klan oath, the world outside the Klan is called "the alien world," and in the eyes of a Klansman like Raymond Cranford, that world is heavily populated by "Communists," "white niggers," and other enemies.

North Carolina has an old and well-earned reputation for moderation in race relations. Nevertheless, as the recent investigation by the House Un-American Activities Committee established, North Carolina's Ku Klux Klan, nonexistent three years ago, is now bigger and better organized than the Klan in any other state. Its membership has been estimated as high as 20,000. The hard core of the Klan is in the flat, sandy, cotton-and-tobacco country in the eastern part of the state, where Negroes make up more than 40 percent of the population. The hard core of this hard core is in Greene County, where Exalted Cyclops Raymond Cranford presides over his klavern.

I owe my introduction to Raymond Cranford to a 33-year-old reporter called Pete Young. Young has spent the last two years covering the mushroom growth of North Carolina's Klan, and he has become a close friend of Exalted Cyclops Cranford, Grand Dragon Robert Jones, and dozens of assorted Klaliffs, Kleagles, Klokkards, Kludds, and just plain Knights. Young had invited me to

have a look at the Klan, and offered to act as my guide. I had accepted, and asked Ted Ellsworth, an old friend, and *Post* photographer Ollie Atkins to go with me.

Cranford was in the marines in World War II, he told us at lunch, and had been wounded and decorated. "A psychiatrist told me I got backward reflexes," he said. "I got no sense of fear. Till I was twelve years old, I couldn't get to sleep at night without a light in the room. But when I'm in danger, I'm *cool*."

Cranford smokes constantly—upwards of four packs a day, he says. His nails are chewed to the quick, and he has bleeding ulcers. He used to drink a lot, but no longer. "When I was in the marines, I used to go out snipin' Japs with one canteen of water and one of alcohol. In the Klan, you can't get drunk, and you can't swear."

Cranford is deeply proud of being a Klansman. "My daddy and my granddaddy were in the Klan," he says. "I was born in the Klan." He is, he says, "a Klansman full time and a farmer part time." He owns a 200-acre farm with a 22-acre tobacco allotment. In most years his tobacco crop alone brings him a net profit of around $11,000. But Raymond Cranford does not think of himself as a prosperous citizen.

"They wouldn't let a poor white like me past the door of the Waldorf-Astoria in New York," he said, as we walked to the parking lot. "So why should a nigger go anywhere he wants?"

Between the bucket seats of Cranford's red late-model car there was a bone-handled pistol and cartridge belt, and a rifle hung in a halter arrangement by the left front door. Cranford demonstrated how he would react if a "nigger or Communist" threatened him in the car. When he opened the door, he could fire his rifle without taking it out of its halter. The hollow-pointed bullets, he explained, would catch a man in the legs or stomach. "Mister, with this little gun," he said, "you can blow a hole through a man, you could walk right through it."

"I can outrun any FBI car in the state—I got a supercharged engine," he said, as we started on the drive to Greene County. "Course, the FBI taps my phone. I got an alibi for every cotton-pickin' minute, but they'll find a way to frame me." To the relief of his passengers, he turned out to be a cautious driver, careful about passing, and stopping at all stop signs.

Cranford is very proud of being Exalted Cyclops, or No. 1 man, of his klavern. A klavern is the basic Klan unit, with membership ranging from a dozen or so to a couple of hundred —Cranford said he had about 60 men in his klavern.

He was also, he said proudly, a major in the "V.I.P. Security Guard" of the Klan. As such, he wears a major's oak leaves, and a helmet liner, uniform, and regulation paratroop boots at the Klan's cross-burning rallies. His job is to guard the Grand Dragon, the Imperial Wizard, and other Very Important Persons.

"Fren, you better keep your hands away from your pockets at a rally. You lay a hand on the Grand Dragon or the Imperial Wizard, and fren, you're *daid*."

As an Exalted Cyclops, Cranford said, he had direct access at any time of the day or night to the Imperial Wizard himself, Robert Shelton of Alabama, to whom he always referred respectfully as "Mr. Shelton."

"I can't get to see 'Light Bulb' Johnson," Cranford said. "I can't get to see the governor. They wouldn't give me the time of day. But I can call *Mr.* Shelton any time of the day or night. There's the number one man in the nation, and he'll take his time and money to talk to me, or come and see me any time."

A man could identify himself as a Klansman if he wanted to, Cranford said, but no other Klansman would identify him, on pain of death. "In some places," he explained, "you got white niggers, they'll fire Klan people —they won't say it's because they're in the Klan, but they'll always find some excuse."

Then there are anti-Klan people in Greene County? "Some, but everybody knows they're just after the nigger dollar."

By this time we had arrived at the motel where we were to stay. When Grand Dragon Jones was in the neighborhood some months earlier, Cranford said, the manager refused to give him a room. Cranford gleefully explained how he dealt with this insult to the Grand Dragon:

"I went to the manager, and I said, 'Now, fren, I'm not threatenin' anybody. But I got twenty niggers working at my place, and they're *real* dirty niggers, why I bet they haven't washed for weeks, and they sure *do* stink. Now I want a public apology to the Grand Dragon, and if I don't get it, I'm gonna register those twenty niggers right here. If you take them you'll have to fumigate the place, maybe burn it down. If you don't take them, I'm gonna prosecute you under the Civil Rights Act.' So he apologized."

That evening we drove over to Raymond Cranford's house for supper and found that quite a little party had been laid on for us. We were introduced to Mrs. Cranford, a strong-faced woman with reddish hair, and to Bob Littleton, the Exalted Cyclops of a klavern in neighboring Pitt County, and his wife. A Kleagle, or recruiter for the Klan, who didn't want to be identified, was there, and so was the Night Hawk of Cranford's klavern. The Night Hawk, whose job it is to organize the Klan's cross-burning rallies, is a sad-faced, monosyllabic farmer called Bennie Earle Oates. Also at the party were Cranford's 19-year-old daughter and 9-year-old son, as well as various in-laws and other children.

The Cranfords live in a small brick house, close to a village street. The furniture is the kind that is meant to be used, not just looked at. There is an old-fashioned front parlor, a dining room and a "family room" at the back. The party moved into the family room. No liquor was served. Somebody put a record on the phonograph. The song's endlessly repeated refrain was: *Move those niggers north, if they don't like our southern ways, move those niggers north.* Cranford pointed to his young son's school book—there was a big KKK scrawled in ink across its cover. "He's born into the Klan too," Cranford said proudly.

When the record stopped, the male members of the party moved into the dining room and were served a good meal of barbecued chicken by the ladies, who ate afterward. The conversation was dominated, as always, by Raymond Cranford. There were a couple of units of the Deacons for Defense, the armed Negro organization in the area, he said, "But we're not scared of them. You start poppin' bullets around a nigger, and their feet's gotta go."

One of the other Klansmen inter-rupted to say that the Klan was "against violence, except in self-defense," which is the official Klan line. "That's right," said Cranford. "We believe in ballots, not bullets—a Klansman gets out of line, and the Grand Dragon will clobber him." But the bullets keep creeping into the conversation.

"I'm not here to shoot a nigger, but if trouble starts, the white nigger's first on my list."

"Sure, the white niggers'll get it first. Say there's a bird on the fence and another bird scrunched down behind the fence. Which one's gonna get shot first?"

How much danger, I asked, was there of some sort of Negro uprising in the area—something like Watts?

"Not a chance," said Cranford, and the others nodded in agreement. "Look, I can have a thousand men in one hour, with air-cooled machine guns and two cases of grenades. There are more combat men in the Klan than in any other organization except the V.F.W. We didn't fight in World War Two just to let the niggers take over the country. That's not a threat. That's a promise."

In the living room, after supper, the guns came out. Everybody seemed to have a gun—all the children had toy guns. Cranford showed the shotgun he had won for recruiting members into the Klan, and Littleton passed around his new highpowered rifle. Then Cranford put on his Exalted Cyclops robes, white with a crimson hood. "They call these robes bedsheets," he said indignantly. "Bedsheets! You just feel that satin. That's the finest quality there is."

We got up to go, and I thanked Mrs. Cranford for the delicious chicken dinner. "Now, when you come to write that article," she said, in a sweet-southern voice, "you be fair. You're not fair, I'm coming to Washington with a machine gun."

All the men piled into cars to inspect Cranford's newly built klavern —permission to show these previously secret Klan meeting halls had apparently come from higher authority. The klavern turned out to be a long, windowless cinderblock hut with a cement floor. In the middle of the floor was the "altar"—a wooden table with a bayonet and a Bible on it, flanked by the U.S. and Confederate flags, backed by a cross lit by bulbs. On the wall behind the "altar" were two signs: FIGHT FOR THE RIGHT, DIE IF WE MUST, BUT ALWAYS REMEMBER, IN GOD WE TRUST, and A MAN NEVER STOOD SO TALL AS WHEN HE STOOPED TO HELP A CHILD. The first is the official Klan motto. Putting up the second, Cranford said proudly, was his own idea.

On a mantelpiece were two long strips of rubber tire, attached to wooden handles. These were used, said the Kleagle who didn't want to be identified, to "teach informers a lesson." The Klan, Cranford explained, has its own system of discipline. A Klansman who "gets out of line"—drinks too much, or "cheats on his wife," or disgraces the Klan in some way—may be tried by a Klan court, and punished appropriately. The Klan is, in fact, a kind of inner government—a Klansman swears allegiance to the Klan above any allegiance to the "alien world."

To us outsiders, the visit to Cranford's klavern was a bit anticlimactic—we had expected something more sinister. Perhaps sensing our disappointment, Cranford seized the bayonet and began demonstrating his "karate," showing how, if a nigger

or a "Communist" made a grab for the bayonet, he would plunge it into his adversary's stomach—"I'll just shove it in, by instinct."

We piled into cars again, to have a look at Bob Littleton's klavern. It is bigger than Cranford's, with seats for more than 100 people. There is also an open coffin—to scare the initiates—and a lot of Klan propaganda tacked up on a post, including a picture of the murdered civil-rights worker, Mrs. Liuzzo, walking with two Negroes. Littleton and the Kleagle both pointed out the damning fact that she was walking barefoot.

There was, we "aliens" agreed at the motel, something very sad about the dreary little klaverns with their kitchen tables masquerading as "altars," and their coffee cans filled with old cigarette butts and their hand-lettered, misspelled signs; and something very sad about the Klan.

The next day, Cranford showed up bright and early with his Klaliff, or No. 2 man. The Klaliff (who didn't want to be identified) turned out to be a pleasant-mannered, freckle-faced young man. He had been in the Korean war, and like most Klansmen we met, he had been a combat soldier.

Cranford took us to the "nigger school" which was, he said, bigger, newer, and more expensive than the white school. I asked if integration of the school had started.

"It started," Cranford said, "but it stopped."

We "aliens" got out to talk to the principal of the Negro school while the Klansmen stayed in the car outside. The principal is a soft-voiced, articulate Negro called Raymond Morris. Yes, he said, it is quite true —the Negro school was newer and better equipped than the white school.

Had integration started? Yes, it had started—three specially chosen Negro children had been sent to the white school, in September. They had got along well for a month.

"But then an unfortunate thing happened," Morris said, in his quiet, singsong voice. "One night, someone shot into the homes of the children who had gone to the white school. No one was hurt, but the parents had a natural reluctance to keep the children in that school." Later we asked Cranford about the shooting incident. He grunted, but for once he said nothing.

That afternoon, we went to the town of Ayden, where, Cranford said, "the niggers are stirring up trouble." Outside a store, a line of Negro children were carrying signs reading NO HIRING NO BUYING or WE'RE TIRED OF BEING BAG-BOYS AND MAIDS. This trouble, Cranford said, had been "stirred up" by the local head of the N.A.A.C.P., an undertaker called Gratz Norcott.

"He stirs up the trouble, and him being an undertaker, if the trouble gets bad, he stands to get all the business. I tole him, if one of my guys gets hurt, I'm not gonna horse around, I'm comin' right after you."

Norcott, it turned out, had his office in a small house across the street from the store. Ted Ellsworth suggested that we call on Norcott, and get his side of the story. The idea of a confrontation with Norcott had clearly never occurred to Cranford. But he interpreted the suggestion as a challenge to his courage. So he squared his shoulders and strode into the little house, followed by the Klaliff, the Night Hawk, and us "aliens."

Norcott's office is tiny, and by the time I elbowed my way into it, what-

ever greetings had been exchanged between Cranford and Norcott had already occurred, and an uncomfortable silence reigned. Norcott, a middle-aged Negro with an expressionless face, was at his desk, with a telephone held against an ear. Occasionally he would mutter something into the telephone, but there were long stretches when he said nothing at all. I shook his hand, and it was wet with sweat, and when he lit a cigarette, the match wavered. But if Norcott was scared by this surprise visit from the Klan, his self-control was remarkable.

For a while, as Norcott held the telephone up to his ear, we white men stood around rather sheepishly—there were only two chairs in the office. Then Norcott held the telephone away from his ear and addressed Cranford in a polite but authoritative tone:

"Mr. Cranford, there are some chairs right across the hall there. Will you fetch a few so these gentlemen can sit down?"

Cranford hesitated a moment, and glared at Norcott, then got the chairs. We all sat down.

At last Norcott put the telephone in its cradle. While he was explaining his side of the "trouble"—the store did most of its business with Negroes, he said, and the Negroes wanted one of the three cashiers' jobs—two young, tough-looking Negroes came into the office, followed by an elderly Negro minister and a Negro doctor. Obviously news of the confrontation had spread rapidly.

The two young men were field workers for Martin Luther King's Southern Christian Leadership Conference. One was a native North Carolinian, the other came from the Bronx. Norcott introduced them, and then introduced Cranford:

"Mr. Cranford here is the Cyclops —is that right, Mr. Cranford? Yes, the *Exalted* Cyclops of the Ku Klux Klan." There was no hint of a smile, only the faint emphasis on the ridiculous adjective.

Cranford, sensing a challenge, glared at the Negro from the Bronx, then addressed Norcott:

"Now, fren, I'm not threatenin' you, I'm just givin' you a bit of advice. You and me, we don't see things the same way, but we'll get along all right, just so long as you don't bring in outsiders to make trouble. If you're gonna bring in outsiders, you could be asking for real *bad* trouble. Now, is that a gamble you want to take?"

"Well, now, Mr. Cranford," said Norcott, his tone polite, almost soothing, "when you had your rallies here last summer, I think I'm right, you brought in Mr. Shelton, the *Imperial* Wizard, I think you call him, from Alabama. And I heard you bring in some *Grand* Dragons, or what is it you call them, from as far away as Ohio. Isn't that right?"

"Well, let me tell you something," said Cranford, "I don't believe in threatenin's a man, or burning crosses to scare him. If I got something I don't like about you, I just walk right up to you in the street and bust you right in the nose."

"Well, now, Mr. Cranford," said Norcott, more soothingly than ever, "I wouldn't walk right up to you and punch *you* in the nose. I'd *discuss* the matter with you. And if we couldn't agree, then I'd put the matter in the hands of the law, because we in the N.A.A.C.P., we believe in the law, we obey the laws of the land."

By this time Cranford was both angry and a little confused, like a bull after the picadors had worked him over.

"I'm against violence," he said, his voice rising, "but I'm gonna protect my rights, and if anybody wants a fight, he can get what he wants. Why, few weeks ago, three niggers pulled up beside my car, I seen they had guns, and I put a clip in my gun, and by God. . . ."

"SHUT UP, RAYMOND," Pete Young said, suddenly and loudly. Cranford subsided. There was some further sparring. Then Cranford said, rather plaintively, "You nigras talk about discrimination. Why, right here, some cops will give a Klansman a ticket just because he's a Klansman."

At this point, Dr. Andrew Best, a Negro physician with a round, good-humored face, intervened for the first time. He spoke with quiet passion:

"But can't you see, that's just what they've been doing to us as long as we've lived, giving us a ticket just because we're Negroes."

"The word 'Negro'," Cranford said, in a Pavlovian reaction, "that's not in my vocabulary. There's colored folk and there's niggers. There ain't no Negroes."

"Mr. Cranford," said Dr. Best, in a tone of infinite earnestness, "I want to ask you to try to imagine something. I want to ask you to try to imagine what your life would be like if my color was your color and your color was my color. Can you imagine what that would be like?"

"Listen, fren," said Cranford, "do you think life's easy for the pore white man in the South?" Cranford got up suddenly and strode out to his car, followed by the Klaliff and the Night Hawk, while we outsiders shook hands with the Negroes and muttered good-byes.

That evening the Exalted Cyclops, the Klaliff, the Night Hawk, and a couple of local Knights joined us "aliens" in a motel room, and we drank a few bourbons and talked. I asked the Klansmen why they hated Negroes. They seemed genuinely surprised. "We don't hate the niggers," the Klaliff said, and others agreed. Cranford told how he supported a family of "no-count niggers" on his place. "We don't hate niggers, long's they behave like colored people," said a Knight. Somebody added that "Northerners don't understand niggers. A nigger's like a dog, he can smell it when you're scared of him."

There was a silence. Raymond Cranford looked musingly at his big hands. "These hands of mine," he said. "They're my secret weapon. By rights they ought to be locked up as a deadly weapon. My hands are like knives—they'll cut a man right across. I can kill a man with the open hand. The tougher the man is, the better I like it."

Cranford had had nothing to drink. He began talking then about a poor white family we had visited that afternoon. The wife and children had come to the door for groceries supplied by the Klan. The man had been lurking somewhere in the house. He was drunk, and he had left his fields untended, and could not hold a job.

"I'm going out there again, maybe tomorrow," Cranford said, "and I'll straighten him out. I'll tell him, 'You straighten out, or I'll bust your tail.' Then maybe I'll shove him up against the wall, and slap him up against the side of a truck, and maybe turn him upside down and shake his brains up a bit. Then I'll tell him, 'Fren, you straighten yourself out, and then we'll go out and get you a job so you can support your family. Course now, I'm not goin' to hurt him, not unless he fights back. If man don't fight back I can't *stand* to whup him. But if he just puts his fists up, man I *love* that. I'll just tear his tail *up*."

There was another silence, as we contemplated Cranford's cure for alcoholism. Then the Klansmen began talking about the rallies the Klan had held every night in the summer—the burning crosses made of big trees dragged out of the forests, the "nigger speeches," the crowds of robed Klansmen. Someone said that the sight of the burning cross gave him a "real religious feeling." Pete Young described a rally at which Collie Leroy Wilkins and the other Alabama Klansmen accused of killing Mrs. Liuzzo had been introduced to the crowd. They were greeted, Young said, with a wild roar of enthusiasm, and the other Klansmen who had been present at the rally nodded happily at the recollection.

It is a reporter's job to listen, to ask questions, to try to understand, to avoid emotional involvement. But suddenly I felt involved, and angry.

"Look," I said to the freckle-faced Klaliff, "you're proud of having fought for your country, and you're right to be proud. But a young man shooting an unarmed woman through the head at a range of ten feet—I don't care what she did, that's a cowardly thing to do, and I just don't see how a brave man like you can shout and clap for a man who did it."

There was a sudden silence in the room. The Klaliff was genuinely shocked—he blushed beet red, as though I had said something obscene.

"Well, now," he said, "I'm not saying I approve of what was done there, but you've gotta remember what she was doing. . . . Anyway, let's face it—this is a war."

There was another silence. Cranford said nothing, but he stared sullenly with his black-rimmed eyes at his big hands, his "secret weapon." For the first and only time, I smelled danger. Then Pete Young changed the subject, and the smell passed. One by one we drifted off to bed. As I was saying good night, the young Klaliff stopped me, and said earnestly, as though trying hard to explain something to me:

"Maybe there's something you don't understand, coming from the North. When it comes to a woman, in the South, why, there's nothing that's respected any more than that."

The next morning Raymond Cranford greeted us bright and early, as usual. The Klaliff was with him, and the Night Hawk. So was a high Klan official, the Grand Klokkard of the Realm, a youngish man with a very thin face, quiet manners, and hard eyes, called Sonny Fischer.

The Grand Klokkard insisted on showing us his klavern. Like Littleton's, Fischer's klavern boasted an open coffin. There were two hand-lettered signs in the coffin—A NIGGER TRIDE A NIGGER DIED, and THIS BOX IS RESERVED FOR MR. BIG MOUTH. Hanging from a wall nearby were two of the long five-cell flashlights which Klansmen carry at rallies—they make very effective clubs, and to make them more effective, they are sometimes lined with lead. One of these flashlights had a deep dent in it. I asked how the dent was made.

"On a burrhead," someone said, and the Klansmen laughed.

Behind the coffin there were two signs which read: OUR GOVERN-

MENT IS DEAD. There was the now familiar picture of Mrs. Liuzzo, walking with two Negroes—again, a Klansman pointed out that she was walking with her shoes in her hand. And hanging from a knob was a little plastic doll of a Negro child.

The doll—it was a girl, in a cotton dress—had a hangman's noose tied around its neck. I asked about this, too, and was told it was "just a joke." I remembered the sign Raymond Cranford had posted in his klavern, and of which he was so proud. A MAN NEVER STOOD SO TALL AS WHEN HE STOOPED TO HELP A CHILD.

Later that day, we said good-bye to Raymond Cranford and his fellow Klansmen. Cranford passed around stickers which read: THE KNIGHTS OF THE KU KLUX KLAN IS WATCHING YOU and BE A MAN JOIN THE KLAN and YOU HAVE BEEN VISITED BY THE KU KLUX KLAN.

"Now, you just stick those on Light-Bulb Johnson's desk when you get up there to Hersheytown," he said, and laughed out loud, for the first time, at his own joke.

Have I been fair to Raymond Cranford? Or would Mrs. Cranford be justified in bringing her machine gun to Washington?

The Kleagle, the Klokkhard, the Night Hawk, Exalted Cyclops Littleton and their wives and children seemed polite, pleasant-mannered people. Raymond Cranford and the other Klansmen were no doubt brave men and patriots by their own lights. And they were all people who wanted very badly, almost desperately, to be understood. Yet, I never did really understand them.

"Maybe there's something you

don't understand coming from the North," the young Klaliff said. Maybe there is. But how *do* you understand people who seem to be moral people, and who feel quite sincerely that a picture of a woman walking with Negroes, with her shoes off, justifies her murder?

Organizer

PETER MATTHIESSEN

The walls at the headquarters of the United Farm Workers Organizing Committee, in Delano, California, are decorated with photographs of Martin Luther King and Mahatma Gandhi; beside them is a blood-red poster of Emiliano Zapata, complete with mustachio, cartridge belts, carbine, sash, sword, and giant sombrero, under the exhortation "*Viva la Revolución.*" All three, in their different ways, are heroes of U.F.W.O.C.'s director, Cesar Chavez. There are also portraits of John Kennedy and Robert Kennedy, black-bordered and hung with flowers, as in a shrine. Here and there is the emblem of U.F.W.O.C., a square-edged black eagle in a white circle on a red background, over the word "HUELGA," which in Spanish means "strike." According to one legend, the eagle appeared in a dream to Chavez; according to another, the inspiration came to Chavez's cousin Manuel

Reprinted by permission of Random House, from "Organizer-II," as it appeared in *The New Yorker* (June 28, 1969), pp. 43, 51, 56, 61.

from the label on a bottle of Gallo Thunderbird wine. The truth is that after Cesar Chavez settled on an Aztec eagle as an appropriate symbol for the union, Manuel sketched one on a piece of brown wrapping paper with the help of Cesar's brother Richard. They then squared off the wing edges so that the eagle would be easier for union members to draw on the handmade flags that are now a familiar sight on picket lines near vineyards in the San Joaquin Valley and elsewhere in California, where for nearly four years U.F.W.O.C. has been conducting a strike to win union contracts for the grape workers.

The organizing work has always gone slowly, and it was especially difficult at first. Manuel Chavez still has his 1963 N.F.W.A. card. On it, along with a green eagle, is printed "Delano Local Number 2. Cesar Chavez, General Director. Manuel Chavez, Secretary-Treasurer." Manuel laughed as he showed it to me. "I guess Cesar was one local and I was the other. We were the membership, too. It's a good thing Richard was still a carpenter—he was kind of supporting us." In this dark period, Chavez, who was penniless, turned down a job, at twenty-one thousand dollars a year, as director of the Peace Corps in a four-country region of South America.

Chavez held on, and by August, 1964, his association had a thousand members. A number of these new members, including Julio Hernandez, who is now a union officer, came from the town of Corcoran, about twenty-five miles northwest of Delano. It was in Corcoran, on October 4, 1933, that five thousand cotton pickers, many of them Mexicans, began a strike that spread up and down the cotton fields of the San Joaquin Valley, and eventually involved eighteen thousand workers. As was customary in the Depression, wages had been drastically pushed down by advertising for many more workers than could be used, then letting starving men with starving families underbid each other for jobs, until the pay ran as low as fifteen cents an hour. When the cotton pickers struck, the growers armed themselves and, after evicting the strikers from their camps, followed them to a rally in Pixley, just north of Delano, where they opened fire on the crowd and killed two workers. A third worker was murdered the same day at Arvin, a town southeast of Delano, in Kern County. Eleven growers were arrested and eleven were acquitted. The strike, which lasted for twenty-four days, won a small wage increase for the workers, but the leaders of the union that ran the strike—the Cannery and Agricultural Workers Industrial Union, an unabashedly pro-Communist organization—were flogged, tarred and feathered, and finally jailed. At the time of the Corcoran strike, an assistant

sheriff was quoted as saying, "We protect our farmers here in Kern County. They are our best people. They are always with us. They keep the country going. They put us in here and they can put us out again, so we serve them. But the Mexicans are trash. They have no standard of living. We herd them like pigs." Like the signs of Chavez's childhood that read "No Dogs or Mexicans Allowed," remarks of this sort are considered poor public relations these days, but the underlying attitude, I was told by members of Chavez's union, is still very much alive.

After a new surge in membership, Mrs. Chavez left the fields to work full time at running the credit union, and Mrs. Huerta took over the bookkeeping and other responsibilities. At about this time, a man named Gilbert Padilla was assigned by the Migrant Ministry to work with Drake on the problem of improving conditions in labor camps run by the counties of Kern and Tulare for migrant workers. A large-scale rent strike organized in the Linnell and Woodville camps of Tulare County by Drake and Padilla and a lawyer named Gary Bellow finally closed them down and led to the construction of new camp buildings. "The county was making a big profit on those camps, which were just slums," Drake told me. "When the workers found out about that profit, it wasn't hard to organize a rent strike." The workers Drake and Padilla had organized during their rent strike came into Chavez's association in February, 1965, and in the summer of that year Padilla led them in a strike at the J. D. Martin Ranch, in Tulare County near Earlimart, and won a pay raise for the grape pickers there. This small victory lifted morale in the new union, and that September what is now known as the California Grape Strike began in earnest.

Chavez eats no breakfast and is careless about lunch. He usually sits down to a modest meal in the evening. During the day, he drinks a great deal of Diet-Rite Cola, and he keeps a supply of dried apricots and prunes and a package of matzos in a drawer in his desk at U.F.W.O.C. headquarters in Delano. On the other hand, he is very fond of Chinese food, and I drove thirty miles with him one evening last summer to eat dinner at his favorite Chinese restaurant in Bakersfield. It was a family outing. Helen Chavez and four Chavez daughters went in one car, with a friend; Chavez and I were in a second car with the youngest daughter, Elizabeth, and the two young Chavez sons, Anthony and Paul. The only child missing was Fernando, nineteen, who was living with his Chavez grandparents in San Jose.

All eight of the Chavez children have nicknames. Elizabeth, who was then ten, had pronounced her own "name as "Titibeth" when she was a baby, and it had stuck; Paul, eleven, who had been an especially rotund infant, started out as Bubble, and the name was later modified to Babo; and Anthony, who had just turned nine, was called Birdie, because of his supposed resemblance to a bird. "My own name was Manzi," Chavez told me. "As a small child, I was supposed to have liked *manzanilla*—you know, camomile tea? So the family always called me Manzi."

The memory made him smile. There is a single silver strand in the black Indian hair that falls across his forehead, and a black mole on the brown skin just below his lower lip

seems to balance a gold tooth in his smile. He went on talking cheerfully about his childhood. His paternal grandfather had been a peon in Mexico, but had come to the United States with his family in 1889 and acquired, as a homesteader, about a hundred and sixty acres of sage and mesquite desert in the Gila River Valley some fifteen miles northeast of Yuma, Arizona. Chavez's parents were both born in Mexico, but Cesar Estrada Chavez entered the world, on March 31, 1927, as a citizen of the United States. According to Chavez, his grandfather, another Cesar, greatly admired the big Mexican haciendas, and since he had nine sons and six daughters, some of whom had families of their own, he designed his house on the same scale. It lasted a half century, and might have lasted indefinitely in that dry climate if the roof had been of tile instead of adobe, because the walls were twenty-four inches thick. The house was cool in summer, warm in winter; it stood on a slope against the hills, with a laundry and a woodshed on one side and a garden on the other side. The farm produced cotton, lettuce, carrots, and watermelon, with maize, grain, and alfalfa for the animals, and it fed not only the Chavez families but many strangers who were wandering up and down the land in the Depression years. "At that time," Chavez said, "my mother's patron saint was St. Edwiges—I think she was a queen who gave everything to the poor— and my mother had made a pledge never to turn away anyone who came for food. And so, you know, ordinary people would come and have the food, and there were a lot of hoboes that used to come, at any time of day or night. Most of them were white. We lived in my aunt's house in Yuma for a while, and my mother sent my brother Richard and me out into the street sometimes to look for *trampitas*—that was our affectionate way of calling the hoboes. I remember the first one. We found him sitting under a retaining wall, right around the corner, and we wanted this one bad, so we could quit looking and go play. But when we told him all about the free food just waiting for him around the corner, that tramp couldn't believe it. 'What for?' he said. 'What are you doing it for?' 'For nothing,' we said. 'You just come with us.' So we hustled him around the corner, and he ate the food, but he still didn't believe it. She'd just give them very simple things—beans and tortillas and hot coffee—but it was a meal, and soon all the hoboes knew about her, because word spreads. We didn't have much, and sometimes there was enough for everybody and sometimes there wasn't."

It is as an organizer, rather than a union leader, that Chavez sees himself, and one afternoon while we were driving back to Delano from some appointments he had had in San Francisco he told me, with cheerful fatalism, that when his union is established and his own people, no longer preoccupied with survival and aspiring to consumer status, find him too thorny for their liking and kick him out, he might like to go and organize somewhere else—maybe in the Mexican slums of East Los Angeles. He always speaks passionately about organizing, but he does not romanticize his work. "There's no trick to organizing, there's no shortcut. A good organizer is someone willing to work long and hard," he said. "Just keep talking to people, and the people will

respond. People can be organized for the most ridiculous things. They can be organized for bad as well as good. Look at the John Birch Society. Look at Hitler. The reactionaries are always better organizers. The right has a lot of discipline that the left lacks. The left always dilutes itself. Instead of merging to go after the common enemy, the left splinters, and the splinters go after one another. Meanwhile, the right keeps after its objective, pounding away, pounding away."

Going south through Oakland toward the freeway, Chavez pointed out St. Mary's Church, in whose hall he had held his first big meeting for the Community Service Organization. "I was green, you know, but we brought in over four hundred people. Oh, I was so happy! I was *happy!*"

By the time we reached the freeway, it was nearly five, and an hour later we were still caught on a belt of noise and ugliness that bored through the sprawling suburbs of the Bay area. The rush-hour traffic was stifling any chance we had of reaching Delano in time for a union meeting that evening, and Chavez said, "Maybe I could stop in San Jose and just say hello to my mother and my dad." Aside from his parents and his son Fernando, he has two sisters and a brother living in San Jose. The brother is a carpenter. One sister is married to a carpenter, the other to a plasterer. "They're pretty good guys," Chavez said. "But they're not interested in what we're doing. I don't see too much of them." Chavez talked a lot about his sister Rita, who became president of the San Jose C.S.O. In a fight to get blacks into her chapter, he said proudly, she had beaten down the prejudice against them that she found among many of the Mexicans. "Oh, Rita's great!" he said. "If she had a choice, she'd be swinging with us right now, down in Delano."

Chavez has always wanted to have his family involved in his organizing work as much as possible. "Of course, I'm lucky to have an exceptional woman," he said. "Even if I come home at four in the morning, I give her a full report on what has happened, and to this day—well, most of the time—she still wants me to do this."

He recalled one Sunday when his wife succeeded in getting him to accompany the family on a picnic. There were so many workers coming to see him on their day off that he planned to leave very early in the morning to avoid refusing them. But a few arrived before he could get away and had to be left unattended to, and Chavez felt so miserable all day that he ruined the picnic for everybody. That evening, he told his wife that he was being pulled apart, that he had to give his full time to the people and just do the best he could with his own family. "It's lucky I have Helen there, because I'm never really home," he said. "I was home when two of the children were born and away for all the rest." He closed his eyes and massaged them with the fingers of one hand—a characteristic gesture of distress. "You know, I always felt that because I really wanted to do something for people this would be all right. But we talk about sacrificing ourselves and often we are sacrificing others. By the time Birdie came, Helen was pretty much used to it, I guess, but . . ." He stopped speaking for a minute, then opened his eyes, and when he spoke again his voice was harsher. "You cannot have it both

ways. Either you concentrate your attention on the people who have claims on you or you say, 'No, I have, to help many more at their expense.' You don't exclude them totally, and they get more attention than anybody else, but they aren't going to get enough. You can't have it both ways. You cannot! Anybody who uses the family as an excuse not to do what he has to do . . ." He stopped again, then resumed, in a quieter voice. "I haven't been home in four nights. Sometimes I'm away for ten nights, maybe more. It hurts me not to be home with my family, you know—I feel it. The whole thing is rough on the children. I know that. They don't like living in poverty, especially when they know that it's intentional on my part. And things get harder as they get older—it's harder to get nice hand-me-down clothes and everything. But they are great, they are just great!" He smiled. "I told them that they were better off than the migrants, that at least they had a purpose in their lives, and they understood this—they really did. Of course, they think I'm pretty old-fashioned. I tease Sylvia about always fixing her hair—the waste of time, you know. I told her that women are prettier the way they are made, that they should leave their hair the way it came. And I make a lot of fun of people who give their spare time to mowing the lawn, or washing their cars, or playing golf. To me, it's such a waste of time. How can you justify doing that sort of thing as long as all these other things are going on—the suffering?"

Severe back pains that had been dragging Chavez down for months finally forced him to take some time off last autumn; and he went to St. Anthony's, a Franciscan seminary in

Santa Barbara, where he could have daily therapy at a hospital. I found him flat on his back in bed. In crisp white pajamas, he looked small. He greeted me cheerfully but made no effort to sit up when he took my hand, his drawn face patched with gray from months of pain. Over his head, three rosaries hung from an extended bar, and with them a Jewish mezuzah on a silver chain, which he always puts on under his shirt when he goes out. "I'm sure Christ wore a mezuzah," he said, with a grin. "He certainly didn't wear a cross." On a wall of the room, as in his office in Delano, there was a Mexican straw crucifix. It was a small room, and the bed, a washstand, two stiff chairs, and a small bureau filled it. On the bureau was a borrowed tape recorder, with tapes of some flamenco music by Manitas de Plata and songs of Joan Baez. There was also a framed photograph of Gandhi.

There had been some bad news from Delano. Mack Lyons, the workers' representative at DiGiorgio, had found two groups of non-union pruners working in DiGiorgio's Arvin vineyards, and when the pruners were questioned they said that the vineyards had been sold. Since the union had been unable to obtain a so-called successor clause in the contract with DiGiorgio, guaranteeing that the contract would bind a new owner, this was a serious blow, and Chavez had called an emergency meeting to discuss how to handle the new threat. The next phase of the long battle was clearly going to be a difficult one, and Chavez would need all his strength for it. (In March of this year, Dr. Janet Travell, who treated President Kennedy, concluded that Chavez's back trouble was not a degenerative-disc condition, as had been thought, but a muscle spasm caused by the fact that one of his legs is shorter than the other and one side of his pelvis is smaller—an imbalance to which, as he grows older and less resilient, his muscles can no longer adjust. Dr. Travell's treatment is the first that has given Chavez any real relief.)

Last fall in Santa Barbara, there was speculation that the long fast Chavez had made earlier in the year might have aggravated his back condition, and in the sun on a porch outside his room I talked with Helen Chavez about the fast. She told me that at the beginning he had kept it secret for about three days. At home, he would pretend that he had already eaten or that he wasn't hungry. Then one day Manuel said to her, "Is he still fasting?" After that, she offered Cesar all his favorite foods, and still he would not eat. Finally, she confronted him in his office, and when he admitted he was fasting she got very upset; she was sure he would harm himself. "The kids were already worried," she said. "And when I told them, they said, 'Dad looks awful. Will he be O.K.?' But after another day or so we got used to the idea and went along with him."

Not everyone went along. The fast, which lasted twenty-five days, split the union down the middle. Mrs. Chavez and Richard and Manuel knew that he had been fasting before he announced it, but even they were stunned by his intention of prolonging the fast indefinitely. So was LeRoy Chatfield, who still speaks with awe of the speech in which Chavez announced his decision. Chavez had called a special meeting for twelve noon on Monday, February 19, 1968, at a hall in Delano, and the strikers and the office staff as well as their families were there. Several acts of violence had been committed by union people, and he talked for an hour and a half about nonviolence. He discussed Vietnam, wondering aloud how so many of his listeners could deplore the violence in Asia and yet promote it in the United States. He said that the Mexican tradition of proving manliness—*machismo*—through violence was in error. *La Causa* must not risk a single life on either side, because it *was* a cause, not just a union, and had to deal with people not as membership cards or Social Security numbers but as human beings, one by one.

"Cesar took a very hard line," Chatfield told me. "He said we were falling back on violence in the strike because we weren't creative enough or imaginative enough to find another solution—because we didn't *work* hard enough. One of the things he said in the speech was that he felt we had lost our will to win—by which he meant that behaving violently or advocating violence, or even thinking that maybe violence isn't such a bad thing, is really losing your will to win, your commitment to win. This seems like a very idealistic position, but there's truth in it. Anarchy leads to chaos, and out of chaos rises the demagogue. That's one of the reasons he is so upset about *la raza*. The same Mexicans that ten years ago were talking about themselves as Spaniards are coming on real strong these days as Mexicans. Everyone should be proud of what he is, of course, but race is only skin-deep. It's phony, and it comes out of frustration—the *la raza* people are not secure. They want to use Cesar as a symbol of their na-

tionalism. But he doesn't want any part of it. He said to me just the other day, 'Can't they understand that that's just the way Hitler started?' A few months ago, a big foundation gave some money to a *la raza* group —they liked the outfit's sense of pride, or something—and Cesar really told them off. He feels that racism will destroy our union faster than anything else—that it plays right into the growers' hands if they can keep the minorities fighting, pitting one race against another, one group against another."

In his speech that day, Chavez discussed the civil-rights movement and how, in its recourse to violence, it had made black people suffer; black homes, not white, were being burned, and black sons killed. The union, he said, had raised the hopes of many poor people. It had a responsibility to those people, whose hopes, along with all the union gains, would be destroyed after the first cheap victories of violence. Finally, he announced the fast. It was not a hunger strike, because its purpose was not strategic; it was an act of prayer and love for the union members, because, as their leader, he felt responsible for the acts of all of them. There would be no vote on the fast, which would continue for an indefinite period, and had, in fact, begun the week before. He was not going into seclusion, and would continue his work as best he could. He asked that the people in the room keep the news entirely to themselves. Since it was difficult to fast at home, and since the Forty Acres was the spiritual home of the union, he would walk there as soon as he had finished speaking, and remain there until the fast was done. "His act was intensely personal,"

Chatfield told me. "And the whole theme of his speech was love. In fact, his last words to us before he left the room and started that long walk to the Forty Acres were something like 'I am doing this because I love you.' "

Helen Chavez followed Cesar from the hall, and everyone sat for some time in silence. Then the meeting was taken over by Larry Itliong, the assistant director, who said straight out that Brother Chavez should be persuaded to come off the fast. Manuel Chavez then declared that Cesar was an Indian, and therefore stubborn, and that once he had made up his mind to do something, nothing anyone could say was going to stop him. Other members made many other comments. One man, for example, dismissed all the talk about striker violence as grower propaganda, and therefore saw no reason for the fast. Some of the Protestants and agnostics in the union, white and brown, still resented the Catholic aura of the Sacramento march of the year before, and now they felt offended all over again. They were supported by some Catholics, who felt that the Church was being exploited, and also by most of the white volunteers, the Jews especially, who disliked any religious overtone whatever. For the first week or so, almost the whole board of directors was against the fast. On the other hand, the membership, largely Catholic, accepted it in apprehensive faith. The people complied with Chavez's request that no one try a fast of sympathy on his own, but he learned later, from the candidly expressed annoyance of their wives, that three young men had taken a vow of chastity for the duration of the fast, and held to it. He speaks of this sacrifice with awe and regret, but it seemed to him a moving example of the farm workers' new spirit.

There were many misgivings and many doubts about what Chavez was trying to accomplish. "When we visited Cesar in his little room at the Forty Acres," Chatfield told me, "he would point at the wall and say, 'See that white wall? Well, imagine ten different-colored balls, all jumping up and down. One ball is called Religion, another Propaganda, another Organizing, another Law, and so forth. When people look at that wall and see those balls, different people look at different balls, and each person keeps his eye on his own ball. For each person, the balls mean different things, but for everyone they can mean something.' I began to see what he meant. My ball was Propaganda, and I kept my eye on that. I could therefore be perfectly comfortable, and understand the fast completely in those terms, and not negate the nine other balls—Organizing, say. And, as a matter of fact, we never organized so many people in such a short time, before or since. The fast gave the lie to the growers' claim that we had no following. Some people came every night to attend Mass at the Forty Acres—came sixty-five, eighty-five miles every night. People stood in line for an hour, two hours, to talk with him. Cesar saw it as a fantastic opportunity to talk to one man, one family, at a time. When that person leaves, he goes away with something. He's no longer a member, he's an organizer. At the Sunday Mass, we had as many as two thousand people. That's what the growers don't understand—we're all over the state. In fact, there's nowhere in this state or anywhere in the Southwest where the people don't know about Cesar Chavez and the

United Farm Workers. And they say, 'When is he coming? Are we next?' "

As the fast wore on through February and into March, many of the farm workers became worried, and a number of strikers came to Manuel and swore that they would never be violent again if he could just persuade Cesar to quit. Other members were made increasingly uncomfortable by the religious implications of the fast, especially after the seventeenth day, when Chavez asked his brother Richard to construct a simple cross— the materials cost a dollar and a half, according to Richard—which was later burned by vandals. The cross was the ultimate affront to at least two volunteers. One dismissed the entire fast as "a cheap publicity stunt." The other, who had once been a priest, accused Chavez of having a Messiah complex. Both soon quit the United Farm Workers for good.

At a Mass of Thanksgiving that concluded the fast, Chavez was too weak to speak, and a brief speech was read for him, in English and in Spanish. After describing the purpose of the fast, he concluded as follows: "When we are really honest with ourselves, we must admit that our lives are all that really belongs to us. So it is how we use our lives that determines what kind of men we are. It is my deepest belief that only by giving our lives do we find life. I am convinced that the truest act of courage, the strongest act of manliness, is to sacrifice ourselves for others in a totally non-violent struggle for justice. To be a man is to suffer for others. God help us be men."

Nightmare Journey

BOB CLARK

My long day's journey into a nightmare began Monday afternoon when I received a phone call from Howard Chapnick of the Black Star Photo Agency. He asked me if I wanted to go to Detroit to cover the riots. I found myself saying yes. Actually, I was in the mood to involve myself in

Reprinted with permission of the publisher from *Ebony*, October, 1967, pp. 121–30.

this kind of experience. I really wanted to know what was going on behind the scenes and I wanted to know it first hand. I had covered a race riot in San Francisco and worked on news stories in the deep South. I once interviewed Stokely Carmichael for a German magazine. I thought I had a feel for the current picture of race relations in America. But Newark and Detroit were a new breed of cat. What was happening in our big city ghettos and how far would it go? Chapnick called me back within an hour and we made final arrangements. Soon I was on an early evening flight to Detroit.

Aboard the plane I kept trying to think of someone I could contact in the city. I knew there wouldn't be time to just roam. Things were happening fast and if I expected to get photographs I would have to be on top of things from the beginning. Being a Negro photographer would present special problems. I could expect rejection and hostility from both whites and blacks. I knew from past experience that black people won't hesitate to attack a "black sellout." I also knew that when violence has taken over a community, police don't always bother to ask questions or check carefully. I told myself I had better move around damn carefully or suffer the consequences.

As the plane banked into Metropolitan Airport I could see clouds of dense smoke drifting up from the city. As I think back now, I realize that even seeing that smoke I did not foresee the massive devastation or the enormous danger ahead of me. I remember tensing up and promising myself I would not be gun-shy. I tried to force myself to relax mentally and I vowed to work real loose.

At the Sheraton Cadillac Hotel there were many reporters and photographers in the lobby. The word at the moment was that there were a great many fires around the city but things seemed to have quieted down. I struck up a conversation with a white man who was standing near by. He was short, stockily built and tough-looking and this appearance matched his trade. An ex-boxer turned promoter, Don Elbaum was in

town for a boxing show that was canceled after the riots began. Elbaum said he was in the midst of the rioting on Sunday because a lot of his boxers were Negroes from the city's ghetto area. Now he was waiting in the lobby in the hope of meeting some of his boys and he wondered whether I would like to talk with them. I thought this was a good idea so I raced up to my room, changed clothes and returned to the lobby in a few minutes. Elbaum and I waited about half-an-hour but no one came. I began to get edgy about losing time.

I tried calling police headquarters and local television stations to find out where the action was, but either the phones were not answered or no one could offer any precise information.

Don Elbaum is one of those fast-talking, fast-moving sort of people who are in the know about what's going on and always have to be where the action is. When I decided to move on, he came with me. Don knew Detroit very well and guessed that the West side was the hot spot at the moment. We used his car and headed that way. The streets were deserted except for patrols of state troopers and national guardsmen. I was surprised to see that even in the downtown area of the city, buildings were burned and ransacked. I saw cars filled with volunteer sheriffs. These private cars raced about the city, shotguns and rifles protuding from the windows. Just the sight of them made my heart slip into my stomach, because I sensed that these men were my biggest menace.

We arrived somewhere; I don't know exactly where or how we got there. All I know is that all hell broke loose. It was a national guard position and snipers were pouring their fire into it. Guardsmen returned the fire with automatic weapons. They had a cross-fire going and it was impossible to know who was firing at whom. The guardsmen fired flares into the darkness and there were lengthy fusillades. I couldn't imagine anyone living through all that fire-power. I crawled out of the car and up into a front position. As I dodged from one point of cover to the next, I yelled out, "I'm press, don't shoot!" It was pitch black. I couldn't shoot pictures without using strobe lights and that would mean blinding some of the guardsmen or exposing their positions. I just squatted—listening and watching—for what seemed like an eternal 20 minutes and then went back to the car.

Don and I cruised around again. We spotted fire on the West side and drove toward it. A large warehouse or factory building was burning furiously and before the fire trucks could get into position the sniper-fire began. A small, three-storey house across an alley from the factory began to burn also. Women and children streamed out of this building carrying what belongings they could. Some men who lived in the neighborhood ran up to the house carrying small lawn hoses. The whole scene was like an unreal movie. Now the house was almost completely ablaze but the men refused to stop trying to put out the fire with those ridiculous hoses. I thought they were pathetic and comical. I ran into the building and on the second floor I was stopped by heat and smoke. A guardsman raced past me heading out of the building. "There's an old man in there," he yelled. "He won't come out. He says this is his home." Outside, high voltage wires began to fall

and whip about, throwing a spray of deadly sparks. A woman screamed, "My baby, my baby! Where is my baby!" A guardsman tried to comfort her. He looked shaken and frustrated. His commander was shouting for the guardsmen to pull out of the area. The fires raged and the flames seemed to cast shadows of despair over these homeless black people. I wondered where they would go now. If they tried walking to find help and shelter they could very well be shot in the dark by a frightened guardsman. I could still hear guardsmen shouting about the man who refused to leave his house and I wondered: how could anyone be willing to die for such a dilapidated old building in such a filthy, hot, stinking neighborhood? I felt helpless and wondered why men are not supposed to cry.

Don and I drove around the burning streets for awhile. We were stopped and searched at almost every block by scared guardsmen with trembling rifles. The rows of burning buildings seemed endless in the night. It struck me at this moment that this was war; that finally America was feeling the destruction and despair of war on her own shores.

I don't know how long we drove around but soon we heard gunfire again and headed for the sound. This time state troopers were being fired upon from a burning building. They returned the fire intensely. A cease-fire was ordered and soon a man emerged from around the corner of the building. He was a tall, dark Negro. His shirt was almost completely ripped off and his body was covered with blood. "Don't shoot! Don't shoot!" he yelled. He was seized and searched. While the troopers frisked him he kept yelling, "Them niggers shot me! Them crazy niggers around the corner, they shot me! Please don't hurt me. I ain't no sniper." I moved in for a photograph and a state trooper stepped in front of me. I moved around him and prepared to shoot again. This time I was shoved by the trooper. "You don't want that picture, do you fella?" he growled. I got the message but I played dumb. "I'm press. I have a right to photograph this situation." I pulled out my press card. "I don't give a goddamned who you are! You get off this f———— street or you'll be treated like the rest," he yelled. I could see he was rattled. As he hollered, he kept slamming me with the shotgun barrel. I moved on. I was trembling inside and I wondered if I should have pushed my argument further. I was upset because I missed the picture. As dawn grew near, police and troopers got tougher to deal with. Don and I were driving around in the dark without lights. Police and guardsmen had shot out all street lamps and were fair game for all. It was almost dawn when we returned to the hotel.

The next morning I called Howard Chapnick in New York and gave him a brief run down on my experiences. I asked him to send me a telegram stating that I was an accredited photo-journalist. Later, armed with this telegram, I went to police headquarters and spoke with the lieutenant in charge. I asked him if I would need any special kind of permit to work in the riot area and what, if any, restrictions were being laid on the press. He told me that the only retsrictions were at night in the vicinity of 12th Street and on Linwood Avenue. These had been among the worst trouble spots and were now completely blocked off to everyone. He checked my telegram from Chapnick, and my press card, and said that I should have no difficulty with these credentials.

I spent the afternoon photographing sporadic fires and sniper action as well as scenes of homeless families. In the late afternoon I was shooting some street scenes when a young guardsman, who looked as though the violent events of the past few days had mad him half-crazed, raced up to me and demanded to see my press pass. Singling out me, he had ignored at least half-a-dozen other photographers—all white—who were also working the same area. We argued, and this was one of the times I pushed the issue. He finally backed off and let me alone. A young Negro who was standing nearby and had been watching this incident sympathetically, came up to me and we began talking. He said he was a Muslim. We spoke about the episode and then he asked me where my sympathies lay. How did I feel about what was happening? I convinced him that I was on the side of Negroes no matter what they did. I expressed the attitude that we are all "soul brothers." I told him I was keenly interested in meeting and talking with young men in the community who were out with the action. The young Muslim said I could walk along with him and he would introduce me to whoever was around.

During our walk I met some youngsters who I later learned were snipers. They laughingly told me that they were spreading rumors that they were planning an attack that night on some suburban communities when in actuality they were going to strike at the downtown district. They told me where they were going to meet later that night and said I could come along if I wished. I photographed these men and then returned to the hotel.

Don Elbaum was still in a mood to stay with the action so we left the hotel together about 9 p.m. We were heading for a meeting with the snipers at a Howard Johnson's somewhere in the downtown district. On our way there, we heard heavy gunfire and followed the sound. As we drew near to the scene our car was fired upon. Shotgun pellets rained on the roof and pelted the windshield. We stopped and crawled to the floor of the car. When the firing died down we identified ourselves and pulled up closer. The position was manned by state troopers and police who were battling snipers. I knew that it's difficult to take pictures during a gun battle but figured I might get some dramatic pictures if any snipers were flushed out and arrested. As Don and I edged closer, the firing started again. The troopers and police were pinned down by a deadly crossfire from the rooftops. The snipers were firing automatic weapons with tracer bullets. We must have stayed pinned for an hour before we were able to sneak away from this skirmish.

We headed for the meeting with the snipers. We found the location but they never showed up. I decided to check with the police department again about my credentials in case the lieutenant on duty during the afternoon had made a mistake about night-time regulations. I was again assured my passes were in order and that I could work during the night.

It was about 10:30 when Don and I left the precinct and saw a fire truck racing to a call. We followed. Our car was stopped and searched many times before we finally arrived at the site of the blaze only to find that the fire truck was returning to its engine house at Warren and Lawton streets. Again, we followed. The area around the firehouse was under heavy sniper attack and the firemen were awfully jumpy. We were checked again and I asked a state trooper at a road block if I could get out of the car and look around. Another fire engine started to pull out of the station and we decided to follow it. We were still near the engine house when we were ordered by guardsmen to halt. We were told to spread eagle against the hood. We showed our press cards and waited. A trooper passed by and called out that he had just checked us and that we were press. The guardsmen ignored the trooper and continued frisking us. Don and I were ordered to lay down on the ground. A young National Guard lieutenant was really giving us a going over. I didn't realize what was happening until another car passed by and someone yelled out, "Halt! Shoot that car! Get them niggers!" There were cries like this all over the place and suddenly shotgun blasts were ringing out everywhere. These fellows were really spooked and acting vicious. They had been under sniper attack all evening without being able to see a thing. I guess they had to take it out on somebody and the somebody was anybody black that passed by in a car.

Don and I were ordered to stand up, hands behind our backs. When I looked up, I froze with terror. There, ahead of us, stood a gauntlet of two long rows of blood-hungry firemen. They were screaming at the top of their lungs: "Kill the black bastards! Castrate those coons! Shoot 'em in the nuts!" A young guardsman crouched before me, his rifle bayonet thrust forward menacingly. His face flushed with fear and excitement and I knew that if I so much as stumbled he would blow a hole in me big enough to put a basketball in. "God-dammit, move!" he hollered. I stepped forward and heard someone scream, "What's that nigger smiling at. Wipe the smile off that monkey's face." A big, red face loomed up in mine. It spit and then suddenly, everyone was spitting, punching, kicking. I don't know how many times I was punched in the groin. I just kept thinking that if I fell I would be shot or stomped to death. I felt the blows on the back of my head. I don't know whether they were rifle butts or what. We must have been far down the gauntlet and near the firehouse door when Don spun around and yelled, "I'll take anyone of you that thinks he's man enough!" I thought they would finish him for sure but a guardsman gave him a crack with a rifle and he was inside the door. We were butted into a small detention room and left with two guardsmen to watch us. The windows were open and the firemen gathered to scream obscenities at us.

My mind was in chaos and couldn't organize what was happening to me. When I had first looked up and seen the gauntlet of firemen standing and screaming before me, I guess a thousand things ran through my mind. I didn't realize I was smiling because certainly I felt a long way from that kind of emotion. I guess I could have been thinking: so this is America! I know that my smug intellectual philosophy about the race problem was destroyed. I kept thinking about the pain, and perhaps even death, on a more real basis than ever before in

my life. I knew they wanted me to cringe and beg and cry out: "Please mista boss man, don't hurt me!" And I wanted to. I wanted to run or plead. But I also knew this wouldn't help, that they would still beat me or kill me and that my pleading would only demonstrate to them how tough they were and add to their violent passions. I know that I don't remember most of the pain. What stands out most in my mind is my struggle then to contain my fear.

We were in the room for about ten minutes when the door flew open and two more "niggers" were shoved into the room. They were badly scared; so scared they couldn't follow orders. "Oh, my God, Oh my God! I'm so scared."

There was more gunfire now outside and the guardsmen ordered us to lie down. The firing lasted for about 15 minutes. We sat for over an hour and I tried to find out why we were being held. No one seemed to know. The guardsmen vaguely said something about a gasoline can and a knife. We did have an empty can of gasoline in the car trunk. It was rusty and I doubt it had ever been used. The knife was of Boy Scout manufacture and I carried it as a tool in my camera bag.

A police wagon arrived and a guardsman escorted each of us out individually. One of them grabbed me by the hair, stuck his 45 caliber automatic in the base of my skull and shoved me out. The firemen were lined up outside the door again and we received more beatings before we were pummeled into the police van. Inside the wagon we waited again. No one seemed to know what to do with us. State troopers brought in another Negro. He was a big, middle-aged man and they said he had a rifle in his car. They kicked and punched him into the wagon and called him all sorts of names. A cop walked up and said, "Is this the black son-of-a-bitch with a rifle? He must be a big man on his block. Let's make him run. The bastard doesn't deserve a cell." They hauled him out of the wagon and three of them beat him without mercy. One just whipped away at his head with a black-jack while two others hammered at him with rifle butts. Someone yelled, "Stop! You'll kill the coon." A shrill voice answered, "I don't give a good f—— if I do!" They laughed as the blood seemed to gush from every part of the man's head. He pleaded and cried and then they threw him back into the wagon. I saw that his face and nose looked as though they were split in two. I couldn't look at this.

During the ride to the police station, a national guardsman sat over me and kept telling me about what they did to niggers in his neck of the woods. We arrived at a police precinct but there was no room. We drove on to another station. This place apparently didn't have an arresting officer to book us on the charges we were to be held for. To simplify matters, the driver was ordered to make out charges and be photographed with us. We were then lined up in a garage and kicked and punched. After being mugged and fingerprinted I was told to sign a card which bore my fingerprints and a charge reading: VIOLATION OF CURFEW. I said I would not sign it without legal counsel and that I didn't understand the charge against me. I showed an officer my press card and Chapnick's telegram. He took them from me and

left the room. When he returned he told me to sign the card or else I would spend a long time in jail. Both Don Elbaum and I refused to sign. We were then marched downstairs into the basement where there is a room which is normally used as a pistol firing range. It was damn cold and dirty with no place to sit or lay. About six women were down there and we were only separated by a small railing. By the next morning the room was filled beyond capacity. We were not permitted to make any phone calls or do anything about obtaining legal counsel. Practically everyone in the room was bloody or had been beaten. Most of the men and youths were gangsters and hustlers and practically all of them boasted about looting or sniping they had done.

I spoke to Eddie Dinkins, the man who had been so brutally beaten outside the fire house for having a rifle in his car. Dinkins is 51 years old, has five children and works for a Ford steel mill as a cleaner. He said he was on his way to work on the number one shift, which starts at 12 p.m. Because of the riot and fires next to his home, Dinkins thought it would be best to keep all his valuables with him. In addition to the rifle, he put in his car just about everything that meant something to him. He wanted to keep the rifle, even though he had never used it and the barrel was rusty.

One easily loses track of time in jail. There were no windows so we couldn't have a feeling of day or night. Some of us had had watches so I know that we were brought downstairs about 12:30 Wednesday morning. We received no food until almost 18 hours later. That meal was two slices of bread and one thin slice of lunch meat. Our next meal was 4 p.m. the next day, Thursday, and this was a repeat of the first feast. We had nothing to drink and no decent toilet facilities.

On Thursday afternoon a young white boy, who was arrested for violation of curfew at the same time I was, had an epileptic convulsion. It was a bad one and I knew the danger because my younger sister suffered from the same illness. Both Don and myself administered what first aid we could. We yelled for help and two guards came. I explained the boy's illness and the danger. They looked down at the boy who was foaming at the mouth and one of the guards said, "Tough s . . t!" Then they both walked out of the room. I begged for some ice to help pull the youth out of it. Another guard brought me two ice cubes wrapped in a paper towel. I finally managed to force open the boy's mouth and then I massaged him until the convulsions left his body. He just lay there in the filth and fell into a deep sleep. The boy usually takes pills to control convulsions. I told a guard that he needed medical attention badly but like all the rest of our pleas this one also went unheeded.

During the second day our impromptu "cell" stank. We had about 50 men and six women cramped together, some covered with caked blood and everyone dirty from two days of being unable to clean themselves after using the toilet. The guards thought it was a great joke to show off "the Zoo" (as they called it) to national guardsmen. We could hear them eating, drinking and joking about breaking some nigger's ass. They spoke without inhibitions because we were animals and it didn't matter what they did to us or said about us. When some of them were bored, they would come into the cell and shove a shotgun or rifle into someone's face and make them beg. Thursday night a short, slim Negro was brought in. He was there for only about five minutes because he was a known sniper. He was beaten badly. His shirt was torn off and he was covered with blood. There was a deep gash in his head which was so swollen and distorted that the man looked as though he was born with a deformity in which one skull had grown out of the original. He was taken into a corridor and beaten until it was unbearable to listen to his pleas. I saw the same man again on Friday and found it hard to believe that he could have lived through such a beating or even be moving around conscious. His entire body looked like one massive wound.

A white youth was brought in either Wednesday or Thursday. He was suspected of being a sniper and while being booked he received a large gash in his skull from a bayonet-wielding national guardsman. They gave him little peace. Every time a cop came near the basement, the guard at our door would bring him in to see the little white sniper.

On Wednesday, I believe, we received another inmate. Still high from a big night of adventure, he was just popping to brag about his sniping. "Man, I got four of them last night! I sat up there with my bottle of wine and they didn't know what was happening. There was about 35 of us and we waited until a group of five cars came into the block. Nobody fired until they were right in the middle and then our guys in the front opened up. Two cars backed out of it but the rest of them were pinned and so scared they didn't even know what to shoot at. We kept 'em like that until reinforcements got there and then we split. They just didn't know what to do with us. I was having a good time!" He was arrested on his way home, he said, because someone had tipped the police that he was a looter. He just had time to hide his gun.

The "cell" became unbearable. We were starving, dirty and needed desperately to talk with someone about getting out. Everytime a guard showed his face near the door, dozens of inmates would rush to the bars and beg for food. Tempers flared and fights erupted. We were not far from becoming the animals our guards believed us to be. At first I thought all I had to do was be calm until Black Star found me but as the days passed I realized that it might well take the agency weeks to locate me. It hit me that I could well end up in a state prison or perhaps even be shot for trying to escape while being transported from one prison to another. I saw the power these men had and suddenly everything seemed futile. Everything I had believed about this country just didn't seem real anymore.

Thursday afternoon we were moved upstairs into a small cell that was approximately 20-feet square and hot as an oven. We were given another baloney sandwich and told that we would either be released or sent to court on Friday. That was good news and everyone's spirits rose. I didn't care what they did to me any longer. I just wanted to talk with someone who had some intelligence. I had been holding everything inside of me for three days and I felt as though I had reached my limit and was ready to explode.

Elbaum, four other men and myself had been there longer than any-

one else in the group. We were so crowded in our new cell that even floor space was at a premium. If you were lucky enough to find space on the floor so you could stretch your legs out, you just didn't move because someone else would grab it. I bought a paper bag from a guy for a dollar so that I could take notes to occupy my mind.

Most of the prisoners knew each other from their neighborhoods. The majority were hustlers and two-bit gangsters. They boasted about how much loot they got. Listening to them I became convinced there was no outside conspiracy or special organization that had welded them together. Their one common point of focus seemed to be a terrific hate for the Detroit police. Their only "organization" was that they would meet and decide to go out and shoot cops.

Friday morning the guard brought us a new inmate. He looked the role of today's young revolutionary. Under his arm he held a recording of the late Malcolm X's speeches. It was apparent that he had been drinking the previous night and the liquor was still talking to him loud and clear: "Hey guard, you stupid white bastards, I want out!" His voice echoed down the corridor and he continued with a long tirade of abuses until we all became quite nervous. Everyone began telling him to shut up and sit down before the guards returned for another head-whipping session. He looked at us scornfully and in the grandest manner possible told us how lowly and whipped we were. He began to expound the glory of Mao Tse-Tung and tried to convince us to overpower the guards and take over the whole damn precinct.

In a quiet moment, a stocky, powerfully built Negro rose from the floor, calmly looked our young revolutionary in the eye and said: "Boy, if you don't sit down and be nice and quiet, and if they don't feed us because of your big mouth, I'm going to break your neck." I called out: "Motion seconded! All in favor say, 'aye'! Everyone grunted approval. The young revolutionary sat.

Friday afternoon they gave us another sandwich, making a grand total of four sandwiches in three days. Now the police were taking greater numbers of people out of cells. When the guard started calling names everyone would run to the door and this would be the only time the cell would be quiet. Soon, there were only a few of us remaining. Most of those who had been arrested for violating the curfew had been released. But Don and I were still there and I was beginning to lose hope. About 5:30 Friday night a detective came to the window and called my name and my heart leaped. He told me that someone was there to see me and opened the cell door. My visitor was Jack Kaufman of Benyas-Kaufman, two free-lance pho-

tographers who also work with Black Star. Jack was thoughtful enough to take a picture of me in the cell before I was released.

As I was being led out, the Chief of Detectives for the Second Precinct stopped me and asked why I had not identified myself when I was brought in. I told him that I had said over and over again that I was from the press and that I had showed my credentials to the patrolman who was standing right next to him. The patrolman, of course, denied it. The Chief said he was releasing me because my arrest was a mistake but he added: "If I should hear of or read of anything detrimental being said about the Detroit police department, you will have the biggest kick back you've ever seen."

The next afternoon, at my hotel, Mayor Jerome Cavanagh called on me personally to apologize for my arrest. He said, "I'm sorry. It should not have happened."

The way I feel about it, nothing in Detroit should have happened and I'm sorry, too.

The Panthers and the Police:
A Pattern of Genocide?

EDWARD JAY EPSTEIN

Between 4:40 and 4:52 a.m. on December 4, 1969, plainclothes police in Chicago, while executing a search warrant for illegal weapons, shot to death Fred Hampton, the 21-year-old chairman of the Black Panther Party of Illinois, and Mark Clark, a member of the party, in Hampton's apartment. Four days later at about the same hour of the morning, the Los Angeles Special Weapons Tactics Team, dressed in black jumpsuits and black hats, moved on the Black Panther Party headquarters in that city with another search warrant for illegal weapons and, in a heated gun battle, shot and seriously wounded three more Panthers.

Commenting on these events, in San Francisco, Charles R. Garry, chief counsel and spokesman for the Black Panther Party, whose membership at the time was estimated at between 800 and 1,200, declared to the press that Hampton and Clark were "in fact the twenty-seventh and twenty-eighth Panthers murdered by the police," and that the deaths and the raids were all "part and package of a national scheme by various agencies of the government to destroy and

Reprinted by permission from *The New Yorker* (February 13, 1971), © 1971 by The New Yorker Magazine, Inc.

commit genocide upon members of the Black Panther Party."

Garry's assertion that 28 members of the controversial black-militant group had been killed by the police was widely reported. On Dec. 7 and Dec. 9, 1969, the New York Times reported as an established fact, without giving any source for the figure or qualifying it in any way, that 28 Panthers had been killed by police since January, 1968 (These stories were disseminated throughout the country to more than 300 newspapers and news agencies that subscribe to the Times wire service.) On Dec. 9, 1969, the Washington Post stated flatly, "A total of 28 Panthers have died in clashes with police since January 1, 1968." In a later article, the Post declared, "Between a dozen and 30 Panthers have been killed in these confrontations." (About 200 newspapers subscribe to the Post's wire service.)

On the basis of what had been reported about the police killings and predawn raids, civil-rights leaders expressed an understandable concern. Roy Innis, director of the Congress for Racial Equality, called for an immediate investigation of "the death of 28 Black Panther members killed in clashes with the police since January, 1968." Ralph Abernathy, who succeeded Martin Luther King, Jr., as the chairman of the Southern Christian Leadership Conference, attributed the death of Panther leaders to "a calculated design of genocide in this country." Julian Bond, a member of the Georgia state legislature, said, "The Black Panthers are being decimated by political assassination arranged by the federal police apparatus." And Whitney Young, executive director of the National Urban League, urgently requested the Attorney General to convene federal grand juries in those "jurisdictions where nearly 30 Panthers have been murdered by law-enforcement officials."

Garry's theory about "a national scheme . . . to destroy" the Black Panthers was also taken up by the press. Pointing to a "growing feeling (particularly in the black community)" that the "Federal Administration has had a hand in the recent wave of raids, arrests and shoot-outs," an article in the Times by John Kifner concluded that statements made by officials of the Nixon Administration "appear to have at least contributed to a climate of opinion among local police . . . that a virtual open season has been declared on the Panthers."

Time reported, on Dec. 12, 1969, that "a series of gun battles between Panthers and police throughout the nation" amounted to a "lethal undeclared war," and concluded, "Whether or not there is a concerted police campaign, the ranks of Panther leadership have been decimated in the past two years." In the very next issue, Time, repeating Garry's claim that "28 Panthers have died in police gunfire," asked, "Specifically, are the raids against Panther offices part of a national design to destroy the

Panther leadership?" The answer was more or less left open.

That same week, Newsweek began a news report entitled "Too Late for the Panthers?" with the same question: "Is there some sort of government conspiracy afoot to exterminate the Black Panthers?" The article then proceeded to portray a "guerrilla war between the gun-toting Panthers and the police," in which the Panther "hierarchy around the country has been all but decimated over the past year," and concluded that "there is no doubt that the police around the nation have made the Panthers a prime target in the past two years . . ."

A few weeks later, Newsweek reported that "the cop on the beat has been joined by Attorney General John Mitchell's Justice Department, which believe the Panthers to be a menace to national security and has accordingly escalated the drive against them" —a drive that "has taken a fearful toll of the Panthers."

The Washington Post, noting in an editorial that the "carnage has been terrible" in the "urban guerrilla warfare" between Panthers and police, concluded that "recent events" had given "added currency" to the Panther charge that "there is a national campaign under way to eradicate them by any means, legal or extralegal."

Picking up the theme in his syndicated column, Carl T. Rowan observed, "We have seen this nationally orchestrated police campaign to turn the guns on the Panthers and wipe them out," and referred to an "obvious conspiracy of police actions across the country that has produced the alleged killing of 28 Black Panthers."

The Nation, in an editorial titled "Marked for Extinction," asserted, "it is becoming increasingly apparent that a campaign of repression and assassination is being carried out against the Black Panthers." Even a paper as cautious as the Christian Science Monitor, after a telephone interview with Garry, cited the Panther charge of "police murder" and "genocide" and expressed "a growing suspicion that something more than isolated local police action was involved."

Confusion about the alleged murders began to set in early, and on Dec. 21, 1969, the Times reported that Garry had put the number of Panthers killed by the police at 12, although it later returned to the figure of 28. While an Associated Press dispatch in the San Francisco Examiner on Dec. 9 reported that 27 Panthers had been killed by police in "Chicago, Denver, San Francisco, Detroit and Indianapolis," the United Press International wire service, on Dec. 12, sent out to its clients a list, provided by the Black Panther Party, of 20 Panthers killed in "cold blood" by police in Los Angeles, Oakland, Seattle, San Diego, New Haven and Chicago. (In the list itself, however, only 16 deaths could actually be attributed to the police.) Life, in a single issue—that of Feb. 6, 1970 —presented three figures: Eldridge Cleaver, the minister of information of the Black Panther Party, was quoted as saying that police "ambush" had led to "28 murders" of Panthers, but at another point the magazine declared, "so far, in the running guerrilla war of rooftop sniping, midnight ambush and mass shoot-outs that the Panthers and police have been waging in a number of cities

. . . at least 19 Panthers are dead," adding, in parentheses, that "it is uncertain that more than a dozen have died of police bullets."

While articles in the New Republic, Ramparts, and the New Statesman have, at various times, put the figure at 20, an article in Newsday by Patrick Owens, who made a conscientious effort to check out Garry's claims, asserted that no more than 10 Panthers had been killed by police.

The executive director of the American Civil Liberties Union in Illinois declared, according to the Washington Post, that 28 Panthers had died in clashes with police since Jan. 1, 1968, while the Los Angeles branch of the same organization said that it was possible to document 12 cases in which Panthers had been killed in such encounters. In a column in the Post a few days earlier, Nicholas von Hoffman had written, "The Panthers alone claim that 28 of their top people have been murdered in the last couple of years, and there is no strong prima-facie reason to disbelieve them."

Even one victim of deliberate police murder would be too many, but if 28 Panthers had been murdered by the police in two years, as Garry claimed and many publications reported, it might indeed represent a pattern of systematic destruction. The implications would be so dreadful that one would expect the figures to be checked out with the utmost scruple. Since the number of Panthers killed would seem to be an ascertainable fact, how can such widely differing figures be accounted for?

When A. M. Rosenthal, the managing editor of the Times, was asked about the discrepancies in his paper, he explained that the Dec. 7 report, which stated, "Twenty-eight Black Panthers have been killed in run-ins with the police since January 1, 1968," was taken from a Dec. 5 story by the same reporter, which said, "According to Charles Garry . . . (Hampton and Clark) were the 27th and 28th Black Panthers killed in clashes with the police since January of 1968," and which was itself based on a telephone conversation with Garry. In the Dec. 7 story, the qualifying phrase "according to Charles Garry" had been deleted, Rosenthal said, because "the reporter probably felt the source was unimportant in the second story"—although Rosenthal, in discussing the matter, said that he personally felt that the reporter should not have turned an assertion by an interested party into a fact. The figure of 28 had subsequently been reported as fact because the reporter "inadvertently referred to the first figure," and this had happened because "no flag was placed on the error." (Whitney Young's assertion that "nearly 30 Panthers have been murdered by law-enforcement officials" was based on the Times, according to his research assistant, and the Times was then able to report in a Sunday summary that the charge of a "national conspiracy" against the Panthers "has been echoed by more moderate civil-rights leaders.")

Ben Bagdikian, the national editor of the Washington Post, also named Garry as the source for his newspaper's assertion that 28 Panthers had been killed by police—though the only "specific documentation" on the subject was the U.P.I. bulletin of Dec. 12. The U.P.I. bulletin, which went out to more than 4,000 subscribing domestic newspapers and broadcasting stations, came from the news agency's San Francisco bureau, which, according to its manager, H. Jefferson Grigsby, obtained the list of "victims of cold-blooded murder by the police" from Panther sources. "There was no further dispatch modifying the Dec. 12 story," Grigsby has noted.

Garry's list apparently provided publications such as the New Republic, Ramparts, and the New Statesman with the "fact" that 20 Panthers had been killed by police (the figure was published without attribution), and Ramparts, in turn, furnished an organization called the Committee to Defend the Panthers—whose letterhead included the names of Norman Mailer, I. F. Stone, Ralph Abernathy, Pete Seeger, Ossie Davis, and Gloria Steinem—with what the committee called the "grim statistic" of 20 Panthers dead. Members of another committee concerned with the treatment that Black Panthers were receiving at the hands of the police— this one set up by former Supreme Court Justice Arthur Goldberg and Roy Wilkins, of the N.A.A.C.P.—were widely quoted as saying that "28" and "nearly 30" Panthers had been "murdered" by police, although Norman C. Amaker, the staff director of the committee, conceded that the list on which these statements were based "was compiled at the behest of their national attorney, Charles Garry."

And so it went. Although Garry was certainly an interested party in the controversy over what came to be called the war between the Panthers and the police, it is clear that his assertions were widely accepted at their face value, so even when modifications were made in the lists of casualties it was Garry's story that was being modified, and practically no independent checking was done.

How, then, did Garry arrive at his figures? In September, 1970, Garry explained to me that he chose the number 28 when newsmen called him for a statement after the shooting of Hampton and Clark because that "seemed to be a safe number"; he added that he believed "the actual number of Panthers murdered by the police is many times that figure." When pressed for the names, however, Garry found he could "document" only "20 police murders" of Panthers. The list of "20 murders," which was sent to me from Garry's office, along with a warning that "the facts are not necessarily empirical," actually comprises only 19 Panther deaths, and one of the 19 deaths— that of Sidney Miller, in Seattle—is attributed by Garry not to police but to "a merchant who claimed he thought Miller was going to rob the store." In the coroner's records, the statement of the Seattle police is that "the deceased and an unknown person were robbing the Seven-Eleven store at 8856 35th Ave. S.W., and in the progress of the robbery the deceased was shot with a .38-calibre snub-nosed Smith & Wesson by the store owner, Donald F. Lannoye." Lannoye does not dispute the statement that he fired the fatal shot.

That leaves 18 "documented" cases involving Black Panthers who Garry claims were murdered by police in pursuance of a conspiracy to "commit genocide upon" the Black Panthers. The way black people in general are treated by the police in our society has become a subject of increasing concern to many citizens,

black and white, and, for a number of reasons—including the deaths of Hampton and Clark in Chicago— the idea of a deliberate police campaign against the Panthers may not seem farfetched. But if there is to be an abatement of the fear and near-hysteria that seem to have developed around the question of the Panthers and the police, surely we must begin by getting the facts straight. For this reason, Garry's list of eighteen Panthers allegedly murdered by the police may be worth examining in some detail.

The Case of Alex Rackley. On May 21, 1969, John Mroczka, a 23-year-old factory worker, stopped his motorcycle near a bridge on Route 147 outside of Middlefield, Conn., and while walking along the edge of a stream looking for trout saw a "set of legs" and "body" partly submerged. State police were called to the scene by Mroczka, and they recovered from the stream the body of a Negro male whose wrists were tied with gauze and whose neck was encircled by a noose fashioned from a wire coat hanger.

An autopsy, conducted immediately afterward, indicated that the man had been severely burned on wide areas of the chest, arms, wrists, buttocks, thighs, and right shoulder and had also been beaten around the face, the groin, and the lumbar region with a hard object before he was shot in the head and chest. The victim, who was subsequently identified by his fingerprints as Alex Rackley, had died, a pathologist concluded, within the preceding twelve to twenty-four hours.

Just after midnight on May 22, New Haven police acted on a tip supplied by an informant who identified a Polaroid photograph of the corpse as a man who had been tortured with scalding water in an apartment that served as Panther headquarters in New Haven. Around 12:30 a.m., they raided the apartment and arrested Warren Kimbro, 35, one of the leaders of the New Haven chapter of the Black Panther Party, and five women members. Eventually, eight other Black Panthers, including Bobby Seale, the national chairman of the party, were arrested, and all of those arrested, except two who were remanded to a juvenile court, were charged with complicity, in varying degrees, in the kidnaping or torture or murder of Alex Rackley, a 24-year-old member of the New York chapter of the Black Panther Party.

Charles Garry immediately charged that "Rackley was killed by the police or by agents of some armed agency of the government." Holding that the murder victim was in "good standing" in the party, he further declared, as quoted in Newsweek, "We have every reason to believe, and we intend to prove, when the time comes, that Rackley was murdered by police agents."

Even without proof, Garry's version of the events gained wide currency. The U.P.I.'s listing to Panthers alleged by a party spokesman to have been killed by the police cites "Alex Rackley" simply as " 'tortured and killed' by the police in New Haven, Conn., in May, 1969."

At Yale, where a national May Day rally was held in the spring of 1970 to support the Panthers charged in the case, William Sloane Coffin, the Yale chaplain, described the trial of the accused Panthers as "Panther repression," and said, "All of us conspired

to bring on this tragedy—law-enforcement agencies by their illegal acts against the Panthers, and the rest of us by our immoral silence in front of these acts." At the same time, the president of Yale, Kingman Brewster, Jr., told striking students—who were demanding, among other things, the release of the Black Panthers awaiting trial for Rackley's murder—that he was "skeptical of the ability of black revolutionaries to achieve a fair trial anywhere in the United States," adding, "In large measure, the atmosphere has been created by police actions and prosecutions against the Panthers in many parts of the country."

At this point, the three Black Panther officers, who were specifically accused of taking Rackley to the stream near Middlefield, Conn., where his body was found had long since admitted their participation in the killing.

George Sams, Jr., a 23-year-old Panther who had once held the rank of field marshal in the national Black Panther Party, pleaded guilty to second-degree murder, which in Connecticut carries with it a mandatory sentence of life imprisonment, and testified that in the early morning of May 21, 1969, he and Warren Kimbro and Lonnie McLucas, using a car that McLucas had borrowed, took Rackley, bound and gagged, from Black Panther headquarters in New Haven to a deserted spot off Route 147; there Kimbro, under Sams' direction, shot Rackley in the head with a .45-calibre pistol, and a few minutes later McLucas fired another shot into the body. Sams testified that he was acting under orders from the "national" party personally given to him by Bobby Seale.

Kimbro pleaded guilty to second degree murder in January, 1970, and testified in open court that he fired the first shot into the back of Rackley's head after Sams said, "Now." Kimbro, however, refused to implicate Seale in the crime, testifying that he himself was asleep at the time Seale was said by Sams to have visited the headquarters.

McLucas, 23, a captain in the Black Panther Party and a founder of the Bridgeport chapter, gave the same general account of the killing to New Haven police detectives and F.B.I. agents two days after he was captured in Salt Lake City in June, 1969. During his own trial, at which he pleaded not guilty to the charge of conspiracy, McLucas testified that he drove Rackley, bound and gagged, along with Sams and Kimbro, from New Haven to Middlefield; after Kimbro had shot Rackley, McLucas said, Sams ordered him, McLucas, "to make sure he was dead." McLucas said he then fired a second bullet into Rackley. McLucas, like Kimbro, has not implicated Seale, although he acknowledged under cross-examination that at the time of the killing he believed he was acting under orders from "national headquarters." (McLucas was found guilty of conspiracy to commit murder and sentenced to 12 to 15 years in prison.)

The testimony of Sams, Kimbro, and McLucas was consistent with physical evidence that has not been contested in various legal proceedings having to do with the case—a .45-calibre pistol that the police found in Panther headquarters on the night of the raid ballistically matched the bullet and the bullet casing found at the scene of the murder, and fingerprints found on the car that McLucas borrowed that night matched those of Sams and Rackley—and also with the statements of other Panthers who were present in the apartment on the night of the killing.

For example, Loretta Luckes, who had stood guard over Rackley while he was tied to a bed in the Panther headquarters for two days, described, in testimony during bail hearings, having helped to dress Rackley on the night of the murder while Sams and Kimbro stood over him with a pistol and rifle (because, one Panther said, "he might go crazy") ; then, she said, "Lonnie (McLucas), Warren Kimbro, and George Sams" went "out the door" with Rackley.

It may be that McLucas, Kimbro, and Sams were acting under orders from Seale or the national Black Panther Party, or it may be, as much of the testimony in the legal proceedings to date indicates, that some wildly irrational suspicions about Rackley turned an interrogation session into torture and murder.

But the fact remains that Rackley was shot not by the police but by two officers of the Black Panther Party, and since both have refused to implicate Seale, the suggestion that they might be "police agents" seems shaky at best. Perhaps Seale's trial for conspiracy now going on in New Haven will shed further light on the motive for the killing, but even at this stage of the legal proceedings it is difficult to take seriously Garry's inclusion of Rackley in his list of Panthers killed by the police.

The Case of Nathaniel Clark. Nathaniel Clark, Jr., a 19-year-old Black Panther, is listed by Garry as having been "killed by a police agent" and by the U.P.I., quoting the Black

Panther Party, as having been "killed by the police in Los Angeles." He was killed by his wife, who told investigating officers that she had shot her husband in self-defense with his revolver after he had, in her words, "shot up with heroin and beat me up." Because of her age, 17 at the time, the case was remanded to a juvenile court, which adjudged the death to have resulted from involuntary manslaughter.

The Case of Arthur Morris. On March 13, 1968, while out on bail on a charge of conspiracy to commit murder, Arthur Glenn Morris (also known as Arthur Coltrale) was killed by a blast from a 12-gauge shotgun in a friend's back yard. According to the friend's wife, Mrs. Henry Daily, Morris and a companion, Donald Campbell, were in the back yard talking with her husband, who had taken his 12-gauge shotgun out there with him. She heard the men arguing, then heard a volley of shots. Rushing out, she found all three men fatally shot. Apparently, there had been a shootout, in which either Morris or Campbell had shot Daily with a .32-calibre automatic (the gun found at the scene) and he had shot both men with his shotgun. None survived to tell their stories.

The Cases of John Huggins, Alprentice Carter, Sylvester Bell, and John Savage. Of the 15 remaining "homicides" on Garry's list, four Panthers—John Jerome Huggins, Jr., Alprentice (Bunchy) Carter, Sylvester Bell, and John Savage—were actually shot to death, according to both the Black Panther Party and California authorities, by members of US, a rival black-militant organization, headed by Ron Karenga, with which the Pan-

thers had once temporarily allied themselves in a lawsuit against the Los Angeles Police Department.

The dispute began at the University of California at Los Angeles in the fall of 1968, when Ron Karenga attempted to select the director of the Black Studies Program through the Community Advisory Board, of which he was a director. A number of Black Panthers, including Huggins and Carter, who were at that time enrolled in the black section of the "high-potential" program, vigorously opposed Karenga's attempt, despite the warning of a Karenga spokesman, who said, "This is not a decision that anybody is going to take out of our hands . . . Anybody that is involved in this is going to have to come back to the community after dark." Leaders of US said that students who accepted Karenga's hand-picked director would be given "protection" against Panther reprisals.

On Jan. 17, 1969, some 150 members of the U.C.L.A. Black Students Union met in Campbell Hall on the U.C.L.A. campus to resolve the dispute over the directorship. Five members of the elite guard of US—known as Simbas, after the word for "lion" in Swahili—were present. Shortly after noon, in the student cafeteria, Huggins and Carter cornered a young Simba named Harold Jones, who had been accused of manhandling a female Panther earlier in the day, and began pummeling him. Suddenly another Simba, dressed in a dashiki, stepped up behind Huggins and fatally shot him in the back. A gun battle ensued, in which Carter was also shot to death before the Simbas fled.

Black Panthers who had been present at the meeting were reluctant to supply information at first, but they cooperated fully with the police and the prosecutor in identifying the assailants and finding witnesses after the prosecutor spoke to Garry, who, the prosecutor later reported, "instructed the local Panthers to help us in our investigation."

Two of the Simbas, George Phillip Stiner and Larry Joseph Stiner, were brought to trial on charges of conspiracy to commit murder, were convicted, largely on the basis of the testimony of the five Black Panther witnesses, and sentenced to life imprisonment. A third Simba, Donald Hawkins, was also convicted of conspiracy to commit murder, and was sentenced to an indefinite term in the detention program of the California Youth Authority. Two other Simbas indicted in connection with the same killings—Harold Jones and Claude Hubert, who are alleged to have done the actual shooting—are still fugitives. (Karenga, who was on a speaking tour of Eastern cities at the time of these shootings, was subsequently arrested and indicted in Los Angeles on torture charges in another case.)

In the aftermath of the gun battle in Campbell Hall, two more Black Panthers were killed by members of the US organization, according to both the Black Panther Party and the police. "At about 3:30 p.m. on May 23rd in San Diego, California, Lt. John Savage, Black Panther Party, was murdered by a whitewashed Karangatang, a member of the US organization led by Ron (Everett) Karenga," the Black Panther newspaper reported, and it went on, "Mr. Karenga, better known as pork chop is leading his culturalized pork chops in a futile attempt to destroy the Black Panther Party."

The US member who shot Savage was eventually arraigned and pleaded guilty to a charge of manslaughter. A few weeks after Savage's death, another Panther, Sylvester Bell, who was selling the Black Panther newspaper in Otto Square in San Diego, was approached by three members of US, who, according to the Black Panther account of the incident, asked him, "Are you talking about us this week?" A fight broke out, during which Bell was joined by two fellow-Panthers, and one of the three members of US drew a gun and fatally shot Bell. The San Diego police arrested three members of US and indicted them for murder. One was convicted of murder, and the two others were convicted as accessories. Since Garry himself and the Panthers assisted the authorities in the identification and prosecution of some of those involved in the killings, his subsequent inclusion of these four names in his list of Panthers murdered by the police appears to be disingenuous.

The Case of Franko Diggs. Franko Diggs, 40, who was a captain in the Black Panther Party, was found fatally shot in the Watts section of Los Angeles on Dec. 19, 1968. No witness to the shooting could be found, but the police identified the murder weapon from the bullets as a foreign-made 9-mm. automatic pistol.

Almost a year later, when the Los Angeles police crime laboratory was doing routine ballistics tests on 18 weapons seized in a raid on Black Panther headquarters early in 1969, it was found that one of the confiscated Panther automatics ballistically matched the bullet that had killed Diggs. The chain of ownership could not be established, however, so the owner at the time Diggs was shot could not be identified.

According to the police, the crime remains unsolved, but Garry, almost a year after Diggs' death, added his name to the list of Black Panthers killed by police. A doubtful matter at best.

The ten remaining Black Panthers on Garry's list were in fact killed by the police—five in 1968 and five in 1969. Whether these deaths were deliberate murders carried out as part of what Garry called a "national scheme" to wipe out the Panthers depends, of course, on the circumstances under which each of the deaths occurred.

The Case of Larry Roberson. In summarizing the deaths of various Black Panthers, the Times quoted "sources in Chicago" as saying that Larry Roberson "died in jail after being wounded in (a) shoot-out during (a) police raid"—a statement suggesting that he was shot during a planned police action against a Panther office.

The picture of what happened that can be pieced together from police records, independent witnesses, and even the Black Panther newspaper is very different. At 2:01 a.m. on July 16, 1969, the Chicago police received a "citizen's complaint" that a fruit stand had been burglarized at 610 California St., in the West Side ghetto. A radio dispatcher routinely recorded this information on a computer card used for statistical analysis of complaints and crime patterns, and dispatched the patrol car that his electronic map indicated was nearest to the scene—Car No. 1124, manned by Officers Kenneth Gorles and Daniel Sampila.

According to Sampila's subsequent report, the officers arrived at the fruit stand at about 2:05 a.m. and were met by Mr. and Mrs. Burman Jenkins, friends of its owner, who pointed out a hole in the door of the stand. The two policemen, led by Mr. and Mrs. Jenkins, then followed a trail of apples and oranges to a passageway, where they found two empty fruit baskets.

While the police were flashing a searchlight around, the group encountered Larry Roberson, 21, and Grady Moore, 28, who identified themselves as "community leaders," and were told by Sampila to "mind your own business."

The group, followed by Roberson and Moore, then returned to the fruit stand, where they were met by the Rev. Edmond Jones, who owned the fruit stand, and another of his friends, the Rev. Clarence Edward Stowers, who was the pastor of the nearby Mars Hill Missionary Baptist Church. A few minutes later, the two policemen and Jenkins were shot.

In a statement Stowers made later, he described what happened this way:

"Reverend Jones, Mr. Jenkins, myself, and the two officers were standing there talking about boarding up the door. Two men walked up and started looking in the hole in the door and asking what had happened. The officers told them that everything was taken care of and they should leave. One of the men had his hand in his pocket, and the officer shined his light on the man. The man asked him why was he shining the light on him and don't be doing that. Then the shooting started. The officers had their guns in their holsters so it must have been the men that were shooting. One of the officers fell down and the other one got hit in the shoulder. I remember it was only one of the two men that was shooting. He turned and ran up the alley. I don't know where the other one went to. Well, anyway the policeman that had fallen to the ground started chasing the man up the alley and lots of shots were fired."

Jones gave a similar account of the incident:

"The policeman and Mr. Jenkins told Reverend Stowers and me that they hadn't found anything and that I could nail a board or something across the door. While we were talking two guys came across the playlot from Flournoy street and started asking a lot of questions. The tall guy (Moore) went and looked in the door and the policeman told them that they had everything under control and for them to go about their business. The tall guy started mouthing at the policeman and then the other guy (Roberson) came up and hollered, "What's happening?" And he started shooting. One of the policemen (Sampila) fell to the ground right at my feet and the two guys started running. The policeman that had fallen by me got up and started chasing the man that was shooting at us. They ran down the alley and I heard more shots."

Mr. and Mrs. Jenkins agreed with this account, Mr. Jenkins adding:

"One man shouted something and started shooting . . . after the first shot one officer fell to his knees, the second shot hit officer Gorles, and the third shot hit me."

Roberson, pursued through the alley, was shot in the ankle, in the thigh, and in the abdomen by Sampila before he surrendered. According to the Chicago crime laboratory, the bullets that struck Gorles (in the left shoulder and collarbone), Sampila (in the head), and Jenkins (in the right side) all came from a .38-calibre snub-nosed Smith & Wesson taken from Roberson. This turned out to be a stolen weapon. Roberson was arrested on charges of attempted murder and was admitted to the Cermak Memorial Hospital, where he underwent surgery. Seven weeks later, he contracted jaundice and died in the Cook County Hospital.

A somewhat different version of the incident was provided by the Black Panther newspaper, which reported, in August:

"On July 17, 1969, two brothers in the Illinois chapter of the Black Panther Party were returning to their community after finishing a day of revolutionary work for the people's party. On this particular night they noticed the pigs had nine brothers on the wall next to a storefront, harassing them. Five of the brothers were in ages ranging from 50—62 years old. The pigs claimed they were answering a burglary in process call. Can you imagine men 50—62 years old burglarizing a store in their own community?

"Well, after investigating the matter and coming to the conclusion that this was just another racist act of harassment committed by the pigs on the people, Larry Roberson and Grady Moore walked over to the scene where the majority of the people had gone and asked an officer what was going on. The pig then demagogically replied "This is none of your damn business." Br. Larry then stated "I am a member of this community and even by your laws I have the right to know what's going on." The crazy pig then said "Smart bastard, you're under arrest for disorderly conduct."

"The people of the community immediately got between Larry and the pigs, and the pig drew his gun and ordered them aside while his pig partner radioed for help. Larry then (with the instructions from the people) was told to go home because the people hadn't seen him do anything, so he and Grady started away and the pig deliberately shot Larry in the leg. Grady grabbed Larry to help him to try to escape with his life.

"This whole area was sealed off with crazy, drunk, inhuman pigs. Larry was then cornered in an alley, unarmed and wounded. As the pig approached him, he oinked "I'll teach you and your partner how to interfere with pig matters." He then aimed at Larry's head. It was true that Larry was unarmed, but being a Panther and a stone revolutionary, he had educated the true power—the people. As the pig was ready to squeeze the trigger, the power of the people was demonstrated. A voice quoted Huey: 'You racist pigs must withdraw immediately from the black community and cease this wanton murder and brutality of black people or face the wrath of the armed people.'

"Then, the shots from the people rang out from everywhere for about 30 seconds; then it ceased. One pig shot in the head and one pig shot in the shoulder. Larry and Grady then started to make it when more pigs arrived. Larry and Grady turned and raised their hands. The pig that was shot in the shoulder raised his gun and shot Brother Larry in the stomach, thigh and leg trying to kill him. Grady evidently escaped death when the people in the community came out to witness the action. . . . Larry Roberson is proven to be a true

revolutionary not by words but by deeds. He has shown his love for the people. He put his life on the line and in return the people released some revolutionary power."

The statements that Roberson was unarmed and that the "people" did the shooting were contradicted by a subsequent report in the Black Panther newspaper, which said that "determined to defend himself even after being shot, Larry managed to get his gun out and wounded two of the attacking maniacs." But the Panther version and the police version actually agree in a number of significant respects: the encounter was accidental: the Panthers approached the police rather than the other way around; and two police officers were shot before Roberson was seriously wounded in the abdomen.

The Case of Bobby Hutton. According to Life magazine, Bobby Hutton, the 17-year-old minister of finance of the Black Panther Party, was killed and Eldridge Cleaver was wounded in an "Oakland police ambush" in 1968. The Times quoted Garry as attributing Hutton's death to a "police ambush."

Shortly after 9 p.m. on April 6, 1968, Officers Nolan R. Darnell and Richard R. Jensen, while on routine patrol in the area of Oakland, Calif., that is predominantly inhabited by blacks, stopped their patrol car on Union street next to a parked 1954 Ford when they caught a glimpse of a man crouching at the curb side of the car. In their report, they said that they suspected he might be trying to steal it.

Moments later, while investigating the situation, both officers were hit by bullets fired from behind them. Afterward, 49 bullet holes were found in the police car, the rear window had "two large areas shot inward," and the side windows and the open door, next to which Darnell was standing at the time, had also been hit numerous times.

According to medical reports prepared by Dr. William Mills, Jr., of Samuel Merritt Hospital, Darnell was wounded in the "upper right back." Jensen, apparently hit by a blast from a 12-gauge shotgun, suffered multiple wounds in the "lower right back," in the "right arm," and in the "right ankle and foot."

According to Darnell, a number of men armed with shotguns and rifles ran from cars parked behind and ahead of the 1954 Ford, some of them through an alley into the block across the street, while Darnell urgently called for help on the police radio.

An account of the incident in the Black Panther newspaper said, "Several Panthers in cars in West Oakland on Saturday night, April 6, were approached by two pigs and menaced with guns. When the Panthers tried to defend themselves, shooting began, and the Panthers ran into a nearby house. . . . Two pigs were wounded slightly." Four Black Panthers gave statements to the police in which they said that they had been patrolling the neighborhood with guns, in three cars, "to protect Negroes against police brutality," and had just parked their cars on Union street in order to stow their weapons in a nearby house when the patrol car pulled up, but the four disclaimed any knowledge of how the shooting began.

Cleaver later said in an interview that was published in the San Francisco Chronicle, "I don't know how those cops got shot. There were so many bullets whizzing around maybe they shot themselves."

In any event, after the two policemen were shot, police from other parts of West Oakland and even from nearby Emeryville, responding to the radio alarm, surrounded a building on 28th street that the Panthers had entered, and there ensued a 90-minute gun battle, in which a third policeman was wounded. Finally, after an exploding tear gas canister had set fire to the building, two Panthers emerged: Cleaver, naked, and wounded by a tear-gas shell, and Hutton, fully clothed.

According to police witnesses, Hutton suddenly bolted down 28th street, whereupon at least half a dozen policemen opened fire, fatally wounding him.

Cleaver, in the Chronicle interview, gave a different version of the shooting of Hutton. He admitted that Hutton had fired some shots at the police, but said that he himself "took Bobby's gun and threw it out"—out the window, that is—and that they both came out unarmed. "The cops told us to get up and start running for the squad car," Cleaver continued. "Bobby started running—he ran about ten yards—and they started shooting him."

The grand jury, after hearing 35 witnesses, concluded that the police had "acted lawfully," shooting Hutton in the belief he was trying to escape.

Eight other Panthers, including Cleaver, who were allegedly involved in the shooting of the policemen were arrested that night and then were released on bail. Two of the eight were subsequently convicted of assault with deadly weapons; one was released to a juvenile court; one was tried and convicted for an unrelated armed robbery and sent to state prison; one, Cleaver, jumped bail and fled the country; two others, with the juvenile, are now on trial in Oakland; and other cases are still pending.

The Cases of Steven Bartholomew, Robert Lawrence and Thomas Lewis. At about 4:45 p.m. on August 5, 1968, in a predominantly Negro section of Los Angeles, three Black Panthers were fatally shot and two policemen were wounded, one critically, in a shootout at Ham's Mobil Service Station.

Fifteen minutes earlier, Police Officers Rudy Limas and Norman J. Roberge were on a routine patrol when, according to their reports, they saw a black 1955 Ford with four men in it start up a private driveway, stop suddenly, then back down the driveway. Finding the movements suspicious, the policemen began following the Ford, whose occupants, Limas noted, kept "looking back." Limas then called the police communications center on the patrol car's radio and gave the Ford's license number, to ascertain whether it had been reported stolen.

Before a reply could be received, the Ford pulled into Ham's service station and stopped by a gas pump. The police car stopped a few feet behind it, and Roberge, according to his statement, asked the driver of the Ford for his license. The driver, Roberge reported, "replied that he didn't have any driver's license," whereupon Roberge "instructed the driver to go back to the police car and place his hands on top of the

police car." Roberge then ordered the three other suspects out of the Ford and over to the police car.

"At this time," Roberge stated, "the suspects were standing in a row facing the police vehicle"—between the two police officers.

Limas gave the following description of what happened next: "Suddenly the guy in front of me, who I think was wearing a yellow shirt and dark pants, spun around and pointed a gun at me, and the others moved at the same time. The guy in the yellow shirt said, 'O.K., m———f———' and then he shot me." According to medical reports and testimony, Limas was shot in the abdomen and the thigh, with a bullet lodging in the hip.

Roberge stated, "As I walked toward the police vehicle, I saw my partner, Officer Limas standing to the left rear of the police vehicle on the other side of the group, facing me. Suddenly I heard some shots and I was knocked to the ground." According to the medical evidence, Roberge was shot in both legs.

In the gun battle that followed, Limas fatally shot "the guy in the yellow shirt" and a second suspect, who was "trying to load a 9-mm. pistol," and Roberge "emptied" his gun at a third suspect. The fourth man who had been in the car fled on foot.

There were two independent witnesses to the shooting—the service-station attendants, Shoji Katayama and Eugene Oba. Katayama, who explained that he was "standing by the pumps . . . a few feet east of the Ford," also stated in a deposition:

"A black (4-door) Ford pulled into the station, pursued by a police car . . . There were 4 Negroes in the Ford.

The driver and front passenger both got out and opened the hood of the car. The two officers immediately got out and ordered all four to the police car with their hands leaning on it. The driver of the Ford looked like to me he hesitated a while and was smoking a cigarette. As the driver with the cigarette came to the car, the Mexican officer (Limas) ordered him not to put out the cigarette (near the pumps), and at that point (I) heard a couple of shots and I looked up and saw the Mexican officer on the ground and the male Negro with the khaki shirt (Army type) with a gun in his hand...."

The other attendant, Oba, had been returning to the office when the shooting began. He gave a similar account of the incident, adding only that after the first round of shots he "saw the Caucasian officer (Roberge) shooting at the Negro men."

When the shooting stopped, a few minutes later, three men were dead or dying—Thomas Melvin Lewis, 18, "the guy in the yellow shirt;" Robert A. Lawrence, 22; and Steven Kenneth Bartholomew, 21. The Black Panther stated that they were all Black Panthers. The fourth suspect, who was subsequently identified by his palm prints on the police car as Anthony Reno Bartholomew, the 19-year-old brother of Steven, later surrendered voluntarily to a judge, and was arraigned on two counts of assault with intent to commit murder.

Anthony Bartholomew's lawyer, Gary Bellow, a well-known civil-rights attorney who has handled a number of Black Panther cases in Los Angeles, noted in a memorandum filed with the court, "There is no dispute that the police officers, Norman Roberge and Rudy Limas, were criminally assaulted on August 5, 1968," but went on to argue that his client had not in fact taken part in the gun battle. Anthony Batholomew was found not guilty.

The Case of Walter Pope. Walter Toure Pope, whom Garry listed simply as "killed by Metro Squad," was shot to death by Officer Alvin D. Moen in a vacant lot across from the Jack-in-the-Box drive-in restaurant in Los Angeles on October 18, 1969.

On that night, Officer Moen and his partner, Officer Don Mandella, were assigned to a robbery stakeout of the Jack-in-the-Box, which had been robbed 14 times in the previous seven months. Sitting in an unmarked car, which they had parked in a lot across the street from the restaurant, the officers began their watch shortly after dark.

At about 10:45 p.m., Moen later testified, he heard a noise behind him and "turned around and saw a man standing with what appeared to be a burp gun ... pointed in my direction." Shouting, "Look-out!" to Mandella, Moen, who was sitting behind the wheel, drew his service revolver. Then, according to his testimony, the man fired a shot, and Moen returned the fire. Suddenly, from the other side of the car, there came what Moen called "another loud explosion," which he identified as a shotgun blast.

According to medical reports, Moen was hit in the back of the right shoulder and the back of the left hand by shotgun pellets. Although he was badly wounded, he managed to get out of the car, empty his revolver at the man with the burp gun, and then run to the restaurant for help. Mandella gave a similar account, testifying that after his partner shouted, "Look out!" two shotgun blasts were fired into the car from the passenger side as the man with the burp gun approached from the opposite side.

Mandella then turned and fired three shots at the assailant with the shotgun, who fled. Picking up the microphone, he urgently requested assistance, saying that he and Moen had been "ambushed." When other policemen arrived, they found Walter Toure Pope, 20, who was subsequently identified by the Black Panthers as their "distribution manager" for Los Angeles, shot to death beside the police car. He had a two-inch revolver tucked in his belt, and there was a .30-calibre carbine, or "burp-gun," lying under his left arm. A sawed-off shotgun, both barrels of which had been fired, was found a few feet behind the police car.

(Another Black Panther, Bruce Darryl Richards, 18, was arrested later that night at the U.C.L.A. Medical Center, where he was being treated for bullet wounds, and was charged with taking part in the assault. He pleaded not guilty but was subsequently convicted on two counts of assault with intent to commit murder.)

The only witnesses to the shooting were those who took part in it, and thus the question of who shot first may be open to doubt—although the medical evidence that Moen was hit by a shotgun blast in the back would seem to suggest that the police were approached from behind.

The Case of Welton Armstead. In Seattle, at about 4:10 p.m. on October 5, 1968, Welton Armstead, 17, was shot to death by a police officer in front of a house at 1706 Melrose Ave. A few minutes earlier, Officers

Erling Buttendahl and Charles Marshall, on a routine patrol, had received a radio message directing them to help Car No. 128 in a stolen-auto case at 1700 Melrose Ave. When they arrived on the scene, they helped the policeman in Car No. 128 apprehend two of three suspects they had been pursuing.

According to Buttendahl, while he was searching for the third suspect he came around the side of a house and was confronted by a man, later identified as Armstead, a Black Panther, standing next to the garage, "holding a rifle with both hands and pointing it" at him. According to the coroner's report, the armed man was asked four times to "drop the rifle" but refused to do so; instead, with one hand he grabbed the barrel of Buttendahl's revolver, raising his rifle with the other, whereupon, Buttendahl says, he himself fired, hitting Armstead in the midsection.

An inquest jury, after hearing 14 witnesses and considering the medical evidence, ruled the shooting "justifiable homicide." Garry does not dispute the fact that Armstead faced Buttendahl with a rifle.

The Case of Spurgeon Winters. On November 13, 1969, Spurgeon (Jake) Winters was shot to death by police on Martin Luther King Drive on Chicago's South Side.

Earlier that evening, James Caldwell, a black prison guard at the Cook County Jail, had told his wife, Ruby, that he needed some money to rent a room for the night, because "some guys are looking for me and they want to kill me." The night before, he had been in a brawl outside the Rumpus Room tavern with Lawrence (Lance) Bell, a Black Panther, and had taken Bell's gun from him, and he feared reprisal from Bell and his friends.

A few hours after Caldwell parted from his wife, someone entered the building where they lived and began pounding on apartment doors and calling Caldwell's name. Looking out a front window after the pounding had stopped, Mrs. Caldwell saw what she subsequently described as "four or five men leaving my building . . . one of them . . . carrying a long gun."

She then went across a connecting porch to her sister-in-law's apartment in an adjacent building, where she asked a friend, Lee Wesley, for advice. Wesley said, she later told police investigators, that she "didn't have any choice but to call the police," because "if James came back they would kill him." Wesley himself then called the police.

At 2:49 a.m., a police dispatcher received a report that there were "men on the street with shotguns," and at 2:53 a.m., according to the police computer cards and radio tapes, the dispatcher ordered the nearest patrol car, No. 226, manned by Officers John Gilhooly and Michael Brady, to 324 East Fifty-eighth St., the sister-in-law's apartment. Three other policemen joined them at the sister-in-law's apartment, which was at the rear of the building, and all five were taken, across the connecting porch, to Mrs. Caldwell's apartment, where, from the front window, Mrs. Caldwell and Wesley pointed out to them three men lurking in an abandoned building across the street.

Leaving by the front door, the policemen crossed over to the vacant building, and Gilhooly started to go in through a gangway. Mrs. Caldwell stated, "We could hear the policeman by the gangway shouting 'Halt!' about three times. Then we heard a loud shot, and it sounded louder than a

pistol shot. Then we saw the policeman come out of the gangway. He was saying 'Oh! Oh!' and he was holding his face.'"

Gilhooly was fatally wounded, a shotgun blast having severed his carotid artery and his jugular vein; Brady had suffered minor lacerations of the forehead from the ricochet of a shotgun blast.

Mrs. Caldwell called the police to report that a policeman had been shot. At 3:04 a.m., the dispatcher put out an emergency call: "Police officer needs help." Twenty-one patrol cars in the area immediately responded.

Another policeman was wounded almost immediately by shotgun blasts, according to police reports, and one police car was "demolished" by carbine fire. One of the gunmen, who was allegedly carrying a carbine, and who was later identified as Bell, was shot in cross fire, and was captured.

Meanwhile, three policemen had chased another man, carrying a shotgun, down an alleyway paralleling Martin Luther King Drive. He wounded all three and, taking refuge under the porch of a house on the Drive, shot another policeman, Frank Rappaport, in the chest and head, killing him, and wounded another. Two policemen, including the one who had just been wounded, emptied their revolvers at him, fatally wounding him.

The dead gunman was later identified as Spurgeon (Jake) Winters. In all, two policemen were killed and seven wounded or hurt. Bell was indicted by a grand jury for murder. The case is pending.

The Black Panther version of the incident was similar to the police version in a number of respects. A "special news bulletin" put out by the Illinois chapter stated:

"On November 13, 1969, Jake Winters stood face to face and toe to toe, his shotgun in his hand, with Pig Daley's murderous task force. He defined political power by blowing away racist pig Frank Rappaport and racist pig John Gilhooly and retired 8 other reactionary racist pigs before he was shot down."

The Black Panther newspaper reported the shootings this way:

"Spurgeon (Jake) Winters, 19, member of the Illinois chapter of the Black Panther party, paid the most that one can pay towards the liberation of oppressed people—his life. At 3:30 a.m., November 13, Jake was murdered in a shoot-out in Chicago where three pigs were killed and seven were wounded. The shoot-out was precipitated by an ambush made by the Standing Army of Chicago (Chicago Police Department) on an abandoned building at 5801 S. Calumet. Arriving on the scene with the armaments and men (more than 1,000 policemen equipped with .12-gauge shotguns, M-1 carbines, .357 magnums, billy clubs, mace, tear gas, paddy wagons, helicopters, and canine units) for domestic warfare against the people in the Black colony, these fanatical pigs started their attack by opening fire on the brother in the building. Party comrade, Lance Bell, 20, was wounded by the pigs as they shot wildly in that area . . . Jake defended himself as any person should do. In essence, he had no choice; it was kill or be killed."

There may be some room for doubt whether the police were in fact mounting an "ambush," as the Panthers claim, or were simply responding to a call originally issued in the belief that James Caldwell's life was in danger, but the Panthers and the police agree that after the police arrived at least eight policemen were shot before Winters was shot.

The Case of Fred Hampton and Mark Clark. The final case on Garry's list is certainly the most important one, since it is the one that prompted Garry to speak of a pattern of "genocide." It involves the fatal shooting of Fred Hampton and Mark Clark by policemen attached to the State's Attorney's office in Chicago on December 4, 1969. While there may be varying degrees of uncertainty about some of the other deaths on Garry's list, these two unquestionably resulted from a deliberately planned raid on a Black Panther headquarters.

On Dec. 3, Sgt. Daniel Groth, a twelve-year veteran of the Chicago Police Department who had been assigned to the State's Attorney's Special Prosecutions Unit, told Assistant State's Attorney Richard S. Jalovec, who was in charge of the unit, that he had received information from a "confidential informer" that a cache of illegal weapons, including sawed-off shotguns, and also riot guns stolen from the Chicago police, was stored in a Black Panther apartment at 2337 West Monroe St. Having received information from the Federal Bureau of Investigation just the day before that the Panthers had recently moved weapons to that address, Jalovec immediately ordered Groth to plan a raid on the Panther apartment, and Jalovec prepared a search-warrant complaint. Circuit Judge Robert Collins signed a warrant later that afternoon.

Groth and 13 other policemen assigned to the Special Prosecutions Unit assembled at the State's Attorney's office at four the next morning. They were heavily armed: five had shotguns, one had a Thompson submachine gun, and one—James Davis, one of five black members of the raiding party—carried with him a .30-calibre carbine of his own. The raid was planned for dawn, to achieve the maximum surprise and minimum potential for neighborhood interference, according to Groth's later testimony.

The raiding party arrived at the West Monroe street apartment in three cars and an unmarked panel truck, and Groth, Davis, and three of the other members proceeded to the front door of the apartment, which was on the first floor; six members went around to the back door; and the three remaining members were stationed at the front of the building. At approximately 4:40 a.m., Groth pounded on the apartment door with his revolver butt. There are markedly different versions of what happened next.

In the police version, which was published in the Chicago Tribune, Groth shouted, "This is the police! I have a warrant to search the premises!" and then, after a delay, had Davis kick the door open. The two men entered a small hallway, where they were faced with another closed door.

Suddenly, the police said, a shotgun blast from inside was fired through this door and "narrowly missed the two policemen."

"Davis then plunged through the inner door into a darkened living room, with Groth behind him, as a "second round went right past" him. Groth fired two shots at a woman who, he said, had fired the second shotgun blast, while Davis, after also firing at the woman and wounding

her, turned and shot to death a man sitting behind him with a shotgun, who was later identified as Mark Clark.

Moments later, three of the members of the raiding party who had gone around to the back broke in through the kitchen door of the apartment. Despite a number of calls for a cease-fire from Groth, the Panthers kept firing shotgun blasts, according to the police version of the events, and a "fierce fire fight" ensued, in which Hampton was killed and four other Panthers and one policeman were wounded.

In the Panther version, as it was reported in the Washington Post, the police burst into the apartment almost simultaneously through the front and rear entrances, without first identifying themselves, and although no Panthers fired any shots whatever, the police opened fire, also without warning. A Black Panther spokesman was reported in the Post to have said that Mark Clark was fatally wounded as he attempted to dodge police submachinegun fire, and others were wounded.

Meanwhile, according to the spokesman, the police entering from the rear went immediately to Hampton's bedroom and fired into it, and Davis then went into the bedroom and fired more shots at Hampton.

In Chicago Today, the Black Panther spokesman added that "Hampton was murdered in bed while he slept" by a policeman who "must have come in the back door and murdered him with a silencer."

A few days later, a private autopsy, performed at the request of Hampton's family, concluded that hours before Hampton was shot to death he had been heavily drugged with

Seconal, a barbiturate, which the spokesman deduced had been administered by a "pig agent" before the raid. The independent autopsy also concluded that the bullet that killed Hampton was missing, for the Panther's pathologist found an entrance wound in the head but no exit wound and no bullet in the head. Lawyers for Panthers intimated that the missing bullet had been secretly extracted and disposed of by the police, because it constituted evidence of murder.

A third version was rendered by a federal grand jury that had been specially empanelled to investigate the Dec. 4 shootings. After having all the physical evidence recovered by both the police and the Panthers analyzed by the F.B.I. Laboratory in Washington and evaluating additional ballistic evidence uncovered by the F.B.I., and after hearing all the witnesses willing to testify, the grand jury concluded, among other things, that the Chicago police investigation of the raid was "so seriously deficient that it suggests purposeful malfeasance."

When Groth and Davis forced their way in through the inner door, according to the grand jury's assessment of the events, a 12-gauge slug was fired from inside the apartment and passed through that door as it swung open to a forty-five-degree angle. There were indications that the shotgun was no more than 15 inches from the opening door. A 12-gauge slug found at the scene proved consistent with a shotgun that was next to Mark Clark's body and was stained with blood of Clark's type; the slug was also found to match the hole in the door. Moreover, an empty shell found nearby was "positively identified" as having come from the shotgun.

Piecing together the physical evidence, the jury posited that Mark Clark, sitting behind the door, fired a shotgun blast through the door just as the police burst in. This, however, was the only shot that could be definitely traced to a Panther weapon.

The grand jury concluded that Groth and Davis apparently came in shooting, for one pistol shot had been fired through the door. Davis shot Clark, who was sitting behind the door holding a shotgun, and a woman then in the room, Brenda Harris, who was holding another shotgun.

Minutes later, after the officers claimed they heard a shotgun blast from a bedroom adjacent to the living room, the wall between the living room and the bedroom was "stitched" with forty-two shots from a carbine and a submachine gun. One of these bullets passed through the first bedroom into a second bedroom, where it fatally wounded Fred Hampton in the right forehead. Another bullet, apparently from the same volley, since it was travelling at the same angle, struck Hampton in the right cheek, and another struck him in the left shoulder. This last, the only bullet recovered from his body, proved to be a .30-calibre bullet from Davis's carbine.

Aside from Hampton and Clark, four of the seven other Panthers in the apartment, as well as one police officer, were wounded by police gunfire in less than 12 minutes after the raid began. Eighty-three empty shells and 56 bullets were recovered from the apartment by the police, the Panthers, and the F.B.I., of which all but one shotgun slug and one shell had been fired from police weapons.

Although the police steadfastly maintained that at least 10 or 15 shots were fired at them by Panthers, a painstaking reconstruction by the grand jury suggests that, following the first shot by Clark, police entering from the back of the apartment mistook Davis's and Groth's shots in the front of the apartment for Panther gunfire, and the police in the front of the apartment similarly mistook the "return" fire from the rear of the apartment for continuing resistance.

According to the grand jury's version, the officers very probably fired through the living-room wall under erroneous impression that they were in a gun battle with Panthers.

The grand jury also attempted to resolve conflicts between the findings of the Panthers' private autopsy and those of the police autopsy by ordering Hampton's body exhumed and yet a third autopsy performed, by an out-of-state medical examiner in the presence of both a Chicago pathologist from the coroner's office and a pathologist retained by the Hampton family.

Two points were clarified by the third autopsy. First, despite the statement of the Panthers' pathologist that there was no exit wound for the fatal bullet that entered Hampton's forehead, this autopsy plainly showed an exit hole in front of the left ear when the sideburns were shaved. Second, the Panthers' claim that Hampton was heavily drugged with Seconal before the shooting was not supported either by this autopsy, which showed "no trace of drugs in the body," or by the report of the F.B.I. Laboratory in Washington, which had also tested the sample used in the Panthers' private autopsy. The toxicologist who performed the analysis for the Panthers told the grand jury that he had not performed the most specific test for Seconal, the gas-chromatography test, but had relied

instead on a less sophisticated test, which required some "subjective evaluation." In performing the gas-chromatography test on the same sample that the Panthers' toxicologist had used, the F.B.I. found no Seconal or other drugs in the sample but did find deterioration in the blood that could have been partially responsible for a mistaken analysis.

On the basis of the grand jury's meticulous investigation of the killings, it seems reasonable to conclude that Hampton was fatally shot not while he was "drugged" or by a policeman standing over him with a silencer, as the Panthers have claimed, but by a bullet fired by a police officer in the living room which had passed through two intervening walls at a time when no Panthers were firing at police.

Are these ten cases of Black Panthers killed by police part of a nationally coordinated pattern? Although Hampton and Clark were the only Panthers killed as a direct result of a planned police raid, or even in a situation in which the police could reasonably be supposed to have had advance knowledge that they would confront Black Panthers, it still might be maintained that the police involved had instructions of some sort to kill Black Panthers whenever the opportunity presented itself.

The theory broached by John Kifner in the Times that the Nixon Administration had, through the statements of public officials, "at least contributed to a climate of opinion among local police . . . that a virtual open season has been declared on the Panthers" seems historically inaccurate, since five of the ten Panther deaths that can be directly attributed to police action occurred before the Nixon Administration took office.

And, as far as I have been able to determine, no Black Panthers have been killed by the police in the period of more than a year that has elapsed since the Hampton-Clark incident.

In all of the ten cases to which Garry's list has been reduced, at least some of the Panthers involved were armed and presented a threat to the police. Six of the ten Panthers were killed by seriously wounded policemen who clearly had reason to believe that their own lives were in jeopardy. In none of these cases, moreover, is there any positive evidence to support a belief that the wounded policemen knew they had been shot by Black Panthers.

According to the evidence that is available, Bartholomew, Lawrence, and Lewis were stopped as burglary suspects; Pope approached a robbery stakeout at night; Winters opened fire when two policemen entered an abandoned building to investigate a citizen's complaint; and although it is agreed that Roberson took it upon himself to challenge the behavior of the police investigating the burglary of a fruit stand, it is not reported that he identified himself as a Black Panther.

In the four remaining cases, the fatal shots were fired by policemen who had not themselves been wounded. A further distinction might be made to take account of the fact that in two of these deaths—those of Armstead and Clark—the police state that in each instance they were confronted by an adversary with a lethal weapon and had reason to presume that their own lives were endangered. Armstead

pointed a rifle at a policeman and refused to disarm himself; Clark confronted a policeman with a shotgun, which, in fact, he had previously fired.

In any event, there are two cases in which Black Panthers were killed by policemen whose lives were not being directly threatened by those men. These are the cases of Hutton, who was shot while allegedly running from the scene of a 90-minute gun battle in which three policemen had been wounded, and Hampton, who was apparently hit by stray bullets in a reckless and uncontrolled fusillade.

Four deaths, two deaths, even a single death must be the subject of the most serious concern. But the basic issues of public policy presented by the militancy of groups like the Panthers and by the sometimes brutal police treatment of angry and defiant black people in general can be neither understood nor resolved in an atmosphere of exaggerated charges—whether of "genocide" against the Panthers or of "guerrilla warfare" against the police—that are repeated, unverified, in the press and in consequence widely believed by the public.

The idea that the police have declared a sort of open season on the Black Panthers is based principally, as far as I can determine, on the assumption that all the Panther deaths cited by Charles Garry—28, 20 or 10 —occurred under circumstances that were similar to the Hampton-Clark raid. This is an assumption that proves, on examination, to be false.

part three

THE
MISEDUCATED

Education of high quality and in great quantity is a requirement for all if our social life is to flourish. One's economic well-being, social status, and life chances are virtually dependent on academic achievement and technical competence. Every individual has good reason for pouring energy and resources into education for himself and his family members. Our educational enterprise, however, has not been able to keep up with the demands of the community or the aspirations of individuals. The educational system has become a source of much frustration, anxiety, and hostility, and it has clearly failed to meet the needs of many individuals.

The educational institution, like other ones, tends to become a slave to its own traditions or to strong individuals who dominate it. In some ways, the activities of the enterprise are related only remotely to the goal of educating individuals to cope with the demands of contemporary social life. Moreover, the educational system is rightly accused of being oriented toward middle-class values, needs, and experiences; the unique needs of those who are born into deprived or minority group status are frequently ignored. The burden is generally placed on the individual to adjust himself to the needs of the institution rather than devising types of settings which can tolerate and maximize individual differences. Education is also a major industry in our society and, as such, it does not escape from the hands of policy-makers and community leaders who permit motivations of self-interest and an investment in the *status quo* to overshadow the need for an effective and equitable system of education for all. The cases presented here illustrate some of the social problems which produce conflict in this arena. The issues involved are many, and their complex interrelations with other community problems inhibit attempts at solutions.

| INDIVIDUAL vs. INDIVIDUAL | INDIVIDUAL vs. ORGANIZATION |

COLFAX, WASHINGTON

LEGACY OF AN ICE AGE

There is no need to describe in great detail the extensive unrest, violence, and turmoil that have hit so many college campuses. The mistrust, misunderstandings, and unusually strong feelings that have been generated around issues relating to our halls of ivy have not only touched the lives of those on campus but have reverberated out into the lives of countless members of our communities. In this article, Mr. Moyers describes an encounter that includes all sorts of people—merchants, politicians, professors, and students—who clash at an informal meeting in a small town close to Washington State University. These individuals and the expressions they give to divergent views display some of the rifts that have opened to divide our communities and our campuses.

Most large urban schools are faced with crucial problems which are part of rapid growth, unexpected changes, and limited resources. However, individuals also play a key role in determining the adequacy of the educational enterprise. The case presented here illustrates the burden that perverted leadership can place on the educational system. Individuals can attain leadership positions and then use them to satisfy their own personal ambition at the expense of the institution. Such leaders leave a legacy which frustrates the good intentions of successors. The prospects for a new superintendent to change the tarnished image of leadership are dim and frustrating. Even a powerful institution, such as the Chicago school system, can be imposed upon and victimized by an individual who places his own interests above the needs of others.

ORGANIZATION vs. INDIVIDUAL	ORGANIZATION vs. ORGANIZATION

HALLS OF DARKNESS: IN THE GHETTO SCHOOLS

Although core city schools have a tendency to attract incompetent and undesirable staffs, this is certainly not true in individual cases. Kozol, a man with obvious compassion for children of poverty and creative interest in teaching such children, reports the difficulties he experienced in the Boston public school system. The educational organization clearly felt it important to prevent him, or at least, it offered him no support in his efforts to deal in special ways with children who bring the problems of economic and social deprivation into the schoolroom. The article portrays well the response of the educational system to individuals who fail to satisfy institutionally defined patterns and who instead pursue solutions to problems which the institution has swept under the carpet.

SPIES ON CAMPUS

The college and university occupy a unique place in our educational system, particularly in respect to the idea of academic freedom. The process of advanced education ideally is one of the free exchange of ideas. Institutions of higher learning, however, are not free from those who would prefer to restrict academic freedom and convert the free market place of ideas into a closed system of ideological indoctrination. Most important of all, those who threaten the educational institution may do so with the support of the federal agencies and under the cloak of such clandestine organizations as the FBI and the CIA. In this article, Donner traces the use of such spies on campus, and he describes how university and college organizations become the victims of organizations which are more concerned with "control" than with education.

Colfax, Washington

BILL MOYERS

By 5:15 every one of the 500 seats is taken and people are sitting on the floor along the walls or standing shoulder to shoulder at the rear of the big room with the concrete floor. Outside another hundred persons have arrived too late to get in. Some of the older men are joking with the deputy sheriff of Whitman County, a stocky man who wears his gun on his left hip for a crossover right-handed draw. The wheat has been harvested and the fairgrounds are surrounded by stubbly hills. The stock barns and the rodeo grounds are as neat and modestly prosperous as the people whose cars and trucks now cover the grassy parking lots.

There is a hum inside the auditorium. Neighbors who have not seen each other for a spell are catching up on their gossip. Something is wrong in one of the local churches and two women seated behind me are certain the preacher made a mistake to take his vacation "right now in the middle of everything." Two women and a man, who I surmise is a school official, are discussing a state-wide poetry contest for grownups. The participants are asked to submit poems that reflect "the goodness of America." One knot of men grumble

Reprinted by permission of Harper & Row, Publishers, Inc., from *Listening to America* by Bill Moyers. Copyright © 1971 by Bill Moyers.

about the latest census figure. Whitman County's population has dropped in ten of its incorporated towns but in Pullman, where Washington State University is located, the population has increased by 50 percent in ten years. "The damn university has grown too fast," one of the men said. The more people you got, the harder it is to control them." Most of the women are dressed as they probably were at church this morning. The men are wearing short-sleeved shirts with open collars except for a few in suits and some who are wearing ties without coats. The rows are dotted with gray crew cuts. The men and women of the towns and farms of Whitman County, in the rich wheat-fields of southeast Washington, are here in goodly numbers to put their university "back on the right track."

About a hundred of their adversaries have come: students and faculty members from Washington State University who have made the thirty-minute drive from Pullman to Colfax "to attend our own lynching," as one of them put it. The students are seated along the left wall of the auditorium facing the stage and in a group in the first few rows of seats. There are several mustaches but few students have really long hair. Most of them are neatly dressed. A beautiful girl with blond hair is walking to her seat in a polka-dotted miniskirt which brings a few stern looks from some women in the audience and more than one furtive glance from the corner of a husband's eye. One student with a rampant beard seats himself beside a middle-aged woman in a print dress who draws her lips tightly and stares ahead. I am not sure whether she is tickled by the adventure, or frightened.

Delbert Logsdon of Cheney, motel owner, has moved to the podium. He is a small, round man in his fifties, with blue eyes set in a full-moon face. He is very nervous. His hands clutch the microphone until they are white as he begins the first meeting of Concerned Citizens:

"I'm happy to see such a crowd today. It means one thing to me, that people are concerned. I've been asked, 'Who's sponsoring this?' There's no particular group. Just a bunch of citizens who are interested in our universities and colleges in this state. It's just what the name implies, Washington *State* University. The taxpayers of the state are the ones who are footing the bill. We're not as a group of citizens trying to raise hay over on the campus. We think there are things that should be done over there and can be, but there are enough rules and regulations over there on the books if they'd be enforced. This is one things that our group is going to insist—that the rules be enforced. This group that is causing a lot of noise and seems to be heard the loudest is a very small minority. You the general public have not taken an active part. This is what has hexed the legislators as well as the board of regents and the college administration. It's happening all over the country. It's not the students, but it is the appeasement, appeasement and ca-

pitulation. I can remember when Chamberlain tried appeasing Hitler. We ended up in World War II. Appeasement didn't work there and I can see no evidence of appeasement working here. It's time to end it."

There is a burst of applause from the audience. None of the students I can see are clapping.

State Senator Elmer Huntley is the first speaker. He is a tall, broad-shouldered man wearing a dark green suit with a modest tie. His forehead runs all the way back to the crown of his head. He begins with a confession:

"Actually I've been in such a quandary for the last week. People have been asking me what the meeting was all about, what I was going to say. Frankly I was called and asked to be here, and that's all I know about it, period."

Delbert Logsdon looks like a man in need of a very strong drink.

"Since I am on the platform," the senator continues, "I'm going to take the prerogative of saying just a few words about what I'm sure you're all interested in today. Living right in the middle of this district, I've been called on many, many times by the citizens of the district to go over and straighten that school out over there. That isn't what I was elected for. I was elected to make laws, not to enforce them. I have spent many hours over on the campus giving them my ideas for whatever they were worth, meeting with students and with the staff. I tried to impress upon them that there are going to have to be some rules and regulations laid down, a code of ethics if you please, and it should come from the regents. We were afraid that if this didn't happen some legislator would take it in his own hands. I would hate like the dickens to see a code of ethics or rules and regulations written into law. You put these things into law and the college staff and the regents don't have any flexibility. I think that I've said about all I have to say."

Delbert Logsdon introduces the next speaker as Representative Robert Goldwater and the audience laughs. His name is Goldsworthy.

"I've been called lots of names [laughter] but this is the first time Goldwater [laughter]," he says. "That's all right; I voted for him [laughter and loud applause]. Not only that, I'd vote for him today [more laughter, more applause—enthusiastic applause]."

Representative Goldsworthy is also tall and he is also wearing green —a checked sport coat and dark slacks. He has a long, square face like a Prussian general. He stands very straight and does not touch the podium or the microphone as he speaks:

"This issue that you're all here for today is going to be one of the biggest issues we're going to face this fall. And I'm saying this knowing that on the ballot there'll be tax reform, the abortion bill, nineteen-year-old voting and all that. But I want to say this is not peculiar to Washington State University, the University of Washington, the state of Washington, or the United States. We're rather newcomers to this problem. For many, many years the students at the University of Mexico, the University of Tokyo, Seoul, in the Philippines—all have made their voices heard and have done it through violent methods. Now we're seeing it spread to this country. We're certainly not pioneering anything new in the United States. I hope this helps you to see that passing more punitive and restrictive legislation is not the an-

swer. Firing the president of the college is not the answer, either. I get many calls and letters to cut the appropriations to the school, and this is not the answer, either. The answer is to keep open the lines of communication. Now this has got to go both ways, not just from me—the middle-class, balding, middle-aged establishment-type person—but from you young folks here who feel strongly on the other side. It's all right for some of you to tell us we've got to listen. But it's got to go both ways. You've got to listen to us, too. The answer to the thing is not a closed mind on either side."

As Robert Goldsworthy sits down he is vigorously applauded by the townspeople and some of the students as well. It is about the last time they will be together. For it is State Senator Sam Guess's turn at the microphone and he is not an equivocal man.

"This is the most serious problem that has faced America since I've been in public office, certainly since I can remember, even back in my high-school and college days," he begins. He has put his left hand on the podium and will leave it there throughout his speech. He is a big man with a crew cut and eyes that peer through black-rimmed glasses directly toward the students. He speaks quietly in a monotone that belies the force of his words:

"We passed a bill in the legislature exactly as the president of Washington University had suggested to give him the power to control uprisings and riots on the campus. Did it stop the situation on the University of Washington's campus? No. Did it stop the situation on Washington State's campus? No. Now if the administrators will not administer, what can you do? The legislature is going to have to do something. I am going to put in a bill that will establish rules and regulations to guide and regulate the conduct of students and faculty members on campus."

[I later obtained a copy of Senator Guess's bill. It provides for the immediate dismissal from the university of anyone "gathering on or adjacent to the campus in a manner which causes damage to public or private property, causes injuries to persons, or interferes with the orderly functioning of the college or university or the normal flow of traffic"; or, among other things, for "inciting students (or faculty) to violate written college or university policies and regulations."]

"I feel that it is my duty as a legislator to furnish the money and the guidelines to the board of regents. I think it is the duty of the board of regents and the administrative staff hired by the board of regents to create on campus a setting in which a student may learn and equip himself in order to be a good citizen of the United States. I do not believe that a university is created by the taxpayers of the state of Washington to be the hotbed of anarchy. I do not believe that we taxpayers pay our money for our children to be infected with bad ideologies and i-de-ologies that are foreign to what has made America great." With the last three words he abandons his monotone and raises his voice for emphasis.

A voice from the crowd: "RIGHT ON!"

There is loud and sustained applause.

"I do not believe that a faculty member violating a professional code has any right to remain on campus."

More applause. A man at the rear shouts: "Give it to 'em, Senator. Let 'em have it."

But Guess returns to his flat way of speaking. "Under this bill any administrator, faculty member, or elected official, including senators and representatives, may submit a written complaint to the board charging any faculty member with unprofessional conduct, specifying the grounds therefor. If the board determines that such complaint merits consideration, the board shall designate three members to sit as a committee to hear and report on such charges. *Upon filing of a complaint* the pay of an accused faculty member shall be suspended until a final determination is made by the board."

Someone behind me shouts: "Guilty until proven innocent, huh?"

Guess: "These are—"

Another voice: "That's a hell of an America."

Guess: "These are conditions that are merited by the situation. The board has the power of subpoena. There will be due process."

A chorus of protesting voices rings from the students.

"What happened to the courts?" a girl asks.

"Jee-sus," another girl says. "I must be having a bad dream."

Guess: "Due process is in here." He has not raised his voice.

Voice from the audience: "Read it to us."

Guess: "You know what it is. This is a time that calls for stern measures." And he sits down to long, hearty applause.

Chairman Logsdon is back at the microphone. "Is there a Thomas Young here?" he asks.

"Yes, right here." A young man stands up behind me.

"Thomas Young contacted me and asked for permission to speak at this meeting and he said that he was a participant in the strike at Washington State last May."

Groans rise from the right side of the auditorium.

The chairman continued: "And I don't know but I think it's right we listen to Tom—or Thomas—and I'd like to have him come up here and let us open-mindedly hear his side of the story."

Two or three people applaud lackadaisically, but Thomas Young does not move. He speaks across the room to the chair: "When I called you, I had a different impression of the meeting, and now that I'm here, I have changed my mind. I do thank you that you responded to my offer, however."

Delbert Logsdon is relieved and hurries to his next introduction: "The past editor of the *Washington State Evergreen*, the college newspaper, Gary Eliassen. Come on up, Gary, and give us a speech."

Angry voices and catcalls from the students are drowned out by applause. The muttering continues after Eliassen, wearing khaki pants and blue shirt, with a straight haircut, his voice cracking nervously while he shifts back and forth on the balls of his feet, says:

"As a student at WSU the past four years I have seen irrational student dissent grow until it reached a climax this spring with the sit-in at the university administration building and the student strike. For the most part, this behavior occurred despite students being allowed an increasing number of freedoms and responsibilities. The president of the university made many attempts to involve students in decisions. Some of the students answered his efforts with ultimatums, demands, and even threats of violence. They made the university

a political arena rather than an educational institute. The student movement at WSU has become an absurdity of generalization, rumor, threats of violence, and oversimplification. Those who didn't participate in the recent student strike were quickly labeled racist by some of the demonstrators. Those merchants who didn't put up WE OPPOSE RACISM signs were simplified as either supporting racism or being ignorant. Anyone who opposed the sit-in at the administration building was called an oppressor of the people's rights to assemble. What about the students who wanted the freedom to attend classes, who protested the president's decision to cancel classes, and whose pleas were ignored by the administration? What about the six hundred students who supported President Nixon's decision to go into Cambodia in a poll taken by my newspaper?"

"That's tellin' it like it is," comes a shout from the audience.

"By God, that boy is right."

Cheers and applause fall upon young Eliassen's ears. His hands are in his pockets and he is rocking back and forth. He still appears very nervous, but I am sure that the turbulent cries of approbation escaping the throats of the majority of his audience at that moment are a sound he will never forget. He is new to the experience. Should he smile? Pause? Raise his arms? He plays it like a professional: he lowers his head and waits for the applause to die away. I wonder if he will ever write another editorial. For in such moments are politicians born. Gary Eliassen has met the people and they are his. His peers only glower.

Now he continues: "If we are not going to allow our college campuses to become an arena simply for political action, irrational dissent, and violence, the taxpayers, students, and most importantly the university administration are going to have to take a long, hard look at the jobs they have been doing. The university must be firm in dealing with both college disrupters whose intent and purpose is not in education but merely to create confusion and bring about confrontation. Taxpayers will have to take even more interest in who they are electing to the legislature [applause]. Students too will have to become even more involved, for I am convinced that we have not seen the end of student unrest at WSU [a few claps from the left side of the room]. In essence, the so-called silent majority must begin speaking. If we stand by we will allow minority rule a free hand on the campuses. Thank you."

And they cheer mightily as Gary Eliassen leaves the stage.

Delbert Logsdon again: "I've been informed that since Mr. Thomas Young will not speak there's another member of the student strike steering committee here who would like to say a few words. Her name is Miss Nola Cross."

Actually it is Mrs. Nola Cross. At first glance I would have guessed her to be a high-school junior, but she is in her early twenties, tall, with hair flowing down to the small of her back. In her manners she is very austere, and I expect to hear a rather harsh voice when she speaks. But it is soft and not at all abrasive.

"I did not intend to give any speech, but due to the nature of this occasion I think it is important that I come and speak now. I was chairman of the strike at WSU and editor of the school paper there in the fall. We've heard a lot of talk about students who want to get a real educa-

tion, who don't want to be disturbed, who want to go to classes and hear lectures and read their books, get their degrees, and go out and make money. But I think there's more to an education than simply going to classes. I know I have rarely missed a class. I know that I have a 3.5 average, but I also know that during the strike I skipped every class that week—"

The students are listening intently to her. There is something about her they respect. Her role last spring must have been commanding. If we ever have a revolution in this country, I conclude, it will be led by women like this wearing baggy old caps and thick cotton jackets storming barricades in the winter snow while their husbands tend the babies.

"—I skipped every class that week and I learned more than I had ever learned in any other week of school [applause]. I learned about political pressures and political ideas and this sort of thing, but I also learned about being an American and how to adjust to being a citizen, a concerned citizen—"

The plagiarism did not go unnoticed among the audience.

"—a concerned citizen, of the United States. I learned that I must speak out as a concerned citizen and do whatever is in my power to change the system, to make the lives and the system, be it in the university itself or in the nation as a whole, more suited to the quality of all those who live within the boundaries [applause]. A democracy means that all citizens should participate in the decisions of the government, and all students should participate in the decisions of the university.

"As far as the strike is concerned, it should be made clear that there were absolutely no threats of violence during the strike by the strike committee. All decisions were made by the strikers in large mass meetings, and there was no bar to attendance. The decisions were made and the actions taken by what one might call a true democracy.

"Please look at the goals of the strike. The people who were striking were striking in particular to support the Black Student Union and the Mexican-American students who live on campus in their struggle to obtain equality with other white students on campus."

There are no blacks in the audience.

"By equality they meant securing classes which were suited to them and would help the rest of the students at the university understand their situation. There are only about sixty black students in a university of thirteen thousand, and that makes them very much of a minority. But that doesn't mean that the white students on campus shouldn't take classes, be allowed to take classes, in Afro-American history so they can learn about the background of black students. The Constitution was intended for a majority of the people in the United States to be able to make decisions but not at the expense of the minority. We were striking in support of the minority and there were no threats of violence by any members of the strike.

"I am troubled by the legislation being discussed here today. When you are talking about whether or not a student is suitable to remain at the university or whether an instructor's conduct is suitable for a professor at a state university, you have to watch the wording in the bill. How vague is it? How specific? What exactly does it mean for a professor to be unsuitable? Does it mean he's not allowed to take part in any kind of protest? Even a legal protest? I think that a number of professors at WSU are not going to try to stay here under those conditions. They are going elsewhere where—"

Loud applause erupts in the center of the room.

"—where they'll have the freedom of expression. You're going to see a decline in the quality of education—"

From the crowd: "That's what we want." More applause. Loud applause.

"—Well, if what you want is a decline in the quality of education this bill is one way to secure it. But the university is no longer going to be a place of freedom of expression. It's no longer going to be an academy. It's going to be a place where you can come to learn cold facts by memory so you can get a job and not to become a citizen of the United States."

"Go home, go home," someone shouts. There is a buzzing through the auditorium. They want her to quit. She does.

As she leaves the stage Delbert Logsdon says: "I think you've got plenty of courage to stand up for what you feel is right and I admire you for it."

There is another angry rumble from the audience and Logsdon, the motel man, does not like it. "It took a lot of nerve for that young girl to come up here and speak," he says angrily. "We don't all have to agree with her, but she still is courageous." His words sting and the audience responds meekly.

Other speakers follow. Mrs. Margaret Hurley, with her brown hair in bangs, wearing large white bracelets, her glasses far down on her nose, is also a state representative and the only

Democrat present. She speaks sweetly:

"People in my district and all over the state are saying that the administrators should keep their place and act responsibly, and the students should keep their place and act responsibly. I think that word 'responsibility' is the key to the whole thing. Act according to your role. If you are acting according to your role, you are keeping your place."

There is a growing murmur from the students and someone asks: "What about the niggers?"

"When I'm not in the legislature, I'm a teacher, and I find that no teacher can teach unless the students are in order, and that order has to be maintained. And the responsibility of the teacher or the administrator is to maintain order. If you students actually really and truly want to learn, you will help to maintain that order."

A titter runs up and down the front row and Mrs. Hurley is nettled. She responds indignantly.

"You children can laugh because you haven't sent any children to college yet. I have sent four to college, and it costs a lot of money. And don't minimize this money thing. It costs a lot in sacrifice by your parents. People who are living out in the districts are darned well fed up with what's happening. . . . Just this last week when I heard over the radio that the University of Washington had named a certain young person as part of their recruitment committee, to go out into other states and into other areas of the nation and bring minority groups into the state to go to college, I thought how ridiculous this is. We have our minority groups. They are welcome at our colleges. I think they deserve an education just as well as any of you down here who are not part of a minority group, but to go out and recruit more minority groups seems to me a very senseless thing to do, and I think that we should demand that this halt immediately."

There is tremendous applause.

The young man sitting in front of me turns to an older woman—I take her to be a member of the faculty—and says: "This is incredible."

"I want to close with this point," Mrs. Hurley says. "It has to do with limiting enrollment. Now I know a number of serious students who really and truly want to get an education and are being eliminated from this because enrollments are limited. Well, I would suggest that they start limiting those people who don't seem to be serious students [applause]. We would cut down the enrollment to where the university could cope with it and we would have students that are interested in getting an education and eliminate those who are not. Thank you very much [applause].

Representative Carlton Gladder, an older man who leans into the microphone, his right hand glued inside his pocket, his left hand moving up and down as he talks:

"I think I was as idealistic as any of you when I was young. But about the time I got out of college—I worked two and a half years between high school and college—there were a bunch of idealistic youths who had been revved up by a bunch of articulate and persuasive politicians in Germany. And when these brown shirts committed their pogroms of the Jewish people of Berlin and all over Germany and Austria, they were motivated by nothing else than idealism. So what I'm saying to you is this, that idealism is a great and wonderful thing, but cherish it a little bit and don't put it clear up on a pedestal and say that this is all that is necessary. . . . The students of America were rightfully and righteously concerned by the Kent State deaths. Violence exploded all over the country. Emotions were wrought up and people were climbing the walls, but I don't downgrade this a bit. But one of the things that does disturb me is that I didn't hear any cries of outrage when Jerry Rubin appeared on campus after campus after campus in this country and said, 'You must be prepared to go home and kill your folks.' Why didn't you rise up? Why didn't you rise up? Why didn't you shout?"

He is shouting.

"When two policemen were killed in one day for doing nothing but performing their duty, where were you? I mean, are you rounded? Are you sincere all the way? I'll tell you this, we're going to try and correct the situation on our campuses. The taxpayers of the state of Washington want us to establish some reasonable ground rules and we're going to. And I'll tell you this, too. Their ideas of what education consists of is going to be adhered to, to quite a degree, rather than what you, in your infinite knowledge, would set up."

"Right on. Right on," a student shouts, facetiously.

Representative James Keenly, a handsome man with graying hair and a ruddy face, dressed in a brown sports jacket and a gold shirt, from Spokane:

"I didn't come down here to put the vigilantes into shape. I didn't come down here to seek any scalp. I'm here as a father . . . and as a taxpayer. . . . I think the key issue of what we're talking about is this business of tax-

payers and who is paying the bill. In the last few years we've seen a number of attempts on the part of some minority groups to rule, to try to gain their goals through anarchism. This scares me half to death. . . . These are rather well-trained, rather well-financed, and rather well-organized young people who aren't on the campus for the purpose of securing an education. They're there for the purpose of stirring up trouble in political ideology, and in the process they are enlisting and rallying up the support of a whole lot of other impressionable young men and women who are there and who do not have the proper background with which they can make intelligent decisions. I don't really think at this point the issues are really important—"

A girl down the row put her head in her hands and said with disgust: "Oh, my God. Oh, my God."

"—and I certainly am not going to talk about them. The issues are being used as subterfuge in many instances. Whether we're talking about Vietnam or Cambodia or final examinations or grades, it makes very little difference; they're subterfuges. If students want to worry about Cambodia, Vietnam, or grades, they can do it on extracurricular time like they do in football. Unfortunately some of our administrators really do feel that some of the theatrical radicals are the architects of a brave and compassionate new world. Some of these theatrical radicals that I refer to are able to spice things up with a little rock music, or a little pot, or a little acid, or the old Marxist idea of dictated equality, and it becomes appealing to some impressionable young people on campus. Some of our administrators and academicians had better learn fast how to contend with this kind of thing because the survival of our colleges and our institutions, the survival of our free-enterprise system, is most certainly at stake. . . .

"I have two fine young daughters. They've told me often what is on their minds and what's going on with their friends and I learned things I did not know. In many instances I changed my manner, I changed my method of doing things. But some place along the line somebody has to call the shots. I'm the guy who pays the bills, and I'm the guy who's going to call the shots in my family. The same thing is going to happen in Washington. The taxpayers of this state, who are putting up the money, are ultimately going to call the shots, whether you people like it or not."

The young man in front of me says to his companion: "In the beginning was lucre, and lucre was God."

"And so," James Keenly is concluding, "if the regents and administrators do not do their duty, we in the legislature will take away the powers of the regents and administrators and place them in the legislature. We may even go further—maybe create a disciplinary board on campus with powers delegated directly from the legislature, to keep discipline. We will also have to let the police go directly onto the campus to deal with these problems. We are not going to hope our way through this or wish our way through. We need action. We want the regents and the administrators to make backbones out of their wishbones—and now."

And the longest applause of the day carries Representative James Keenly back to his seat. Not once did he raise his voice.

As the next speaker—a woman who teaches in the political-science department of Washington State—begins to lecture the students that the goals (of the strike) did not justify the means (of the strikers) someone in the audience shouts: "Then how do you justify Vietnam?"

"I did not come here to discuss the war," she replies, "and I remind you that I have the floor." The audience is on her side, but it is late. Delbert Logsdon moves back to the podium and she concludes hastily. Several students raise their hands to seek recognition. He looks past them and says: "This has drug on long enough. If you want to meet with individual legislators afterwards, you can get to them when we've adjourned. This debate could go on for hours and hours. We all know what we came for today and I hope you all realize something from it."

The students shout: "Let us speak. Let us speak. Don't stop now."

Delbert Logsdon of Cheney ignores them. He leans into the microphone as if he is applying mouth-to-mouth resuscitation and asks: "Is the silent majority ready to be heard?"

The roar that reverberates in the hall momentarily stuns even Delbert Logsdon: what has he loosed? He stands there, three-fourths of his short, round frame hidden by the podium, sweat running from his face, and suddenly he is no longer nervous. For the first time during the afternoon he is not gripping the microphone. His hands are on his hips.

"What about the minority?" a young voice cries from the floor. A professional-looking man turns to a student with long hair and says: "Now you see what we're up against."

Delbert Logsdon leans into the microphone and says: "I said you can come up here and speak to any one of the legislators you want to, but we're not going to stay here all night and listen to you. Goodbye." And he walks triumphantly away from the microphone.

They did stay. Small groups of students cornered the representatives and some engaged the townspeople. One young man in the midst of about twelve adults was asked if things were going to get worse. "Yes," he said, "I think they will." Another man, about thirty, with very short hair, said to the student: "You better watch out then, because if it get worse, it's gonna get worse for YOU." A much older man with a slight European accent said he had heard that there were twenty outsiders now using official university rooms to plan next fall's riots. The student replied: "Look, man, we've come here. You've got to come to the university to see that that just isn't true." The man's wife said: "I'd be afraid to go and I'd be afraid to let my husband go."

On stage a young woman in a tight white blouse and a red miniskirt talked to the representative from Spokane. "Why did you bring up the war without saying that it should stop?" she asked. "It's immoral for anyone to mention the war without saying in the next breath that we must stop it. Don't you realize that for everyone who dies over there, Vietnam or American, this whole country dies? Some of my friends have died over there but I don't mean just them. The whole country is dying." She began to cry. The legislator answered: "I mentioned the war because it was one of the reasons for the protest. That's why I brought it up. But the real reason for the meeting here was what the taxpayers think about the

university and not about the war." And she replied: "I am goddamn sick and tired of hearing about the taxpayers this and the taxpayers that. I am a taxpayer and I am an orphan and I own my parents' property and I bet I pay more taxes than anyone else in this room tonight. And I am goddamn sick and tired of paying taxes for these goddamn farmers not to grow wheat. Why didn't you mention that tonight? Why? I'll tell you why. The reason you didn't mention that was because the room was full of wheat farmers and you're a politician and you haven't got the goddamn guts." And the man from Spokane who had said issues were not really important managed to get out of there.

I located Mr. Logsdon. His eyes were bluer than they had seemed from the audience. He was quite happy. "I never said more than five words in public in all my life," he confessed. "Until today. And they said, 'Del, we got no chairman; you'll have to moderate it.'"

How did this meeting come about?

"Some of us was just having coffee one morning and lamenting what was happening to Washington State. The kids were destroying it. There had been this strike and the administration just threw up their hands and ran. When they got through running, they capitulated. I didn't go to Washington State but I have a niece over there and my father did and I belong to the Cougar Club. I've always boosted 'em in sports. And I just don't want to sit over at Cheney and watch the university get torn apart the way Harvard and those other places back east have been.

"I went over to the campus after the coffee session and asked a lot of questions, but I got no answers. We began to hear there's gonna be trouble in the fall and we decided to let the regents and the legislature know that it isn't just a small group of businessmen who are upset—lots of other people are, too. So we decided to have this meeting. I just didn't believe we'd have this many people, but I'll tell you—this is all the proof I need. Folks are fed up to their teeth." And he turned to receive the congratulations of his neighbors, who were coming forward with outstretched hands.

Legacy of an Ice Age

CHARLES AND BONNIE REMSBERG

Eight months ago James F. Redmond, a lean chain-smoker with leonine head and slow, dry wit, left the quietude of the school's superintendency in Syosset, New York, to assume a post in the field of public service. Yet for all his $48,500 a year . . . Dr. Redmond is among the least envied of public servants. His new job has put him squarely in the biggest hot seat—some say electric chair—in American education. And the future of the nation's second city may be sitting beside him.

His responsibilities as general superintendent of Chicago schools are awesome. Although 30 percent of Chicago's children attend parochial schools, the public system still enrolls some 600,000 students, employs 23,000 teachers, and occupies more than 600 classroom buildings. In short, Chicago

Reprinted by permission of the publisher and authors from Charles and Bonnie Remsberg, "Chicago: Legacy of an Ice Age," *Saturday Review*, May 20, 1967, pp. 73–75, 91–92.

has more population inside its schools than Denver or Minneapolis have within their city limits.

But what is more critical than size to Redmond's—and the city's—future is the state of the system's health. In the words of Robert Havighurst, a University of Chicago educator who exhaustively investigated Chicago schools at the request of the Board of Education, the system "is sick and getting sicker." Adds school board member Warren Bacon, "If this system were an industry dependent upon the quality of its products for survival, it would have gone bankrupt long ago."

For thirteen stormy years before Redmond took over, Chicago schools were in the iron grip of a superintendent whom sociologist Philip Hauser, another of the system's analysts, has characterized as "a giant of inertia, inequity, injustice, intransigence, and trained incapacity." Under this superintendent, Benjamin C. Willis, schools became the most controversial aspect of life in the Windy City.

What critics termed "his defensiveness, belligerence, hostility, and total lack of respect for the dignity of any person who dares even to ask him a question" led to the loss of progressive members from the school board at times when they were desperately needed. His consistent refusal to proceed with plans for racial integration gave birth to the nation's first school boycotts and to an increasingly militant civil rights movement which, experience has already demonstrated, is on a collision course with major violence. His contempt for parents' concern about quality of education accelerated the middle class's flight to the suburbs and shattered some racially mixed neighborhoods that were struggling for stability. His insistence that he could run a "problem-free" system stifled creative experimentation and bred among teachers a morale of fear. And his failure to confront mounting classroom crises produced, in the words of former school board member James Clement, "tragic consequences for all our children." "It is quite correct to say," Warren Bacon adds, "that Ben Willis virtually sank the Chicago public schools."

Yet, in attempting to salvage the system, Redmond faces not only the Augean stables Willis left behind but the political realities of the city as well. For all the well documented damage Willis wrought before he reached retirement age last fall, he and his policies were loyally supported by the city administration, the influential business community, and the most powerful press, all of which remain in positions to affect the changes Redmond is able to make. What is more, many needed improvements will

require big money, and Redmond finds himself in the state that ranks forty-ninth in the percentage of its per capita income allotted to education and a state where the fiscal fate of major metropolitan areas rests in the hands of a rural-dominated legislature.

Says a Chicago teacher: "I look at Dr. Redmond and I get impatient because nothing is different at the classroom level from before he came here. Then I look at the problems and I say, 'God help this man because this city's schools are doomed.'"

Because of an old scandal in which the school system was exposed as a haven for patronage hacks, the running of Chicago schools today, in theory, is buffered from politics. Yet, like everything else in the city that hosts the last great political machine, the schools are, in the final analysis, politically influenced. Understanding the forces that permitted a Ben Willis and will now help shape Redmond's efforts requires some knowledge of the nature of Chicago's political power.

Since its first settler opened a trading post in the 1790s, Chicago has been first and foremost a businessman's town, and no machine mahatma has taken shrewder advantage of this fact than Democratic Mayor Richard J. Daley, who was just overwhelmingly elected to his fourth term. Daley, one City Council member explains, "is essentially a broker," catering to the needs and desires of big business and finance, in trade for their political support. The exchange works so effectively that in this spring's mayoral elections the Republican party had to search for a sacrificial lamb who would finance the bulk of his own campaign while otherwise Republican business brahmins ran full-page ads for Daley and even the right-wing Chicago *Tribune* backed him.

The schools superintendent, like other potential movers-and-shakers in the city's superstructure, must be compatible with both the Daley machine and its business angels, and the mechanics to see that he is compatible have been provided. Members of the Board of Education, which hires the superintendent and is supposed to set policy, are appointed by Mayor Daley. The fact that he draws exclusively from a list of nominees drafted by a twenty-member commission "representing civic and professional organizations and educational institutions" allegedly inoculates against "politics." But the commission, itself appointed by Daley, is chaired by Dr. Eric Oldberg, the Mayor's Health Board president, and remains in existence only at the Mayor's discretion.

Not surprisingly, the school board in composition is almost a Lilliputian reproduction of the Daley-controlled City Council. Token representation is given to minority groups; two of the board's eleven members are Negro (though more than 50 per cent of the public school population is colored). Frequently, Negro appointees have been compliant, but currently one, Warren Bacon, an Inland Steel executive, is doubling in another role characteristically provided for on the board, that of vocal liberal dissenter. The majority of the board, which includes the father of a former Democratic alderman, a judge active in Democratic politics, and personal friends of the Mayor, remain, in Bacon's words, "votes the Daley administration can control."

Thus, even though Willis dictatorially usurped the board's powers—

effecting pocket vetoes, indulging in acid petulance, resigning briefly at one point to get his way—his four-year contract was three times renewed and then extended until his retirement. The reason, believes James Clement, a respected patent attorney who quit the board in 1965 to protest what was happening to the schools, was simply that Willis served the city's power structure, despite his divisive effect on the populace.

For one thing, the detail-minded Willis loved to build, and was rumored to know the location of every brick in every school building in the city. He acquired the nickname Ben the Builder after launching a multi-million-dollar school construction program soon after his arrival from Buffalo in 1953. Moreover, Willis's phobia about federal aid to education won him the unflagging loyalty of the *Tribune*, still Chicago's most powerful newspaper. Largely because he made himself a symbol of racial segregation, he also was lionized by whites in the city's blue-collar population. This group has traditionally attached the the least importance to quality education, and it is perhaps the most valuable grassroots buttress to the Daley machine, particularly in light of the usually lethargic Negro vote.

Finally, and perhaps most important, Clement explains, "He convinced the business community that Chicago could get quality education at bargain-counter rates."

Critics argue that the business interests have never demanded much from Chicago schools. Ringed by some of the best suburban school systems in the nation, home of a dozen major colleges and universities, still a magnet for the talented young of the Midwest and the Great Plains, Chicago has not been threatened by any letup in the steady stream of professionals and aspirants to the executive suite feeding in from the outside. With their own children by and large attending parochial, private, or suburban schools, "the principal concern of influential business leaders for Chicago schools," contends Alderman Leon Despres, a liberal lawyer elected to the City Council from the University of Chicago area of Hyde Park, "has been keeping costs—and taxes—down." In the context of the system's size, Willis's budgets were always relatively appealing.

Daley, a savvy oldtime "pol," said by experts to be the second-most powerful Democrat in the country, has always been careful overtly to keep hands off school matters. Whenever Willis and the system were under attack, he dragged forth his familiar "great-city-of-Chicago" speech but did not tangle openly with the specific issues. Behind the scenes, though, he worked to stifle criticism with time-tested machine tactics, many of them still in operation. Parents planning to keep their children home to protest conditions in inner-city schools have been quickly visited by welfare workers, public housing officials, and Democratic precinct captains and threatened with rent increases or removal from public-aid rolls if they joined the boycott. Boycott leaders suddenly have been offered jobs, reportedly including positions with the federal antipoverty program (a creature of the city administration in Chicago), which they have interpreted as bribes for silence. In the fall of 1965, when HEW froze some $30,000,000 in federal aid to Chicago schools until a "full investigation" could be made of charges that the system is deliberately segregated by race, the funds were thawed within a matter of hours after Daley allegedly telephoned the White House. Interestingly, the Mayor's Commission on Human Relations, established to combat racial injustice in the city, has an "education expert" but will not accept complaints about the Chicago public schools.

In keeping the power structure convinced that he was doing an adequate job for relatively little money, Willis enjoyed a crucial advantage over his critics: The way he ran the school system, they found it virtually impossible to establish statistically that quality in the schools was jeopardized. Willis, in effect, made Chicago the system that could not be tested.

Among other things, he changed the method of recording students' achievement scores, substituting for a system of *national* norms—which has a nine-point stanine scale—one of *intra-city* norms. "As a consequence," complained a statement issued by a group of high school teachers, "we are no longer able to tell how our students rate in comparison to those in other school systems, and neither can their parents or public." In 1965 Willis flatly refused to permit achievement tests and background information quizzes to be administered to Chicago pupils in a nationwide survey by the U.S. Office of Education. A few months later, he ordered Chicago principals not to answer questionnaires from the OE regarding this survey, and successfully urged the school board to decree that all future contacts between the school system and Washington officials "shall emanate from the general superintendent." A local TV station has found that Chicago school children even have been repeatedly forbidden to participate in a televised "quiz bowl!"

program which would put them against suburban and parochial students. In this atmosphere, claims James Clement, "The feeling has grown up that it is just not polite to speak the truth about Chicago schools."

The longer Willis is gone from the scene, however, the more the grim realities of what Redmond faces seem to be coming to light.

Besides political and economic pressures and a paralyzingly centralized administrative bureaucracy, he has, for one thing, inherited the effects of Willis's fanatical commitment to the "neighborhood school" policy. Civil rights leaders such as ex-teacher Al Raby charge that this has been nothing more than a professional disguise for perpetrating school segregation, especially since Chicago is residentially one of the most segregated cities extant. Whatever the motive, the policy led Willis to present his building proposals in five-year packages, denying Chicago any long-term citywide school planning and resulting in such ultimately costly anachronisms as buildings with as few as twelve classrooms.

In public hearings before the school board last month, parents from a number of middle-class white districts complained that their schools are so small that curriculum is weakened. Unlike larger counterparts, for instance, Norwood Park Elementary School on the far Northwest Side offers no foreign language or art instruction. The size of Bret Harte Elementary School on the South Side, parents claim, prevents it from having a music teacher, a full-time gym instructor, a full-time librarian, or an adjustment teacher for counseling and tutoring.

The tone of the recent hearings and other public statements indicates that one of Redmond's biggest problems will be mending a schism of growing cynicism and despair between parents and the schools. Although the new superintendent has stated publicly that he seeks a lively interplay between schools and community, the atmosphere of arrogance and hostility toward anyone outside the four walls of the school that flourished under Willis is still the prevailing one in most schools.

During Willis's reign, the city PTA president for two years was refused an appointment with him to discuss school issues, and many principals still actively discourage PTA activities by banning evening meetings—a death knell, of course, in inner-city areas where many mothers work during the day. At some schools, teachers have been told that they may not, even on their own time, belong to community organizations without their principals' okay. Volunteers willing to come into the schools from the community to relieve teachers of time-consuming lunchroom duty, truancy calls, and routine record-keeping were, until recently, discouraged. Even the telephone numbers of Chicago schools are unlisted, and one West Side kindergarten teacher recalls that when she mentioned to her principal that a visiting mother had observed that there were fifty-seven children in the class, the principal shouted: "Parents have no business in your room!"

Undoubtedly, Redmond's major challenge, however, is correcting classroom deficiencies that have become an accepted way of life because of what more than one teacher calls "Willis's reign of fear."

Because of conditioning caused by the ex-superintendent's long and vehement insistence that the system suffers no major ills, the premium in Chicago schools, teachers say, is on "not presenting any problems to the person above you." Thus teachers have found that the best way to receive good performance ratings from their principals, many of whom personally visit classes a maximum of once or twice a year, is to bring no discipline cases to their attention. "In many classrooms, kids are in an atmosphere of control only, no teaching whatsoever," says a North Side teacher. At year's end, it is an unwritten rule that a teacher flunk no more than 3 per cent of her students. "You have to keep them moving," explains a first grade teacher at an inner-city school, "or you destroy the image."

Principals, in turn, are often desperately anxious that their schools not be identified by superiors as trouble spots. Parents complain that even sex crimes against their children have not been reported to the police, and many incidents of violence against teachers go unrecorded.

Innovative teaching, which is likely to have rocky moments, has become anathema to many principals. A celebrated case involves Jo Ann Bowser, who during the Willis regime was a sixth-grade teacher at the slum-area, all-Negro Jenner School, largest elementary school in Chicago. Young Miss Bowser developed imaginative techniques to overcome the environmental apathy of her pupils and persuaded them to come to school an hour early each day, to work on science projects, prepare speeches, write plays and operettas—"anything to stimulate them." Their enthusiasm spread to their regular class work to the extent that they even refused recess. IQs increased markedly. Reading levels skyrocketed, with only five of

the twenty youngsters scoring below the sixth-grade-seventh-month level. All scored at seventh grade in math. The class swept the district in awards at science and speech contests, although in competition with white schools. "For the first time," Miss Bowser says, "I was producing a middle-class class in a low-income area." Then her principal, highest paid elementary principal in the system (in Chicago principals are salaried according to number of children under their command), ordered her to stop—because the rulebook issued by the superintendent's office says children are forbidden in the building before the regular class hour. Despite vociferous parent protest, the administrative hierarchy backed the principal. Miss Bowser resigned.

Hundreds of her colleagues in recent years have fled to the suburbs, where many consider educational methods to be "thirty years ahead of Chicago's." Indeed, the exodus of seasoned teachers and the increasing reluctance of talented novitiates to accept Chicago assignments, particularly in light of the fact that most must start in hard-core slum schools without benefit of any orientation or inservice training, has left many schools bereft of personnel.

The Chicago Teachers Union has estimated that 300 to 700 classrooms each day have no teachers whatever, with the concentration of teacherless rooms particularly heavy in Negro areas. One survey showed that in a district encompassing seventeen schools 83 per cent of the teacher absences were not covered. In others, as many as 80 per cent of the teachers on any given day are substitutes. In some schools, libraries are closed down weeks at a time because librarians must be drafted for classroom duty. Likewise, gym classes in some schools have been suspended as long as eighteen months.

Dr. B. J. Chandler, dean of Northwestern University's college of education and a member of the Mayor's commission for school board nominations, estimates that twenty-five out of every 100 teachers who *are* in class are not certified. A person may teach in Chicago without certification if he is willing to forego tenure, assignment security, and the normal salary increments. In some slum areas it is not unknown for a school to have but one or two certified teachers, and many of the uncertifieds are Negroes who themselves have been educated in woefully inadequate Southern schools and whose principal alternative to handling classes in teacher-hungry Chicago is domestic work.

Because the system has been unwilling to confront its problems, Chicago is graduating an inordinate and increasing proportion of "miseducated" and "uneducated" youngsters. Talk among high school teachers seems to focus with ever greater frequency on the alarming number of functional illiterates being promoted from the grades—"kids," one teacher put it, "who not only don't know their multiplication tables but can't mix a bowl of Jello by reading the package directions." A survey of records from the Forrestville North Upper Grade Center, which a complaint to the OE claims "may well be indicative of the entire system," shows that the *median* reading level of the eighth grade graduating class in a recent year was fifth grade, with many students ranging as low as second grade.

In a system so large there are, of course, traditional islands of excellence, the most touted probably being the North Side's Von Steuben High School, to which experienced teachers have gravitated and where a predominantly Jewish student population arrives in class strongly motivated. Scattered around the city, too, are individual teachers and principals who have been willing to run the risks of innovation. Experts have observed that tucked away in various sections of Chicago one can find in progress nearly every kind of educational experiment. But these are not widely discussed nor by any means broadly applied. In fact, says Redmond, "I am told some of these efforts are surreptitious."

The difficulties of functioning as an educator in such circumstances are evident to Northwestern University sociologist Raymond Mack, who recently captained a probe of Chicago schools for the OE's Equality of Educational Opportunity report. He notes that a deepening "don't-care" philosophy among personnel seems to be seeping throughout the system. "Wherever they are located, in white neighborhoods or black," confirms James Clement, "most of Chicago's schools today are second- or third-rate."

The third-rate schools are most likely to be Negro, and the color controversy, ignored by the school administration since the 1964 Hauser report proved the existence of de facto segregation, is one of the first Redmond will be forced to tackle. He has been ordered by the OE to answer charges by the Coordinating Council of Community Organizations, Chicago's civil rights federation, that school boundary lines have been deliberately drawn to promote segregation, that Negro teachers by and large are banned from white schools, and that vocational and trade schools and apprentice training programs practice discrimination in their admissions policies.

CCCO's exhaustively documented complaint states that 90 per cent of Chicago's Negro youngsters attend all-Negro schools (97 per cent attend majority-Negro) and that, rather than diminishing, segregation has actually intensified in recent years. "Chicago is in the forefront of the segregated systems," says Sanford Sherizen, education researcher for the Chicago Urban League. "It is segregated as solidly as the South."

In response to the school board's excuse that the color of students in Chicago's neighborhood schools merely reflects the city's housing pattern, the CCCO complaint points out that the board historically opposed and has never complied with a 1963 state law forbidding the location of new schools in a way that promotes racial separation. Instead, schools have been constructed in the very hearts of Negro ghettos and white enclaves, and district boundary lines have been obviously gerrymandered to preserve racial imbalance as housing patterns changed. Meyer Weinberg, author of the complaint and editor of *Integrated Education* magazine, charges that it is naïve not to recognize that school board decisions have been strongly influenced by the desires of the city's powerful anti-integration real estate interests.

Since 1961, sporadic and limited transfer and school cluster plans have been in effect, with the presumed potential for increasing integration. But, according to a national report on racial isolation in public schools

published this year by the U.S. Commission on Civil Rights, the Chicago plans have been "incapable of facilitating any substantial number of transfers" from Negro to white schools. Most school critics contend that the plans were designed to fail. Some, for example, were not launched until midterm, after students were already settled in their neighborhood schools. Also, transfer permits are temporary, subject to revocation at any time, and some Negro students have been told, incredibly, that credits from courses in their schools in some cases will not be accepted by the white schools to which they wish to transfer.

Residents of some areas see the school system's reluctance to effect strong and permanent transfer plans as a major threat to community stability. For instance, Marynook, a suburb-like settlement of modest new homes on the far South Side, has fought hard—and so far successfully—to maintain residential integration. "But the schools," says Hugh Brodkey, past president of an area community organization, "have been our worst enemy."

In public statements, Redmond has talked of meeting the civil rights crisis "honestly and intelligently" and of building "ahead [of] the movement of people . . . to help stabilize the existing integrated neighborhoods and make possible experiences of multiracial, multicultural education." Refreshingly, he has also conceded that the Chicago system is "staggering under severe educational handicaps," and he has spoken with heretofore heretical candidness about the need to "create effective dialogue with the communities," to "make decentralization work," to "encourage" teaching innovations knowing "that not all tries will be successful," to bring teacher aides into schools, to "give more than lip service" in developing the maximum potential of each child, and to "feel free" professionally at all levels in the system.

As yet, no significant strides have been made in these directions. According to Redmond's press aide, David Heffernan, the reason is that the superintendent has been devoting full time to budget and collective bargaining problems. Both these matters are indeed critical. Soon after his arrival last October, Redmond discovered there was "not one penny of local or state money to enlarge one single item in our operation." Indeed, he was heading into the new budget with a multimillion-dollar shortage.

"Over the last two years," Redmond has said, "the school board has known we were going to need money, but did not take this into account in their planning. New York spends about $800 a year per pupil. Suburban areas with acknowledged good schools spend less than $1,200 a year. Chicago spends less than $600. Yet not until last November did the board decide to ask for a local tax increase to help the schools. I suggest this is not very good planning."

With the tax increase approved last February and, possibly, with some additional state aid, Redmond hopes at least "to stand still." But, he says, "to do things we know how to do—including reduced class size (which has been rising)—we could use an additional $100 million tomorrow."

Unless the legislature does an abrupt about-face, this is pie-in-the-sky dreaming . Illinois, third among the states in income, supports only 22 per cent of the expenses of the public schools, compared to a national average of about 40 per cent. Some school districts in the state are so strapped that they have begun paying teacher salaries in script.

In Chicago, most school critics still are taking a wait-and-see attitude toward the new superintendent. Optimistic observers expect that Redmond will move to clean out the Willis underlings and progressively reorganize the system's administration in the near future. Massive plans for decentralization are said to be afoot and presumably will be aided by a study in preparation by management consultants Booz-Allen & Hamilton. A recent contract negotiated by the Chicago Teachers Union and the Board of Education, providing grievance procedures, policy-making, and improved communication, is being hailed as a big step in the right direction.

But, says a federal official in Chicago, to judge how much of a revolution in policy can be expected one must measure the concern of the city's business elite. "And education as an issue is not even before these people. It has not challenged the basic power structure the way the threat of open occupancy has. They do not know the facts about the schools, and they certainly are not convinced that anything needs to be done about them."

Increasing militancy within the civil rights movement may quicken the pace. Much of the local support for Dr. Martin Luther King grew up around concern about the quality of the schools—for black and white—and King has said that the reason he chose Chicago as his Northern base of operations is because it possesses the political machinery to effect change if it chooses to do so. That the Establishment has not so chosen since King's arrival, however, is leading rights leaders to predict privately that Watts-like rioting and burning will erupt in Negro districts this summer on a scale that will dwarf last year's bloody West Side eruption.

"Maybe then," says the federal offi-cial, "the business-political tandem here will see the connection between quality of education and society and realize that, the way things stand now, guaranteed rioters are being produced by the education factories of Chicago."

Halls of Darkness:
In the Ghetto Schools

JONATHAN KOZOL

The school was built seventy years ago and rises along the side of an un-distinguished hill. Fifty years ago, the neighborhood in which it stands was solidly white Protestant. Twenty years ago, it was Jewish. Today it is 80 per cent Negro and moving quickly to-ward 100 per cent. In a matter of years, five, six, or seven at most, there will not be ten white faces in a school which holds six hundred children.

From outside, the school seems morbid, desolate, crumbling. Inside, it overpowers one with a sense of heavi-ness and darkness. Gloom pervades the atmosphere. Children file in lines of silence. Teachers are present in the manner of overseers: watchful, sternfaced, guarded. They stand at corners, at the tops and bottoms of stairways. They laugh to each other

Published in *Death at an Early Age* (Houghton Mifflin Company, 1967); also, in the *Harvard Educational Review*, XXXVII, Summer, 1967, pp. 379–94. Copyright © 1967, Jonathan Kozol.

sometimes or smile in whispered con-fidences, but they do not laugh or smile at the children. "Keep your mouth shut"—"Please walk more quietly"—"Get back in line where you belong" are the expressions of morn-ing welcome most commonly heard.

Two years ago, I was a fourth-grade teacher in this school. My class was located on the second floor, on the street side, in the corner of an auditorium. Severe overcrowding and the school system's refusal either to bus or to redistrict had obliged the school for several years to pack two classes into the corners of this audito-rium while still using the central por-tion for other activities. Singing, sew-ing, conferences, drama, and remedial work of various kinds all took place simultaneously on many mornings. Torn curtains, rotted window-sashes, broken blackboards, and a faded U.S. flag highlight my memories of that classroom: these, and the dirt on the panes, the cardboard covering over broken windows, desks without tops, walls of peeling paint and, over it all, above it all, looking down upon it all in dark and mocking daguerrotype, a portrait of Abe Lincoln.

The atmosphere within the cellar of the school had qualities belonging to a Dickens novel: rank smells, angry shouts, a long grim corridor leading out into the schoolyard. I remember one teacher who used to post himself down there next to the toilets and coal-furnace every morning during the beginning of recess. There, in the gloomy half-light, he would stand watching the lines of herded children, holding a long thin rattan ever at the ready in his hand. If a small boy walked too slowly, took too long peeing, laughed to another child, or did any other little thing that might be wrong, that bamboo rod began to threaten. I've seen him whip at a boy on several occasions and I've also seen him do this: He would grab a child, one who was *really* little, maybe only three and a half or four feet tall, and swinging him by the collar, actually bash him up against the wall. Whatever the pretext, the vehemence of the rebuke was always a hundred times too strong. One day I noticed him virtually hurling a first-grade pupil down the length of the long corridor in the general direction of the door.

There were also teachers who forgot themselves occasionally while we were sitting together in the downstairs teachers' smoke-room and let out the forbidden but, evidently, not yet forgotten terms that one might have believed by now to have been banished from the doors of a schoolhouse, if not from the national memory altogether. Suddenly, as if in total oblivion of all around us, as if in a kind of unknowing and unaware

reversion to the habits, vocabulary, and practices of another part of the country, or of a generation long past, the teachers would be speaking of the children in their classes in the language of casual hate and satire. The children, their parents, their people, their ministers, became the "jigs," the "niggers," the "bucks," the "black stuff." And, all at once, within the schoolhouse of an American city, the teachers were speaking with the same words, scoring with the same scorn, hating with the same hate, as those who wear the robes and burn the crosses and stand in angry crowds to shout at Negro children in Mississippi and Alabama whose families have somehow had the temerity to want to send them to an integrated school.

Of all the forms that injustice took within that schoolhouse, the most enduring and enveloping seemed to stem from the cruelty and condescension that were engendered within the attitudes of many teachers. This was as true, I felt, for the quietly reserved and gentle older lady who patted the little children on their heads and then withdrew with immense relief to her home in a white suburb as it was for the outright redneck and head-slamming bigot who would not hesitate to call the kids within the classroom jigs and niggers. In a way, I think, those gently smiling older ladies were even more dangerous and more self-compromising, for it is they, after all, who make up the backbone of almost any urban system; and it is they, in the long run, who are most responsible for the perpetuation of its styles and attitudes.

No one teacher can stand for thousands, but sometimes one teacher can represent in her views and ways a great deal that is most familiar and most disturbing in many others. One such teacher, with whom I had a close involvement in my building, was a lady to whom I will refer here as the Reading Teacher. Unlike many others, this woman was seldom consciously malevolent to anyone. She worked hard, gave many signs of warmth to various children, and spoke often of her deep feelings for them. She was precisely the sort of person whom an outside observer would instantly have designated as a "dedicated teacher," if for no other reason than because she herself and dozens of others in the school would tell him that she was. There is no doubt that she was dedicated, if by dedication one means absorption in the job of teaching. She cared deeply about teaching, about the children, their progress, and the things that they were learning. She also cared, in a highly public and self-conscious manner, about the whole area of fair play and equal rights and racial justice. She would go on at great lengths describing and bemoaning the many forms of open or half-suppressed race prejudice which were, according to her confidences, very nearly universal in the building. It came, however, as a shock, or an insult, or perhaps even at moments as a marginal revelation for her to consider the possibility that she herself might share a few fragments of the same feelings.

One morning she came up to see me in my classroom during lunchtime. She was, as I remember, in one of her familiar moods—making fun of the bigotry of others while at the same time, and almost unknowingly, congratulating herself upon her freedom from such attitudes. "Others may be prejudiced," was the content of her message. "So and so downstairs uses

the word 'nigger,' I know, I've heard him say it with my own ears. It makes me sick every time I hear him say that. If a person feels that way, I don't know what he's doing teaching at this school. You wouldn't imagine the kinds of things I used to hear. . . . Last year there was a teacher in this school who used to call them 'black stuff.' Can you imagine somebody even thinking up a phrase like that? If people are prejudiced, they should not be teaching here."

Another time, she spoke of the same matter in these words: "Others may be prejudiced. I know that I am not. There are hundreds like me. Thank God for that. Some teachers are prejudiced. The majority are not. We are living in a time when everything is changing. Things are going along, but they must not change too fast."

I felt astonished at her certainty. I told her, for my own part, that I would feel very uneasy in making that kind of absolute statement. I said that on many occasions I had become convinced that my thinking was prejudiced, sometimes in obvious ways and sometimes in ways that lay deeper and would not have been so easy for other people to observe. Furthermore, I said, I also was convinced that I was prejudiced in a manner hardened over so many years that some of that prejudice undoubtedly would always be within me.

"Well I'm not," she replied with much emotion.

I did not try to turn any accusation toward her. Everything I said was directed at "people in general," at "white society," and mainly at myself. I said to the Reading Teacher that, so far as my own feelings were concerned, I had little doubt of what I was saying. I had learned, in much of the work I'd done in ghetto neighborhoods, that more than once I must have hurt somebody's feelings badly by an undercurrent or an unconscious innuendo in my talk or else the people I was talking to just would not have winced the way they had. I said I was certain, from any number of moments like that, that there was plenty of regular old-time prejudice in me, just as in almost every other white man I ever saw.

To this, however, the Reading Teacher snapped back again, and now with an absolute self-confidence: "In me, there is none."

We stood together in the doorway. The children sat in their chairs. It was almost the end of lunchtime. Each child was having milk except the ones who couldn't afford it. Sometimes white and Negro children chattered with each other, but there were not sufficient white children for this to happen freely enough. The Reading Teacher looked out at the children and said, "Roger over there, I think, is the most unhappy boy in this class." Roger was one of only three white boys in my class. He was sitting behind a boy named Stephen. Stephen, a Negro child who was regularly harassed and punished all year long, was a ward of the state, an orphan who had been placed in a dismal and unfriendly home and who had been having serious psychiatric problems for some time. The difference between his situation and that of the white child was so enormous that I could not imagine a teacher ever balancing the difficulties of two such children within a single scale. Yet the Reading Teacher not only threw them both into the same scale, but judged Roger's case to be more serious. She said to me, "When I look

at them, I do not see white or black." But I felt really that she saw white much more clearly than she saw black. She saw the somewhat unhappy and rather quiet little white boy. She did not see Stephen in front of him, his hands welted from rattannings and his face scratched and scarred with scabs. "I see no color difference," she told me. "I see children in front of me, not children who are black. It has never made a difference to me. White skin or black skin, they are all made by God."

Another day she told me about a trip she had made to Europe during the summer before. She told me that one evening a man on the boat had come across the floor to dance with her. But the man's skin was black. "I knew it was wrong but I honestly could not make myself say yes to that man. It was because he was a Negro. I just could not see myself dancing with that man."

I didn't know if anyone could be condemned for being honest. "What if I fell in love with a Negro girl?" I asked her.

She told me the truth: "I would be shocked."

I said I didn't see why she couldn't dance with a Negro passenger.

"I could not do it."

She also said, "If you married a Negro girl, I have to admit that I would feel terribly sad."

I did not have that in my mind, but I found I was still puzzled about what she had been saying. "Would you have Negroes visit you or come and have dinner with you?"

To that, the answer was clear, elucidating, and exact: "They could come and visit if I invited them to come but not as you could come to see me. They could not feel free to just drop in on me. I would have to draw the line at that."

Hearing that, I asked myself what this kind of feeling meant in terms of one teacher and one child. This woman had drawn the line "at that" just as the city had drawn the line of the ghetto. A Negro was acceptable, even lovable, if he came out only when invited and at other times stayed back. What did it do to a Negro student when he recognized that his teacher felt that she had to "draw the line at that"? Did it make him feel grateful for the few scraps that he got, or did it make him feel embittered instead that there ought to be any line at all? The Reading Teacher apparently was confident that the line did not descend, in her feelings, to the level of the children—or that, if it did, it would not be detected by them. I gained the impression, on the contrary, that the line was very much in evidence in the classroom and that many of the children were aware of it.

There were two ways in which I thought the Reading Teacher unknowingly but consistently revealed the existence of that line. One of these ways, certainly the less important, was in the occasional favors that she showed and in the kinds of arrangements that she would make for various children. She gave a really fine and expensive children's book to one of my pupils. I recall that she presented it to the child before the whole class and spoke of how much the little girl deserved it and of how warmly she admired her. For a poor boy from a large family, she tried to arrange a stay at summer camp. In the case of a third child, she made a friendly contact with his parents, invited them on a couple of occasions to come over and visit in her home, and in general

took a warm and decent interest in his up-bringing. The point of this account is that all three of these children were white and, while all may well have deserved her help and fondness, nonetheless it is striking that there was a definite minority of whites within that class of thirty-five, and, during the course of the entire year in which I was teaching them, I did not once observe her having offered to do anything of that sort for any child who was black. When I took it on my own initiative to do something similar for a couple of the Negro children in my class, she heard about it immediately and came up to advise me that it was not at all a good idea.

In November, I began giving one of the children a lift home after class. In December, I also started to make occasional visits to see Stephen on the weekends, and one day I took him over to my old college to visit for an afternoon. On Christmas Eve, I brought him some crayons and some art paper and visited for a while in his home. From all of these trivial actions, but especially from the last, I was seriously discouraged. It was not good practice. It was not in accord with teaching standards. It could not but ruin discipline if a teacher got to know a pupil outside class. Yet the person who offered me this criticism had just done many things of a similar nature for a number of white children. It seemed evident to me, as it must by now be evident also to her, that the rule or the standard or the policy or the pattern that defines the distance between a teacher and his pupil was being understood at our school, and was being explicitly interpreted, in precisely such a way as to maintain a line of color. The rule was there. It was relaxed for white children. It was enforced rigorously for Negroes. In this way, the color line grew firm and strong.

There was another way in which the Reading Teacher showed her preference. It was in the matter of expectations—what you could even hope to look for "in these kinds of children," meaning children who were Negro. Directly hooked onto this, often expressed in the same sentence, was a long and hard-dying panegyric to the past. The last, the panegyric, was one of the most common themes and undercurrents in our conversations all year long. Even at moments when she knew it to be inappropriate almost to the point of cruelty, still she could not suppress it. Several of the other teachers in the school expressed the same idea frequently, but the most vivid conversations of this sort that I remember from the first part of the year were those with the Reading Teacher.

In the early part of winter, I had to ask the Reading Teacher for permission to take my pupils on a trip to the Museum. I spoke to her of the fact that we would soon be studying Egypt and the desert and said I thought a morning's visit to the Museum of Fine Arts to see the Egyptian collection and also to wander around and look at some of the paintings would be a good idea. The Reading Teacher's manner of reacting to this request anticipated the way in which she and certain of the other teachers would respond to many other requests that I was to make later in the year. Her first reaction was to turn me down flatly. Then she paused for a moment—and, finally, feeling suddenly the need to justify her refusal, she added, "With another sort of child, perhaps. The kind of chil-

dren that we used to have. . . ." The moment of panegyric: "Oh we used to do beautiful work here. Wonderful projects! So many wonderful ideas. . . ." The present tense again: "Not with these children. You'd take a chance with *him*? or *her*? You'd take a group like them to the museum?"

In a similar vein, I made a suggestion for another child—not for Stephen, because I knew in advance that it would have been doomed to her refusal—but for a little girl. "I thought about next summer. She's one of the best in drawing. I wanted to try to get her into an art class somewhere starting in June."

The Reading Teacher grilled me about it skeptically. "Where?"

I told her that I had two places in mind. One was the school attached to the Art Museum. A summer class for young children was conducted there. Another class that sounded more exciting was located near the university. The latter program, situated in a converted loft, was being spoken about with much excitement by many of the people interested in art education, and it had already won a lively reputation for its atmosphere of openness and freedom. The children of some friends of mine were taking classes there.

"How would she get there?"

I answered that I knew someone who would drive her.

"Who'd pay for it?"

I said the same person had offered to pay for the lessons.

The very idea of this little Negro girl bridging the gap between two worlds seemed inconceivable or mechanically unfeasible to the Reading Teacher. To hear her voice, you might well have thought that it was an arrogant proposal. It was as if I were suggesting a major defiance of nature and of all proper relations and proportions. A moment's pause for thinking and then this answer, finally: "I wouldn't do anything for Angelina because I just don't like her. But if you're going to do anything, the Museum School's plenty good enough for a child like her."

Because she respected herself as highly as she did, I wonder if the Reading Teacher would have been astonished if somebody had told her that she sounded rather ungentle? Perhaps she would not have been astonished—because she probably would not have believed it. She was surely one of the most positive persons whom I have ever known, and she also had an amazing capacity to convince herself of the justice of her position on almost any issue at all. At any moment when she was reminded, by herself or someone else, that she was being less than Christian or less than charitable to kids who already did not have very much in life, she was apt to question whether there was really so much suffering here as people liked to say or whether things were really all that bad. With Stephen, for example, there were only rare moments when she would come face to face with his desperate position. Characteristic of her response to him was the attitude expressed the time she pointed to the white boy in the seat in back of him and called him the most unhappy child in the class. I remember that when I said to her, "What about Stephen? He doesn't even have parents!" the Reading Teacher became instantly defensive and irritated with me and replied, "He has a mother. What are you talking about? He has a foster mother and she is paid by the state to look

after his care." But I said maybe it wasn't like having a real mother. And also, I said, the state didn't seem to have time to notice that he was being beaten up by his foster mother while being thoroughly pulverized and obliterated in one way or another almost every day at school. "He has plenty," was her answer. "There are many children who are a great deal worse off. Plenty of white people have had a much harder time than that." Harder than he had? How many? I didn't believe it. Besides, when it got to that point, did it very much matter who, out of many suffering people, was suffering a little bit less or a little bit more? But the Reading Teacher became impatient with the direction of my questioning and she ended it at this point by telling me with finality, "He's getting a whole lot more than he deserves."

It was this, her assumption that people don't deserve a great deal in life, and that a little—even a very, very little for a Negro child—is probably a great deal more than he has earned, which seemed the most disturbing thing about her. Yet, at the same time, she enjoyed delineating to me the bigotry of others, attacking certain of her associates ruthlessly when she was not chatting with them, and making hash out of the Principal when she was not making hash out of someone else. I came into that school as a provisional teacher in October, but it was four months before I had the courage to begin to speak to her with honesty.

One of the other fourth grades within our school building was located in a room across the stairs from me. In this room, for almost an entire year, there was a gentle teacher on the apparent verge of mental breakdown. Instead of being retired or given the type of specialized work in which he might have been effective, the man had simply been shunted from one overcrowded ghetto school into another. His assignment in our school was unjust both to him and to the children. The classroom was filled with chaos, screams, and shouting all day long. The man gave his class mixed-up instructions. He was the sort of mild, nervous person who gives instructions in a tone that makes it clear in advance he does not really expect to be obeyed. He screamed often but his screams contained generally not force but fear. Bright children got confused; all children grew exhausted. There was little calm or order. Going in there on an errand during the middle of the morning, you were not always immediately able to find him. You could not see him in the midst of the shouting, jumping class. On rare occasions, the children, having no one else to blame for this except their teacher, would rise up in angry instant and strike back. I remember one cold day in the middle of January, when the teacher went out onto the fire escape for a moment—perhaps just to regain his composure and try to calm himself down. One of the children jumped up and slammed the door. It locked behind him. "Let me in!" the man started screaming. It was unjust to him but he must have seemed like Rumpelstiltskin, and the children, not ever having had a chance at revenge before, must have been filled with sudden joy. "Let me in! How dare you?" At last they relented and someone opened the door.

After I went into his classroom the first time in November, I began to find my attention drawn repeatedly to two of the children. One of them was a bright, attractive, and impatient Negro girl who showed her hatred for school and teacher by sitting all day with a slow and smouldering look of cynical resentment in her eyes. Not only was she bright but she also worked extremely hard, and she seemed to me remarkably sophisticated, even though she was still very much a little child. I thought that she would easily have been a sure candidate for one of the local girls' schools of distinction had she not been Negro and a victim of this segregated school. For two years, she had had substitute teachers, and this year a permanent teacher in a state of perpetual breakdown. Her eyes, beautiful and sarcastic, told that she understood exactly what was going on. She possessed enough shrewdness and had a sufficient sense of dignity to know where to place the blame. She was one of thousands who gave the lie, merely by her silent eloquence, to all the utterances of those who have defined the limits and capabilities of Negro children. Five years from now, if my guess was correct, she would be out on the picket lines. She would stand there and protest because, after so much wasting of her years, there alone would be the one place where her pride and hope would still have a chance.

The other child whom I noticed in that fourth-grade room was in an obvious way far less fortunate—he was retarded. For Edward there was no chance at all of surviving inwardly within this miserable classroom, still less of figuring out where the blame ought to be applied. The combination of low intelligence with a state of emotional confusion resulted in behavior which, though never violent, was unmistakably peculiar. No one could have missed it—unless he wanted to, or needed to. The boy walked upstairs backward, singing. Many teachers managed not to notice. He walked with his coat pulled up and zippered over his face; inside, he roared with laughter, until a teacher grabbed him and slammed him to the wall. Nobody said, "Something is wrong." He hopped like a frog and made frog-noises. Occasionally, a teacher would not be able to help himself and would come right out and say, "Jesus, that kid's odd." But I never did hear any-one say that maybe also, in regard to the disposition of this one child at least, something in the system of the school itself was wrong or odd.

Edward was designated a "special student," categorized in this way be-cause of his I. Q. and hence, by the expectation of most teachers, not teachable within a normal, crowded room. On the other hand, because of the overcrowding of our school and the lack of special teachers, there was no room for him in our one special class. Because of the refusal of the city either to redistrict or to bus Negro children to white neighborhoods, he could not be sent to any other school which might have room. The conse-quence of all of this, as it came down through the chancery of the system, was that he was to remain a full year mostly unseen and virtually forgotten, with nothing to do except to vegetate, cause trouble, daydream, or just silently decay. He was unwell. His sickness was obvious, and it was im-possible to miss it. He laughed to near crying over unimaginable details. If you didn't look closely, it seemed often that he was laughing over nothing at all. Sometimes he smiled wonderfully with a look of sheer ecstasy. Usually it was over something tiny: a little dot on his finger or an imaginary bug upon the floor. The boy had a large head and very glassy, rolling eyes. One day I brought him a book about a little French boy who was followed to school by a red balloon. He sat and swung his head back and forth over it and smiled. More often he was likely to sulk, or whimper, or cry. He cried in reading because he could not learn to read. He cried in writing because he could not be taught to write. He cried because he couldn't pronounce words of many syllables. He didn't know his tables. He didn't know how to subtract. He didn't know how to divide. He was in the fourth-grade class, it seemed to me, by an admin-istrative error so huge that it appeared an administrative joke. The joke of HIM was so obvious it was hard not to find it funny. The children in the class found it funny. They laughed at him all day. Sometimes he laughed with them since it's quite possible, when we have few choices, to look upon even our own misery as some kind of desperate joke. Or else he started to shout. His teacher once turned to me and said quite honestly and openly, "It's just impossible to teach him." And the truth, of course, in this case, is that the teacher *didn't* teach him; nor had he really been taught since the day he came into the school.

In November, I started doing spe-cial work in reading with a number of the slowest readers from all the fourth grades. It was not easy to pick them, for few children at our school read near grade-level. Only six or seven in my own class were fourth-grade readers. Many of them were at least a year, frequently two years, be-hind. Those who had had many sub-stitutes in the previous two years tended to be in the worst shape. In selecting this special group of children, it seemed to me that Edward deserved the extra help as much as anyone. He wanted it too—he made that apparent. For he came along with excitement and with a great and optimistic smile. He began by being attentive to me and seemed very happy for a while. The smiling stopped soon, however, because he could not follow even the extremely moderate pace that we were keeping. The other children, backward as they had been, were too far ahead of him. He soon began to cry. At this point, the Reading Teacher came rushing on the scene. Her reaction was predictable. Rather than getting angry at either the school or the city or the system for this one child's sake, her anger was all for him; and her outrage and her capacity for onslaught all came down upon his head. "I will not have it," she said of him and of his misery and then, virtually seething with her decision-making power, she instructed me that I was not to teach him any longer. Not taught by me and not by his regular teacher. I asked her, in that case, by whom he would be taught from now on, and the answer in effect was, "Nobody." The real decision, spoken or unspoken, was that he would not be taught at all. In this, as in so many of the other things that I have described, I was reluctant at that time to argue forcefully. Instead, I acquiesced to her authority; I quietly did as I was told. For the duration of the fall and for the major portion of the winter, the little boy with the olive smile would ask me, it seemed, almost every morning, "Mr. Kozol, can I come to reading with you?" And almost every morning, I pretended that his exclusion was only temporary; and I lied to him and told him, "I'm sorry, Edward. Just not for today."

There is a tendency in a great many teachers in all kinds of schools to attribute lies to children who in fact did not lie and had not lied and about whom the teacher may know very little. In a ghetto neighborhood especially, the assumption of prior guilt seems at times so overwhelming that even a new teacher with strong affiliations to the Negro community, and sometimes even a teacher who is Negro, will be surprised to discover the extent to which he shares it. It seems at moments to require an almost muscular effort of the imagination to consider the possibility in a particular case that a Negro child might actually *not* have done it, that he might *not* be telling any lie. I remember several incidents of this kind when a pupil whom I knew for certain to be innocent was actually brought around to the point of saying, "Yes, I did it" or, "Yes, I was lying," simply from the force of an adult's accusation.

One morning the Mathematics Teacher—another among the ranks of dedicated and high-powered older teachers—came rushing into the fourth-grade across the stairs from mine when the regular teacher was not present and when I was taking his class while somebody else was filling in with mine. The children had done an arithmetic assignment the day before. All but two had it graded and passed back. The two who didn't get it back insisted to me that they had done it but that the substitute teacher who had been with them the day before must have thrown it aside or lost it. I had been in and out of that room long enough to know those two boys and to believe what they were saying. I also knew that in the chaos of substitute changes there was continual loss and mislaying of homework and of papers of all sorts. Despite this, the Math Teacher came sweeping into the room, delivered a withering denunciation to the whole class on their general performance, then addressed herself to the two boys whose papers had not been given back. She called them to the front and, without questioning or qualification, she *told* them that they were lying and that she knew they were lying, and furthermore, that she did not want contradictions from them because she knew them too well to be deceived. The truth is that she did not know them at all and probably did not even know their names. What she meant was that she knew "children who are like them"—in this case, "Negro nine-year-old boys who like to tell lies." Knowing them or not, however, she swept down upon them and she told them that they were liars and did it with so much vigor that she virtually compelled them to believe it must be so.

A somewhat different incident of this sort concerned another boy and involved one of the male teachers in our school. One day while I was working, I saw this teacher coming toward me and holding a boy named Anthony rather firmly by the arm. I asked the class to sit still a moment while I went out behind the portable blackboard to find out what was going on. The teacher continued to hold Anthony by the arm. He stood Anthony before me. Anthony looked down at the floor. I knew him only slightly. He was one of the slow readers who met with me for extra work from time to time.

"ANTHONY," said the teacher,

"I WANT YOU TO TELL MR. KOZOL NOW THE SAME THING THAT YOU TOLD ME."

It was spaced out like that, exactly, with a caesura of intensity and measured judgment and of persuasive intelligence in between every parceled word: "I WANT YOU TO GO ON NOW AND SAY TO MR. KOZOL WHAT YOU WANT TO TELL HIM, AND I WANT YOU TO SAY IT IN A VOICE WHICH IS LOUD AND CLEAR, AND I WANT YOU TO LOOK UP AT MR. KOZOL."

When he spoke this way, it was as if every child, or every person, in the whole world might be an isolated idiot and that, if the words did not come out so slowly and carefully, nobody in the world might every truly find out what any other person believed.

"ANTHONY," the teacher continued, "MR. KOZOL IS A VERY BUSY MAN. MR. KOZOL HAS A WHOLE CLASS OF CHILDREN WAITING NOW WE DON'T WANT TO KEEP MR. KOZOL STANDING HERE AND WAITING FOR YOU, ANTHONY, DO WE? AND WE WOULDN'T WANT MR. KOZOL TO THINK THAT WE WERE AFRAID TO SPEAK UP AND APOLOGIZE TO HIM WHEN WE HAVE DONE SOMETHING WRONG. WOULD WE WANT MR. KOZOL TO THINK THAT, ANTHONY?"

Anthony kept his eyes on the floor. My students poked and peered and stared and craned their necks around from behind the broken blackboard. At last I could see that Anthony had decided to give in. With one of the most cynical yet thoroughly repentant looks of confession that I have ever seen in any person's eyes, he looked up first at the teacher, then at me, and said decently, "I'm sorry." And the teacher said to him, "I'm sorry— WHO?" And Anthony said nicely, "I'm sorry, Mr. Kozol." And the teacher said, "Good boy, Anthony!" or something of that sort and he touched him in a nice way on the arm. Now the truth is he *had* been a good boy. He had been a very good boy indeed. He had been a good boy in exactly this regard: he had gone along with the assumption of one white man about one Negro; he had done nothing at all to contradict or to topple that conception; and he even had acted out and executed agreeably a quite skillful little confessional vignette to reinforce it. To this day, I haven't the slightest idea of what it was about.

When something as crazy as this happens, it seems important to try to find out how it could be possible. How can an adult so easily, so heedlessly, and so unhesitatingly attribute to a child the blame for a misdemeanor about which the child has so little information and about which, in fact, he may know nothing? I am sure the reasons are mainly the same as those for the use of corporal punishment: haste and hurry, fear on the part of teachers, animosity and resentment, and the potentiality for some sort of sudden insurrection by certain children. The atmosphere at times gets to seem so threatening to many teachers that they dare not risk the outbreak of disorder which might occur if they should take time to ascertain gently, carefully, and moderately the nature of what is really going on. It always seems more practical and less risky to pretend to know more than you do and to insist on your omniscience. When you assume a child is lying and

tell him so without reservations, he is almost inclined to agree with you, and furthermore it is often to his advantage to do so since, in this way, he is likely to minimize his punishment. A child, of course, who begins by pretending to accept blame may end up *really* accepting it. If one pretends something well, and if that pretense becomes a habit, and if that habit in time becomes the entire style and strategy with which one deals with the white world, then probably it is not surprising if at last it gets into the bloodstream too. Naturally all children don't react in the same way. Among the children at my school there were many different degrees of blame-acceptance or resignation or docility. There were also children who did not give in at all. It was not these —not the defiant ones—but the children who gave in to their teachers most easily and utterly who seemed the saddest.

One day I was out in the auditorium doing reading with some children. Classes were taking place on both sides of us. The glee club and sewing class were taking place at the same time in the middle. There was also a fifth-grade remedial math group, comprising six pupils, and there were several other children whom I did not know simply walking back and forth. Before me were six fourth-graders, most of them from the disorderly fourth grade and several of whom had had substitute teachers during much of the previous two years. It was not their fault; they had done nothing to deserve substitute teachers. And it was not their fault now if they could not hear my words clearly; I could barely hear theirs. Yet the way that they dealt with this dilemma, at least on the level at which I could observe it, was to blame, not the school but themselves. Not one of them would say, "Mr. Kozol, what's going on here? This is a crazy place to learn."

This instead is what I heard:

"Mr. Kozol, I'm trying as hard as I can, but I just can't even hear a word you say."

"Mr. Kozol, please don't be angry. It's so hard—I couldn't hear you."

"Mr. Kozol, please, would you read it to me one more time?"

You could not mistake the absolute assumption that this mess was not only their own fault but something to be ashamed of. It was a triumph of pedagogic brainwashing. The place was ugly, noisy, rotten. Yet the children before me found it natural and automatic to accept as normal the school's structural inadequacies and to incorporate them, as it were, right into themselves: as if the rotting timbers might not be objective calamities but self-condemning configurations of their own making and as if the frenzied noise and overcrowding were a condition and an indictment not of the school building itself but rather of their own inadequate mentalities or of their own incapacitated souls. Other children were defiant, but most of them were not. It was the tension between defiance and docility, and the need of a beleaguered teacher to justify something absolutely unjustifiable, which created the air of unreality, possible danger, intellectual hypocrisy, and fear. The result of this atmosphere was that too many children became believers in their own responsibility for being ruined; and they themselves, like the teachers, began somehow to believe that some human material is just biologically better and some of it worse. A former chairman of the school committee of this city, a man of extreme conservative leanings and well-known segregationist beliefs, has publicly given utterance to this idea in words he might regret by this time. "We have no inferior education in our schools," he has let himself be quoted. "What we have been getting is an inferior type of student." Is it any wonder, with the head of a school system believing this, that after a while some of the children come to believe they are inferior too?

Spies on Campus

FRANK DONNER

In comparison with most student protests held before and since, the one staged on the evening of February 9, 1967, at State University College at Brockport in Upstate New York was singularly uneventful. Instead of a prolonged marathon involving hundreds of students, the demonstration—in the form of a sit-in, held at the student union—attracted only a handful of students and lasted a scant 15 minutes. Sponsored by members of a group called the Campus Committee of Concern, the sit-in protested nothing so lofty as Vietnam, civil rights or academic freedom. The students involved simply wanted the union to remain open a while longer at night so they could drink Cokes and talk there. Even the local press, knowing a nonstory when it saw one, devoted only a short item to the action the next day.

But before the month was over, it was clear that this minidemonstration had, like the first element in an elaborate Rube Goldberg device, set in motion a series of more complicated events that ended in the exposure of an extensive network of FBI spying and political surveillance on the Brockport campus.

The story of the snooping—perhaps even more alarming because Brockport is hardly known as a hotbed of political activism—was brought to the surface by the widely respected Reverend John Messerschmitt, ecumenical chaplain to the college and a faculty advisor to the group that sponsored the sit-in. Speaking on February 23 to a hushed meeting of the local American Association of University Professors, Messerschmitt revealed that the morning after the sit-in, a member of the Brockport administrative staff, during a conversation with Messerschmitt about the Campus Committee of Concern, began making remarks about Dr. Ernst A. Wiener, then associate professor of sociology and also a faculty advisor to the C. C. O. C. The administrator asked if Messerschmitt was aware of Wiener's involvement with civil rights, the peace movement and various New Left groups that the staff member "knew" to be Communist fronts. When Chaplain Messerschmitt protested that without evidence such accusations were irresponsible, the administrator confided (according to the chaplain's notes, recorded shortly after the conversation): "John, I know I can trust you with this information. I'm in regular contact with the FBI. There are four or five of us on the campus—two with the FBI and three with the CIA. We've been asked to watch Wiener very closely. Believe me when I tell you he has quite a background. Be careful." Messerschmitt responded by telling the man he could hardly believe he was actually working for the FBI and that if he was, his position "was in contradiction to what the university stood for and extremely dangerous to the civil liberties of all the individuals he was keeping under surveillance."

For a half hour, the two men argued the subject. "Wouldn't you do this FBI work if your country requested it of you?" asked the nameless administrator. "How can you attack the FBI when it's only trying to protect you? . . . This surveillance work is occurring on every campus in the country . . . Those who are being watched shouldn't have anything to hide if what they are doing and saying is aboveboard. . . . Don't think I get paid for this; I don't. I was asked to do this and I agreed as a service to my country."

From the conversation, the surprised chaplain learned not only that such campus spying was common but that both the FBI and CIA were regularly in touch with friendly Brockport faculty members, who were instructed—in the words of the administrator—"to kind of keep an eye on things on a permanent basis."

"Finally," Chaplain Messerschmitt concluded, "I told him our conversation had left me no less shocked at his disclosure. I was sorry he had assumed a confidence of me without first asking, but because this news was absolutely incompatible with what I understood higher education to be, I could not be quiet about it."

Nor was he. With the fuse lit by his subsequent disclosures, reactions exploded in swift succession. Convinced and outraged by what they had heard but prevented from direct legal action by the fact that the conversation was unwitnessed, the Brockport chapter of the American Association of University Professors passed a resolution strongly condemning undercover operations on the campus—as threat of "faculty intimidation" and "thought control." Within the next month, the Brockport faculty senate and the State University Federation of Teachers at Brockport passed similar resolutions. The CIA responded by labeling the Brockport charges "nonsense" and stated that it "does not engage in spying in the United States." The FBI's authority is not so circumscribed, however. A few weeks later, FBI Director J. Edgar Hoover, in a letter to Chancellor Samuel Gould, the administrative head of the New York State University system, admitted the charges. "I would never permit the FBI," Hoover wrote, "to shirk its responsibilities. I feel certain that you, as a responsible educator and citizen, would never condone this Bureau's failure to handle its obligations in the internal security field, or that you would have us ignore specific allegations of subversive activity in any segment of our society, including college campuses."

Professor Ernst Wiener—whose activities and views had sparked all the commotion—seemed less surprised at the discovery of a campus spying network than at the fact that it should be concerned with someone as harmless as himself. "I have never attempted to conceal the nature of my political beliefs," he announced. And in what many felt was a moving document, indeed (a letter published March 17 in the Brockport college paper), he described his participation in the 1965 Selma-Montgomery march, his concern for the local problems of integration, his opposition to the Vietnam war and his membership in various groups supporting these and similar beliefs. He closed his letters by quoting Socrates: "For of old I have had many accusers who have accused me falsely to you during many years. . . . Hardest of all, I do not know and cannot tell the names of my accusers . . . and therefore I must simply fight with shadows in my own defense, and argue when there is no one who answers."

Professor Wiener must have thought a good bit about Socrates in the month that followed; for on April 20, he committed suicide. In a letter found after his death, he had written: "It is too painful to continue living in a world in which freedom is steadily being constricted in the name of freedom and in which peace means war, in which every one of our institutions, our schools, our churches, our newspapers, our industries are being steadily engulfed in a sea of hypocrisy."

The events that grew from the Brockport affair would be tragic enough even if it were an isolated incident, conceived in the overzealous mind of a local FBI agent of his regional chief. But as Director Hoover's letter makes clear, the FBI regards campus spying as a near-sacred obligation. Just about the same time Dr. Wiener killed himself, *Ramparts* magazine—following up its disclosure that President Ngo Dinh Diem's intrigue-ridden regime in South Vietnam had relied heavily on the expertise of CIA-sponsored faculty members from Michigan State University—exposed a labyrinth of CIA front groups, notably the National

Student Association. During the same month, a pseudo coed at the Madison campus of Fairleigh Dickinson made headlines by announcing that she had been planted there by county detectives to spy on a fellow student; and the president of Brigham Young University reluctantly admitted that a group of students had been used to spy on liberal professors. In the past two years, disclosures such as these have appeared with what the agencies involved must find embarrassing regularity, and they provide a small glimpse through the curtain that up to now has concealed a nationally organized, centrally coordinated, undercover campus intelligence operation.

Apologists for this collegiate spying frequently adopt the position of the nameless Brockport vigilante: "Those who are being watched shouldn't have anything to hide if what they are doing and saying is aboveboard." Because the agencies engaged in snooping have yet to use in a court case the mass of information they have gathered, they can easily be viewed as concerned—and relatively ineffective—voyeurs. We are only trying to find out the facts, say the surveiller-informers; we neither enjoin nor punish political expression or association.

But even if the snooping were as benign and nonrestrictive as the agencies suggest, there would still remain the thorny question of academic freedom. In theory, colleges are supposed to be open market places of ideas, where students and teachers are free to say and think what they please. Government agencies violate this principle simply by listening in on what is said, even if they never use the information. Their presence—or just the possibility of their presence—

can stimulate a self-censorship far more damaging to freedom and learning than most of the restraints against individual liberty currently on the statute books. If a student or a teacher has reason to suspect that Big Brother —or anyone, for that matter—is surreptitiously listening to or recording what he says, he will surely be more circumspect than he would be in complete privacy. Firmly committed students tend to accept political sleuthing as a predictable risk and often use it to support their alienation from society. But it is measurably daunting to the large number of timid, uncommitted but curious students—the samplers, sippers and tasters of the various causes offered on campus. These are the students who most need the opportunity to experiment and examine, an opportunity that our Bill of Rights—and our concept of academic freedom—was designed to protect. As the Brockport student paper asked editorially last March: "How may academic freedom thrive in a classroom in which the instructor may be the patriotic, rightwinged informer to the FBI and the CIA? The students are not so naïve as to believe that liberal or left-wing sentiments go unnoticed by the FBI." The result is that snooping yields maximum returns of control for a minimum investment of official power; it drastically curbs dissent and, in so doing, it evades judicial review in an area for which the courts have shown a special and commendable concern.

The surveillance-informing system is marvelously efficient because life in American society—particularly on the campus—makes the average "subject" extremely vulnerable to fear when he learns his politics are under scrutiny by the Government, especially by the

FBI. The undercover character of the surveillance, the benighted standards of the investigators, the assumed guilt of the subject, the denial of an opportunity to face charges or to offer a defense and the inability to understand the reasons for the investigation can be shatteringly Kafkaesque. Reputations, brittle as glass, are easily smashed beyond repair. "Of what crime was Ernst Wiener guilty," inquired the Brockport campus paper, "to allow the smearing of his name in a local newspaper as 'under investigation'? This is just more evidence of implying guilt by innuendo, while the investigators and smearers are well covered under a muffling cloak of silence."

Critics of campus spying—and they are legion—claim not only that collegiate surveillance is ethically questionable but that there's little legal justification for it as well. Neither the CIA nor any of the state and local vigilante groups described below can cite a single law permitting the sort of political snooping they engage in as a matter of routine. Even the legality of the FBI's activities in this area is suspiciously ambiguous. In 1956, Don Whitehead, J. Edgar Hoover's Boswell, published in *The FBI Story* a private directive—sort of a "Dear Edgar" letter—sent to Hoover by President Roosevelt in 1939. This letter—which was *not* an Executive Order—authorized the FBI to engage in "intelligence activities" incidental to its newly acquired domestic spy-catching authority. This informal and obscure note—at best intended as a stopgap measure in an atmosphere of impending war—has become the tail that wags the enormous dog of a permanent FBI surveillance apparatus. Hoover seems to have expanded the vague terms of the directive to confer upon the FBI the power, in Hoover's language, "to identify individuals working against the United States, determine their objectives and nullify their effectiveness." These "individuals," Hoover would say, are those whose activities involve "subversion and related internal security problems." With this murky justification, the FBI has assumed the power to police not acts but opinions, speech and association— and not for the purpose of preparing evidence for presentation at a trial but merely to keep track of nonconformists.

No act of Congress has ever authorized the FBI to exercise these powers. In fact, an act permitting the FBI to trail campus radicals, take their photographs, open their mail, record their license-plate numbers, bug their conversations, penetrate their meetings and associations through decoys and informers and assemble extensive dossiers that include tips and complaints supplied by private (and frequently anonymous) individuals would be about as constitutional as a law creating a hereditary monarchy.

Only since 1960 or so has the security establishment zoomed in on the college campus. According to the snoopers' logic, this new focus makes eminent sense. In the 1960s, the campus has emerged as the spawning ground of the most vigorous—and the most radical—antiwar and political movements. The campus is where the action is. As a group, college teachers now dominate the New Left intellectual community. In faculties and student bodies alike, the young, the restless and the militant abound, openly activist and publicly disdaining what they see as the hang-ups and

the subterfuges of their elders. These activists can provoke the messianic instincts in the snoopers themselves, many of whom believe they have a patriotic obligation to "save" students from "mistakes they might regret later on." This protective reasoning expresses the quasi-Freudian thesis that political preferences and attitudes are irrevocably fixed before the age of 20 and that unless a youthful subject subsequently defects or informs, he'll bear watching the rest of his life. On a more practical level, the university has also moved up in the intelligence peeking order because of its increasing financial involvement with the Federal Government, particularly in the area of security-related research projects.

Since 1960, the House Un-American Activities Committee, at least in its public and semipublic endeavors, has been inordinately preoccupied with youth and the college scene. The California Burns Committee— HUAC's Golden State equivalent— has "protected" California by issuing four extensive reports (the first based on files apparently stolen from the offices of a New Left student group at Berkeley) on the activities of California's young. But the most ambitious campaign to unearth subversion in collegiate militancy has been mounted by Hoover and the FBI. Since 1963, Hoover has vainly tried to ban Communist speakers from college campuses, justifying his concern on grounds that even some FBI sympathizers found offensive: that seductive Communist propaganda is too treacherous for naïve student ears. Hoover's campaign reached a high pitch of passion in his annual report for 1966: "In its cynical bid to gain an image of respectability, the Party is directing an aggressive campaign at American youth, claiming to perceive a new upsurge of 'leftist' thinking among the young people."

So it's not surprising that when an admitted Communist visits a college campus, the FBI photographs not only him but his host—and keeps careful watch over anyone who visits either of them. An avowed Communist is presumed to be a conspirator, so anyone who breaks bread with him bears scrutiny, too. All too often, even more tenuous relationships attract the FBI. In 1963, for instance, John McAuliff, then a junior at Carleton College in Northfield, Minnesota , was investigated after he had sent a check to Dan Rubin, a Communist youth leader who had visited Carleton to speak on a program organized by a campus group (organized for the purpose of presenting controversial speakers of every political stripe) that McAuliff happened to head. The path of this investigation led an FBI agent to one of McAuliff's friends in Indianapolis. The friend was questioned about McAuliff's politics and then urged to keep quiet about the investigation. Nonetheless, *The Minneapolis Tribune* eventually found out about it, published all the facts and wondered editorially how the FBI knew that McAuliff had sent a check to Rubin—unless it had opened Rubin's mail.

In view of the FBI's overpowering obsession with protecting innocent youth from being duped by the wily Communists, it's also not surprising that FBI agents are now familiar figures in the halls of academe. In their legitimate functions—probes to which the student presumably consents, such as to clear him for Federal employment or to support his con-

scientious objector claim—FBI agents have routine access to student transcripts (which are not always confined to grades) and also to personal files that may contain political or psychological data. Much of the material in these files is quite unrelated to security matters, but increasingly, colleges keep data on a student's political activities, associations and opinions—because administrators have learned in the past few years that they probably will be asked about these matters.

The presumably legitimate FBI investigations of students and former students have institutionalized the relationship between the Bureau and the universities. The intelligence agent who majors in campus spying develops a soft, friendly relationship with the college staff members with whom he works. The deans, registrars and their assistants know that the agent has "chosen policework as his career" because it is so "challenging." They know that the agent is as concerned as the next man with academic freedom. Didn't he attend college himself, sometimes the very college at which he now spends most of his time? Doesn't he have college-bound youngsters of his own? And, after all, isn't he "only doing his job"?

But when the investigating agents are on a sympathetic, first-name basis with those who keep the records, the shadowy line between legitimate and illegitimate surveillance is not always observed. Early in 1967, Berkeley's admissions officer, David Stewart, admitted that in "three or four cases in the last few months," student records were given to the FBI. These were records of students who had not applied for any Government position, students who had manifestly *not* consented to a *sub rosa* examination of their personal histories and political preferences. And even at universities that strive to maintain the distinction between legitimate and illegitimate investigations, the agent's explanation of the reasons for his investigation is almost invariably taken at face value —on trust.

Since the Government itself now keeps dossiers on literally millions of individuals, information from a student's college files frequently finds its way into the Government's master file. Unhappily, the accuracy of the resultant hodge-podge of facts and observations is far from unimpeachable. At a time when the Government is the nation's largest employer and when some sort of security clearance is practically *de rigueur* for many of the most interesting jobs, the dossier system develops a formidable economic influence. An inaccurate or slanted report of an individual's campus activities—political or otherwise—recorded indelibly in a file the Government consults but that the student can never see, can haunt him with preternatural persistence throughout his life.

As a small but perhaps revealing example: Joseph Tieger, who graduated near the top of his class at Duke in 1963, was denied conscientious-objector status by his New Jersey draft board. The board, it turned out, had referred to a 5000-word biography of Tieger, anonymously written but apparently prepared by the FBI, mostly from information compiled on Tieger while he was at Duke. This revealing document, which Tieger subsequently had the unique good fortune of obtaining from his draft board, does not record that a Duke religion professor had signed a state-

ment asserting that Tieger deserved C. O. status "beyond question." It does mention, however, that Tieger in high school "failed to participate in extracurricular activities which is required to make a well-rounded personality"; that he once showed up at a tea party at Duke "in shorts with his shirttail out and wearing tennis shoes"; and that the university library once "addressed a postcard to the registrant indicating that a book concerning the writings of Trotsky was overdue." As we go to press, Tieger, now a law student, has just received a deferment for one year.

Although the once-invisible CIA is confined by statute to intelligence operations outside the United States, its activities, too, spill over into the groves of academe. Students and professors who receive grants for foreign travel or study are frequently approached by CIA representatives, who request that the prospective travelers do a little moonlighting as unofficial intelligence agents during their sojourn abroad. Returning students are also interviewed and often invited to report or answer questions of interest to the CIA; if they have taken photographs, they might be asked for copies. The CIA stimulates such voluntary contributions by offering a generous "consultation fee"—as well as the prospect of a new grant. Some veterans of these sessions have taken to voluntarily stopping by the CIA office for a "debriefing" after sojourns to such places as Africa, Indonesia or India.

This might seem harmless enough, as long as the moonlighting scholars don't take their role as spies too seriously. But foreign-study grants are also used more directly, as a cover for regular CIA agents with legitimate or fraudulent academic credentials. While such a gambit is undoubtedly very useful to the CIA, its effects on the academic discipline involved are somewhat less salubrious. A weighty report recently published by the American Anthropological Association states that in many parts of the world American anthropologists are suspected of being spies. "There is some basis for these suspicions and beliefs," the report notes, adding that as a result, legitimate anthropological research has been severely handicapped. Some anthropologists, the report continues, after failing to get research grants for projects they view as worth while, "have been approached by obscure foundations or have been offered supplementary support from such sources, only to discover later that they were expected to provide intelligence information usually to the Central Intelligence Agency."

A rather similar example involved an instructor at an Eastern university, who in 1963 was turned down for a Fulbright grant for study overseas. The CIA, which seems to keep good track not only of those who get such grants but of those who don't, approached the disappointed instructor and asked him if he'd like to study abroad anyway. He'd receive the same stipend as a Fulbright fellow and, in return, he would only have to report details about the host country and about the activities of the actual Fulbright scholars there. The instructor reluctantly agreed; but before the deal was closed, he attended an antiwar demonstration, where a student was seen taking pictures of him. The instructor subsequently learned that the CIA had assigned the student to check on the instructor's feelings about the war in Vietnam. The instructor

apparently failed his CIA 'entrance' exam, because he never did receive his pseudo Fulbright grant.

Others have been luckier, if you want to call it that. A former Ivy League student who is now a journalist parlayed his impeccable credentials in the Young Republican Organization—which the CIA seems to regard as "safe"—into a jaunt to Europe and then into a free trip around the world. He didn't realize the first trip was at the CIA's expense —until after he returned and was quizzed about it. He reported that all was safe overseas, which must have pleased the CIA, because it sent him back again. After his second return, the CIA never contacted him, so he didn't bother to report at all.

This may be nice work if you can get it, but many of those who succumb to the lure of free travel are not quite as cynical as this chap. Junketeers typically feel they ought to report *something*, if only to justify the CIA's expense. Many also feel that the juicier the information they give, the more likely they are to receive another "foundation grant" in the future. There are no facts to support this assumption, but it's not beyond belief that some of these part-time agents have filed fabricated or greatly exaggerated reports—perhaps to the disadvantage of whatever individuals and groups about which they were reporting.

Besides the CIA and the FBI, there is a surprising number of local surveillance agencies. These are called "Red Squads" or "Bomb Squads" and most of them sprang up in the early years of this century to keep track of Bolsheviks, anarchists, wobblies and the like. While these particular foes are nowadays hardly more than names out of the history books, the forces that once engaged them in battle are still emphatically alive. In fact, campus demonstrations, student antiwar activities and big-city racial disturbances have made them more robust than ever. On campuses in Berkeley, Chicago and New York City—to name a few—political-surveillance bureaus, directly or indirectly related to local police bodies, have taken it upon themselves to watch leftist opinions and associations.

As an example: On the eve of the 1966 National Student Association Convention, a St. John's (New York) University coed, Gloria Kuzmyak, was visited by detectives from New York City's Bureau of Special Services, known as BOSS. Miss Kuzmyak, then an officer in the N. S. A., was planning to attend the convention to be held at the University of Illinois, and the BOSS men solicited her help "to keep a check on demonstrations that were going to take place." Her help in this instance would be confined to giving BOSS the names of all New York N.S.A. students and representatives "associated with the liberal caucus." Miss Kuzmyak declined. After she returned from the convention, she was visited twice, first by the same detectives with a similar plea and subsequently by another of their number, with the request that she "forget all about" the earlier attempts to extract names from her.

Some local Red Squad agents are so well known that they inspire an emotion similar to camaraderie among those they're paid to spy on. Not too long ago, a student "undercover" agent at the University of Texas, whose affiliation with the Texas Department of Public Safety was an ill-kept secret, was elected honorary chairman of the local chapter of Students for a Democratic Society—in recognition of his exemplary attendance record and the attentiveness with which he followed the proceedings.

The dean of all campus Red Squad operatives, until his recent retirement, was an inspector at Berkeley who has become something like Mr. Chips to a generation of Berkeley radicals. "This affable, balding gentleman," recalls one nostalgic Berkeley grad, "was so familiar to us that he would come up on the platform ahead of a meeting and ask for a list of speakers." The inspector claimed to have the authority to attend whatever Berkeley meetings he wished, but according to our informant, he usually left when asked to—"in order not to make a scene."

But indulgent sentiment for operatives such as this one, coupled with student notions of the ultimate harmlessness of the activities they engage in, sometimes conceals the fact that the Red Squad wings of local police forces are particularly useful to the higher security establishment, if only because of the ease with which they disregard state curbs on wire tapping and bugging. The authorities have allowed FBI agents to "tune in" only when national security is at stake (though the FBI tends to see national security threatened more frequently than most of us might); but local police tap phones routinely, without recourse to any high-sounding justifications. When discovered engaging in political bugging, they frequently explain their actions in terms of some conventional police function. In recent years, they have magically transformed what objective observers would construe as out-and-out political surveillance into investigations of such nonpolitical offenses as drug or morals violations.

Completing our roster of agencies that engage in campus snooping are the Army and Navy counterintelligence crews (who probe draft-connected security risks) and the R.O.T.C. For years, the Berkeley Navy R.O.T.C. has conducted systematic surveillance of New Left campus groups. Whether such work earns academic credits isn't clear but Berkeley undoubtedly provides enough radicals and anarchists to keep the N.R.O.T.C. busy. Much of their work involves compiling dossiers and maintaining files of leftish handbills, which are kept in folders marked CONFIDENTIAL—NAVAL INTELLIGENCE —TWELFTH NAVAL DISTRICT.

Recently the Army R.O.T.C. tried to extend the intelligence operation to encompass the eight Western states in the Sixth Army area. R.O.T.C. instructors at each school in the area were provided with "confidential" educational training kits, which made it easy for cadets to sniff out the bad guys. When a group of professors at the University of Washington learned about the kits, R.O.T.C. officials admitted that the kits had been distributed—but denied that cadets were instructed to snoop. Any spying that had occurred, said the officials, had been done by cadets on their own initiative. But the local chapter of the American Association of University Professors, which perhaps has learned the hard way that students don't usually undertake spare-time projects if they don't count toward the final grade, commended the university for its action against "political propagandizing" and charged the Army with "serious intrusions into academic life."

As both the R.O.T.C. groups and the CIA seem to have perceived, the best people to do spying work on campus are students themselves. If the student agent keeps his cool, the risks of exposure are minimal. He has perfect protective coloring, because, unlike the more conventional agent, his background, life style and appearance are just like everyone else's. And the role is much less demanding than being a decoy for drug pushers or homosexuals, or other after-school jobs for which students have been recruited. Students whose politics lean to the right tend to regard informing as a civic duty, like giving blood to the Red Cross.

Students who cannot be induced to spy on their cohorts by appeals to patriotism or the lure of free travel will often succumb to the more tangible blandishment of hard cash. Not too long ago, testimony in a court trial revealed that Charles Benson Childs, a student at the University of North Carolina, earned $100 a month, plus expenses—and he received a draft deferment as well.

Today the pay is not as niggardly. When the tiny Advance Youth Organization was on trial in 1963 and 1964 (the Government was trying to compel the group to register as a Communist-front organization), 11 youthful informers testified they had received a total of over $45,000 for brief periods of undercover work. The highest-paid was one Aaron Cohen, whose take from the FBI totaled $6571.65. The sum presumably reflected his extra value as an officer of the organization. Officers, especially secretaries, keep the membership lists, and thus are prime targets for intelligence sleuths. During the 1965 passport-violation trial of three young people who were part of a student delegation that had visited Cuba, several informers—recruited from campuses as far-ranging as San Francisco State and Columbia—surfaced long enough to testify for the prosecution. All admitted they were well paid. One student testified the FBI had given him a $300 bonus for going to Cuba. Another of the informers wasn't even Government sponsored: He turned out to be in the employ of anti-Communist lecturer Gordon Hall, who had planted him in the delegation in order to arm himself with fresh material for the luncheon circuit.

Almost as good a recruit as an actual member is a student who joins a target organization and then leaves it for ideological reasons. As soon as the FBI learns of his defection, he is often offered the opportunity to avenge himself, usually at the expense of his former colleagues. A few defectors become chronic Government witnesses, zealously denouncing their former beliefs and associates. Others, who might be less willing witnesses, are induced to inform more out of a feeling of panic. One day they impulsively join an organization and after weeks of sober reflection, they're stricken with profound regrets. A visit from the FBI at the right moment—or a telephone call by the student himself to the local FBI office—results in a get-together. The experienced FBI agent is predictably adept at manipulating hesitant subjects. He overcomes reluctance to inform by a promise that the information will be kept secret, by patriotic appeals ("Don't you want to help your country?"), by the assurance that "all the kids are doing it," by hints that the agent already possesses compromising information and by expressing sympathy for the

humanitarian impulses that led the student into his political lapse. The agent scrupulously avoids the term "informer"; his plea is for "cooperation." The usual result is that the hesitant defector finally identifies other members of his group or pledges to stay on as an informer.

If the soft sell fails, agents do not scorn cruder methods—especially if the potential stoolie seems a worthwhile recruit. If the subject has a job, an agent has been known to confront him there—and threaten to report a refusal to cooperate to the subject's employer. With law and prelaw students, a threat to report them to the bar association's character committee —which must approve all admissions to the bar—can sometimes turn the trick. A similar ploy can be used with students who plan teaching careers. And when all else fails, there's always the possibility of appealing to the subject's parents, to warn them that their offspring is associating with the wrong people on campus.

The recruiter's life is no bed of roses, however: Even though he concentrates on likely prospects, he is often indignantly rebuffed. To the continuing dismay of security types, most students regard informing as betrayal and they regard the invitation to engage in it as a personal insult. Furthermore, student groups persistently refuse to react in ways the security agents are most familiar with. Students, for instance, are unwilling to adopt the closed, Communist-cell-like political associations that agents are so adept at penetrating. Openness is the key to the students' political style. Students feel they have nothing to hide and—especially in their political associations—are largely repelled by secrecy. But the security establishment finds this attitude both perplexing and disconcerting, since it expects its targets to be guiltily concealing everything they do. After all, secret political machinations—loosely interpreted as "conspiracies"—are a key justification for the surveillance system.

The colleges themselves have responded to snooping activities in a variety of ways. A disturbing number of universities have been tacitly cooperative—in ways that greatly transcend the cozy personal relationships that often grow up between Federal agents and the college administrative staffs. Documented evidence supports the charge that some universities —Duke, Illinois, Indiana, Kansas, Michigan State, Ohio State and Texas, for instance—have actively collaborated with the FBI. In these institutions, a highly security-conscious bureaucracy compiles data about their students' politics from such sources as deans, faculty, staff, faculty advisors of campus organizations, fraternity officers, judicial boards, housemothers, housemasters, maids, the press and the police—both campus and local. Often this information is not only compiled but interpreted. At Duke, for example, Dean Robert Cox keeps an extensive set of dossiers that have been called "potentially the most explosive of all" by a special university committee headed by Professor John Curtiss, president of the Duke chapter of the American Association of University Professors.

Fortunately, most colleges aren't quite this zealous in lending aid and comfort to the surveillance establishment. But even sins of omission can be grievous enough. Two summers ago, the House Un-American Activities Committee sent subpoenas to Michigan and Stanford universities, requesting lists of officers of campus groups that had criticized the U.S. Vietnam policy. (Many universities require organizations to file membership lists to qualify for registration as an official campus body.) Both schools complied with these subpoenas —though many critics of HUAC, both within the schools and outside, thought that the HUAC action could be challenged as unconstitutional. Similar attempts to secure membership lists from the NAACP had been rebuffed by the Supreme Court, which had held that such enforced disclosures may "constitute as effective a restraint of freedom of association" as more direct forms of interference. The "inviolability of privacy," the Court had said, is "indispensable to the preservation of the freedom of association, particularly where a group espouses dissident beliefs." Despite what seemed a perfect precedent for refusal, or at least challenge, neither of the universities even protested or in any way questioned HUAC's mandate. And neither of the universities seemed to realize that they were collaborating in what amounted to a punitive exposure of the individuals on the lists. Whether or not those listed were summoned as witnesses (some were), all the names were permanently dossiered in the Committee's file and reference service—available to security bloodhounds and even to the constituents of any Congressman who might ask for them.

To be sure, a few colleges have courageously resisted the intrusions of the surveillance establishment. And with several sorry exceptions—such as California until 1963 and North Carolina and Ohio State until 1965—

they successfully resisted the snoopers' attempts to bar Communist speakers from campus. The general response to these two challenges left room for hope that painful memory of the abuses done to dissenting professors in the Fifties would quicken a determination not to collaborate in intimidating the burgeoning student protest movements of the Sixties. But only a handful have lived up to this promise. Following an S.D.S. peace demonstration at Wesleyan University (Connecticut) in the spring of 1966, an FBI agent appeared and asked that college authorities hand over the S.D.S. membership list. College Dean Stanley J. Idzerda refused, saying, "We keep no such lists of any organizations." He added, "We consider the student's activity his own affair. At the same time, it's unfortunate that a climate of suspicion can be created by such activities that might lead some students to be more circumspect than the situation requires. Things like this can be a danger to a free and open community if men change their behavior because of it." The resultant furor brought the FBI agent back to the campus, where he told the dean that there had been a "misunderstanding." No probe of the S.D.S. had been contemplated, but only of "possible infiltration of the S.D.S. chapter by Communist influence."

Another agent involved in the case thoughtfully added that the FBI "makes inquiries every day on campuses throughout the country—we investigate 175 types of violations, security as well as criminal." When a Wesleyan student committee subsequently wrote J. Edgar Hoover that the investigation constituted a gross infringement of academic freedom, Hoover replied that the charge was

"not only utterly false but also is so irresponsible as to cast serious doubt on the quality of academic reasoning or the motivation behind it."

When the director of the FBI can hint, without too much subtlety, that uncooperative colleges are themselves flirting with subversion or conspiracy, it's not too surprising that the colleges try to avoid such conflicts—even when their vital interests are at stake. Reluctant to act unless absolutely forced to do so, most colleges unwittingly invite the very pressures they seek to avoid—and then respond to these with more evasion and more compromise. Their caution is reinforced by the inbred conformity that seems common to all bureaucracies— collegiate or otherwise—a conformity that assures not only that accommodation to the demands of the security establishment will be mindless and irresponsible but that it will be uniform. As one student correspondent—who must remain anonymous, since he's still in school—puts it:

"Most university administrators operate on the principle of inertia —it's easier to go along with inquiries than to refuse. Why run the risk of being labeled a Commie-hippie school? Most of them cheerfully give out some information, although not all, without ever thinking they may be creating a serious problem. Once they are made aware that they also have a prerogative to refuse, many agree it would be fine if all universities refused, but why should one university risk being labeled 'oddball'?"

But unless it is willing to take this risk, the university will soon find itself on a collision course with "national security." It will not be enough for the university to make informing or secret political surveillance—by faculty or students alike—grounds for immediate censure, discharge or explosion, though this would certainly be a good beginning. In the long run, it is fatuous, or at least diversionary, to attempt to reconcile academic freedom with national security. They simply cannot be reconciled. The university must reconstruct, on the foundation of academic freedom, an ethos that—no matter what the risks or temporary costs—rejects surveillance altogether. If the university is disturbed by nonstudent attempts to gain a voice in its affairs (as in the Berkeley outbreak), then it should feel all the more threatened by the actions of Big Brother. At a time when the life and values of the university are being subjected to unprecedented stress by "security" pressures, the university, if it is to survive at all, must simply learn to say no—to the FBI, the CIA, the R.O.T.C., the Red Squads, the Congressional committees and the tribe of spies, spooks, snoops, surveillants and subpoena servers they have spawned. In the last analysis, the only real threat to our national security is the mutilation of academic freedom that will inevitably result if the security establishment continues to flourish on our nation's campuses.

part four

THE SICK

Medical care and those who render it have traditionally been regarded with both respect and mystery by community members. Health care also involves complex human relationships between those who render care and those who need it. The nature, scope, and quality of these relationships and the context of medical practice is critical to the fate of patients. To the outsider, it may seem that the medical practitioner is above the strains which enter other human endeavors, but this simply is not so. The norms of the economic market place and the political and social strivings of persons in the health field have resulted in serious inequities in the provision of services. Many Americans receive less than highest quality care—care inferior to that given in other parts of the world.

There is disagreement on what constitutes the boundaries of health care. For example, many say obesity is as much a sickness as pneumonia; some claim that most bizarre criminal behavior is a form of illness. Clearly emotional as well as physical troubles plague our population. Not only do the emotionally disturbed suffer themselves, but their conditions often disrupt the lives of family and friends. The behavior of mental patients is disturbing primarily because of its bizarreness, the occasional person who is destructive (in the sense of harming community members) creates fear and anxiety in many of us about the emotionally disturbed and the illnesses of the mind.

This chapter presents examples of the social conflicts that confront us in the treatment and prevention of illness. Some problems are related to sick individuals' demands on the medical profession—demands that cannot be met or are not in keeping with "professional" notions of good care. Other problems stem from preferential treatment in the provision of medical care, reflecting processes which operate in other areas of social life. In some instances, individual practitioners take advantage of their almost unassailable status abusing patients for the sake of personal gain, as do industries whose products are detrimental to life and good health. These are some of America's troubles in its efforts to maintain physical health, treat mental illness, and prolong life.

| INDIVIDUAL vs. INDIVIDUAL | INDIVIDUAL vs. ORGANIZATION |

DIET PILLS

All occupational groups who deal with the public have their share of unscrupulous people. In most consumer-seller contexts, we almost expect disreputable behavior and stand somewhat prepared to deal with it. A mark of the professions, however, is an emphasis on scrupulous behavior. The physician is held up as an epitomy of integrity because of the helplessness of the patient. Yet most medical care is rendered in privacy where the behavior of the doctor depends largely on self-discipline and personal honesty. There are those who are willing to break the trust, who take advantage of community members concerned and worried about their well-being. "Diet Pills" describes charlatans taking advantage of individuals who seek them out and believe in their therapeutics.

CHARLIE MANSON: ONE MAN'S FAMILY

The great majority of the mentally ill are not dangerous either to their close associates or the general run of community members. Rather, they are disruptive to society for what they do to themselves. Manson is unusual. His illness is manifested by attracting, corrupting, and influencing to murder a group of alienated, isolated, and troubled girls—his so-called "family," his victims. Since this article was written, Manson and several of his group have been tried and convicted for murder. While their eventual fate is open to question, the case illustrates another critical point, the varying definitions of what constitutes mental illness. He and those in his group were responsible for their crime from a legal standpoint, but many experts would argue they are psychologically sick. Who are the victims? Clearly *both* the micro-organization of "Manson's family" and the community as a whole.

| ORGANIZATION vs. INDIVIDUAL | ORGANIZATION vs. ORGANIZATION |

SIXTY-TWO YEARS FOR VAGRANCY

Hospital care for mental illness has become more humane, if not more effective. There still exist, however, institutions so inadequate and harsh that they bring disgrace to all community members; perhaps the most notorious of these are for the so-called criminally insane. Half jails, half mental hospitals, they have the worst features of both. Persons in these institutions in many cases would have been better off in prison, where most sentences at least have an endpoint; persons committed to criminal hospitals are at the mercy of an inadequate and sometimes incompetent staff. Bridgewater Hospital has been a dumping ground for generations. While it now has a more enlightened staff, only partial success has been achieved in remedying the situation. The impact of prolonged commitment on the individuals described in Richard's article is irreversible. The consequences of their hospitalization is a shameful burden to be borne by persons responsible for mental health care and by the entire community.

ANNALS OF ADVERTISING: CUTTING DOWN

The self-interests of organizations are apparently superordinate to such basic concerns as optimum health. Despite the accumulation of evidence over several decades that cigarette smoking is deleterious to health, the tobacco industry continues to make the cigarette appear attractive to young and old alike. Over the years there has been a continual battle, involving the Federal Trade Commission and the Federal Communication Commission, regarding the use of mass media to sell the cigarette. In this conflict between a government organization and the tobacco industry, the difficulties of imposing socially desirable controls in the face of lucrative profits are clearly demonstrated. The selection from the *Congressional Record* indicates how important the economic motive is to industry. We find characteristics at an organizational level similar to those of the corrupt, money-hungry individual physicians in the case of the "diet-pills."

Diet Pills

SUSANNA McBEE

No one has ever called me fat. A little on the hippy side perhaps. But never fat. I am a reliable size 10, and my weight, without clothes, is 124 to 125, respectable enough for my 5'5" frame.

By ordinary standards I would flunk out as a candidate for obesity treatments. But in a recent six-week period, traveling to nearly every section of the country, I went to 10 doctors who treat weight problems and instead of bouncing me out of their offices as I had expected, they welcomed me. Although three of them said I had no weight problem and another even congratulated me for catching the problem early (that is, before it developed), they all, every last one of them, gave me diet pills. My "haul" was 1,479 pills.

The pills, analyzed later by a chemist, included amphetamines, barbiturates, sex hormones, diuretics, thyroid and digitalis. They came in various sizes and colors, some of them very pretty and all of them—for me, at least—completely unnecessary. Even though I had undergone an arduous eating program—several buttered rolls with every meal, gobs of sour cream on my baked potatoes and enough cheesecake to supply a White House banquet I had gained only five

Life, January 26, 1968. © Time Inc., 1968.

or six pounds and was definitely not a "medical overweight problem."

The first doctor I visited was an osteopath. Dr. Edward A. Devins, whose drab suite on the third floor of the Altman Building in Kansas City, Missouri had been raided less than a month earlier. Agents of the Food and Drug Administration's Bureau of Drug Abuse Control and a deputy U.S. marshal had confiscated 2.5 million pills most of them amphetamines and some barbiturates. The pills were seized on the basis of a civil complaint alleging that Dr. Devins had failed to keep accurate records of the pills he received and dispensed.

At Dr. Devins' office, as at the others, I gave my correct name, made up a local address and occupation, and said only that I wanted to lose weight, never asking for pills. The day I appeared, a girl handed me a form with 195 questions, starting out conventionally enough with eyesight, hearing, nose and throat conditions, and progressing to my mental condition, which was hardly improved by the queries: "Do you feel alone and sad at a party?" "Do you often cry?" "Does life look entirely hopeless?" "Do you often wish you were dead and away from it all?"

A girl read over my questionnaire, asked if I were allergic to medicine and if I were nervous. "What is the highest your weight has ever been?"

she asked; then she weighed me with my clothes and shoes on. I came to 130½ pounds. Not bad, considering I had just gorged myself at a late lunch.

"You should weigh 120 to 125." she said reprovingly, "and we'll get you down to 120." She took my blood pressure, pulse and measurements. When she got to my waist, which normally is about 25 inches, it measured 28 because I stuck out my stomach. She seemed not to notice but recorded the statistic. Then she asked who had referred me. I said I'd heard about Dr. Devins at a party from a woman whose name I couldn't remember.

"I've never heard that one before," the girl said cheerfully, "but one lady said she heard about us at a bus stop." Obviously, this girl *wanted* to believe me. She then announced: "I'm going out now and prepare your medication."

Several minutes later Dr. Devins entered, carrying a box of pills which he had picked up before even seeing me. He did not examine me but said I would feel different after taking his pills "because, after all, you're on diet medicine."

Talking rapidly, Dr. Devins said, "We don't advise going on a diet." He then read me the instructions on my pillbox, which contained 140 tablets—pinks, browns, tans and grays. "If you're not nervous (my questionnaire indicated I was not), they won't make any difference." He said I might not sleep too well with the pink pills but not to worry about it.

I asked what was in the pills. He did not tell me but said only that the pinks would suppress the appetite, the browns would keep me from being constipated ("People tend to get constipated when they lose weight") and

the others would work with the pinks to reduce me. They contained, it turned out, amphetamines, laxatives and thyroid.

Dr. Devins said he would see me in a month and directed me to the receptionist, who looked at my chart and said, "Ten dollars."

That was easy, I thought, but the Rubel clinic in Decatur, Illinois, which attracts the heavy set from all over the state, might be difficult. Perhaps, if I were rejected as a patient there, a fat man posing as my husband could go through the clinic and tell me about it. A friend in Decatur said he'd locate one, and while waiting I realized I would need a gold ring, too.

At the local Woolworth's a clerk showed me a large tray of rings. She pointed to some with stones.

"No, I just want a gold ring."

She pointed to gold rings with stones.

"No, no. Just a plain gold ring," I said, trying to smile.

Her eyebrow arched toward her scalp. Her eyes narrowed. She knew exactly what kind of woman she was dealing with. Coldly, she displayed a section of gold bands. I grabbed one, paid $1.05 and started to put it in my purse. "Don't you even want to try it on?" the clerk asked as I hurried out.

I did not find a fat husband and went alone. In the Rubel waiting room a nurse called my name over a microphone and gave me a one-page, 136 questions form to fill out. It asked about my current physical condition, past illnesses and eating habits. I saw several women go beyond the reception desk, presumably for their monthly checkup, and come out again, carrying a little white sack of pills— all in less than five minutes.

The clinic, which is one of three in the Midwest run by Dr. Louis L. Rubel, has an array of tests for new patients: weight, measurements, blood pressure, pulse, urinalysis, blood sample from a finger, an electrocardiogram. There is also the ankle-jerk test, which most internists and endocrinologists regard only as a measure of hypothyroidism, and an inconclusive one at that. I took it sitting on my knees on a cushion beside a machine called an "Achilleometer," and after a technician tapped my Achilles tendon and saw the indicator on the machine jump into the middle range, she told me this meant I could take an average dose of their medicine. Of which medicine? "Of all our medicine."

Dr. William K. Franta, who saw me after my tests, is one of four osteopaths at the clinic working for Dr. Rubel, also an osteopath. "You're not really overweight," said Dr. Franta, who has a weight problem of his own. He reviewed my tests, which came out normal, and my weight 129½. He asked if I took any medication. Just vitamins, I said.

"Well, we'll give you our own vitamins so you won't have to take the others if you don't want to." He wrote a prescription, and I asked what the pills were. He said one kind was a "gland substance" and the others were vitamins and minerals. He made no effort to examine me, not even to listen to the heart or feel the impulse over the chest both considered part of a complete heart examination.

Instead he gave me a little talk. Weight control, he said, is a matter of glandular balance. Since I was in the normal weight range, which for me he said is 119 to 129, I might not make too much progress. We would try the pills for a few months and see how I did.

Dr. Franta spent three to four minutes with me discussing my diet, handed me the prescription and told me to drop it in the wicker basket at the front desk. When I did, the office manager put it on a dumb-waiter pulley behind her and it was lifted upstairs. Shortly, a white paper bag with three small envelopes inside slid down the pulley, and after I paid $15 and was told that each succeeding visit would cost $10, I was given the bag. It housed 84 pills, 28 each of vermilion vitamins, magenta vitamins and lime-green thyroid. There was also a brochure explaining the Rubel program and beginning with the words that fatties love to hear: "Overweight or obesity is a very common disorder which can be corrected without dieting."

When I telephoned the office of Dr. C. C. Mendenhall in Gardena, California, the first thing the girl said was that visit and medication would cost $15. That's cash; no personal checks, she said. When I arrived, a girl led me to a small room with an ankle-jerk machine, this one called a "Photomotograph." While the machine was warming up, she quizzed me about my physical condition, even about how my liver and spleen were doing, as if a layman could know. She said I looked slim and asked what I wanted to weigh. I had just hit 132½; the cheesecake obviously had gotten to me. I said I wanted to weigh 120 to 125. She tapped my Achilles tendon, measured me and took my pulse and blood pressure. (Later, Dr. Mendenhall's services to new patients were expanded to include a physical exam, electrocardiogram, urinalysis and blood tests.) The girl gave me a brochure which urged patients to follow a high-protein, low-fat diet, and she told me not to eat fried foods, salad oils or soft drinks.

Dr. Mendenhall appeared, looking tired, perhaps because he sees 60 or more patients a day. He reviewed my medical history, put a stethoscope to my heart in two places, felt the front and back of my neck and checked my ankles for possible swelling. I asked how much a person of my height and build should weigh.

"It wouldn't do any good to tell you because you people aren't going to get down to the weight you should weigh anyhow," he said.

You people?

He said he was just trying to get people down to a weight where they would be happy. "I'm not trying to reform the world. Very few fat people get down to their ideal weight and stay there."

I asked about medication, and he told me I would be getting an appetite depressant, a laxative to take if I needed it, some protein, thyroid and something for my hips (which I said I wanted to reduce). I asked what the hip medication was. "My own preparation." It turned out to be prednisone, an anti-inflammation hormone.

I left Dr. Mendenhall with 364 pills to consume in a *month*, and the next day, after a visit with Dr. Myron F. Babcock in the Los Angeles office of Raymond A. Landis, D. O., I had 84 more pills, including amphetamines. After several tests (weight, measurements, ankle jerk, blood), Dr. Babcock said, "You're not overweight, honey," then congratulated me on "catching the problem in time." The pills? "Things to make you lose weight." And, after I persisted: "This

one's a thyroid-acting substance—something you could put young children on."

From there I went to San Diego, where Dr. Orville J. Davis' patients receive a 10-page mimeographed notebook which begins, "WELCOME ABOARD!.... FIRST, if you are NOT overweight by average standard I DO NOT WANT YOU TO WASTE YOUR MONEY AND MY TIME WITH EVEN AN INITIAL VISIT" and concludes, "I do not consider you to have ANY medical overweight problem at all unless you are 15% or more over your average weight."

My average standard was 125. That day I was 130 with my clothes on, only 4% over—an honest-to-God test case for Dr. Davis. Technicians first put me through a physical exams procedure—urinalysis, blood drawn from the vein in my left arm, weight, measurements, blood pressure, pulse and electrocardiogram and then I saw Dr. Davis. He said, "You're in great shape, kid. You have no weight problem," then he prescribed progesterone, which is a sex hormone, and 234 pills, including diuretics, thyroid and appetite suppresants. I paid $40 and wondered how many pills Dr. Davis would give someone *with* a medical overweight problem.

In Denver I saw Dr. Charles William Brietenstein, and after being weighed and measured—nothing else —paid $12 for a 28-day supply of appetite suppressants and tablets containing thyroidlike material. Then I went to the office of Chester M. Rasmussen and Duane A. Thompson, D.O.s, in Hillsboro, Oregon, where a brown-haired woman with glasses, a white dress and the sweetest of voices told me she wanted to check my hemoglobin count. She jabbed the side of my third finger, right hand, but couldn't draw enough blood, then rubbed my finger, trying to push something, anything, out of the capillary. She apologized, gave up and tried the third finger, left hand. Only an insignificant drop or two came. As she kept rubbing and apologizing, her hands got sweaty and so did mine. Now very flustered and very contrite, she attacked my middle finger, right hand. Same result. She kept saying, "You just don't know how sorry I am." She had no idea just how sorry *I* was.

Finally, she called in another woman who noted that jabbing should be done at the tip of the finger, not the side. She demonstrated on me, and she was right: there was all kinds of blood.

The first woman, still apologizing, resumed the testing—urinalysis, ankle jerk, pulse, blood pressure, measurements, weight. In a heavy suit and shoes I came to 131¾ pounds.

Then she posed a medical history quiz, replying: "Real good," whenever I indicated I had no problem. She asked if I had any swollen extremities—hands, feet. I told her I had some swollen fingers.

After she left, Dr. Thompson discussed my diet, said, "We don't want to make you look like Twiggy, Ha, Ha, Ha," but nevertheless prescribed the sex hormone, progesterone, and other pills, including digitalis, thyroid, amphetamine—268 in all for the month.

My next stop was the Manhattan office of Gordon L. Green, M.D., one of the most prosperous "fat doctors" in the country. He has 19 offices and grosses just under a million dollars a year. Here, I encountered machine-age medicine. The receptionist told me to listen to a tape recording, which said that the pills I'd receive would not affect any illness I might get one way or the other. You can lose weight without pills, said the voice, but you came to me for an easy way to reduce.

After listening to the tape, I asked the receptionist where Dr. Green was. She said he was not in any of the 19 offices. "He just runs the business." I asked if that voice on the tape was his. "Oh, no. We got a disc jockey to do that."

She weighed me (129 with clothes on), took measurements and asked about my medical history. She took a plastic box of capsules and tablets off a shelf and directed me to the doctor's office, where she put the pillbox on his desk. Then Dr. Sam Provenzano checked my blood pressure, listened to my heart, asked some questions about my medical history and explained how I should take the pills—46 for the week, including amphetamine-thyroid combinations.

In Falls Church, Virginia, Dr. Julius Seymour Siegel said I weighed 129 pounds and that he could tell, "by the size of your arm," that I ought to weight 115. "Eat and drink anything you want," he said. "All you have to do is take the pills I'm going to give you" three a day until I got down to 115, then one a day as "maintenance medicine." He took my blood pressure and pulse rate, listened to my heart, said, "Ah, perfect," asked no questions about medical history, current illnesses or allergies to medicine. Then he picked up a wall phone that was a direct line to a pharmacy, said he wanted pills for, uh, "Hey, what's your name?" and, hanging up, gave me directions to the Falls Church Drug Center. "Can I get the prescription filled at my own pharmacy?" I asked the secretary-nurse. "Oh, no," she answered. "You *must* go to the Drug Center." I paid her $3 and left to pick up 150 amphetamine-barbiturate-thyroid combinations for $7.50. I had spent three minutes with Dr. Siegel.

Dr. Siegel set the record for short office calls, and my next doctor, Harry Needelman, M.D. of Miami Beach, Florida, the record for long ones. Dr. Needelman holds another record. In 1955 he was convicted of illegal sales of narcotics, was later pardoned and is still battling the Dade County Medical Association for reinstatement.

Despite his legal difficulties, Dr. Needelman has a booming weight-control practice, seeing, according to one report, 750 patients a week. When I joined the ranks, I brought along a LIFE photographer who said he was my husband and asked if he could watch. "Sure," said the receptionist, "we'll be glad to let him go through the factory, too."

I was weighed (130¼), measured and tested (blood pressure, temperature, hemoglobin, urine), then directed through a door that said "Doctor's office" and opened into a small auditorium. The room was remarkable. The doctor's elaborate, crescent-shaped desk was on a platform a step higher than where the patients, or audience, sat on 11 large black leatherette chairs arranged in three rows.

The thick carpet was Kelly green, with standing ashtrays sunk into it. The doctor's desk had a camera (for taking before-and-after pictures of patients), a tape recorder and a rotary slide projector.

Three of us "fatties" had settled into the audience chairs by the time Dr. Needelman, a small, overweight man in his mid-fifties, bounced into the room, smiling frequently and talking very much like Eddie Cantor, though with a slight lisp. He took his place onstage, at his desk, and for an opener told us we could, if we wanted, eat six turkey sandwiches a day. "Doesn't that sound like a fairy tale?" All we had to do was to follow his advice on eating the right foods and we would lose five to seven pounds the first week and three to five pounds a week thereafter.

Then, amazingly enough, he called each of us up to his desk, one by one, and discussed our individual cases in front of the other patients. I listened, for example, as he interviewed one woman who loses weight under his program but gains it back when she returns home to New York. She had been going, off and on, to Dr. Needelman for four years. When she first came, her weight was 128; it was now 148. I asked her later about her downhill progress, and with the loyalty fat patients characteristically have for their "fat doctors," she said huffily, "Dr. Needelman can't help it because I'm a pig."

It was my turn. "You're a young woman," he told me. "Would you like to get down to 120?" He promised to get me down to that in two weeks, then put me on a maintenance program of one pill a day for a month. In front of everyone, he reviewed the state of my kidneys, hemoglobin and blood pressure. He listened briefly to my heart and asked about any swelling. But he took no medical history.

He proudly proclaimed that we were about to see "the longest-running show in the world," that he had been giving the same lecture, with variations, for 14 years. "Now," he said, "we'll put our little show on the road." He flicked on the tape recorder and sat silently as his voice came down at us from a loudspeaker in the ceiling.

The tape went on and on and on as the slide projector flashed "before-and-after" pictures of patients. The voice would name the patients and tell where they worked. It mentioned a local lawyer, shoe salesman, grocer, hotel employee, even a local bookie. "You see, I give all the local businesses a little plug." explained the voice. "With my pills, you can eat 3,000 to 4,000 calories a day and lose weight." After an hour or more, Dr. Needelman, in person, allowed questions from the audience, even asked himself questions, answered them and reviewed what he had already said. "Aren't we having fun this afternoon?" he beamed. He kept calling himself the "talkingest doctor in the world."

Finally it was time for our weekly shot, which he explained only by say-ing it was the first gear in revving up the body machinery. I was reluctant, but he overwhelmed me with, "Try it this time. If you don't like it, you won't have to take it next time." I took it. I also received 26 pills for the week—diuretics, barbiturates and a combination of amphetamine, laxative and thyroid—and paid $15. A sign at the desk advised that after Jan. 1 prices were going up: $20 for the first visit and $10 a week thereafter. Dr. Needelman told us our capsules contained thyroid, adding that he would be able to determine the following week if we were getting the correct dosage. The "show" was over. It had run three hours, 15 minutes.

Among the "fat doctors" I visited, there was no consensus on diet— some said eat anything you want; others offered elaborate programs. They did not agree on exercise, or on liquor consumption. Their physical examinations ranged from several tests to merely a weight and measure-ment check. There was consensus, though, on one point: pills, pills, pills.

Charlie Manson:
One Man's Family

STEVEN V. ROBERTS

LOS ANGELES.

The day had been soft and bright, the sort of glistening Saturday that fills the beaches and the tennis courts and the gardens of Southern California with ruthlessly robust, pleasure-pursuing multitudes. In midmorning, police were called to an isolated, expensive home on Cielo Drive, back in the wooded hills above Hollywood. What they found was a scene of unimaginable horror: Five people had been brutally murdered, including Sharon Tate, a stunning blond film actress who was eight and a half months pregnant. The word "pig" had been scrawled in blood on the front door.

Terror streaked through the beaches and the tennis courts, clawing at the August sun. Angelenos feverishly bought guns and watchdogs, private police and burglar alarm, and behind their padlocked doors they traded theories and rumors about the murders with morbid fascination.

Meanwhile, Hollywood carried on. The victims were buried with the obligatory number of weeping movie stars and harassed press agents in attendance. Screen director Roman

Reprinted by permission from the *New York Times Magazine* (January 4, 1970), pp. 11, 29–35. © 1970 by the New York Times Company.

Polanski, Miss Tate's husband, called a press conference to defend his wife's reputation and say that her unborn baby "had been her greatest picture." Before leaving, he found time to pose for photographs in their blood-stained living room.

But even Polanski's performance could not still the rumors: The murderer was a drug pusher, a victim of past sexual abuses, "rough trade" picked up on Sunset Strip for fun and games, a friend who had freaked out on speed and turned violent. All the stories had a common thread—that somehow the victims had brought the murder on themselves, that they were responsible for the violence. The attitude was summed up in the epigram: "Live freaky, die freaky."

For months, police made little headway. They announced the discovery of a "major" clue—a pair of eyeglasses that limited the suspects to several million myopic men with bullet-shaped heads. Then they started hearing rumors about a roving "family" of young people—mostly of middle- or upper-middle-class background, slavishly devoted to a bearded guru—who had been arrested in the desert near Death Valley for stealing cars. A member of a motorcycle gang gave the police some leads, and then one of the girls who had been arrested in the desert, Susan Denise Atkins, told a cellmate about the band's lethal activities.

On Dec. 1, police announced they had issued warrants for the arrest of three young people: Linda Kasabian, 20, Patricia Krenwinkel, 21, and Charles (Tex) Watson, 24. A week later, a grand jury, after deliberating for 20 minutes, indicted the three, plus Miss Atkins and Charles Manson, the 35-year-old leader of the nomads, for the Tate murders. They also indicted the five, plus Leslie Van Houten, 19, for the murder of Leno and Rosemary La Bianca, wealthy grocery-store owners, who had been killed the day after Miss Tate and her friends.

The arrests evoked a new surge of public panic. Suddenly, all the rumors appeared to be wrong. A national magazine had to scrap a feature detailing 20 theories about the Tate murders. According to Miss Atkins, the killers did not even know who their victims were; the deaths were arbitrary, random. Dying "freaky" could happen to anyone.

The police are convinced that Miss Atkins is telling the truth, since she is supposed to know details only the murderers could have known. Her explanation of the motive behind the crimes, however, remains murky. Manson ordered his followers to commit the murders, she said in a copyrighted newspaper article, "to instill fear in man himself, man, the establishment." The Tate house was chosen because a previous occupant, Terry Melcher, a record producer and the son of Doris Day, had not kept a promise to help Manson get a recording contract. At another point, Miss Atkins said the group hoped to foment a race war between blacks and whites.

Whether Miss Atkins is telling the truth, and whether Charlie Manson and his "family" did commit murder, is a question that can be answered only after what is likely to be a lengthy and highly publicized trial. (The pretrial publicity has been so extensive that the judge has ordered all principals not to make any public comments that might prejudice a jury.) But what cannot be denied is the existence of Manson and his strange family of wandering young people. Living on the fringes of a hostile society, they posed just by their presence a basic challenge to the values and institutions of their parents. Where did they come from? What were they like? What road did they travel to that crowded courtroom in which a nervous assistant district attorney formally told them that they were charged with murder?

The most compelling, but in some ways the most understandable, member of the family is Manson himself, a man whose life stands as a monument to parental neglect and the failure of the public correctional system. Charles Milles Manson was born in Cincinnati on Nov. 11, 1934, the son of a teen-age prostitute named Kathleen Maddox and one of her boyfriends, a man remembered only as "Colonel Scott." In order to give her child a name, the pregnant girl had married William Manson, an older man who quickly left the scene. In 1939, Mrs. Manson was arrested for robbery, and the boy was sent to live with his grandmother and an aunt near Wheeling, W. Va. Charles later remembered his aunt as a "harsh disciplinarian," but his uncle secretly gave him money for the movies and took him on hunting and fishing trips. When the uncle became ill with tuberculosis, Mrs. Manson, then out of jail, reclaimed her son and moved to Indianapolis.

Mrs. Manson recalled in later years that people fell in love with her personable little boy. She promised herself to provide him with a good home, but every vow was soon broken by liquor and men. She would put him to bed, say she was only going out for an hour, and then leave him all night by himself. When the remorse flooded in, she gave the child 50 cents and yet another promise. At other times, she abused him.

Mrs. Manson tried to place Charlie in a foster home, but the arrangements fell through. Then she sent him to the Gibault School in Terre Haute, a boys' school run by Catholic priests. She could not keep up the payments, however, and Charlie came home, but not for long. "I didn't want to stay where mother lived in sin," he told juvenile authorities. Only 14, he rented his own room, and supported himself with odd jobs and petty thievery. His mother turned him in to the city's juvenile center, where he met the Rev. George Powers, a Catholic priest. "This particular boy seemed very lonesome, just craving attention and affection," recalled Father Powers, who arranged for Charlie to go to Boys Town near Omaha, Neb.

Even then, the youth displayed one of his marked adult traits, a charismatic personality. "He was a beautiful kid for his age, a warm and friendly boy; he won everybody over," the priest remembered. ("Charlie had to be persuasive," a friend said recently; "it was the only way he could survive. Otherwise, he would have been dead long ago.")

Charlie stayed a total of three days in Boys Town before running away with an accomplice named Blackie Nielson. The pair were arrested for robbing a grocery store in Peoria, Ill., and when he was returned to Indianapolis, Charlie was sent to the Indiana Boys School in Plainfield. He ran away 18 times before he was arrested in Beaver City, Utah, for stealing a car. He wound up in the National Training School for Boys in Washington, D.C.

After his release in 1954, Charlie went back to West Virginia and within months married a local girl, Rosalie Jean Willis. She became pregnant, and he started stealing cars. By the time the baby was born, Manson was in jail in Los Angeles.

Rosalie moved to California to be near her husband. Kathleen Manson displayed an uncommon streak of maternal sympathy and came to help care for her grandchild. But by the time Charlie was released in August, 1958, his wife and mother had gone, leaving him alone again. Several arrests for car theft and pimping followed; in 1960, he was convicted of forging Government checks and was given a 10-year sentence. During his stay in McNeil Island Penitentiary in the state of Washington, Manson dabbled in philosophy, took up the guitar and taught himself to sing and compose songs. As a habitual probation violator, he was not eligible for parole, and served seven years until his release in March, 1967.

The long stretch had left its mark. "If Charlie has any roots, it is in the penal system," said one acquaintance. "Inside, you have to be aware of everything, and when he came out, Charlie was like a cat. Nothing got by Charlie. If something happened within 100 miles of him, he made sure he knew about it. Every time he came into a room, he cased it, like an animal. Where were the windows?

What was the quickest way out? He never sat with his back to the door." A man who served 10 years himself said: "I knew lots of guys like Charlie in jail—little magicians with eyes that really psych you out. Doing time strengthens you, you know. You learn how much you can take and how much you can give."

Soon after his release, Manson made his way to Haight-Ashbury, the district in San Francisco where the hippie movement was in brief, bright flower. The true hippies, the gentle folk who believed in peace and love and sharing with others, who had some sense of themselves and their direction, were like a primitive African tribe suddenly exposed to civilization. As the news media spread their story, the hippies were quickly overwhelmed by runaway teenyboppers, motorcycle gangs and a wide variety of mentally deranged types who found their openness all too inviting.

Manson's probation officer remembers he was "shaken" by the friendliness of the natives—but, before long, he learned how to exploit it. A slight man, about 5 feet 7 inches tall, with chestnut hair and burning eyes, Manson started to collect a harem of young, impressionable girls who had fled to the Haight in search of the community of love advertised by the press and TV. A guitar, a pleasant voice, a boyish smile, sinuous mannerisms, a smooth line of talk—these were the ingredients of Manson's appeal.

"He was magnetic. His motions were like magic, it seemed like," said one of his girls. Susan Atkins recalled: "One day, a little man came in with a guitar and started singing for a group of us. . . . Even before I saw him, while I was still in the kitchen,

his voice just hypnotized me—mesmerized me. Then when I saw him, I fell absolutely in love with him." One observer of Manson's courtships said: "You either hated Charlie or had a strong attraction to him. He cut right to it; he cut through the pitter-patter. It was sex, and the women knew it; there was no foreplay involved."

To his girls, Charlie Manson was a "beautiful man" who "loved us all totally." To many outsiders, he was a relentless recruiter who came on very strong with every girl he met, a cynic who treated his harem like possessions and seldom showed any real affection. "In a way, he was very frank and truthful," a close friend explained, "but in a way he was very treacherous with his words—there was no meaning behind them." To Dr. David Smith, the founder and director of the Haight-Ashbury Free Clinic, these two sides of Charlie Manson were not really contradictory:

"To take one example, if you get to know any paranoid schizophrenics it won't puzzle you at all. The schizophrenic usually believes in a mystical system in which he is right, and he can plan in the most calculating and cunning way possible. He himself does not really know whether he is a con man, or whether he really does love the girls. He vacillates between one emotion and the other; one of the characteristics of a schizoid personality is the inability to sustain one emotion. It doesn't confuse me that he would be able to convey sincere emotion and carry on in a very plotting way. Of course, he would hide the cunning side as much as possible from those he wanted to involve in his system."

As the Haight was increasingly

taken over by the hard-dope pushers, the psychotics and the rapists, Charlie packed his crew into a converted school bus and headed south in the spring of 1968. The group of 14—nine girls and five boys—were arrested near Oxnard for sleeping nude in a field; one of the girls, the mother of a newborn infant, was also charged with endangering the health of a child. But the charges were dropped when the group agreed to leave Ventura County.

Once in Los Angeles, they "crashed" in Topanga Canyon, originally a haven for many stable hippies, which, like the Haight, has been overrun with itinerant panhandlers. For a while, the group lived with Gary Hinman, a musician, in his Topanga home (Hinman was dead last July and Susan Atkins and another family member, Robert Beausoleil, have been charged with the murder). Then one of the girls met Dennis Wilson, a member of the Beach Boys singing group, who invited the family to stay in his luxurious home in Pacific Palisades. But Wilson never quite gave in to Manson's demands for total loyalty and the family left after several months.

They finally settled at Spahn's Ranch, an old movie set in the craggy, desolate Santa Susana Mountains, just north of the San Fernando Valley. The ranch's owner, 83-year-old George Spahn, was blind and feeble and desperately afraid of Manson. But he also liked the attention of the girls, who cooked and cleaned for him, and the group was allowed to stay. The family lived at the ranch for about a year, leaving this fall after deputy sheriffs staged several raids, looking for stolen cars and motorcycles. It was then that they decamped for the desert, where they made their last home before the arrests in October.

Once Manson succeeded in making recruits, he tried to eradicate their "hang-ups" about conventional society. By "hang-up," he essentially meant anything he did not like, and their removal was not a very difficult process. He was dealing with lonely, insecure people in need of a father figure, people who did not have much ego to begin with. What he did, in effect, was to tear down that ego and substitute himself, thus achieving enormous control over his followers. They became empty vessels for whatever he poured in. As Susan Atkins said bleakly: "I never questioned what Charlie said. I just did it."

Probably the major hang-up most girls brought to the group was sex. But Charlie was so persuasive, and so brutal when necessary, that any girl who stayed quickly accepted the idea of having sex with him, or any other member of the group, on demand. He preached that women should be totally submissive to men, an idea he put into a song that was recorded by the Beach Boys. Charlie's title for the song was "Cease to Resist," and although the Beach Boys changed it to "Never Learn Not to Love," they kept this lyric: "Submission is a gift, give it to your lover." Recurring throughout the song is a pleading, wailing voice singing: "I'm your kind, I'm your kind, I'm your kind."

Once he controlled the girls, Manson was able to use them in his ceaseless pursuit of new acolytes. "The women around the place were always his property," recalled one boy who lived at Spahn's Ranch. "You were always welcome to share them, but then you became his property, too." Charlie's technique, another acquaintance said, was "to put you under some obligation and then milk it dry." Four or five boys became somewhat permanent members of the family, but those with some measure of self-confidence resented Charlie's desire for total mastery and drifted away.

The girls were offered to visitors who were in a position to help Manson, as well as ranch hands at Spahn's (at least one cowboy who accepted the gift ended up with venereal disease). Sometimes, one of the girls recalled, "Charlie had to chase guys away and remind them we weren't running a whore house." But Sandra Good, one of the few family members not in jail, found nothing wrong with the arrangements. "If a guy wanted to use women, or play power games, the girls said, 'Uh, uh,'" she said. "Charlie treated us right; he loved us totally. And the fellows in the family were supergentle and right with the girls. They loved us; they didn't use us. And there aren't too many men like that."

Manson's ability to "psych people out" and discern their hang-ups was so acute that some of his disciples believed he could read minds. "He could play any role you wanted him to—a father, a lover, a little boy, anything," said Sandy Good. A man who was close to Manson for several months added: "Charlie was a man of a thousand faces; he had a different one for everybody. That's why he didn't grow a beard for so long: He felt it would reduce his ability to communicate with people."

Manson knew what to say to make people feel good, to bring them out of themselves. Sharon Rayfield, a girl who lived near the Spahn Ranch and rode horses there, said: "I always thought I was ugly, but Charlie made me feel beautiful." Another girl recalled the time when the family was having one of its frequent songfests. The girl was "playing inhibited" and refusing to join in, convinced she could not sing. Charlie sat down next to her and yelled at her to sing. "I started to cry," she recalled, "but after he yelled a few more times I finally started to sing. It was a tremendous relief. It was what I had always wanted to do, but I didn't have the nerve. I was just making myself miserable by not singing."

Then there is the story about Dean Morehouse, a former Methodist minister who met Manson in San Jose several years ago. Manson gave Morehouse his first LSD and the two became friends—until Manson ran off with Morehouse's beautiful 15-year-old daughter (who remained a member of the family to the end). Morehouse and another man, who had given Manson a Volkswagen bus, took off after the family. After three days, they found them near Los Angeles; Morehouse approached Manson, burning with fury. "You're just angry because you want to do to your daughter what I'm doing," Manson told the irate father.

"Then he told me he loved me, and all the girls said, 'We love you, Dean,' and I realized I was angry only because of my own hang-ups," recalled Morehouse, who is now in state prison for giving LSD to minors. Several months later, Morehouse returned to Los Angeles and found the family living at Dennis Wilson's house. "Charlie said I would be a prophet," said Morehouse, who wants to start his own sect, The Universal Order of Metaphysics, when he gets out of jail.

"Then he said to Dennis, 'Isn't Dean beautiful?' and he got down and kissed my feet."

Manson was adept at picking up and playing on the dissatisfactions of his followers. One of his favorite lines was: "People spend too much time worrying about the moon and not enough making love." He gloried in nature and denounced the evils of urban life. A man who lived with the family for a while said: "Charlie's ability to speak was really something. He could point to a black wall and say it was white and you would almost believe it. Anyone with some intelligence can point out the wrongs in society, and if he can talk convincingly, he can atract a following. I remember he used to say that giving acid to kids was no worse than sending them to military school, and that made sense, even to me.

"He once took me out to a new housing tract in Chatsworth, near the ranch. It was all finished, but no people had moved in. We got out and walked around. He asked me what the place reminded me of, and I knew right away—a graveyard. That is what he was against—stone-cold, ugly houses. It was just horrible. I'm sure he took other people there; it was all very effective."

Fantasy always played a large role in the life of the family. They were frequent users of LSD, when they could get it, but often their fantasies took the form of childish games. "When we were at the ranch, we would play cowboy and cowgirl, and talk Okie talk to each other," said Sandy Good. "Out there in the mountains, we became mountain folk and the city people were the flatland foreigners. Sometimes, we'd put on long dresses and play like it was a long time ago, back in the pioneer days."

To get to the Spahn ranch from Los Angeles, you drive through the western end of the San Fernando Valley, a farming area before World War II that now harbors more gasoline pumps than orange trees. Huge signs proclaim the virtues of new housing tracts with names like Vista Del Norte and Hidden Lake. But when you climb off the valley floor and into the hills, you cross into a different world.

The Spahn Ranch, a cluster of dilapidated buildings arranged like a Western street, complete with board sidewalk, is still used occasionally for B-minus movies, but most of its meager income comes from renting horses to day-riders or movie companies. The family squatted where it could—in the jail and the saloon on the movie set, in an old bunkhouse back in the woods, or outside during the warm months.

They foraged for food in garbage cans—they once startled a grocery-store owner by collecting refuse in Dennis Wilson's Rolls-Royce—and ate huge communal meals cooked by the girls. They shared the few clothes they had, when they bothered with them at all. Manson hated the hang-up of material possessions and his attitude permeated the group.

But he also used possessions, as he used the girls, to win over recruits. A master of the dramatic gesture, he once gave a new boy his favorite shirt and told him to defecate on it. "It took away the ego thing the kid had," Morehouse recalled. When Sandy Good joined the family, another girl gave her a beautiful ring that had once belonged to the girl's grandmother. "Isn't that expensive?"

Sandy asked. "What does expensive mean?" the girl replied.

People often gave the family presents, and the family was not above asking for them. One day, several of the girls were hitchhiking to the beach. They started talking to the man who picked them up, and one of the girls said: "Can we have your car?" The man, somewhat flustered, said he had an old Studebaker with a busted transmission that did not run. The girls asked him for the keys, and one of the boys, an expert mechanic, put the car back in working order. One girl gave Manson $5,000 she had in stocks, and another donated $10,000; a third girl is said to have stolen $5,000 from friends on Manson's orders.

But Charlie was also generous with what he had. He gave Dean Morehouse money to meet some overdue car payments, and George Spahn enough to cover taxes and a horse-feed bill. Manson also donated $2,000 to the Fountain of the World, a religious retreat near the Spahn Ranch where the family occasionally went for meals and Saturday evening musical shows. "Charlie didn't want any physical possessions," Morehouse insisted. "The only thing Charlie wanted was people—and their souls. He wanted to deliver their souls."

As time went on, Charlie seemed to consider himself something of a prophet and even a savior. He preached an electric and confused doctrine that all people are one person and part of God. "I am Charlie and Charlie is me," is a line used by many of his followers. In this sense, Manson maintained, there can be no death, since the oneness of God endures. Indeed, he considered all things part of an inseparable whole. One day,

walking through the woods, he picked up a stick and started stroking it. "That is making love," he said. Another time, one of his girls was collecting brightly colored stones in the desert and he handed her a plain gray one. "Take this one, too," he said. "This is just as beautiful as the others."

Doctors familiar with paranoid schizophrenics and habitual users of LSD—who often share similar symptoms—find many of Manson's attitudes quite understandable. Such people they point out find it difficult to distinguish between fantasy and reality and have delusions about their own grandeur. Moreover, an LSD trip makes a person aware of a consciousness apart from his physical body, and imparts a feeling of oneness with the universe. This experience, the doctors believe, could lead a person to believe there really is no death.

In the past eight months or so, people detected a change in Charlie Manson. While he could be loving and warm with his followers, he could explode with anger at those who crossed him. George Spahn recalls having a fierce argument with Charlie because the family's motorcycles were scaring the horses. When Spahn finally called the police, Charlie hid outside. After they left, he came back screaming. "He said, 'Open your eyes, you goddamn son of a bitch. You're a liar: You really can see,'" Spahn recalled, sitting in a fly-covered ranch house littered with dogs and Western saddles. "He called me every foul name you could think of and made me say over and over, 'I can see, I can see.' He held me hostage the better part of an hour. Every once in a while, he'd throw a fist past my eyes thinking I would blink. Then he threatened to cut my throat. Finally, he sat down and got real quiet. There were two girls with him, I think, and he never said a word. That got me even more scared than before. I don't know much about dope, but they had to be full of it; they were shaking and shaking, like a horse does before he died. Then, before they left, Charlie said, 'George, I love you.' "

Charlie's control over the group grew more rigid and intolerant. "You were either for him or against him," recalled one friend, and Susan Atkins has said, "We belonged to Charlie, not to ourselves." Friends of the family noticed a vacant passivity in some of the most avid followers. Clem Tufts, one of the boys, once took Dennis Wilson's Ferrari for a joy ride and smashed it up. When he returned, unhurt, and was asked why he had taken the car, Tufts just shrugged and said: "I wanted to see how fast it could take a curve."

Manson was not satisfied with preaching to his small circle of disciples. He wanted to carry his message to the world and he deeply admired the Beatles for their influence on young people. He even had a fantasy that he would some day meet the Beatles and they would greet him as a comrade. The main reason he wanted to get a recording contract was not for the money, but for the chance to make new converts. (Manson apparently has some musical talent and some tapes he made of his own songs may now be put into an album.)

Susan Atkins has testified that Manson was angry with Terry Melcher for not helping him get such a contract, but Charlie's hatred of the Establishment went much deeper than that. Juan Flynn, a ranch hand at Spahn's, put it this way: "He got

stepped on quite a few times, and when he cried out, no one paid any attention. You have to live at the bottom in order to know who's stepping on you. Charlie often said he wasn't successful to the Establishment, but he felt he was successful to himself in love."

Manson's feelings about society showed in his attitude toward children. He often preached that the power structure corrupted young minds, and he urged his girls to have babies they could raise in their own way. At least four of the girls did have babies, including Sandy Good, who was feeding her three-month-old son, Ivan, as she talked:

"In the city, where I was before I met the family, everyone was having abortions. The first girl I met in the family was pregnant and she wasn't married, but she was happy about it. Babies are perfect, if you don't let them grow up with all that garbage in their heads. They're total love. If you don't teach them that certain things are wrong or dirty, they'll have a pure mind."

Recently, Manson's resentment against the Establishment began to blend with a growing phobia about Negroes, particularly the Black Panthers. He claimed that he had been beaten up by a group of Panthers and that they were coming to the ranch to kill him. He believed in the law of karma, the Eastern religious idea that all events come in cycles and have previous causes—and he was convinced that the black man would revolt and oppress the white man in the way that whites had previously oppressed the blacks. And he saw the signs of the coming revolt in a rather unlikely place—an album recorded by the Beatles.

A song called "Blackbird," he be-lieved, was really referring to black militants when it said: "Blackbird singing in the dead of night/Take these broken wings and learn to fly/All your life/You were only wait-ing for this moment to arrive." He theorized that in "Helter-Skelter" the Beatles were actually describing the coming race war when they sang: "Look out, helter-skelter, helter-skelter/Helter-skelter/Look out, 'cause here she comes." And to Charlie, the song "Revolution 9," a lengthy caco-phony of odd sounds and snippets, was pointing to the ninth chapter of the Book of Revelations. That chapter describes an angel who unleashed "locusts upon the earth: and unto them was given power, as the scor-pions of the earth have power." The locusts were commanded to harm "only those men which have not the seal of God in their foreheads."

Manson's fear of the blacks drove him to start collecting cars—the fam-ily has been charged with stealing some of them—and converting them into dune buggies. He believed that his group could survive the revolu-tion in the desert if properly prepared, and might become the last link to white civilization. The girls sewed clothes designed for rugged desert life. Guns started appearing at the ranch and the men frequently took target practice. Guards were posted. A girl remembers dropping someone off at the ranch at 2 A.M., and being greeted by a menacing machine gun.

Escape routes to the desert were plotted. Caches of gasoline and other necessities were buried all over the Death Valley area. Charlie tried to recruit some motorcycle types to act as guards but was unsuccessful.

Shortly after the Tate murders,

police raided the Spahn ranch look-ing for stolen vehicles, and a week later Charlie decided to get out. He led his followers to the deserted Barker Ranch near Death Valley, the place where he wanted to make his last stand and where he was ulti-mately arrested, despite an elaborate look-out system complete with walkie-talkies.

The inevitable question remains, however: Why? What caused the void, the terrible emptiness that drove so many young people to Haight-Ashbury, the East Village and dozens of other places, seeking refuge from the culture of their parents? What is still sending them out into the world, so lost and confused? And what makes these troubled adolescents so vulner-able to spiritual gurus like Charlie Mason?

Charlie Manson's family was only part of a much broader phenomenon, but the reasons behind it are neither clear nor easy. Even the sketchy hints that are discernible remain unsatis-factory; many youngsters from back-grounds similar to Charlie's girls' never run away and still think LSD is a college football team. But one factor seems to be the breakdown of the family and the community as structured units in which children can find security, affection and ideals. This is particularly true in California, where one out of every two marriages ends in divorce, and where the past ends at the eastern slopes of the Sierra Nevada. Here there is only the rest-less present—new communities sunk no deeper into the earth than a tum-bleweed, a personal freedom that is as corrosive as it is liberating, a flailing-about for meaning and identity.

Almost every girl in Charlie Man-son's family came from a disrupted home. Susan Atkins was 15 when her mother died and her father left home in San Jose to look for work. When she got into trouble with the police, her father complained that the courts were "too lenient" because they let her out of jail. "She once did some beautiful things," he told a hometown reporter recently, "but that was a long time ago. I don't know what went wrong."

Linda Kasabian's parents were married only briefly, if ever. She grew up in Milford, N.H., and saw her father, a bartender in Miami, only twice in 15 years. She was married at 16, divorced within months. She had a child by her second husband, who brought her to California and then abandoned her. Now she is pregnant again. "She was ensnared," her lawyer said, "by what she thought was a loving group of hippies." Her mother said when she was arrested: "There is no hate in her, at all. She was searching, searching for love."

Sandra Good is the daughter of a wealthy stockbroker in San Diego who divorced her mother when the girl was 2. Sandra and her brother and sister were sent away to school most of the time. "All my mother cared about was her social climbing," recalled Sandra, a soft, pretty girl with reddish-brown hair. "She'd do anything to get in the social column. I was scared of her; I was terrified." After Sandra was arrested in the Death Valley raid, her baby was placed in a foster home, and she asked her father to post bail so she could recover the child. He did so, reluctantly, and she went to live with him when she got out of jail. She stayed a week. "My stepmother had this expensive tea in the house and I kept drinking it, so she hid it," Miss

Good said. "My father gave me $200 when I left, and said that was it: he wouldn't give me 'anymore.'"

A girl who has lived in the hippie world for years tried to explain the situation this way: "Sure, the girls were obviously weak, but it's not that hard to be fooled, especially if a woman expects to be led by a man. He was offering not just a physical living situation, but sex, a family, everything a woman is looking for. Love is blind, you know." Another girl added: "Women have been falling for the wrong men for years."

But the girls' backgrounds are only part of the story. "We can't be dismissed as uneducated or deprived kids, or the products of tormented childhoods. We're pretty typical. A lot of parents can identify with us as their kids," insisted Sandy Good, who has been cleared of all criminal charges. She is now living with her baby on welfare in a shabby motel room in Independence, Calif., the little mountain community where some of the girls are still in jail. She hopes, against all odds, that the family can be reunited and will help her raise her baby. She has nowhere else to go.

To support her point, Sandy ticked off the occupations of the girls' fathers: stockbroker, scientist, psychologist, realestate man, insurance salesman, auctioneer, minister. Many of the parents had some college education; so did some of the older girls. One girl with a master's degree had been a librarian. Sandra had been studying marine biology. Leslie Van Houten, a legal secretary, had been a high-school homecoming princess. "You can't categorize us," said Sandra, with a look of triumph. "We're going to blow people's minds."

Dr. David Smith believes part of the explanation for the girls' rebellion lies in the state of the society that raised them. "If you're going to believe in the institutions and conventions of a society, then you have to believe in that society, and that is very difficult," said the doctor, who also teaches toxicology at the University of California and recently finished an academic paper on the Manson family. "Things like the Vietnam war and environmental pollution are just as important in adolescent alienation as family background.

"The thing that is different now, as opposed to the thirties, is the instant information environment. There were pollution and graft and unpopular wars years ago, but people didn't find out about them right away. Today, youth gets an instant feedback about what's happening. It makes them question the quality of American life and institutions, and this questioning comes at a very vulnerable period."

There is also a third possible explanation. Simply put, Charlie Manson gave the girls a chance to do something, even if it was only the most rudimentary of tasks. Neither their family lives, nor school, nor their jobs had enabled them to say: "I have accomplished something; I am worth something."

Marx predicted the alienation of the assembly line, but that same sense of incompleteness has permeated many areas of modern life. Perhaps the society needs to provide new rites of passage for the young, new tests and opportunities in which they can earn their adulthood and a higher sense of themselves and their possibilities. As Sandra Good explained her experience:

"When I joined the family, I just didn't think I could do anything. But after a while, I made a dress from an old piece of cloth. Then I started cooking without recipes. I got pretty damn creative. I could cook, sew, sing, play the guitar. You don't have to learn; it's in you. You have to believe you can do it, and not be afraid to let it out."

A fourth factor is the yearning to "be simple," to "get back to nature," to escape the "hassle" of city life, of stultifying school work, of the "instant feedback"—news pollution—of crisis and disaster. "I used to think I had to read a million books a day," Sandy said with a smile. "Now, what I want to do is watch the sun come up. When I came into the family, it was like I had walked into a dream. Maybe you get the same feeling on an isolated Greek island. There were no clocks, no radios, no papers, no books."

Whatever the causes, there are thousands of young people just like Charlie's girls who have broken with their families and are looking for a new home and new values. Dr. Smith understands the positive side of their protest, but he also senses a danger. "The second leading cause of death among adolescents is suicide," he declared angrily. "There is an incredible increase in drug use. There is a great rise in things like the hippie subculture and youthful activism. And through it all there is a common thread—the alienation of young people from the central core of American society. Yet the leaders say nothing is different, we don't have to change, we don't have to resolve the alienation of these kids."

Did Charlie Manson and his family commit murder? Only a jury can decide that. Whether or not such a group is *capable* of violence is another matter. Dr. Smith believes the possibility for violence exists in any group in which individuals are totally committed to the righteousness of their leader, and thus give up their own ability to think independently— in other words, the "I was only following orders" syndrome.

"If you set up infant consciousness as an objective [Manson preached that a child's mind, unsullied by society, is perfect], you have to strip away all the social controls you've learned from your parents and society," the doctor said. "You can thus see where the mechanism for violence might come from. If the delusional system turns hostile, and you're committed to whatever your spiritual leader says is right, and he says: 'Kill,' you can kill. I think the mechanism of violence that can operate in these groups is the same as what is indicated by the recent stories from Vietnam. What you do with soldiers is strip away all normal social controls, and you substitute a form of nationalism. Then you get involved in an emotional situation, and if the leader says to shoot women and children, they shoot women and children."

62 Years for Vagrancy

RAY RICHARD

A weary old man of 83 years sleeps peacefully on a canvas-covered mat in his cell at the State Hospital now, his mind no longer tortured by the sadness of being forgotten for 62 years.

No longer does this man, arrested as vagrant and committed to the criminal hospital for a two-year sentence in 1905, ask himself, as he probably had done for decades, "Why could this happen to me?"

No longer can his mind try to reason why, since the day he was admitted, July 7, 1905, he has never had

Reprinted with the permission of the Boston Globe from *The Boston Sunday Globe*, February 12, 1967, p. 66.

a visitor, never had a letter, a package or a message from outside his prison walls.

His mind is gone now. As far as living is concerned, his life is all wrapped up. His reason, his memory can never be regained. Nor can he ever tell his story of being a forgotten man.

Even his identity is almost erased. The officers who care for him know it, and maybe some of the other troubled men who spend their fading years in the same geriatric ward at the hospital have enough of senses left to remember his true name, but hospital regulations, set by law, order that the identity of patients cannot be publicized. So we will call him George.

He has spent more years at Bridgewater State Hospital than any other of the 650 inmates now there.

But he's not the only forgotten man.

A man named John has been committed there since November 6, 1909. His crime, the commital papers reveal, was "Breaking and entering a building with intention to steal."

Another patient, named Charles, has been confined as a criminal in Bridgewater since February 2, 1910. His crime was breaking and entering, the maximum penalty for which was two years at the time he was committed.

A fourth patient has been committed to Bridgewater since 1910. His crime was vagrancy.

Still another man, now elderly like these others, has spent 56 years committed to the hospital for the criminally insane because on August 17, 1911, some judge ruled him "a tramp."

These are the men who have felt the back of society's hand. These are the patients for whom help, although late, may be on the way. The superintendent of the hospital, The Massachusetts Medical Society, the Massachusetts Bar Association and a special legislative commission updating our mental health laws all are fighting decades of apathy to help men like George and prevent others like him from being committed as criminals, then forgotten, for more than half a century after their sentences ran out.

Life once was exciting for George. He was 13 years old when he sailed into Boston Harbor, a shouting, waving, exhilarated young Swiss coming to the "promised land."

"He has been most carefully brought up by his grandmother," reads a plaintive, bewildering message written in longhand for hospital records in behalf of George's real mother in 1906.

"I am writing this because she does not know English," a clergyman, apparently from Lausanne, wrote.

"His mother says he drank, but she never knew him to drink to intoxication," reads another aged message in the files at the hospital, records which cast one weak ray of light into the darkened world of George, the forgotten man.

Why was he committed to Bridgewater?

The records tell all—or all that was required in those years to commit a young man of 22 to the institution which was officially known then as "The Massachusetts State Asylum for Insane Criminals."

Carefully preserved within the records are his commitment papers, his medical records, records of any visitors he might have received, a listing of any packages or other mail which may have been sent to him, the findings of psychiatrists and medical doctors who have examined him from time to time.

They all are carefully preserved under his name and his distinguished, unenviable number: Inmate 1304.

Inmate numbers are allocated consecutively as men are admitted as patients.

The last inmate to be admitted Saturday got number 9835.

The commitment papers, all properly signed by two physicians as required by law in these days, tell why this young immigrant who had been in the United States only eight years and in Massachusetts four months, was committed.

"He does not seem to comprehend questions" was the reply of the physicians to "Why was the patient admitted?"

Other reasons for George's being confined also were clearly delineated in the long questionnaire the physicians had to answer to make his commitment legally complete.

The questions included: The patient's appearance and mannerisms?

The doctors replied, "Dull, imbecilic; from appearances he would be unable to take care of himself."

An accurate knowledge of the previous history of the patient?

"At the age of six years," is the penciled reply, "a needle was introduced on his neck and the soul of his foot and produced no pain."

Under the question, facts indicating insanity personally observed by me (the physician) there was no answer, only 16 empty lines.

The answer to the next query was more specific: What the patient did? (Here state what the patient did in the presence of each examiner separately, unless it was done in the presence of both.)

The reply reads "Nothing special."

"Has he ever been insane before?" is the next question on the formal commitment paper.

"No," reads the reply, "except he was never normal."

The most detailed descriptions of George's shortcomings are explained in response to the instruction to the doctors. "Describe any disease, accident or change of circumstances that seem to have caused this attack."

He was sentenced for vagrancy in Somerville, other affidavits show.

Other documents describe the man, then 22, as he was seen at the time by relatives and neighbors, who replied to routine questionnaires sent acquaintances of men committed to Bridgewater in that era.

"At the last meeting with his mother (before being arrested for vagrancy) he offered her a dollar, which the mother wouldn't take," wrote one respondent. "She admonished him to buy clothing with it. This shows he was never angry at his mother. He listened always, silently to advice and to reproach and promised to do better."

But once committed, George was cast aside by our commonwealth. His file at the hospital has, almost mockingly, as its first entry: CRIME: vagrancy. SENTENCE BEGAN: July 1, 1905. SENTENCE EXPIRED: July 7, 1907.

Subsequent medical reports on the man detail almost inexplorably, his mental and emotional decline. A few years later, words like "regression" are noted in doctors' reports.

His downhill plunge is clearly noted by reports, each of which contains the statement: "STATEMENT: CUSTODIAL CARE."

From his mattress on the cold floor of his cell, George sat up Saturday evening in response to a friendly pat from an officer. It was plain that George had had it. His only response was an incoherent mumbling with a hauntingly rhythmic beat while he waved his right hand back and forth, then sideways, first like a trombone player, then as though he were leading a band.

His condition has regressed, the medical reports show. From the man committed because he "did not seem to comprehend questions," George was described recently in a psychiatric report in these terms:

"A mumbling, restless, growling,

muttering, chanting, humming, drowsy, incongruous, hyperkinetic, ill-at-ease white male."

Others among oldtimers at Bridgewater who have been forgotten by the law have similarly distressing records.

A former Brockton shoe worker who was sentenced in 1910 for a two-year term, and is still there, had his "insanity" blamed, according to his records, on "poor heredity and alcohol."

The plight of these men distresses the staff of officers and medical personnel at the hospital.

"Please don't blame us for keeping them here for so long," one officer pleads. "We've had to. The laws required us to."

"These men cannot be saved now," Charles W. Gaughan, superintendent, says, "but they should not be in a criminal institution. They should be in a civil mental hospital which has many more comforts than we can offer here."

The president of the Massachusetts Bar Association, Attorney Paul Tamburello of Pittsfield, vigorously agrees and is leading his 6000-member organization in an effort to help these forgotten men.

"This man had a life to lead, but our commonwealth took it away from him," Tamburello said. "It's too late now to salvage his life, but we can't let this happen to any more men."

Annals of Advertising:
Cutting Down

CONGRESSIONAL RECORD

HON. FRANK E. MOSS of Utah in the Senate of the United States, *Friday, November 20, 1970.*

Mr. Moss. Mr. President, last week Warren Braren, formerly manager of the New York office of the National Association of Broadcasters Code, filed a petition relating to cigarette advertising. In his petition, Mr. Braren documents fairly, but unsparingly, the cigarette companies' ex-

Congressional Record, November 20, 1970.

cesses and abuses of the advertising media and calls upon the Federal Trade Commission to issue firm, restrictive rules eliminating such abuses. The merit and persuasiveness of his case appear to me to be beyond question.

Because the situation he describes must trouble the conscience of every American concerned with the public health, I ask unanimous consent that the text of Mr. Braren's letter to the Trade Commission be printed in the Extensions of Remarks.

There being no objection, the letter was ordered to be printed in the *Record*, as follows:

New York, N.Y.,
November 12, 1970.
Federal Trade Commission,
Washington, D.C.

Gentlemen. The enormity of the public health problem relating to cigarette smoking compels the undersigned to respectfully petition the Commission to set forth prior to January 2, 1971:

(1) Its enforcement policy with regard to all themes and representations in cigarette advertising, promotions and on packages, which have the capacity to deceive or mislead the public, and

(2) Its procedures with respect to carrying out this enforcement policy.

By way of identification, the petitioner is the former manager of the New York Office of the Code Authority, National Association of Broadcasters. He directed Code activities relating to the content of commercials and particularly was responsible for supervising the only broadcast industry study on cigarette advertising. The study culminated in a report critical of many themes employed in promoting cigarettes. The report was publicly released by him in June 1969 prior to his testimony before Congress and this Commission on broadcast self-regulation and cigarette advertising.

NATURE OF PROBLEM

A look at cigarette advertising as it prepares to shift to non-broadcast media as of January 2 reveals that:

(1) Expenditures in print and other nonbroadcast media will jump in some cases 300 or more per cent, possibly reaching $150 million.

(2) The industry's Cigarette Advertising Code disbanded as of August 1, leaving not even that weak form of regulation overseeing the claims and appeals used in cigarette promotions.

(3) Themes and representations implying health benefits that were once prohibited under self-regulation are now being widely and extensively circulated.

(4) The public's concern for pollution of the environment is being exploited by some brands as a marketing tool.

(5) Previously unused promotional gimmicks have emerged, including direct tie-ins with clothing manufacturers and salons.

(6) Newly introduced pictorial and other representations on cigarette packages are diluting or negating the required health warning.

(7) The FTC has failed to act upon the many criticisms of cigarette advertising and promotion contained in its own Reports to Congress.

The petitioner's request for Commission action is necessitated by the wide range of deceptions or misrepresentations, direct or implied, that exist in cigarette advertising and labeling. Most of the themes involved are not unknown to the Commission. They are of the same nature or closely parallel those extensively criticized in the Commission's Reports to Congress which led in part to the passage of the Public Health Cigarette Smoking Act of 1969.

The action requested is required regardless of the status of the Commission's proposed trade regulation rule requiring tar and nicotine content disclosure in cigarette advertising.

PUBLIC HEALTH CIGARETTE SMOKING ACT OF 1969

Under the old Cigarette Labeling and Advertising Act which expired in July, 1969, the Commission was in a delicate position with regard to policing cigarette advertising. The tacit understanding was that the Commission should be patient while the tobacco industry and media were given the opportunity to self-regulate. That situation no longer exists under the new legislation.

The two most publicized features of the 1969 Act relate to the revised health warning on packages specifying that "... cigarette smoking is dangerous to your health" (emphasis supplied) and to the ban of all broadcast cigarette commercials effective January 2, 1971.

But the Act contains an equally important feature which, if given incomplete attention, has the capacity of substantially lessening the public health benefits that are intended to result from the first two provisions. Specifically the statute makes positively clear that the FTC has full authority to act with respect to unfair or deceptive practices in all remaining advertising of cigarettes. This includes the issuance of trade regulation rules and affirmative disclosure statements (except that a health warning in advertising is precluded at least until July 1973).

Quite clearly the success of this Public Health Act depends in no small measure on the Commission assuming its full responsibility in policing the themes and representations employed in the promotion of cigarettes. If these themes and representations enjoy unfettered license, they can readily negate and offset the new health warning and broadcast ban.

TIMING FOR ENFORCEMENT CRITICAL

It is essential that the Commission move at once to correct the many abuses which exist in cigarette advertising and labeling. January 2, 1971, represents a turning around period. Advertisers are gearing up for the change to non-broadcast media effective that date. These media, as discussed later, will experience large jumps in the amount of cigarette advertising. Now clearly is the time to set up warning flags so all parties concerned are fully aware of the Commission's enforcement policies.

REPORT TO CONGRESS

The Commission in its four Reports to Congress[1] on cigarette advertising and labeling was emphatic in its finding that cigarette advertising creates the impression that cigarette smoking is a healthy activity. The Reports raise many serious questions with respect to the nature of individual themes and representations. These criticisms fall into three prime areas of concern:

(1) Satisfaction theme—smoking and the kind of taste derived from it are satisfying,

(2) Associative theme—smoking associated with that which is desirable or even good, and

(3) Assuaging of anxiety—smoking is relatively free of hazard.

Thus the 1969 Report concludes in

[1] 1964, 1967, 1968, 1969.

part that the "net effect (of cigarette advertising) is to portray smoking as socially desirable, healthful, youthful and contributing to, or reflecting, material success. The health hazards of smoking are ignored or denied, usually by means of indirect references . . . (the) risk, to the extent that it exists, can be reduced through the presence of a filter."[2]

These same types of themes and representations, with the possible exception of tar and nicotine claims, continue unchecked. In fact some have been elaborated upon, and new themes capitalizing on the public's interest in pollution and the environment have been introduced.

EFFORTS TO MOTIVATE SELF-REGULATION OF CIGARETTE ADVERTISING

The Commission, as well as members of Congress and health officials, made its criticisms known to self-regulatory authorities seeking to spur industry and media to take more meaningful actions.

In November 1965, the Commission wrote to cigarette and broadcast industry officials calling attention to the need to eliminate "advertising which tends to negate, contradict, obscure, undermine, or dilute the cautionary statement on cigarette packages." It went on to state that "the provisions of the Codes appear to be inadequately designed to achieve Congress' objectives that the public should in no way be misied, or lulled into a false sense of security, with respect to the health hazards of cigarette smok-

[2] The findings and conclusions in these Reports are remarkably similar to those contained in the aforementioned broadcast industry report on cigarette advertising conducted in 1966.

ing." The request essentially went unheeded, the rationale being that both the cigarette industry and broadcast Codes were being responsive in dealing with this problem.

The Commission wrote the Code Authority again in March 1967 indicating that the "showing (of) handsome and attractive men and women smoking and enjoying cigarettes" appeared to violate the Television Code cigarette standard. The response was non-committal.

In both of these instances, the Commission indirectly affirmed the criticisms and conclusions contained in its Reports to Congress.

CIGARETTE ADVERTISING CODE AND PRINT MEDIA

Every informed person knows that cigarette advertising enjoyed considerable leeway under the self-regulatory programs. The Commission concluded that its Reports "amply demonstrate the futility in relying upon voluntary regulation of cigarette advertising to achieve any significant changes in the content and meaning of cigarette advertising."

Today there is no administrated self-regulation of cigarette advertising. The Cigarette Advertising Code (CAC) fumbled and finally closed its door on August 1 of this year. It exists now only on paper. The industry has discretely avoided a public announcement.

As for print and other advertising media, outside broadcasting, they do not even pretend to standards affecting the content of cigarette promotions. The only restraint is found in the few publications that do not accept such advertising.

From another vantage point, the

advertising column in the October 10, 1970 Sunday New York Times described the pressures on media from advertisers and agencies. Referring to "advertising standards that give a little" implied that it is only human for media standards to become flexible when confronted with advertising budgets.

This is the situation which prevails as well over $100 million in cigarette revenue lines up to be spent next year in non-broadcast media. Consequently, now more than ever, the public must look to the Commission to control cigarette advertising representations.

INEFFECTIVE SELF-REGULATION MORE EFFECTIVE THAN THE FTC

Paradoxically the collapse of the CAC has not resulted in more effective control of the themes and representations employed by cigarette manufacturers. Rather the situation has grown worse. Claims and depictions implying health benefits which had been precluded by the industry's own Code now run rampant.

Under section 3 of that Code, a cigarette's filter could not be highlighted nor could there be emphasis placed on a filtration process. Descriptive names for the filter (e.g. micronite) were taboo. Diagrams, full shots of the filter and the like were minimized or eliminated altogether. Claims of innovation for a filter were unacceptable without proof of medical significance.

Under section 4, "mildness" claims had to be qualified to refer to "taste." Even that euphemism is often omitted today. "Activated charcoal" was ruled out. Discussion of gases in cigarette smoke was unacceptable. Menthol cigarettes were unable to be displayed on ice or snow. References to "fresh air" would never have made the grade, not to mention the claim "stop smogging" and references to "modern science."

These sections of the tobacco Code were rescinded after the Commission policy statement of March 1966 allowing tar and nicotine representations in advertising.

FTC FAILS TO CONTROL HEALTH CLAIMS

At one point, it appeared that the FTC was going to exercise its statutory authority in cracking down on the whole range of health claims not directly related to a cigarette's tar and nicotine content. Two articles appeared in the Wall Street Journal issues of January 16 and March 18, 1969 disclosing an FTC investigation begun in December 1968—almost two years ago! The articles cited a two-page questionnaire which had been sent to tobacco companies requesting scripts and substantiation of health claims made in all ads.

Reference is made in these articles to the charcoal filters of Tareyton and Lark and the gas phase of cigarettes; to other filter descriptions and representations relating to a filter process; and to the complicated inner workings of filters—all in terms of implying "comparative safety." The later article clearly indicates that the ensuing FTC staff report concluded that such implied health claims should be halted. The report apparently was before the Commission in March 1969. A year and a half later the Commission has failed to act to control such deceptive representations.

LARK'S GAS-TRAP FILTER CAMPAIGN

The Lark "gas-trap filter" campaign is an example of advertising running wild unchecked by any kind of reasonable public interest regulatory standards.

One current ad shows a road sign reaching out at you with the blue sky as background—the sign title reads "STOP SMOGGING." The copy reads "start smoking Lark. You see modern science uses a special type of charcoal to clean air" and so on. Another shows a city bus spewing exhaust blackening its backside and the surrounding air while the bus prominently displays a billboard conveying the solution—"why don't they put Lark's gas trap filter on me?" The implication of health benefit could not be clearer.

In still another, four people are shown grimacing while the ad title reads—"Just what does gas in cigarette smoke taste like?" The solution, of course, is Lark. Finally, Lark's filter is named "The GAS MASK" and is directly equated with one—"it actually works just like a gas mask." The contention gains support through the aseptic display of an oversized Lark cigarette with dissected wrapper attractively showing the magic charcoal granules.

A gas mask cleans air and makes it safe for you to breathe! The gas-trap filter cleans smoke and makes it safe for you to inhale. As an added plus it stops "smoggy taste." Then for the crowning touch, some of these ads show the Lark package diagram of the filter which, in addition to the gas filter, points to tar and nicotine filters #1 and #2. According to the latest FTC test Lark 85 mm contains 17.2 mg. tar; 100 mm 17.6 mg. tar. ranking 31 and 38, respectively.

These representations constitute blatant deception, unabashedly taking advantage of the public's concern over pollution and the quality of air,

while cynically disguising the real nature of the health hazards presented by smoking.

On February 13, 1969, the Code Authority wrote to the Commission seeking clarification of its enforcement policy relative to the effects of gases in cigarette smoke. Despite the statements in the Wall Street Journal, the Commission responded on April 17, 1969 advising that it had "decided to await the action of Congress before the Commission addresses itself to the subject." Now Congress has acted and the Commission has remained silent even though it criticized the gas phase advertising in its 1969 Report to Congress. As a result, the public— even under the new FTC provision in the Public Health Cigarette Smoking Act of 1969—is being subjected to the worst sort of confusion and abuse in this vital public health area.

ACTIVATED CHARCOAL AND THE GAS THEME

Tareyton likewise has been touting its "activated charcoal" ever since the CAC deleted its health claims sections. Typical copy now reads "Tareyton is better, charcoal is why . . . activated charcoal delivers a better taste. A taste no plain white filter can match." The taste qualification notwithstanding, the emphasis is on supplying protection and allaying the smoker's fears related to his health.

Multifilter, a comparatively new brand, pictorializes its charcoal filter in much the same aseptic way as Lark. The display of the filter has a medical, space-age technology feeling. It reassures as the copy reads "Activated Charcoal Granules; highly absorbent of selected gases to smooth out flavor." The brand also takes advantage of the fresh air problem, calling attention to its "Fresh Air

System: acetate fibers reduce tar, while fresh air injection surrounds and freshens flavor." The implication of health benefit is overt. The name of the brand alone would not have been approved under the industry's own Code.

FRESH AIR BECOMES MARKETING TOOL

The public's concern with the quality of air it is being forced to breathe has become fair game for cigarette advertising. There can be no vestige of scruples when that which pollutes your lungs is tagged with a "fresh air" label. Cigarette advertising used to hint at fresh air through the display of open spaces and the feeling of freshness. Now it has become overt. Multifilter is a case in point. Then there is Belair, which lets you "start fresh" showing a couple in the beautiful, cool blue of a shoreline and open sky.

A new brand, Maryland 100's actually has been introduced around a fresh air theme. It claims "100% fresh air cured tobacco (for) fresher menthol flavor" while its package is displayed in the open, fresh air countryside. Preparation is your safeguard. Tobacco is treated to "fresh air for up to eight long weeks." The removal of noxious substances is clearly implied.

Lucky Filters, a brand relatively high in tar, ranking in the upper 70's out of 118 brands last tested by the FTC, takes full advantage of this custom-made diversionary tactic. It speaks of "air-cured tobacco (giving) you a lighter taste . . . you'll like the fresh change." This kind of terminology clearly keeps the public off-guard. It misleads by creating a false sense of security and by confusing the public as to the real meaning of tar and nicotine levels.

OTHER TYPE FILTER REPRESENTATIONS

Parliament claims "it works just like a cigarette holder works." Some ads show Parliament selected from a dozen cigarette holders. The health promise is plain—"the filter is recessed, tucked back away from your lips. So you only taste the good, clean Parliament flavor. The Parliament cigarette holder. It works." To do what?

New Kent Menthol 100's has "got it all together!", with a "Wow!" no less. And what does "all together" mean?—"a new kind of menthol refreshment. Brisk, breezy flavor . . . Kent's exclusive micronite filter . . . good rich taste." These are "all the good things of a Kent." The "good things" of a Kent consist of terminology and portrayals which substantially mask the health hazards attendant to smoking the product.

Another new brand, Mark VII, highlights its "puff-control filter" according to press reports. Still another, New Leaf, scheduled for an $8 million campaign in November and December of this year alone, has as its principal theme the phrase "gives you a tingle." Without seeing the ads, it is hard to imagine now this promise of sensation will contribute to the smoker's awareness of the health hazards attendant to smoking.

MILDNESS

Raleigh Filter Longs let you "spend a milder moment" with its "quiet taste." A beautiful golden sunset and romance complete the milder moment with the reader assured that ". . . special treatment softens the tobacco for a smoother, milder taste." The words milder, quiet, smoother are as reassuring as the serene beauty of the moment depicted in the ads. The feeling is that the product is good for you.

Chesterfield 101 promises "gentle flavor for the mildest of taste." The deceptive nature of the words is brought home when you realize that the brand ranks an incredible 90th in the most recent tar listing.

Other brands take advantage of mildness and similar references. Advertisers simply use these reassuring words as part of their jargon without hindrance from the Commission.

BEAUTIFUL PEOPLE IN BEAUTIFUL PLACES DOING BEAUTIFUL THINGS

Cigarette smoking most often does not represent a rational choice on the part of the smoker. It is tied up with many emotional and peer group considerations. The themes in cigarette advertising take full advantage of these very human frailties and susceptibilities. These themes divert attention from considering the real consequences of smoking.

The three Chesterfield brands in a coupon campaign use the theme "Chesterfield the beautiful giver." Bold copy reads "beautiful taste, beautiful gifts, beautiful new packs. Everything is beautiful with Chesterfield." Not just the taste, not just the gifts, not just the packs—everything! Including one's health?

Current Viceroy ads show an attractive young lady in a modern boutique. Clad in a mini dress, she is just the kind of girl that catches your eye. "Her clothes? Anything goes. In a smashing size 7. Her cigarettes? Nothing short of Viceroy

Longs. She won't settle for less." A young couple "famous" for their dinner parties is seen in a specialty foods shop "searching out the unusual. Their cigarette? Viceroy. They won't settle for less. It's a matter of taste." To be in good taste in all things includes smoking Viceroy!

The romance and sexual attractiveness themes continue in many ads. Kent's "good time" generally features a couple enjoying life. Meeting, getting together, doing things is made complete through smoking.

Salem carries the romance theme into "springtime." A youngish man and woman look at each other as if they have discovered true love for the first time. Purity of love, purity of springtime. New life. "You can take Salem out of the country, but . . ." It ranks 89th on the latest tar scale!

No one can contend that the man who "walks a mile for a Camel" is not a rugged individualist. The copy rightfully should go on to read "he likes his tar strong." Regular size non-filter Camel almost hits the jackpot at 105th. Old Gold Filter, also promoted for "independent people," stands in the same league at 101st on the scale. Marlboro individuality and rugged outdoor themes still leave you with a cigarette which, depending upon the size, ranks 71st to 91st in tar content.

The number of unfeminine or unattractive women who have appeared in cigarette commercials can be counted on both hands. But it took Virginia Slims to help make the American woman what she is today. Comparing today's woman with her drab counterpart of yesteryear, copy stress "we made Virginia Slims especially for women because women are dainty and beautiful and sweet and generally different from men." Femininity, up-to-date appearance, become equated with smoking.

Beautiful people in the kind of places people enjoy, doing the kinds of things that give people satisfaction. These themes and others related to them have been amply documented and criticized in the Commission's Reports to Congress. There has been no change for the better in 1970. What has proved successful in TV obviously will set the tone for promotions in print and other media. Clearly the Commission's repeated criticisms require action in the form of enforcement.

OTHER PROMOTIONAL ACTIVITIES

Both Lark and Pall Mall have found yet another way to enhance the attractiveness of cigarette smoking and to allay any fears smokers may have.

Elizabeth Arden has now introduced the "Lark Collection . . . fashions that are a lark to wear and a lift to live in." Chic fashion and the salon are interwoven with "today's distinctive taste in cigarettes." At Elizabeth Arden you can be massaged, bathed, exercised, etc. With the admonition to "surround yourself with beautiful things" and "be perfectly proportioned from head to toe," Lark becomes an integral part of the cultured up-to-date woman.

Pall Malls tie-in is with the latest fashions sold to stores by Ann Fogarty. The theme is "Pall Mall Gold . . . longer yet milder. Ann Fogarty . . . longer yet wilder." The clothes compliment the cigarette. The cigarette compliments the clothes.

These types of tie-in arrangements could prove to be a natural for print media. Directly associating cigarettes with products and services which do not involve health considerations

might well comprise an unfair trade practice since the hazards of cigarette smoking through these tie-ins are rendered inconsequential or non-existent.

In still another media, a United States Lawn Tennis Association tournament took place in Houston this September. Its name—Virginia Slims. Women players were featured at the tournament. The identity of the cigarette with the sport seems implicit.

Point of purchase devices use terminology urging the shopper not to leave before purchasing a brand of cigarettes. These pleas can be of no help to persons looking for support to shake the smoking habit or not to begin. What better than impulse buying of cigarettes? These appeals contain no tar and nicotine information which might at least guide some purchasers in their choice of brand.

CIGARETTE LABELING

More than ever, the package is becoming a form of advertising. Colorful, pictorial representations wrap around the package itself creating an aura and image clearly in conflict with the warning on the side panel. The warning tends to become lost or at least insignificant.

The Chesterfield Menthol pack is covered by a picture of a babbling brook running through a beautiful green forest—a couple is seen relaxing and smoking. Chesterfield 101 shows a beautiful golden sunrise with a couple on a sailboat in calm waters enveloped by the sun. Chesterfield King Size Filters portrays a couple on horseback riding contentedly in reddish warmth of dusk passing a beautiful overhanging tree.

The appeal of bright red fall foliage is the setting for a couple walking arm and arm through the woods on the L & M Filter Kings pack. L & M Filter 100's takes advantage of rustic fall foliage reflecting in a crystal clear lake which bubbles over a waterfall as a couple looks on. The L & M Menthol pack shows the couple standing on a rock as beautiful, blue water swirls by with green trees overhanging in the foreground and as background.

The types of representations on the Chesterfield and L & M packs clearly suggest moods conducive to relaxing, unwinding, and enjoying. All tension, anxiety and frustration are absent. The cigarette is portrayed as one of the vital dimensions which exist between male and female.

Other cigarette labels, such as Lark and Doral, employ graphic filter diagrams; or, as True, portray the filter prominently conveying an aseptic, space age technology feeling. The Multifilter label uses two circular designs graphically symbolizing the protection features of its filter.

Failure of the Commission to make known its enforcement policy with respect to promotional representations on cigarette packages allows manufacturers to use these packages to deceive and mislead the public.

ONE HUNDRED AND FIFTY MILLION DOLLARS TO PROMOTE CIGARETTES IN 1971

Cigarette advertisers have been rushing to introduce new brands prior to the legislative ban on radio and television commercials for cigarettes commencing January 2, 1971. According to an article in the September 16, 1970 Wall Street Journal, plans have been made for next year to more than triple the advertising budget for newspapers to a new high of $50 to $75 million; magazine advertising revenue will rise more than $10 million to a high of $40 million; billboard advertisements will triple to an approximate $6 million.

Later reports show even these figures to be too low. An October 16, 1970 Advertising Age article authoritatively projects outdoor ads in the $30 to $40 million range with Brown and Williamson alone spending $7 million in this medium for 1971. The same article projects magazines "far above $50 million."

Advertising Age the following week indicated that American Brands was seeking guaranteed positions (52 week, 5 day per week schedules) in newspapers to the tune of $15 to $30 million in small-space ads" with the deal hinging on "fixed position above the TV log." American clearly seeks to offset the loss of TV penetration.

The figures could well add up to $150 million used to promote cigarettes in non-broadcast media during 1971. It is quite obvious that cigarette manufacturers are dramatically increasing their budgets in these other media. In so doing, they are ignoring the pleas of Senators Moss and Magnuson, and of other members of the Senate Commerce Committee who worked so diligently to pass the 1969 Public Health Cigarette Smoking Act. The nature and volume of this promotion makes the third provision of the act pertaining to the responsibilities of the FTC all the more important. According to the Wall Street Journal of November 5, 1970 cigarette sales are "looking stronger lately," so much so that "some analysts predict per capita consumption will show a gain for 1970."

TAR AND NICOTINE CONTENT DISCLOSURE IN ADVERTISING

The Commission's statement of March 25, 1966 opened the way for tar and nicotine claims in advertising. The Commission clarified its enforcement policy with respect to such claims in two additional letters on October 25, 1967 and October 8, 1969. These actions clearly establish precedent for the Commission to issue statements covering its enforcement policies pertaining to the full range of potential deceptions and misrepresentations in cigarette advertising.

The proposed trade regulation rule requiring disclosure of tar and nicotine content in all cigarette advertising does not deal with what is being said and shown in the ads and on the packages. Such disclosure, prominently made, is necessary to inform the public. Unfortunately its utility risks are being negated, diluted or rendered inconsequential in the absence of Commission action dealing with the themes and representations used to convey a positive, healthy image for cigarette smoking. Claims employing health benefits clearly must be delimited to those relating to tar and nicotine levels—at least until such time as medical science clearly recognizes other aspects of smoking as being important to the health of the smoker.

THEMES AND REPRESENTATIONS REQUIRING ISSUANCE OF ENFORCEMENT POLICIES

This petition is to request the Commission to set forth its enforcement policies with respect to all themes and representations employed in cigarette advertising promotions and on packages which have the capacity to deceive or mislead the public particularly in matters which bear on the smoker's health. These themes and representations include but are not necessarily limited to the following:

(1) Effect of gases in cigarette smoke and attendant claims.

(2) Use of terms and descriptions identified with the public's concern over pollution and the environment.

(3) Promotion of filters including the use of descriptive devices, names and terms which state or imply unique or special benefits.

(4) Claims for the subjective quality of the smoke, e.g. mild, cool, light, smooth.

(5) Representations of satisfaction, including enjoyment, refreshment, quiet relaxation and uplift.

(6) Association of smoking with the latest "in" styles of dress, demeanor and surroundings.

(7) Relating the special qualities of femininity, rugged masculinity, individuality and overall physical attractiveness to smoking.

(8) Implications that romance and sexual attraction go hand in hand with smoking.

(9) Equating smoking with the beauties and serenity of nature, e.g. springtime, bubbling brooks, sunsets.

(10) Employing symbols and copy identified with popular causes related to youth.

(11) Tie-ins of smoking with fashions, or other products and services, which do not involve health considerations.

(12) Promotion of athletic and other sports activities, including identifying the brand or company name with a sports event.

(13) Use of placards, counter cards, window decals and other devices directly urging people at point of purchase to buy a particular cigarette brand.

(14) Employing the package as promotion in a manner which distracts from or negates the impact of the required health warning, e.g. pic-

torial representations, cross-sectional and other filter depictions implying benefits other than those related to the level of tar and nicotine content.

MONITORING OF ANTI-CIGARETTE SMOKING MESSAGES

In its July 22, 1969, testimony before the Consumer Sub-Committee of the Senate Commerce Committee, the Commission committed itself to periodically reporting back to Congress on "the effectiveness of cigarette labeling, of anti-cigarette commercials, and of the voluntary discontinuance of television and radio advertising." The inclusion of anti-cigarette commercials is extremely pertinent in light of the Commission agreeing, and the 1969 Act stating, that it will take no action prior to July 1971 on its proposed trade regulation rule requiring a health warning in advertising.

Anti-smoking messages to be effective must receive extensive repeat exposure. A record as to the volume of this exposure must be accurate and readily available to facilitate determination of effectiveness. The responsibility for seeing that such a record exists falls with the Commission. This requires planning and setting up a monitoring program covering all media.

ALLOCATION OF RESOURCES AND STAFF INADEQUATE

For years now the Commission has failed to allocate sufficient resources and to assign adequate staff to handle cigarette advertising and promotions. In fact, not one attorney has been assigned to cigarettes full time throughout the year. Rather one or more staff members give part time attention to cigarettes with the number increasing at Report times.

The Commission cannot pretend to be effectively policing cigarette advertising and promotions until it assigns an adequate number of qualified staff members full time to the task; and until it establishes procedures which realistically are capable of carrying out meaningful and significant enforcement policies.

PROCEDURES SHOULD INCLUDE SUBMISSION OF ALL ADS AND PROMOTIONS

Copies of all ads, promotions and labeling should be submitted to the Commission staff simultaneously with the first publication or exposure date. They should be available for immediate public inspection. To facilitate such inspection, a copy of each item should be forwarded to the main FTC field offices throughout the country.

Documentation in support of any new product claims should accompany these ads and labels.

CONCLUSION

The Commission should promptly make public by January 2, 1971, its enforcement policies and implementing procedures. To serve the public interest, these should:

(1) Prescribe the permissible limits for cigarette advertising and promotions.

(2) Prescribe the permissible limits for representations on cigarette labeling.

(3) Establish procedures for the submission and review of all new cigarette advertising promotions and labels.

(4) Establish procedures for the

submission and review of documentation for all claims in advertising, promotions and on labeling.

(5) Establish a monitoring program of anti-cigarette smoking messages covering all media.

The Commission must place cig-arettes on a new level of priority commensurate with the awesome epidemic of death and overall public health problems attendant to cigarette smoking.

Respectfully submitted.

WARREN BRAREN.

part five

THE
DISENFRANCHISED

Social relationships are regulated by systems of norms that define appropriate behaviors and the acceptable personal characteristics for participating in various social activities. It is possible for individuals and groups to deviate from the norms to some degree without provoking negative reactions from community members; but some deviations, in either behavior or social identity, are not tolerated. Certain types of extreme behavior or unusual attributes may result in a denial of access to normal social relationships and in discrimination that limits opportunities, and may also occasion interpersonal responses that make the disenfranchised feel extremely uncomfortable, uneasy, and stigmatized. Feelings of stigma in the individual or group have important consequences for the totality of their social behavior.

If we were to ask social scientists to identify the single social characteristic that most sharply differentiates persons' responses to each other, neither social class nor age would be mentioned most frequently. Rather, the answer would be sex. The sex you are, the sexual practices in which you engage, and your legal status as a sex partner operate to place you in positions of advantage and disadvantage.

The articles in this section discuss the social conflicts faced by individuals and organizations because they are sexually unusual in behavior or status. The first three articles describe groups of individuals who, by their behavior, have rejected the norms regulating sexual conduct—homosexual men and divorced men and women. Even today, in our so-called sexually permissive and promiscuous milieu, such individuals are disenfranchised and limited in their social negotiations. The fourth article considers the problems faced by women in their struggle for occupational and social equality. Disenfranchisement because of being a woman, perhaps even more than being sexually unusual, is a persistent and pervasive problem.

INDIVIDUAL vs. INDIVIDUAL	INDIVIDUAL vs. ORGANIZATION

TEAROOM TRADE

Sexual activity between persons of the same or opposite sex is often surrounded by the mysticism of romantic love; at least, most persons in American communities like to think that it is only in such an atmosphere that orgasmic gratification can take place. We know this is hardly so in terms of relationships between prostitutes and their customers, or the way many couples, hetero- and homo-sexual, married and unmarried, behave. Humphreys, however, describes a setting for homosexual encounters that would be regarded by large numbers of individuals, no matter what their predispositions for sexual gratification are, as unusual, sterile and, while perhaps functional to the other aspects of their lives, not rewarding sexual experiences. In the description of these individuals one is struck with how organized and routinized such relationships are. At least some of them are each others' victims.

STRANGE COURTSHIP CUSTOMS OF THE FORMERLY MARRIED

Values on matters of family break-up and divorce have changed considerably over the last few decades. Today, divorce is not likely to affect the individual's job status or opportunities for participation in community affairs. In fact, it may not present even a serious barrier to one's chances for being elected President. The divorced person, however, bears a stigma in the community in regard to certain activities. Communities do not generally prescribe ways or places for divorced persons to develop heterosexual relationships, and consequently the means by which they meet dates and prospective mates are special ones. Hunt describes the unique relationship which develops between divorced persons who pursue courtship and romance. The interpersonal behavior between the parties involved is at least somewhat a result of their unusual marital status.

ORGANIZATION
vs.
INDIVIDUAL

ORGANIZATION
vs.
ORGANIZATION

WHAT IT MEANS TO BE A HOMOSEXUAL

Merle Miller is a distinguished man of letters who is well-off economically and has the opportunity to enjoy the recognition and social life of a well-regarded contributor to the arts and the world of entertainment. In this extremely sensitive article, Miller discusses what it means for him to be a homosexual. In many ways the changes in the legal codes and the lessening of strict enforcement of laws against homosexuals, as well as the greater tolerance of persons whose homosexual activities are confined to encounters with other homosexuals, have made the lot of persons like Miller much less difficult. Nevertheless, as his article recounts, like the adulterer of several centuries ago, he carries his reputation with him virtually wherever he goes. Needless to say, the very publication of this article increased the negative sanctions of straight society and the differential responses that are received by gay people, regardless of their other accomplishments.

'SISTERHOOD IS POWERFUL'

The development of strong group identification and militant collective actions have been a strategy of many minority groups in order to achieve recognition of their inequitable treatment and social change to improve their status. Women have used this tactic before, usually to achieve very specific goals, such as the right to vote. The woman's liberation movement, which began in the late sixties has broader objectives: namely, a struggle to achieve equity on a variety fronts—political, occupational, and social, using the term equity in the broadest sense. Brownmiller's article discusses the genesis of a New York Women's liberation group. She records some of the conflicts and struggles of this organization of women against the community, but she also describes some of the infighting, the splintering, the intra-organizational conflicts that inevitably accompany the development of a social movement. The various struggles within the movement slow down their accomplishments in conflicts with the larger community.

Tearoom Trade

LAUD HUMPHREYS

At shortly after five o'clock on a weekday evening, four men enter a public restroom in the city park. One wears a well-tailored business suit; another wears tennis shoes, shorts and teeshirt; the third man is still clad in the khaki uniform of his filling station; the last, a salesman, has loosened his tie and left his sports coat in the car. What has caused these men to leave the company of other homeward-bound commuters on the freeway? What common interest brings these men, with their divergent backgrounds, to this public facility?

They have come here not for the obvious reason, but in a search for "instant sex." Many men—married and unmarried, those with heterosexual identities and those whose self-image is a homosexual one—seek such impersonal sex, shunning involvement, desiring kicks without commitment. Whatever reasons—social, physiological or psychological—might be postulated for this search, the phenomenon of impersonal sex persists as a widespread but rarely studied form of human interaction.

There are several settings for this type of deviant activity—the balconies of movie theaters, automobiles, behind

bushes—but few offer the advantages for these men that public restrooms provide. "Tearooms," as these facilities are called in the language of the homosexual subculture, have several characteristics that make them attractive as locales for sexual encounters without involvement.

Like most other words in the homosexual vocabulary, the origin of *tearoom* is unknown. British slang has used "tea" to denote "urine." Another British usage is as a verb, meaning "to engage with, encounter, go in against." According to its most precise meaning in the argot, the only "true" tearoom is one that gains a reputation as a place where homosexual encounters occur. Presumably, any restroom could qualify for this distinction, but comparatively few are singled out at any one time. For instance, I have researched a metropolitan area with more than 90 public toilets in its parks, only 20 of which are in regular use as locales for sexual games. Restrooms thus designated join the company of automobiles and bathhouses as places for deviant sexual activity second only to private bedrooms in popularity. During certain seasons of the year—roughly, that period from April through October that midwestern homosexuals call "the hunting season"—tearooms may surpass any other locale of homoerotic enterprise in volume of activity.

Public restrooms are chosen by those who want homoerotic activity without commitment for a number of reasons. They are accessible, easily recognized by the initiate, and provide little public visibility. Tearooms thus offer the advantages of both public and private settings. They are available and recognizable enough to attract a large volume of potential sexual partners, providing an opportunity for rapid action with a variety of men. When added to the relative privacy of these settings, such features enhance the impersonality of the sheltered interaction.

In the first place, tearooms are readily accessible to the male population. They may be located in any sort of public gathering place: department stores, bus stations, libraries, hotels, YMCAs or courthouses. In keeping with the drive-in craze of American society, however, the more popular facilities are those readily accessible to the roadways. The restrooms of public parks and beaches—and more recently the rest stops set at programmed intervals along superhighways—are now attracting the clientele that, in a more pedestrian age, frequented great buildings of the inner cities. My research is focused on the activity that takes place in the restrooms of public parks, not only because (with some seasonal variation) they provide the most action but also because of other factors that make them suitable for sociological study.

There is a great deal of difference in the volumes of homosexual activity that these accommodations shelter. In some, one might wait for months before observing a deviant act (unless solitary masturbation is considered deviant). In others, the volume approaches orgiastic dimensions. One summer afternoon, for instance, I witnessed 20 acts of fellatio in the course of an hour while waiting out a thunderstorm in a tearoom. For one who wishes to participate in (or study) such activity, the primary consideration is finding where the action is.

Occasionally, tips about the more active places may be gained from unexpected sources. Early in my research, I was approached by a man (whom I later surmised to be a park patrolman in plain clothes) while waiting at the window of a tearoom for some patrons to arrive. After finishing his business at the urinal and exchanging some remarks about the weather (it had been raining), the man came abruptly to the point: "Look, fellow, if you're looking for sex, this isn't the place. We're clamping down on this park because of trouble with the niggers. Try the john at the northeast corner of [Reagan] Park. You'll find plenty of action there." He was right. Some of my best observations were made at the spot he recommended. In most cases, however, I could only enter, wait and watch—a method that was costly in both time and gasoline. After surveying a couple of dozen such rooms in this way, however, I became able to identify the more popular tearooms by observing certain physical evidence, the most obvious of which is the location of the facility. During the warm seasons, those restrooms that are isolated from other park facilities, such as administration buildings, shops, tennis courts, playgrounds and picnic areas, are the more popular for deviant activity. The most active tearooms studied were all isolated from recreational areas, cut off by drives or lakes from baseball diamonds and picnic tables.

I have chosen the term "purlieu" (with its ancient meaning of land severed from a royal forest by perambulation) to describe the immediate environs best suited to the tearoom trade. Drives and walks that separate a public toilet from the rest of the park are almost certain guides to deviant sex. The ideal setting for homosexual activity is a tearoom situated on an island of grass, with roads close by on every side. The getaway car is just a few steps away; children are not apt to wander over from the playground; no one can surprise the participants by walking in from the woods or from over a hill; it is not likely that straight people will stop there. According to my observations, the women's side of these buildings is seldom used at all.

WHAT THEY WANT, WHEN THEY WANT IT

The availability of facilities they can recognize attracts a great number of men who wish, for whatever reason, to engage in impersonal homoerotic activity. Simple observation is enough to guide these participants, the researcher and, perhaps, the police to active tearooms. It is much more difficult to make an accurate appraisal of the proportion of the male population who engage in such activity over a representative length of time. Even with good sampling procedures, a large staff of assistants would be needed to make the observations necessary for an adequate census of this mobile population. All that may be said with some degree of certainty

is that the percentage of the male population who participate in tearoom sex in the United States is somewhat less than the 16 percent of the adult white male population Kinsey found to have "at least as much of the homosexual as the heterosexual in their histories."

Participants assure me that it is not uncommon in tearooms for one man to fellate as many as ten others in a day. I have personally watched a fellator take on three men in succession in a half hour of observation. One respondent, who has cooperated with the researcher in a number of taped interviews, claims to average three men each day during the busy season.

I have seen some waiting turn for this type of service. Leaving one such scene on a warm September Saturday, I remarked to a man who left close behind me: "Kind of crowded in there, isn't it?" "Hell, yes," he answered, "It's getting so you have to take a number and wait in line in these places!"

There are many who frequent the same facility repeatedly. Men will come to be known as regular, even daily, participants, stopping off at the same tearoom on the way to or from work. One physician in his late fifties was so punctual in his appearance at a particular restroom that I began to look forward to our daily chats. This robust, affable respondent said he had stopped at this tearoom every evening of the week (except Wednesday, his day off) for years "for a blow-job." Another respondent, a salesman whose schedule is flexible, may "make the scene" more than once a day—usually at his favorite men's room. At the time of our formal interview, this man claimed to have had four orgasms in the past 24 hours.

According to participants I have interviewed, those who are looking for impersonal sex in tearooms are relatively certain of finding the sort of partner they want. . . .

You go into the tearoom. You can pick up some really nice things in there. Again, it is a matter of sex real quick; and, if you like this kind, fine—you've got it. You get one and he is done; and, before long, you've got another one.

. . . . and when they want it:

Well, I go there; and you can always find someone to suck your cock, morning, noon or night. I know lots of guys who stop by there on their way to work—and all during the day.

It is this sort of volume and variety that keeps the tearooms viable as market places of the one-night-stand variety.

Of the bar crowd in gay (homosexual) society, only a small percentage would be found in park restrooms. But this more overt, gay bar clientele constitutes a minor part of those in any American city who follow a predominantly homosexual pattern. The so-called closet queens and other types of covert deviants make up the vast majority of those who engage in homosexual acts—and these are the persons most attracted to tearoom encounters.

Tearooms are popular, not because they serve as gathering places for homosexuals but because they attract a variety of men, a *minority* of whom are active in the homosexual subculture and a large group of whom have no homosexual self-identity. For various reasons, they do not want to be seen with those who might be identified as such or to become involved with them on a "social" basis.

SHELTERING SILENCE

There is another aspect of the tearoom encounters that is crucial. I refer to the silence of the interaction.

Throughout most homosexual encounters in public restrooms, nothing is spoken. One may spend many hours in these buildings and witness dozens of sexual acts without hearing a word. Of 50 encounters on which I made extensive notes, only in 15 was any word spoken. Two were encounters in which I sought to ease the strain of legitimizing myself as lookout by saying, "You go ahead—I'll watch." Four were whispered remarks between sexual partners, such as, "Not so hard!" or "Thanks." One was an exchange of greetings between friends.

The other eight verbal exchanges were in full voice and more extensive, but they reflected an attendant circumstance that was exceptional. When a group of us were locked in a restroom and attacked by several youths, we spoke for defense and out of fear. This event ruptured the reserve among us and resulted in a series of conversations among those who shared this adventure for several days afterward. Gradually, this sudden unity subsided, and the encounters drifted back into silence.

Barring such unusual events, an occasionally whispered "thanks" at the conclusion of the act constitutes the bulk of even whispered communication. At first, I presumed that speech was avoided for fear of incrimination. The excuse that intentions have been misunderstood is much weaker when those proposals are expressed in words rather than signalled by body movements. As research progressed, however, it became evident that the privacy of silent interaction accomplishes much more than mere defense against exposure to a hostile world. Even when a careful lookout is maintaining the boundaries of an encounter against intrusion, the sexual participants tend to be silent. The mechanism of silence goes beyond satisfying the demand for privacy. Like all other characteristics of the tearoom setting, it serves to guarantee anonymity, to assure the impersonality of the sexual liaison.

Tearoom sex is distinctly less personal than any other form of sexual activity, with the single exception of solitary masturbation. What I mean by "less personal" is simply that there is less emotional and physical involvement in restroom fellatio—less, even, than in the furtive action that takes place in autos and behind bushes. In those instances, at least, there is generally some verbal involvement. Often, in tearoom stalls, the only portions of the players' bodies that touch are the mouth of the insertee and the penis of the insertor; and the mouths of these partners seldom open for speech.

Only a public place, such as a park restroom, could provide the lack of personal involvement in sex that certain men desire. The setting fosters the necessary turnover in participants by its accessibility and visibility to the "right" men. In these public settings, too, there exists a sort of democracy that is endemic to impersonal sex. Men of all racial, social, educational and physical characteristics meet in these places for sexual union. With the lack of involvement, personal preferences tend to be minimized.

If a person is going to entangle his body with another's in bed—or allow his mind to become involved with another mind—he will have certain standards of appearance, cleanliness, personality or age that the prospective partner must meet. Age, looks and other external variables are germane to the sexual action. As the amount of anticipated contact of body and mind in the sex act decreases, so do the standards expected of the partner. As one respondent told me:

I go to bed with gay people, too. But if I am going to bed with a gay person, I have certain standards that I prefer them to meet. And in the tearooms you don't have to worry about these things—because it is just a purely one-sided affair.

Participants may develop strong attachments to the settings of their adventures in impersonal sex. I have noted more than once that these men seem to acquire stronger sentimental attachments to the buildings in which they meet for sex than to the persons with whom they engage in it. One respondent tells the following story: We had been discussing the relative merits of various facilities, when I asked him: "Do you remember that old tearoom across from the park garage—the one they tore down last winter?"

Do I ever! That was the greatest place in the park. Do you know what my roommate did last Christmas, after they tore the place down? He took a wreath, sprayed it with black paint, and laid it on top of the snow—right where that corner stall had stood. . . . He was really broken up!

The walls and fixtures of these public facilities are provided by society at large, but much remains for the participants to provide for themselves. Silence in these settings is the product of years of interaction. It is a normative response to the demand for privacy without involvement, a rule that has been developed and taught. Except for solitary masturbation, sex necessitates joint action; but impersonal sex requires that this interaction be as unrevealing as possible.

PEOPLE NEXT DOOR

Tearoom activity attracts a large number of participants—enough to produce the majority of arrests for homosexual offenses in the United States. Now, employing data gained from both formal and informal interviews, we shall consider what these men are like away from the scenes of impersonal sex. "For some people," says Evelyn Hooker, an authority on male homosexuality, "the seeking of sexual contacts with other males is an activity isolated from all other aspects of their lives." Such segregation is apparent with most men who engage in the homosexual activity of public restrooms; but the degree and manner in which "deviant" is isolated from "normal" behavior in their lives will be seen to vary along social dimensions.

For the man who lives next door, the tearoom participant is just another neighbor—and probably a very good one at that. He may make a little more money than the next man and work a little harder for it. It is likely that he will drive a nicer car and maintain a neater yard than do other neighbors in the block. Maybe, like

some tearoom regulars, he will work with Boy Scouts in the evenings and spend much of his weekend at the church. It may be more surprising for the outsider to discover that most of these men are married.

Indeed, 54 percent of my research subjects are married and living with their wives. From the data at hand, there is no evidence that these unions are particularly unstable; nor does it appear that any of the wives are aware of their husbands' secret sexual activity. Indeed, the husbands choose public restrooms as sexual settings partly to avoid just such exposure. I see no reason to dispute the claim of a number of tearoom respondents that their preference for a form of concerted action that is fast and impersonal is largely predicated on a desire to protect their family relationships.

Superficial analysis of the data indicates that the maintenance of exemplary marriages—at least in appearance—is very important to the subjects of this study. In answering questions such as "When it comes to making decisions in your household, who generally makes them?" the participants indicate they are more apt to defer to their mates than are those in the control sample. They also indicate that they find it more important to "get along well" with their wives. In the open-ended questions regarding marital relationships, they tend to speak of them in more glowing terms.

TOM AND MYRA

This handsome couple live in ranch-style suburbia with their two young children. Tom is in his early thirties—an aggressive, muscular and virile-looking male. He works "about 75 hours a week" at his new job as a chemist. "I am *wild* about my job," he says. "I really love it!" Both of Tom's "really close" friends he met at work.

He is a Methodist and Myra a Roman Catholic, but each goes to his or her own church. Although he claims to have broad interests in life, they boil down to "games—sports like touch football or baseball."

When I asked him to tell me something about his family, Tom replied only in terms of their "good fortune" that things are not worse:

We've been fortunate that a religious problem has not occurred. We're fortunate in having two healthy children. We're fortunate that we decided to leave my last job. Being married has made me more stable.

They have been married for eleven years, and Myra is the older of the two. When asked who makes what kinds of decisions in his family, he said: "She makes most decisions about the family. She keeps the books. But I make the *major* decisions."

Myra does the household work and takes care of the children. Perceiving his main duties as those of "keeping the yard up" and "bringing home the bacon," Tom sees as his wife's only shortcoming "her lack of discipline in organization." He remarked: "She's very attractive ... has a fair amount of poise. The best thing is that she gets along well and is able to establish close relationships with other women."

Finally, when asked how he thinks his wife feels about him and his behavior in the family, Tom replied: "She'd like to have me around more —would like for me to have a closer relationship with her and the kids." He believes it is "very important" to

have the kind of sex life he needs. Reporting that he and Myra have intercourse about twice a month, he feels that his sexual needs are "adequately met" in his relationships with his wife. I also know that, from time to time, Tom has sex in the restrooms of a public park.

As an upwardly mobile man, Tom was added to the sample at a point of transition in his career as a tearoom participant. If Tom is like others who share working class origins, he may have learned of the tearoom as an economical means of achieving orgasm during his navy years. Of late, he has returned to the restrooms for occasional sexual "relief," since his wife, objecting to the use of birth control devices, has limited his conjugal outlets.

Tom still perceives his sexual needs in the symbolic terms of the class in which he was socialized: "about twice a month" is the frequency of intercourse generally reported by working class men; and, although they are reticent in reporting it, they do not perceive this frequency as adequate to meet their sexual needs, which they estimate are about the same as those felt by others of their age. My interviews indicate that such perceptions of sexual drive and satisfaction prevail among respondents of the lower-middle to upper-lower classes, whereas they are uncommon for those of the upper-middle and upper classes. Among the latter, the reported perception is of a much higher frequency of intercourse and they estimate their needs to be greater than those of "most other men."

AGING CRISIS

Not only is Tom moving into a social position that may cause him to reinterpret his sexual drive, he is also approaching a point of major crisis in his career as a tearoom participant. At the time when I observed him in an act of fellatio, he played the insertor role. Still relatively young and handsome, Tom finds himself sought out as "trade," i.e., those men who make themselves available for acts of fellatio but who, regarding themselves as "straight," refuse to reciprocate in the sexual act. Not only is that the role he expects to play in the tearoom encounters, it is the role others expect of him.

"I'm not toned up anymore," Tom complains. He is gaining weight around the middle and losing hair. As he moves past 35, Tom will face the aging crisis of the tearooms. Less and less frequently will he find himself the one sought out in these meetings. Presuming that he has been sufficiently reinforced to continue this form of sexual operation, he will be forced to seek other men. As trade he was not expected to reciprocate, but he will soon be increasingly expected to serve as insertee for those who have first taken that role for him.

In most cases, fellatio is a service performed by an older man upon a younger. In one encounter, for example, a man appearing to be around 40 was observed as insertee with a man in his twenties as insertor. A few minutes later, the man of 40 was being sucked by one in his fifties. Analyzing the estimated ages of the principal partners in 53 observed acts of fellatio, I arrived at these conclusions: the insertee was judged to be older than the insertor in 40 cases; they were approximately the same age in three; and the insertor was the older in ten instances. The age differences ranged from an insertee estimated to be 25 years older than his partner to an insertee thought to be ten years younger than his insertor.

Strong references to this crisis of aging are found in my interviews with cooperating respondents, one of whom had this to say:

Well, I started off as the straight young thing. Everyone wanted to suck my cock. I wouldn't have been caught dead with one of the things in my mouth!...So, here I am at 40—with grown kids—and the biggest cocksucker in [the city]!

Similar experiences were expressed, in more reserved language, by another man, some 15 years his senior:

I suppose I was around 35—or 36—when I started giving out blow jobs. It just got so I couldn't operate any other way in the park johns. I'd still rather have a good blow job any day, but I've gotten so I like it the way it is now.

Perhaps by now there is enough real knowledge abroad to have dispelled the idea that men who engage in homosexual acts may be typed by any consistency of performance in one or another sexual role. Undoubtedly, there are preferences: few persons are so adaptable, their conditioning so undifferentiated, that they fail to exercise choice between various sexual roles and positions. Such preferences, however, are learned, and sexual repertories tend to expand with time and experience. This study of restroom sex indicates that sexual roles within these encounters are far from stable. They are apt to change within an encounter, from one encounter to another, with age, and with the amount of exposure to influences from a sexually deviant subculture.

It is to this last factor that I should

like to direct the reader's attention. The degree of contact with a network of friends who share the actor's sexual interests takes a central position in mediating not only his preferences for sex role, but his style of adaptation to—and rationalization of—the deviant activity in which he participates. There are, however, two reasons why I have not classified research subjects in terms of their participation in the homosexual subculture. It is difficult to measure accurately the degree of such involvement; and such subcultural interaction depends upon other social variables, two of which are easily measured.

Family status has a definitive effect on the deviant careers of those whose concern is with controlling information about their sexual behavior. The married man who engages in homosexual activity must be much more cautious about his involvement in the subculture than his single counterpart. As a determinant of life style and sexual activity, marital status is also a determinant of the patterns of deviant adaptation and rationalization. Only those in my sample who were divorced or separated from their wives were difficult to categorize as either married or single. Those who had been married, however, showed a tendency to remain in friendship networks with married men. Three of the four were still limited in freedom by responsibilities for their children. For these reasons, I have included all men who were once married in the "married" categories.

The second determining variable is the relative autonomy of the respondent's occupation. A man is "independently" employed when his job allows him freedom of movement and security from being fired; the most

obvious example is self-employment. Occupational "dependence" leaves a man little freedom for engaging in disreputable activity. The sales manager or other executive of a business firm has greater freedom than the salesman or attorney who is employed in the lower echelons of a large industry or by the federal government. The sales representative whose territory is far removed from the home office has greater independence, in terms of information control, than the minister of a local congregation. The majority of those placed in both the married and unmarried categories with *dependent* occupations were employed by large industries or the government.

Median education levels and annual family incomes indicate that those with dependent occupations rank lower on the socioeconomic scale. Only in the case of married men, however, is this correlation between social class and occupational autonomy strongly supported by the ratings of these respondents on Warner's Index of Status Characteristics. Nearly all the married men with dependent occupations are of the upper-lower or lower-middle classes, whereas those with independent occupations are of the upper-middle or upper classes. For single men, the social class variable is neither so easily identifiable nor so clearly divided. Nearly all single men in the sample can be classified only as "vaguely middle class."

As occupational autonomy and marital status remain the most important dimensions along which participants may be ranked, we shall consider four general types of tearoom customers: 1) married men with dependent occupations, 2) married men with independent occupations, 3) unmarried men with independent occupations, and 4) unmarried men with dependent occupations. As will become evident with the discussion of each type, I have employed labels from the homosexual argot, along with pseudonyms, to designate each class of participants. This is done not only to facilitate reading but to emphasize that we are describing persons rather than merely "typical" constructs.

TYPE I: TRADE

The first classification, which includes 19 of the participants (38 percent), may be called "trade," since most would earn that appellation from the gay subculture. All of these men are, or have been, married—one was separated from his wife at the time of interviewing and another was divorced.

Most work as truck drivers, machine operators or clerical workers. There is a member of the armed forces, a carpenter, and the minister of a pentecostal church. Most of their wives work, at least part time, to help raise their median annual family income to $8,000. One in six of these men is black. All are normally masculine in appearance and mannerism. Although 14 have completed high school, there are only three college graduates among them, and five have had less than 12 years of schooling.

George is representative of this largest group of respondents. Born of second-generation German parentage in an ethnic enclave of the midwestern city where he still resides, he was raised as a Lutheran. He feels that his father (like George a truck driver) was quite warm in his relationship with him as a child. His mother he describes as a very nervous, asthmatic

woman and thinks that an older sister suffered a nervous breakdown some years ago, although she was never treated for it. Another sister and a brother have evidenced no emotional problems.

At the age of 20 he married a Roman Catholic girl and has since joined her church, although he classifies himself as "lapsed." In the 14 years of their marriage, they have had seven children, one of whom is less than a year old. George doesn't think they should have more children, but his wife objects to using any type of birth control other than the rhythm method. With his wife working part time as a waitress, they have an income of about $5,000.

"How often do you have intercourse with your wife?" I asked. "Not very much the last few years," he replied. "It's up to when she feels like giving it to me—which ain't very often. I never suggest it."

George was cooking hamburgers on an outdoor grill and enjoying a beer as I interviewed him. "Me, I like to come home," he asserted. "I love to take care of the outside of the house. ... Like to go places with the children—my wife, she doesn't."

With their mother at work, the children were running in and out of the door, revealing a household interior in gross disarray. George stopped to call one of the smaller youngsters out of the street in front of his modest, suburban home. When he resumed his remarks about his wife, there was more feeling in his description:

My wife doesn't have much outside interest. She doesn't like to go out or take the kids places. But she's an A-1 mother, I'll say that! I guess you'd say she's very nice to get along with—but don't cross her! She gets aggravated with me—I don't know why.... Well, you'd have to know my wife. We fight all the time. Anymore, it seems we just don't get along —except when we're apart. Mostly, we argue about the kids. She's afraid of having more.... She's afraid to have sex but doesn't believe in birth control. I'd just rather not be around her! I won't suggest having sex anyway—and she just doesn't want it anymore.

While more open than most in his acknowledgement of marital tension, George's appraisal of sexual relations in the marriage is typical of those respondents classified as Trade. In 63 percent of these marriages, the wife, husband or both are Roman Catholic. When answering questions about their sexual lives, a story much like George's emerged: at least since the birth of the last child, conjugal relations have been very rare.

These data suggest that, along with providing an excuse for diminishing intercourse with their wives, the religious teachings to which most of these familes adhere may cause the husbands to search for sex in the tearooms. Whatever the causes that turn them unsatisfied from the marriage bed, however, the alternate outlet must be quick, inexpensive and impersonal. Any personal, ongoing affair—any outlet requiring money or hours away from home—would threaten a marriage that is already shaky and jeopardize the most important thing these men possess, their standing as father of their children.

Around the turn of the century, before the vice squads moved in (in their never-ending process of narrowing the behavioral options of those in the lower classes), the Georges of this study would probably have made regular visits to the two-bit bordellos. With a madam watching a clock to limit the time, these cheap whorehouses provided the same sort of fast, impersonal service as today's public restrooms. I find no indication that these men seek homosexual contact as such; rather, they want a form of orgasm-producing action that is less lonely than masturbation and less involving than a love relationship. As the forces of social control deprive them of one outlet, they provide another. The newer form, it should be noted, is more stigmatizing than the previous one—thus giving "proof" to the adage that "the sinful are drawn ever deeper into perversity."

George was quite affable when interviewed on his home territory. A year before, when I first observed him in the tearoom of a park about three miles from his home, he was a far more cautious man. Situated at the window of the restroom, I saw him leave his old station wagon and, looking up and down the street, walk to the facility at a very fast pace. Once inside, he paced nervously from door to window until satisfied that I would serve as an adequate lookout. After playing the insertor role with a man who had waited in the stall farthest from the door, he left quickly, without wiping or washing his hands, and drove away toward the nearest exit from the park. In the tearoom he was a frightened man, engaging in furtive sex. In his own back yard, talking with an observer whom he failed to recognize, he was warm, open and apparently at ease.

Weighing 200 pounds or more, George has a protruding gut and tattoos on both forearms. Although muscular and in his mid-thirties, he would not be described as a handsome person. For him, no doubt, the aging crisis is also an identity crisis. Only with reluctance—and perhaps never—will he turn to the insertee role. The threat of such a role to his masculine self-image is too great. Like others of his class with whom I have had more extensive interviews, George may have learned that sexual game as a teen-age hustler, or else when serving in the army during the Korean war. In either case, his socialization into homosexual experience took place in a masculine world where it is permissible to accept money from a "queer" in return for carefully limited sexual favors. But to use one's own mouth as a substitute for the female organ, or even to express enjoyment of the action, is taboo in the Trade code.

Moreover, for men of George's occupational and marital status, there is no network of friends engaged in tearoom activity to help them adapt to the changes aging will bring. I found no evidence of friendship networks among respondents of this type, who enter and leave the restrooms alone, avoiding conversation while within. Marginal to both the heterosexual and homosexual worlds, these men shun involvement in any form of gay subculture. Type I participants report fewer friends of any sort than do those of other classes. When asked how many close friends he has, George answered: "None. I haven't got time for that."

It is difficult to interview the Trade without becoming depressed over the hopelessness of their situation. They are almost uniformly lonely and isolated: lacking success in either marriage bed or work, unable to discuss

their three best friends (because they don't have three); en route from the din of factories to the clamor of children, they slip off the freeways for a few moments of impersonal sex in a toilet stall.

Such unrewarded existence is reflected in the portrait of another marginal man. A jobless Negro, he earns only contempt and sexual rejection from his working wife in return for baby-sitting duties. The paperback books and magazines scattered about his living room supported his comment that he reads a great deal to relieve boredom. (George seldom reads even the newspaper and has no hobbies to report.) No wonder that he urged me to stay for supper when my interview schedule was finished. "I really wish you'd stay awhile," he said. "I haven't talked to any one about myself in a hell of a long time!"

TYPE II: AMBISEXUALS

A very different picture emerges in the case of Dwight. As sales manager for a small manufacturing concern, he is in a position to hire men who share his sexual and other interests. Not only does he have a business associate or two who share his predilection for tearoom sex, he has been able to stretch chance meetings in the tearoom purlieu into long-lasting friendships. Once, after I had gained his confidence through repeated interviews, I asked him to name all the participants he knew. The names of five other Type II men in my sample were found in the list of nearly two dozen names he gave me.

Dwight, then, has social advantages in the public restrooms as well as in society at large. His annual income of

$16,000 helps in the achievement of these benefits, as does his marriage into a large and distinguished family and his education at a prestigious local college. From his restroom friends Dwight learns which tearooms in the city are popular and where the police are clamping down. He even knows which officers are looking for payoffs and how much they expect to be paid. It is of even greater importance that his attitudes toward—and perceptions of—the tearoom encounters are shaped and reinforced by the friendship network in which he participates.

It has thus been easier for Dwight to meet the changing demands of the aging crisis. He knows others who lost no self-respect when they began "going down" on their sexual partners, and they have helped him learn to enjoy the involvement of oral membranes in impersonal sex. As Tom, too, moves into this class of participants, he can be expected to learn how to rationalize the switch in sexual roles necessitated by the loss of youthful good looks. He will cease thinking of the insertee role as threatening to his masculinity. His socialization into the Ambisexuals will make the orgasm but one of a number of kicks.

Three-fourths of the married participants with independent occupations were observed, at one time or another, participating as insertees in fellatio, compared to only one-third of the Trade. Not only do the Type II participants tend to switch roles with greater facility, they seem inclined to search beyond the tearooms for more exotic forms of sexual experience. Dwight, along with others in his class, expresses a liking for anal intercourse (both as insertee and insertor), for group activity, and even for mild forms of sadomasochistic sex.

A friend of his once invited me to an "orgy" he had planned in an apartment he maintains for sexual purposes. Another friend, a social and commercial leader of the community, told me that he enjoys having men urinate in his mouth between acts of fellatio.

Dwight is in his early forties and has two sons in high school. The school-bound offspring provide him with an excuse to leave his wife at home during frequent business trips across the country. Maintaining a list of gay contacts, Dwight is able to engage wholeheartedly in the life of the homosexual subculture in other cities—the sort of involvement he is careful to avoid at home. In the parks or over cocktails, he amuses his friends with lengthy accounts of these adventures.

Dwight recounts his first sexual relationship with another boy at the age of "nine or ten":

My parents always sent me off to camp in the summer, and it was there that I had my sexual initiation. This sort of thing usually took the form of rolling around in a bunk together and ended in our jacking each other off. . . . I suppose I started pretty early. God, I was almost in college before I had my first woman! I always had some other guy on the string in prep school—some real romances there! But I made up for lost time with the girls during my college years. . . . During that time, I only slipped back into my old habits a couple of times—and then it was a once-only occurrence with a roommate after we had been drinking.

Culminating an active heterosexual life at the university, Dwight married the girl he had impregnated. He reports having intercourse three or four times a week with her throughout their 18 married years but also admits to supplementing that activity on occasion: "I had the seven-year-itch and stepped out on her quite a bit then." Dwight also visits the tearooms almost daily:

I guess you might say I'm pretty highly sexed [he chuckled a little], but I really don't think that's why I go to tearooms. That's really not sex. Sex is something I have with my wife in bed. It's not as if I were committing adultery by getting my rocks off—or going down on some guy—in a tearoom. I get a kick out of it. Some of my friends go out for handball. I'd rather cruise the park. Does that sound perverse to you?

Dwight's openness in dealing with the more sensitive areas of his biography was typical of upper-middle and upper-class respondents of both the participant and control samples. Actual refusals of interviews came almost entirely from lower-class participants; more of the cooperating respondents were of the upper socioeconomic ranks. In the same vein, working-class respondents were most cautious about answering questions pertaining to their income and their social and political views.

Other researchers have encountered a similar response differential along class lines, and I realize that my educational and social characteristics encourage rapport with Dwight more than with George. It may also be assumed that sympathy with survey research increases with education. Two-thirds of the married participants with occupational independence are college graduates.

It has been suggested, however, that another factor may be operative in this instance: although the upper-class deviants may have more to lose from exposure (in the sense that the

mighty have farther to fall), they also have more means at their disposal with which to protect their moral histories. Some need only tap their spending money to pay off a member of the vice squad. In other instances, social contacts with police commissioners or newspaper publishers make it possible to squelch either record or publicity of an arrest. One respondent has made substantial contributions to a police charity fund, while another hired private detectives to track down a blackmailer. Not least in their capacity to cover for errors in judgment is the fact that their word has the backing of economic and social influence. Evidence must be strong to prosecute a man who can hire the best attorneys. Lower-class men are rightfully more suspicious, for they have fewer resources with which to defend themselves if exposed.

This does not mean that Type II participants are immune to the risks of the game but simply that they are bidding from strength. To them, the risks of arrest, exposure, blackmail or physical assault contribute to the excitement quotient. It is not unusual for them to speak of cruising as an adventure, in contrast with the Trade, who engage in a furtive search for sexual relief. On the whole, then, the action of Type II respondents is apt to be somewhat bolder and their search for "kicks" less inhibited than that of most other types of participants.

Dwight is not fleeing from an unhappy home life or sexless marriage to the encounters in the parks. He expresses great devotion to his wife and children: "They're my whole life," he exclaims. All evidence indicates that, as father, citizen, businessman and church member, Dwight's behavior patterns—as viewed by his peers—are exemplary.

Five of the 12 participants in Dwight's class are members of the Episcopal church. Dwight is one of two who were raised in that church, although he is not as active a churchman as some who became Episcopalians later in life. In spite of his infrequent attendance to worship, he feels his church is "just right" for him and needs no changing. Its tradition and ceremony are intellectually and esthetically pleasing to him. Its liberal outlook on questions of morality round out a religious orientation that he finds generally supportive.

In an interview witnessed by a friend he had brought to meet me, Dwight discussed his relationship with his parents: "Father ignored me. He just never said anything to me. I don't think he ever knew I existed." [His father was an attorney, esteemed beyond the city of Dwight's birth, who died while his only son was yet in his teens.] "I hope I'm a better father to my boys than he was to me," Dwight added.

"But his mother is a remarkable woman," the friend interjected, "really one of the most fabulous women I've met! Dwight took me back to meet her—years ago, when we were lovers of a sort. I still look forward to her visits."

"She's remarkable just to have put up with me," Dwight added:

Just to give you an idea, one vacation I brought another boy home from school with me. She walked into the bedroom one morning and caught us bare-assed in a 69 position. She just excused herself and backed out of the room. Later, when we were alone, she just looked at me—over the edge of her glasses—and said:

"I'm not going to lecture you, dear, but I do hope you don't swallow that stuff!"

Although he has never had a nervous breakdown, Dwight takes "an occasional antidepressant" because of his "moodiness." "I'm really quite moody, and I go to the tearooms more often when my spirits are low." While his periods of depression may result in increased tearoom activity, his deviant behavior does not seem to produce much tension in his life:

I don't feel guilty about my little sexual games in the park. I'm not some sort of sick queer.... You might think I live two lives; but, if I do, I don't feel split in two by them.

Unlike the Trade, Type II participants recognize their homosexual activity as indicative of their own psychosexual orientations. They think of themselves as bisexual or ambisexual and have intellectualized their deviant tendencies in terms of the pseudopsychology of the popular press. They speak often of the great men of history, as well as of certain movie stars and others of contemporary fame, who are also "AC/DC." Erving Goffman has remarked that stigmatized Americans "tend to live in a literarily-defined world." This is nowhere truer than of the subculturally oriented participants of this study. Not only do they read a great deal about homosexuality, they discuss it within their network of friends. For the Dwights there is subcultural support that enables them to integrate their deviance with the remainder of their lives, while maintaining control over the information that could discredit their whole being. For these reasons they look upon the gaming encounters in the parks as enjoyable experiences.

TYPE III: GAY GUYS

Like the Ambisexuals, unmarried respondents with independent occupations are locked into a strong subculture, a community that provides them with knowledge about the tearooms and reinforcement in their particular brand of deviant activity. This open participation in the gay community distinguishes these single men from the larger group of unmarrieds with dependent occupations. These men take the homosexual role of our society, and are thus the most truly "gay" of all participant types. Except for Tim, who was recruited as a decoy in the tearooms by the vice squad of a police department, Type III participants learned the strategies of the tearooms through friends already experienced in this branch of the sexual market.

Typical of this group is Ricky, a 24-year-old university student whose older male lover supports him. Ricky stands at the median age of his type, who range from 19 to 50 years. Half of them are college graduates and all but one other are at least part-time students, a characteristic that explains their low median income of $3,000. Because Ricky's lover is a good provider, he is comfortably situated in a midtown apartment, a more pleasant residence than most of his friends enjoy.

Ricky is a thin, good-looking young man with certain movements and manners of speech that might be termed effeminate. He is careful of his appearance, dresses well, and keeps an immaculate apartment, furnished with an expensive stereo and some tasteful antique pieces. Seated on a sofa in the midst of the things his lover has provided for their mutual comfort, Ricky is impressively self-assured. He is proud to say that he has found, at least for the time being, what all those participants in his category claim to seek: a "permanent" love relationship.

Having met his lover in a park, Ricky returns there only when his mate is on a business trip or their relationship is strained. Then Ricky becomes, as he puts it, "horny," and he goes to the park to study, cruise and engage in tearoom sex:

The bars are o.k.—but a little too public for a "married" man like me.... Tearooms are just another kind of action, and they do quite well when nothing better is available.

Like other Type III respondents, he shows little preference in sexual roles. "It depends on the other guy," Ricky says, "and whether I like his looks or not. Some men I'd crawl across the street on my knees for—others I wouldn't piss on!" His aging crisis will be shared with all others in the gay world. It will take the nightmarish form of waning attractiveness and the search for a permanent lover to fill his later years, but it will have no direct relationship with the tearoom roles. Because of his socialization in the homosexual society, taking the insertee role is neither traumatic for him nor related to aging.

Ricky's life revolves around his sexual deviance in a way that is not true of George or even of Dwight.

Most of his friends and social contacts are connected with the homosexual subculture. His attitudes toward and rationalization of his sexual behavior are largely gained from this wide circle of friends. The gay men claim to have more close friends than do any other type of control or participant respondents. As frequency of orgasm is reported, this class also has more sex than any other group sampled, averaging 2.5 acts per week. They seem relatively satisfied with this aspect of their lives and regard their sexual drive as normal—although Ricky perceives his sexual needs as less than most.

One of his tearoom friends has recently married a woman, but Ricky has no intention of following his example. Another of his type, asked about marriage, said: "I prefer men, but I would make a good *wife* for the right *man.*"

The vocabulary of heterosexual marriage is commonly used by those of Ricky's type. They speak of "marrying" the men they love and want to "settle down in a nice home." In a surprising number of cases, they take their lovers "home to meet mother." This act, like the exchange of "pinky rings," is intended to provide social strength to the lovers' union.

Three of the seven persons of this type were adopted—Ricky at the age of six months. Ricky told me that his adoptive father, who died three years before our interview, was "very warm and loving. He worked hard for a living, and we moved a lot." He is still close to his adoptive mother, who knows of his sexual deviance and treats his lover "like an older son."

Ricky hopes to be a writer, an occupation that would "allow me the freedom to be myself. I have a religion [Unitarian] which allows me freedom, and I want a career which will do the same." This, again, is typical: all three of the Unitarians in the sample are Type III men, although none was raised in that faith; and their jobs are uniformly of the sort to which their sexual activity, if exposed, would present little threat.

Although these men correspond most closely to society's homosexual stereotype, they are least representative of the tearoom population, constituting only 14 percent of the participant sample. More than any other type, the Rickys seem at ease with their behavior in the sexual market, and their scarcity in the tearooms is indicative of this. They want personal sex—more permanent relationships—and the public restrooms are not where this is to be found.

That any of them patronize the tearooms at all is the result of incidental factors: they fear that open cruising in the more common homosexual market places of the baths and bars might disrupt a current love affair; or they drop in at a tearoom while waiting for a friend at one of the "watering places" where homosexuals congregate in the parks. They find the anonymity of the tearooms suitable for their purposes, but inviting enough to provide the primary setting for sexual activity.

TYPE IV: CLOSET QUEENS

Another dozen of the 50 participants interviewed may be classified as single deviants with dependent occupations, "closet queens" in homosexual slang. Again, the label may be applied to others who keep their deviance hidden, whether married or single, but the covert, unmarried men are most apt to earn this appellation. With them, we have moved full circle in our classifications, for they parallel the Trade in a number of ways:

1. They have few friends, only a minority of whom are involved in tearoom activity.
2. They tend to play the insertor role, at least until they confront the crisis of aging.
3. Half of them are Roman Catholic in religion.
4. Their median annual income is $6,000; and they work as teachers, postmen, salesmen, clerks—usually for large corporations or agencies.
5. Most of them have completed only high school, although there are a few exceptionally well-educated men in this group.
6. One in six is black.
7. Not only are they afraid of becoming involved in other forms of the sexual market, they share with the Trade a relatively furtive involvement in the tearoom encounters.

Arnold will be used as the typical case. Only 22, Arnold is well below the median age of this group; but in most other respects he is quite representative, particularly in regard to the psychological problems common to Type IV.

A routine interview with Arnold stretched to nearly three hours in the suburban apartment he shares with another single man. Currently employed as a hospital attendant, he has had trouble with job stability, usually because he finds the job unsatisfactory. He frequently is unoccupied.

Arnold. I hang around the park a lot when I don't have anything else to do. I guess I've always known about

the tearooms . . . so I just started going in there to get my rocks off. But I haven't gone since I caught my lover there in September. You get in the habit of going; but I don't think I'll start in again—unless I get too desperate.

Interviewer. Do you make the bar scene?

Arnold. Very seldom. My roommate and I go out together once in a while, but everybody there seems to think we're lovers. So I don't really operate in the bars. I really don't like gay people. They can be so damned bitchy! I really like women better than men—except for sex. There's a lot of the female in me, and I feel more comfortable with women than with men. I understand women and like to be with them. I'm really very close to my mother. The reason I don't live at home is because there are too many brothers and sisters living there. . . .

Interviewer. Is she still a devout Roman Catholic?

Arnold. Well, yes and no. She still goes to Mass some, but she and I go to seances together with a friend. I am studying astrology and talk it over with her quite a bit. I also analyze handwriting and read a lot about numerology. Mother knows I am gay and doesn't seem to mind. I don't think she really believes it though.

Arnold has a health problem: "heart attacks," which the doctor says are psychological and which take the form of "palpitations, dizziness, chest pain, shortness of breath and extreme weakness." These attacks, which began soon after his father's death from a coronary two years ago, make him feel as if he were "dying and turning cold." Tranquilizers were prescribed for him, "but I threw them out, because I don't like to become dependent on such things." He quoted a book on mental control of health that drugs are "unnecessary, if you have proper control."

He also connects these health problems with his resentment of his father, who was mentally ill.

Arnold. I don't understand his mental illness and have always blamed him for it. You might say that I have a father complex and, along with that, a security complex. Guess that's why I always run around with older men.

Interviewer. Were any of your brothers gay?

Arnold. Not that I know of. I used to have sex with the brother closest to my age when we were little kids. But he's married now, and I don't think he is gay at all. It's just that most of the kids I ran around with always jacked each other off or screwed each other in the ass. I just seemed to grow up with it. I can't remember a time when I didn't find men attractive. . . . I used to have terrible crushes on my gym teachers, but nothing sexual ever came of it. I just worshipped them, and wanted to be around them all the time. I had coitus with a woman when I was 16—she 22. After it was over, she asked me what I thought of it. I told her I would rather masturbate. Boy, was she pissed off! I've always liked older men. If they are under 30, I just couldn't be less interested. . . . Nearly all my lovers have been between 30 and 50. The trouble is that *they* always want sex—and sex isn't really what I want. I just want to be with them—to have them for friends. I guess it's part of my father complex. I just want to be loved by an older man.

Few of the Type IV participants share Arnold's preference for older men, although they report poorer childhood relationships with their fathers than do those of any other group. As is the case with Arnold's roommate, many closet queens seem to prefer teenage boys as sexual objects. This is one of the features that distinguishes them from all other participant types. Although scarce in tearooms, teenagers make themselves available for sexual activity in other places frequented by closet queens. A number of these men regularly cruise the streets where boys thumb rides each afternoon when school is over. One closet queen from my sample has been arrested for luring boys in their early teens to his home.

Interaction between these men and the youths they seek frequently results in the sort of scandal feared by the gay community. Newspaper reports of molestations usually contain clues of the closet queen style of adaptation on the part of such offenders. Those respondents whose lives had been threatened by teen-age toughs were generally of this type. One of the standard rules governing one-night-stand operations cautions against becoming involved with such "chicken." The frequent violation of this rule by closet queens may contribute to their general disrepute among the bar set of the homosexual subculture, where "closet queen" is a pejorative term.

One Type IV respondent, an alcoholic whose intense self-hatred seemed always about to overflow, told me one night over coffee of his loneliness and his endless search for someone to love:

I don't find it in the tearooms—although I go there because it's handy to my work. But I suppose the [hustler's hangout] is really my meat. I just want to love every one of those kids!

Later, this man was murdered by a teen-ager he had picked up.

Arnold, too, expressed loneliness and the need for someone to talk with. "When I can really sit down and talk to someone else," he said, "I begin to feel real again. I lose that constant fear of mine—that sensation that I'm dying."

STYLES OF DEVIANT ADAPTATION

Social isolation is characteristic of Type IV participants. Generally, it is more severe even than that encountered among the Trade, most of whom enjoy at least a vestigial family life. Although painfully aware of their homosexual orientations, these men find little solace in association with others who share their deviant interests. Fearing exposure, arrest, the stigmatization that might result from a participation in the homosexual subculture, they are driven to a desperate, lone-wolf sort of activity that may prove most dangerous to themselves and the rest of society. Although it is tempting to look for psychological explanations of their apparent preference for chicken, the sociological ones are evident. They resort to the more dangerous game because of a lack of both the normative restraints and adult markets that prevail in the more overt subculture. To them, the costs (financial and otherwise) of operating among street corner youths are more acceptable than those of active participation in the gay subculture. Only the tearooms provide a less expensive alternative for the closet queens.

I have tried to make it impossible for any close associate to recognize the real people behind the disguised composites portrayed in this article. But I have worked equally hard to enable a number of tearoom players to see themselves in the portrait of George, and others to find their own stories in those of Dwight, Ricky or Arnold. If I am accurate, the real Tom will wonder whether he is trade or ambisexual; and a few others will be able to identify only partly with Arnold or Ricky.

My one certainty is that there is no single composite with whom all may identify. It should now be evident that, like other next door neighbors, the participants in tearoom sex are of no one type. They vary along a number of possible continua of social characteristics. They differ widely in terms of sexual career and activity, and even in terms of what that behavior means to them or what sort of needs it may fulfill. Acting in response to a variety of pressures toward deviance (some of which we may never ascertain), their adaptations follow a number of lines of least resistance.

In delineating styles of adaptation, I do not intend to imply that these men are faced with an array of styles from which they may pick one or even a combination. No man's freedom is that great. They have been able to choose only among the limited options offered them by society. These sets of alternatives, which determine the modes of adaptation to deviant pressures, are defined and allocated in accordance with major sociological variables: occupation, marital status, age, race, amount of education. That is one meaning of social probability.

THE SOCIOLOGIST AS VOYEUR

The methods employed in this study of men who engage in restroom sex are the outgrowth of three ethical assumptions: First, I do not believe the social scientist should ever ignore or avoid an area of research simply because it is difficult or socially sensitive. Second, he should approach any aspect of human behavior with those means that least distort the observed phenomena. Third, he must protect respondents from harm—regardless of what such protection may cost the researcher.

Because the majority of arrests on homosexual charges in the United States result from encounters in public restrooms, I felt this form of sexual behavior to provide a legitimate, even essential, topic for sociological investigation. In our society the social control forces, not the criminologist, determine what the latter shall study.

Following this decision, the question is one of choosing research methods which permit the investigator to achieve maximum fidelity to the world he is studying. I believe ethnographic methods are the only truly empirical ones for the social scientist. When human behavior is being examined, systematic observation is essential; so I had to become a participant-observer of furtive, felonious acts.

Fortunately, the very fear and suspicion of tearoom participants produces a mechanism that makes such observation possible: a third man (generally one who obtains voyeuristic pleasure from his duties) serves as a lookout, moving back and forth from door to windows. Such a "watch-queen," as he is labeled in the homosexual argot, coughs when a police car stops nearby or when a stranger approaches. He nods affirmatively when he recognizes a man entering as being a "regular." Having been taught the watchqueen role by a cooperating respondent, I played that part faithfully while observing hundreds of acts of fellatio. After developing a systematic observation sheet, I recorded fifty of these encounters (involving 53 sexual acts) in great detail. These records were compared with another 30 made by a cooperating respondent who was himself a sexual participant. The bulk of information presented in *Tearoom Trade* results from these observations.

Although primarily interested in the stigmatized behavior, I also wanted to know about the men who take such risks for a few moments of impersonal sex. I was able to engage a number of participants in conversation outside the restrooms; and, eventually, by revealing the purpose of my study to them, I gained a dozen respondents who contributed hundreds of hours of interview time. This sample I knew to be biased in favor of the more outgoing and better educated of the tearoom population.

To overcome this bias, I cut short a number of my observations of encounters and hurried to my automobile. There, with the help of a tape recorder, I noted a brief description of each participant, his sexual role in the encounter just observed, his license number and a brief description of his car. I varied such records from park to park and to correspond with previously observed changes in volume at various times of the day. This provided me with a time-and-place-representative sample of 134 participants. With attrition, chiefly of those who had changed address or who drove rented cars, and the addition of two persons who walked to the tearooms, I ended up with a sample of 100 men, each of whom I had actually observed engaging in fellatio.

At this stage, my third ethical concern impinged. I already knew that many of my respondents were married and that all were in a highly discreditable position and fearful of discovery. How could I approach these covert deviants for interviews? By passing as deviant, I had observed their sexual behavior without disturbing it. Now, I was faced with interviewing these men (often in the presence of their wives) without destroying them. Fortunately, I held another research job which placed me in the position of preparing the interview schedule for a social health survey of a random selection of male subjects throughout the community. With permission from the survey's directors, I could add my sample to the larger group (thus enhancing their anonymity) and interview them as part of the social health survey.

To overcome the danger of having a subject recognize me as a watchqueen, I changed my hair style, attire and automobile. At the risk of losing more transient respondents, I waited a year between the sample gathering and the interviews, during which time I took notes on their homes and neighborhoods and acquired data on them from the city and county directories.

Having randomized the sample, I completed 50 interviews with tearoom participants and added another 50 interviews from the social health survey sample. The latter control group was matched with the participants on the bases of marital status, race, job classification and area of residence.

This study, then, results from a confluence of strategies: systematic, firsthand observation, in-depth interviews with available respondents, the use of archival data, and structured interviews of a representative sample and a matched control group. At each level of research, I applied those measures which provided maximum protection for research subjects and the truest measurement of persons and behavior observed.

Strange Courtship Customs
of the Formerly Married

MORTON M. HUNT

What on earth is ailing Raymond Hartwell, Esq.? Three times today, his secretary entered his office and found him staring out of the window, lost in thought, a pile of briefs still unread in front of him. Two of those times, she asked him questions about documents he had dictated yesterday and was met with a blank look that yielded to comprehension only after some effort; the third time, he sharply told her to use the head God gave her and sent her off with eyes brimming over. This past hour, he has been thumbing through a little guidebook of some sort and making phone calls; between-times, he has played with paper clips, paced the floor in thought and stared at his reflection in the glass doors of the law-reports bookcase, frowning at the gray in his temples and the slight bulge at his waist. His twenty-four-year-old secretary assumes there is some weighty legal problem on his mind; but if she knew what was troubling him, her tears would give way to a fit of derisive giggles: Raymond Hartwell, Esq. (the name is

fictitious), is going out tonight on his first date as a formerly married man and, quite simply, he is nervous.

Yet it is nothing to laugh about. This momentous occasion was preceded by a great deal of anxiety, fear, hope and just plain effort, much of which centered about the problem of finding a suitable woman for his first postmarital adventure. Where did Raymond Hartwell find her?

A resident of the World of the Formerly Married (an "FM") is not likely, as we have seen, to find a prospective new partner through the good offices of his married friends, helpful as they may try to be. But the World of the Formerly Married offers the newcomer a number of other, and often more efficient, ways of finding and appraising potential partners. These range from the slightly unconventional to those that ignore middle-class proprieties. The majority of FMs are torn between their desire to use more effective ways of finding partners and a contrary desire to respect the rules of middle-class society; as a result, they favor methods with an acceptable façade concealing the fact that what they offer is a chance to shop around among strangers for new partners.

One such informal, pseudoconventional mechanism is the grapevine.

This is an invisible, spontaneous network of communication along which passes the news that such and such a desirable person is now available; the message results in phone calls and other approaches from persons not known to the FM being called but known to a mutual friend. This mention of a mutually known name is the nod to convention; when the man phones the woman, it reassures her and makes it acceptable for her to talk to a stranger; and when she phones the man, it gives her some flimsy pretext for phoning (she may say, for instance, that she is having open house the following week and had heard from their mutual friend So-and-So that he might be available).

At first, newcomers are astonished by the grapevine, and some view it sourly: "The men just seemed to appear like vultures. I couldn't get over it. It never occurred to me that men would give my name to other men all over the place, and I resented it." Other women either have no objection or learn to make the most of the situation. Men, though they are less apprehensive about such phone calls, are astonished to find women taking the initiative, even under the guise of legitimate business: "Somehow, the word got around that I was separated, and they just came zooming in on me. And this in a Southern town, too! I was amazed, but I soon got to like it. I've met quite a few women that way."

The grapevine is not only accepted as a windfall by some, but diligently cultivated. The newly separated person sometimes starts back in circulation by calling friends, both married and unmarried, and asking them to pass his or her name around. One is not usually this blunt with the married (though it is easy to be so with fellow FMs), but mentions in passing that he or she is starting to get around; or one may say something like, "Know anyone just right for me?"—adding a little chuckle as though it were only a joke, although none but a clod could misinterpret the message. But these obeisances to convention are being abandoned more and more. One veteran man of seven years' standing says that half a dozen years ago a middle-class FM woman would ask her friends if they knew a man for her and suggest that perhaps she could meet him at their place some evening, while nowadays many such women say merely, "If you know anyone I might like, please give him my name."

Such boldness and willingness to try new methods are increasingly common among FMs hunting for partners, even though they still cling to some shred of semiconcealing convention. How tiny that shred can become—and yet be retained—is indicated by an unusual communique from a divorcée in Scarsdale, New York: "The latest thing is for a girl to make up a list of men she's heard about or seen and send them invitations to a cocktail party she has no intention of giving. Then she phones each one a few days later to apologize and gives some reason for canceling. And if she's a good conversationalist, she can wind up with half a dozen different dates with new guys." Even if this particular contrivance is a local idiosyncrasy, it expresses the general need of FM women to take unusual and daring action because they are so much less free to initiate contacts openly.

A more familiar pseudoconventional

mechanism is the club or association that has some unimpeachable stated purpose but also, and more importantly, happens to serve as a market place for FMs.

Parents Without Partners is a fast-growing national organization, which now has 166 chapters and 18,500 members, with the stated purpose of enabling single parents "to learn better ways of helping themselves and their children cope with life in the one-parent or divided family."

Chapter presidents and membership directors of Parents Without Partners continually make public avowals such as this: "Now, bear in mind that we are *not* a marriage bureau and not basically a social club. It happens that we do socialize, but that's only incidental. We're here to help you adjust to life as single parents; we're here to make you better and stronger than when you walked in that door." Privately, however, the very officer who makes that pious statement concedes that the primary motive of nine tenths of the incoming members is to look for eligible partners.

The disinterested observer can recognize this at any monthly meeting. Before the meeting starts, men and women—most of them secretaries, teachers and housewives or salesmen, businessmen and lower-echelon executives—drift into the rented auditorium in somewhat of a party mood: they mill about, talking, laughing, searching, speculating, maneuvering themselves a little closer to someone who looks interesting. The chairman raps for order, but has great difficulty in getting everyone to sit down and be silent.

At last the meeting begins; there are the usual committee reports, an-nouncements of activities, followed by the speaker of the evening; but during all this, scores of eyes roam the room, necks crane, whispers rustle in the background. When the speech is over, applause is duly rendered and the meeting is adjourned for coffee and cookies. Now the real business of the meeting begins. Female faces don the bright, welcoming look, and male faces a studied indifference or an equally studied air of appraisal. Little groups form, disintegrate and re-form; wall-flowers stand immobilized around the margins or wander slowly about, trying to look as though they were going somewhere; the more daring men cut through the throng to speak to some woman they have spotted; the more daring women openly smile at some man they hope to interest; and those who are neither wallflowers nor daring talk to someone of their own sex, protecting each other against ioslation but keeping a lookout on all sides for any better possibility.

Yet perhaps that is only how it looks to one who has no personal stake in the goings-on. To those who do, the meetings, parties and dances may be a trifle bleak and somewhat competitive, but at least they do bring together large numbers of men and women who have the same basic problem.

Numerous other organizations and groupings exist whose stated aims have nothing to do with being a market-place for unattached adults; they thrive, nevertheless, because this is what they are. They run the gamut of literary discussion clubs, bowling leagues, bridge circles, skiing associations, summer-home groups (cooperative renters), tennis leagues, and the like. Any excuse for gathering the unmarried together will do; often the excuse itself is something worthwhile —an art-appreciation course, a health club, dancing instruction—but newcomers seldom return for a second or third visit if the people present are not eminently suitable as potential dates. Many such groups are ephemeral and last only very briefly; but others go on year after year, with a membership that changes continually except for a small, hard core of the intractably unmarriageable.

The pretext of some of these pseudo-conventional devices often becomes thin to the point of transparency— and still they are retained in order to save face. But the thinner the pretext and the more evident the real motive, the harder it is for some users to stomach, as one young divorcée makes plain: "I tried a Caribbean cruise last winter. It was a total waste of time and money—seventy-eight girls and eleven men. And what men, at that! My God, they were impossible! Either real drips or attractive enough but insufferably egotistical—as they could well afford to be. It was awful. We girls were just there to be picked over, and most of us ended up on the scrap heap."

The same situation prevails at those large resort hotels that attract mobs of unattached hopefuls on weekends, especially on advertised "singles weekends." Most women who go to such hotels seeking to meet men cannot help feeling almost naked under constant scrutiny; if they are continually passed by, their embarrassment is superseded by shame and depression. But it is not altogether a lark for the men, either; aside from a minority who are cheerfully predatory, many men are made uncomfortable by the continual appraisal or hopeful signaling of so many eyes and by their own fear of entrapment by some undesirable woman.

All this is probably true to a greater degree for FMs than for never-married people. The Formerly Married have lived for years in social tranquility, away from the turmoil and stress of open competition; it is unsettling to be thrust back into it and to see one's own needs so transparently mirrored on so many hopeful, over-eager faces. Most of the formerly married men and women who go to such resorts candidly say that they detest doing so, even though it sometimes proves useful.

A 53-year-old man is a case in point: "I avoided going to resort hotels for a long while, and when I finally tried, in a desperate period of my life, I found it very unpleasant. The congregation of women—the hungry, eager, slightly shopworn women—at those places seem to me terribly sad. It was a freak bit of luck that I found Audrey [his present wife] there."

A 34-year-old divorcée is even more vehement: "I hate being on the open market. It isn't fear of competition— I think I'm more attractive than most of the women at those places—but the men are so *awful* in their manner. They're all looking for something quick and easy and they think all the women are, too. It's really disgusting. But I go because how many legitimate ways are there to meet men anyhow? You have to try."

This willingness to take a chance is a key feature of the emergent philosophy of the Formerly Married. Though most are unable at first to tolerate any but the conventional means of seeking new partners, the inadequacy of those means and the permissiveness of the subculture cause many of them to adopt new and more venturesome methods and take chances they had not imagined they ever would.

The outstanding case is that familiar way of meeting new partners known as the pickup. Although it has long been casually accepted at the lower levels of society as a legitimate and natural way for male and female to meet, the middle class has always frowned on it. The "nice" girl is taught to shun it altogether; the "nice" boy, uneasy about it, is more likely to use it to seek a quick sexual encounter with a lower-class girl than to make the acquaintance of a girl he would like to date regularly.

This remains more or less true among unmarried adults; most pickups in public places are intended to result in a quick and uninvolved sexual connection rather than a serious relationship. But nowadays many middle-class FMs are borrowing the pickup technique in their search for suitable dates and potential love-partners.

"I've learned to keep my eyes open wherever I am," a 37-year-old woman says. "I now have no prejudice against any avenue of meeting. I even met a very fine man on a subway platform one time. You have a number of disappointments that way, and sometimes I am even frightened, but I feel I must take every chance. You never know when or where you'll meet someone."

More promising than the subway platform are the sites where the pickup is common procedure. Just as a favorite locus of the pickup among the lower class is the corner saloon, so among the middle class it is the cocktail lounge or bar, or at least those that have spontaneously become known as rendezvous for unattached adults.

Many a newly separated person, on first hearing about this, is startled at the thought of openly searching for a pickup date in public places. The first time he visits one of the pickup bars or watches the commerce on a busy beach, he may find the whole scene vulgar and cheap—a reaction which helps combat the alarming thought that maybe he ought to try it, too. But time, need and exposure to the customs of the subculture gradually make the pickup seem a less crass and distasteful procedure, even to female FMs, and fear of it diminishes with increasing experience of unconventional methods until the pickup is only the next and not very giant step.

The bar or restaurant, as a pickup site, is not totally outside the conventions; the very woman who will allow a strange man to talk to her in such a place might rebuff him if he tried to talk to her on the street. Even so, the bar or restaurant is used by only about one out of ten women and one out of six men, and then rather infrequently. For some reason, about twice as many of each sex feel that a pickup in a plane or train is acceptable. Like planes or trains, beaches, museums, libraries and business or professional conventions have their own small coteries of adherents.

Nevertheless, even some who grow accustomed to the pickup continue to dislike it and feel nervous about it. A slim, debonair, 40-year-old actor from Los Angeles explained his feelings: "During my years as a divorced man, I found that a much more productive way for me to meet new girls than through friends or at parties was to pick them up on the beach. I did so for years, but I always hated it. I always feared the possibility of being rejected and looking like a jackass. I had to force myself to do it."

Most women seem to accept the method grudgingly, out of sheer necessity. Says an attractive 32-year-old legal secretary from a medium-size city in the Southwest: "I thought it wouldn't be too easy to meet men. It turned out to be completely impossible. The people I know don't give parties with single people present, and I couldn't afford to go alone to public events. After nearly a year, I still have found no way other than going to a 'joint' alone where I can meet anyone. Pretty shocking for a girl raised as a good Baptist, isn't it?"

But surprisingly enough, some middle-class women actually come to accept the practice of pickups without misgivings. A successful writer of children's books, 37 years old and quite pretty, says: "One of the main surprises was pickups—conversations begun while walking, traveling, shopping, et cetera, which often turned out to produce some delightful dates. I think it's just a myth that this is not a 'nice' way of meeting people. One just has to be careful, that's all."

Basic to all the genuinely unconventional methods is their lack of pretense. There is, for example, a species of unconventional get-together that might be called the "open party"; there is no guest list, but by word of mouth all kinds of friends, acquaintances and strangers hear of it and come—the only requirement being that each man bring a bottle, the only purpose being to prospect for new partners.

Open parties vary greatly, but most are given by people with bohemian or shabbily furnished apartments (none with decent furnishings would risk it). While sometimes the guests may be well dressed and well-bred, more often they are either flashily or ill dressed, and most of them are manifestly undesirable in one way or another—physically, psychologically or socially. They are, by and large, the leftovers and discards of the dating-and-mating process.

Some open parties are run by individual proprietors, "friendship clubs" or nonprofit social organizations; they are open in the sense that the only impediments to entrance are a door fee and, sometimes, a suggested age bracket.

Such open parties—which usually take the form of dances, to make meeting and breaking away easier—have recently proliferated like Mayflies. In New York City on a typical winter weekend, roughly 150 public parties and dances are held, some being advertised in the papers and others by direct mail to "members" (anyone who pays a door admission, at most of these so-called clubs, becomes a mailing-list member). Here are excerpts from listings in one New York newspaper:

THE DIVORCED SET
Call_____
Sundays at 6 p.m.

Dance: The Second Quarter Club—a co-ed group of select singles, 25–40. Total contribution $1.25.

Lecture & Ladies Nite Dance, for singles 25–40. "Communication between the Sexes." by Dr. Irving Delugatch. Stan Kaye & His Orchestra. Adm. $1.75.

DOCTORS & TEACHERS, you are cordially invited to_____'s exclusive HOUSE PARTY, Friday 9 p.m., ages 21–36, Saturday 9 p.m., ages 23–37. Call _____for invit.

Previous Married People.
4 Select Socials.

Saturday	8 p.m.	ages 27–37
Sunday	3 p.m.	ages 25–40
Sunday	6 p.m.	ages 28–45
Sunday	9 p.m.	ages 30–50
	Call_____	

One can pick and choose, according to his own age, pocketbook and interests and according to his preference for dancing or talking, crowds or small groups, the intelligentsia or the hoi polloi.

But the idea is far from being special to New York; indeed, it originated in Milwaukee in the early 1930s with the first so-called "friendship club"—a public dance, with a modest admission charge (50 cents at that time; $1.50 to $3 today), where unattached people could meet. Public dance halls were nothing new, as far as lower-class people were concerned; what was new was the application of the idea on a lower-middle- and middle-class level in the guise of a "club." It quickly met a need of FMs and other unattached adults and spread from the Midwest to the West and the East.

If it is rather unconventional to pay a small fee to make an introduction unnecessary, it is far more unconventional to pay a larger fee to somebody to select a partner for one and arrange a meeting. Such an intermediary may call himself a marriage adviser, a matrimonial consultant or a social adviser, or label his business a date bureau, introduction service, friendship service or matrimonial agency; but no matter what euphemism he uses, he is practicing the ancient profession of the marriage broker or matchmaker. No one knows how many matchmakers there are in the United States; the most recent published figure dates back to 1951, when Dr. Clyde Vedder, a sociologist at the University of Florida, reported that there were 800 marriage brokers in this country. They have an active clientele of several hundred thousand, and probably about a quarter to a third of these are FMs.

Some matrimonial agencies are highly ethical, service-minded and devoted to the often substantiated proposition that widely dissimilar backgrounds in marriage partners spell trouble. The Scientific Marriage Foundation, a nonprofit organization based in Mellott, Indiana, was started by George W. Crane, a Chicago physician, and uses electronic sorting techniques to match prospective partners according to such things as age, education, race, religion, marital status, hobbies and habits.

According to Dr. Crane, it works beautifully. With an active clientele of about 50,000—each of whom pays $25 for the service—the foundation manages about 20,000 introductions each year, and Dr. Crane guesses that about a quarter of all the clients eventually marry as a result. It is too bad that there has been no study of the ratio of success to failure in these marriages; one would like to know whether the use of the machine produces more happiness than human beings have managed to achieve on their own.

Quite different in its approach but equally dedicated is a small agency in Los Angeles called Friends Finders Institute. Two sisters, Mrs. Marjorie Richmond and Miss Alice Thornton, both with some training in counseling, founded and operate the organization; they give their clients a good deal of individual personal attention and therefore restrict themselves to a total case load of some 350. Each applicant is interviewed for one or two hours, fills out detailed biographical-data sheets and takes a set of sociometric tests of tastes and attitudes. Mrs. Richmond and Miss Thornton then weigh the results, and having found two people seemingly compatible in most of their habits, likings and experiences, the sisters introduce them at one of the institute's socials and later do some premarital counseling with them if they become serious about each other.

Over a ten-year period, the institute has married off about ten per cent of the enrolled clients. Recently, however, the rate has gone far higher, due to a new policy of requiring a one-year enrollment, which costs $102; with this much time to work on a case, Mrs. Richmond and Miss Thornton married off nearly eighteen per cent of their enrollees in 1964. Forty-two per cent of all the clients who have gotten married through their services were divorced persons.

Marriage brokers or introduction services are looked on askance by most middle-class FMs and are thus a very small part of the present marketplace; but as the unconventional aspects of FM life become more and more acceptable and commonplace, it is quite possible that matchmakers or their modern equivalents will become a more important part of it. The subculture tolerates and even encourages a great deal of unconventionality in the search for partners, because any avenue by which the FM can hasten on the way to dating, courtship and remarriage is assumed to be the right road.

The resumption of dating is as difficult and filled with anxiety for the FM as are the first shaky steps a patient takes after a serious illness and prolonged confinement to bed. The very word "date" may make him wince: it sounds so juvenile, and so artificial. Dating implies behavior he thinks would look silly in him—dancing to records in the living room, going to the movies and a hamburger joint, necking in a parked car, grappling on a couch. Even getting dressed up, going out for a drink and dinner with someone new and making conversation for a couple of hours may, in advance, seem awkward, unnatural and mechanical.

Among other uncertainties, the man is unsure what sort of evening to offer the woman. He may think that dinner, dancing and a round of drinks are almost obligatory; but what with alimony and child support, he is reluctant to spend forty or fifty dollars merely to get acquainted. He may want to invite her just for a drink, as the veteran FM suggested, but is embarrassed to propose it, rightly feeling that his motives would be transparent and wrongly fearing that such an invitation would be unacceptable. He may want to suggest that they spend the evening quietly at her home, talking and playing music, but fears she would think him cheap. He may think of inviting her to come help him make dinner at his place, but wonders if she would take it to mean that he intended to play the wolf.

The woman as a beginner, is uncertain whether to accept a date for cocktails only or to be offended and refuse. But if she is invited to dinner, should she let him spend freely or show a kindly—and perhaps belittling—regard for his wallet? If she invites him to spend the evening at her place, will he assume he needn't ever take her anywhere? And if he wants her to go to his place, would her acceptance be construed as agreeing to seduction?

Once the FM actually starts dating, he rapidly finds there is great flexibility among the Formerly Married and that he can arrange the details of his dating in whatever way best suits his own personality, age, means and taste. The prevailing philosophy of the subculture, as he soon realizes, is thoroughly permissive. No one need consent to any suggestion he or she dislikes, but it is not impermissible for the other to have made it. If a man wants to invite a woman just for cocktails, it is not improper for him to do so. If he wants to have dinner with her and then go dancing, she, as the early-rising mother of schoolchildren, is perfectly within her rights to suggest a shorter evening. An invitation to his apartment is allowable and is possibly, but not necessarily, an advance notice of an attempt at seduction; an acceptance on her part is no guarantee that she will comply—although she well might. But in either case, there is nothing dreadful about his attempt or her refusal. The emotional needs of FMs are so imperious and their haste is so great that, short of misusing or damaging another person, almost nothing is disallowed.

If the FM woman has children, she has still other problems to solve when she begins to date. She must wrestle with the complexities of finding a reliable babysitter (she worries more about a sitter's reliability than she did when married), feeding the children, issuing instructions about homework and lights-out time, and getting herself ready in time. The children, if they are not infants, are bound to see her going out with a man, and she will have to explain it to them—but how?

If they are very young, she may get away with saying almost nothing ("A friend of ours is coming here tonight"); if they are a bit older, she may try a plea for sympathy ("Mommy needs to have some fun, too") or even appeal to their self-interest ("I'm going out with a gentleman because I'm trying to find a new daddy for you"); and if they are teenagers, she may make no explanation at all, but merely announce it casually at the breakfast table, hoping not to be questioned.

The reactions, especially from small children, can be disconcerting. One correspondent writes that although she had explained about her dating to her five-year-old son, he waited until the man arrived before firing off this barrage of questions: "Won't Daddy be angry? Can I go with you? Are you going to marry him? Is he sleeping here tonight?" Small children also sometimes stage last-minute rebellions, after Mother's date arrives, in the form of temper tantrums, throwing up or crying spells; older ones suddenly fight with each other or announce a crisis over a missing homework assignment that is due the next day; teenagers may unsettle their mother's nerves by acting sullen and churlish toward the new competitor for her attention or, conversely, competing with her for his attention. (One woman says that her buxom teen-age daughter put on her tightest sweater and openly flirted with the caller, thereby making the mother feel at the very outset like an old crone.)

If men do not have the special problem of resident children, they nevertheless share with women one other problem—stage fright, like that afflicting Raymond Hartwell, Esq. The anxiety before a first date is so strong as to produce diarrhea, hives and other disorders in some FMs and to make others phone at the last moment and cancel the date on some pretext. But the great majority, despite their deep discomfort, go through with it because they must—and because, too, they have a feeling of anticipation and hope. Three out of four FMs do begin dating within the first year, and over nine out of ten do so before the end of the second.

A minority of FMs have only indifferent or even distressing experiences when they first begin dating; but most FMs are surprised and pleased to find how communicative and outgoing they can be on a date.

They freely dwell on their own and the others' feelings with the unabashed self-absorption of adolescents. They may discuss neutral topics now and again, but gravitate automatically toward themselves and toward a comparison of attitudes and emotions about their state. After a while, perhaps, feeling perilously exposed, they veer off to some other topic—only to return soon, as if hypnotized, to the incomparably fascinating subject of themselves. Within the first half dozen dates, therefore, most FMs begin to see themselves as relatively open, communicative and responsive persons with social skills.

A 37-year-old woman was surprised at herself: "I realized, after dating awhile, that I am much more outgoing and warm than I had thought. I seem to inspire confidence. Men really open up to me, maybe because I offer so much of myself without guile."

A 40-year-old man who had avoided dating for a long while says "I found it very exciting that I could seem to interest almost any woman—that I could talk about myself in a way that almost always got through to them. At the same time, I found that I could draw almost any woman out and get her to open up and reveal herself. It was a revelation to me that I could do this. I'd hate to think of the total amount of money I spent in bars that first year charming the bejeezus out of dozens of different girls."

The exchange of biography between two people on a first date has a special fascination that most conversations between husband and wife cannot have. It is also true that what seems so fascinating and exciting at first may become burdensome and tedious after many a repetition.

A tart-tongued young advertising woman puts it this way: "I'm sick of the whole business of 'explaining myself to each new man on the first date or two. Sometimes I think I ought to make a résumé for them, listing my college, major subject, degree, favorite composers, favorite books, how long married, reasons for breaking up, favorite foods, attitudes toward sports, religion and sex. I could mimeo the whole thing and just shove it across the cocktail table. It would be a funny bit, but I don't really have the guts to do it."

But for most FMs the process of mutual exploration and discovery remains fascinating for a long while, and there is nothing they more urgently need to tell about than their own broken marriages. Sometimes they offer a superficial formula, but more often FMs are likely to talk about their experience in some depth —not necessarily with insight, but with bits and scraps of reminiscence that evoke sympathy and tenderness and convey the nature of their fears and what they hope to avoid in a new relationship.

A recently divorced man tells a new friend: "It's so good talking to you—after eleven years of living with someone I could hardly talk to. All that interested her was clothes and money and possessions. Every time I wanted to invite people over who were interested in books and ideas, she'd find some way to cancel the party, or she'd say she had a headache and stay upstairs the whole evening, and then be so furious that she wouldn't talk to me for a week."

A young divorcée says: "My parents can't understand why I left him, and I can't tell them. . . . Well, you tell me —you're a man. Do you think a man should insist on it even when his wife isn't in the mood? I mean, insist that she let him *use* her? I think sex is a beautiful thing—but when it was like that, it was so ugly I wanted to scream."

Such disclosures concerning the broken marriages can be viewed as a special form of courtship; they are nearly always meant to show the speaker as a fine, decent, wounded human being who deserves to be loved and has been wronged.

Behind all these complaints and confessions of one's recent agony is a plea: "Listen to my story and pity me, and that will make us love each other."

Among the Formerly Married, all this happens at a greatly accelerated pace; the result is what we might call "instant intimacy." Since instant intimacy requires a sense of kinship and a fund of common experience, many of the Formerly Married find that dating never-married or widowed people is far less satisfactory than

dating other FMs. Among the people I queried, fellow FMs were preferred as dates about two to one over the other two categories of unattached people combined; this preference was particularly marked among people in their upper thirties and older.

The formerly married man suspects that the never-married girl of thirty or more has deep emotional problems —fear of men, fear of sex, and so on. Even if this is not the case, or if she is younger, he finds that many of his most significant recent experiences are not particularly meaningful or interesting to her. He may talk about his children, or about married life, or about the strangeness of returning to single ways; but instead of responding with complete understanding, as a formerly married woman would, she listens and replies with obvious effort, as though he were speaking in a foreign tongue she had studied but was not fluent in. She does, of course, have the great advantage of being a more convenient date—there are no baby-sitting or scheduling problems, and she can easily go with him, stay out late, even remain at his place without advance planning. Yet even these advantages are outweighed by the sense of fellowship and understanding he finds in women who have been married before.

And FM women, in their turn, have equally strong suspicions and reservations about unmarried men in their thirties or older. Most of these men, even if attractive, agreeable and well-off, seem incomplete or unreachable to FM women who date them. As one 32-year-old woman of considerable experience summed them up: "Bachelors in their thirties and forties talk and act supervirile, but most of them are Mama's boys and sexually very feeble. Sometimes they think they're very passionate, and I never have the heart to tell them that they're really nothing. They're so self-centered you can't make real contact on any level."

Widows and widowers, though they have been married, seem to most FMs even less satisfactory as dates than do the never-married. The formerly married man going on a date with a widow is aware in a matter of minutes that it is a distinctly different experience from dating a formerly married woman. The widow may be friendly and talkative on the surface, but she wears her loyalty to the dead man like a mask over her face; it is as though any show of interest or warmth would be a betrayal of her own love—especially if directed toward a man who had broken up his marriage instead of having it broken up, as hers was, by fate. At best, her attitude seems to be: "See if you can possibly make me like you. I doubt that you can, but I dare you to try."

Similarly, many an FM woman, on meeting or dating a widower, finds him condescending toward her, emotionally chilly, passive rather than outgoing. This is a sample comment: "Widowers seem to think there is something lacking, or something wrong, with the divorcée, or else she would have been able to work it out. They have no understanding and no sympathy. They sit in judgment on you, rather than try to make you feel desirable."

Undoubtedly, many widows and widowers do not act like this, and it is true that the Formerly Married and the widowed do mingle, date and enter into affairs. But the fact remains that, by and large, they are somewhat antagonistic toward one another and prefer to date their own kind. The preference is neither temporary nor superficial; much later on the Formerly Married and the widowed will show the same inclinations when they come to select partners for remarriage.

The Formerly Married, in their initial dating experiences, gain new skills, a sense of identity and a comforting familiarity with the practices of the world they now live in. But even more important than these are the aid and stimulus they get in their task of revaluing themselves and repairing their egos. In a collapsing marriage, a man or woman may feel worthless, unsexed, prematurely old; out of that marriage and beginning to date, the same person may perceive himself or herself as valuable, sexual and youthful.

This is how two of them have expressed it: A woman of 37 who manages a perfume store: "Dating as an ex-married person was a whole new experience. I learned to enjoy the fact of being a woman—a condition I think I had never really appreciated until I met men who really *liked* women." A 41-year-old psychologist, male: "I discovered that I had drastically underestimated my own appeal to woman and my ability to be both tender and manly at the same time."

This regained respect and liking for oneself, though it may seem somewhat superficial and vain, is a prerequisite for more profound experiences that are to follow, and a significant advance toward the recapture of emotional health. Dating, though it may sometimes look like an adolescent and contrived form of heterosexual interaction, is an effective way for the FM to reappraise and reconstruct himself, even while exploring and testing the qualities that he needs in a potential love-partner.

Postmarital dating differs in various respects from premarital dating, and nowhere more sharply than in the area of the sexual overture. The main differences lie in the far greater speed and frankness with which such overtures are made and in their permissibility very early in the acquaintance of the dating couple. "Permissibility" does not mean that the woman routinely acquiesces, but that, in the World of the Formerly Married, it is within the bounds of convention for the man to try. It is common, almost standard, for the man to make an overture—verbal or physical, jestingly or seriously—within the first few dates and, in many cases, on the first or second date. Over half the women I queried said that all or most of the men do so on the first or second date, and the men confirm it.

Second, though it is not standard, it is fairly common for women to acquiesce to propositions made so early in an acquaintance; possibly half of these very early propositions are accepted, without there being any need for the intermediate stages of necking, petting and emotional attachment. Of those women who refuse, moreover, the majority do so pleasantly and conditionally, indicating a possibility that they will change their minds in the future.

Women new to the World of the Formerly Married find the prevalence of these attitudes and practices not only startling, but frightening and degrading. Even some of those who think of themselves as sophisticates are not emotionally prepared for the sexual expectations and unabashed approaches of many of the men.

A woman copywriter in an advertising agency, who had always considered herself knowledgeable and emancipated, felt like this when first thrown into the arena: "It's kind of horrible. They're a bunch of nuts, all trying to prove something. After my first few dates, I wouldn't go out with anyone new for a long while— I just didn't want to have to face that inevitable try, and the inevitable anger that my refusal produced."

A Midwestern homemaker in her early thirties had this to say: "I was so shocked the first time that I cried. The second time, I got mad. The third time, I was waiting for it, and I got the giggles. That was the worst—it made him absolutely livid with rage."

Only after a while does such a woman adjust to the climate of opinion in the world she now lives in. She may still choose to be chary of awarding her favors, but she is no longer upset or angry at the frequency or seeming casualness of solicitation.

Men are less likely to be sharply taken aback; the initiative, after all, is theirs most of the time, and they are therefore not often taken unawares or propositioned against their will. Yet this does happen more frequently than it did in their younger years, and a man new to the World of the Formerly Married may well be surprised and rather uneasy when certain looks or a gentle pressure of the hand seem to indicate that it is high time for him to make a move. Even more surprising to him may be the broad hints dropped by the somewhat bolder female who senses that she is dealing with a slow-moving novice and seeks to arouse him, in order to reassure herself of her feminine appeal.

He may be skittish the first time this happens; but unless he is one of the very badly damaged, he will soon get used to the milieu and feel freer to act according to his own wishes and needs, without undue fear of offending or creating an unpleasant scene. Whether he becomes a fast operator or chooses to hold back until he knows a woman well and genuinely desires her, he will cease being overly anxious about the subject; he will learn to handle the come-on with equanimity, even if he continues to prefer a woman who allows him to be in charge.

The veteran FM man, if he is sensitive to a woman's mood, can usually tell in advance whether or not a degree of rapport exists between himself and the woman that will make an overture welcome, and if it does exist, he hardly need put the suggestion in words. One man of savoir faire explains: "I never suggest sex verbally or try to see how far I can get with a girl. Only boors and bores make passes of that sort. When I am with a woman who appeals to me sexually, I indicate to her by my whole manner how I feel—but only if I really feel that way. And she sends signals back in kind—a glint in the eye, a *moue* at the corner of the mouth, a little pressure of her hand on mine or of her thigh against mine while dancing. Sometimes it's even subtler than that, and I just know from her overall attitude toward me. If I don't see or feel it in her, I don't try. But if I do see or feel it, I don't have to 'ask'—it happens with hardly a word."

The FM woman just beginning to date is lucky if she goes out with such a man; he will sense her unreadiness and will take her home and bid her good-night with a kiss. But to judge from what women have to say about it, such refinement is not the general rule. The fault is only partly that of the men.

Though FMs communicate most marvelously about many things, many women—especially newcomers—hide or disguise their sexual feelings; they are as likely to act falsely flirtatious as falsely reluctant. This makes it difficult for the man to read the message correctly; besides, he is either in the process of rebuilding his self-confidence or anxious to keep it rebuilt by achieving continued conquests. Many FM men therefore fall into the habit of making a routine suggestion on a first or second date, whether or not they have been getting positive signals.

Whatever form of approach he uses, the man justifies it to himself: "She needs, I need, we're both adults, so why beat around the bush?" "She feels flattered as hell, even if she doesn't want to give in." "I'm not lying when I speak of love on a first or second date—I do feel a kind of love at the time." Still other men say they try to bed their dates on little acquaintance because sex is intensely pleasurable, or necessary to the soul, or the only way a man and woman can really get to know each other. Of all their reasons, this last one touches closest to home; most FM men, whatever they think they want, are desperately anxious to find the temporary reassurance of a few hours of intimacy, to replace the lost intimacy of their shattered marriages.

What It Means
To Be a Homosexual

MERLE MILLER

Edward Morgan Forster was a very good writer and a very gutsy man. In the essay "What I Believe," he said: "I hate the idea of causes, and if I had to choose between betraying my country and betraying my friend, I hope I would have the guts to betray my country. Such a choice may scandalize the modern reader, and he may stretch out his patriotic hand to the telephone at once and ring up the police. It would not have shocked Dante, though. Dante places Brutus and Cassius in the lowest circle of Hell because they had chosen to betray their friend Julius Caesar rather than their country Rome."

It took courage to write those words, just as it does, at times, for anyone else to repeat them. In the early nineteen-fifties when I wanted to use them on the title page of a book on blacklisting in television that I wrote for the American Civil Liberties Union, officials of the A.C.L.U. advised against it. Why ask for more trouble, they said. Being against blacklisting was trouble enough. Those were timorous days. "What I Believe" was included in a book of essays used in secondary schools, but it disappeared from the book around 1954

From *The New York Times Magazine*, January 17, 1971. © 1971 by the New York Times Company. Reprinted by permission.

and was replaced by something or other from the Reader's Digest. When I protested to the publisher, he said—it was a folk saying of the time—"You have to roll with the tide." The tide was McCarthyism, which had not then fully subsided—assuming it ever has or will.

Forster was not a man who rolled with the tide. I met him twice, heard him lecture several times, was acquainted with several of his friends, and knew that he was homosexual, but I did not know that he had written a novel, "Maurice," dealing with homosexual characters, until it was announced last November. On top of the manuscript he wrote. "Publishable—but is it worth it?" The novel, completed in 1915, will, after 55 years and the death of Forster, at last be published.

Is it worth it? Even so outspoken a man as Forster had to ask himself that question. It is one thing to confess to political unorthodoxy but quite another to admit to sexual unorthodoxy. Still. Yet. A homosexual friend of mine has said, "Straights don't want to know for sure, and they can never forgive you for telling them. They prefer to think it doesn't exist, but if it does, at least keep quiet about it." And one Joseph Epstein said in Harper's only last September: "...however wide the public tolerance for it, it is no more acceptable privately than it ever was . . . private acceptance of homosexuality, in my experience, is not to be found, even among the most liberal-minded, sophisticated, and liberated people. . . . Nobody says, or at least I have never heard anyone say, 'Some of my best friends are homosexual.' People do say —I say—'fag' and 'queer' without hesitation—and these words, no matter who is uttering them, are putdown words, in intent every bit as vicious as 'kike' or 'nigger.' "

Is it true? Is that the way it is? Have my heterosexual friends, people I thought were my heterosexual friends, been going through an elaborate charade all these years? I would like to think they agree with George Weinberg, a therapist and author of a book on therapy called "The Action Approach," who says, "I would never consider a person healthy unless he had overcome his prejudice against homosexuality." But even Mr. Weinberg assumes that there is a prejudice, apparently built-in, a natural part of the human psyche. And so my heterosexual friends had it, maybe still have it? The late Otto Kahn, I think it was, said, "A kike is a Jewish gentleman who has just left the room." Is a fag a homosexual gentleman who has just stepped out? Me?

I can never be sure, of course, will never be sure. I know it shouldn't bother me. That's what everybody says, but it does bother me. It bothers me every time I enter a room in which there is anyone else. Friend or foe? Is there a difference?

When I was a child in Marshalltown, Iowa, I hated Christmas almost as much as I do now, but I loved Halloween. I never wanted to take off the mask; I wanted to wear it

everywhere, night and day, always. And I suppose I still do. I have often used liquor, which is another kind of mask, and, more recently, pot.

Then, too, I suppose if my friends have been playing games with me, they might with justice say that I have been playing games with them. It took me almost 50 years to come out of the closet, to stop pretending to be something I was not, most of the time fooling nobody.

But I guess it is never easy to open the closet door. When she talked to the Daughters of Bilitis, a Lesbian organization, late last summer, Kate Millett, author of "Sexual Politics," said: "I'm very glad to be here. It's been kind of a long trip. . . . I've wanted to be here, I suppose, in a surreptitious way for a long time, and I was always too chicken. . . . Anyway, I'm out of the closet. Here I am."

Not surprisingly, Miss Millett is now being attacked more because of what she said to the Daughters of Bilitis than because of what she said in her book. James Owles, president of Gay Activists' Alliance, a militant, nonviolent organization concerned with civil rights for homosexuals, says: "We don't give a damn whether people like us or not. We want the rights we're entitled to."

I'm afraid I want both. I dislike being despised, unless I have done something despicable, realizing that the simple fact of being homosexual is all by itself despicable to many people, maybe, as Mr. Epstein says, to everybody who is straight. Assuming anybody is ever totally one thing sexually.

Mr. Epstein says, "When it comes to homosexuality, we know, or ought to know, that we know next to nothing"—and that seems to me to be true.

Our ignorance of the subject is almost as great now as it was in 1915 when Forster wrote "Maurice," almost as great as it was in 1815 or, for that matter, 1715. Freud did not add much knowledge to the subject, nor have any of his disciples, none that I have read or listened to, none that I have consulted. I have spent several thousand dollars and several thousand hours with various practitioners, and while they have often been helpful in leading me to an understanding of how I got to be the way I am, none of them has ever had any feasible, to me feasible, suggestion as to how I could be any different.

And that includes the late Dr. Edmund Bergler, who claimed not only that he could "cure" me but get rid of my writer's block as well. He did neither. I am still homosexual, and I have a writer's block every morning when I sit down at the typewriter. And it's too late now to change my nature. At 50, give or take a year or so, I am afraid I will have to make do with me. Which is what my mother said in the beginning.

Nobody seems to know why homosexuality happens, how it happens, or even what it is that does happen. Assuming it happens in any one way. Or any thousand ways. We do not even know how prevalent it is. We were told in 1948 by Dr. Alfred C. Kinsey in "Sexual Behavior in the Human Male" that 37 per cent of all males have had or will have at least one homosexual experience between adolescence and old age. And last year a questionnaire answered by some 20,000 readers of Psychology Today brought the same response. Thirty-seven per cent of the males said that they had had one homosexual experience. (I will be speaking in what follows largely of male homosexuality, which has been my experience.)

Voltaire is said to have had one such experience, with an Englishman. When the Englishman suggested that they repeat it, Voltaire is alleged to have said, "If you try it once, you are a philosopher; if twice, you are a sodomite."

The National Institute of Mental Health says that between 3,000,000 and 4,000,000 Americans of both sexes are predominantly homosexual, while many others display what the institute delicately calls occasional homosexual tendencies.

But how do they know? Because the closets are far from emptied; there are more in hiding than out of hiding. That has been my experience anyway. And homosexuals come in all shapes and sizes, sometimes in places where you'd least expect to find them. If Jim Bouton is to be believed, in big league baseball and, if we are to go along with Dave Meggysey, in the National Football League. Nobody knows. The question as to who is and who isn't was not asked in the 1970 census.

A Harris survey indicates that 63 per cent of the American people feel that homosexuals are "harmful" to American society. One wonders, I wondered anyway, how those 37 per cent of the males with one admitted homosexual experience responded to the question. After how many such experiences does one get to be harmful? And harmful in what way? The inquisitive Mr. Harris appears not to have asked. Harmful. Feared. Hated. What do the hardhats find objectionable in the young? Their lack of patriotism and the fact that they are all faggots. Aren't they? We're in the midst of a "freaking fag revolution," said the prosecutor in the Chicago conspiracy trial. At least that seems to be the politically profitable thing to say in Chicago.

In the nineteen-fifties, McCarthy found that attacking homosexuals paid off almost as well as attacking the Communists, and he claimed they were often the same. Indeed, the District of Columbia police set up a special detail of the vice squad "to investigate links between homosexuality and Communism."

The American Civil Liberties Union recently has been commendably active in homosexual cases, but in the early fifties, when homosexuals and people accused of homosexuality were being fired from all kinds of Government posts, as they still are, the A.C.L.U. was notably silent. And the most silent of all was a closet queen who was a member of the board of directors, myself.

Epstein, a proclaimed liberal, said in Harper's: "If a close friend were to reveal himself to me as being a homosexual, I am very uncertain what my reaction would be—except to say that it would not be simple.... If I had the power to do so, I would wish homosexuality off the face of this earth."

I could not help wondering what Epstein, who is, I believe, a literary critic, would do about the person and the work of W. H. Auden, homosexual and generally considered to be the greatest living poet in English. "We must love one another or die." Except for homosexuals?

> Beleaguered by the same
> Negation and despair,
> Show an affirming flame.

The great fear is that a son will turn out to be homosexual. Nobody seems to worry about a Lesbian daughter; nobody talks about it anyway. But the former runs through every level of our culture. In the song Peggy Lee recently made popular, "Love Story," part of the lyric has to do with the son she and her husband will have, *"He's got to be straight/ We don't want a bent one."** In the Arpège ad this Christmas: "Promises, husbands to wives, 'I promise to stop telling you that our youngest is developing effeminate tendencies.' "

And so on, and on. I should add that not all mothers are afraid that their sons will be homosexuals. Everywhere among us are those dominant ladies who welcome homosexuality in their sons. That way the mothers know they won't lose them to another woman.

And, of course, no television writer would feel safe without at least one fag joke per script. Carson, Cavett and Griffin all give their audiences the same knowing grin when *that* subject is mentioned, and audiences always laugh, though somewhat nervously.

Is homosexuality contagious? Once again, nobody seems to know for sure. The writer Richard Rhodes reports that those tireless and tedious investigators, Dr. William Masters and Mrs. Virginia Johnson of St. Louis, have got into the subject of homosexuality. And Masters *hinted* to Rhodes that his clinical work had shown that "homosexual seduction in adolescence is generally the predetermining factor in later homosexual choice."

* © Copyright 1967 by the January Music Corp., a division of the A. Schroeder Music Corp. International copyright secured. All rights reserved. Used by permission.

One should not hold the indefatigable doctor to a "hint," but the Wolfenden Committee set up by the British Government in the fifties to study homosexuality and prostitution found the opposite.

It is a view widely held, and one which found favor among our police and legal witnesses, that seduction in youth is the decisive factor in the production of homosexuality as a condition, and we are aware that this condition has done much to alarm parents and teachers. We have found no convincing evidence in support of this contention. Our medical witnesses unanimously held that seduction has little effect in inducing a settled pattern of homosexual behavior, and we have been given no grounds from other sources which contradict their judgment. Moreover, it has been suggested to us that the fact of being seduced often does less harm to the victim than the publicity which attends the criminal proceedings against the offender and the distress which undue alarm sometimes leads parents to show.

Martin Hoffman, a San Francisco psychiatrist who has written a book about male homosexuality called "The Gay World," said in a recent issue of Psychology Today:

Until we know about the mechanisms of sexual arousal in the central nervous system and how learning factors can set the triggering devices for those mechanisms, we cannot have a satisfactory theory of homosexual behavior. We must point out that heterosexual behavior is as much of a scientific puzzle as homosexual behavior. . . . We assume that heterosexual arousal is somehow natural and needs no explanation. I suggest that to call it natural is to evade the whole issue; it is as if we said it's natural for the sun to come up in the morning and left it at that. Is it possible that we know less about human sexuality than the medieval astrologers knew about the stars?

I know this. Almost the first words I remember hearing, maybe the first words I choose to remember hearing, were my mother's, saying, "We ordered a little girl, and when you came along, we were somewhat disappointed." She always claimed that I came from Montgomery Ward, and when I would point out that there was no baby department in the Monkey Ward catalogue, she would say, "This was special."

I never knew what that meant, but I never asked. I knew enough. I knew that I was a disappointment. "But we love you just the same," my mother would say, "and we'll have to make do."

We had to make do with a great many things in those days. The Depression came early to our house, around 1927, when my father lost all his money in the Florida land boom, and once we got poor, we stayed poor. "You'll have the wing for supper, because this is a great big chicken and will last for days, and tomorrow you can take a whole leg to school in your little lunch pail and have it all to yourself." Day-old bread, hand-me-down clothes that had once belonged to more prosperous cousins, holes in the soles of my shoes—all of it. I was a combination of Oliver Twist and Little Nell.

They say that the Depression and the World War were the two central experiences of my generation, and that may be. I certainly had more than enough of both, but I was never really hungry for food. It was love I craved, approval, forgiveness for being what I could not help being. And I have spent a good part of my life looking for those things, always, as a few psychologists have pointed out, in the places I was least likely to find them.

My baby blankets were all pink, purchased before the disaster, my birth. The lace on my baby dress was pink; my bonnet was fringed with pink, and little old ladies were forever peering into the baby buggy and crib, saying, "What an adorable little girl." They kept on saying that until I got my first butch haircut, at 4, just before I started kindergarten. Until then I had long, straight hair, mousebrown, lusterless, and long hair was just as unpopular in Marshalltown then as it is now.

Not until college did I read that Oscar Wilde's mother started him down the garden path by letting his hair grow and dressing him as a little girl. As Oscar said, "Children begin by loving their parents; as they grow older they judge them; sometimes they forgive them."

I was 4 years old when I started school. My mother had told them I was 5; I was somewhat precocious, and she may just have wanted to get me out of the house. But butch haircut or not, some boys in the third grade took one look at me and said, "Hey, look at the sissy," and they started laughing. It seems to me now that I heard that word at least once five days a week for the next 13 years, until I skipped town and went to the university. Sissy and all the other words—pansy, fairy, nance, fruit, fruitcake, and less printable epithets. I did not encounter the word faggot until I got to Manhattan. I'll tell you this, though. It's not true, that saying about sticks and stones; it's words that break your bones.

I admit I must have been a splendid target, undersized always, the girlish voice, the steel-rimmed glasses, always bent, no doubt limp of wrist, and I habitually carried a music roll. I studied both piano and violin all through school, and that all by itself was enough to condemn one to permanent sissydom.

When I was doing a television documentary of Harry Truman's life, he said at one point: "I was never what you'd call popular when I went to school. The popular boys were the athletes with their big, tight fists, and I was never like that. . . . I always had a music roll and wore thick glasses; I was wall-eyed, you know. . . . I stopped playing the piano when I was 14 years old. Where I come from, playing the piano wasn't considered the proper thing for a boy to do."

I said, "Mr. President, did they ever call you 'four-eyes' when you were a little boy?"

"Oh, yes," he said, " 'four-eyes,' 'sissy,' and a lot of other things. When that happens, what you have to do is, you have to work harder than they do and be smarter, and if you are, things usually turn out all right in the end."

As a child I wanted to be the girl my mother had had in mind—or else the All American boy everybody else so admired. Since sex changes were unheard of in those days, I clearly couldn't be a girl; so I tried the other. I ate carloads of Wheaties, hoping I'd turn into another Jack Armstrong, but I still could neither throw nor catch a baseball. I couldn't even see the thing; I'd worn glasses as thick as plate-glass windows since I was 3. ("You inherited your father's eyes, among other weaknesses.") I sold enough Liberty magazines to buy all the body-building equipment Charles

Atlas had to offer, but it did no good. I remained an 89-pound weakling year after year after year. And when the voices of all the other boys in my class had changed into a very low baritone, I was still an uncertain soprano, and remained that until I got to the University of Iowa in Iowa City and, among other disguises, lowered my voice at least two octaves so that I could get a job as a radio announcer on the university station.

I also became city editor of The Daily Iowan and modeled myself after a character out of "The Front Page," wearing a hat indoors and out, talking out of the corner of my mouth, never without a cigarette, being folksy with the local cops, whom I detested, one and all. I chased girls, never with much enthusiasm I'm afraid, and denounced queers with some regularity in the column I wrote for the Iowan. What a fink I was—anything to avoid being called a sissy again.

I was afraid I would never get into the Army, but after the psychiatrist tapped me on the knee with a little hammer and asked how I felt about girls, before I really had a chance to answer, he said, "Next," and I was being sworn in. For the next four years as an editor of Yank, first in the Pacific and then in Europe, I continued to use my deepest city editor's-radio announcer's voice, ordered reporters and photographers around and kept my evenings to myself, especially in Paris.

After the war, I became as much a part of the Establishment as I had ever been, including servitude as an editor of Time. I remember in particular a long discussion about whether to use the picture of a British composer on the cover because a researcher had discovered that he was.

. . . I am sure if there was a vote, I voted against using the picture.

A little later, after finishing my first successful novel, "That Winter," which became a best seller, I decided there was no reason at all why I couldn't be just as straight as the next man. I might not be able to play baseball, but I could get married.

Peter Ilich Tchaikovsky had the same idea. Maybe marriage would cure him of what he called "The." But, afterwards, in a letter to his friend Nadejda von Meck, he wrote, ". . . I saw right away that I could never love my wife and that the *habit* on which I had counted would never come. I fell into despair and longed for death. . . . My mind began to go. . . ."

Peter Ilich's marriage lasted only two weeks. My own lasted longer and was not quite so searing an experience, but it could not have succeeded.

Lucy Komisar says in Washington Monthly that this country is obsessed by what she calls "violence and the masculine mystique," which is certainly true enough. "The enemies of national 'virility' are called 'effete,' a word that means 'sterile, spent, worn-out,' and conjures up the picture of an effeminate pantywaist." Also true, but Americans are certainly not the first people to get uptight about "virility."

Philip of Macedon was forever fussing at Olympias because he claimed she was making their son Alexander effeminate. And, to be sure, Alexander turned out to be at least bisexual, maybe totally homosexual. How else could one explain his grief at the death of his lover, Hephaestion? According to Plutarch, "Alexander was so beyond all reason transported that, to express his sorrow, he immediately ordered the manes and tails of all his horses and mules cut, and threw down the battlements of the neighboring cities. The poor physician he crucified, and forbade playing on the flute or any other musical instrument in the camp a great while. . ."

Gore Vidal has been quoted as saying: "The Italians are sexual opportunists. Anything that feels good, they're for it." Which may be true, but I cannot imagine an Italian father who would not be devastated if he found that his son was homosexual. Or, for that matter, a father in any country in Western society. In England, where the Sexual Offenses Act has been on the law books since 1967, 10 years after the recommendations of the Wolfenden Committee, Anthony Gray, director of an organization that helps sexual minorities, says that even today ". . . the briefest experience is enough to convince one that discrimination against known homosexuals is still the rule rather than the exception." Gray notes that homosexuals still cannot belong to the Civil Service and are still likely to lose their jobs if "found out."

Most members of the Gay Liberation Front appear to believe that Marxism is the answer, which is odd because in Communist China homosexuals are put in prisons for brainwashing that are called "hospitals for ideological reform." Chairman Mao has said: "Our object in exposing errors and criticizing shortcomings is like that of a doctor in curing a disease." In Cuba homosexuals have been placed in concentration camps. Still, as Huey P. Newton, Supreme Commander of the Black Panther Party, has said, there is no reason to think a homosexual cannot be a revolutionary. Late last summer, shortly after the New York chapter of the Gay Liberation Front gave a $500 donation to the Panthers, Newton in a rambling, rather tortured statement said:

What made them homosexual? Some people say that it's the decadence of capitalism. I don't know whether this is the case; I rather doubt it. . . . But there's nothing to say that a homosexual cannot also be a revolutionary. . . . Quite the contrary, maybe a homosexual could be the most revolutionary.

On the other hand, Eldridge Cleaver in "Soul on Ice" gives what I am sure is a more prevalent view among the Panthers: "Homosexuality is a sickness, just as are baby rape or wanting to become head of General Motors."

Of course, the Soviet Union claims not to have any homosexuals. I cannot comment on the validity of that claim, never having been there, but I do know that when one of the Russian ballet companies is in town, you can hear a great many Russian accents on West 42d Street and in various gay bars.

Growing up in Marshalltown, I was allowed to take out as many books as I wanted from the local library, and I always wanted as many as I could carry, 8 or 10 at a time. I read about sensitive boys, odd boys, boys who were lonely and misunderstood, boys who really didn't care all that much for baseball, boys who were teased by their classmates, books about all of these, but for years nobody in any of the books I read was ever tortured by the strange fantasies that tore at me every time, for instance, my mother insisted I go to the "Y" to learn how to swim. They swam nude at the Y, and I never went. Lead me not into temptation. In gym—it was required in high school—I always tried to get in and out of the locker room before anybody else arrived.

And in none of the books I read did anybody feel a compulsion, and compulsion it surely was, to spend so many hours, almost as many as I spent at the library, in or near the Minneapolis & St. Louis railroad station where odd, frightening things were written on the walls of the men's room. And where in those days, there were always boys in their teens and early 20's who were on their way to and from somewhere in freight cars. Boys who were hungry and jobless and who for a very small amount of money, and sometimes none at all, were available for sex; almost always they were. They needed the money, and they needed someone to recognize them, to actually see them.

That was the way it happened the first time. The boy was from Chicago, and his name was Carl. He was 17, and I was 12 and the aggressor. I remember every detail of it: I suppose one always does. Carl hadn't eaten, said he hadn't eaten for two days. His father was a plumber, unemployed, and his mother was, he said rather vaguely, "away, hopefully forever." I remember once I said, "But why don't you go home anyway?" And he said, "Where would that be?"

Years later a boy I met on West 42d Street said it best, about the boys in my childhood and the boys on all the streets of all the cities where they wait. He was the next-to-youngest child in a very poor family of nine, and once he ran away from home for two days and two nights, and when he got back, nobody knew that he had been gone. Then, at 19, he discovered The Street, and he said, "All of a sudden here were all these men, and they were looking at me."

The boys who stopped by at the M. and St. L. in Marshalltown all had stories, and they were all anxious to tell them. They were all lonely and afraid. None of them ever made fun of me. I was never beaten up. They recognized, I guess, that we were fellow aliens with no place to register.

Like my three friends in town. They were aliens, too: Sam, whose father ran a grocery store my mother wouldn't patronize. ("Always 'buy American, Merle, and don't you forget it. We don't know *where* Jews send the money you spend in one of their stores.") A girl in a wheel chair, a polio victim; we talked through every recess in school. And there was the woman with a clubfoot who sold tickets at the Casino, a movie house, and let me in for free—tickets couldn't have been a dime then, but they were —until I was 16, and, as I say, skipped town.

The black boy and the black girl in my high school class never spoke to me, and I never spoke to them. That was the way it was. It never occurred to me that that was not necessarily the way it was meant to be.

There were often black boys on the freight trains, and we talked and had sex. Their stories were always sadder than anybody else's. I never had any hangups about the color of somebody's skin. If you were an outcast, that was good enough for me. I once belonged to 22 organizations devoted to improving the lot of the world's outcasts. The only group of outcasts I never spoke up for publicly, never donated money to or signed an ad or petition for were the homosexuals. I always used my radio announcer's voice when I said "No."

I was 14 when I happened on a

book called "Winesburg, Ohio." I don't know how. Maybe it was recommended by the librarian, a kind and knowing woman with the happy name of Alice Story. Anyway, there at last, in a story called "Hands," were the words I had been looking for. I was not the only sissy in the world: "Adolf Myers was meant to be a teacher ... In their feeling for the boys under their charge such men are not unlike the finer sort of women in their love of men."

Sherwood Anderson's story ended unhappily. Of course. How else could it end? "And then the tragedy. A half-witted boy of the school becomes enamored of the young master. In his bed at night he imagined unthinkable things and in the morning went forth to tell his dreams as facts. Strange, hideous accusations fell from his loose-hung lips. Through the Pennsylvania town went a shiver. Hidden, shadowy doubts that had been in men's minds concerning Adolf Myers were galvanized into beliefs."

I must have read "Hands" more than any story before or since. I can still quote it from beginning to end. "They had intended to hang the schoolmaster, but something in his figure, so small, white, and pitiful, touched their hearts and they let him escape."

Naturally. If you were *that way*, what else could you expect? Either they ran you out of town or you left before they got around to it. I decided on the latter. I once wrote that I started packing to leave Mashalltown when I was 2 years old, which is a slight exaggeration.

As he ran into the darkness, they repented of their weakness and ran after him, swearing and throwing sticks and great balls of soft mud at the figure that

screamed and ran faster into the darkness.

"Winesburg" was published in 1919, and one of the terrifying things is that the people in any town in the United States, quite likely any city, too, would react very much the same way today, wouldn't they?

Look what happened only 15 years ago, in 1955, in Boise, Idaho, when a "homosexual underworld" was uncovered. The "upright" citizens panicked, and some people left town, some were run out of town, and others were sentenced to long prison terms.

In a perceptive and thorough account of what happened. "The Boys of Boise," John Gerassi reports that a lawyer told him that during the height of the hysteria the old American custom of a night on the town with the boys disappeared entirely:

You never saw so many men going out to the bars at night with their wives and girl friends ... we used to have poker games once a week. Well for a few weeks we canceled them. Then one of the guys got an idea: "We'll invite a girl to play with us. You know, it's not very pleasant to play poker with women, not when you're in a serious game. But that's what we had to do."

I have been back to Marshalltown only briefly in all the years since my escape, but a few years ago, I did return to a reunion of my high school class. I made the principal speech at the banquet, and at the end there was enough applause to satisfy my ego temporarily, and various of my classmates, all of whom looked depressingly middle-aged, said various pleasant things, after which there was a dance.

I have written about that before, but what I have not written about, since I was still not ready to come out of the closet, is that a little while after the dance began, a man whose face had been only vaguely familiar and whose name I would not have remembered if he had not earlier reminded me came up, an idiot grin on his face, his wrists limp, his voice falsetto, and said, "How about letting me have this dance, sweetie?" He said it loud enough for all to hear.

I said, "I'm terribly sorry, but my dance card is all filled up." By no means the wittiest of remarks, but under the circumstances it was the best I could manage.

Later, several people apologized for what he had said, but I wondered (who would not?) how many of them had been tempted to say the same thing. Or would say something of the kind after I had gone. Fag, faggot, sissy, queer. A fag is a homosexual gentleman who has just left the room.

And the man who said it was a successful newspaper executive in Colorado, in his mid-40's, a father of five, I was told, a grandfather. After all those years, 27 of them, was he still ... what? Threatened by me? Offended? Unsettled? Challenged? No children or grandchildren around to be perverted. Was his own sexual identity so shaky that ...? A closet queen at heart? No, that's too easy. And it's too easy to say that he's the one who needs treatment, not me. George Weinberg says,

The "homosexual problem," as I have described it here, is the problem of condemning *variety* in human existence. If one cannot enjoy the fact of this variety, at the very least one must learn to become indifferent to it, since obviously it is here to stay.

The fear of it simply will not go away, though. A man who was once a friend, maybe my best friend, the survivor of five marriages, the father of nine, not too long ago told me that his eldest son was coming to my house on Saturday: "Now please try not to make a pass at him."

He laughed. I guess he meant it as a joke; I didn't ask.

And a man I've known, been acquainted with, let's say, for 25 years, called from the city on a Friday afternoon before getting on the train to come up to my place for the weekend. He said, "I've always leveled with you, Merle, and I'm going to now. I've changed my mind about bringing— [his 16-year-old son]. I'm sure you understand."

I said that, no, I didn't understand. Perhaps he could explain it to me.

He said, "— is only an impressionable kid, and while I've known you and know you wouldn't, but suppose you had some friends in, and....?"

I suggested that he not come for the weekend. I have never molested a child my whole life through, never seduced anybody, assuming that word has meaning, and, so far as I know, neither have any of my homosexual friends. Certainly not in my living room or bedroom. Moreover, I have known quite a few homosexuals, and I have listened to a great many accounts of how they got that way or think they got that way. I have never heard anybody say that he (or she) got to be homosexual because of seduction.

But then maybe it is contagious, floating in the air around me, like a virus. Homosexuals themselves often seem to think so. How else can you explain the self-pitying "The Boys in the Band"?

Martin Hoffman, the San Francisco therapist I mentioned earlier, says:

Self-condemnation pervades the homosexual world and, in concert with the psychodynamic and biological factors that lead toward promiscuity, makes stable relationship a terrific problem. In spite of the fact that so many homosexuals are lonely and alone, they can't seem to find someone with whom to share even part of their lives. This dilemma is the core problem of the gay world and stems in large measure from the adverse self-definitions that society imprints on the homosexual mind. Until we can change these ancient attitudes, many men—including some of our own brothers, sons, friends, colleagues and children yet unborn—will live out their lives in the quiet desperation of the sad gay world.

Perhaps. None of my homosexual friends are any too happy, but then very few of my heterosexual friends—supposed friends, I should say—are exactly joyous, either. And as for the promiscuity and short-term relationships, neither of those has been quite true in my case, and only recently I attended an anniversary party of two homosexuals who had been together for 25 years, reasonably happy. They still hold hands, though not in public, and they are kind to each other, which is rare enough anywhere these days.

Late in October members of the Gay Activists' Alliance staged an all-day sit-in at Harper's to protest the Epstein article, surely the first time in the 120-year history of the magazine that that has happened. And as Peter Fisher, a student at Columbia who helped organize the sit-in, kept saying, "What you don't understand is that there's been a revolution."

I'm not sure it's a full-scale revolution yet, but there's been a revolt, and for thousands of young homosexuals, and some not so young, the quiet desperation that Hoffman talks about is all over. They are neither quiet nor desperate.

The whole thing began with an event that has been compared to the Boston Tea Party or the firing on Fort Sumter: the Stonewall Rebellion. On June 28, 1969, the police started to raid a gay bar in the West Village, the Stonewall Inn. The police are forever raiding gay bars, especially around election time, when they also move in on West 42d Street. And in the past, what you did was, you took the cops' abuse, and sometimes you went off with only a few familiar epithets or a hit on the head. And sometimes you were taken to the station on one charge or another and, usually, released the next morning. But that is not what happened on June 28, 1969. A friend of mine who was there said.

It was fantastic. The crowd was a fairly typical weekend crowd, your usual queens and kids from the sticks, and the people that are always around the bars, mostly young. But this time instead of submitting to the cops' abuse, the sissies fought back. They started pulling up parking meters and throwing rocks and coins at the cops, and the cops had to take refuge in the bar and call for reinforcements. . . . It was beautiful.

That was the beginning, and on the anniversary last summer between 5,000 and 15,000 gay people of both sexes marched up Sixth Avenue from Sheridan Square to the Sheep Meadow in Central Park for a "gay-in." Other, smaller parades took place in Chicago and Los Angeles, and all three cities survived the sight and sound of men with their arms around men and women kissing women, chanting, "Shout it loud, gay is proud," "3-5-7-9, Lesbians are mighty fine," carrying signs that said, "We Are the People Our Parents Warned Us Against," singing "We Shall Overcome."

And something else perhaps even more important happened last June. When Arthur J. Goldberg paid what was to have been a routine campaign visit to the intersection of 85th and Broadway, more than three dozen members of the G.A.A. were waiting for him. They shook his hand and asked if he was in favor of fair employment for homosexuals and of repeal of the state laws against sodomy. Goldberg's answer to each question was, "I think there are more important things to think about."

But before the election Goldberg had issued a public statement answering yes to both questions, promising as well to work against police harassment of homosexuals. Richard Ottinger and Charles Goodell also issued statements supporting constitutional rights for homosexuals. Of course, Rockefeller and Buckley, the winners, remained silent on those issues, but Bella Abzug, one of the earliest supporters of G.A.A., won, and so did people like Antonio Olivieri, the first Democrat elected in the 66th Assembly District in 55 years. Olivieri took an ad in a G.A.A. benefit program that served to thank the organization for its support.

Marty Robinson, an extremely vocal young man, a carpenter by profession, who was then in charge of political affairs for G.A.A., said that "this election serves notice on every politician in the state and nation that homosexuals are not going to hide any more. We're becoming militant, and we won't be harassed or degraded any more."

John Francis Hunter, one of the alliance's founders, said:

G.A.A. is a political organization. Everything is done with an eye toward political effect. . . . G.A.A. adopted this policy because all oppression of homosexuals can only be ended by means of a powerful political bloc.

For an organization only a little more than a year old and with only 180 paid-up members, G.A.A. has certainly made itself heard. And that, according to Arthur Evans, another fiery member, is just the beginning. He said: "At the end of June we had a statement that gay is good. We had a joyous celebration, as is right. But today we know not only that gay is good, gay is angry. We are telling all the politicians and elected officials of New York State that they are going to become responsible to the people. We will make them responsible to us, or we will stop the conduct of the business of government." Well.

Small wonder that the Mattachine Society, which for 20 years has been trying to educate straight people to accept homosexuals, is now dismissed by some members of G.A.A. and the Gay Liberation Front as "the N.A.A.C.P. of our movement."

Laws discriminating against homosexuals will almost surely be changed. If not this year, in 1972; if not in 1972, in 1976; if not in 1976. . . .

Private acceptance of homosexuals and homosexuality will take somewhat longer. Most of the psychiatric establishment will continue to insist that homosexuality is a disease and homosexuals, unlike the blacks, will not benefit from any guilt feelings on the part of liberals. So far as I can make out, there simply aren't any such feelings. On the contrary, most people of every political persuasion seem to be too uncertain of their own sexual identification to be anything but defensive. Fearful. And maybe it is contagious. Prove it isn't.

I have never infected anybody, and it's too late for the head people to do anything about me now. Gay is good.

Gay is proud. Well, yes, I suppose. If I had been given a choice (but who is?), I would prefer to have been straight. But then would I rather not have been me? Oh, I think not, not this morning anyway. It is a very clear day in late December, and the sun is shining on the pine trees outside my studio. The air is extraordinarily clear, and the sky is the color it gets only at this time of year, dark, almost navy blue. On such a day I would not choose to be anyone else or any place else.

Sisterhood Is Powerful

SUSAN BROWNMILLER

There is a small group of women that gathers at my house or at the home of one or another of our 15 members each Sunday evening. Our ages range from the early twenties to the late forties. As it happens, all of us work for a living, some at jobs we truly like. Some of us are married, with families, and some are not. Some of us knew each other before we joined the group and some did not. Once we are settled on the sofa and the hard-backed chairs brought in from the kitchen, and the late-comers have poured their own coffee and arranged themselves as best they can on the floor, we begin our meeting. Each week we explore another aspect of what we consider to be our fundamental oppression in a male-controlled society. Our conversation is always animated, often emotional. We rarely adjourn before midnight.

From *The New York Times Magazine*, March 15, 1970.© 1970 by the New York Times Company. Reprinted by permission.

Although we are pleased with ourselves and our insights, we like to remind each other now and then that our small group is not unique. It is merely one of many such groups that have sprung up around the city in the last two years under the umbrella of that collective term, the women's liberation movement. In fact, we had been meeting as a group for exactly four Sundays when one of us got a call from a representative of C.B.S. asking if we would care to be filmed in our natural habitat for a segment on the evening news with Walter Cronkite. We discussed the invitation thoroughly, and then said no.

Women's liberation is hot stuff this season, in media terms, and no wonder. In the short space of two years, the new feminism has taken hold and rooted in territory that at first glance appears an unlikely breeding ground for revolutionary ideas: among urban, white, college-educated, middle-class women generally considered to be a rather "privileged" lot by those who thought they knew their politics, or knew their women. From the radical left to the Establishment middle, the women's movement has become a fact of life. The National Organization for Women (NOW), founded by Betty Friedan in 1966, has 35 chapters across the country. Radical feminist groups—creators of the concept of women's liberation, as opposed to women's *rights*—exist in all major cities side by side with their more conservative counterparts.

Without doubt, certain fringe aspects of the movement make "good copy," to use the kindest term available for how my brethren in the business approach the subject matter. ("Get the bra burning and the karate up front," an editor I know told a writer I know when preparing one news magazine's women's liberation story.)

But the irony of all this media attention is that while the minions of C.B.S. News can locate a genuine women's liberation group with relative ease (they ferreted out our little group before we had memorized each other's last names), hundreds of women in New York City have failed in their attempts to make contact with the movement. I have spoken to women who have spent as much as three months looking for a group that was open to new members. Unclaimed letters have piled up at certain post office box numbers hastily set up and thoughtlessly abandoned by here-today-and-gone-tomorrow "organizations" that disappeared as abruptly as they materialized. The elusive qualities of "women's lib" once prompted the writer Sally Kempton to remark, "It's not a movement, it's a state of mind." The surest way to affiliate with the movement these days is to form your own small group. That's the way it's happening.

Two years ago the 50 or so women in New York City who had taken to calling themselves the women's liberation movement met on Thursday evenings at a borrowed office on East 11th Street. The official title of the group was the New York Radical Women. There was some justification at the time for thinking grandly in national terms, for similar groups of women were beginning to form in Chicago, Boston, San Francisco and Washington. New York Radical Women came by its name quite simply: the women were young radicals, mostly under the age of 25, and they come out of the civil rights and/or peace movements, for which many of them had been fulltime workers. A few years earlier, many of them might have been found on the campuses of Vassar, Radcliffe, Wellesley and the larger coed universities, a past they worked hard to deny. What brought them together to a women-only discussion and action group was a sense of abuse suffered at the hands of the very protest movements that had spawned them. As "movement women," they were tired of doing the shopping and fixing the food while "movement men" did the writing and leading. Most were living with or married to movement men who, they believed, were treating them as convenient sex objects or as somewhat lesser beings.

Widely repeated quotations, such as Stokeley Carmichael's wisecrack dictum to S.N.C.C., "The position of women in our movement should be prone," and, three years later, a similar observation by Black Panther Eldridge Cleaver had reinforced their uncomfortable suspicion that the social vision of radical men did not include equality for women. Black power, as practiced by black male leaders, appeared to mean that black women would step back while black men stepped forward. The white male radical's eager embrace of *machismo* appeared to include those backward aspects of male supremacy in the Latin culture from which the word *machismo* is derived. Within their one-to-one relationships with their men, the women felt, the highly touted "alternate life style" of the radical movement was working out no better than the "bourgeois" life style they had rejected. If man and wife in a suburban split-level was a symbol of all that was wrong with plastic, bourgeois America, "man and chick" in a Lower East Side tenement flat was hardly the new order they had dreamed of.

In short, "the movement" was reinforcing, not eliminating, their deepest insecurities and feelings of worthlessness as women—feelings which quite possibly had brought them into radical protest politics to begin with. So, in a small way, they had begun to rebel. They had decided to meet regularly —without their men—to talk about their common experience. "Our feminism was very underdeveloped in those days," says Anne Koedt, an early member of the group. "We didn't have any idea of what kind of action we could take. We couldn't stop talking about the blacks and Vietnam."

In Marxist canons, "the woman question" is one of many manifestations of a sick, capitalist society which "the revolution" is supposed to finish off smartly. Some of the women who devoted their Thursday evening meeting time to New York Radical Women believed they were merely dusting off and streamlining an orthodox, ideological issue. Feminism was bad politics and a dirty word since it excluded the larger picture.

But others in the group, like Anne Koedt and Shuli Firestone, an intense and talkative young activist, had begun to see things from a different, heretical perspective. Woman's oppressor was Man, they argued, and not a specific economic system. After all, they pointed out, male supremacy was still flourishing in the Soviet Union, Cuba and China, where power was still lodged in a male bureaucracy. Even the beloved Che wrote a guidebook for revolutionaries in which he waxed ecstatic over the advantages to a guerrilla movement of having women along in the mountains—to prepare and cook the food. The heretics tentatively put forward the idea that feminism must be a separate movement of its own.

New York Radical Women's split in perspective—was the ultimate oppressor Man or Capitalism?—occupied endless hours of debate at the Thursday evening meetings. Two warring factions emerged, dubbing each other "the feminists" and "the politicos." But other things were happening as well. For one thing, new women were coming in droves to the Thursday evening talk fest, and a growing feeling of sisterhood was permeating the room. Meetings began awkwardly and shyly, with no recognized chairman and no discernible agenda. Often the suggestion, "Let's sit closer together, sisters," helped break the ice. But once the evening's initial awkwardness had passed, volubility was never a problem. "We had so much to say," an early member relates, "and most of us had never said it to another woman before."

Soon *how* to say it became an important question. Young women like Carol Hanisch, a titian-haired recruit to the civil rights movement from a farm in Iowa, and her friend Kathie

Amatniek, a Radcliffe graduate and a working film editor, had spent over a year in Mississippi working with S.N.C.C. There they had been impressed with the Southern-revival-style mass meeting at which blacks got up and "testified" about their own experience with "the Man." Might the technique also work for women? And wasn't it the same sort of thing that Mao Tse-tung had advocated to raise political consciousness in Chinese villages? As Carol Hanish reminded the group, Mao's slogan had been "Speak pain to recall pain"—precisely what New York Radical Women was doing!

The personal-testimony method encouraged *all* women who came to the meeting to speak their thoughts. The technique of "going around the room" in turn brought responses from many who had never opened their mouths at male-dominated meetings and were experiencing the same difficulty in a room full of articulate members of their own sex. Specific questions such as, "If you've thought of having a baby, do you want a girl or a boy?" touched off accounts of what it meant to be a girl-child—the second choice in a society that prizes boys. An examination of "What happens to your relationship when your man earns more money than you, and what happens when *you* earn more money than him?" brought a flood of anecdotes about the male ego and money. "We all told similar stories," relates a member of the group. "We discovered that, to a man, they all felt challenged if we were the breadwinners. It meant that we were no longer dependent. We had somehow robbed them of their 'rightful' role."

"We began to see our 'feminization' as a two-level process," says Anne Koedt. "On one level, a woman is brought up to believe that she is a girl and that is her biological destiny. She isn't supposed to want to achieve anything. If, by some chance, she manages to escape the psychological damage, she finds that the structure is prohibitive. Even though she wants to achieve, she finds she is discouraged at every turn and she still can't become President."

Few topics, the women found, were unfruitful. Humiliations that each of them had suffered privately—from being turned down for a job with the comment, "We were looking for a man," to catcalls and wolf whistles on the street—turned out to be universal agonies. "I had always felt degraded, actually turned into an object," said one woman. "I was no longer a human being when a guy on the street would start to make those incredible animal noises at me. I never was flattered by it, I always understood that behind that whistle was a masked hostility. When we started to talk about it in the group, I discovered that every woman in the room had similar feelings. None of us knew how to cope with this street hostility. We had always had to grin and bear it. We had always been told to dress as women, to be very sexy and alluring to men, and what did it get us? Comments like 'Look at the legs on that babe' and 'would I like to—her.' "*

"Consciousness-raising," in which a woman's personal experience at the

---

* My small group has discussed holding a street action of our own on the first warm day of spring. We intend to take up stations on the corner of Broadway and 45th Street and whistle at the male passersby. The confrontation, we feel, will be educational for all concerned.

hands of men was analyzed as a *political* phenomenon, soon became a keystone of the women's liberation movement.

In 1963, *before* there was a women's movement, Betty Friedan published what eventually became an American classic, "The Feminine Mystique." The book was a brilliant, factual examination of the post-World War II "back to thé home" movement that tore apart the myth of the fulfilled and happy American housewife. Though "The Feminine Mystique" held an unquestioned place as *the* intellectual mind-opener for most of the young feminists—de Beauvoir's "The Second Sex," a broad, philosophical analysis of the cultural restraints on women, was runner-up in popularity—few members of New York Radical Women had ever felt motivated to attend a meeting of Friedan's National Oranization for Women, the parliamentary-style organization of professional women and housewives that she founded in 1966. Friedan, the mother of the movement, and the organization that recruited in her image were considered hopelessly bourgeois. NOW's emphasis on legislative change left the radicals cold. The generation gap created real barriers to communication.

"Actually, we had a lot in common with the NOW women," reflects Anne Koedt. "The women who started NOW were achievement-oriented in their professions. They began with the employment issue because that's what they were up against. The ones who started New York Radical Women were achievement-oriented in the radical movement. From both ends we were fighting a male structure that prevented us from achieving."

Friedan's book had not envisioned

a movement of young feminists emerging from the college campus and radical politics. "If I had it to do all over again," she says, "I would rewrite my last chapter." She came to an early meeting of New York Radical Women to listen, ask questions and take notes, and went away convinced that her approach—and NOW's—was more valid. "As far as I'm concerned, we're *still* the radicals," she says emphatically. "We raised our consciousness a long time ago. I get along with the women's lib people because they're the way the troops we need come up. But the name of the game is confrontation and action, and equal employment *is* the gut issue. The legal fight is enormously important. Desegregating The New York Times help-wanted ads was an important step, don't you think? And NOW did it. The women's movement *needs* its Browns versus Boards of Education."

Other older women, writers and lifetime feminists, also came around to observe, and stayed to develop a kinship with girls young enough to be their daughters. "I almost wept after my first meeting. I went home and filled my diary," says Ruth Herschberger, poet and author of "Adam's Rib," a witty and unheeded expostulation of women's rights published in 1948. "When I wrote 'Adam's Rib,' I was writing for readers who wouldn't accept the first premise. Now there was a whole roomful of people and a whole new vocabulary. I could go a whole month on the ammunition I'd get at one meeting."

In June of 1968, New York Radical Women produced a mimeographed booklet of some 20 pages entitled "Notes from the First Year." It sold for 50 cents to women and $1.00 to men. "Notes" was a compendium of speeches, essays and transcriptions of tape-recorded "rap sessions" of the Thursday evening group on such subjects as sex, abortion and orgasm. Several mimeographed editions later, it remains the most widely circulated source material on the New York women's liberation movement.

The contribution to "Notes" that attracted the most attention from both male and female readers was a one-page essay by Anne Koedt entitled, "The Myth of Vaginal Orgasm." In it she wrote:

"Frigidity has generally been defined by men as the failure of women to have vaginal orgasms. Actually, the vagina is not a highly sensitive area and is not physiologically constructed to achieve orgasm. The clitoris is the sensitive area and is the female equivalent of the penis. All orgasms [in women] are extensions of sensations from this area. This leads to some interesting questions about conventional sex and our role in it. Men have orgasms essentially by friction with the vagina, not with the clitoris. Women have thus been defined sexually in terms of what pleases men; our own biology has not been properly analyzed. Instead we have been fed a myth of the liberated woman and her vaginal orgasm, an orgasm which in fact does not exist. What we must do is redefine our sexuality. We must discard the 'normal' concepts of sex and create new guidelines which take into account mutual sexual enjoyment. We must begin to demand that if a certain sexual position or technique now defined as 'standard' is not mutually conducive to orgasm, then it should no longer be defined as standard."

Ann Koedt's essay went further than many other women in the move-

ment would have preferred to go, but she was dealing with a subject that every woman understood. "For years I suffered under a male-imposed definition of my sexual responses," one woman says. "From Freud on down, it was *men* who set the standard of my sexual enjoyment. *Their* way was the way I should achieve nirvana, because their way was the way it worked for them. Me? Oh, I was simply an "inadequate woman.' "

By September, 1968, New York Radical Women felt strong enough to attempt a major action. Sixty women went to Atlantic City in chartered buses to picket the Miss America pageant. The beauty contest was chosen as a target because of the ideal of American womanhood it extolled —vacuous, coiffed, cosmeticized and with a smidgin of talent.

But New York Radical Women did not survive its second year. For one thing, the number of new women who flocked to the Thursday evening meetings made consciousness-raising and "going around the room" an impossibility. The politico-feminist split and other internal conflicts—charges of "domination" by one or another of the stronger women were thrown back and forth—put a damper on the sisterly euphoria. An attempt to break up the one large group into three smaller ones—by lot—proved disastrous.

Several women felt the need for a new group. They had become intrigued with the role of the witch in world history as representing society's persecution of women who dared to be different. From Joan of Arc, who dared to wear men's clothes and lead a men's army, to the women of Salem who dared to defy accepted political, religious mores, the "witch" was pun-

ished for deviations. Out of this thinking grew WITCH, a handy acronym
that the organizers announced, half
tongue-in-cheek, stood for Women's
International Terrorist Conspiracy
from Hell.

Much of WITCH was always
tongue-in-cheek, and from its inception its members were at great pains
to deny that they were feminists. The
Yippie movement had made outrage-
ous disruption a respectable political
tactic of the left, and the women of
WITCH decided it was more compatible with their thinking to be
labeled "kooks" by outsiders than to
be labeled man-haters by movement
men.

In the WITCH philosophy, the
patriarchy of the nuclear family was
synonymous with the patriarchy of
the American business corporation.
Thus, four women took jobs at a
branch of the Travelers Insurance
Company, where a fifth member was
working, and attempted to establish
a secret coven of clerical workers on
the premises. (For the Travelers' project, WITCH became "Women Incensed at Travelers' Corporate Hell.")
In short order, the infiltrators were
fired for such infractions of office rules
as wearing slacks to work. Undaunted,
a new quintet of operatives gained
employment in the vast typing pools
at A.T.&T. "Women Into Telephone
Company Harassment" gained three
sympathizers to the cause before Ma
Bell got wise and exorcised the coven
from her midst. Two WITCHes were
fired for insubordination; the rest were
smoked out and dismissed for being
"overqualified" for the typing pool.

WITCH's spell over the women's
movement did not hold. "At this
point," says Judith Duffet, an original
member, "you could say that WITCH

is just another small group in women's
liberation. We're concerned with consciousness-raising and developing an
ideology through collective thinking.
We don't do the freaky, hippie stuff
any more."

While WITCH was brewing its unusual recipe for liberation, another
offshoot of New York Radical Wom-
en emerged. The new group was
called Redstockings, a play on *blue-
stockings*, with the blue replaced by
the color of revolution. Organized by
Shuli Firestone and Ellen Willis, an
articulate rock-music columnist for
the New Yorker and a serious student
of Engels's "Origins of the Family,"
Redstockings made no bones about
where it stood. It was firmly committed to feminism and action.

Redstockings made its first public
appearance at a New York legislative
hearing on abortion law reform in
February, 1969, when several women
sought to gain the microphone to
testify about their own abortions. The
hearing, set up to take testimonoy
from 15 medical and psychiatric
"experts"—14 were men—was hastily
adjourned. The following month,
Redstockings held its *own* abortion
hearing at the Washington Square
Methodist Church. Using the consciousness-raising technique, 12 wom-
en "testified" about abortion, from
their own personal experience, before
an audience of 300 men and women.
The political message of the emotion-
charged evening was that *women* were
the only true experts on unwanted
pregnancy and abortion, and that
every woman has an inalienable right
to decide whether or not she wishes to
bear a child.

Redstockings' membership counts
are a closely held secret, but I would
estimate that the number does not

exceed 100. Within the movement, Redstockings push what they call "the pro-woman line." "What it means," says a member, "is that we take the woman's side in *everything*. A woman is never to blame for her own submission. None of us need to change ourselves, we need to change men." Redstockings are also devout about consciousness-raising. "Whatever else we may do, consciousness-raising is the ongoing political work," says Kathie Amatniek. For the last few months, the various Redstocking groups have been raising their consciousness on what they call "the divisions between women that keep us apart"—married women *vs.* single, black women *vs.* white, middle class *vs.* working class, etc.

While Redstockings organized its abortion speak-out, the New York chapter of NOW formed a committee to lobby for repeal of restrictive abortion legislation. These dissimilar approaches to the same problem illustrate the difference in style between the two wings of the women's movement.

But within New York NOW itself, a newer, wilder brand of feminism made an appearance. Ti-Grace Atkinson, a Friedan protégée and the president of New York NOW, found herself in increasing conflict with her own local chapter and Friedan over NOW's hierarchical structure, a typical organization plan with an executive board on top. Ti-Grace, a tall blonde who has been described in print as "aristocratic looking," had come to view the power relationship between NOW's executive board and the general membership as a copycat extension of the standard forms of male domination over women in the society at large. She proposed to NOW that all executive offices be abolished

in favor of rotating chairmen chosen by lot from the general membership. When Atkinson's proposal came up for a vote by the general membership of the New York chapter in October, 1968, and was defeated, Ti-Grace resigned her presidency on the spot and went out and formed her own organization. Named the October 17th Movement—the date of Ti-Grace's walkout from NOW—it made a second debut this summer as The Feminists, and took its place as the most radical of the women's liberation groups. (New York NOW suffered no apparent effects from its first organizational split. Over the last year it has *gained* in membership as feminism has gained acceptability among wider circles of women.)

The Feminists made anti-elitism and rigorous discipline cardinal principles of their organization. As the only radical feminist group to take a stand against the institution of marriage they held a sit-in at the city marriage license bureau last year, raising the slogan that "Marriage Is Slavery." Married women or women living with men may not exceed one-third of the total membership.

Differences over such matters as internal democracy, and the usual personality conflicts that plague all political movements, caused yet another feminist group and another manifesto to make their appearance this fall. In November, Shuli Firestone and Anne Koedt set up a plan for organizing small groups—or "brigades," as they prefer to call them—on a neighborhood basis, and named their over-all structure the New York Radical Feminists. Eleven decentralized neighborhood units (three are in the West Village) meet jointly once a month.

The Radical Feminists coexist with

the Feminists and the Redstockings without much rivalry, although when pressed, partisans of the various groups will tell you, for instance, that Redstockings do too much consciousness-raising and not enough action, or that the Feminists are "fascistic," or that the Radical Feminists are publicity hungry. But in general, since interest in the women's liberation movement has always exceeded organizational capacity, the various groups take the attitude of "the more the merrier."

Despite the existence of three formal "pure radical feminist" organizations, hundreds of women who consider themselves women's liberationists have not yet felt the need to affiliate with any body larger than their own small group. The small group, averaging 8 to 15 members and organized spontaneously by friends calling friends has become *the* organizational form of the amorphous movement. Its intimacy seems to suit women. Fear of expressing new or half-formed thoughts vanishes in a friendly living-room atmosphere. "After years of psychoanalysis in which my doctor kept telling me my problem was that I wouldn't accept—quote— *my female role*," says a married woman with two children who holds a master's degree in philosophy, "the small group was a revelation to me. Suddenly, for the first time in my life, it was *O.K.* to express feelings of hostility to men." Says another woman: "In the small group I have the courage to think things and feel feelings, that I would never have dared to think and feel as an individual."

The meetings have often been compared to group therapy, a description that most of the women find irritating. "Group therapy isn't political and what we're doing is highly politi-cal," is the general response. In an early paper on the nature and function of the small group, Carol Hanisch once wrote, "Group therapy implies that we are sick and messed up, but the first function of the small group is to get rid of self-blame. We start with the assumption that women are, really 'neat' people. Therapy means adjusting. We desire to change the objective conditions."

The groups are usually leaderless and structureless, and the subjects discussed at the weekly meetings run the gamut of female experience. The Radical Feminists offer to new groups they organize a list of consciousness-raising topics that includes:

Discuss your relationships with men. Have you noticed any recurring patterns? Have you ever felt that men have pressured you into sexual relationships? Have you ever lied about orgasm?
Discuss your relationships with other women. Do you compete with women for men?
Growing up as a girl, were you treated differently from your brother?
What would you most like to do in life? What has stopped you?

"Three months of this sort of thing," says Shuli Firestone, "is enough to make a feminist out of any woman."

The kind of collective thinking that has come out of the women's liberation movement is qualitatively different from the kinds of theorems and analyses that other political movements have generated. "Women are different from all other oppressed classes," says Anne Koedt. "We live in isolation, not in ghettos, and we are in the totally unique position of having a master in our own houses." It is not surprising therefore, that marriage and child care are two subjects that receive intensive scrutiny in the small group.

If few in the women's movement are willing to go as far as the Feminists and say that marriage is slavery, it is hard to find a women's liberationist who is not in some way disaffected by the sound of wedding bells. Loss of personal identity and the division of labor within the standard marriage (the husband's role as provider, the wife's role as home maintenance and child care) are the basic points at issue. "I have come to view marriage as a built-in self-destruct for women," says one divorcée after 12 years of marriage. "I married early, right after college, because it was expected of me. I never had a chance to discover who I was. I was programed into the housewife pattern." Many married women's liberationists will no longer use their husbands' last names; some have gone back to their maiden names, and some even to their mothers' maiden names.

One paper that has been widely circulated within the movement is entitled "The Politics of Housework," by Pat Mainardi, a Redstocking who is a teacher and painter. "Men recognize the essential fact of housework right from the beginning," she wrote. "Which is that it stinks. You both work, you both have careers, but *you* are expected to do the housework. Your husband tells you, 'Don't talk to me about housework. It is too trivial to discuss.' MEANING: *His* purpose is to deal with matters of significance. *Your* purpose is to deal with matters of insignificance. So *you* do the housework. Housework trivial? Just try getting him to share the burden. The measure of his resistance is the measure of your oppression."

Not only the oppression of housework, but the oppression of child care has become a focus of the women's movement. Much of the energy of young mothers in the movement has gone into setting up day-care collectives that are staffed on an equal basis by mothers and fathers. (Thus far they have proved difficult to sustain.) "Some of the men have actually come to understand that sharing equally in child care is a political responsibility," says Rosalyn Baxandall, a social worker and an early women's liberationist. Rosalyn and her husband, Lee, a playwright, put in a morning a week at an informal cooperative day nursery on the Lower East Side where their 2-year-old, Finn, is a charter member.

In November, at the Congress to Unite Women, a conference that drew over 500 women's liberationists of various persuasions from the New York area, a resolution demanding 24-hour-a-day child care centers was overwhelmingly endorsed. Women in the movement have also suggested plans for a new kind of life style in which a husband and wife would each work half-day and devote the other half of the day to caring for their children. Another possibility would be for the man to work for six months of the year while the woman takes care of the child-rearing responsibilities—with the roles reversed for the next six months.

The "movement women" who did not endorse the separatism of an independent radical feminist movement last year and chose to remain in what the feminists now call "the male left" have this year made women's liberation a major issue in their own political groups. Even the weatherwomen of Weatherman meet separately to discuss how to combat male chauvinism among their fellow revolutionaries. The women of Rat, the farthest out of the underground radical newspapers, formed a collective and took over editorial management of their paper last month, charging that their men had put out a product filled with sexist, women-as-the-degraded-objects pornography. Twenty-two-year old Jane Alpert, free on bail and facing conspiracy charges for a series of terrorist bombings, was spokesman for the Rat women's *putsch*. A black women's liberation committee functions within S.N.C.C., and its leader, Frances M. Beal, has said publicly, "To be black and female is double jeopardy, the slave of a slave."

The new feminism has moved into some surprisingly Establishment quarters. A spirited women's caucus at New York University Law School forced the university to open its select national scholarship program to women students. Women's caucuses exist among the editorial employes at McGraw-Hill and Newsweek. Last month, 59 women in city government sent a petition to Mayor Lindsay demanding that he actively seek qualified women for policy-making posts.

The movement is a story without an end, because it has just begun. The goals of liberation go beyond a simple concept of equality. Looking through my notebook, I see them expressed simply and directly. *Betty Friedan: "We're going to redefine the sex roles." Anne Koedt: "We're going to be redefining politics."* Brave words for a new movement, and braver still for a movement that has been met with laughter and hostility. Each time a man sloughs off the women's movement with the comment,

"They're nothing but a bunch of lesbians and frustrated bitches," we quiver with collective rage. How can such a charge be answered in rational terms? It cannot be. (The supersensitivity of the movement to the lesbian issue, and the existence of a few militant lesbians within the movement once prompted Friedan herself to grouse about "the lavender menace" that was threatening to warp the image of women's rights. A lavender herring, *perhaps*, but surely no clear and present danger.)

The small skirmishes and tugs of war that used to be called "the battle of the sexes" have now assumed ideological proportions. It is the aim of the movement to *turn men around*, and the implications in that aim are staggering. "Men have used us all their lives as ego fodder," says Anne Koedt. "They not only control economics and the government, they control us. There are the women's pages and the rest of the world." It is that rest of the world, of course, that we are concerned with. There is a women's rights button that I sometimes wear and the slogan on it reads, "Sisterhood is Powerful." If sisterhood were powerful, what a different world it would be.

Women as a class have never subjugated another group; we have never marched off to wars of conquest in the name of the fatherland. We have never been involved in a decision to annex the territory of a neighboring country, or to fight for foreign markets on distant shores. Those are the games men play, not us. We see it differently. We want to be neither oppressor nor oppressed. The women's revolution is the final revolution of them all.

How does a sympathetic man relate to a feminist woman? Thus far, it has not been easy for those who are trying. The existence of a couple of *men's* consciousness-raising groups— the participants are mostly husbands of activist women—is too new to be labeled a trend. "When our movement gets strong, when men are forced to see us as a conscious issue, *what are they going to do?*" asks Anne Koedt. And then she answers: "I don't know, but I think there's a part of men that really wants a human relationship, and that's going to be the saving grace for all of us."

part six

TROUBLED
ADOLESCENTS

An adverse view of "the younger generation" is held apparently by each successive adult generation about those soon to enter adulthood. Conflict between generations is interpreted in many ways: Some hold it to be essential to social development and the taking on of adult roles; others regard it as evidence that the "in charge" generation is only partially successful in handing down its ideas, values, and solutions to the problems of life; and still others suggest that it reflects the dissatisfaction of youth with contemporary social life and our social order. Apparently, the young in the United States have always been more willing than the old to reject the *status quo* and to challenge values accepted by the adult community member.

The United States is now confronted with particularly sharp conflicts between adults and adolescents. The extensive conflict between generations is attributed to a number of different characteristics of contemporary social life, including the delayed entry of the younger generation into full adult status because of extended requirements for education and training, an emphasis on permissiveness and freedom of expression for the child in his family life, and increased exposure to pleasuristic values and diversity through the mass media. Moreover, the strong association between personal power, prestige, and economic wherewithal is appreciated by the adolescent, and he realizes more than ever before how it affects his own present social relationships and future life chances. The conflict between generations, while perhaps a necessary ingredient of a rapidly changing social order, does produce casualties. The search for new experiences, the rebellion against family norms and the testing of new ideas take their toll on both youths and their families. The cases in this chapter are of adolescents whose behavior is seen by many as having both immediate and long-run undesirable consequences.

INDIVIDUAL	INDIVIDUAL
vs.	vs.
INDIVIDUAL	ORGANIZATION

WE BURNED A BUM FRIDAY NIGHT

Taking the life of another community member is the gravest of all offenses, yet under certain circumstances, it is possible to understand that it could happen. For example, revenge, jealousy, self-defense, or even rage during a personal interchange are generally regarded as mitigating motives for murder. The most difficult of all crimes to understand, however, is that of senseless murder. Some lives are taken for no apparent reason and seem to result from a desire to destroy, rather than from a conflict between the killer and his victim. The story of Leonard Benton, Jr.'s death is one of cruelty. It is particularly difficult to understand because of the youth of the perpetrators and the helplessness of the victim.

REPORT FROM TEENY-BOPPERSVILLE

Often in expressing their rebellion against the adult world, teenagers end up in situations that make them even *more* dependent on the adult world. Thus, the pregnant girl or the youth apprehended by the police for a felony are confronted with the immediate need for resources only the adult world can provide. Other adolescents discover safe avenues for exercising their hostility—that is, they engage in deviant behavior but they minimize their chances for getting caught. Kirk Sale and Ben Appelbaum describe a place where teenagers gather to participate in behavior that would be unacceptable in the adult world. The place provides them anonymity and protection from the adult world, and condones their desire to behave in defiance of adult rules. While the term "teeny-bopper" may go out of style to describe such individuals, the phenomenon seems destined to continue.

ORGANIZATION vs. INDIVIDUAL	ORGANIZATION vs. ORGANIZATION

IN RE GAULT

In the eyes of the adolescent, the world is organized and operated by adults, for adults. Young people often feel powerless either to participate in the shaping of their environment or in instigating the changes they feel would bring it closer to the way they believe things ought to be. Not only are they often ignored as participants in the community, but in many ways they are not accorded the same individual rights as other citizens. Gerald Gault's experience in court as a juvenile delinquent, the later appeals on his behalf to the state court, and the verdict in his favor illustrate how the legal system has discriminated against the juvenile. Rights which are carefully protected by legal statute for adults have not been considered equally important for adolescents in the United States.

A HARD COP AND HIS PATIENT PARTNER ON A MENACING BEAT

The 1960s saw the street people, the flower children, and the hippies become commonplace in most major American cities. In many cities, like San Francisco, they carved out their own neighborhoods where they dominated the social life and the economy. While not particularly accepted by "middle America," adolescent groups in unusual dress, doing their own thing, getting kicks in their own ways, managed to create for themselves a special place on the American scene. But, like other such social movements, their endurance has been short. Many of the neighborhoods once occupied by hippies and drop-outs who go by other names, have turned into areas of deprivation, violence, hard drugs, and high crime rates. Haight Ashbury, the famous West Coast home of hippieism, is now such a place. This article describes the conflict between the police—an organization dedicated to the maintenance of the prevailing social order—and the persons who have grouped themselves outside of that order. Are the police victims of their occupational role, or are the victims those in the adolescent culture who face them?

We Burned a Bum Friday Night

NICHOLAS PILEGGI

It was dark outside when the bar-and-grill's owner looked up and saw "a yellow ball of fire" reflected in his plate-glass window. He remembered seeing some children run past the bar and suddenly he realized that the ball of fire was bounding across Mercer Street and that it was a man. The man appeared to be suspended for a moment; as though caught in the middle of a brilliant leap, and then, touching the ground, he began to scream. The man threw himself onto the street and, as he rolled about, an arm, a leg, the back of his head would become visible for an instant and then, again, would be lost in the flames. Seconds later the figure of another man was silhouetted against the light and then a blanket fell over the flames. A fireman, who had been on duty a hundred fifty feet away, fell upon the blanket and tried to halt the spastic jerks of the figure beneath him. Other firemen raced toward the pair with wet sheets and more blankets and they all began to strip the man of his burning clothes. The man's screams soon turned to moans and, though the flames he inhaled had

burned the inside of his throat and part of his windpipe, he managed to rasp:

"Some kids set me on fire."

Leonard Benton, Jr., was from eastern Kentucky, an ordained Protestant minister and a fifty-one-year-old Bowery derelict. He had sustained second- and third-degree burns over 40 percent of his body and the skin of his face, neck, back, chest, stomach and buttocks was completely charred. "His hair, lashes, lids and ears seemed to be gone," one fireman later recalled. "He was burned so badly that it was impossible to tell whether he was a white man or colored," another added. Benton lived six painful days after his burning—long enough to describe to the police his own immolation and the boys who set him on fire.

Benton had come to the Bowery in 1953. He usually paid $1.10 a night to sleep on a narrow cot in a sunless cubicle at the Sunshine Hotel, at 241 Bowery. He earned what little money he needed for lodgings and wine by collecting wastepaper in a pushcart supplied by a lower East Side waste dealer. It is common practice among local rag and paper dealers to lend pushcarts to derelicts they know to be "regulars." In addition, Benton earned a few cents from sympathetic motorists by wiping automobile windshields at the corner of Houston and Lafayette Streets. When drinking his thirty-three-cents-a-pint Linda Lee muscatel, Benton would sometimes forego his hotel room and spend a night or two, during the warm weather, sleeping outdoors. He would find a doorway in a deserted loft and warehouse district near the Bowery, a part of what the Fire Department calls "Hell's Hundred Acres." The area, which separates the Bowery from the southern tip of Greenwich Village, has long been used by many of the Bowery's thousands of homeless men as a "doorway flop." The largely uninhabited district is thought by derelicts to be comparatively safe from the Bowery "hawks" who strip them of their clothing and shoes while they sleep.

The three or four nights before his burning, Benton had been drinking heavily and he did not have enough money for the Sunshine Hotel. The weather was still warm and the pressure to sleep indoors had not yet struck the Bowery. During cold spells in New York, the city's morgue van routinely visits the street each morning to haul away the bodies of derelicts frozen to death the night before. At approximately six o'clock Monday night, September 19, 1966, Benton sat down on some collapsed cardboard cartons in the doorway of a loft building at 147 Mercer Street, seven blocks west of the Bowery. He had with him a day-old newspaper with which he intended to read himself to sleep.

Benton was a very private man and what it was that took him from Eastern State Teachers College and Grayson Christian College—both in Kentucky—to the doorway on Mercer Street no one knows. According to Benton's father, a retired conductor with fifty years on the Louisville & Nashville Railroad, he had no idea

what his son did in New York. He did say, to The New York *Times,* that Benton, an ordained minister in the Christian Churches (Disciples of Christ), a predominantly Southern denomination of nearly two million members, had preached in some small churches in eastern Kentucky before World War II. During the war, the elder Benton recalled, his son joined the Merchant Marine and became a meatcutter, an electrician and a painter, but not a chaplain. He said that Benton had been married, but did not know what had happened to his son's wife.

"He got in with the wrong crowd and got to drinking. We haven't heard from him in a long time."

Benton was the second derelict in three days to be set on fire by a fourteen-year-old blond boy and his thin twelve-year-old companion. Both boys were residents of the small Italian tenement neighborhood on the southern tip of the Village. Their first victim was burned after the boys had finished classes at St. Anthony's of Padua parochial school. This earlier burning, however, was not brought to the attention of the police because doctors at St. Vincent's Hospital assumed the man was just another wine-fogged derelict who had set himself on fire. They performed an emergency tracheotomy on the street and when they transferred the man to the hospital they refused detectives permission to talk to him. They said it would be too painful to talk to anyone in that condition.

"There was no way of knowing it was kids that first time," one of the detectives explained later. "Even though we didn't talk to the guy until after Benton was burned, we did smell his clothes and there was no gasoline smell on any of them. On that first night the idea that neighborhood kids had found themselves a new hobby was the least likely of many possibilities."

The boys, however, were not pleased by the lack of attention they received as a result of their first victim, a sixty-seven-year-old ex-sandhog named Frank Cassidy. They had burned him on Friday after school by pouring gasoline from a Coke bottle on to his head and setting him on fire. All day Saturday and Sunday, the boys, especially the blond boy, whispered to friends what they had done. At school all day Monday, while nuns and brothers taught classes, knots of children gathered in corners around the blond boy.

"We burned a bum Friday night," the blond boy calmly told every kid who would listen. "We burned a bum Friday night and we're going to burn another one tonight," he boasted.

The boy's claims were greeted, for the most part, with derisive hoots, not because of the horror of his boast, police later learned, but because the children thought he was a liar. His schoolmates later told police that they doubted his story of burning the man because they did not hear it on the radio news or see it on television. At one point during the day a nun saw a little girl giggling in class. She called the girl to the front of the room and demanded to know what was so funny. The girl told her that she had heard some of the boys talking about burning bums. The nun took the girl to the parish priest, but apparently no further action was taken that day. Both the police and the church refuse to discuss what steps were taken as a result of the girl's revelation. The police did say, however, that as the day progressed the blond boy became more and more frustrated by the fact that none of his friends seemed to take his boast seriously and at one point he told three or four local boys, "Yeah, well come with us tonight, smart guys, and watch us burn another bum. You'll find out."

Even before the first burning, incidents of derelict harassment had been reported to the police. Youngsters from the neighborhood would go into the warehouse district and throw rocks at derelicts. Sometimes they would creep up on a sleeping man, kick him and run. It seems to have been accepted, if not as a local sport, at least as a way of keeping the derelicts from getting too close to the section in which the children lived. Local youngters had been seen spilling gasoline and lighter fluid in puddles on the sidewalk of the warehouse district and watching it burn. A variation of the game was to pour gasoline in a stream along the street, light one end of it and watch the flames travel the track of fuel. To some detectives the burning of Cassidy on Friday night was no more than the next step on a regular progression of violent street pranks. They had seen wanton violence before. It was not until the second burning, three nights later, of Benton, that the police became worried and very anxious to capture the children before, as one detective said, "we had an epidemic of bum burnings spread through the whole neighborhood."

The blond boy lived on the top floor of a seven-story walk-up tenement. He had a reputation around the neighborhood for being a bit odd. He was considered somewhat spoiled and willful, and on one occasion, a local story goes, he is supposed to have dangled from the seventh-floor fire escape until his parents capitulated to his wishes. The boy's father was a taxicab driver, and there was enough money in the house for a color television and a set of expensive drums. The furniture in his house was new and his mother had a washing machine in her kitchen. The family was, by the standards of the working-class community, well-off. The boy's mother, who was pleased that he showed an interest in music, insisted that he be considerate of their neighbors and not practice on his drums after six in the evening. He agreed. He was vain about his hair. His mother told police that it often took her son fifteen minutes to arrange his elaborate coiffure. When newly combed, one of the detectives said, the boy's hair looked as though it had been poured on his head by a cake decorator.

His thin twelve-year-old companion, who lived just a few doors away, had difficulty sleeping without a night-light, stuttered slightly and liked to draw. His mother described him to detectives as "sensitive," and pointed out that he had been working "very hard" on a painting of John F. Kennedy on the days of both burnings. She told people that she was pleased that the boy wanted to become an artist, and she said she encouraged him to continue his drawing and painting studies. The boy's father, a longshoreman who lost a leg in a dockside brawl, was less enthusiastic about his son's ways. One of the things which annoyed the father was the fact that his wife had to go to bed with their son before the boy could fall a-sleep. While the mother attributed this to his "high-strung and sensitive" qualities, his father disapproved but

could not stop the practice. As soon as her son fell asleep she would get up and go to her own bed. However, the night-light could not be turned off.

On Monday, after a day of derision at school, the blond boy and his friend met again. This time they were joined by three other boys who would serve as witnesses to the act. The five set out with a distinct intention to burn another man. Detectives established that it was the blond boy who started the group toward a garage. As they were walking it was also the blond boy who, after looking in garbage heaps in vain for a Coke bottle, finally settled on a waxed milk container. The difference in the amounts of gasoline about to be thrown on a man—the Coke's six ounces compared to the milk carton's thirty-two—was the difference between life for Frank Cassidy and death for Leonard Benton. At the garage the blond boy filled the waxed container with the gasoline left in an extra-long truck-service hose. There is always gasoline left in a pump hose, and the youngsters knew that in the truck-length hoses sometimes a quart of gasoline could be found. In the doorway at 147 Mercer Street, two blocks away from the garage, they found Benton asleep on a cardboard mattress. The twelve-year-old took the gasoline from the blond boy and the two of them approached the brown metal doorway as the three witnesses hovered in the rear. They all shouted and whooped in an effort to wake up Benton, and one of them yelled: "Hey, mister, wake up, hey mister, what time is it?"

They all laughed and jumped about, the thin twelve-year-old careful not to spill any of the gasoline. Benton did wake and drowsily told the boys that he did not have a wristwatch and did not know the time. He later told police, "I tried to shoo them away." The twelve-year-old ran some gasoline along the ground to Benton's foot. The blond boy lit a match and the flames moved toward the man's shoe and then went out. It is no longer clear in the minds of the five boys how long the harassment of Benton continued. Memory returns solidly only with the vision of the twelve-year-old boy leaning over Benton and tipping the milk container onto his head. He remembered later how easily the gasoline poured out of the container. He told police that it poured out in a steady stream. It had been more difficult, he recalled, getting the gasoline out of the Coke bottle onto Cassidy's head on Friday night. The blond boy, who was standing next to him, waited until Benton was thoroughly drenched, then took a book of matches from his pocket, struck one and touched it to Benton's hair.

The doorway in which Benton had been sleeping when he suddenly burst into flames showed no sign of having been scorched. Neither did the hand-lettered signs, Jamie Togs Inc. and Peta-Pat Inc., directly over Benton's head. The collapsed cardboard mattress showed no sign of having been burned. It was all too obvious, according to the firemen who first saw the scene, that the center of the fire was Benton himself.

At the hospital, in what detectives came to think of as a heroic effort on Benton's part, he managed to rasp out a few words about what had happened to him. Doctors and nurses, working nearby, moved as quietly as possible, and the detective who listened had his ear close to Benton's mouth. Doctors

had performed a tracheotomy on Benton in order that he might breathe more easily, so a nurse had to hold a compress against the breathing hole in his neck in order for him to speak. After four or five words, the nurse would release the compress and Benton would gasp for air through the hole in his neck. It was a long and painful session for Benton, but when it was over the detectives had a clear picture of what had taken place.

"I was reading a paper," Benton stated.

"I got tired of reading.

"I tried to get some sleep.

"Some kids came by.

"They woke me up.

"They asked me for the time.

"One was a big kid.

"One had a lot of blond hair.

"I shooed them away.

"I didn't have a watch.

"Then I felt something wet.

"On my head.

"On my shoulders.

"I saw a milk container.

"I heard a high-pitched voice yell.

"It said, 'Oh my God, Vinnie.'

"I was on fire."

Accompanied by doctors, detectives went to a ward upstairs, and there sixty-seven-year-old Cassidy, having spent a weekend in silence, confirmed that it was a blond boy who had set him on fire and added that he could identify the boy who poured the gasoline.

The morning after Benton's burning there was no one in that small, closely knit community who did not know that a man, perhaps two men, had been critically burned by neighborhood children. With the description of the youngsters—especially the blond boy—detectives had started moving about the tenements, explaining, cajoling, lying, tempting, even vaguely threatening, doing, in other words, everything detectives do when they want information. The nature of detective work is not the following of a circuitous though rational route through threats, clues and hints that leads finally to one neat, tidy suspect who is simply taken away and "booked." At its most subtle it has to do with making as many people as possible feel they personally have something to gain by turning stool pigeon. A detective involved in the investigation said he knew it would be difficult. He described the neighborhood as filled with "hard working, suspicious, religious and close-mouthed people. It is strictly an interfamily neighborhood," he went on. "They settle their own problems with the help of their church. The police are considered strangers and are not trusted. The people are basically law-abiding, but they kind of follow their own rigid morality. That entire neighborhood knew the whole story about the burnings, but no one would call the police."

One of the detectives who was of Italian descent, like most of the people in the neighborhood, tried to explain the insularity of the community:

"Do you know, for instance, that the apartments in the neighborhood are handed down from family to family? In some buildings you have three and four generations of the same family. It's a neighborhood they know. They feel safe in it. There are no locks on any of the doors. When one man's son gets married to a neighbor's daughter, the whole neighborhood starts looking for someplace for the couple to live. They're protective toward each other and toward each other's children. No matter how hor-

rible they might think the burning of those men was, you've got to remember, it would be a very, very difficult thing for them to turn in someone else's son."

The first reaction detectives met among most of the neighborhood residents was one of horror at the deed, but at the same time anger at their questioners.

"Why are you asking us?"

"How do you know the kids didn't come from somewhere else?"

"We've been having a lot of trouble with the coloreds."

To Lieutenant Albert Dandridge, who is colored, they said, "We've been having a lot of trouble with the Puerto Ricans." It is a neighborhood that clings to its own heritage and the people who live there identify all other people by either racial, national or religious stamps. In such a situation the tip of an outsider is often all the detectives can hope for.

By noon Tuesday, less than twelve hours after detectives began expressing interest in the blond boy, the telephone call for which they all had been waiting came through. The call was from "a friend" of one of the detectives. The caller said, "The kid you're looking for lives at—Sullivan Street." When Lieutenant Dandridge and two other detectives got to the Sullivan Street building they asked people downstairs where the blond boy lived. They climbed the six flights and knocked on the door. The blond boy's mother answered. The detectives identified themselves. The apartment was clean, neat and well-organized. There was a full set of drums in the living room, and seated at the kitchen table doing arithmetic homework was the blond boy, bent over a loose-leaf binder. The boy's father was not home, but a roast was in the oven.

"We know that last night a fellow was burned at Mercer and Prince Streets and we're looking for help," Dandridge said. "Have you heard anything from any boys you know?"

"Oh no!" the blond boy's mother answered immediately. "Oh no! They're all good boys."

"Do you know a boy named Vinnie?" Dandridge asked, using the name Benton had mentioned.

The blond boy shuffled about, detectives recalled, and then said, "Yeah."

"Where is he?"

"I don't know. Sometimes he goes to Staten Island."

"Where does he live?"

"Down the block."

"Do you know anything you can tell us about the burning?"

The blond boy simply shrugged.

"Anything at all?" the detectives asked.

"Nah. I haven't heard anything about it in the neighborhood. Just what I heard on the radio."

This is what detectives call "the wedge." There had been no news broadcasts about the burning at that time.

"Who was with you when you heard it on the radio? Maybe they can help us."

"I don't know. I don't remember. Just some of the guys."

"Well, when did you hear it. Maybe that'll make you remember who you were with."

"I guess it was around nine o'clock."

(One of the detectives remarked later that in questioning children in front of their parents there is always a period of uncertainty when the parent doesn't know what the child is going to say next. The parent's facial expressions and unaccustomed atten-tion to the exact wording of the child's reply always reveal his own uneasiness and apprehension.)

"Where were you when you were listening to the radio?"

"I don't remember."

"Well, who was with you at nine o'clock last night?"

Here the blond listed the names of several boys, including Vinnie. The detectives walked into the hallway and when they returned they asked the blond boy's mother if she and her son would mind accompanying them to the station house for further questioning.

"Well, I don't see why," was her first answer. "He's told you all he knows. He's only a boy. But if you think it will help any, we will."

At that point, all the detectives agreed, the mother had no idea that her son was guilty. In fact, as they were on their way to the station house, she kept trying to help him remember where he was when he might have heard the news on the radio. He continued to rattle off the names of friends, but detectives noted that Vinnie and a name which turned out to be that of the twelve-year-old boy were repeated most frequently.

Within a few hours all five boys and their parents were in the Beach Street station house being apprised of their rights. The boys sat beneath a row of the F.B.I.'s Ten-Most-Wanted posters in Dandridge's office. The room is painted a municipal green, has heavy wooden furniture and screened windows. The parents, for the most part stood around their children as if to shelter them from any harm. The arrests of their sons had surprised the parents; the men arrived in their work clothes and the women wore the cotton housedresses in which they had been cooking the evening meal. The lack of formality seemed to give the parents courage—as though they understood that nothing really very bad can happen to you when you are wearing everyday clothes. It was at the court appearance the next day when the men wore dark suits and the women dark crepe dresses and no makeup that the parents first seemed to recognize fully the import and deadliness of what their sons had done. At the police station, however, there were many tears that evening, not necessarily for the burned men.

"Gee, he's only twelve years old," the mother of the boy who poured gasoline on both men pleaded. "What do you want to pick on him for?"

"His voice," she kept repeating. "His voice. My son has the best singing voice in his school."

The boy's father, the one-legged longshoreman, was the only parent who attempted to strike his son during the questioning. A detective standing next to him said the man went through an elaborate ritual of unstrapping his belt and shouting threats about whipping the boy within an inch of his life. He was, of course, restrained.

The boy's mother, meanwhile, paid very little attention to her husband's rage.

"How could he do this?" she kept asking. "He wouldn't step on a bug."

It was after the threat of his father's strap that the twelve-year-old made his first admission:

"I guess we shouldn't have done it," he said. "We just got nothing to do." And then, brightly, he asked, "Will I be able to go to school tomorrow?"

Outside Dandridge's office the blond boy's mother told a reporter: "I don't know why in the name of God the boys did a thing like this. I always told my boy I'd give him anything in my power and I asked only one thing from him. I asked him never to disgrace me. I wonder now if he knows what he has done to me."

She told the reporter that she had shopping to do, but was "too ashamed" to be seen in the streets. She said she would have to go home and stay home. She had a dental appointment the next day, but she would not keep it because she could not face her neighbors.

The mother of one of the boys who acted as a witness was outraged. "They were only bums," she kept insisting. "Everybody talks about how bad the bums are and how we should get rid of them; the children did something about it. But it was just a stupid mistake—nothing wrong. Why did the cops have to pick on these children and put their names in the record? Because the cops wanted a fast arrest and a solution to the crime so they could get a promotion, that's why," she said.

"I feel bad about the bums who were burned," she admitted, "but what about my son's life? That's the important thing to me and now he's marked."

At the end of the night all of the youngsters had admitted either to witnessing or taking part in the burning. Statements were taken by the District Attorney and a stenographer. The boys were all charged with "juvenile delinquency," with the specification in parentheses, "Felonious Assault." In New York, cases involving children under sixteen are tried in Children's Court and no public record is permitted of the hearings, nor is the Court's disposition of the case revealed. The case of Cassidy's and Benton's burning, in fact, would have been handled in just this manner except that on Sunday afternoon, six days after he was burned, Benton died. This altered the city's position in the case entirely and the prosecution of the five boys was turned over to the Corporation Counsel by the District Attorney's office. The police department rearrested the boys—who had been allowed to go home with their parents after their first arraignment—and the specific charge against them was changed to homicide.

Joseph Halpern, who acted as the prosecutor for the city, said he was convinced the youngsters were not impressed at all by what they had done. Halpern insists they were neither contrite nor remorseful when they walked into the court charged with homicide. For whatever reasons, Halpern said, the lawyers for the children had apparently convinced the parents that they would be able to take their children home after the homicide hearing. Now the lawyers pleaded with the judge that keeping the boys in jail until the formal trial date would make them miss two weeks of school. Halpern objected strenuously and the judge ordered the children to remain in jail.

It was then that the twelve-year-old's mother fainted and the other mothers began to cry and wail. It was also then, according to Halpern, that the children began for the first time to show some concern.

"They were evidently able to comprehend the seriousness of their actions only through the distress of their mothers, and the mothers seemed to regard the action of their sons as serious only to the extent that their sons were being kept from them."

Children's Court is on the second floor of a midtown municipal office building. Every attempt is made to keep the youngsters who appear there from freezing at the awesome "dignity" of the court. The judge, for instance, though he wears judicial robes, does not sit on a raised platform, but behind a desk in a room which looks very much like an office. The children, however, are usually unaware of the court decor. A clerk who has watched many of these confrontations says that it is the sight of their parents in "Sunday clothes" during the week —a father standing uncomfortably in a suit—to which the child most often will respond.

"The most heinous crimes in the past few years," Halpern states flatly, "have all been committed by kids."

He pointed specifically to the blond boy and his friend:

"We must remember that they came back. They burned Cassidy on Friday night, they heard his screams, they saw he was on fire, they knew what fire does, they knew what they had done, and they came back again and did it all over again on Monday night to Benton. The whole horror here is that they came back. The blond boy's mother even said that her son had seen a woman in an apartment across the street burned to a crisp in a fire. He knew what fire did. And yet, the two of them came back."

Never, from the very first time Halpern read of the case until its conclusion, was he able to understand why the pair had burned the two men. The boys were never able to give a response to that question which anyone felt was meaningful. Halpern suspects that any youngster in that particular neighborhood could have become involved as a witness to the burning. He insists, however, that the two boys who did pour the gasoline and light the match, especially the blond boy, had to be a very special type of child. He said he was struck during the testimony by how facile the pair were in telling about the steps involved in burning the men. The two boys spoke as though they were not participants, Halpern said, a trait common among persons confessing to a crime. Halpern felt that there should have been some final recognition by the two boys of what they had done, but there never was. The three boys who witnessed the burning were allowed to return home with their parents twenty-two days after Benton died. The blond boy and his friend were given preliminary psychiatric examinations while jailed at Youth House. When the report was returned with the prison psychiatrist's suggestion that the twelve-year-old boy, not the blond, be given a full-scale examination at Bellevue Hospital, the attorney and detectives connected with the case became suspicious that somehow the reports had gotten mixed up. When the psychiatrist was questioned about the possibility of an error

he became immediately defensive, according to an attorney who spoke to him, and started muttering about privileged communication. He refused to disclose anything about his findings or even to discuss them. The sentence finally imposed on the pair ordered that both boys be remanded to Youth House for an indeterminate period. Their parents returned to the insular safety of their neighborhood and became convinced, more and more each day, that their sons were the victims of police and judicial zeal. Benton's body, after an autopsy, was released by the city and flown to Kentucky at his father's expense. Cassidy, after being treated for three months at St. Vincent's hospital, was finally well enough to leave.

"He just checked out one day and was gone," a detective said. "He probably went back to the Bowery. He didn't have anyone, you know. Usually when someone's injured we get calls from friends, relatives, somebody. With Cassidy a guy by the name of Gallagher called. No first name, just Gallagher. He said he thought maybe he knew Cassidy. He never called back."

Report from Teeny-Boppersville

J. KIRK SALE/BEN APFELBAUM

There is no urgency. They move slowly, languidly, along the crowded sidewalks. Brightcolored bell-bottoms, miniskirts, long hair falling straight down the back, a sagging pocketbook swung lazily by its straps, pastel sandals shuffling. Paisley shirts with puffed sleeves and open to the third button, tight cuffless trousers flaring slightly at the ankles, long sideburns flowing into carefully coiffed hair brushing gently on the collar, boots clicking in long, loping strides. Milling and ambling, like a rush-hour crowd in slow motion, they absorb the sights and sounds of the street. From a garishly painted basement cage, the heavy, shivering, electronic pulse of a band sets an imperceptible rhythm.

"Free admission, come on in, join our show, just starting. . . . Yeah, Dylan's dead, I'm hip. . . . My hair isn't short, that's just school rules, look at this. . . . Oh, yeah, she wears her face that she keeps in the jar by the door. . . . Hey, baby, so what's happening? "

A piece of pizza at the corner, eaten slowly and carefully, back against the counter, casually appraising the scene. In the window of the Rienzi, boys in

Reprinted by permission from J. Kirk Sale and Ben Apfelbaum, "They've Got the Generation Gap Blues: Report From Teeny-Boppersville," *New York Times*, May 28, 1967. Copyright by The New York Times Company.

full plumage assessing their reflections, a comb from nowhere patting the bobs in place. Strolling past Googie's and the Tin Angel, then, leisurely, drifting up to the park. Eventually back to the crowded heart, outside the Cafe Wha? and the Cock-'n'-Bull, an orange drink at the newsstand, some new faces gossip, moving back as the cops push wearily through, then leaning easily, knee bent, against the wall, humming softly with the rhythm of the bands, and the crows, and the laughter, lots of laughter.

Down in the basement of the Wha? on Macdougal Street, a long and narrow, low-ceilinged cavern, the Raves are into their last set, stark on the blazingly lighted stage, surrounded by huge amplifiers, speakers, microphones and wires. The noise is infectious: both young guitarists on the stage are dancing, shuffling, smiling broadly, and just below them the regulars at the center booths are singing along, yelling to the drummer, pulling on the wires, swaying in their seats, while in the back, against the far wall, two girls, a vinyl miniskirt and a plaid pants suit, are dancing, easily, relaxed, absorbed. The music is satisfying and exhilarating, everyone in the room from ticket-taker to tourist is caught up in it, in the good time the band is having, loose, untroubled, free, and when the last electronic chord fades there is a laughing cheer and a sad, sated, little audible sigh that fills the room.

This is a warm spring Saturday night in the center of New York's Greenwich Village, which in the last two years has become the magnet for the newest, and liveliest, subdivision of New York's teen-age world: the teeny-bopper. Along these special eight blocks teeny-boppers from the entire metropolitan area find a world apart, a world dedicated to them and their pleasures, and every evening, every weekend, they fill it; when they can't make the Village scene they dream of it, or wait for the time, or pretend they are *there*. There are teeny-bopper scenes, of course, all across the country—in Chicago's Old-town, on West Hollywood's Sunset Strip, even Denver and Philadelphia and Toronto, for the teeny-boppers have sprung up wherever the young congregate and electronic bands pulsate. But the Village is special.

"I feel free to do whatever I want down here. I mean, where I live there's nothing to do, no excitement. Here you can do what you want." That, the statement of a young boy from Queens, is the teeny-bopper testimonial to the Village. "I wanted to be a teacher," says a miniskirted girl from the Bronx, "but I changed my mind. Since I came down here, I have no time for school, I want to come here all the time. I want to live here.... I love it down here, it's my kind of people. I'm so comfortable."

"I was a teeny-bopper and I used to come down once a year," said one Village regular, "and then every weekend, and soon you like it so much that you don't want to leave at all." The Village magnet is powerful—and the pull is self-perpetuating. One high-

school senior, a boy very close to the teeny-bopper world, talks about its attraction to the girls he knows:

They take a friend and they come crawling into the Village from Forest Hills and Canarsie, dress the way they see in pictures, talk the way they've learned to, and go and sit in the Cock-'n'-Bull with other kids who are exactly like them in every way. And then they all go home and feel proud that they 'hung out in the Village.' They think it's great, and they say to their friends, "I hung out in the Village—can you top that?" After all, the Village is famous all over the world. I mean, could you go to Paris and say, "I hung out in Borough Park?"

Barbara, a 16-year-old from the Bronx and a student at Evander Childs High School, is a regular at the Cafe Wha? Like most, she makes the standard disclaimer, afraid of being put down, hating the imprisonment of the press's label: "Me? I'm not a teeny-bopper; that's that kid over there." We asked her what she does on Saturday morning.

"I get ready to come down here to the Village at night," she laughed embarrassed.

"And what do you do?"

"Well, first I do all my homework, I do all the things I have to around the house. Then I call my friends and we talk about what we're going to wear—and then we come down the Wha?" ("Down the Wha?," incidentally, is a signal part of the teeny-bopper lexicon.)

"What time do you get here?"

"It starts at 7:30, and we get here at 8:30. We don't want to be the first ones; we have to make our entrance, you know." She laughs at her own frankness. "Then we walk down the aisle, and sometimes if you're lucky you get a wave, you know, from the guys in the group. And then when the set is over, they come down. Then we sit and watch them and wave, and yell, and all that.

"And then we watch the whole show, and after it's over we go out in the lobby. And like last night we were talking with some other kids, and you get to know about them, what they think about the Wha?, you know, and then how old they are, and what *we* think about it. You get to exchange ideas.

"And then at the end, we come back in, the band does its last set, the crazy set, and we're there in the back, singing and joking, and they yell at us to shut up. We sit all the way in the back next to the wall; we can dance there, and crack up and everything." She sighs and smiles and squirms a little.

No easy definition of "teeny-bopper" is possible, for the perimeters of the word change as fast as the Top 10, and as the general press picks it up it is used to describe practically anyone who is not senile. (The word "bopper" itself comes from the old Negro argot "bebopper" of the forties, the bebop jazz enthusiast who dressed oddly and dug the then far-out music.)

But, roughly, the teeny-boppers range from 10 to 19, though the majority are of high-school age, between 14 and 17. They are caught up in the simple fact of being young, scorn the pretense of "acting grownup" or trying to be an adult, and audaciously, aggressively, parade their youthfulness. They are intellectually as well as emotionally set against their parents' standards on sex, drugs, music, clothes, behavior, hair and politics. The word "teeny-bopper" at first seemed to re-

fer to girls, but no special term has been coined for the male of the species, so "teeny-bopper" now applies to both sexes.

They are the kids who deliberately involve themselves in more than just a radio-listening way with the current pop-music world, who spend their weekends and summer vacations religiously visiting the cafes where the bands play, who are friendly, or try to be, with the musicians (who are generally of, or close to, their own age), who can tell gossip from truth in the teen magazines and, in fact, make rock'n'roll the focus of their interest and energy, the theme of their conversations and dreams.

Even in the larger cities, where the teeny-boppers become identifiable as a group, they probably represent no more than a minority of the teen-age population, though a very distinct, involved and articulate minority. Not just any teen-ager with longish hair and a pair of boots is a teeny-bopper. Coexisting with them are the *hippies* —the descendants of the beats, usually the older teens, somewhat scornful of the youthful musicians, more involved with drugs, usually living away from home and perhaps working at odd jobs, tolerant of the teenies but living in a more adult, though thoroughly anti-Establishment, world; the *screamies*—younger children, usually girls, from 9 to 12, who are only beginning to awaken to the world around and have not yet developed any cool about themselves, screaming and fainting at the few big-name concerts they are allowed to go to; and the *squares*— the straitlaced, short-haired, penny-loafer, crew-cut set, football players and A-students.

In a way, the teeny-boppers partake of all these worlds and may have square characteristics along with their hip ones; they may be reading "Silas Marner" and the East Village Other, looking up to both Longfellow and Leary, gossiping about the senior prom as well as last night's party. For teeny-bopperism is a stage, part of a loose evolutionary process of adolescence that connects with other stages. Thus, it is possible for a screamie to become a bopper, or a bopper a hippie—this last is fairly frequent in the Village, where the two worlds overlap—for the categories are loose, and the entries easy.

Although the teeny-boppers resemble earlier teen-age groups in some ways—rebellious, self-centered, questioning—there is a difference of degree so great as to be a difference of kind between them and the flappers of the twenties, the bobby-soxers of the forties or the Presleyites of the fifties. For one thing, they are more obvious, more aggressive, less inhibited, continually play-acting their youthful roles in public, "goofing on" (putting-on-putting-down) the squares and the adults: panhandling the tourists in the Village streets and reveling in their embarrassment, gaily yelling, "Let's go shoot up" in front of policemen and grownups just for the effect, making fun of the blank unsmiling faces in the subways.

But the music they create and listen to tells most about them. The lyrics of today have come a long way from Patti Page's "How Much Is That Doggie in the Window?" Listen to this rather blunt but accurate sentiment from 15-year-old Janis Ian:

If you think I'm hating grownups, you've got me all wrong.
They're very nice people when they stay where they belong. /

But I'm the younger generation.
And your rules are giving me fixations.
I've got those younger generation, re-gurgitating blues.*

And another:

Her mother plays on the golf course ev'ry day
And her Daddy sits at home and plays with the maid
They've found the perfect alibi:
Stay together for the sake of the child,
Divorce don't fit
And they're too young to split.
Think they're martyrs but they're killing the kid.*

It's not unusual for the teeny-boppers' music to be written and played by their contemporaries. A group called the Raves, for example, who are very big with the teeny-bop set at the Cafe Wha? and who recently cut a record of their own composition that is moving up on the charts, are led by Michael Jimenez, all of 19, and his brother David, 17. These contemporaries are touchable and talkable to —on the street after their show, in the coffeehouse down the street, at the party on Saturday. It is the everyday quality of these idols that differentiates this generation from those past. Peter Tork of the Monkees, mooned over by girls across the country and probably worth half a million dollars, is right there walking along Macdougal Street and will even stop to talk; Brian Jones of the Rolling Stones, a group nearly as successful and rich as the Beatles, can be seen in the Village restaurants.

John Emelin, a tall, serious young singer of 21, who is a member of a

* From "Younger Generation Blues," and "Janey's Blues," copyright 1966, Dialogue Music, Inc.

popular new band called Lothar and the Hand People (Lothar is the nickname they have given their theremin, an electronic instrument played by moving the hands along a tubular electrode, hence the "hand people") sums up the attitude of a special group of his generation:

The difference between 1940 and now is amazing. We don't have a major war, but we have a lot of very strange little ones. We have the memory of an assassination which is still getting fantastic publicity. We have a tremendous race scene that is getting a tremendous amount of publicity. We have a fantastic drug scene that's getting a lot of attention. We have an amazing music scene which was just not happening in the forties the way it's happening now. We have an amazing science scene—fantastic! In the forties they were discovering nylon, or something. We're about to embark for the moon.

What sets the teeny-bopper apart is a special awareness of, and dissatisfaction with, the adult world, and a deliberate attempt to create a separate free-and-easy world through a rough hedonism of music, companionship, emotionalism, sex, drugs and, as the teeny-boppers say, "anything that turns you on, makes you happy."

At the Rienzi, a coffeehouse where boppers and post-boppers mingle, we asked a boy named David, 17, neatly dressed and with well-groomed hair curling under his ears, about his parents. He snorted, "My father wants me to be rich," and made a face. "My father wants me to grow up to be exactly like him. He's a champion bridge player and he goes down to the bridge club all night. And I say, 'I'm going down to Macdougal Street,' and he says, 'You're just hanging around down there.' So I say, 'I'm just going to be with my friends. *You* go to the bridge club: what do you go *there* for?' Every—night he goes to the bridge club!" And a young girl echoes: "You rarely find a girl who can talk to her parents. Her parents are always putting her down."

Iris, a pretty high-school senior who has made the Village scene for some years, argues that the big problem is that the teeny-boppers have to lead double lives because they can't get through to their parents. "They say, 'Oh, Mom, I'm going to hang around at the corner,' and they come down here and smoke [that's not tobacco] and have sex and it's all very teeny. And they go home and they're Miss Goody-Goody again, and comes Friday night, it's 'I'm going to the corner of the park' again. Because they can't say to their parents, 'This is what I am and what I want to do.' So a lot of them lead a kind of double life. How can you go home and when your mother says, 'What did you do tonight, dear?' say, 'Ma, tonight I smoked grass?' "

This generational gap showed itself one night recently in the Village when a big Lincoln pulled up in front of the Cafe Wha? and a large matron stormed out, went up to the doorman and screamed: "Where's my daughter? Get her up here, you bum! Get her out of this evil place!" She then marched inside and found her daughter talking to a longhaired youth of perhaps 15: "You spend all your time with these disgusting queers?" The daughter took one look and ran off down Macdougal Street. Her mother went tearing after her at a remarkable speed and in a few minutes reappeared, dragging the girl, in tears, back to the car.

An hour later, much to the amusement of the regulars on the street, the daughter was back, strolling casually. She explained: "I ran into the subway and lost the—bitch."

In reaction to the world of their parents which they think they understand and don't want to be a part of, the teeny-boppers run away into a world of their own where they can be young and revel in their childish enthusiasms without anybody tsk-tsking over their shoulders. They want to be left alone in an arena where they can maintain their own mores and values, however flimsy, which they regard as no worse than their parents'. They ask very little from the outside—except money from home and passing grades from school, both usually given easily —and certainly not meaning or guidance or companionship. These they get from their contemporary heroes in the bands and on the streets, from group experience of emotional music shared at fever pitch, and from being a part of a scene that's "happening." The dominant note of this world is amplified twang of an electronic guitar: rock'n'roll is the lingua franca, musical involvement the passport. Frank Zappa, a member of a new group of talented musicians called the Mothers of Invention, whose wild black curls and black anklelength coat have made him a Macdougal Street standout, sees a kind of patriotism in this involvement. "The only real loyalty that exists in the American teenager today is to his music. He doesn't give an actual damn about his country or his religion. He has more actual patriotism in terms of how he feels about his music than in anything else. And this just has never happened before."

Part of the exhilaration, of course, comes from the incredible noise level at which the music is played, thanks to the complicated electronic gadgetry that has turned a guitar from a sweet accompanying instrument into a blaring siren and a weak teen-age tenor into an echo-chamber scream. John Emelin, whose own group's theremin is one of the loudest electronic creations of them all, argues that "it's a lot of noise only in the same way that Indian music is a lot of noise sometimes, or symphonies are a lot of noise. It makes you peak out emotionally." Hearing the signers and memorizing the songs—it means buying the records ($250-million worth a year), reading the teen magazines (50 million copies a year), and above all talking, talking about the world of the rock'n'roll stars. On the streets, in the cafes, over the sausage sandwiches, the conversations are heavily rock-centered: "Hey, d'you see that that Russian guy—what's it? Yevtushenko?—made the Monkees concert in Hawaii?" Or: "You know the Animals where they say, 'Have you ever been so hungry that you had no pride?' Like that's where I'm at now about Eric Clapton, I told you I saw him at the Tin Angel the other night: he's so beautiful." Even gossip and putdowns are couched in these terms: "Oh, no, man, let's stay away from that chick. You know her bag? Like she sits around and watches the Beatles on Ed Sullivan, she just sits there and screams, or sometimes like she'll take pictures of the screen just to have pictures of *them*. She's got this picture of Paul McCartney, it's all distorted, with no focus, and she'll say, 'This is a picture of Paul.' You know, what kind of—?"

Naturally enough, through this process the culture heroes for the teeny-boppers are in large measure the rock'n'roll musicians of any stripe—not just the locals who have made good like Lothar and the Hand People and the Mothers of Invention or the famous ones who make the scene like the Rolling Stones and the Animals, but also—and especially—Bob Dylan and, still, the Beatles. Even today when a Beatles song comes on in a Village diner, there is a modified hush, everyone listening with one ear. And Dylan, who was the first to turn many of these kids on to some serious ideas and a glimpse of poetry, represents for many a kind of supreme figure, a kid who dropped out of the parental world, made good, got rich, scored whenever he wanted to, and then dropped out again, a mysterious, beautiful figure proving to the teeny-boppers that they must be on to something great.

In the same way the professional dropouts around the Village, seeable and knowable, are culture heroes: Allen Ginsberg especially ("Oh, what a beautiful life, I mean beautiful"), Timothy Leary and Andy Warhol: There is something about the way they are "goofing on" the square world and yet making a go of it that embodies all the teeny-bop ideals. This "grooving with" the hip dropout spills over to such groups as homosexuals and Negroes who while they are not themselves teeny-boppers—the Village scene has no more than a handful of Negro teeny-boppers, largely because Negro youths apparently don't need such a scene to declare their freedom from and hostility to the Establishment power structure—represent the kind of sentiment the boppers feel they are into.

If there is hedonism in the music, there is also hedonism in the life that surrounds it. The sights and sounds of rock'n'roll are enough for most of the teeny-boppers, but there is no question but that the twin revolutions of the adult world in sex and drugs have also filtered down to become a part of their world as well.

We talked to one girl of 18 who had been coming to the Village regularly for four years—she was pretty, shy, and except for her unusual dress could have been any suburban girl—and asked her about sex.

"Well, I'd meet boys, and like, you know I'd ... I'd *love* them, not just like them. So I stayed with them. And then the summertime, I stayed down here, I smoked a lot, and ... I didn't just go to *anybody*; I really liked these boys. But they used me. Like I'd tell them I liked them and wanted to be with them, and they'd use me and then say, 'Goodby now, that's it.' And I was very hurt. . . ."

"How do you feel about all that now?"

"I don't know. I think it was a good experience. I mean, I'm better now, I learned. I don't think everything I did was right, but I don't feel guilty. I mean it's just a misfortune that it went wrong. I learned about things and how to handle them.

"But even now, I meet boys and the first thing they say is, 'Come on, let's go to bed.' And I want to show the boy that I like him, but now ... I don't know what to do."

The confusion is natural enough. "My mother knows I wouldn't go with anybody," one girl told us. "Though sometimes I feel that I would. But I know that when it really comes down to things, I'd be scared witless. I feel that if I ... went with somebody, I couldn't look them in the face afterward, I really couldn't." In addition to the simple fear of the unknowns of sex, most of the teeny-boppers seem to be aware of the other difficulties—the possibilities of pregnancy, venereal disease, emotional turnmoil and "a bad reputation." "This may be old-fashioned," says 16-year-old Barbara, "but I think a boy respects you better if the first time you meet him you don't say, 'How about it?,' you know?" She laughs at the exaggeration. "I think it's not good, that you should know what you're doing better, when you're 20 or so."

There are enough sad stories of girls who have slept around to indicate that sex is a real—if troublesome—part of the liberality of this world (but whether it is more so than in the corn belt no one knows). "I know this one girl," admits a young teeny, "she was going with this guy in a band, and she went to bed with him. And after that he wouldn't talk to her, and she felt funny. So then pretty soon everybody in the group had her. She's walking around now like she's lost."

The fact is that with the sexual mores of the teeny-boppers the possibilities, and the pitfalls, are much more open than in the past.

Marijuana, too, is more or less routine, though of course it is not confined to the teeny-boppers ("I can get more grass in East Orange than I can down here," said one girl in the Village). By the time they are 16 probably most of the teenies have experimented with marijuana, and quite a number may smoke regularly— "They don't think marijuana is a drug, they think it's normal," one teenie says—and a sizable minority is "into the acid scene," i.e., taking LSD occasionally. But it appears that very few go on to amphetamines—"Stay away from A, man," one boy warns— and almost none to heroin.

Marijuana is obviously a convenient release for some of the teeny-bopper set, most of whom are too young to get a drink legally (their hangouts are all liquor-free and the only thing stronger than Coke is the music) and many of whom profess to be rather repulsed by what they have seen of adult use of alcohol, anyway. ("I came home about 2:30 in the morning when my mother was having a party," one boy told us, "and I saw all these disgusting middle-aged people, all drunk and doing all these foolish disgusting things.") Marijuana is a way, they say, of getting high without being either sloppy or particularly noticeable (losing cool); it is simple and inexpensive; and it serves to heighten rather than diminish the sights and sounds of the scene.

Though marijuana is considered normal enough, the teeny-boppers are keenly aware that possession of it is against the law. "Like, I *know*, man, you can get busted for smoking and sometimes I get up tight when I see these plainclothes guys come with their badges. But I've read all the stuff; I know it can't hurt you—pot, that is—and all that about how it can lead to stronger stuff—well, no one believes that anymore except maybe in Indiana." And they also know the dangers of the stronger drugs—like music, this is a subject on which they seem well-informed—and pretty religiously steer away from them. For though there is indeed a dangerous drug scene in the Village (as elsewhere) and a few of the teenies do get sucked into it—either through some older teen-ager who is pushing drugs for a living or just as a result of youthful experimentation—there is also a powerful built-in correction in the Village: the wasted, empty men you can see around in the darkened doorways who have been hooked. The teeny-boppers can know, perhaps better than their suburban friends, just how evil the addiction scene is.

And so what, in the end, is to be made of this strange new world? What will become of it?

It is really too early to tell. Some of the teeny-boppers will probably simply fade from the scene as they reach 17 and 18—maybe bored, or choosing to go away to college, or settling into a job and its square responsibilities. Some will surely go into the hippie life, find a pad in the East Village, try to live along the Village fringes as long as they can. But whatever happens, it is unlikely that the years of bopperhood will have failed to make their mark.

There is no question about what today's teeny-boppers and those around them believe: "We're on to something new, and wonderful." The singer John Emelin says, "A whole return to a simple philosophy is what's happening. A whole group of kids is now rediscovering the concept of love —and not a romantic love, it's like *agape* or whatever. It's like Christian love without any of the hang-ups of the church scene."

Or, in the words of a 16-year-old boy: "There's one thing the adult generation in this country doesn't dig, man: we are the future generation." "Yeah, I can see our next President with long hair and a beard," said one youngster. Another added, "Look at us. The society has changed so much since we were 6 years old. Some day you'll see a long-haired cat sitting in Congress saying, 'Fourscore,' right?"

Phil Leone, a 19-year-old drummer with the Raves and very much a part of the subculture of the new generation, says: "Let's put it this way. The teeny-boppers now are going to be the future leaders of the world. And like if they're still thinking the way they are now it's going to be a beautiful place to live in."

And so what, in the end, is to be made of this strange new world? What will become of it?

In Re Gault

THE PRESIDENT'S COMMISSION ON LAW ENFORCEMENT AND ADMINISTRATION OF JUSTICE

Mr. Justice Fortas delivered the opinion of the Court.

Reprinted from The President's Commission on Law Enforcement and Administration of Justice: Task Force Reports: Juvenile Delinquency and Youth Crime, Appendix A, In re- Gault, pp. 57–76. Footnotes have been deleted.

This is an appeal under 28 U.S.C. § 1257(2) from a judgment of the Supreme Court of Arizona affirming the dismissal of a petition for a writ of habeas corpus. 99 Ariz. 181, 407 P.2d 760 (1965). The petition sought the release of Gerald Francis Gault, petitioners' 15-year-old son, who had been committed as a juvenile delinquent to the State Industrial School by the Juvenile Court of Gila County, Arizona. The Supreme Court of Arizona affirmed dismissal of the writ against various arguments which included an attack upon the constitutionality of the Arizona Juvenile Code because of its alleged denial of procedural due process rights to juveniles charged with being "delinquents." The court agreed that the constitutional guarantee of the due process of law is applicable in such proceedings. It held that Arizona's Juvenile Code is to be read as "impliedly" implementing the "due process concept." It then proceeded to identify and describe "the particular elements which constitute the due process in a juvenile hearing." It concluded that the proceedings ending in commitment of Gerald Gault did not offend those requirements. We do not agree, and we reverse. We begin with a statement of the facts.

I.

On Monday, June 8, 1964, at about 10 a.m., Gerald Francis Gault and a friend, Ronald Lewis, were taken into custody by the Sheriff of Gila County. Gerald was then still subject to a six months' probation order which had been entered on February 25, 1964, as a result of his having been in the company of another boy who had stolen a wallet from a lady's purse. The police action on June 8 was taken as the result of a verbal complaint by a neighbor of the boys, Mrs. Cook, about a telephone call made to her in which the caller or callers made lewd or indecent remarks. It will suffice for purposes of this opinion to say that the remarks or questions put to her were of the irritatingly offensive, adolescent, sex variety.

At the time Gerald was picked up, his mother and father were both at work. No notice that Gerald was being taken into custody was left at the home. No other steps were taken to advise them that their son had, in effect, been arrested. Gerald was taken to the Children's Detention Home. When his mother arrived home at about 6 o'clock, Gerald was not there. Gerald's older brother was sent to look for him at the trailer home of the Lewis family. He apparently learned then that Gerald was in custody. He so informed his mother. The two of them went to the Detention Home. The deputy probation officer, Flagg, who was also superintendent of the Detention Home, told Mrs. Gault "why Jerry was there" and said that a hearing would be held in Juvenile Court at 3 o'clock the following day, June 9.

Officer Flagg filed a petition with the Court on the hearing day, June 9, 1964. It was not served on the Gaults. Indeed, none of them saw this petition until the habeas corpus hearing on August 17, 1964. The petition was entirely formal. It made no reference to any factual basis for the judicial action which it initiated. It recited only that "said minor is under the age of 18 years and in need of the protection of this Honorable Court [and that] said minor is a delinquent minor." It prayed for a hearing and an order regarding "the care and custody of said minor." Officer Flagg executed a formal affidavit in support of the petition.

On June 9, Gerald, his mother, his older brother, and Probation Officers Flagg and Henderson appeared before the Juvenile Judge in chambers. Gerald's father was not there. He was at work out of the city. Mrs. Cook, the complainant, was not there. No one was sworn at this hearing. No transcript or recording was made. No memorandum or record of the substance of the proceedings was prepared. Our information about the proceedings and the subsequent hearing on June 15, derives entirely from the testimony of the Juvenile Court Judge, Mr. and Mrs. Gault and Officer Flagg at the habeas corpus proceeding conducted two months later. From this, it appears that at the July 9 hearing Gerald was questioned by the judge about the telephone call. There was conflict as to what he said. His mother recalled that Gerald said he only dialed Mrs. Cook's number and handed the telephone to his friend, Ronald. Officer Flagg recalled that Gerald had admitted making the lewd remarks.

Judge McGhee testified that Gerald "admitted making one of these [lewd] statements." At the conclusion of the hearing, the judge said he would "think about it." Gerald was taken back to the Detention Home. He was not sent to his own home with his parents. On June 11 or 12, after having been detained since June 8, Gerald was released and driven home. There is no explanation in the record as to why he was kept in the Detention Home or why he was released. At 5 p.m. on the day of Gerald's release, Mrs. Gault received a note signed by Officer Flagg. It was on plain paper, not letterhead. Its entire text was as follows:

Mrs. Gault:
Judge McGHEE has set Monday June 15, 1964 at 11:00 A.M. as the date and time for further Hearings on Gerald's delinquency

/s/Flagg

At the appointed time on Monday, June 15, Gerald, his father and mother, Ronald Lewis and his father, and Officers Flagg and Henderson were present before Judge McGhee. Witnesses at the habeus corpus proceeding differed in their recollections of Gerald's testimony at the June 15 hearing. Mr. and Mrs. Gault recalled that Gerald again testified that he had only dialed the number and that the other boy had made the remarks. Officer Flagg agreed that at this hearing Gerald did not admit making the lewd remarks. But Judge McGhee recalled that "there was some admission again of some of the lewd statements. He—he didn't admit any of the more serious lewd statements." Again, the complainant, Mrs. Cook, was not present. Mrs. Gault asked that Mrs. Cook be present "so she could see which boy had done the talking, the dirty talking over the phone." The Juvenile Judge said "she didn't have to be present at that hearing." The judge did not speak to Mrs. Cook or communicate with her at any time. Probation Officer Flagg had talked to her once—over the telephone on June 9.

At this June 15 hearing a "referral report" made by the probation officers was filed with the court, although not disclosed to Gerald or his parents. This listed the charge as "Lewd Phone Calls." At the conclusion of the hearing, the judge committed Gerald as a juvenile delinquent to the State Industrial School "for the period of his minority [that is, until 21], unless sooner discharged by due process of law." An order to that effect was entered. It recites that "after a full hearing and due deliberation the Court finds that said minor is a delinquent child, and that said minor is of the age of 15 years."

No appeal is permitted by Arizona

law in juvenile cases. On August 3, 1964, a petition for a writ of habeas corpus was filed with the Supreme Court of Arizona and referred by it to the Superior Court for hearing.

At the habeas corpus hearing on August 17, Judge McGhee was vigorously cross-examined as to the basis for his actions. He testified that he had taken into account the fact that Gerald was on probation. He was asked "under what section of . . . the code you found the boy delinquent?"

His answer is set forth in the margin. In substance, he concluded that Gerald came within ARS § 8—201—6(a), which specifies that a "delinquent child" includes one "who has violated a law of the state or an ordinance or regulation of a political subdivision thereof." The law which Gerald was found to have violated is ARS § 13—377. This section of the Arizona Criminal Code provides that a person who "in the presence of or hearing of any woman or child . . . uses vulgar, abusive or obscene language, is guilty of a misdemeanor. . . ." The penalty specified in the Criminal Code, which would apply to an adult, is $5 to $50, or imprisonment for not more than two months. The judge also testified that he acted under ARS § 8—201—6(d) which includes in the definition of a "delinquent child" one who, as the judge phrased it, is "habitually involved in immoral matters."

Asked about the basis for his conclusion that Gerald was "habitually involved in immoral matters," the judge testified, somewhat vaguely, that two years earlier, on July 2, 1962, a "referral" was made concerning Gerald, "where the boy had stolen a baseball glove from another boy and lied to the Police Department about

it." The judge said there was "no hearing," and "no accusation" relating to this incident, "because of lack of material foundation." But it seems to have remained in his mind as a relevant factor. The judge also testified that Gerald had admitted making other nuisance phone calls in the past which, as the judge recalled the boy's testimony, were "silly calls, or funny calls, or something like that."

The Superior Court dismissed the writ, and appelants sought review in the Arizona Supreme Court. That court stated that it considered appellants' assignments of error as urging (1) that the Juvenile Code, ARS § 8—201 to § 8—239, is unconstitutional because it does not require that parents and children be apprised of the specific charges, does not require proper notice of a hearing, and does not provide for an appeal; and (2) that the proceedings and order relating to Gerald constituted a denial of due process of law because of the absence of adequate notice of the charge and the hearing; failure to notify appellants of certain constitutional rights including the rights to counsel and to confrontation, and the privilege against self-incrimination; the use of unsworn hearsay testimony; and the failure to make a record of the proceedings. Appellants further asserted that it was error for the Juvenile Court to remove Gerald from the custody of his parents without a showing and finding of their unsuitability, and alleged a miscellany of other errors under state law.

The Supreme Court handed down an elaborate and wide-ranging opinion affirming dismissal of the writ and stating the court's conclusions as to the issues raised by appellants and other aspects of the juvenile process.

In their jurisdictional statement and brief in this Court, appellants do not urge upon us all of the points passed upon by the Supreme Court of Arizona. They urge that we hold the Juvenile Code of Arizona invalid on its face or as applied in this case because, contrary to the Due Process Clause of the Fourteenth Amendment, the juvenile is taken from the custody of his parents and committed to a state institution pursuant to proceedings in which the Juvenile Court has virtually unlimited discretion, and in which the following basic rights are denied:

1. Notice of the charges;
2. Right to counsel;
3. Right to confrontation and cross-examination;
4. Privilege against self-incrimination;
5. Right to a transcript of the proceedings; and
6. Right to appellate review.

We shall not consider other issues which were passed upon by the Supreme Court of Arizona. We emphasize that we indicate no opinion as to whether the decision of that court with respect to such other issues does or does not conflict with requirements of the Federal Constitution.

II.

The Supreme Court of Arizona held that due process of law is requisite to the constitutional validity of proceedings in which a court reaches the conclusion that a juvenile has been at fault, has engaged in conduct prohibited by law, or has otherwise misbehaved with the consequence that he is committed to an institution in which his freedom is curtailed. This conclusion is in accord with the decisions of a number of courts under both federal and state constitutions.

This Court has not heretofore decided the precise question. In *Kent* v. *United States*, 383 U.S. 541 (1966), we considered the requirements for a valid waiver of the "exclusive" jurisdiction of the Juvenile Court of the District of Columbia so· that a juvenile could be tried in the adult criminal court of the District. Although our decision turned upon the language of the statute, we emphasized the necessity that "the basic requirements of due process and fairness" be satisfied in such proceedings. *Haley* v. *Ohio*, 332 U.S. 596 (1948), involved the admissibility, in a state criminal court of general jurisdiction, of a confession by a 15-year-old boy. The Court held that the Fourteenth Amendment applied to prohibit the use of the coerced confession. Mr. Justice Douglas said, "Neither man nor child can be allowed to stand condemned by methods which flout constitutional requirements of due process of law." To the same effect is *Gallegos* v. *Colorado*, 370 U.S. 49 (1962). Accordingly, while these cases relate only to restricted aspects of the subject, they unmistakably indicate that, whatever may be their precise impact, neither the Fourteenth Amendment nor the Bill of Rights is for adults alone.

We do not in this opinion consider the impact of these constitutional provisions upon the totality of the relationship of the juvenile and the state. We do not even consider the entire process relating to juvenile "delinquents." For example, we are not here concerned with the procedures or constitutional rights applicable to the prejudicial stages of the juvenile process, nor do we direct our attention to the post-adjudicative or dispositional process. See note 48, *infra*. We consider only the problems presented to us by this case. These relate to the proceedings by which a determination is made as to whether a juvenile is a "delinquent" as a result of alleged misconduct on his part, with the consequence that he may be committed to a state institution. As to these proceedings there appears to be little current dissent from the proposition that the Due Process Clause has a role to play. The problem is to ascertain the precise impact of the due process requirement upon such proceedings.

From the inception of the juvenile court system, wide differences have been tolerated—indeed insisted upon—between the procedural rights accorded to adults and those of juveniles. In practically all jurisdictions, there are rights granted to adults which are withheld from juveniles. In addition to the specific problems involved in the present case, for example, it has been held that the juvenile is not entitled to bail, to indictment by grand jury, to a public trial or to trial by jury. It is frequent practice that rules governing the arrest and interrogation of adults by the police are not observed in the case of juveniles.

The history and theory underlying this development are well-known, but a recapitulation is necessary for purposes of this opinion. The juvenile court movement began in this country at the end of the last century. From the juvenile court statute adopted in Illinois in 1899, the system has spread to every State in the Union, the District of Columbia, and Puerto Rico.

The constitutionality of juvenile court laws has been sustained in over 40 jurisdictions against a variety of attacks.

The early reformers were appalled by adult procedures and penalties, and by the fact that children could be given long prison sentences and mixed in jails with hardened criminals. They were profoundly convinced that society's duty to the child could not be confined by the concept of justice alone. They believed that society's role was not to ascertain whether the child was "guilty" or "innocent," but "What is he, how has he become what he is, and what had best be done in his interest and in the interest of the state to save him from a downward career." The child—essentially good, as they saw it—was to be made "to feel that he is the object of [the State's] care and solicitude," not that he was under arrest or on trial. The rules of criminal procedure were therefore altogether inapplicable. The apparent rigidities, technicalities, and harshness which they observed in both substantive and procedural criminal law were therefore to be discarded. The idea of crime and punishment was to be abandoned. The child was to be "treated" and "rehabilitated" and the procedures, from apprehension through institutionalization, were to be "clinical" rather than punitive.

These results were to be achieved, without coming to conceptual and constitutional grief, by insisting that the proceedings were not adversary, but that the State was proceeding as *parens patriae*. The Latin phrase proved to be a great help to those who sought to rationalize the exclusion of juveniles from the constitutional scheme; but its meaning is murky and its historic credentials are of dubious relevance. The phrase was taken from chancery practice, where, however it was used to describe the power of the State to act in *loco parentis* for the purpose of protecting the property interests and the person of the child. But there is no trace of the doctrine in the history of criminal jurisprudence. At common law, children under seven were considered incapable of possessing criminal intent. Beyond that age, they were subjected to arrest, trial, and in theory to punishment like adult offenders. In these old days, the State was not deemed to have authority to accord them fewer procedural rights than adults.

The right of the State, as *parens patriae*, to deny to the child procedural rights available to his elders was elaborated by the assertion that a child, unlike an adult, has a right "not to liberty but to custody." He can be made to attorn to his parents, to go to school, etc. If his parents default in effectively performing their custodial functions—that is, if the child is "delinquent"—the state may intervene. In doing so, it does not deprive the child of any rights, because he has none. It merely provides the "custody" to which the child is entitled. On this basis, proceedings involving juveniles were described as "civil" not "criminal" and therefore not subject to the requirements which restrict the state when it seeks to deprive a person of his liberty.

Accordingly, the highest motives and most enlightened impulses led to a peculiar system for juveniles, unknown to our law in any comparable context. The constitutional and theoretical basis for this peculiar system is—to say the least—debatable. And in practice, as we remarked in the

Kent case, *supra*, the results have not been entirely satisfactory. Juvenile court history has again demonstrated that unbridled discretion, however benevolently motivated, is frequently a poor substitute for principle and procedure. In 1937, Dean Pound wrote: "The powers of the Star Chamber were a trifle in comparison with those of our juvenile courts. . . ." The absence of substantive standards has not necessarily meant that children receive careful, compassionate, individualized treatment. The absence of procedural rules based upon constitutional principle has not always produced fair, efficient, and effective procedures. Departures from established principles of due process have frequently resulted not in enlightened procedure, but in arbitrariness. The Chairman of the Pennsylvania Council of Juvenile Court Judges has recently observed: "Unfortunately, loose procedures, high-handed methods and crowded court calendars, either singly or in combination, all too often, have resulted in a denial of due process."

Failure to observe the fundamental requirements of due process has resulted in instances, which might have been avoided, of unfairness to individuals and inadequate or inaccurate findings of fact and unfortunate prescriptions of remedy. Due process of law is the primary and indispensable foundation of individual freedom. It is the basic and essential term in the social compact which defines the rights of the individual and delimits the powers which the State may exercise. As Mr. Justice Frankfurter has said: "The history of American freedom is, in no small measure, the history of procedure." But in addition, the procedural rules which have been fashioned from the generality of due process are our best instruments for the distillation and evaluation of essential facts from the conflicting welter of data that life and our adversary methods present. It is these instruments of due process which enhance the possibility that truth will emerge from the confrontation of opposing versions and conflicting data. "Procedure is to law what "scientific method' is to science."

It is claimed that juveniles obtain benefits from the special procedures applicable to them which more than offset the disadvantages of denial of the substance of normal due process. As we shall discuss, the observance of due process standards, intelligently and not ruthlessly administered, will not compel the States to abandon or displace any of the substantive benefits of the juvenile process. But it is important, we think, that the claimed benefits of the juvenile process should be candidly appraised. Neither sentiment nor folklore should cause us to shut our eyes, for example, to such startling findings as that reported in an exceptionally reliable study of repeaters or recidivism conducted by the Stanford Research Institute for the President's Commission on Crime in the District of Columbia. This Commission's Report states:

In fiscal 1966 approximately 66 percent of the 16- and 17-year-old juveniles referred to the court by the Youth Aid Division had been before the court previously. In 1965, 56 percent of those in the Receiving Home were repeaters. The SRI study revealed that 61 percent of the sample Juvenile Court referrals in 1965 had been previously referred at least once and that 42 percent had been referred at least twice before. *Id.*, at 773.

Certainly, these figures and the high crime rates among juveniles to which we have referred (*supra*, note 26) could not lead us to conclude that the absence of constitutional protections reduces crime, or that the juvenile system, functioning free of constitutional inhibitions as it has largely done, is effective to reduce crime or rehabilitate offenders. We do not mean by this to denigrate the juvenile court process or to suggest that there are not aspects of the juvenile system relating to offenders which are valuable. But the features of the juvenile system which its proponents have asserted are of unique benefit will not be impaired by constitutional domestication. For example, the commendable principles relating to the processing and treatment of juveniles separately from adults are in no way involved or affected by the procedural issues under discussion. Further, we are told that one of the important benefits of the special juvenile court procedures is that they avoid classifying the juvenile as a "criminal." The juvenile offender is now classed as a "delinquent." There is, of course, no reason why this should not continue. It is disconcerting, however, that this term has come to involve only slightly less stigma than the term "criminal" applied to adults. It is also emphasized that in practically all jurisdictions, statutes provide that an adjudication of the child as a delinquent shall not operate as a civil disability or disqualify him for civil service appointment. There is no reason why the application of due process requirements should interfere with such provisions.

Beyond this, it is frequently said that juveniles are protected by the process from disclosure of their deviational behavior. As the Supreme Court of Arizona phrased it in the present case, the summary procedures of juvenile courts are sometimes defended by a statement that it is the law's policy "to hide youthful errors from the full gaze of the public and bury them in the graveyard of the forgotten past." This claim of secrecy, however, is more rhetoric than reality. Disclosure of court records is discretionary with the judge in most jurisdictions. Statutory restrictions almost invariably apply only to the court records, and even as to those the evidence is that many courts routinely furnish information to the FBI and the military, and on request to government agencies and even to private employers. Of more importance are police records. In most States the police keep a complete file of juvenile "police contacts" and have complete discretion as to disclosure of juvenile records. Police departments receive requests for information from the FBI and other law-enforcement agencies, the Armed Forces, and social service agencies, and most of them generally comply. Private employers word their application forms to produce information concerning juvenile arrests and court proceedings, and in some jurisdictions information concerning juvenile police contacts is furnished private employers as well as government agencies.

In any event, there is no reason why, consistently with due process, a State cannot continue, if it deems it appropriate, to provide and to improve provision for the confidentiality of records of police contacts and court action relating to juveniles. It is interesting to note, however, that the Arizona Supreme Court used the confidentiality argument as a justification for the type of notice which is here attacked as inadequate for due process purposes. The parents were given merely general notice that their child was charged with "delinquency." No facts were specified. The Arizona court held, however, as we shall discuss, that in addition to this general "notice" the child and his parents must be advised "of the facts involved in the case" no later than the initial hearing by the judge. Obviously, this does not "bury" the word about the child's transgressions. It merely defers the time of disclosure to a point when it is of limited use to the child or his parents in preparing his defense or explanation.

Further, it is urged that the juvenile benefits from informal proceedings in the court. The early conception of the juvenile court proceeding was one in which a fatherly judge touched the heart and conscience of the erring youth by talking over his problems, by paternal advice and admonition, and in which, in extreme situations, benevolent and wise institutions of the State provided guidance and help "to save him from a downward career." Then, as now, goodwill and compassion were admirably prevalent. But recent studies have, with surprising unanimity, entered sharp dissent as to the validity of this gentle conception. They suggest that the appearance as well as the actuality of fairness, impartiality and orderliness—in short, the essentials of due process may be a more impressive and more therapeutic attitude so far as the juvenile is concerned. For example, in a recent study, the sociologists Wheeler and Cottrell observe that when the procedural laxness of the "*Parens patriae*" attitude is followed by stern disciplining, the contrast may have an adverse effect upon the child, who feels that he has been deceived or enticed. They conclude as follows: "Unless appropriate due process of law is followed, even the juvenile who has violated the law may not feel that he is being fairly treated and may therefore resist the rehabilitative efforts of court personnel." Of course, it is not suggested that juvenile court judges should fail appropriately to take account, in their demeanor and conduct, of the emotional and psychological attitude of the juveniles with whom they are confronted. While due process requirements will, in some instances, introduce a degree of order and regularity to juvenile court proceedings to determine delinquency, and in contested cases will introduce some elements of the adversary system, nothing will require that the conception of the kindly juvenile judge be replaced by its opposite, nor do we here rule upon the question whether ordinary due process requirements must be observed with respect to hearings to determine the disposition of the delinquent child.

Ultimately, however, we confront the reality of that portion of the juvenile court process with which we deal in this case. A boy is charged with misconduct. The boy is committed to an institution where he may be restrained of liberty for years. It is of no constitutional consequence—and of limited practical meaning—that the institution to which he is committed is called an Industrial School. The fact of the matter is that, however euphemistic the title, a "receiving home" or an "industrial school" for juveniles is an institution of confinement in which the child is incarcerated for a greater or lesser time. His world becomes "a building with white-washed walls, regimented routine and institutional laws...." In-

stead of mother and father and sisters and brothers and friends and classmates, his world is peopled by guards, custodians, state employees, and "delinquents" confined with him for anything from waywardness to rape and homicide.

In view of this, it would be extraordinary if our Constitution did not require the procedural regularity and the exercise of care implied in the phrase "due process." Under our Constitution, the condition of being a boy does not justify a kangaroo court. The traditional ideas of juvenile court procedure, indeed, contemplated that time would be available and care would be used to establish precisely what the juvenile did and why he did it—was it a prank of adolescence or a brutal act threatening serious consequences to himself or society unless corrected? Under traditional notions, one would assume that in a case like that of Gerald Gault, where the juvenile appears to have a home, a working mother and father, and an older brother, the Juvenile Judge would have made a careful inquiry and judgment as to the possibility that the boy could be disciplined and dealt with at home, despite his previous transgressions. Indeed, so far as appears in the record before us, except for some conversation with Gerald about his school work and his "wanting to go to . . . Grand Canyon with his father," the points to which the judge directed his attention were little different from those that would be involved in determining any charge of violation of a penal statute. The essential difference between Gerald's case and a normal criminal case is that safeguards available to adults were discarded in Gerald's case. The summary procedure as well as the long commitment were possible because Gerald was 15 years of age instead of over 18.

If Gerald had been over 18, he would not have been subject to Juvenile Court proceedings. For the particular offense immediately involved, the maximum punishment would have been a fine of $5 to $50, or imprisonment in jail for not more than two months. Instead, he was committed to custody for a maximum of six years. If he had been over 18 and had committed an offense to which such a sentence might apply, he would have been entitled to substantial rights under the Constitution of the United States as well as under Arizona's laws and constitution. The United States Constitution would guarantee him rights and protections with respect to arrest, search and seizure, and pretrial interrogation. It would assure him of specific notice of the charges and adequate time to prepare his defense. He would be entitled to clear advice that he could be represented by counsel, and at least if a felony were involved, the State would be required to provide counsel if his parents were unable to afford it. If the court acted on the basis of his confession, careful procedures would be required to assure its voluntariness. If the case went to trial, confrontation and opportunity for cross-examination would be guaranteed. So wide a gulf between the State's treatment of the adult and of the child requires a bridge sturdier than mere verbiage, and reasons more persuasive than cliché can provide. As Wheeler and Cottrell have put it, "The rhetoric of the juvenile court movement has developed without any necessarily close correspondence to the realities of court and institutional routines."

In *Kent* v. *United States, supra,* we stated that the Juvenile Court Judge's exercise of the power of the State as *parens patriae* was not unlimited. We said that "the admonition to function in a 'parental' relationship is not an invitation to procedural arbitrariness." With respect to the waiver by the juvenile court to the adult of jurisdiction over an offense committed by a youth, we said that "there is no place in our system of law for reaching a result of such tremendous consequences without ceremony—without hearing, without effective assistance of counsel, without a statement of reasons." We announced with respect to such waiver proceedings that while "We do not mean . . . to indicate that the hearing to be held must conform with all of the requirements of a criminal trial or even of the usual administrative hearing; but we do hold that the hearing must measure up to the essentials of due process and fair treatment." We reiterate this view, here in connection with a juvenile court adjudication of "delinquency," as a requirement which is part of the Due Process Clause of the Fourteenth Amendment of our Constitution.

We now turn to the specific issues which are presented to us in the present case.

III.

Notice of Charges. Appellants allege that the Arizona Juvenile Code is unconstitutional or alternatively that the proceedings before the Juvenile Court were constitutionally defective because of failure to provide adequate notice of the hearings. No notice was given to Gerald's parents when he was taken into custody on Monday, June 8. On that night, when Mrs. Gault went to the Detention Home, she was orally informed that there would be a hearing the next afternoon and was told the reason why Gerald was in custody. The only written notice Gerald's parents received at any time was a note on plain paper from Officer Flagg delivered on Thursday or Friday, June 11 or 12, to the effect that the judge had set Monday, June 15, "for further hearings on Gerald's delinquency."

A "petition" was filed with the court on June 9 by Officer Flagg, reciting only that he was informed and believed that "said minor is a delinquent minor and that it is necessary that some order be made by the Honorable Court for said minor's welfare." The applicable Arizona statute provides for a petition to be filed in Juvenile Court, alleging in general terms that the child is "neglected, dependent, or delinquent." The statute explicitly states that such a general allegation is sufficient, "without alleging the facts." There is no requirement that the petition be served and it was not served upon, given, or shown to Gerald or his parents.

The Supreme Court of Arizona rejected appellants' claim that due process was denied because of inadequate notice. It stated that "Mrs. Gault knew the exact nature of the charge against Gerald from the day he was taken to the detention home." The court also pointed out that the Gaults appeared at the two hearings "without objection." The court held that because "the policy of the juvenile law is to hide youthful errors from the full gaze of the public and bury them in the graveyard of the forgotten past," advance notice of the specific charges or basis for taking the

juvenile into custody and for the hearing is not necessary. It held that the appropriate rule is that "the infant and his parent or guardian will receive a petition only reciting a conclusion of delinquency. But no later than the initial hearing by the judge, they must be advised of the facts involved in the case. If the charges are denied they must be given a reasonable period of time to prepare."

We cannot agree with the court's conclusion that adequate notice was given in this case. Notice, to comply with due process requirements, must be given sufficiently in advance of scheduled court proceedings so that reasonable opportunity to prepare will be afforded, and it must "set forth the alleged misconduct with particularity." It is obvious, as we have discussed above, that no purpose of shielding the child from the public stigma of knowledge of his having been taken into custody and scheduled for hearing is served by the procedure approved by the court below. The "initial hearing" in the present case was a hearing on the merits. Notice at that time is not timely; and even if there were a conceivable purpose served by the deferral proposed by the court below, it would have to yield to the requirements that the child and his parents or guardian be notified in writing, of the specific charge or factual allegations to be considered at the hearing, and that such written notice be given at the earliest practicable time, and in any event sufficiently in advance of the hearing to permit preparation. Due process of law requires notice of the sort we have described—that is, notice which would be deemed constitutionally adequate in a civil or criminal proceeding. It does not allow a hearing to be held in which a youth's freedom and his parents' right to his custody are at stake without giving them timely notice, in advance of the hearing, of the specific issues that they must meet. Nor, in the circumstances of this case, can it reasonably be said that the requirement of notice was waived.

IV.

Right to Counsel. Appellants charge that the Juvenile Court proceedings were fatally defective because the court did not advise Gerald or his parents of their right to counsel, and proceeded with the hearing, the adjudication of delinquency and the order of commitment in the absence of counsel for the child and his parents or an express waiver of the right thereto. The Supreme Court of Arizona pointed out that "there is disagreement [among the various jurisdictions] as to whether the court must advise the infant that he has a right to counsel." It noted its own decision in *State Dept. of Public Welfare* v. *Barlow,* 80 Ariz. 249, 296 P. 2d 298 (1956), to the effect that *the parents* of an infant in a juvenile proceeding cannot be denied representation by counsel of their choosing." (Emphasis added.) It referred to a provision of the Juvenile Code which it characterized as requiring "that the probation officer shall look after the interests of neglected, delinquent and dependent children," including representing their interests in court. The court argued that "The parent and the probation officer may be relied upon to protect the infant's interests." Accordingly it rejected the proposition that "due process requires that an infant have a right to counsel."

It said that juvenile courts have the discretion, but not the duty to allow such representation; it referred specifically to the situation in which the Juvenile Court discerns conflict between the child and his parents as an instance in which this discretion might be exercised. We do not agree. Probation officers, in the Arizona scheme, are also arresting officers. They initiate proceedings and file petitions which they verify, as here, alleging the delinquency of the child; and they testify, as here, against the child. And here the probation officer was also superintendent of the Detention Home. The probation officer cannot act as counsel for the child. His role in the adjudicatory hearing, by statute and in fact, is as arresting officer and witness against the child. Nor can the judge represent the child. There is no material difference in this respect between adult and juvenile proceedings of the sort here involved. In adult proceedings, this contention has been foreclosed by decisions of this Court. A proceeding where the issue is whether the child will be found to be "delinquent" and subjected to the loss of his liberty for years is comparable in seriousness to a felony prosecution. The juvenile needs the assistance of counsel to cope with problems of law, to make skilled inquiry into the facts, to insist upon regularity of the proceedings, and to ascertain whether he has a defense and to prepare and submit it. The child "requires the guiding hand of counsel at every step in the proceedings against him." Just as in *Kent* v. *United States, supra,* at 561–562, we indicated our agreement with the United States Court of Appeals for the District of Columbia Circuit that the assistance of counsel is essential for purposes of waiver proceedings, so we hold now that it is equally essential for the determination of delinquency, carrying with it the awesome prospect of incarceration in a state institution until the juvenile reaches the age of 21.

During the last decade, court decisions, experts, and legislatures have demonstrated increasing recognition of this view. In at least one-third of the States, statutes now provide for the right of representation by retained counsel in juvenile delinquency proceedings, notice of the right, or assignment of counsel, or a combination of these. In other States, court rules have similar provisions.

The President's Crime Commission has recently recommended that in order to assure "procedural justice for the child," it is necessary that "Counsel . . . be appointed as a matter of course wherever coercive action is a possibility, without requiring any affirmative choice by child or parent." As stated by the authoritative "Standards for Juvenile and Family Courts," published by the Children's Bureau of the United States Department of Health, Education, and Welfare:

As a component part of a fair hearing required by due process guaranteed under the 14th Amendment, notice of the right to counsel should be required at all hearings and counsel provided upon request when the family is financially unable to employ counsel. Standards, at p. 57.

This statement was "reviewed" by the National Council of Juvenile Court Judges at its 1965 Convention and they "found no fault" with it. The New York Family Court Act contains the following statement:

This act declares that minors have a right to the assistance of counsel of their own

choosing or of law guardians in neglect proceedings under article three and in proceedings to determine juvenile delinquency and whether a person is in need of supervision under article seven. This declaration is based on a finding that counsel is often indispensable to a practical realization of due process of law and may be helpful in making reasoned determinations of fact and proper orders of disposition.

The Act provides that "At the commencement of any hearing" under the delinquency article of the statute, the juvenile and his parent shall be advised of the juvenile's "right to be represented by counsel chosen by him or his parent . . . or by a law guardian assigned by the court. . . ." The California Act (1961) also requires appointment of counsel.

We conclude that the Due Process Clause of the Fourteenth Amendment requires that in respect of proceedings to determine delinquency which may result in commitment to an institution in which the juvenile's freedom is curtailed, the child and his parent must be notified of the child's right to be represented by counsel retained by them, or if they are unable to afford counsel, that counsel will be appointed to represent the child.

At the habeas corpus proceeding, Mrs. Gault testified that she knew that she could have appeared with counsel at the juvenile hearing. This knowledge is not a waiver of the right to counsel which she and her juvenile son had, as we have defined it. They had a right expressly to be advised that they might retain counsel and to be confronted with the need for specific consideration of whether they did or did not choose to waive the right. If they were unable to afford to employ counsel, they were entitled in view of the seriousness of the charge and the potential commitment, to appointed counsel, unless they chose waiver. Mrs. Gault's knowledge that she could employ counsel is not an "intentional relinquishment or abandonment of a fully known right."

V.

Confrontation, Self-Incrimination, Cross-Examination. Appellants urge that the writ of habeas corpus should have been granted because of the denial of the rights of confrontation and cross-examination in the Juvenile Court hearings, and because the privilege against self-incrimination was not observed. The Juvenile Court Judge testified at the habeas corpus hearing that he had proceeded on the basis of Gerald's admissions at the two hearings. Appellants attack this on the ground that the admissions were obtained in disregard of the privilege against self-incrimination. If the confession is disregarded, appellants argue that the delinquency conclusion, since it was fundamentally based on a finding that Gerald had made lewd remarks during the phone call to Mrs. Cook, is fatally defective for failure to accord the rights of confrontation and cross-examination which the Due Process Clause of the Fourteenth Amendment of the Federal Constitution guarantees in state proceedings generally.

Our first question, then, is whether Gerald's admission was improperly obtained and relied on as the basis of decision, in conflict with the Federal Constitution. For this purpose, it is necessary briefly to recall the relevant facts.

Mrs. Cook, the complainant, and the recipient of the alleged telephone call, was not called as a witness.

Gerald's mother asked the Juvenile Court Judge why Mrs. Cook was not present and the judge replied that "she didn't have to be present." So far as appears, Mrs. Cook was spoken to only once, by Officer Flagg, and this was by telephone. The judge did not speak with her on any occasion. Gerald had been questioned by the probation officer after having been taken into custody. The exact circumstances of this questioning do not appear but any admissions Gerald may have made at this time do not appear in the record. Gerald was also questioned by the Juvenile Court Judge at each of the two hearings. The judge testified in the habeas corpus proceeding that Gerald admitted making "some of the lewd statements ...[but not] any of the more serious lewd statements." There was conflict and uncertainty among the witnesses at the habeas corpus proceeding—the Juvenile Court Judge, Mr. and Mrs. Gault, and the probation officer—as to what Gerald did or did not admit.

We shall assume that Gerald made admissions of the sort described by the Juvenile Court Judge, as quoted above. Neither Gerald nor his parents was advised that he did not have to testify or make a statement, or that an incriminating statement might result in his commitment as a "delinquent."

The Arizona Supreme Court rejected appellant's contention that Gerald had a right to be advised that he need not incriminate himself. It said: "We think the necessary flexibility for individualized treatment will be enhanced by a rule which does not require the judge to advise the infant of a privilege against self-incrimination."

In reviewing this conclusion of Arizona's Supreme Court, we emphasize again that we are here concerned only with proceedings to determine whether a minor is a "delinquent" and which may result in commitment to a state institution. Specifically, the question is whether, in such a proceeding, an admission by the juvenile may be used against him in the absence of clear and unequivocal evidence that the admission was made with knowledge that he was not obliged to speak and would not be penalized for remaining silent. In light of *Miranda* v. *Arizona*, 384 U.S. 436 (1966), we must also consider whether, if the privilege against self-incrimination is available, it can effectively be waived unless counsel is present or the right to counsel has been waived.

It has long been recognized that the eliciting and use of confessions or admissions require careful scrutiny. Dean Wigmore states:

The ground of distrust of confessions made in certain situations is, in a rough and indefinite way, judicial experience. There has been no careful collection of statistics of untrue confessions, nor has any great number of instances been even loosely reported ... but enough have been verified to fortify the conclusion, based on ordinary observation of human conduct, that under certain stresses a person, especially one of defective mentality or peculiar temperament, may falsely acknowledge guilt. This possibility arises wherever the innocent person is placed in such a situation that the untrue acknowledgement of guilt is at the time the more promising of two alternatives between which he is obliged to choose; that is, he chooses any risk that may be in falsely acknowledging guilt, in preference to some worse alternative associated with silence.

"The principle, then, upon which a confession may be excluded is that it is, under certain conditions, *testi-monially untrustworthy* .... [T]he essential feature is that the principle of exclusion is a testimonial one, analogous to the other principles which exclude narrations as untrustworthy. ..."

This Court has emphasized that admissions and confessions of juveniles require special caution. In *Haley* v. *Ohio, supra,* where this Court reversed the conviction of a 15-year-old boy for murder, Mr. Justice Douglas said:

What transpired would make us pause for careful inquiry if a mature man were involved. And when, as here, a mere child—an easy victim of the law—is before us, special care in scrutinizing the record must be used. Age 15 is a tender and difficult age for a boy of any race. He cannnot be judged by the more exacting standards of maturity. That which would leave a man cold and unimpressed can overawe and overwhelm a lad in his early teens. This is the period of great instability which the crisis of adolescence produces. A 15-year-old lad, questioned through the dead of night by relays of police, is a ready victim of the inquisition. Mature men possibly might stand the ordeal from midnight to 5 a.m. But we cannot believe that a lad of tender years is a match for the police in such a contest. He needs counsel and support if he is not to become the victim first of fear, then of panic. He needs someone on whom to lean lest the overpowering presence of the law, as he knows it, crush him. No friend stood at the side of this 15-year-old boy as the police, working in relays, questioned him hour after hour, from midnight until dawn. No lawyer stood guard to make sure that the police went so far and no farther, to see to it that they stopped short of the point where he became the victim of coercion. No counsel or friend was called during the critical hours of questioning.

In *Haley,* as we have discussed, the boy was convicted in adult court, and not a juvenile court. In notable decisions, the New York Court of Appeals and the Supreme Court of New Jersey have recently considered decisions of juvenile courts in which boys have been adjudged "delinquent" on the basis of confessions obtained in circumstances comparable to those in *Haley*. In both instances, the State contended before its highest tribunal that constitutional requirements governing inculpatory statements applicable in adult courts do not apply to juvenile proceedings. In each case, the State's contention was rejected, and the juvenile court's determination of delinquency was set aside on the grounds of inadmissibility of the confession. *In the Matters of Gregory W. and Gerald S.*, 19 N.Y. 2d 55,—N.E. 2d—(1966) (opinion by Keating, J.), and *In the Interests of Carlo and Stasilowicz*, 48 N.J. 224, 225 A. 2d 110 (1966) (opinion by Proctor, J.).

The privilege against self-incrimination is, of course, related to the question of the safeguards necessary to assure that admissions or confessions are reasonably trustworthy, that they are not the mere fruits of fear or coercion, but are reliable expressions of the truth. The roots of the privilege are, however, far deeper. They tap the basic stream of religious and political principle because the privilege reflects the limits of the individual's attornment to the state and —in a philosophical sense—insists upon the equality of the individual and the State. In other words, the privilege has a broader and deeper thrust than the rule which prevents the use of confessions which are the product of coercion because coercion is thought to carry with it the danger of unreliability. One of its purposes is to prevent the State, whether by force

or by psychological domination, from overcoming the mind and will of the person under investigation and depriving him of the freedom to decide whether to assist the State in securing his conviction.

It would indeed be surprising if the privilege against self-incrimination were available to hardened criminals but not to children. The language of the Fifth Amendment, applicable to the States by operation of the Fourteenth Amendment, is unequivocal and without exception. And the scope of the privilege is comprehensive. As Mr. Justice White, concurring, stated in *Murphy* v. *Waterfront Commission*, 378, U.S. 52 (1964), at 94:

The privilege can be claimed in *any proceeding*, be it criminal or civil, administrative or judicial, investigatory or adjudicatory . . . it protects *any disclosures* which the witness may reasonably apprehend *could be used in a criminal prosecution or which could lead to other evidence that might be so used.* (Emphasis supplied.)

With respect to juveniles, both common observation and expert opinion emphasize that the "distrust of confessions made in certain situations" to which Dean Wigmore referred in the passage quoted above is imperative in the case of children from an early age through adolescence. In New York, for example, the recently enacted Family Court Act provides that the juvenile and his parents must be advised at the start of the hearing of his right to remain silent. The New York statute also provides that the police must attempt to communicate with the juvenile's parents before questioning him, and that a confession may not be obtained from a child prior to notifying his parents or relatives and releasing the child either to them or to the Family Court. In *In the Matters of Gregory W. and Gerald S.*, referred to above, the New York Court of Appeals held that the privilege against self-incrimination applies in juvenile delinquency cases and requires the exclusion of involuntary confessions, and that *People* v. *Lewis*, 260 N.Y. 171 (1932), holding the contrary, had been specifically overruled by statute.

The authoritative "Standards for Juvenile and Family Courts" concludes that, "Whether or not transfer to the criminal court is a possibility, certain procedures should always be followed. Before being interviewed [by the police] the child and his parents should be informed of his right to have legal counsel present and to refuse to answer questions or be fingerprinted if he should so decide."

Against the application to juveniles of the right to silence, it is argued that juvenile proceedings are "civil" and not "criminal," and therefore the privilege should not apply. It is true that the statement of the privilege in the Fifth Amendment, which is applicable to the States by reason of the Fourteenth Amendment, is that no person "shall be compelled in any *criminal case* to be a witness against himself." However, it is also clear that the availability of the privilege does not turn upon the type of proceeding in which its protection is invoked, but upon the nature of the statement or admission and the exposure which it invites. The privilege may, for example, be claimed in a civil or administrative proceeding if the statement is or may be inculpatory.

It would be entirely unrealistic to carve out of the Fifth Amendment all statements by juveniles on the

ground that these cannot lead to "criminal" involvement. In the first place, juvenile proceedings to determine "delinquency," which may lead to commitment to a state institution, must be regarded as "criminal" for purposes of the privilege against self-incrimination. To hold otherwise would be to disregard substance because of the feeble enticement of the "civil" label-of-convenience which has been attached to juvenile proceedings. Indeed, in over half of the States, there is not even assurance that the juvenile will be kept in separate institutions, apart from adult "criminals." In those States juveniles may be placed in or transferred to adult penal institutions after having been found "delinquent" by a juvenile court. For this purpose, at least, commitment is a deprivation of liberty. It is incarceration against one's will, whether it is called "criminal" or "civil." And our Constitution guarantees that no person shall be "compelled" to be a witness against himself when he is threatened with deprivation of his liberty—a command which this Court has broadly applied and generously implemented in accordance with the teaching of the history of the privilege and its great office in mankind's battle for freedom.

In addition, apart from the equivalence for this purpose of exposure to commitment as a juvenile delinquent and exposure to imprisonment as an adult offender, the fact of the matter is that there is little or no assurance in Arizona, as in most if not all of the States, that a juvenile apprehended and interrogated by the police or even by the juvenile court itself will remain outside the reach of adult courts as a consequence of the offense for which he has been taken into custody. In Arizona, as in other States, provision is made for juvenile courts to relinquish or waive jurisdiction to the ordinary criminal courts. In the present case, when Gerald Gault was interrogated concerning violation of a section of the Arizona Criminal Code, it could not be certain that the Juvenile Court Judge would decide to "suspend" criminal prosecution in court for adults by proceeding to an adjudication in Juvenile Court.

It is also urged, as the Supreme Court of Arizona here asserted, that the juvenile and presumably his parents should not be advised of the juvenile's right to silence because confession is good for the child as the commencement of the assumed therapy of the juvenile court process, and he should be encouraged to assume an attitude of trust and confidence toward the officials of the juvenile process. This proposition has been subjected to widespread challenge on the basis of current reappraisals of the rhetoric and realities of the handling of juvenile offenders.

In fact, evidence is accumulating that confessions by juveniles do not aid in "individualized treatment," as the court below put it, and that compelling the child to answer questions, without warning or advice as to his right to remain silent, does not serve this or any other good purpose. In light of the observations of Wheeler and Cottrell, and others, it seems probable that where children are induced to confess by "paternal" urgings on the part of officials and the confession is then followed by disciplinary action, the child's reaction is likely to be hostile and adverse—the child may well feel that he has been led or tricked into confession and that

despite his confession, he is being punished.

Further, authoritative opinion has cast formidable doubt upon the reliability and trustworthiness of "confessions" by children. This Court's observations in *Haley* v. *United States*, are set forth above. The recent decision of the New York Court of Appeals referred to above, *In the Matters of Gregory W. and Gerald S.*, deals with a dramatic and, it is to be hoped, extreme example. Two 12-year-old Negro boys were taken into custody for the brutal assault and rape of two aged domestics, one of whom died as the result of the attack. One of the boys was schizophrenic and had been locked in the security ward of a mental institution at the time of the attacks. By a process that may best be described as bizarre, his confession was obtained by the police. A psychiatrist testified that the boy would admit "whatever he thought was expected so that he could get out of the immediate situation." The other 12-year-old also confessed. Both confessions were in specific detail, albeit they contained various inconsistencies. The Court of Appeals, in an opinion by Keating, J., concluded that the confessions were products of the will of the police instead of the boys. The confessions were therefore held involuntary and the order of the Appellate Division affirming the order of the Family Court adjudging the defendants to be juvenile delinquents was reversed.

A similar and equally instructive case has recently been decided by the Supreme Court of New Jersey. *In the Interests of Carlo and Stasilowicz*, *supra*. The body of a 10-year-old girl was found. She had been strangled. Neighborhood boys who knew the girl were questioned. The two appellants, aged 13 and 15, confessed to the police, with vivid detail and some inconsistencies. At the Juvenile Court hearing, both denied any complicity in the killing. They testified that their confessions were the product of fear and fatigue due to extensive police grilling. The Juvenile Court Judge found that the confessions were voluntary and admissible. On appeal, in an extensive opinion by Proctor, J., the Supreme Court of New Jersey reversed. It rejected the State's argument that the constitutional safeguard of voluntariness governing the use of confessions does not apply in proceedings before the juvenile court. It pointed out that under New Jersey court rules, juveniles under the age of 16 accused of committing a homicide are tried in a proceeding which "has all of the appurtenances of a criminal trial," including participation by the county prosecutor, and requirements that the juvenile be provided with counsel, that a stenographic record be made, etc. It also pointed out that under New Jersey law, the confinement of the boys after reaching age 21 could be extended until they had served the maximum sentence which could have been imposed on an adult for such a homicide, here found to be second degree murder carrying up to 30 years' imprisonment. The court concluded that the confessions were involuntary, stressing that the boys, contrary to statute, were placed in the police station and there interrogated; that the parents of both boys were not allowed to see them while they were being interrogated; that inconsistencies appeared among the various statements of the boys and with the objective evidence of the crime; and that there were

protracted periods of questioning. The court noted the State's contention that both boys were advised of their constitutional rights before they made their statements, but it held that this should not be given "significant weight in our determination of voluntariness." Accordingly, the judgment of the Juvenile Court was reversed.

In a recent case before the Juvenile Court of the District of Columbia, Judge Ketcham rejected the proffer of evidence as to oral statements made at police headquarters by four juveniles who had been taken into custody for alleged involvement in an assault and attempted robbery. *In the Matter of Four Youths,* Nos. 28—776—J, 28—778—J, 28—783—J, 28—859—J, Juvenile Court of the District of Columbia, April 7, 1961. The court explicitly stated that it did not rest its decision on a showing that the statements were involuntary, but because they were untrustworthy. Judge Ketcham said:

Simply stated, the Court's decision in this case rests upon the considered opinion—after nearly four busy years on the Juvenile Court bench during which the testimony of thousands of such juveniles has been heard—that the statements of adolescents under 18 years of age who are arrested and charged with violations of law are frequently untrustworthy and often distort the truth.

We conclude that the constitutional privilege against self-incrimination is applicable in the case of juveniles as it is with respect to adults. We appreciate that special problems may arise with respect to waiver of the privilege by or on behalf of children, and that there may well be some differences in technique—but not in principle— depending upon the age of the child and the presence and competence of parents. The participation of counsel will, of course, assist the police, juvenile courts and appellate tribunals in administering the privilege. If counsel is not present for some permissible reason when an admission is obtained, the greatest care must be taken to assure that the admission was voluntary, in the sense not only that it has not been coerced or suggested, but also that it is not the product of ignorance of rights or of adolescent fantasy, fright or despair.

The "confession" of Gerald Gault was first obtained by Officer Flagg, out of the presence of Gerald's parents, without counsel and without advising him of his right to silence, as far as appears. The judgment of the Juvenile Court was stated by the judge to be based on Gerald's admission in court. Neither "admission" was reduced to writing, and, to say the least, the process by which the "admissions" were obtained and received must be characterized as lacking the certainty and order which are required of proceedings of such formidable consequences. Apart from the "admission," there was nothing upon which a judgment or finding might be based. There was no sworn testimony. Mrs. Cook, the complainant, was not present. The Arizona Supreme Court held that "sworn testimony must be required of all witnesses including police officers, probation officers and others who are part of or officially related to the juvenile court structure." We hold that this is not enough. No reason is suggested or appears for a different rule in respect of sworn testimony in juvenile courts than in adult tribunals. Absent a valid confession adequate to support the determination of the Juvenile Court, confrontation and sworn testimony by

witnesses available for cross-examination were essential for a finding of "delinquency" and an order committing Gerald to a state institution for a maximum of six years.

The recommendations in the Children's Bureau's "Standards for Juvenile and Family Courts" are in general accord with our conclusions. They state that testimony should be under oath and that only competent material and relevant evidence under rules applicable to civil cases should be admitted in evidence. The New York Family Court Act contains a similar provision.

As we said in *Kent* v. *United States*, 383, U.S. 541, 554 (1966), with respect to waiver proceedings, "there is no place in our system of law for reaching a result of such tremendous consequences without ceremony. . . ." We now hold that, absent a valid confession, a determination of delinquency and an order of commitment to a state institution cannot be sustained in the absence of sworn testimony subjected to the opportunity for cross-examination in accordance with our law and constitutional requirements.

VI.

Appellate Review and Transcript of Proceedings. Appellants urge that the Arizona statute is unconstitutional under the Due Process Clause because, as construed by its Supreme Court, "there is no right of appeal from a juvenile court order. . . ." The court held that there is no right to a transcript because there is no right to appeal and because the proceedings are confidential and any record must be destroyed after a prescribed period of time. Whether a transcript or other recording is made, it held, is a matter for the discretion of the juvenile court.

This Court has not held that a State is required by the Federal Constitution "to provide appellate courts or a right to appellate review at all." In view of the dismissal of the writ of habeas corpus for other reasons, we need not rule on this question in the present case or upon the failure to provide a transcript or recording of the hearings—or, indeed, the failure of the juvenile court judge to state the grounds for his conclusion. Cf. *Kent* v. *United States, supra,* at 561, where we said, in the context of a decision of the juvenile court waiving jurisdiction to the adult court, which by local law, was applicable: "... it is incumbent upon the Juvenile Court to accompany its waiver order with a statement of the reasons or con-

siderations therefor." As the present case illustrates, the consequences of failure to provide an appeal, to record the proceedings, or to make findings or state the grounds for the juvenile court's conclusion may be to throw a burden upon the machinery for habeas corpus, to saddle the reviewing process with the burden of attempting to reconstruct a record, and to impose upon the juvenile judge the unseemly duty of testifying under cross-examination as to the events that transpired in the hearings before him.

For the reasons stated, the judgment of the Supreme Court of Arizona is reversed and the cause remanded for further proceedings not inconsistent with this opinion.

It is so ordered.

A Hard Cop and His Patient Partner on a Menacing Beat

L. H. WHITTEMORE

Patrolman Colin Barker waded in. To the tune of *Here Comes the Bride,* someone in the crowd of disheveled young people began to sing: "Here comes the pig, here comes the pig. . . ."

"Hey, he looks even younger than me."

"Gestapo!"

"I could be his mother."

"Then you should have had an abortion." Colin Barker, who wore a crew cut beneath his police hat, indeed looked much younger than his 23 years. His uniform appeared a bit stiff, especially with the walkie-talkie resting awkwardly on his chest. Out of self-consciousness he adjusted it from time to time.

To several young men lounging on the hood of a convertible, the cop yelled, "Is this your car?"

"No."

"Then get off it!"

His suddenly asserted authority, plus the chorus of hisses that followed, brought fresh color to Colin's face.

"Hi, officer," said a pretty young girl. "Want to buy a necklace?"

"No . . . no thanks."

"There's a pig in our midst!"

The patrolman paused before a doorway, where three unkempt young men sprawled.

"This isn't your doorway, is it?"

"Nope."

"Then get on your feet."

As they picked themselves up, a wine bottle sheathed in a paper bag rolled off the top step and bounced to the pavement. Colin picked it up and poured the wine between two parked cars, to a chorus of boos and hisses.

On the sidewalk ahead, several boys and girls were kneeling over a lovely design in multicolored chalk. A huge set of flowers had been drawn in pink, purple, blue and white; and a message was printed below the flowers: "I, YOU, WE ARE GOD."

"All right," said Colin. "Get some water and scrub this off."

"We worked hard on this. Is it really against the law?"

"You're blocking the entrance to this man's establishment," said Colin, looking in the window of the Laundromat. The middle-aged storekeeper shrugged from behind the glass. A crowd gathered and watched as the youngsters, supplied with buckets of water and brushes from the Laundromat, scrubbed off the chalk design.

Colin continued his stroll. A girl with bare feet jumped in front of him, held a flower to his face and danced backward. "Have a flower, officer."

"No thanks, but thanks."

The girl stared defiantly and shouted, "TAKE THE FLOWER!" Suddenly the patrolman's hand shot out and batted the flower away. The sound of his hand smacking hers seemed too loud. Red-faced, he turned and began walking back. "That wasn't very nice," the girl called after him.

Colin heard someone following him, whistling. The faces he passed were smiling, expectant. The whistling grew louder at the back of his head. Colin stopped. The whistler continued on one long high note; then silence. Colin heard the person breathing behind him, but refused to turn around.

"ATTENTION!"

The sound hurt Colin's ears. Turning abruptly, he faced a tall young man with flowing blond hair, dirty face and frazzled clothing. Colin whispered: "What did you say?"

"I said, 'F——— you, cop!' That's what I said."

Colin threw the young man against the wall and flayed at him with his fists. The young man screamed and kicked. Colin tried to grab his shirt, but the young man reached up and tore off the patrolman's badge. The crowd cheered and Colin smashed his nightstick down—once, twice, a third time. The mob surged in, but Colin already was on his walkie-talkie calling for help. The young man on the sidewalk shouted, "Revolution, now! Kill him!" Colin folded his arms.

"I hope," screamed the young man, "that somebody jumps on *you* some day."

"Cool off, fella."

"Next time, brother, you'll be in

front of my gunsight. You pig!"

At last the paddy wagon rolled up and two patrolmen helped Colin drag the screaming young man into the back.

"What's the trouble, Colin?"

"I think he's on LSD or something. He's out of his head."

Behind the paddy wagon, in an unmarked car, sat four members of the San Francisco tactical patrol. One of them jumped from the car and stood, legs apart, challenging anyone to provoke him. The crowd seemed to fear him, because the heckling stopped abruptly. Colin hopped into the cab of the paddy wagon as it rolled down the foggy street to the station house in Golden Gate Park.

Colin Barker had arrived at Park Station, his first and only police post, in early 1967. Already there was resentment among working people, Negro and white, toward Haight-Ashbury hippies, who had caused an increase in rents and a decline in property values as a result of the publicity they generated.

Colin said, "If the whole thing hadn't been publicized, the original hippies and the store owners probably could have gotten along. They weren't really happy about each other, but I think they would have made it all right. Before, when we had a robbery suspect, it was never a hippie. But the scene is all changed now. We're getting a lot of shootings, some stabbings—two people killed last week—robbery, assault.

"There are only a few Flower Children left. Now you've got the juveniles, maybe 16 through 19. They're pitiful, really pitiful. And then there are the political activists who want to overthrow the government, the older guys who sell dope and chase

some of the young girls, and the mentally ill. I would say at least 15% of the people I've arrested for one thing or another have either been in a mental institution or were outpatients from some psychiatric clinic. And some of these nuts are on drugs!

"Then the Negro kids from the Fillmore bring phony drugs onto the street. For every piece of legitimate narcotics sold up here, there's four or five times as much phony stuff. If you buy from a stranger, you're either gonna get done in—beat up or your money taken or both—or you'll wind up with phony stuff.

"The hippies just wanted to be left alone. Now it's fashionable to grow a beard and wear weird clothes and say you're a hippie. They're dirty people, that's all."

Unlike his brother, a poet who teaches literature at Harvard, Colin Barker studied economics at a California junior college. "Believe it or not, I *asked* to work on Haight Street, maybe because I'm dealing with my own generation. I wanted to see what it was like to walk the beat. I've even made friends with guys I've busted for felony charges. Guys say, 'Hey, Colin, what's going on?' and 'Don't bust me again this week, not again'—that kind of thing."

But Colin quickly became more defensive and even hostile on the job. One night he and a 22-year-old patrolman named Fred Rennie were walking through the park shortly after 11 p.m. when they heard footsteps in the darkness beyond some foliage. Colin started to his left and Fred to his right, so that they would approach the person from two sides. Suddenly there was a shotgun blast. Shining his flashlight, Colin saw Fred Rennie lying dead on his back. The blast had caught him directly in the face. Ten minutes later the tactical squad picked up two Negro teen-agers as suspects. They also found the shotgun nearby.

Colin's hardening attitude was influenced by his association with Gary Cummings, who was assigned to share his beat. Together they walked the 4 p.m.-to-midnight and midnight-to-8 a.m. shifts in and around Haight Street, occasionally covering a wider area in a prowl car. One night they had an argument in the locker room at Park Station. Gary Cummings, reading a newspaper story about the two youths charged with killing Fred Rennie, remarked, "The two boys are pleading self-defense."

"Self-defense?" Colin cried. "It was outright murder!"

"You know," Gary Cummings said, "there's always the *possibility* that self-defense might be a valid claim."

"It's plain and simple: Fred was killed by two colored punks, both of whom were known to peddle narcotics in The Haight."

"But there is the *possibility*," Gary insisted, "that the cop who gets shot by some Negro maybe *had* threatened the black guy. You don't know if Fred had stopped those same Negro guys two or three times before that night and told them, 'Niggers, if I ever stop you again, I'm gonna blow your heads off.' "

"Look, Gary, what are you trying to say? That Fred Rennie *should* have been shot? What the hell kind of kick are you on?"

"You know as well as I do!" Gary said. "Fred was famous for planting phony stuff on his prisoners. And you know that when he got shot in the park they looked through his clothing and found about a dozen needles in his pocket. Now, he wasn't using them on himself. And the chances are *very*

good that those two Negro guys knew this about him, and they maybe figured he was going to plant stuff on them illegally."

"Well, why don't you go to court and testify in their behalf?" Colin shouted. "Sounds to me like you're on the opposite side."

Gary Cummings, 26, had been on the force two years before being transferred to Park Station. In appearance and outlook he differed from most of the policemen around him. He wore his black curly hair longer than the other officers and sprinkled his speech with "hip" lingo.

"I became a cop almost on a dare," he said. "I knew a guy from Boston, a very bright guy, and yet he had this sadistic personality. And the cat wanted to be a policeman!

"I was working at a part-time job in San Francisco, and when that got to be too much I quit and went on unemployment. And then that friend of mine from Boston was trying the police department there. He sent me letters about himself, and I thought about it. I didn't really think I could make it. I thought I was too thin. I took the test anyhow, and before I knew it I was in the Police Academy. Next thing I knew I was out in the car, scared to death. I remember the guy I was with trying to tell me, 'Hey, relax, it's not that bad.'

"And it really *isn't* that bad. Obviously, insurance clerks don't get killed proportionately to policemen, but I'm a little fatalistic about it now."

Before being transferred to Park Station, Gary Cummings was in a San Francisco police station when three white patrolmen from the tactical squad brought in a Negro prisoner. The black man kept saying, "Get your hands off me, you white bastards." The officers said nothing to him, but among themselves, and to Gary, they expressed desire to "kick his ass."

The prisoner asked to make a call and was allowed to use a public telephone in a corner of the room.

After about five minutes, the sergeant said, "Hey, that guy's been on the phone a long time."

"Then," Gary said, "I saw the cops putting on their lead gloves and they stood there like vultures." As Gary recalled it, one officer went to the booth and said, "Let's go. Hey, hey! Let's go—get off that phone!"

Startled, the Negro said, "Hey, hold it. Wait a minute, I'm almost through."

Gary said, "As soon as he said, 'Wait a minute,' that was enough." They dragged him out of the phone booth and, according to Gary, five policemen jumped on the prisoner, punching and kicking until he could no longer move.

"I just stood there," Gary remembered, "and at first I was so shocked that I couldn't say anything. Then I found myself shouting at the sergeant. He just looked at me like I was a traitor or something and walked away."

When he was transferred to Park Station, says Gary, "The word was already here. Some sort of reputation had preceded me."

Gary's transfer put him with Colin Barker on foot patrol. Colin explained to his new partner that a foot patrolman in Haight-Ashbury can almost regulate the amount of "business" he generates. "For me," Colin said, "it's an exception to walk through The Haight and not send at least one guy back to the station. The old-timers avoid trouble. A lot of them see something and look the other way."

"Why don't *you* look the other way?" Gary asked. "You like putting people in jail?"

"No, but it's a matter of selectivity. Sometimes, like I've told guys to move off the steps or out of the street and they've gotten angry. And if they get mean, I *have* to grab 'em. It's a personal matter, sometimes. With each partner I tend to act differently, because each guy has a special kick, you know?"

"I'll let you know when I find my kick."

"Like one guy I walked with used to be a bus driver, so he always gave out tickets to cars parked in bus zones. When I wasn't with him, I'd never bother with any of that stuff."

The two patrolmen emerged from the winding path of Golden Gate Park and entered the cool sunshine of an uphill lawn, where four Navajo Indians were sprawled on the grass. A young Negro man and a girl with long blonde hair were with the Indians. Some in the group were sleeping, others were eating French fries that had been dumped on a blanket.

Colin and Gary walked up to the group, but no one moved or spoke. Colin pulled back a blanket, revealing a fifth Indian who was embracing a gallon jug of wine. Colin emptied the jug on the grass. "Get up," he said to the Indian. "I want to see you walk." The Indian adjusted his orange headband, stood up and walked a few steps, then stumbled. One by one, Colin made the Indians rise and then take seats on a park bench, where they slumped against each other.

"Look at them," said Colin. "I've locked two of them up before."

Gary said, "Why arrest them? They're not bothering anybody."

"They've helped ruin this park,

for one thing," Colin said. "I hope you noticed back there, the way they've left their crud right on the pathways. And look at all that food. No wonder there are rats in the park now."

About 30 yards down the pathway a young man began shouting, "Pig, pig, pig!" His long, sandy hair curled at the shoulders and he wore an unkempt beard. Another young man, dressed in a gray windbreaker and blue jeans, was holding him by the shirt. "Get your hands offa me, goddam narko pig!" The plainclothes narcotics agent slapped him. He fell down and the cop picked him up again. "Nark! Pig!" Colin rushed over and helped bring the screaming young man back to the bench.

The blonde girl gave a dollar bill to each Indian. Strolling away with her Negro companion, she remarked to no one in particular, "My daddy doesn't know it but he just gave his first donation to the American Indian."

The wagon rolled up. One of the Indians, wrapped in a faded pink blanket, began wandering aimlessly away. "Hey!" shouted Colin, grabbing him and steering him back to the wagon. "Get in there, Sam Running Drunk."

"What did this cat do?" Gary asked the narcotics agent, who was pushing his prisoner into the back of the wagon with the Indians.

"He offered to sell me LSD."

Colin and Gary took another pathway near a small pond. Walking toward them was a young Negro who stopped as if he were waiting for the cops to pass. Colin said, "What are you doing in here?"

"Walking, man."

"Put your hands out."

"Oh, no, man . . ." He put his arms straight out. "What was I doing just now 'cept standing, huh?" The black man's voice betrayed a feeling of helplessness. "I ain't done nothing, so I stopped and did *absolutely* nothing. And still you stop me."

Concluding his frisk, Colin said, "Now, get out of here!"

"I'm going. But I don't know what I'm gonna do with you."

As they walked on, Gary said, "You just made that guy hate your guts, you know that?"

"So what? That's the same type of guy who killed Fred. I've stopped many guys and found guns on 'em. As I've said, the love generation is dead around here."

"Well, exactly how long could *you* say 'I love you' when you're getting beat by the cops?"

Colin glared. "Sounds like you'll be out there with them next time, throwing the rocks at us."

The evening had been extremely quiet and Colin and Gary were assigned to investigate a complaint that a "noisy party" was going on in the Fillmore, an all-black area.

"Man," Gary exclaimed, "what kind of police call is that?"

"A noisy party could be just about anything," Colin said. "It could be anything from a family fight to a riot."

The patrolmen parked outside a two-story wooden building containing only two apartments. Dozens of young black men, in their late teens and early twenties, were milling about the lawn and sitting on the small wooden porch, drinking wine and beer.

"You know what I really think about this deal?" Colin asked.

"No. What?"

"I think we shouldn't even get out of the car."

"Keep cool, man," Gary urged. "Did you ever think of something like this as an opportunity?"

"An opportunity for what? To get killed?"

"Calm down. I mean an opportunity to give these cats a feeling that all cops really aren't so bad, you know? Just act friendly to them."

"For how long? Listen, we're just gonna walk into trouble. Nothing but black militants out there."

"Come on," Gary said. "We've got to talk to the complainant."

The two cops got out of their car while the black youngsters watched stoically. "Don't walk on the grass," Gary commanded Colin in a near whisper. "You wouldn't do that in a white neighborhood."

They entered a dark hallway with a flight of stairs at the far end, leading to the apartment where the party was taking place. A "soul" record reverberated through the building. Gary knocked on the downstairs apartment door and an elderly Negro woman opened it as far as the chain would allow.

"Police, ma'am. May we come inside?"

"Yes, just a second." She undid the door chain and the cops entered her small living room. "My husband is in the other room," the woman said, "and he can't sleep for the noise up there. He has to be up at four o'clock in the morning for his job. They been having these parties up there every week, it seems to me. Me and my husband are too old, and . . ."

"Look," Gary interrupted. "I'll go up there and talk to whoever is giving the party, and I'll *ask* him if he'll turn down the noise a little bit. Do you know the name of the guy who lives up there?"

"His name is Robert Ellis."

"Bobby Ellis?" Colin asked.

"Yeah, I know 'cause I seen his mail."

Colin turned to Gary and said, "Bobby Ellis is head of that black student union. He's militant as hell." Gary said nothing.

Starting for the stairs in the hall, Gary said, "Come on, will you?"

When they reached a landing, Gary paused to look out the side window. Down in the darkness he saw two young black men leaning against the patrol car.

"Oh, man," Gary said. "I left the doors unlocked. I just hope to hell they haven't taken the shotgun out of the car."

"Boy, you *are* an idiot, you know that?" Colin felt his gun. "If I see one of these guys with that shotgun . . ."

"What will you do? Start a shootout, like the Wild West? Come on, we'll just go down to the car and check it."

Some 25 young men were outside, watching. Gary looked in the back seat; the shotgun was there.

"Okay," he said. "I'll lock the doors and then we'll go back."

"Forget it," said Colin. "I'm not going up there again. If something breaks out we wouldn't have a chance."

"Okay, buddy, I'll tell you what. Put in a call and ask for one more car to back us up while we go upstairs."

Colin hesitated, then slipped into the driver's seat and reached for the microphone under the dashboard. "They've cut it out of the car! They've cut the goddam microphone! It's gone! We can't even call for help!"

"Colin, buddy, we don't need any help—not yet, anyway, so relax a minute, will you?"

"Let's get out of here."

"So they cut out the microphone, what's the big deal? It was done in a Halloween spirit."

"You must be kidding," Colin said from inside the car.

"Hey, hey! Before I was a policeman, then I was a kid? And when I saw an empty police car? Listen, I had to resist like hell so as not to take the car for a ride or something. It's the same with these guys."

Colin got out of the car and looked at the Negro youngsters, who seemed unconcerned. Almost to himself, Gary said, "Goddam, now when we go back to the station tonight I'll have to make a report explaining why that microphone got cut out of the car."

"Well, let's just get out of here," Colin urged.

Gary handed Colin a dime and said, "Go across the street to that bar and call Communications. Ask for another car."

"All right," Colin muttered, taking the dime and running across to the tavern. In minutes the car radio crackled and Gary heard the dispatcher saying, "Attention all units, all units, we got a 904 Code Two, all units . . ." Gary stood in shock as he heard his location cited as a major trouble spot.

As Colin emerged from the tavern, sirens could already be heard. Then came the whirling red lights as five cars pulled into the block.

"What the hell's going on?" Gary screamed to Colin. A sixth car and

a seventh rolled up. "What the hell did you tell them?"

"I just said we needed help right away."

"Well, damn! Those guys are coming from everywhere!" Almost crying with embarrassment, Gary said, "All these cars—and nothing has happened!" Then from the house came Bobby Ellis, a slightly-built, clear-eyed young man in a yellow windbreaker. Gary walked up and began to apologize, but Ellis, his black beret tipped forward proudly, shook his head.

"Nobody talks to nobody," Ellis said, "not with all this pig out here. What is all this?"

Gary swallowed: "Uh, you got a noisy party up there."

"Well, God damn," Bobby Ellis said, "you didn't have to call out the whole police force, did you?" The other black youngsters began yelling, "Honkies! Pigs!"

Almost whispering, Gary said, "Listen, man, this was a mistake. I apologize."

The heckling grew more angry in tone, but Ellis seemed in complete control. "What do you want?" he asked.

"Nothing," said Gary. "Just a little less noise. This ain't a bust or anything."

"Okay. I'll quiet the party down if you can get all these cops out of here. Can you do that?"

After a moment, Gary said, "Yeah, I'll get 'em out of here." He walked back to the car where Colin was talking to the sergeant. "God damn it, Sergeant," Gary yelled. "Get those policemen out of here!"

"You sure everything's okay?"

"It won't be okay if these guys stay here much longer."

The sergeant returned to his car,

went on the air and told all the units to return to wherever they had come from. The patrolmen, almost reluctantly, walked back to their cars, a chorus of jeers at their backs.

The next day, Gary placed a phone call to Bobby Ellis. "Ellis told me," Gary said, "that there were still a couple of those patrol cars riding around that area for hours, harassing every goddam kid who left that party."

There was at least one thing about which Gary and Colin had similar feelings: next to members of the Tactical Patrol Force, both men felt like sensitive social workers. Unlike the two young patrolmen, both weighing under 160 pounds, the tactical police are mostly above average in height and weight. They wear impressive black leather jackets, white crash helmets and big gun belts with equipment that jangles as they stride. They cruise in unmarked cars, two men in front and two in back; in the station house they stay together, enjoying their status as an elite group.

Early one evening Gary and Colin were in a corner of the station house watching three tactical cops getting ready to charge outside for the beginning of a shift. They were waiting impatiently for a fourth to come down from the locker room. One was clapping his hands together and rocking up and down on his feet. A partner suddenly threw him a black leather glove and barked, "Think fast!" The cop caught the glove, shouted "Hey!" and tossed it back.

"They have so much damn energy," Colin said. "I went to a house call with that guy," he said, pointing to the cop who was smacking his hands together. "He doesn't walk upstairs; he *runs*."

The fourth member of the squadron nimbly descended the stairs and shouted, "Ready?"

"Right!"

They put on their white helmets and strode outside.

"They act like they're constantly on riot duty," Gary said.

"They're great for riots, though," said Colin. "If you want a display of force, if you *need* that display, they're it. But I have to agree— they're kind of like animals."

"Well," Gary admitted, "they probably do serve a need. Obviously, in certain tough situations you don't need a bunch of policemen who are as disorganized as the rioters. My only complaint is that they don't have enough emphasis on restraint."

"Well, whenever I'm in trouble I'm glad to see them around," said Colin.

A tactical patrol returned. A young Negro, arms handcuffed behind his back, sailed headfirst into the room, landing on the floor. His friend, also handcuffed, was shoved down on the bench so hard that his head snapped against the wall. His dark glasses fell from one ear and dangled on his face. A huge tactical cop took one step and kicked the man on the floor.

"Take these cuffs offa me!" he screamed. "I'll fight!"

Three members of the patrol smiled as their prisoner managed to stand. "Why don't you shoot me!" he pleaded. "If I had a gun I'd shoot *you*." He was thrown toward the window and held there while another cop felt through his clothing.

"How old are you?" asked the sergeant from behind the window.

"I'm 18! White man! Knocking me down, for nothing! Never in my life . . . ! If you're gonna kill me, why don't you just kill me!"

He was thrown toward the bench. He fell, still shouting, alongside his friend. He stood up, struggling with the handcuffs behind him, and charged at the tactical police. Again he was hurled against the bench.

"YOU'RE A PRISONER, CLOWN! YOU DO WHAT YOU'RE TOLD."

Gary walked over to the tac police. "What's going on, fellas?"

"What's it to you?"

"Hey, man, I'm a policeman like you. I just thought I'd find out why you're kicking this guy's ass." Gary added, "I just want to find out what side I'm on."

"Listen, Cummings," said the sergeant, "there's only one side of the story—*our* side."

The middle-aged restaurant proprietress seemed glad to see Gary and Colin. She had been held up a few nights before "by three Mexican-Indian types."

"How much did they get?" asked Gary.

"About $90. If you boys had come in here, they would have killed you. You wouldn't have had a chance."

"Did all three have guns?"

"Two of 'em did for sure."

The two patrolmen ate a large, inexpensive dinner of chicken and rice. As they left the restaurant, a girl came up and informed the patrolmen that a man in a parked car was exposing himself. She led them to a small red car on Haight Street. Colin rapped at the window and motioned for the well-dressed man to step out. "He's the kind who make speeches about young people being sick," said the girl. "And look at him! He's perverted!" Colin politely asked the man what he was doing in Hip-

pieville. The man shrugged. "Arrest him!" the girl demanded.

Colin said, "The girl says you were exposing yourself."

"No, I didn't do that."

"Liar!" the girl yelled.

"I think you'd better leave this area," Colin said as the man jumped back into his car.

"We could have arrested that guy," Gary said.

"I checked his driver's license," Colin said. "Lots of credit cards. He might be a big shot. A perverted big shot. He'd be out on bail and we'd be in hot water."

The cops heard a call, "Officer! Officer!" From a side street ran a squat, middle-aged woman.

"Take your time," Gary said.

She caught her breath: "I heard a girl yelling. Just a block down."

"On the street, was she?"

"No, no. Up in the house. Something about a man holding a gun on her."

"Okay, okay," said Colin. "We'll follow you." The woman nodded, still breathing heavily as she led the way. She pointed to the second floor of a Victorian home and said, "Up there."

The cops went to the second floor. They heard a girl's voice: "I see my mother. Hello, Mom! Don't let the bad man take me away. La, la, la." Colin knocked on the door and the girl screamed, "They're coming!"

Colin tried to push open the door, but it was locked. "Open up! Police!"

A bearded, shirtless man with a medallion around his neck greeted them. The girl screamed again.

"What's going on?" Gary asked.

"She's high, man. Real high. She's not harming anyone." The girl screamed again. White and naked, she was dancing about and apparently having drug-induced hallucinations. "Don't go near her," the man pleaded.

"Shut up," Colin ordered. "Hey," he called to the girl. "Are you all right?"

The girl stopped dancing—there was no music—and stared at Colin. She turned away, looked back at Colin's uniform and rushed straight into a window, splashing glass. Instantly Colin was behind her, pulling her by the legs back over the broken glass. Gary covered her with a shirt and helped her to stand. Colin called for a patrol car and an ambulance.

"You shouldn't have gone in there," said the bearded man. "You had no right. She wasn't harming anybody."

"Not much," Colin snapped.

"You had no . . ."

"Shut your fat head!"

Somehow the girl managed to wriggle into a sacklike dress. Blood dripped down her legs. The man demanded to be taken with the girl in the ambulance.

"You're going to the station," Colin told him.

"What for? You won't find any acid on me, man!"

"Then get the hell out of here!" Colin said. "No, stay here!"

The two patrolmen searched the apartment but found no drugs.

Back on the street Colin angrily kicked the sidewalk. "These kids," he said. "Sometimes they don't even know what they've put inside themselves. I asked a kid once and he said, 'No, I don't know what I shot up with. If it kills me so what? Dying might be a good trip.'"

Four young men were sitting on stairs, almost hidden by shadows. Colin splashed his flashlight beam across their faces. "How're you doing, fellas?" There was no answer, so he added, "I'd like to see your IDs." Three of the young men immediately reached for their wallets, while the fourth, wearing a bright-gold blouse and shoulder-length hair, seemed upset. Gary checked the identification cards of the other three and the nervous boy walked to the sidewalk, fishing a crumpled pink paper from his pocket.

Colin trained his flashlight on the pink sheet and the boy said, "You can't arrest me."

Colin had no intention of arresting him, but he asked, "Why can't I?"

"Because I'm a juvenile."

Without warning the boy sprinted across the street. Instantly Colin was on his heels. Gary ordered the others to get off the steps and stand facing the wall as he watched Colin's pursuit. The fleeing boy reached a small grass embankment, tripped and fell. He wheeled and Colin drew his gun. The boy, luckily for himself, froze.

After Colin had called for the wagon, he asked the handcuffed boy some questions.

"Where do you live?"

"Anywhere."

"What's your name?"

"Jingle Bells."

"Occupation?"

"I'm a tourist attraction."

"Are you a student?" Colin shouted the question.

"No! I'm a juvenile!"

Colin pushed his hand against the back of the boy's head, smashing his face into a garage door.

"And on the side," the boy said defiantly, "I keep a lookout for police brutality."

"I should have shot your face off over there," Colin told him.

Later Colin said, "We had had two murders in the week and, for all I knew, this was the kid that did it. He could have had a gun. How would I know?"

Next evening, Colin and Gary returned to the same cafe to order the same meal of chicken and rice. Right down the street, a plainclothes narcotics agent was "buying" some acid from two black dealers from Oakland. As soon as the transaction was made, he said, "You're under arrest." The agent moved quickly, handcuffing the men together and using a box nearby to call for a patrol car.

The dealers broke loose and ran around the corner, ducking into a saloon. The black owner told them to leave. Then the radio car pulled up and two officers, plus the undercover man, attempted to drag the prisoners out of the bar.

In 30 seconds most of the Haight knew something big was on. Colin and Gary heard the sirens and dashed toward the crowd, leaving their half-eaten dinner behind.

Colin went to a rooftop to prevent people from throwing things and Gary mingled with the people on the street, trying to calm things down. "I'm up there watching the action," Colin said later, "and as soon as the cops left, the crowd started throwing more bottles, bricks, sticks—every kind of thing—at cars . . . they hit a couple of buses real good. The most frustrating thing is to be in a position where you can see people doing things that are absolutely wrong, and being totally helpless.

"Many people were just spectators. So one group started smashing windows in the store directly underneath

me! What was I gonna do? Shoot 10 people standing down below because they're burglarizing a store?"

The riot ended with a "sweep" by tactical cops. Afterwards Gary brought the following allegation, printed in an underground paper, to Colin's attention: "The cops who had arrested us took us into the interrogation room, closed the door and proceeded to methodically, carefully and skillfully beat us up. . . . The cops concentrated on my kidneys, chest and groin."

"The other side to that story," Colin said, "is that the kids *wanted* the police to beat them up. Many of them tried their best to make the police break the law."

To Gary it had been "a bad scene." He said, "These kids have made police brutality a part of their lives. I think it helps them to identify with black people.

"And here we get into the personality of the cop, which is something that's not supposed to matter. But some guys, they don't care if it's a Negro or not. Some guys just like to whip a guy's head.

"They have to put caliber people in these kinds of areas who are willing to take whatever crap is flying and try to apply some imagination to it and turn it around. A cat you send to any area that is explodable should be your most talented person, not your most off-balance.

"Meanwhile," Gary sighed, "it's as if Haight-Ashbury was an arena, with the kids on one side and the cops on the other, while the rest of society just sits back and chooses sides."

part seven

THE
SELF-ABUSERS

One function of society is to protect the self-interests of its members. Not only does the state protect the individual from other members of society, but it also places barriers before individuals who would abuse, injure, or destroy themselves. For example, social control mechanisms are employed when there is clear-cut evidence of the self-destructive character of individual or group actions. This is the case with suicide: The community or individuals stand in the person's way if he decides to destroy himself even if circumstances of excessive pain or confirmed feelings of futility characterize his life. In other instances, laws and norms are imposed because certain behaviors are contradictory to dominant moral values and seem to threaten long-standing social patterns for conduct, such as certain sexual behaviors. In still other instances, certain activities of community members are held to be undesirable because of myths or the lack of experience with the consequences of the actions involved. For example, scientific evidence does not support the view that marijuana is habituating or that it calls forth bizarre or undesirable behavior to any greater extent than other substances which are freely available in the community. Its use, however, remains illegal, for it is defined as harmful to the individual.

Condemnation of certain behaviors often runs counter to the value of the right of individuals to make their own decisions with respect to personal behavior. Groups in society often regard methods of control as an invasion of individual freedom and privacy. Controversies recur in many areas because of the incompatibility of the values of the right of the community to regulate individual behavior and the right of the individual to act as a free agent. The four cases presented here vary in the extent of self-abuse inflicted as well as the degree of community consensus on the impropriety of the behavior involved.

| INDIVIDUAL vs. INDIVIDUAL | INDIVIDUAL vs. ORGANIZATION |

SUICIDE

Death is a part of life, and unless the party involved is an intimate, the event is usually treated in a rather routine fashion. Physicians particularly are often bland in the face of death because they are constantly confronted by it. However, the moral imperatives against taking one's own life are strong in the western world, and such a death has a different effect. "Suicide" is a personal account by a physician who attended another doctor, a close friend, during his last hours of life after a suicide attempt. The case portrays the ultimate act of self-abuse and the hostility and guilt felt by one who attended in both a professional and a personal role. The reader must decide for himself who is the protagonist and who the victim in this account.

THE FANTASTIC LODGE

Heroin addiction is viewed with great alarm in American society, perhaps because of the difficulty in reversing the habit once it is formed. Few community members feel that the individual should have the option to elect a life of drug use for himself. Consequently, a variety of methods exists to limit the access that individuals have to drugs, and a range of therapeutic regimens are applied to addicts in spite of the slim chance for cure. The confirmed drug addict can be seen as a protagonist of the social order who breaks the rules and opposes the attitudes of the community. The selection here is part of an edited account of a young girl drug addict and her rejection of a number of community norms in the face of coping with her "monkey."

ORGANIZATION vs. INDIVIDUAL	ORGANIZATION vs. ORGANIZATION

TWILIGHT OF THE WCTU

Community members often mobilize individuals into a structured organization in order to focus on and control what they regard as self-abusive activities of individuals. Alcohol, at least in moderation, is regarded by many as an appropriate substance that inspires conviviality and relaxation. But there are also those who hold that *any* use of alcohol is self-destructive and that it should not be available to the individual. Although the WCTU today is an anemic organization compared to its once powerful status, it still operates to harass the consumer and purveyor of alcohol. Kloman's report of the activities of the WCTU demonstrates how the organization impinges on the lives of individuals in an area of activity that a minority regards as self-abusive.

THE LIFE AND DEATH OF ATLANTA'S HIP STRIP

While there is no way of knowing whether more or fewer persons are "dropping out," hippie communities at least as ordinarily characterized in the 60's appear to be waning in size and cohesiveness. They may be losing their own momentum; life in them perhaps is less fun and rewarding than the participants thought. But in addition to internal reasons for their diminished robustness, in most places the larger community and their police organizations have at least failed to protect hippies, if not themselves harrassing them, and destroying the neighborhoods and the social organization of persons living there. Wooten describes the Atlanta experience, where powerful "bike gangs" were allowed to completely "do in" a hippie community. The carnival-like, crowded, and warm, if anormative, neighborhood by conventional standards, known as "The Wall," has been reduced to a depressing, cold, dull place—a frightening and dangerous place to live.

Suicide

HOWARD M. FEINSTEIN, M.D.

November 2—, 195—
4:30 p.m.

Dr. B—— was found unconscious at about 3:30 p.m. He had lacerations of both wrists and neck which were self-inflicted with broken window glass. He lost an undetermined amount of blood. Efforts to maintain blood pressure with fluids failed. Respirations ceased at about 4:05 and he was pronounced dead.

The high-pitched screech of the telephone operator rasped against my drums. "They need you here in a hurry doctor—it's urgent—an emergency!" I mumbled something about it being a hell of a way to spend Thanksgiving and charged out of the door into gray deserted streets. I tried to keep the meaning of "emergency" hidden from myself, but I couldn't. In our hospital it most often meant suicide. I stopped for a light. The dull red brick hospital came into view as I turned the corner. It stood solid, complacent and ugly. There were lights in most of the windows but no faces. I pulled up to the entrance between two "No Parking" signs and stopped the car.

The powder-caked face of the operator looked even whiter and more masklike than usual. "They're in the operating room!" she yelled, but I

Reprinted with permission of the author and the publisher from *Community Mental Health Journal,* III, 3 (Fall 1967), pp. 259–61.

didn't need to hear. I was off following a thin trail of blood spattered over the freshly waxed asphalt tile floor.

He was stretched out limply on the table. The resident in shirt sleeves bent over a flaccid arm, tensely probing for a vein. "Lost lot of blood . . . broken window . . . wrists . . . neck." I looked at the ashen face. He was a handsome young man with blonde hair still neatly combed. Ice-blue eyes stared vacantly at the ceiling. A jagged necklace of clotted blood and torn flesh hung about his throat.

"Give me a stethoscope and blood pressure cuff," I demanded, trying to force down the revulsion that mounted within me. The nurse searched the room fruitlessly, looked up as if to excuse herself, and ran off to the ward. His pulse beat faintly but regularly against my cold fingers. He breathed shallow sighs. "Maybe I can do something . . . I'm supposed to be able to do something!" I reached for things once known. The infusion dripped briskly. I looked at the lemon-yellow face and knew that would never be enough. We had no blood bank. He needed extensive surgical repair. "Better call an ambulance and warn the General that he's coming." The male attendant pushed his horn-rimmed glasses up on the bridge of his nose and disappeared.

I looked around the prison-gray tile room noticing the others drawn by the blood of a near-headless man. A crew-cut medical student hovered over the end of the table pecking away at a cold ankle with a needle trying to start another infusion. I wondered at his calm and then remembered the comfortable feeling of learning in a situation where someone else was responsible. He missed a third time and droplets of sweat joined us together. The young nurse with tight black curls ran through the door waving the cuff and stethoscope triumphantly, as if they really mattered.

There was no measurable blood pressure. I moved the black bell onto his chest, dutifully searching for parts of the body that might still be alive. The sallow chest shuddered and a hand pushed the bell away. I looked toward the head of the table. The eyes pleaded. Parched lips formed voiceless words: "Let ... me ... be."

I turned away so that he could not sense my rage. I fought the urge to raise my fist and bring it smashing down on his face, then pushed the helpless hand out of my way and pressed the black thorn into the flesh.

The male attendant peered over the glasses which had once again slipped down his nose. In a respectful, apologetic whisper he told me that the police had sent a squad car by mistake. They just left to get an ambulance. They would come back in a hurry. Both infusions were running now. The chest still rose and fell mechanically with the tide of unwanted air. I put some gauze pads in place to hide his wounds.

A cop, stuffed in a soiled uniform with tarnished brass buttons, entered. His cap was shoved back on his head. As he looked over the resident's shoulder, the tough professional veneer peeled away revealing horror and

fright. He wrinkled his nose at the sweet smell of fresh-cut meat. I asked for the stretcher, and he turned to the three others that had filed in behind him. There was none. He ran out. He came back carrying a gray canvas stretcher. They each held one corner and moved alongside the table. The blonde head turned slowly and glared at the buttons. We grabbed hold to move him to the waiting stretcher. He shrugged loose. I asked for a sheet and we spread it out to wrap around him. He bellowed like a trapped animal and sat up. The resident grabbed one bloody wrist and I took hold of the other. Another raucous, outraged bellow filled the room. He pulled and tugged to break free. His head balanced precariously like a ping-pong ball on a pencil. Blood ejaculated from his wounds. He began to laugh. Then he sagged back onto the table. He clutched his throat.

"Give me the tracheotomy set," I demanded. The nurse with tight curls ran to the instrument cabinet. It was locked. She fled to get the nursing supervisor.

She came back nervously fingering a jingling mass of unfamiliar keys. As she tried them one by one, the supervisor commented in an oily smooth voice, "We don't use this room very often, you know." The nurse brought over the jar with scalpel blades resting on the bottom. She couldn't find a forceps so I reached into the viscous preservative and fished out a blade.

By now the young man lay motionless. None of us wanted to put the knife to his throat. I offered the instrument to the resident. He turned away. The student said that he had never done a tracheotomy. Instead of extending the minutes of his life, it felt like one of us would finish with steel what he had started with jagged glass. I fingered the bare cartilage of his neck and shoved the blade down with a twist. The student pushed in on the chest to breathe for him, but it was useless. Again I pressed the ball against him, but this time there was no sound. He was dead.

We turned from the body to ourselves. A gray-headed attendant with a thick Irish brogue told how worried she had been. After the resident put him in seclusion, she had checked on him frequently. Surely there was nothing more she could have done. "Why I spoke with him at three-fifteen ... No, I remember now it was three-twenty."

The charge nurse, an old hand, confirmed this and grumbled, "I told his doctor two days ago that he was sick. But did he listen to me? Oh no. The trouble with these young residents is they're too wrapped up with talk. What he needed was shock treatment."

The resident and I bent over the sink washing our hands. He had spent half an hour talking with Dr. B——— when he made rounds in the afternoon. He had seemed okay then. "He gave me his word that he would let me know if he felt the urge to harm himself."

I listened but I was intent on what I was doing. I soaped my hands for the third time and scrubbed vigorously. The preservative had fixed brown flecks of blood on my fingers. They wouldn't wash off.

There were forms to fill out and procedures to follow. They fell in place easily, like grains of sand erasing his path. With this finished, I made a note in the chart as I had been trained to do.

AFTERMATH

This is the context in which the word "suicide" became meaningful to me. Dr. B———'s suicide touched us all. In the many group meetings that were held with residents, patients, and staff to discuss our dismay at his death, there was never any discussion of the nature of professional responsibility vis-à-vis a man intent on taking his own life. The upset of the hospital was treated as a pain that needed amelioration—like a boil that wants lancing rather than an ethical dilemma to be thought through. I suspect this was no accident or peculiarity of a particular hospital. Rather, it was to be expected in the medical training setting. Unfortunately, psychiatrists still begin their specialty training hobbled by the medical materialism of earlier training more suitable for the internist or the surgeon. Our education begins with death as an event that has significance primarily as a cause, the effect of which is to produce dissection material. By the time the smell of formaldehyde has given way to the nameless odors of the hospital corridor, the psychiatrist-to-be has also been taught that suicide is the act of a diseased machine that he is responsible for labeling and impounding before it runs off a cliff. We undertake to stamp out suicide like one would stamp out poliomyelitis. A problem that involves human choice is misunderstood with the mental equipment more suitable to the solution of physicochemical problems.

With the image of Dr. B———'s suicide fresh in mind, I would like to make a distinction that seems obvious to me now but was not then. The word "suicide" can refer to a medical emergency and also to an existential problem. One needs to understand that the assumptions and actions of a physician acting to restore physiological integrity are quite different (or should be) from those of a psychotherapist working with someone contemplating suicide. I have no quarrel with medical training that places the physician reflexly on the side of perpetuating the body in an emergency— even that of a man who has tried to end his own life. A man who attempts to kill himself should expect that a doctor called to the scene would attend to his circulation. In so doing, the doctor is acting on behalf of the professional ethic of physicians, which places him uncritically on the side of prolonging bodily function.

The psychotherapist is in a quite different situation. But because he has had training experiences like the one described here, the differences may be obscured. A man contemplating suicide is a human being weighing the choice of life or death. Dr. B—— decided that his life was no longer worth living, and he might have been right. As a physician I pushed this question out of sight. As a psychotherapist, I find it is a central concern. Weighing the value and meaning of one's life is not a question of

physiology. A psychotherapist has, I believe, a contractual commitment to help that man in his attempt at self-understanding and self-mastery. Talk of suicide is an invitation to inquiry, not a reason for intrusive action.

To withhold intrusive action is not the same as being disinterested in the outcome. This too is a distinction that it is hard for the physician psychotherapist to make. Action on behalf of the preservation of life is the doctor's function. Such action may conflict with the work of the psychotherapist. He cares about the outcome but insists that he cannot perform his function as a therapist when the possibility is ever present that he may act to interfere with another's action if the patient's decision does not coincide with his own. The therapist cannot help another examine his life if he sits in judgment. His concern shows itself in a respect for another's powers to manage his own life or his own death. Though he may choose life, the therapist can see that for some death may be more desirable and he acknowledges their right to choose.

As I think back over Dr. B——'s death, I am troubled that so many of us were ready to force him onto a stretcher but none even thought of taking his hand.

The Fantastic Lodge

HELEN MacGILL HUGHES

They had to send me down to see how much bread I had. Well, when I first went down there, she looked at me and she said, "Two dollars." "Two dollars!" I said.

"Well, you've got a three-dollar book."

I said, "Well, cash it in." And that's what she did, thank God, which gave me five whole wonderful dollars!

I didn't realize just how much it meant to me to leave the place, and how much tension I had been under during the time that I had been there, until I started to get into the station wagon that was to drive me to town, and I was lifting my suitcase. All of a sudden, my legs started shaking uncontrollably—I had heels on. I was all dressed up. It felt marvelous to be dressed up again. And I couldn't stop them from shaking. I just lost all control. I got into the station wagon and started to light a cigarette, and it's the same thing: I had to hold both hands to get the cigarette up to my mouth and then, just as we were driving out the gate, I started crying. I didn't know why it should have been so tremendous, but it was.

Meanwhile, I was thinking fast. I knew I couldn't take a train home: I

Reprinted by permission of the publisher from Helen MacGill Hughes, *The Fantastic Lodge* (Boston: Houghton Mifflin Company, 1961), Chapter Eleven, pp. 229–44. © 1961 by the Chicago Area Project.

didn't have enough bread. Also, I knew I had to get out of town. About eight hours, I think they give you, after you sign your AMA papers, or else you'll be picked up.

There wasn't a train until eight or eleven, or something fantastic like that, that night. There was a bus, and so I decided to take a bus as far as I had bread for. I got to the bus station, said good-by to the cab, and walked in feeling like, you know, everyone knew what kind of a station wagon I had gotten out of and where I came from. I couldn't get used to looking at the people in the station, and they'd look at me and I'd think they were staring at me. I finally had to get up and go in the washroom and sit there for a while, while I calmed myself down and talked myself out of all these jitters.

I bought a ticket and bought some candy. I hadn't had anything to eat all day. And a pack of cigarettes—ah, they tasted good! And got on the bus and went.

I had the strangest feeling all that day until I got back home. I had been used to whatever existence Lexington had meant to me. I'd just begun to get used to the routine—and yet, it had been so foreign to me that I had hardly gotten over the newness. And then, to be confronted suddenly with all these strange towns, just nowhere, with no money, and no real means of getting anywhere for sure. Yet I enjoyed it, perversely, in some fashion. I felt: "Well, here I am. I don't have any money. I can't get any junk for at least twelve hours. I'll be a normal person for that long, anyway." Incidentally, since I got on the bus I *knew* that I would be making it as soon as I got back into town. In fact, I felt that that would be the first thing I would do.

Now, when I got as far as I could, to this strange city, I tried to call Bob, collect. And there was no answer, at first. I hadn't thought of that. And I was hungry, and I was down to a couple of pennies. It was really very bad. So, finally, I went to Travelers' Aid and laid this story on them, and asked them what they suggested, and they said call Bob back. And this time he was in. When I heard his voice, I burst into tears again. And he, of course, he asked me how I would like to have the money sent. Well, there was a Western Union strike on, but in spite of the strike, the service was supposedly still on.

So I sent a telegram, and I was to wait. A hard old bench. Nothing was happening. Nothing was happening. And four hours had gone by. My mother had, supposedly, wired the money to me, and it still hadn't come. I was sounding the chick every five minutes now. I made another frantic phone call to Bob. The last quick bus that would take me home in a reasonable amount of time was due to leave in another hour and a half, and I *still* hadn't gotten the money. So then Bob's people were going to run frantically down to Travelers' Aid there and leave some more bread, and do it that way. Finally, just at the last possible minute—the way those things always work out—the wire came through. And they stopped the

other money coming from Travelers' Aid. And I thanked everybody and I trotted off on the bus.

I hadn't had any sleep now for over thirty hours. I hadn't had anything to eat outside of one sandwich for twenty-four hours. I was feeling all the effects of kicking the habit, right all over again. And I couldn't sleep, I was so worked up emotionally.

It was all so unreal, driving through all these strange towns. Bus travel is crazy, even if it is tiring and sweaty and everything else. At nights, there's nothing like it. And I was plenty sick, but I still enjoyed it.

Bob met me at the bus station. And then we went over to my mother's house. And already it had begun. Why had I done this? Actually, why had I? I came out without any money, made a big scene out of it, so that his parents were aware, my mother was aware I was a complete failure, in all of their eyes. Even Bob was disappointed with me, I knew. I was disappointed with myself. We had no place to stay. We'd given up our pad. It was all just very ridiculous and very typical of me. And on top of that, I was trying to cope with the feelings that I got from Lexington. Must've been from Lexington, because that was the only experience I've had. It changed me.

I had the idea, then, when I first got out of the treatment center, for the first time in my life that I was an incurable junkie. For the first time, I could see myself. Always before, I had thought of myself as, well, someday, someday, somehow, I'll kick this. But I felt beaten. "Why am I fighting it and spending money, and hanging up and going two flips, and why don't I just accept it and do the best I can? Because that's the way it is. I'll never change." Well, of course, this feeling nearly broke my heart. It's not an easy thing, I mean, to accept that. It would be like accepting cancer, I guess.

And because I just accepted it and had no urge to fight it, or anything else, I felt terrible, as far as Bob was concerned. We went through quite an emotional scene. I wanted him to leave me, because I felt more and more an awareness of how I was dragging him down. And that when I came back each time from some sort of an escapade it would be *me* that was really the instigator, as far as getting back on again was concerned.

I couldn't actually go so far as to say that I hated him, didn't want any part of him, or anything. And that's all he wanted to know . . . was how I felt about him. So for two days I didn't take anything. But it was just tooth and nail, every minute of the day. I felt very weak, physically, which didn't help. But I just felt there was no reason at all to be doing this, that I was with my own kind down there, and I saw how things were with them, and that's what I would be in another fifteen or twenty years. And time in joints across the nation, being locked up for years, didn't seem to make any difference to them. Why should I expect that it would make any difference with me? I stayed in bed most of the time and cried, and felt miserable. So naturally, I made it again.

Then we got a pad, furnished place, and went into there, and started making it pretty regularly. The rent was expensive, the fact that we were making it again meant Bob would become dependent on his parents again for money. Ah, the same routine! Into it just like it was an old fairy tale we both knew our parts in completely

well, you know. And everybody just sort of fell into line, you know. I mean, his people, and my mother, they all seemed the same role to me. Well, of course, with them, that's the role they *want* to play. With us, it's sort of half-and-half; we do and we don't. We do, and we can't seem to be strong enough to get out of it.

I don't even like to think about those days. We moved out into a hotel for a week, still downhill. Then we got a sixth-story monstrosity in a tenement. I had plans. I was thinking about getting furniture and straightening it up and then, once I had straightened up, of doing something about all this.

We had begun scoring at the Hill Hotel, and since it was much too hot to have Bob over there, I was doing most of the trips. We were scoring from a spade cat, who had a fay chick who was his old lady, and he was pimping for her, and they were constantly hitting on me: either go to work for Bob through the connection, or do some free-lance work or something. It was silly—all this money to be run down; I was a white girl; I was attractive; if I had to have it, I might as well be realistic about it and face it. The world at the Hill Hotel, I mean, it's a world of small pimps and whores and small-time dope-peddlers and petty thieves and boosters. It's just a little section of the underworld, the dirty end of the underworld, the small-time rackets. We were frantic for money, naturally, to score with, and here was all this money to be made, and I thought, This is what I'm going to be eventually, anyway. And these are eventually my people. And for what am I holding back? But, of course, this made me so terribly unhappy at the same time. I think it was all an urge on my part to really just wallow in it. I was going to play this game and play it the whole way, instead of messing around and playing it halfway and still trying to pretend that I was different. Or that I was a sensitive person or something—anything that would distinguish me, you know, from the run of junkies.

I even tried to talk Bob into letting me hustle,* and I was serious about it, and of course, this nearly broke his heart. And I think I, inside, must have enjoyed hurting him as much as I was hurting myself. That's only one aspect of our relationship, anyway, that's been forged in neurotic fires. And at the same time, I had become so despondent. We weren't getting good junk. We didn't have the *bad* habit, but I had thrown myself so completely into the mechanisms of being hooked—of waking up feeling horrible, of having to have the first fix, of copping frantically, you know— the pace and the misery that go with real addiction. It was more the externals than the internals, really, but nonetheless, just as big and just as high. And we were so high up—six floors.

I thought, one day when I was sitting out on the fire escape, of how easy it would be just to stop everything. I was in so much pain, and I was putting Bob in so much pain. At the same time, I was being pressed very definitely by Zimpert to come to a decision. And Bob and I seemed to grow farther and farther apart, because of all our arguments and so forth and so on. We had some terrible fights during this period, I mean, regular physical fights. Once he chased me down the street, then knocked me

down on the ground. There were some people there—they were on his side. And he was on my side, telling me he wasn't a gentleman, and what was he doing this thing for? And I grew very angry at them for interfering and we marched off together.

And I did think about taking my life then. Bob fought me one night when I tried. And another night, while he was gone out to work I went out and sat on the fire escape and I was smoking a cigarette and I threw it down, and I watched. You know, when you watch little objects. And I thought how I would feel if I were going down. And I thought that wouldn't be so hard. It was almost as though I were hypnotized by the ground and by hitting. I could feel myself hitting it. But I waited.

And then came the night that started all of the events of the last bust. Bob and I had had another big fight that evening, and I threw a glass of water at him and threw a shoe at him that missed him and went through the glass door of the apartment and broke it. I think the thing that started it, if I remember correctly, was that he thought we shouldn't score. And I was saying, in effect, "Why try? Why try to do anything?" And so he said, "All right! *You* can go to the Hill Hotel, and get the junk." And he took the money and he cut out.

I waited for a while, and he didn't come back. I waited for a little while longer and he still didn't come back. I knew the trip should take him an hour at the outside. And he still hadn't come back. So I went down to the drugstore to make the phone call. I phoned the police, thinking that maybe Bob had gotten picked up. No, he wasn't down there. I couldn't

* Be a prostitute.

figure that out. Where would he be? So then I called the connection's house, but he never got there. So then I was *really* puzzled. I thought maybe Bob had come in while I was gone, so I decided to go back upstairs. I was walking up the narrow stairs in the hall and I happened to look down the stairs. I thought I heard my name. I thought, God, I'm hearing things.

And I looked down, and there was my mother coming up the stairs. I thought, Now, what in Christ's name is she doing on the scene? Then I started to say hello to her. And then I saw two cats coming up behind her. And I thought, Uhh-oh, what is this? They were right behind me. I was cut off. So I just kept going up the stairs, past our floor, which was the top floor, and went across the narrow boarding that was up at what would have been the seventh floor and was out on the roof. And hung there, and watched them go into my pad, the two cats and my mother.

I tried to hear what they were saying, got my head next to the door, and I thought I heard one of the cats say, "I'm a police officer. I'm only a police officer," or something. And I was so right! But I didn't know at the time. And Phil Schaefer, meantime, was just coming up the stairs, from the drugstore. So I yelled down the elevator shaft: I said, "Phil! get out!" And he didn't need any further word. He went—like that! So then I met him downstairs, and we went and called the police station, thinking I might be able to find out if Bob had been picked up, and maybe they just weren't telling me, or something.

I don't think I would have gone back if I had known where Bob was. I still went cautiously. I went up the

fire escape and hung outside the window. And then I became aware of the fact that she was alone in the pad. Now she was in the kitchen doing the dishes. So I came in the window. I said, "What's going on? Who were these two cats?" And so forth and so on. And she gave me a story a yard long: "Well, oh, they just had a flashlight. I couldn't find your apartment. And they gave me the flashlight, and they were showing me upstairs."

"Well, what were they doing in the apartment, talking?"

"Well, I broke down when I got up here, and saw the broken glass and the door, and I didn't know what happened. I thought you may have committed suicide. Janet. I was so upset! And I started crying and they were very sympathetic. And then they left." She said, "And I'm sorry to be so emotional. I was just a mother."

And she lied beautifully—superbly —I must say not so much in what she did as how she said it. My mother's never been good at lying to me.

And then I said, "Well, have you heard from Bob?"

She said, "Well, yes, yes, yes. He called our house. He's going to meet you at my place. You come home with me now. To my place." And I said, "Uuh-uuh. I'll wait here for him. But I will go downstairs and we'll call your house, and see if he's there."

All right. So we went downstairs together and she called. She was talking on the phone, when this cat came up behind me. And just stood there for a couple of minutes first. He didn't really look like the man, frankly. He was a tall, thin, dark-haired cat; almost looked more like a junkie then he did the man. And then I realized what the score was, all right.

"Come on. You're under arrest."

And I said, "What? On what grounds?" You know, I really gave him a good argument, at this point, still believing in our Bill of Rights. And he said, "Why? Because you're a drug addict."

I said, "Because I'm a drug addict?" I said, "Even saying that I was, and I'm not saying that I am, there's no law that says you can't be a drug addict in this state or in this city."

And he told me, "Yes, there is!" And then he starts reading off the number—and I know the number; that's the law putting narcotics addicts in jail.

And I said, "Well, that's nothing. A little two-hundred-bond state disorderly-loitering narcotics-addict op." I said, "You can't even take me in for that, because you're arresting me in my own home. I'm minding my own business. There's nothing you can do." He said, "Well, your mother has signed a complaint against you." And I turned around, and I said, "Why, you dirty bitch!" And I lunged at her, you know. And then he grabbed me.

And she says, "Oh, I know you feel this way, Janet." She's standing there. She says, "But this is all for the best. I'm doing it for you, Janet." And the tears are pouring out of her eyes.

I said, "You fucking bitch! You lousy cocker!" I'm screaming at her, and the neighbors were coming out, meantime—"Oh, look at the cops! Look at the junkie! Look at the mother!" You know.

And I said, "Well, let's talk outside. I don't want to make a scene." And we cut outside, and then there was this little pause. What's the proper decorum in this sort of situation? She pulls out a cigarette and lights it. And I remember at that time, I thought: This is not going to happen to me

again! I am not going through this. And I saw all the implications, you know. There's no feeling worse than the point when you're just arrested. I knew I had to go through it. I knew how sick I was going to be. I knew the Main Station deal.

And so I waited until he relaxed, and I was off, down the street, as fast as I could go. I had the idea that he would take out a gun and try to shoot me, you know, the way they do in the movies. And I just thought, Well, at least, then, they'll take me to a hospital. That's the only thing I can remember running through my mind. I took him completely off guard, so I had a good head-start. But he was young and a pretty fast runner. And the other cat tried to run, too; but he gave up. In fact, if he'd been there by himself (he was a little fat bastard), he never would make it in a million years. As he said, "I wouldn't have run after you. It'd wear me out."

So I was doing pretty good, you know, keeping a couple of yards between us. And I was making it toward these buildings, where I figured I could dodge in and out of the doors and throw him off, and then cut through an alley. And that's when I made that fatal little stumble over a piece of glass, and went down and couldn't get up on my ankle. And he was on top of me. But I still wouldn't go of my own volition. They had to bring cops and drag me to the car, and everything. And then I found out they had another cat stationed at my mother's house. It had all been very complete.

At the station started the usual pseudo questioning. First, the young cat, the thin one, the one who caught me, started giving this little routine about "Give us your man, and I won't kick you." This is the man-to-man talk, as distinguished from the man-to-rat talk you get from some of 'em. And he says, "We know you been going to the Hill Hotel. And we know a lot about you. Now, you know and I know that if you talk, we'll protect you, and we can get the man behind this, we can drive our own car."

I let him talk and agreed with him and everything, and then when he got to the end, I looked at him. I said, "Well, you know I won't do that. Call it honor among thieves, if you will," I said, "but I have a certain amount of ethics. I simply couldn't. It would be against everything that I believe in. So let's not talk about it any more."

"Well, I'm disappointed, Janet," he says, "I knew you wouldn't."

Then they started filling out the sheet. They got a new sheet they're using around at all the stations. Very funny. It's junkie sheet. Like, "Why did you first use dope?" When he asked me that, I had to laugh. What could you possibly say? I looked at him for a couple of minutes and I said, "Sure got me." That was the only thing I could think of.

So we went through that. And my mother very kindly and magnanimously—the victor, you know—sends in a hamburger and a cup of coffee.

It's a little like a class. You all sit around and they say, "Janet, you're a good-looking girl." The young one: "You look like my wife." "I do?" "Yes, you do. Why, but what you need is carnies and beer. Go to a tavern. Have a drink. Meet a nice boy. Stay away from these musicians. They're no good, no good at all. They got to have stuff to beat those instruments the way they do." And the cat says, "Eat steaks. Buy yourself clothes. And love your mother."

Love your mother! All mothers are good. All these cats have mother complexes, I have heard this from every mother-fucking cop, practically, that I have ever talked to. You know, when they're scratching their heads and figuring "Now what the hell can you tell this kid to do? What's gonna save her?" This is the obvious answer.

And naturally, all I wanted to do was just get in a room with my mother for two minutes. Man! It was like a piece of iron inside me, hard and warped. Every time they just mentioned the word "mother," I wanted to regurgitate. But I mean, I played it cool.

"Now, my mother, after she died," he says, "I thought of the things that she did for me. Things that nobody else would do. Mothers take everything." So, anyway, he said he'd buy me a steak when I got out.

I waited for the wagon to come. And it was all sort of incongruous—I was right in my own neighborhood there. There was a street—a very familiar street. There was the movie. I could be over there in that movie! I was thinking of all kinds of things like that. I felt like trying to make another break for it, but I knew I wouldn't get anywhere.

Soon as I get to the Main Station and they're fingerprinting me, there's a broad in the cell right even with the little place where they sign in. It's four thirty in the morning, and here was this broad, standing up there, quacking in a storm. This is my first introduction to the opera singer. She was an older-looking Polack, or something, about forty-five years old and husky. Then she started singing operatic arias, and patriotic American songs, and Polish and oh, my God, what she didn't sing! That woman could sing anything.

They took me way down to the end and locked me up. And that's where I met another girl who was going to be with me for some time, Muriel Lane, an older junkie. And, later on, a young pickpocket, shoplifter, who used to use junk. So we talked, with slight interruptions for Muriel and I to be sick.

And there we were—hung up. What can you say about that, except that it happened? I was supposed to be booked and processed Wednesday and go to court Thursday. Every time they'd come down and take somebody to the Narcotics Unit and processed them that day, I'd say, "Me? Now, me?" I was afraid I was just going to be hung up there a couple of days.

And the opera singer was singing all this time, all day and all night and all day and all night. They finally took her out. We had four blissful hours in the afternoon of utter silence, except for our quacking. And then they bring in the grande dame. She was worse. She'd say, "I don't know why I'm in here. I know the Monsignor. My brother-in-law owns a furniture company. I'm a voting citizen! I don't know why they brought me down here. I'm just here as a witness for the FBI." And then all these gloomy stories. There was constantly that voice in your ear. It was enough to drive you mad. And then she'd cry. When she cried, she didn't cry silently; she bawled.

Everyone in the cell started yelling, "Shut up, bitch!" You know, all these hard bitches off Madison Street called her everything. And the grande dame: "Oh, oh, Mother of God," she said, "Oh, Jesus Christ! That they should be talkin' this way! These common scum, these bums, these low women!" And then, "Speak to me! What's the matter?" and then someone would say,

"Up you, sister." And she'd say, "Oh, oh, my God, did you hear that? Did you hear that? Mary, Mother of God, did you hear that?"

This would keep on all day and all night. Well, she finally slipped completely before I left the joint. That was the worst yet. It was on my last day. I'll never forget that as long as I live. She'd been quiet for two hours. We should have known something was happening.

It was absolutely quiet—no sound —everybody was sleeping. All of a sudden, she lets out the most horrible scream. Nobody paid any attention to her. By this time, the matron and everybody figures, you know, that she is completely cracked. She said, "They're in here! They're in here! They're in the cell! Matron! Matron! My God! They're in the cell! Oh Mary, Mother of God!" You know she was praying—getting up and down and screaming.

I said, "Muriel, can't you do something? What's she yelling about?" Muriel said, "I don't know. Something's in the cell." Then the grande dame said, "There like a little mesh screen on the bars. Watch the screen! There it is, there it is! I'm watching!" There on in, for about eight hours, this is all we heard. Like she was a pilot talking on an intercom system to somebody else. "I'm watching! I'm watching!" Muriel said she moved her mouth like she was talking through a microphone. "There he is! There we are! There it is, on the screen! I'm watching! They're coming from the left, the left, the left. . . ." She'd say nothing but "the left," for instance, for five minutes. "It's dark, it's dark on the bottom of the screen. There they are! There they are! I'm watching them!" She kept that up until we left the next day. We swore we'd kill her, but of course we never got a chance.

At any rate, I was booked that night, after I'd been processed. I went to the Narcotics Unit. It was a mere nothing. The usual, even less than last time.

I made the phone call to Roy. And Roy said he didn't have the bread to bail me out. Could I wait, since it was just a couple of hours to court? And I thought, Sure! It's only a couple of hours and I'll be out! I was so sure that there would be no hang-ups in court and that everything would go cool and that I would be free.

Twilight of the WCTU

WILLIAM KLOMAN

Shortly before last Christmas a brisk matronly shopper stopped in front of a display of candied fruits arranged in small plastic tubs in the S. S. Kresge store in Evanston, Illinois, and paid twenty-nine cents for a jar of brandy sauce which was being sold for use on holiday puddings. The sale would have been routine in another town or to another customer, but Evanston is the home of the Woman's Christian Temperance Union and the customer was Mrs. Fred J. Tooze, its president.

Mrs. Tooze returned with her purchase to her office where she fired off indignant letters to the mayor and chief of police of Evanston and to the Illinois Liquor Control Commission

Reprinted by permission of CURTIS BROWN, LTD. from William Kloman, "Can the Forces of Virtue Defeat John Barleycorn?" *Saturday Evening Post*, March 11, 1967, pp. 85–89. Copyright © 1967 THE CURTIS PUBLISHING COMPANY INC.

in Chicago, charging that minors were buying the brandy sauce "for beverage purposes" and demanding "criminal prosecution of these selling activities by this store." The Liquor Control chairman, accustomed to such correspondence from Chicago's nearest northern suburb, telephoned the Kresge store manager, Dwain Tubbs, and told him to remove the item from sale.

Old S. S. Kresge himself, who was a ranking member of the tough-minded Anti-Saloon League, would have understood perfectly well what was happening but the manager of his Evanston branch reacted as if he had been hit by a sniper. "I wouldn't know the lady if I seen her," he said later. "She bought the stuff and did everything under the cloak of anonymous." The sauce itself, he claimed, was harmless enough. "We just bought it for fruitcake."

Tubbs isn't the only Evanston merchant to run afoul of the WCTU in recent years. Two years ago, also at Christmas time, Mrs. Tooze, accompanied by a local Baptist minister, made a small but successful raid on a Walgreen's drug store which had attracted her attention by offering for sale a battery-powered contrivance called the Charley Weaver Bartender Toy.

Mrs. Tooze recalled the incident recently. "It was a cute little gadget, really. There was this little old guy sat there at the bar shaking a cocktail, putting it in a glass, and drinking it down. Now we went after the Walgreen's to get it out of there because they had put it out where the kids could get to it and get the idea of shaking the cocktail and so on. Well, when we went in to remonstrate with them about it, the manager, he said, 'Well, that isn't for children. That's a gadget for adults.' But you see, that's why we went in there. Because it was a toy that had been produced for children, in order to build up a . . . what? . . . a *brainwashing* or psychological something in their minds about how this thing can be shaken up and so on. So the pastor said to the manager, 'Well, then. What have you put it down *here* for? There, look at the kids—they're the ones that are looking at it. The adults aren't paying any attention to it.' And you see, the manager went over and grabbed the thing off the shelf, and we never saw it in Walgreen's any more." Before the bartender toy incident, it was cooking sherry in the Kroger store.

Evanston, Illinois, is one of the last strongholds of a crusade for total abstinence from alcoholic beverages that began in the nineteenth century and which by the end of the First World War had succeeded in getting its legislative demands written into the

Constitution of the United States. Although the Prohibition Amendment was repealed in 1933, Evanston remains bone-dry and the WCTU means to keep it that way, not only in fact, but also in spirit.

Evanston's dry laws, which antedate national prohibition by more than half a century, are a classic case of what might be called legislative Overkill. The town was born dry since the state-enforced Charter of Northwestern University, written twelve years before Evanston was incorporated, includes a permanent injunction against the sale of alcoholic beverages within four miles of the campus—roughly the distance of the town's perimeter. There is also a city ordinance against selling beverage alcohol, backed up, in turn, by a state law making it a crime to sell beer or whiskey where local law forbids it.

As an added guaranty of permanent sobriety the original University trustees, who held title to most of the land that later became Evanston, planted clauses in their property deeds automatically invalidating the documents should future owners countenance trade in spirits. As one local lawyer put it, "If the town fathers had been able to arrange for a Doomsday Machine to activate itself the day the first highball was sold in Evanston, they probably would have done it."

The Woman's Christian Temperance Union, which continues to exercise surveillance over the morals of Evanston under a self-imposed mandate which it calls "home protection" is a national organization which was born in a spontaneous flurry of energy and indignation on Christmas Eve, 1783, in Hillsboro, Ohio. That morning seventy-five of the leading ladies of the community marched on the local saloons and, with much singing and praying and a smattering of modest civil disobedience, extracted promises from the proprietors that they would give up their trafficking in liquor and beer. These first raids were remarkably successful, and the distilleries in nearby Cincinnati quickly sent in reinforcements to buy up the available licenses and thus salvage some of their previously profitable trade.

The target of the first protests were immigrant saloon-keepers who insisted on selling beer from immigrant-owned breweries to their immigrant customers. In the nineteenth century teetotaling was the mark of the solid native middle-class respectables. And much of the impetus behind national prohibition, when it came, was the determination of the white, rural, Protestant, Anglo-Saxon majority to enshrine their personal values in the Constitution for all time. Come what may in the way of foreign scum to swell the urban proletariat, the newcomers would be forced to recognize as sacred writ the prevailing customs of the sturdy yeoman farmer who made the country what it is, etc., etc. It is not accidental that Prohibition was finally passed in 1918 and that the temperance propaganda of the time made good use of the anti-German sentiments aroused by the World War.

The original motto of the WCTU was "For God and Home and Native Land," and the organization remained a parochial cabal of small-town do-gooders until it was taken in hand by its second president, Frances E. Willard, an authentic organizational genius who was raised on a Wisconsin farm where applications of freshwater were considered a proper specific for all ailments from sore throats to broken legs. Before Miss Willard took over the WCTU in 1879, she had been a teacher in the Evanston College for Ladies, which later merged with Northwestern in a daring experiment in co-education. Miss Willard stayed on as dean of women in the university and taught a course in aesthetics (which was thought rather too avant-garde by her dowdy male superiors) but soon left teaching to devote all of her time to the Movement. Once in office, she set about streamlining its jumbled structure, expanding its membership rolls, and broadening its perspective to include women's suffrage, minimum wage legislation, and laws against white slavery.

She also founded the World WCTU. Returning to her hotel room after a tour of San Francisco's Chinatown, Miss Willard came to a conclusion notable for both its social and its geographic insight: "But for the intervention of the sea," she said, "the shores of China and the Far East would be part and parcel of our fair land. We are one world of tempted humanity." The motto of the WCTU was then changed to "For God and Home and Every Land," and the already receding values of rural America were made available on a global scale.

* * *

The WCTU is organized in every state in the Union, and while policies and activities—down to what is discussed in local meetings each month —are set in Evanston, the organizational pattern roughly follows a federal scheme. Each state has its own president (California and Washington for some reason each have two) and each county has a district president. The smallest unit, usually consisting of about thirty members, is the local "union."

The organization is technically non-sectarian, but the bulk of the members belong to Protestant churches of the fundamentalist variety. As one national officer put it, "We're a Christian organization right down the line. Of course we do have a few Catholic members as well."

In four states—Maryland, North Carolina, Tennessee, and Oklahoma—there are parallel groups for Negroes, who, in those states, elect their own officers and send their own delegates to national conventions. These groups are called Sojourner Truth unions, in honor of Sojourner Truth, an escaped female slave who had the distinction of being the first Negro to win a slander suit against a white man in an American court of law. Sojourner Truth died in 1883. One of her favorite phrases—she was, from all reports, a fiery platform-speaker—was "Chillun, I talk to God and God talks to me," which is approximately the same feeling Frances Willard had about her own work among the upper-middle-class whites of her day. Alabama had a Sojourner Truth group, but it died out a few years ago. Kentucky's has recently been incorporated into the regular WCTU, a step which the ladies at national headquarters believe to be indicative of social progress

Mrs. Herman Stanley, a deep-bosomed, regal, and completely dedicated WCTU lady who serves as promotional secretary, is in charge of keeping track of the local unions and, if possible, attracting new members. She told me that she had no idea how many local unions there were, although she is in the process of creating an organizational chart by which she hopes to keep better track of things in the future. She estimates that there are perhaps five or six thousand local organizations, ranging in size from seven or eight members to five hundred. Each member pays a dollar a year to belong to the WCTU, of which ten cents is forwarded to national headquarters. The rest remains in the state, most of it going to finance state newspapers. There are also more honorific forms of membership, such as the Rock of Ages member, whose dues are "a penny a day and a prayer."

The WCTU national officers are decisive and outspoken on practically every topic except the number of members the organization has. Mrs. Stanley didn't know. Some of the ladies put the estimate as high as half a million, she said, but "I think that's overdoing it a bit." Mrs. Tooze said a quarter of a million, "in round figures." The round figures include the children, but as to how many children and how many adult ladies they involved, she said, "I can't tell you that right now. I don't even know really. It's a shame. We're trying to get that straightened out this year so we can . . . right now I can't break that down for you. We just say in round figures a quarter of a million. Total."

A district president in a Western state was more direct. "Membership?" she said. "That is information I have been instructed never to give. At national headquarters they feel that information on membership has been misused in the past." How misused? "Just misused." Also referring to the national officers another member told me, "They're cagey about those numbers. They'll never tell."

The reason for the caginess can be

found tucked away in the annual Treasurer's Report presented to the national convention. According to "income from dues" figures in these reports, the WCTU currently has 164,184 members. This is not a paltry number for a national protest organization, but a year-by-year comparison for the past five years shows that the movement has been going down, and the decline has been sharp. For the past five years, the WCTU has been losing members at a rate of 8420 a year, a trend which would totally deplete the membership of the group within twenty years.

Not all states are losing members. When there are net gains—usually in the South and Midwest—they are conspicuously and joyfully marked with an asterisk in the convention minutes each year. The incentives to the local unions also tell the story: Holdfast Unions (granted a certificate recognizing them as such) are those which retain all their living resident members on the rolls. Steadfast Unions (same reward) are those which have as many members this year as last—in other words, those which replace deceased members with new living ones. Fruitful Unions are those which show a net gain of one or more, and Life-line Unions—the significance of the honorary title is not lost on the ladies—are those which gain new members and contribute to the various fund-raising projects set up by national headquarters. "We had almost four hundred Life-line Unions last year," Mrs. Stanley told me. "We were very, very proud of them."

The Evanston union is one of about one hundred-fifty Iota Sigma chapters in the country, which means that it is designed especially for professional women and working girls. The WCTU has long believed that women

"out in the world" face especially fierce temptations, so in 1934 it was decided that their specific needs could best be met by separate organizations. Iota Sigma means "To Prevail with a Sane Mind."

The professional women who comprise Evanston Iota Sigma are the thirty-two officers and staff members of the national headquarters, and they meet in Rest Cottage at noon on the second Tuesday of each month. Each lady brings her own sandwich, but dessert and coffee are provided by the Dessert Committee. After lunch comes a business session and business is followed by an educational program appropriate to a specific monthly theme. I was invited to sit in on a recent meeting. The theme was Character Building.

At Rest Cottage I was taken in hand by Mrs. Stanley, the promotion secretary, who acts as sort of an information officer for the WCTU and handles their usually unsatisfactory relations with the press. She asked me if I had brought my lunch along. I had not, and word was passed back to the kitchen, from which a roast-beef sandwich done up in Saran-Wrap was presently brought.

The ladies were seating themselves at folding card-tables, in foursomes, and I was asked to sit at a table which had already acquired two occupants—the only other men in the room. "I'll just sit over here with the boys," Mrs. Stanley explained to no one in particular. "The boys" turned out to be Mrs. Stanley's husband, Herman, who works around the headquarters building (locking up at night and delivering packages and the like) and Mr. Paul Wright, who has worked in the headquarters mail-room for the past fifteen years.

"I can remember when William

McKinley was elected," Mr. Wright said. "How about that?" Mr. Stanley, a mild-mannered man, somewhat shorter than his wife, said that he remembered the day McKinley was assassinated but that the election was before his time. Mrs. Stanley smiled and said that it was time to stand for grace-before-meals. Grace, which was sung, was led by a large woman who wore orthopedic shoes and kept time with both arms. The singing was loud and spirited.

During lunch Mr. Stanley told me of a recent trip to Washington, D.C., which he and his wife had taken. Inside the Capitol there had been a large mural of the Battle of Lake Erie which he had wanted to photograph. A Capitol policeman, however, told him that taking pictures inside the building was against regulations. "It was the right thing for the policeman to have done," Mrs. Stanley told her husband. "Some people will distort pictures to make them show things which aren't there." Stanley said that he had meant no harm.

"Our national shrines should be sacred," Mrs. Stanley told us. "And we should have a Sacred Patriotism where our nation's traditions are concerned, too." She was warming to her topic. "You take the Supreme Court. They're supposed to preserve the Constitution and yet they change it around to mean things it's not supposed to mean. They interpret and distort and ... and ... why, the first thing you know it doesn't mean *anything* any more." Mr. Stanley sat very straight, listening, while Mr. Wright ate his lunch and ignored the conversation. "The churches do it too," Mrs. Stanley said, "change our documents and water them down until we have nothing left to hold on to."

Mr. Stanley recalled that in a recent *National Geographic* he had read that Andrew Johnson had asked to be buried with his head resting on a copy of the Constitution. "Ach," said Mrs. Stanley. "Buried with the Constitution. Sentimentality. That's not what I'm talking about. Not at all."

Mr. Wright interrupted his lunch to ask what she *was* talking about and Mrs. Stanley told him that she had hoped to see the cherry blossoms in Washington, but that the city had been too crowded. "There were people all over the place," she said.

Just then a heavy-set Negro wearing a dark blue suit and black tie entered the room. He was about forty-five, and was accompanied by a slightly younger woman in a tan suit and light blue coat. Her skin was lighter than her companion's and she wore a furry pill-box hat which matched her coat. Miss Allen, the Narcotics Education lady, crossed the room to meet them and showed them to two seats at a table near the door which had been left vacant. Several of the ladies present apparently knew the newcomers and nodded greetings, which were returned. The gentleman was later introduced as the Reverend King L. Mock, a graduate of the WCTU narcotics Education course in Chautauqua, New York, and today's guest speaker. The woman was his wife, Charlotte.

As coffee was poured and the Dessert Committee served slices of Sara Lee cheesecake a woman announced that everybody should look at the underside of his teaspoon. One spoon at each table was marked with a strip of tape and the person with the marked spoon was to be allowed to keep the cloth flower which had served as the center-piece for each table. No one at our table had a marked spoon and Mrs. Stanley suggested that Mr. Wright take the flower on our table home to his wife, who had been visiting her sister in South Bend and therefore had missed the meeting. "Don't want to," he replied. "You take the thing. You're the woman." Mrs. Stanley thanked him, and with everyone's assent pinned the flower to her dress and ate her dessert.

When Mr. Wright had finished eating he folded up the table leg on his right and held the table in place with his hand until the rest of us were done and the remaining dishes had been cleared away. Then Mr. and Mrs. Stanley and I each folded a table-leg and Mrs. Stanley carried the table away. The chairs were then placed in a semi-circle two or three chairs deep; Mrs. Tooze took a seat in the back row (she does not hold office in the local chapter). A bust of Frances Willard on a pedestal behind Mrs. Tooze's chair peered over her shoulder and looked as if it were in attendance at the meetnig. The monthly meeting of the Evanston WCTU was then called to order.

The business part of the meeting took twelve minutes. The treasurer reported a balance of $82.93 in the kitty and announced that "almost ten dollars" had been spent on books for the Haven Junior High School, the health director of which was reported to be delighted by the gift of anti-alcohol propaganda. The acquisition of seven new card tables (the ones we had used at lunch) and thirty-six new folding chairs (on which we were sitting) was announced. The tables and chairs had been purchased with green stamps the chapter members had accumulated.

It was announced that several White Ribbon Recruits were ready to

be presented to the chapter but that their induction ceremony would be postponed until the national convention so that they could be shown to the delegates. White Ribbon Recruits are children under the age of six dedicated to total abstinence and purity by their mothers. A white ribbon is tied around their wrists to symbolize their dedication, and it is expected that at the age of six the Recruits will join the Loyal Temperance Legion and sign the pledge for themselves.

Under new business it was moved that any remaining premium stamps be used to get a portable ice chest to prevent the candy bars which are sold in the headquarters building to raise money for Iota Sigma from "going limpy" during the summer. The measure aroused some controversy: one lady thought that hard candy or gumdrops would answer the problem more economically, but was informed that some of the members preferred Hershey Bars, even in the summer. Another member suggested keeping the candy in the basement during hot spells, but her proposal was met by general derision. "You don't expect us to go traipsing all the way down the basement just to buy a candy bar?" one lady said. The original motion was re-stated and passed unanimously.

After the business meeting was adjourned the lady in the orthopedic shoes who had earlier led the singing rose to deliver an inspirational message on the theme of Mother. She cited several Biblical mothers and grandmothers as evidence of God's particular interest in motherhood, and went on to generalize her theme to apply to women in general. "You don't have to bear the child to be a mother," she said, "or to share in the special grace which God has showered upon the holy estate of motherhood. For God has raised up Woman to have, I shall not say a sixth sense, but to have a heart of compassion and love not only for this child which may be her own, but for all of mankind." Several of the ladies nodded vigorously. "Amen," one of them said.

It was Hannah Whitall Smith, a prominent Philadelphia Quaker and the mother-in-law of both Bertrand Russell and Bernard Berenson, who called the WCTU Organized Mother-Love. Frances Willard herself, of course, was not a mother, and neither is the present WCTU national president, which perhaps suggests that Mother-Love is most potent when it is vicarious. Miss Willard, as a result of her association with the WCTU, became known as the Uncrowned Queen of American Womanhood.

Now, in Evanston, Charlotte Mock, as a representative of Woman, was asked to make a few remarks in advance of her husband's address. "I'd rather let my husband do the talking," Mrs. Mock said. "He's the one you want to hear." "Ladies first," said one of the ladies, and the rest laughed lightly as Mrs. Mock rose to speak.

"Well," she said. "I should like to thank you ladies for inviting us up here this afternoon to share some of our experiences with you." She looked around the room at the ladies, who were smiling in anticipation, and smiled back at them. "I am reminded of my home in Kansas," she told them. "I grew up in a house much like this one, a lovely Victorian cottage with gingerbread on the eaves and lovely shade trees in the front yard and grass. I couldn't help but

think on the way up here that Evanston and Rest Cottage are a long way, not only in miles, from the concrete and steel which is the basic design of the South Side of Chicago. My home now is in a high-rise and the problems of the families who live in those places are different from the problems we knew as children. My husband and I are seeking answers to those problems and that is why we have turned to you. We heard that you offered a course in narcotics education, and that's what we needed—narcotics education. Those who try to do something about narcotics on the South Side find that nobody is willing to teach them."

She drew a short breath; she had been talking rapidly. "There is also an alcohol problem on the South Side and it is not limited to adults. There are children who drink and children who take dope and we are looking for the answer to problems like these. We know of children, even those whose families can afford to give them money for lunch at school, who rather than buy that lunch will kitty up their money and buy liquor. The teachers tell me they can spot the ones who do. They droop in class. They droop and sleep because they have gotten liquor or had older children get it for them and have been drinking that liquor even before the school day has begun."

Several of the ladies exchanged wide-eyed glances. Some shook their heads.

"We have found a strange thing," Mrs. Mock continued. "We have found, or teachers have found and told us, that there are many bright children among their pupils. Children who will work and in many cases over-excel, but only until they get to the fourth grade. That seems to be the cut-off point and even the bright ones seem to give up by the time they're in the fourth grade. Now we don't know what causes this but we have our suspicions, and it all has to do with the way these children and their families live.

"It is said that the poor you will always have with you," Mrs. Mock said. Several of the ladies smiled appreciatively, nodding their heads. "And we have found this to be true. Even when you work to instill pride in these people—for pride is the secret ingredient—and your work is crowned with success, why, the next thing you know the people become middle-class and move out of the high-rise and others move in to fill their places and it's with them that you have to start all over again." Mrs. Mock stopped abruptly. "But please," she said, "here I am running on. My husband is the one who knows this thing first-hand. He must tell you. Thank you for your kind attention."

The ladies applauded and nodded vigorously to Mrs. Mock, who smiled and sat down.

King Mock, a powerfully built and serious man with deep lines in his full face, is a graduate of the Chicago Baptist Institute and an ordained minister in the Baptist church. Until 1958 Mr. Mock had been pastor of the Beersheba Baptist Church, on the South Side, but resigned his pastorate and took a job as a high-rise apartment house supervisor. "To get closer to people's lives," he says.

He now stood before the Evanston WCTU holding a packet of six large filing cards, a bulging manila envelope, a small worn brown paper bag, and a rolled-up square of black fabric. Without acknowledging the applause, which had trailed off after his wife sat down and which was now reviving for him, he opened the square of cloth and draped it over a small table which stood in the front of the room. Then he laid the file-cards flat on the cloth to form a U.

"These cards represent our high-rise complexes on the South Side," he said. "They have laundries and playgrounds and every other thing you can think of. Even some grass is beginning to grow in some cases." The ladies were amused by this comment and the atmosphere of the room grew more relaxed. Mr. Mock opened his manila envelope and peered inside. He turned it upside-down over the high-rise cards and several hundred pennies clattered onto the table. The pennies formed a mound which spilled over the cards, partly obscuring them. "These pennies represent people and how they spill over," he said.

The ladies looked intently at the pennies. Mr. Mock opened his paper bag and emptied twenty or so hypodermic syringes and several small pharmacy vials on top of the pennies. There was now heavy breathing in the room and some audible gasps. Several of the women shifted uneasily in their folding chairs. Mr. Mock continued. "And this is what happens to the people when they spill over. Each of these syringes I have personally taken away from a narcotics addict in the neighborhood where I live. I have scared some of them into turning them over; some I have taken from small children whose older brothers or sisters have led me to them hoping I could do some good before it was too late."

He surveyed his audience. "Those of you who have not been exposed to this problem, I can't say that you're blessed because it gives you a feeling of humanness and compassion for a fellow human being to know such things and to enter into them, and we have a while ago heard some very fine sentiments expressed concerning compassion and the instincts of love which God has put into mothers." Attention shifted briefly to the lady in the Dr. Scholl's shoes, who smiled brightly.

"But you *are* blessed because your nerves are not torn apart by some kid who has gotten to you and kept you awake at night wondering *why?*" Mr. Mock had shouted the question. His voice now became gentle and conversational. "You and I have been brought up to respect the gray hair and to have reverence for the woman." There was a general nodding of heads. "Uh-huh," said Mr. Stanley, nodding. "You and I have been taught to think of dope pushers as hardened male criminals." Quizzical looks were exchanged. "But I am here to tell you that there are some women who will lead children astray. Many of those who sell the dope to the young people in the South Side of Chicago are women, and some of them are not young women." "No," said one of the ladies, "no." "Tsk," said another.

"So the question arises, what to do? And the fact is that there are no simple answers to this question. How many of you have read *The Ugly American?*" Mr. Mock asked. "I read part of it," one lady volunteered. "I read a review," said another. "Well, from studying the story of that American diplomat, faced every day with situations nobody had ever faced before and for which his training had not prepared him, we see that I cannot take solutions from one area over into the next one. Instead of being so ready with our cut-and-dried answers, we must look deeply into the causes of things, and in coming to understand the causes—what causes people to lose their pride in the first place, for instance—there comes a great frustration.

"There is a great incursion of rural people into the cities. You go down any day to the Illinois Central railroad and see them coming in from the South." "Mmm, yes," someone said. "There are not sufficient jobs for these people. We don't even have enough jobs for the people already *here*. And the government won't let them work for their relief checks. There's work enough to be done, but they have to take the relief money like a hand-out and that's part of what kills people's pride in themselves. I say put them to work cleaning vacant lots, cleaning up alleys or fixing up the parks. Anything, so they can say they earned that money they get from the government. But here you run up against the labor unions and they want to protect themselves and what they've got, so they want their people to get whatever jobs there are. And if there isn't enough money to pay union wages they would rather see the job not done at all.

"Then there is the entire attitude of the housing people. I have been working for eight years trying to get them to take the name project out of the housing. Think of living in a 'project.' A project is something experimental. Something not completed. These are our *homes*, so leave the name project out of it. If you call us project people then we must be here for manipulation and experiment. And I say to the housing people, if you have something else in mind for us, let's hear it. Otherwise don't call it a project."

Mr. Wright, who had taken a front seat, was now asleep.

"There was a day," Mr. Mock continued, "and you all remember it, when the family dwelling was passed down from one generation to the next. Grandfather or Grandmother was there to advise the young ones as they came up, and the father was the head of the family. We are in a new age, groping our way. And we are fast arriving at a situation where there is a head of nothing.

"Adults greedy for money are waiting to lead our children astray. And it isn't just the little old woman who's pushing the stuff. Take her away and three like her are waiting to take her place. It's a business. There is no dope grown in America. It all has to be imported, so it comes on somebody's ship or in somebody's plane. That's business. The government spends millions every year to keep it out, but someone's making millions on it and they have the money to protect their investment. I don't know where it comes from and I don't *want* to know. People who know get killed. But it comes all the same.

"Like I say, I don't have the answers. I just want to tell you what the problem is like. Maybe you have the answers. I don't." Mr. Mock turned to gather up his illustrative materials. He picked up a small bottle from among the syringes and read its label. "Looks like someone robbed Saul's Pharmacy," he said.

The ladies clapped vigorously and nodded to one another. Miss Allen smiled broadly and formed a silent "thank you" for Mr. and Mrs. Mock. A woman in the back of the room tapped her cane on the carpet and asked if a question were in order, and as the speaker gathered his file card housing development together the woman with the cane delivered a brief speech in which she pointed out that she had learned, while doing volunteer work in the Welfare Office, that people on ˎrelief were lazy and unappreciative and that they lacked self-respect. She said that they didn't really want to work so long as the government was feeding them. Mr. Mock answered that his experience had been different and that maybe we shouldn't draw firm conclusions from only a few cases.

A second woman suggested that Mr. Mock go to speak with the labor leaders in Chicago and convince them "to open their doors more freely to Negroes." Mr. Mock thanked her for her suggestion.

A third lady, perhaps recalling the story of Miss West and the thousand opium pipes, wanted to know if Mr. Mock had reformed all of the drug addicts whose syringes he had brought with him. Mock looked blankly at his questioner for a moment, then looked at his wife, who smiled gently and lowered her eyes. "Ma'am, perhaps we'd better explain something to you," he began.

Several days later I asked Mrs. Tooze her impression of Mr. Mock's talk. "I thought that maybe he would have something there he would leave us. Some literature or something," she said. She seemed disappointed, a little puzzled. "But he didn't seem to have any literature."

It was late afternoon and Mrs. Tooze had put in a hard day struggling against the rich and crafty legions of King Alcohol. This dope addiction business—it seemed to keep cropping up. Was it meant to lure the ladies into dividing their forces? If so, it wouldn't work. Organized Mother-Love would not be diverted from its purpose. "There's nothing that the liquor people would like to see us do any better than to go off on a tangent," she said firmly. "Our main line is alcohol. We were organized to fight the liquor traffic, and that's where we'll stay."

The Life and Death of Atlanta's Hip Strip

JAMES T. WOOTEN

Like Moslems to Mecca, they once came to The Wall, and The Neighborhood hummed with their crowded cameraderie. The Wall belonged to them. It was theirs exclusively, a creation of their contradistinctive culture: an entire, windowless side of a long brick building on which was splashed a great, garish mural of a giant Jesus and a chorus of surrealistic disciples—and it was there at The Wall on the corner of Peachtree and 10th Streets in the heart of this city's hippie colony that all the lost children gathered in the evenings to bind up the day in a communion of castaways.

Others were drawn there as well, creeping curiously along in their cars and cabs, gawking and pointing and staring like kids at the zoo ("Look at that, Mildred. The place is crawling with hippies!") and shaking their

Reprinted from *The New York Times Magazine*, March 14, 1971. ©1971 by The New York Times Company. Reprinted by permission.

heads as they wondered aloud about the future of this country's youth, what with the drugs and long hair and strange attire ("And my God, Marvin, all that free love!"), and the Chamber of Commerce, taking note of the frequent traffic jams, announced with only half a smile that the place was one of Atlanta's most popular attractions.

That is how it was yesterday: a gay, gaudy carnival, noisy and naughty and with all the makings of a Greenwich Village South.

But today The Wall is a big, black, blank blotch. The colossal Christ and his chatoyant coterie are gone, obliterated by the same young artists who had painted it. Tired of their creation, they had petulantly covered it, and now The Wall looms darkly vacant, an ebony symbol of what has happened to The Neighborhood.

In the evenings, the street stands starkly still, nearly empty. Those who once came to watch or be watched, or to watch those being watched watch those watching them, do not come any more. "Some say it's the weather, the winter scene, you know, but it's more than that," a shaggy inhabitant observes sadly. "We really had it all together here. Really had it going, and now it's gone—just gone." And only those whose imaginations run to extremes believe it can ever be the same again.

The cause of the alteration of Atlanta's once happy hippie colony is fear—a fear spawned in violence. It began last summer (perhaps even before that: perhaps in the very conception of a community of gentle tolerance, the antithesis is also conceived). Riots and near riots and rumors of riots; kidnappings, murders, tortures, rapes, assaults, robberies, shootouts—and all of this has ripped at the fabric of the colony, multiplying the tensions with the larger community. The police, who were already anxious, have become even more unnerved, and now the fear flows freely, like the sweet smell of hemp becoming ash, seeping into the very bricks and mortar, lurking malevolently around the corner of every day.

There was once an élan in its streets that fairly captured those who walked them, and now, to say the least, it is not what it once was. Substantial numbers of longtime residents are moving, and the rate of immigration has slowed to nearly zero, and those who still come discover that it is not what they were told by those who passed through a few months ago.

Perhaps it is the bikers, a horde of incredibly lawless men and women on motorcycles who moved into the area last summer and have remained. Perhaps it is the presence of a small cadre of political radicals, committed both to a violent revolution and to a zealous, missionary pursuit of others

not quite convinced their methods are wise. Perhaps it is the almost constant friction between the colony and the local government, or perhaps it is the drugs that make some of the residents both criminals and victims, caught up in their habit and set upon—beaten, raped and robbed—by those who know they will not and cannot go to the police; or perhaps it is the apathy of the people who choose to live there—a charming, comfortable, careless attitude that has its debilitating effects. Or perhaps it is simply that what was happening among the hippies at Peachtree and 10th Streets cannot happen at all.

This section of town has always had an abundance of names, The Area or The Neighborhood or The Strip or The Hip Strip, and some still refer to it as Tight Squeeze, a designation born generations ago when the width of Peachtree as it headed northward out of town would not accommodate two carriages passing side by side.

A few blocks from where it begins deep in the core of the city, Peachtree divides into eastern and western thoroughfares. After that, the cross streets begin to have numbers instead of names and when the eastern segment reaches 8th or 9th Streets, about a mile or so from the gleaming newness of Atlanta's downtown, The Neighborhood begins.

A few years ago, at the beginning of the last decade, it was a collection of small stores, bars and large old homes that had seen better days and were being used as rooming houses for the young men and women freshly arrived from all across the South. They were Dixie's ambitious sons and daughters, tired of the farms and dull little towns and the meager pay and the predictable future—and so they came because Atlanta was swinging into a new era of prosperity. The rent was cheap and the location convenient. Branch banks were opened, along with a few delicatessens, service stations and pharmacies, and its attractiveness to young people multiplied as more of them moved in.

But in the middle of the decade, the area began to attract a new breed. The youth revolution was rolling full steam and the word spread that Atlanta was a free city, that their thing could be done there, and the disciples of the new life style began pouring in —and The Neighborhood changed again.

The shops on one side of Peachtree went with their new clientele, while those across the way began catering to the tourists until, after a few months, the center stripe down Peachtree Street became the dividing line between hip and straight. On one side were art theaters, boutiques and the snack shops and craft shops that attracted the hippie; on the other were the "redneck" bars and strip joints.

Many of the original hippies were Atlantans, drawn, like thousands of other young people across the country, to a life that rejected contemporary standards and values. The first to arrive minded their own business and went about their pursuits with a quiet diligence; there was a freedom in The Neighborhood that soon became relatively famous. Former Mayor Ivan Allen Jr. told police to leave them alone unless they broke the law. They had a right, Allen insisted, to live the way they chose, as long as it was within the law—and the word got around.

By the summer of 1970, it was estimated that as many as 5,000 hippies had taken up permanent residence in The Neighborhood, and in addition to them, there were the hundreds of "street people," the passers-through, on their way from nothing to nowhere, looking only for a new experience, asking only for a bed and an occasional meal.

By then, it was a genuine community. An underground newspaper, The Great Speckled Bird, was formed in 1967 and soon became one of the best, if not the best, of its genre in the country. Arts and crafts projects began and cooperative outlets were established for distribution. .Health clinics and drug rehabilitation centers sprang up and nearby Piedmont Park, a sprawling expanse of lawn and lakes, became their unofficial retreat. There were art festivals, pop festivals, love parades, peace marches and women's liberation demonstrations.

Any growing community inevitably generates problems, and The Neighborhood was no exception. Drugs became commonplace (in late 1969, for example, a hippie leader estimated that about 10 per cent of the residents were heroin addicts). Venereal disease was rampant, hepatitis frequent, malnutrition an everyday discovery, and the crime rate soared with the influx of junkies, pushers and others whose not so gentle life style was nourished by the free and easy aura of The Neighborhood.

Leaders in The Neighborhood recognized what had happened; moreover, they were appalled by the prospects of thousands of other jobless and homeless young people taking up residence there, threatening their relative peace. At an Atlanta Community Relations Commission meeting last May, the hippies conceded that they needed housing, jobs, better sanitation—and police protection. The commission returned a month later and said it planned to provide some assistance in the first three areas, and Mayor Sam Massell Jr. responded to the fourth plea on his own.

On the evening of June 4, in a televised address, he declared The Neighborhood to be "an intensive care area" and announced he was dispatching a special force of 64 policemen into the locale. They were headquartered in an old storefront building immediately dubbed "the pigpen" by the youngsters, but the initial reaction within the enclave was one of cautious approval. There were those who had their doubts, among them David Durrett, then the director of the Midtown Alliance, one of the many groups formed to assist in the building of the community. He said he liked the Mayor's speech (Massell had talked about making certain the rights of all were protected) but wondered "if that many cops, all coming in at once, are really needed for the protection we requested."

On the back streets and frequently on brightly lighted Peachtree itself, many of the area's more experienced residents had been victims of the robberies and rapes, and for a while they were happy with the increased police presence. So were many of the merchants who had been complaining that the hippies had so hurt their businesses that they were thinking of moving away. After the police patrols were expanded, the customers started coming back and the merchants stopped complaining.

"But the coming of the cops was the thing that started the real change," Durrett said later. "It didn't take long for the tensions to build. The cops harassed the kids and the kids harassed the cops." Soon, there was a striking bitterness among the residents of the area and a growing radical sentiment. At issue were the arrests police had made for such charges as jaywalking, loitering or maintaining a dive, which were sometimes drug-related and were viewed as pure hassling by the community.

The new breach between the hippies and the police grew wider. The kids were persuaded that while the cops were diligent about busting drug users, they made little effort to protect hippies from those who preyed on their tolerance and on the loose discipline of the area. "The cops are busting all those little grass dealers," one of the residents said then, "but they're not touching the red necks who beat on us like drums."

When an arrest took place, a crowd would gather at the scene and, as other police began to move down the street to assist, a following of hippies would fall in behind them. The bystanders wrote down badge numbers and physical descriptions, anticipating abuse on the part of the police. The pattern was predictable and so was the result: about two weeks after the large contingent of officers had been sent to the area, police were making a midnight arrest on the street when about 400 irate youngsters gathered around—and out of the crowd flew a collection of bricks and bottles and stones.

"It was precisely what we had been trying to avoid and what we had feared most," remembers Clarence Greene, an employe of the city who serves as the Mayor's liaison with The Neighborhood. The Great Speckled Bird refers to Greene as "Massell's hip-pig," but there are many residents of the area who do not share that antagonism. The 53-year-old Greene and his wife, Dorothy, spend almost every evening in The Neighborhood, talking, giving advice, settling disputes between police and hippies, and attempting to, as he puts it, "just keep the lid on."

In three months, nearly 1,000 arrests were made. The largest number was for public drunkenness (325), with the next most frequent charge being violations of drug and narcotics laws (315). Since most hippies do not drink and drug users with any experience seldom get caught, Greene concluded then that much of the "law and order" problem in The Neighborhood was a product of outsiders.

Both Greene and the Mayor heard midsummer rumors that thousands of other "outsiders" would be coming to the city. Some of them were expected because of a rock festival at nearby Byron, Ga. On June 20, Massell submitted an advertisement to 12 underground newspapers across the country. "Unless you have bread and a pad, please find your thing somewhere else—or face a bad scene" in Atlanta, the advertisement said. The Great Speckled Bird ran The Mayor's ad along with the paper's own response, which called it "typically silly." The editors also asked other underground papers not to print the advertisement or, if they did, to publish a statement from hippie leaders beside it.

The festival at Byron on July 4 did not produce the immense influx of outsiders that had been predicted and neither did the rest of the summer. The "pigpen" was closed and the number of policemen in the area reduced. But what the summer and the festival had brought were the bikers, and their swaggering presence soon made itself known.

Although there were some bikers in The Neighborhood as early as last spring, hundreds more were drawn to Georgia by the Byron festival, where they were hired as security guards. Some were paid in beer, just as a number of them had been rewarded for their services at an earlier festival in Altamont, Calif., where, with Mick Jagger of The Rolling Stones on stage, a cadre of bikers went berserk, killing a black man. After the Byron festival, about 300 of them and their girl friends headed for Atlanta. They liked what they found, and they stayed. The beginning of the end was evident.

A long-time resident of the area says: "The biker has this kind of attitude—they see what they want and they take it, period."

The merchants on Peachtree are terrified of them. "They come in and browse around and all of a sudden they're picking up handfuls of trinkets and walking out," one of the businessmen says. "I say to them, 'What are you doing?' and they say, 'We're shopping,' and they tell me that if I call the cops they will burn the store. I do not call the cops." Other shopowners along The Strip relate similar stories, and so do the street people.

"I'm walking down the street with this girl, see," one remembers. "Up comes these two guys on bikes and one of them says he really digs my jacket —it was suede with fringes, you know —and I told him thanks and then he tells me to give it to him. I told him no and he just up and beat hell out of me with the other one standing there holding a tire wrench on the girl. He took the jacket and they left."

At least four distinct gangs of bikers now exist in The Neighborhood, with a combined membership of approximately 500, including the bikers' numerous girl friends. Although most are believed to have migrated from Florida, some are natives of Atlanta, and these different geographic loyalties are one source of feuds between the gangs. Like almost all of the hippies, the bikers are white.

They are a subculture, caught up in the glory of their machines and the delight of a life unimpeded by the law. Many are master machinists capable of dismantling and reassembling their cycles with the sure art of an infantryman repairing his weapon. Astride their behemoths, they go where they please, when they please, and perhaps the power of their mounts is too much for their psyches —the roar, the speed, the throbbing may infuse them with a notion that they, like their machines, are beyond mortal limitations.

They live in many of the old houses originally revamped for the influx of the youngsters, often in filth that exceeds even the level usually attributed to the hippies. They look much like their machines: greasy, and studded with chrome against black leather. In each group, at least one "mother" is sexually available to every male member. Theirs is a "give-and-take" community, one hippie says. "They give everybody hell and take what they want."

Many are involved heavily in narcotics traffic, stocking their shelves with drugs stolen from hippie pushers, some of whom are forced to give up their wares after beatings. The bikers, in turn, sell to the transients on the streets, those whom Greene calls the "unlearned, unhappy pseudo hippies." If a customer shows the biker-pusher money, he is likely to lose it all without getting the drugs he wants to purchase.

The police are genuinely disturbed by the bikers' presence and attitudes, but they are inhibited, they say, by the demand for fairness. "Sure, they are bad," one policeman says, "but you can't arrest bikers for just being bikers. You have to prosecute them for particular crimes within the law, and believe me, not many crimes by bikers are ever reported."

The hippies reply that they do not notice the police enforcing loitering, jaywalking and other "nuisance" ordinances against the bikers. There are many in The Neighborhood who are persuaded that the attitude of the local police is similar to that of law-enforcement authorities in most of the South toward crime within the black community. "They say, 'What the hell, it's just a bunch of hippies and bikers,'" a hippie complained recently. "That's the way they are about the blacks. They say, 'What the hell, it's just a bunch of niggers.'"

Greene tried to put it together. "It was already tense, you know, between the street people and the cops after they started their crackdown and the number of arrests mushroomed. That was when the real radicalism began. A lot of the kids became hawks as far as the police were concerned. They were the ones who threw the rocks. Then comes the bikers and the tension just doubled. They are getting it, the street people think, from both sides— the cops and the bikers—and a lot of them told me that they had bought guns or were going to. I knew it was building. You could tell. There was too much violence around them. It was bound to happen."

On the evening of Oct. 10, police arrested two girls at the corner of Peachtree and 11th Street on charges of creating a turmoil, aiding and abetting another girl to escape and violating the state narcotics law. One of the girls screamed, the officer called for assistance, and a fellow policeman, on his way, was hit on the head by a brick. Young people tore his uniform and grabbed the badge from his shirt, and for a moment the situation was almost out of control. But the police closed Peachtree near 10th Street and for a time order was restored. Then suddenly the tension Greene had been describing erupted in full force into open violence.

Rocks were hurled at the police. Bricks zinged through the air, shattering windows and car windshields. Fire bombs landed in the streets and some witnesses reported that shots were fired both by the police and at the police. "We are lucky that we are not today mourning the death of a dozen people in last weekend's riot," The Atlanta Constitution editorialized on Monday morning.

The violence had finally broken through, and shots and firebombs echoing through the night became almost commonplace.

Then, on Dec. 30, Barney Leigh McSherry, a giant biker with the nickname of "Tree," was shot to death by a young hippie as he forced his way into one of the dozens of big homes converted into rooming houses in The Neighborhood.

When the police searched the old mansion where the 6-foot-7, 250-pound McSherry was slain (it was once the residence of the French consul), they found 18 bottles of gasoline rigged as firebombs, a stick of dynamite, two shotguns, seven rifles and four pistols. They arrested the 17 residents, including Robert W. T'Souvas, one of those accused of murder at Mylai, and charged them all with murder.

The charges were dismissed a day later by a municipal judge who said there had been too many threats and too much violence in the area to warrant a murder charge. He ruled that the youth who had shot McSherry —18-year-old John Wesley Roberts— had acted in self-defense: Just before Roberts had opened fire on McSherry, the biker had placed his hand in his pocket, and the police found a loaded revolver there when they searched the body.

What had impressed the judge was the testimony he had heard. Harvey Parks, the man who leased the house and rented it to hippies, said its residents had been "ripped off" (robbed) and terrorized time and again by the bikers. Two weeks before the night McSherry was killed, three armed women who were part of a motorcycle gang robbed a group of the residents and threatened to kill anyone who called the police or gave them any trouble.

Three days later, Parks continued, more bikers came to the house and took one hippie away at gunpoint. He broke loose, returned to the house for a weapon and began firing at the bikers. They returned his shots and at least 15 rounds of gunfire were exchanged before the bikers left. The hippies demolished a car the bikers had left in the yard, decided to arm themselves, and established a "no visitors" policy at the house.

The day after the McSherry shooting, moreover, the body of a Tampa, Fla., man was found 45 miles south of Atlanta after a wounded companion had made his way to help. With two other Florida men, the pair had been visiting in The Neighborhood, where all were beaten, tortured and kidnapped by a gang of 11 men and women who wore bikers' garb. Before the week was out, another abduction by bikers had been reported to Atlanta police—and in the next two weeks, there were two more murders and several rapes, robberies and beatings in The Neighbohood.

Police Chief Herbert Jenkins told Atlanta residents it was dangerous to venture into the area. All of the magic seemed gone and Greene confirmed that the exodus was on.

Now there are still about 3,000 permanent residents in the area, with a fluctuating, transient population of between 300 and 500, and, of course, the bikers.

"It's a bummer here now," a black-bearded young man says. "Bad scene after bad scene. Everybody who can is splitting, and those who aren't want to and will when they are able. Pigs on every corner, every night, all night. The bikers hassle them and hassle us and hassle everybody and hassle themselves. It could have been great—but it's over, I think."

Perhaps it could have been.

There always were quite a few folks in this town who really rather liked the idea of having those strange young people around. They didn't say that, of course. If you asked them directly, they would purse their lips like everybody else and moan a lament about the death of decency.

But somehow they had mined some metaphysical *mystique* from the presence of the hippies which gave them a certain pride. "This is the New York City of the South," the taxi drivers were wont to say on the way in from the airport, and there were many in Atlanta who liked that idea. Enter-

taining the hippies was a symbol of urbanity, their way of saying that Atlantans are neither rural nor provincial, something to show off, like the brassy new buildings downtown or their big-league sports teams.

The trouble was that theirs was a minority report, and besides, it was never read.

The fact is that right from the time the hippies began to converge on Atlanta about four years ago, the prevailing attitude of the rest of the city toward them has been negative. The kids rubbed against the genteel grain of a city that suited Scarlett O'Hara and Coca-Cola just fine, and they sensed it. There was a certain sadness in all their good times, like tots caught up in some forbidden pleasure knowing that sooner or later it would be taken from them.

Now that time seems to have come; yet there is still a certain stubbornness in The Neighborhood. The Great Speckled Bird persistently preaches that nothing is wrong and that anyone who suggests such a possibility is merely intent on hastening the day when something will be wrong. "There is no feud" between the hippies and the bikers, The Bird says, it is merely the creation of the straight world. "Stay together," is The Bird's advice—and perhaps that indomitable spirit is contagious. The Wall, where they once gathered at the feet of the Messiah, is still an ebony void, but there is a small notation at one side which promises that another mural will soon be painted.

part eight

THE
MARKS OF CRIME

It is impossible to be uninformed of the pervasiveness of crime in the United States today. Many parts of our cities are literally out of bounds in daytime as well as at night, unless one is willing to risk life, serious injury, or, at the very least, economic loss. Thefts of household property and of automobiles are so commonplace that the police, insurance companies, and even the victims regard them with relative unconcern and are apathetic about anything being done about the situation. Moreover, as community members are aware, in the course of the routine of daily life, much of the business of the community is conducted on an extra-legal basis. Crimes that involve bodily harm or weapons are perhaps the only ones that consistently raise the wrath of community members, and result in calls for increased measures of prevention and detection. Other violations of the legal norms, such as petty thefts, are tolerated, and certain illegal behavior, such as gambling, affronts but a small proportion of the population and is often allowed to prosper openly.

While most Americans in the abstract subscribe to the principles of law and order, they are often uncommitted to these principles in their own behavior, allow many types of illegal acts to continue as long as they are unaffected by them or benefiting from them, and fail to vigorously support the police and the courts in their efforts to control and prevent illegal activities. One result of this state of affairs is a weak, sometimes corrupt, legal system with our police, prison, and court officials behaving as criminally as those they are supposed to apprehend, punish, and rehabilitate. The cases here indicate some of the dimensions of a problem currently occupying considerable attention at both a federal and local level.

INDIVIDUAL
vs.
INDIVIDUAL

INDIVIDUAL
vs.
ORGANIZATION

THE MANY FACES OF MURDER

FRANKIE CARLIN, THE BOOKIE

This case is about a man with an apparently ordinary childhood and adolescence, a farm boy with a father who perhaps drank too much. He was a popular student during high school, an outstanding athlete, and achieved well academically. A "shotgun" wedding eliminated the chances of a college education and the dream for a career in conservation, and from then on his life apparently turned to hell. His first marriage ended; a second turned out even worse. The result—a hunting rifle and the deaths of his estranged wife, his father-in-law, his sister-in-law, and a fifteen-year-old baby sitter. These individuals were victims of a man who crumbled under the weight of failure; he is, nevertheless, a murderer. The case is instructive not only for its insight into the psychology of a man, but because it illustrates the most common type of mortal crime—a close intimate making a victim of another.

Some laws seem to exist primarily as an expression of an unrealistic moralism or as attempts of virtuous men to save supposedly lesser men from sin and vice. These laws are usually enforced because of the demands of a few, rather than because of a widespread community feeling that the conduct involved is improper and ought to be suppressed. Gambling is illegal in most communities, but many otherwise relatively obedient citizens participate in it. The majority of community members is simply unconcerned and undisturbed about gambling as a crime. Frankie Carlin, the bookie, is a man whose occupation is to help others gamble; his customers are more than willing "victims." His occupation offends but a virtuous few in the community, and it is very much a part of ordinary life.

ORGANIZATION
vs.
INDIVIDUAL

ORGANIZATION
vs.
ORGANIZATION

A WOMAN'S STORY OF JAIL

Various punishments have been devised to promote law-abiding behavior and to keep in check those who violate our legal code. Threat of confinement is a major ploy in the United States to discourage illegal behavior. Some argue that the modern prisons should not only be a place to punish misdeeds, but also should serve as a setting where criminals can be rehabilitated. The success of most prisons and jails as rehabilitation centers is highly questionable. In fact, it seems that prison communities are places where illegal behavior is taught and encouraged. Moreover, some of those responsible for our prisons and jails are as corrupt and ruthless as the inmates in their charge. This account of a woman's experience in jail indicates how an organization that is supposed to correct the behavior of an individual may have the opposite effect.

WINCANTON: THE POLITICS OF CORRUPTION

Beyond causing grief for victims, crime can make great demands on the economic resources of the community. A murder, for example, involves not only loss of a life; in addition, the community must bear the cost of apprehending, adjudicating and finally caring for the offender. Yet the costs of such crimes actually may be negligible in comparison with those incurred through corruption of the community's civic and political structures. When the offices of the community are subtly subverted to plunder its coffers or victimize its citizens, the loss is often too great and far-reaching to calculate. Wincanton is a community which was victimized by its own municipal organization, and the account of organized crime gives penetrating insights into some of the intricacies of such corruption.

The Many Faces of Murder

BRUCE PORTER

Even if you press him hard, Jim McBrair still isn't sure which one he shot first. In court, the police said it must have been his 15-year-old sister-in-law, Barbie. But all Jim remembers is being dressed in his tan-plaid hunting parka, holding the .22-caliber semi-automatic rifle he'd picked up back at the house and standing in the darkened kitchen, not quite knowing why he was there. Suddenly, he spotted a shadowy figure moving toward him from the living room and he shot at it. He heard a scream and the kitchen filled with light and someone was coming through the door and Jim wheeled and fired again. Then he fired again and again, the bullets punching the figure back over the telephone table. The tiny cabin exploded. People were running about, wailing and yelling, trying to get away from the man with the gun. And as if it were one of those little shooting galleries in a penny arcade, where a bear with the light in his shoulder lurches in and out of cardboard trees, Jim automatically pulled the trigger every time something came into view. Finally, his 15-shot magazine spent, he walked out the kitchen door into the chilled winter night, jamming fresh rounds into his rifle as he went.

That's when his wife, Carol, came

This article originally appeared in *Playboy Magazine*, October, 1970. © 1970 by *Playboy*.

to him, sobbing. "Please, Jim," she said, "let me get you some help." McBrair slipped and fell on the ice in the driveway. Still pleading, Carol grabbed the gun barrel and began wrestling with her husband.

"Every time I pulled on it," Jim remembers, "it seemed like the gun was going off. She said, 'You've hit me,' and she put her hands on top of her head and kneeled down and she said to finish her off." Instead, Jim went back toward his car. But as he watched Carol limp into the cabin, he remembered a rule his father had laid down on their first hunting trips: Never leave a wounded animal to suffer. So Jim returned to the cabin, where he found Carol leaning on an ironing board, her back to him, and it all began again. This time, he didn't stop shooting until he felt something tugging at his hunting pants.

He looked down and saw his seven-year-old daughter, Kristie. "Daddy, Daddy," she said, "please don't shoot any more." At that, Jim McBrair finally quit, tucked his two children into bed and went to tell his father what he'd done.

The only sound then was from the wind as it swept across the frozen lake into the trees. In the cabin, four people were dead: Jim's 24-year-old wife, Carol; her father, Marv, who ran the Pontiac agency in town; her sister, Barbie; and a fourth girl police couldn't identify until they took Jim back to look. She was Cheryl Oleson, a 15-year-old baby-sitter. She was found lying face down in one of the beds, her head cradled in her arm. Beside her, where Jim had put them before he'd left, were the children, Kristie and Kathy, who was five. They were unharmed and fast asleep when the police arrived.

The bodies were barely cold that March Sunday in 1967 when the news began rolling out into the tiny farm community of Wautoma, Wisconsin. Bodie Severins, who knew Jim as well as anyone, said that he and the rest of the fellows were at a roadhouse called Camp Waushara that afternoon, drinking beer and watching a television set behind the bar. It was there they'd last seen Jim the night before. He was standing in front of the picture window that looks out over Silver Lake and he seemed then as if nothing were wrong. Bob Leitz remembers talking to him about a dog Leitz had sold him and Severins remembers asking Jim if he planned to stop off for a party at a place called the Coop after the bar closed. The jukebox was blaring with the usual Saturday-night din of rock 'n' roll and the place was filled with shouts and great whoops of laughter. The only untoward thing was an incident with Carol's brother, who came in around midnight and poked Jim hard in the shoulder. There were some angry words, but nobody heard what was said. Severins remembers someone remarking, "Oh, oh, looks like we got somethin' goin' here." But Carol's brother left and Jim went back to listening to his friends talk.

Now, the next day, Sheriff Virgil Batterman had let just enough news seep out, so that as the fellows drifted in to watch the game, they could add their own special pieces to the story. "Everyone," said Severins, "was just sitting around, and one guy would come in and say this and another, that. No one really knew all about it, only the part about Carol. We just stood around, shaking our heads; that's all we did. The first reaction, I would say, was just shock."

At the time, shock seemed the most logical reaction to the crimes of 27-year-old James Dennis McBrair. Blond, straight, fairly tall, with close-cropped hair—his mother called him Butchie—he had the good looks of a Kirk Douglas but with a softer gaze and gentle blue eyes. He came from strong Scotch-Irish stock; his father's family had been farming in the central part of Wisconsin for 100 years. As a boy, he worked hard, helping his father and mother till the family's 400 acres of cucumbers, which they sold for pickles. Jim, his mother said, "could plow like a charm." And often he'd work from four in the morning until ten at night, especially when his father was drunk and couldn't do his share of the work. No one in town held it against Jim, Sr., that he drank. He was a hard man and a good one, people thought, but he had a rage in him and sometimes, when he was drinking, he would abuse his family. Jim remembers getting mad at his father, but only once or twice, when he was "hurting Mom." But he never struck his father, he is quick to add— not once.

If life was grueling on the farm, it was eased by the hunting and fishing trips Jim would take with his father and by his daytime escape to Tri-County High School nearby. His high school coach, Chet Schraeder, who thought highly of him, recalled that the only unusual thing about Jim was that he had no particular goals in life. And he had no abiding interests other than hunting, which he thought he might be able to indulge in by getting into conservation work. One thing he was good at was being popular and in this he excelled—a B student all four years, vice-president of his class each year and king of the junior prom. In his junior year, he sang the lead in a Forties-style high school play about going to college and wearing beanies and raccoon coats. It was called *The Singing Freshman* and Jim was the freshman.

He was also a football hero, a basketball hero and a baseball hero. This is what Wautoma remembers best about Jim McBrair. And, as he sits in his cell in the Wisconsin State Prison at Waupun, Jim remembers fondly the time in high school he scored 36 points in the 1958 basketball play-off with Winneconne High but saw victory snatched from his team in the last three seconds of the game, when a Winneconne player in desperation hurled the ball from center court and scored a miraculous winning basket. And he remembers the time, during the fall of his last year in high school as all-conference right end on the football team, that Johnny McAlpin, the Blatz Beer distributor, came over after a game and offered to help pay Jim's way through the state university.

Johnny McAlpin was the last nice thing to happen to Jim McBrair. From the girl he got pregnant and married that year, canceling his hope of going to college, through his quick divorce the following fall, the jobs he couldn't seem to keep, an Army stint he hated so much his mother had to get him a discharge with a hardship plea and, finally, to his marriage to Carol, he seemed caught in a chaotic downdraft that swept him, relentlessly, to the final tragedy.

In the countdown months leading up to the murders, McBrair was going through personal hell. The relationship with his wife, Carol, begun five years earlier as a casual flirtation during a Saint Patrick's Day party, was always in a precarious state near misery for both of them. They were separating constantly; it got to be so often that McBrair can still rattle off the pattern. "First there would be family fights," he says, "started with little or no reason. Then she would begin the anti-Jim campaign with her mother. The third step would be filing papers for divorce and then she'd be seen in public with other men." McBrair was so afraid of a second divorce that he was incapable of asserting himself. He thought he knew where the blame lay—it was, in his eyes, always his own fault. "Maybe I was causing the trouble," he remembers thinking.

His wife, on the other hand, continued to go out with other men; and whenever he confronted her with evidence of her affairs, she flicked them back at him like darts, daring him to object. Once, when Carol was working at the Moose Inn as a barmaid and she and Jim were living at his parents' house, it was Jim's mother who threw her out when she came home from her job at three in the morning.

"I don't know, it seemed like wherever I turned, there were problems," says McBrair. "The house payments, the car payments, the telephone and electric bills. I'd try to think things out, but they all seemed so big and I'd try to solve one thing and a bigger one would take its place." It was then he experienced the "tired" feeling. "It was not sleepy-type tired," he recalls, "but the sick type, like I wanted to vomit—but not from the stomach, from the brain." Even wild escape attempts provided no relief. Once, he took Carol and fled to a small town in Canada with $1700 he'd taken from his and his father's joint checking account. He was planning to set up a resort bar and somehow make a break to freedom. They were back within a week. What's more, there was trouble about the $1700 check.

Finally, around Christmas 1966, Carol was instituting her last set of divorce papers. Bills were mounting. Jim had bought her a cottage on Fox Lake, in the woods. There were payments on that to be made. He injured his back on the job at a local sand-and-gravel company and after that, just didn't bother going in to work. He lost 20 pounds within a few months. Along with the tired feeling then came thoughts of suicide, of lying down in the middle of the highway and letting a truck run over him. He tried to talk to someone—the family court commissioner, the judge, the district attorney, the social worker and the priest. His friends in town, meanwhile, noticed little. Bodie Severins, of course, knew that Jim always seemed to be getting into one kind of mess or another, but the depths were unsuspected. As for the others, they wouldn't even listen. Working all week on the farms, they had no thought on Saturday night but to go into town and drink and get a girl. "The guys around here," explained one paunchy crewcut farmer who said he, too, was one of Jim's friends, "they don't want to hear a guy crying the blues on their shoulder

all the time, telling them what a bad time he's having and this and that. When we come into town, we want to have fun."

The day before the murders, though, even Jim's father noticed that he was acting strange. The two were to go ice fishing up at Devil's Elbow on the Wisconsin River. Jim dragged himself along, but instead of going down to the river with his father, he stayed in the camper truck and slept. "He stayed there all day," his father remembers. "I sent a boy back to tell him his dad wondered where he was. But he never came down."

The next day, Jim got up and worked inattentively on his income-tax return. This time, he told his father he didn't want to go fishing. In the afternoon, he went over to the cottage to see Carol and talk about their income tax and about what to do with the children. She was in a bad mood and baited him and picked at him. At one point, she answered the telephone and Jim heard her talking to one of the men she'd been going with. Jim told Carol that he hadn't thought she was still seeing him. Carol said she couldn't stop him from calling. Jim left and went over to the man's house. The man denied seeing Carol. Jim stopped in a phone booth on the way back and watched the man drive by with Carol's brother. He followed them to the cabin, then crept up to a window to watch. He saw the man stand behind Carol and put his arm around her. Then he nuzzled her with his cheek and they kissed. After the two men left, Jim walked in and confronted Carol with what he'd just seen. Didn't he notice that advances were made by the man? Carol asked. Jim said yes, but insisted that she could have turned him away. Then Carol got angry. She asked him who he thought her real lover was. "I think then I just blurted it out," says Jim. " 'I think it's your attorney,' I said."

It was a wrong guess and it encouraged Carol to sharpen her taunts. "What happened to the 'great detective'?" she asked. "Didn't the great detective notice that on Thursday night I wasn't wearing any underpants?" Jim and Carol had made love on Thursday night. "Where do you think I was all the rest of the evening?" she asked. Even to Jim, the answer was clear. Then Carol asked: "And how do you like seconds on the old punching bag, dear?"

Jim spun his car out of the driveway and drove over to Camp Waushara. He remembers Severins asking him something about stopping off at the Coop after closing, then Carol's brother poking him in the shoulder and accusing him of causing trouble between Carol and the other man. Jim remembers telling him he'd been out at the cabin and had seen it all, so there was no use lying about it. Carol's brother left. Jim finished his beer and got into his car to drive to his parents' home. "I was going 90 miles an hour and I remember looking down at the speedometer and thinking it was like I wasn't even moving." When he got there, he went into the house to get his hunting clothes—insulated underwear and boots, the tan-plaid jacket. "Colleen [his sister] asked me where I was going and I said something about a snowmobile party. I remember taking the .22 and taking shells out of the cabinet. I remember feeling along the stock to see if there was a loading ramp." Jim drove into town and bought some beer and then drove

around some more, ending up in a parking lot across from the restaurant in Wautoma run by Carol's mother. "I could see through the window and could see Carol working in there. There was something crazy going through my head, something about going in and shooting myself in front of her mother and all the people. It was something about letting everyone see what these people had driven me to and bleeding all over the restaurant floor."

Then Carol came out and got into a car with some other people. Jim followed them to the cabin by the lake. And that's when the shooting began.

At the trial, the jury found Jim McBrair guilty of premeditated murder and, since Wisconsin has no capital punishment, he was sentenced to life imprisonment. This means, says his lawyer, a state legislator named Jon Wilcox, that if things work out, Jim could be free by 1979. In the meantime, he is happy where he is. He works as a nurse in the prison infirmary. During his spare time, he reads psychology books and when he gets out, he says, he's thinking of becoming a social worker and helping other people in trouble. As for Carol, he still loves her. "But, and maybe this sounds funny," Jim says, "since that day, I can't remember her face. I don't have a picture, but you'd think after being with someone for that long, you'd remember. But I don't. I don't remember what she looked like."

His father said that friends had been very good to the family since the tragedy. When Mr. McBrair went into the hospital more than a year ago, he got maybe 100 get-well cards from neighbors. But Jim's father didn't get well. He died last fall of stomach cancer. Before he died, he talked a little bit about his son. "I've asked myself why a thousand times," he said, "but I still don't have the answer. We go up to see Jim whenever we can, and he seems more relaxed now. He's earning a dime a day and I guess he feels no one is after him anymore."

Frankie Carlin, the Bookie

JOE FLAHERTY

It was 10:45 Saturday morning and Frankie Carlin was finishing his soft-boiled eggs and his second cup of Irish home-brewed tea. His squat wife sat in a kitchen chair, dressed in drab wool slippers and a flowered smock, looking like a familiar house plant. He rose and slipped a light tan topcoat over his large frame and with fleshy hands molded his chocolate-brown hat into shape. It was time to go to work.

On the molding of the front door hung a blue plastic holy-water font with a sculptured crucifix. With his right hand he took some water and made the sign of the cross, his protection against evil spirits. Carlin's devils dress in blue. He's a bookmaker.

Recently United States Attorney Robert M. Morgenthau, functioning as the Dow-Jones of the underworld, stated that the annual business of bookmakers in the metropolitan area was $100-million. Recently also, New York State announced that it would

Reprinted by permission of the author and publisher from *The New York Times*, April 2, 1967. © 1967 by The New York Times Company.

run a quarterly series of lotteries based on horserace results, the idea being to channel some of that money into the state coffers. So contrary to the tenets of free enterprise, the state has set out to create unemployment in one of the oldest and most skilled trades in the history of man.

Of course this is all laughable to the people inside the trade. The trouble with reformers is that they equate their need for action with that of the general public, and envision themselves as Nick the Greek every time they wager a quarter at a church bazaar. Mark Twain once said the world was made up of turtles and goats, and no matter how much you explained, the turtles would never understand the depravity of the goats. The turtles in the State Assembly passed their Mock Reformation on the theory that a gambler needs action only quarterly. It is the same as saying that if we put everyone in the Yankee Stadium over the Fourth of July weekend for an orgy, the city would remain celibate for the rest of the year.

Carlin (a fictional name) runs his

operation in the Prospect Park area of Brooklyn. He walks to work through quiet tree-lined streets. The houses are mostly brownstone and limestone, and the occupants fall in the lower-middle- to middle-class income level.

Bookmaking, like everything else in our graduated society, adheres to economic class levels. The underprivileged bookie, like his clientele, usually hustles the street, taking action on a catch-as-catch-can basis: street corners, playgrounds, hallways. The middle-class bookie (Carlin's level) operates out of a permanent location. And those bookies who cater to the rich give all the advantages to the beautiful people: tell-a-phone credit card action.

Carlin paused outside the window of a bar bearing an Irish name. He stood lighting a cigarette while he casually viewed the interior. The bartender waved a greeting. Carlin nodded. His office was safe, his workday was about to begin.

The bar was one of those classic Irish "made bars" that exist only in Brooklyn and Queens. It was strictly a no-nonsense joint, no frills, no extras, you came here to drink. A long mahogany bar dominated the room. Workmanlike whisky bottles, without pouring spouts, formed a shapeup on the back bar. John Fitzgerald Kennedy's memory was encased on the wall between Irish and American flags. A shuffleboard stood against the side window like a low, sleek schooner in a bottle. The white marble floor gave a regimental click to every footstep. The only feminine-appearing thing in the place was a garishly made-up jukebox, but even that was denied: it was not plugged in.

Carlin draped his coat over a wooden booth. A guy in his 20's wearing a windbreaker, his slick hair sweeping back like jet streams, called down to the end of the bar, "Hey, Frankie, how about an eye-opener?" "Sure, Richie, first today." Faking enthusiasm, Carlin turned to the bartender. "Make it a creme de menthe on the rocks, Lenny." Carlin turned and muttered. "I haven't even digested breakfast—Christ, this slop will kill me." Why take it then, I asked. "Look, if you don't booze with your players, they think you're playing it sober and trying to hustle them."

"Frank, mind if I join you?" The windbreaker was trying to feel out my presence. "Sure, glad to have you —I want to introduce you to a friend of mine." I shook hands with my new acquaintance. Still unsure of my presence, he played it cool. "Frank, let me pay you the 15 I owe you from the other night." Carlin smiled, "It's all right, Richie, you can talk—he's all right." Richie still seemed uncomfortable. "Here's the dog I owe you and give me 20 to win on Advocator." Richie moved back to the bar and began to mingle among the patrons. This was the last time anybody approached Carlin with trepidation all day; the word was out—I was all right.

All operations like Carlin's give their clients the benefit of the "dog" or the "marker," inside names for credit. Carlin explained: "The average working stiff is tapped out by Tuesday or Wednesday so I let them place their action on the cuff. Come Saturday, he has his pay and he straightens out his tab. If they legalize bookmaking is Rockefeller going to let the bettor hold a marker on the state till Saturday?" He frowned slightly, registering his displeasure at the Governor's inhumanity.

It was 12:30 now and the bar began to become more crowded, Saturday is a big day for Carlin and this one in all probability would be bigger than most. At 4:30 every Saturday Channel 5 televises two horse races. This week the action was from Hialeah, and the feature was the Widener Handicap, a mile-and-a-quarter race with the value placed at $125,000 added. Hundred-grand races always stimulate the bankroll of the bettors; they have a mystique about them that is similar to a championship prize-fight.

The projected star of the production, the incomparable Buckpasser, was sidelined with an injury on the West Coast. But this was lamentable only to the big-money boys who delight in picking up 20 cents on every $2 wagered—for the average bettor. Buckpasser's payoffs are as exciting as a dividend check on one share of A.T.&T. Carlin's clientele likes action, a quick turnover. So, with Buckpasser's absence, the field was reduced to eight mediocrities, all going off at a decent price. In short, the Widener became a "good betting race."

Carlin was now drinking highballs. He moved among the drinkers like a social butterfly at a cocktail party. But there was a lot more happening than chit-chat. The action was being taken at all times, but even when you were looking for it, it was almost impossible to spot.

His performance was perfected by years of repetition. First he approaches the client and then bellows to the Bartender, "Lenny, give this deadbeat a drink on me." The client feigns anger. "Lord, if you're buying I'd better go to confession; the world must be coming to an end." A great curtain opener.

Scene two: the fabled Irish politician's "personal" touch. "How's Mary, Tim?" "Fine, Frankie, just grand." "The Pope will canonize that woman for living with a scoundrel like you." Some light jabbing and mock scuffling. The action is passed. Carlin gently slides the slips with the bet on it and the money into his pocket.

Find an exit line. "Tim, what are your Mets going to do this year?" "First division, absolutely." "My God, Carmine, did you hear what this crazy Mick just said?" A young Italian kid seated two stools away smiles and answers, "All Micks are crazy." Carlin booms, "Hell, Lenny, I'll buy a drink to that." What transition! Exit lines lead into new entrances. Right here in a Brooklyn gin mill, techniques Shakespeare couldn't master.

Ethnic joking is a big thing in bars like this. "That crazy clown thinks the Mets will wind up in first division." Carlin places his highball glass on the bar. Tony slides a $10 bill with his bet slip folded inside toward the glass. "Mets, what Mets?" Theatrical outrage. Carlin takes the 10 and slips it into his pocket. Tony adds, "This is the year of the Yankees, with that beautiful Italian kid Joe Pepitone in center field. A new DiMag."

Carlin displays weary frustration. "Pepitone? Why do I bother with you when there's a good squarehead in the bar? Fred, drink up."

An old man drinking whisky with an orange juice chaser delivers a stage imitation of a Swede. "Min-na-sota will win the pen-nant by seven games, by Yim-a-nee." The bar roars with laughter. It's all familiar, it's been in the repertory for years. The drinkers love the safeness of its familiarity. And Carlin moves along the length of the bar majestically. Not a line is missed, the interplay is beautiful. Alfred Lunt playing to revolving Lynn Fontannes.

Carlin now has many slips in his pocket. This is known as his "work" and a good bookie always protects his work. Checking everyone at the bar, he slowly moves to the back of the saloon. The back room is used only on special occasions like bachelor parties or an affair for some local kid going into the service. From it a large mahogany door leads to the cellar. Carlin opens it and disappears. The cellar is where his "bunk" or "stash" is located. His bunk is where he hides his work.

When Carlin disappeared through the door not a head at the bar would take note of his movement. It was as if Lady Godiva were riding through Coventry; there was a religious dedication to blindness. The bunk is the most important factor in the bookie's business. And for a good bookie there are two unbreakable commandments about his work: (1) Don't let the police seize it. (2) Never destroy it.

In actuality, it is preferable—and less expensive—to let the cops confiscate the work than destroy it. To be caught with wager slips is only a misdemeanor under Section 986 of the New York State Penal Law, but the destruction of one's work could mean grave financial losses. A bookmaker of Carlin's stature takes in up to $1,500 a week and as much as $500 on a given Saturday. If the word gets out that he has been raided and had to destroy his work many of these bets miraculously become winning ones. The client, realizing that the bookmaker has no record of the transactions, claims he wagered on winning horses, winning teams or what have you. The bookmaker, no matter how doubtful of the validity of the claims, must pay off the conjured wager to protect his reputation.

When a bookmaker gets the reputation of a deadbeat or a welcher, his action dwindles till he finally has to close shop.

By 3:50 the action started to ebb. Carlin's work for the most part was done for the day. Late stragglers still approached him with bets on the televised races. Carlin kept moving from the bar to the cellar to deposit any new action. He seemed tired.

"Doesn't this get you down day after day?" I asked. He smiled. "I don't get any wearier than a guy working a regular job and I earn a hell of a lot more. Thirty years ago before I got into this I worked as a clerk in a small brokerage house earning three thousand a year. It seemed to me then that my laundry bill for white shirts was about two thousand. Where would I be today with them? Eight-nine thousand a year. Now I put in about five hours a day and I'm good for anywhere from 30 to 40 thousand a year. No, when I think of that I don't tire of it."

"What about the pressure, the aggravation of the business?" He patted his full head of hair. "It may be white but it's still there and I'm nearly 60. Sure you have to be on the lookout for the cops all the time but guys with regular jobs come in here to booze and you swear to God they were the Fugitive the way their bosses hound them. Everybody's got aggravation."

He ordered another highball and raised it to me. "Do you know of anybody who has these working conditions? Besides the cops, what do I really have to worry about? Certainly not a lack of supply and demand. Some clown with a crazy longshot isn't going to break me. I've got enough collateral to cover me and if any action is too big I can always hedge off."

The term "hedge off" means that if a bookmaker is receiving too much money on a certain horse he can call another bookie (usually a wire-room set-up) and place a good part of the bet with a fellow operative. This eliminates the chance of taking a severe financial beating on a particular bet. The "hedge off" system also protects the bookmaker from being the sole target of a "sure thing."

Carlin deals only with flat horse races. He will take action on any flat horse on any track in the country. When a large bet materializes on a horse running at a bush track (a small out-of-town track), it is time to hedge off. Big money appearing on an obscure horse at an obscure track usually means the bettor has information, thus the danger of the "sure thing."

Carlin will handle only horses. "I'm no sportsman," he said. "That's where the big action is today, but I leave that to the big-money boys, the syndicate crowd. I operate alone. Besides, sports are too easy to rig. Who in their right mind would take action on college basketball? Those kids are so hungry they're easy pickings for any sharpie who waves a couple of hundred under their noses for a dump."

"What about the trotters?" I asked. "If the college kids are looking for spending money," he said, "those old men driving the trots must be looking for retirement pensions. I wouldn't touch them. I stick strictly to the flats."

A man no bigger than 5 foot 2, wearing a gray peaked cap, approached Carlin and handed him a slip with $2. Carlin read the slip and laughed. "Big Joe, are you still trying to break me with your crazy longshot parlays?" The little man grinned. "I'll get you yet, you big lug," he said.

As the small man retreated, Carlin motioned for the bartender. "Lenny, send Big Joe down a drink." Carlin turned back to me. "You see that little guy? He's a real sweetheart. He wouldn't bet a horse under 20-to-1. I always like to see him catch a couple of long ones. He's been playing with me now for about 20 years."

Carlin excused himself and disappeared into the cellar again. No matter how small the ticket, he didn't want it on his person. When he returned he laughed and said, "I'm going to have them build an escalator down to that place."

Looking at the clock on the wall, he said, "Four-ten—that should be about it for the day." He looked at my near-empty glass. "Come on—drink up."

"How much does it cost you buying drinks on a day like this?"

"I never count, these people are my friends. I've been operating out of this place nearly 30 years. I saw most of these kids you see here christened. Their fathers played with me, even some of their grandfathers. This very bar, I've been paying the rent in this place as long as I have been using it as a location. There are hundreds of set-ups like this around the boroughs.

"You know, John Q. Public thinks guys like me scoop in all the money and run home and bank it in the sugar bowl. Hell, I love to gamble as much as the next guy; that's how I got into this business in the first place. I always liked the horses. When I was with the brokerage house over 70 per cent of the employees liked to bet on one thing or another. We used to have this runner come around and pick up the action, but he was unreliable. Most days he was late and others he never showed. So I got myself a small bankroll and started to handle the action myself. I was single then and I lived in a small rooming house a couple of blocks from here and in the evening and Saturdays I would come here to drink. The guys at the bar were always talking about betting and how hard it was to find a bookie so I got together with the owner and I set up shop. After about a year things went so well I quit the brokerage house and I've been here ever since."

"Do you still gamble?" I asked. "Hell, I chase the ponies down to Florida a couple of weeks a year and in August, I chase them up to Saratoga. You know what the cops call us? Degenerate gamblers." He snorted. "You know something? They're right! Very few bookies can stay away from the action themselves."

He was completely relaxed now and he began to enjoy the whisky. Sitting back in the booth, he talked of how television with its extensive coverage of sports has aided gambling. "The average guy sits down to watch a football game and he likes to back his rooting interest with a five or a ten." When I asked him what events take the most money today his answer sounded more like Daniel Moynihan than a bookmaker. "The Jews like baseball and basketball, but especially baseball. That's the biggest play today. The big-money boys like the one-to-one situation of the starting pitchers. Guys today follow Koufax and Marichal like guys years ago would follow Man o' War and Dan Patch. The Irish and the Italians like the horses and pro football. The Negroes and the Puerto Ricans, because they don't have the bread, play the numbers—

sucker odds at 500-to-1; they get a pipe dream for two bits."

"Have you had much trouble over the years?" I asked. "In any business there is always trouble. I had guys give me bets and welch. About eight years ago a couple of kids I knew since they were babies fleeced me for about $1,700. One of them would drive to Bowie in Maryland and watch the races and wait for a big pay-off. When the pay-off was official he would run out of the track and call his buddy here in Brooklyn with the name of the horse. Then the kid would charge over here and dump $30 to $40 on the sure thing. It's called past posting. Normally I wouldn't touch a ticket like that, but hell, like I said, I knew the kids all their lives. I wasn't going to refuse a bet with a neighborhood kid because he was about four minutes late. They strung me about four times then I got wise."

"What did you do when you caught on?" "What was I going to do? Beat them? Kill them? They took me and that was that. I let everyone here know what they pulled, they never showed their faces here again. I have a lot of friends here, but I wouldn't let anyone lay a hand on them. I don't run that kind of operation, my friend—I'm no mobster."

"The kind of trouble I was really talking about was the cops," I said. Carlin started to laugh. He told of how six years ago the cops began to lean on him. Every day there was a plainclothesman or two dressed as mail carriers or longshoremen standing at the bar. Carlin couldn't move. Then a brilliant idea struck him.

Since he couldn't circulate among the patrons and most certainly the patrons couldn't walk down to the basement to place their slips in his bunk, he decided to have the men's room redecorated. The bathroom is one of those museum pieces with gigantic marble urinals that Toulouse-Lautrec could have used for a shower stall. Carlin decided to replace the old plaster ceiling with a Cello-Tex one. The idea was that he would leave one Cello-Tex square loose and his clients, by mounting the urinal, could stash their action and their cash in the false ceiling. Carlin would remove his work late at night when the bar was no longer under surveillance.

The operation worked great for about three days till the plainclothesmen began to wonder if the bar patrons were plagued by kidney disease. Finally, his curiosity aroused, one plainclothes man decided to follow a patron to the men's room. Giving the guy a few minutes headstart, the cop pushed in the door and saw his suspect standing on the urinal with his arms stretched upward. Unable to explain his peculiar form of toilet training, the bettor wound up in cuffs while the cop mounted the urinal and flushed out the evidence. Carlin had tears of laughter running from his eyes at the completion of the story.

"What happened?" I asked. "Let's just say it cost me plenty to get out of that one." Pointing to the end of the bar at a lanky guy in a sports jacket, Carlin said, "That's him. Since then we baptized him 'Johnny Highchair.'" His laughter was rich, and the best kind—self-directed.

"You seem like a contented man," I said.

"I am."

"No regrets?"

"I'll lay you 7 to 5 no one can say that."

I laughed. "No bet."

The television set was now turned on. The voice of Fred Caspella nasally intoned, "It is now post time." George Widener's Ring Twice was an easy winner under a front-running ride by Billy Boland. Carlin was pleased by the results. Most of the big money he had taken in this race was on Advocator, the favorite, who finished down the track. But he wouldn't know how his day came out till he heard all the results from around the country that evening at 6:30 on FM radio. Then he would balance his books. Sunday afternoon at 1:30 after the 12:15 mass at the parish church, he would wait for the winning bettors inside the bar. Their winnings would be in white sealed envelopes with their names on them inside his topcoat pocket. Every bet paid precisely, rounded off to the nearest dollar.

Saturday's results were now turf history. But come Sunday the papers would list the entries for Monday. And come Monday the bettors would be back again. Why? You looked up at the electronic picture and television truly became educational.

There they were in the winner's circle. Ring Twice worth $24.40 to his believers. Seventy-seven-year-old George Widener winning his ancestor's race. Seventy-eight-year-old Wilbert "Bert" Mulholland training the winner. Dynasty! Continuity! Ring Twice, whose sire was Gallant Man, the Belmont Stakes winner, his stock reaching back to mysterious Arabia. Widener, Mulholland, Arabia —permanence, history. Carlin talking of generations of bettors. Man's passage through life. His history, his need to test overwhelming odds. His need for action.

This historic need. Why? One of their own, Nick the Greek, said it as neat as an inside straight. "The next best thing to winning—is losing."

'An Absolute Hell':
A Woman's Story of Jail

DONALD JONJACK / WILLIAM BRADEN

Cook County Jail has been described as a jungle. But that is the wrong word, according to a North Shore matron who was a prisoner there.

"A jungle is a dark and dangerous place," said Mrs. Jean Macdonald. "That much is true. But it is also a thing of nature, and it can be beautiful. County Jail to me is a hell . . . an absolute hell."

The 57-year-old Evanston woman, mother of nine, told the story of her 1964 confinement this week to The Sun-Times—and to the state's attorney's office. She will testify before a grand jury that is investigating charges of terror and corruption at the jail.

Mrs. Macdonald said she went to jail to defend a principle. She was cited for contempt of court when she refused to allow a bank to assess her home in connection with a complicated inheritance suit dating back to 1938.

If recent stories coming out of jail are accurate, the conditions she describes have not changed since then— except perhaps to become even worse.

Mrs. Macdonald is a widow and a

Reprinted with permission of the publisher from Donald Jonjack and William Braden, " An Absolute Hell': A Woman's Story of Jail," *Chicago Sun-Times*, XX, No. 264, December 6, 1967.

1931 graduate of the University of Illinois, where she was voted most popular co-ed during her senior year. She owns a games company and with her late husband James she created a card game, based on the U.S. Constitution, that won an award from the Freedoms Foundation.

After routine processing at the jail, she said, she was examined by a doctor.

"I told him I was a heart patient," she said. "But he wouldn't let me keep the prescription medicine I had in my purse. It might be dope, he said. But he assured me the medicine would be checked out, and he said I would be supplied with the drug later."

Mrs. Macdonald said she was taken then to the women's section.

"As I walked through the gates," she said, "I saw female prisoners in this open room, which was a compound. They were walking around without any tops on—nude from the waist up in view of the male guards. I couldn't believe it."

She was greeted, she said, by prisoners who told her immediately that she would be in trouble if she didn't supply them with cigarettes and candy. Said one of the women:

"You had better provide, baby."

Mrs. Macdonald said she was directed next to the "barn boss," a prisoner in charge of that section of the jail.

"She was a very stout Negro woman who was in jail on a murder charge. She seemed nice enough, and she never threatened me. She gave me a pair of smelly shoes and a filthy dress. She also gave me a dirty towel and a cup.

"The barn boss could shift people around, and she was the person who decided where I would stay. She showed me a cell intended for four persons, but there was only one woman in it—a woman named Judy.

"Judy was in jail on a dope-peddling charge. She did a lot to protect me, and I don't know what I would have done without her."

"In the cell, the sheets were practically black and had bed bugs. The toilet didn't work, and the air had a terrible odor. I learned later that the 68 women on my tier had only three workable toilets and the rest of them had been shut off for a long time.

"I wasn't to say anything about this, I was told, or I would be severely punished—and not by the guards.

"The reason was, the empty pipes were used to transport things from the first floor. I was told that candy and narcotics were pulled up by strings through the pipes.

"On the very first day, I noticed many kinds of strange behavior. When I'd ask Judy what was wrong with a person, she'd say: 'Oh, she's high.' Which meant she was on dope.

"Everything was so out in the open there. It was unbelievable. In the compound, women would take off their clothes and climb on top of the table and molest each other. They would touch each other and cry out. They never even bothered to clean the tables when they were finished,

and then later they would eat at those same tables."

Mrs. Macdonald said there was a disregard on the part of jail personnel for basic sanitary procedures. It started with the processing physical examination, she said.

Before she was assigned to a tier, Mrs. Macdonald and six other women were taken into a room where a matron ordered her and the others to remove all their clothing.

"The matron had a vaginal tool," said Mrs. Macdonald. "She said she had to examine us with it to see if we were concealing narcotics.

"Then she started to examine the second girl, without sterilizing the tool. I was shocked. And I protested. The matron looked at me and said: 'just for that, you are going to be last.'

"I was the last one she examined, and the women before me included prostitutes and murderers."

Mrs. Macdonald tried to keep her own cell clean, she said, and that earned her a nickname with the other prisoners. They called her the Wipe Lady.

"There was a catwalk running all around the section," she said. "At night the guards would walk around to make sure everybody was accounted for. But during the day they never walked around, and the prisoners were left to themselves. So you were helpless. Everybody was at the mercy of the strong and violent ones.

"There was nothing to do, nothing to read, and you couldn't go outside —not even in the summer. Dope was the only thing. Dope and perversions.

"You'd hear a woman screaming lewd conversations with men prisoners. I have raised nine children, and I have an idea what life is about. But these people raved and screamed the most ugly, dirty things they would like to do with each other—sadism and masochism—every filthy thing that can be imagined they screamed back and forth, back and forth.

"What really hurt me was hearing about the young boys who were molested. The male prisoners forced them into homosexual acts under threat of stabbing, beatings, starving. The boys were frightened and defenseless. The guards just pretended not to hear, or were not around."

On the second day, said Mrs. Macdonald, the barn boss transferred her to another cell where she was approached by two formidable looking women. They laughed, she said, and one of them told her:

"I'm Queenie from 63d St., and I never had a white woman before. Are we going to have fun with you tonight!"

Said Mrs. Macdonald:

"I never prayed so much in my life. I told them if they would leave me alone I would buy them cigarettes and candy or whatever they wanted. I also mentioned Judy, who apparently was close to the barn boss. And so they did leave me alone, except for insults and threats."

Then there was the shower room at the end of the cell block.

"The entrance is wide enough for only one person," said Mrs. Macdonald. "I went in on my second day to take a shower and I found two women in the middle of a perverted act. Later I learned that the shower room was used only for acts of perversion, and it was a place where new women were often attacked sexually. After my one experience which was a close call, I decided it wasn't worth the risk to be clean."

Mrs. Macdonald did not care for the jail food.

"It was served on trays that were caked with old food," she said. "The potatoes we got were orange. If I had 30 cents a day, I could serve better food."

She told of narcotics addicts going through withdrawal.

"These unfortunate persons had no help, no pity. Sometimes they were preyed upon by other prisoners who would sexually assault them even while they were in their terrible agony. They rolled around on the concrete floor, trying to keep cool during the worst of it. And then afterward they would have a great craving for sugar, which they would steal or fight for."

Mrs. Macdonald said a fellow inmate at that time was Mrs. Irwinna Weinstein, convicted of slaying her husband in a celebrated murder case. (The charge against her was dropped this year after a successful appeal for a new trial.)

"I hardly ever saw her," said Mrs. Macdonald. "I was told she was never in her cell, except at night. Once I did see her, and she looked as if she'd just come from Elizabeth Arden. Her hair had been done—that's something a woman knows and her nails had been manicured. She never talked to anyone, and she kept apart from the other prisoners.

"Her cell was beautiful, filled with satins and silks, and there was even perfume. It was the difference between heaven and hell. I asked the other prisoners how it was possible, and they told me: 'Well, Wipe Lady, money talks; if you've got money, you can get anything.'"

There was another prisoner—named Shirley.

"What happened to her was inhuman," said Mrs. Macdonald. "If it had happened in a jail 500 years ago, somebody would have stopped it."

"Shirley was mentally ill. She thought she had killed her husband after catching him in an affair with her maid.

"There were two women in the next cell. They started to torment her. They yelled things like: 'Hey, honey, show us how you found your husband and the maid,' 'Were your husband and she real close, loving?'

"The woman was reeling, tortured. And the more she reacted, the more they tortured her. She begged. She pleaded with them to stop. She hit her head against the wall. And they said: 'That's good. Do it once more—once for your maid.'

"Finally she put her head in the bowl of her toilet and tried to drown herself, flushing the toilet over and over again while the animal women screamed and laughed.

"I couldn't stand it any more.

"I'd been warned never to call a guard under any circumstance, unless I wanted a beating. But I called now. I screamed for a guard.

"Nobody came.

"I grabbed a broom and shoved it through the bars. I pushed her away from the toilet. And then I kept pushing with the broom to keep her away.

"Finally somebody came. The guards strapped her to her bed and then left. As soon as they were gone the women started again, redoubling their efforts. Shirley thrashed and cried out. She broke the springs in her bed, and they were cutting her back.

"That day Shirley was given no food. She cried that she would do anything the women wanted—would emulate what the maid had been do-ing with her husband—if only they would leave her alone. But of course they wouldn't, and didn't. What finally happened to her I don't know.

"I thought I would be punished for calling the guards. But I wasn't. A cart came around once a day, and I was able to buy things for the other prisoners to keep them from attacking me.

"What I couldn't buy was my medicine. I asked for it repeatedly, but I never got it. The doctor didn't keep his promise.

"One day in the compound two women got into a fight, and one of them threw a large container of scalding water. It spilled over me and burned me. But none of the prisoners tried to get any help, and nobody came for 10 minutes. Then they smeared Vaseline on the burns, and that was all. I never saw a doctor, never once after that first time.

"On the sixth day I was nursed by a woman named Helen, in her 70s, who was in jail for bad checks. She brought me cold towels for relief, and she brought me water. But I couldn't eat, and I couldn't sleep.

"Then my daughter Jeanette came to the jail to visit me, and she begged me to obey the court order. She told me a dear friend of our family had just been killed in an auto accident. And I had become a grandmother again.

"So I obeyed the order, and I left the jail. After seven days.

"I saw what happens there. And I don't see how any person who has the slightest connection with the jail can be ignorant about all the hate, torture and terror there. I don't see how it is possible."

Wincanton: The Politics of Corruption

JOHN A. GARDINER, WITH THE ASSISTANCE
OF DAVID J. OLSON

In general, Wincanton represents a city that has toyed with the problem of corruption for many years. No mayor in the history of the city of Wincanton has ever succeeded himself in office. Some mayors have been corrupt and have allowed the city to become a wide-open center for gambling and prostitution; Wincanton voters have regularly rejected those corrupt mayors who dared to seek reelection. Some mayors have been scrupulously honest and have closed down all vice operations in the city; these men have been generally disliked for being too straitlaced. Other mayors, fearing one form of resentment or the other, have chosen quietly to retire from public life. The questions of official corruption and policy toward vice and gambling, it seems, have been paramount issues in Wincanton elections since the days of Prohibition. Any mayor who is known to be controlled by the gambling syndicates will lose office, but so will any mayor who tries completely to

From the President's Commission on Law Enforcement and Administration of Justice: Task Force Reports: Organized Crime, Appendix B, John A. Gardiner, with the assistance of David J. Olson, Wincanton: The Politics of Corruption, pp. 61–70, 78–79. Footnotes omitted.

clean up the city. The people of Wincanton apparently want both easily accessible gambling and freedom from racket domination.

Probably more than most cities in the United States, Wincanton has known a high degree of gambling, vice (sexual immorality, including prostitution), and corruption (official malfeasance, misfeasance and nonfeasance of duties). With the exception of two reform administrations, one in the early 1950's and the one elected in the early 1960's, Wincanton has been wide open since the 1920's. Bookies taking bets on horses took in several millions of dollars each year. With writers at most newsstands, cigar counters, and corner grocery stores, a numbers bank did an annual business in excess of $1,300,000 during some years. Over 200 pinball machines, equipped to pay off like slot machines, bore $250 Federal gambling stamps. A high stakes dice game attracted professional gamblers from more than 100 miles away; $25,000 was found on the table during one Federal raid. For a short period of time in the 1950's (until raided by U.S. Treasury Department agents), a still, capable of manufacturing $1 million in illegal alcohol each year, operated on the banks of the Wincanton River. Finally, prostitution flourished openly in the city, with at least 5 large houses (about 10 girls apiece) and countless smaller houses catering to men from a large portion of the state.

As in all cities in which gambling and vice had flourished openly, these illegal activities were protected by local officials. Mayors, police chiefs, and many lesser officials were on the payroll of the gambling syndicate, while others received periodic "gifts" or aid during political campaigns. A number of Wincanton officials added to their revenue from the syndicate by extorting kickbacks on the sale or purchase of city equipment or by selling licenses, permits, zoning variances, etc. As the city officials made possible the operations of the racketeers, so frequently the racketeers facilitated the corrupt endeavors of officials by providing liaison men to arrange the deals or "enforcers" to insure that the deals were carried out.

The visitor to Wincanton is struck by the beauty of the surrounding countryside and the drabness of a tired, old central city. Looking down on the city from Mount Prospect, the city seems packed in upon itself, with long streets of red brick row houses pushing up against old railroad yards and factories; 93 percent of the housing units were built before 1940.

Wincanton had its largest population in 1930 and has been losing residents slowly ever since. The people who remained—those who didn't move to the suburbs or to the other parts of the United States—are the lower middle class, the less well educated; they seem old and often have an Old World feeling about them. The median age in Wincanton is 37 years (compared with a national median of 29 years). While unemployment is low (2.5 percent of the labor force in April 1965), there are few professional or white collar workers; only 11 percent of the families had incomes over $10,000, and the median family income was $5,543. As is common in many cities with an older, largely working class population, the level of education is low—only 27 percent of the adults have completed high school, and the median number of school years completed is 8.9.

While most migration into Wincanton took place before 1930, the various nationality groups in Wincanton seem to have retained their separate identities. The Germans, the Poles, the Italians, and the Negroes each have their own neighborhoods, stores, restaurants, clubs and politicians. Having immigrated earlier, the Germans are more assimilated into the middle and upper middle classes; the other groups still frequently live in the neighborhoods in which they first settled; and Italian and Polish politicians openly appeal to Old World loyalties. Club life adds to the ethnic groupings by giving a definite neighborhood quality to various parts of the city and their politics; every politician is expected to visit the ethnic association, ward clubs, and voluntary firemen's associations during campaign time—buying a round of drinks for all present and leaving money with the club stewards to hire poll watchers to advertise the candidates and guard the voting booths.

In part, the flight from Wincanton of the young and the more educated can be explained by the character of the local economy. While there have been no serious depressions in Wincanton during the last 30 years, there has been little growth either, and most of the factories in the city were built 30 to 50 years ago and rely primarily upon semiskilled workers. A few textile mills have moved out of the region, to be balanced by the construction in the last 5 years of several electronics assembly plants. No one employer dominates the economy, although seven employed more than 1,000 persons. Major industries today include steel fabrication and heavy machinery, textiles and food products.

With the exception of 2 years (one in the early 1950's, the other 12 years later) in which investigations of corruption led to the election of Republican reformers, Wincanton politics have been heavily Democratic in recent years. Registered Democrats in the city outnumber Republicans by a margin of 2 to 1; in Alsace County as a whole, including the heavily Republican middle class suburbs, the Democratic margin is reduced to 3 to 2. Despite this margin of control, or possibly because of it, Democratic politics in Wincanton have always been somewhat chaotic candidates appeal to the ethnic groups, clubs, and neighborhoods, and no machine or organization has been able to dominate the party for very long (although a few men have been able to build a personal following lasting for 10 years or so). Incumbent mayors have been defeated in the primaries by other Democrats, and voting in city council sessions has crossed party lines more often than it has respected them.

To a great extent, party voting in Wincanton follows a business-labor cleavage. Two newspapers (both owned by a group of local businessmen) and the Chamber of Commerce support Republican candidates; the unions usually endorse Democrats. It

would be unwise, however, to overestimate either the solidarity or the interest in local politics of Wincanton business and labor groups. Frequently two or more union leaders may be opposing each other in a Democratic primary (the steelworkers frequently endorse liberal or reform candidates, while the retail clerks have been more tied to "organization" men); or ethnic allegiance and hostilities may cause union members to vote for Republicans, or simply sit on their hands. Furthermore, both business and labor leaders express greater interest in State and National issues—taxation, wage and hour laws, collective bargaining policies, etc.—than in local issues. (The attitude of both business and labor toward Wincanton gambling and corruption will be examined in detail later.)

Many people feel that, apart from the perennial issue of corruption, there really are not any issues in Wincanton politics and that personalities are the only things that matter in city elections. Officials assume that the voters are generally opposed to a high level of public services. Houses are tidy, but the city has no public trash collection, or fire protection either, for that matter. While the city buys firetrucks and pays their drivers, firefighting is done solely by volunteers—in a city with more than 75,000 residents. (Fortunately, most of the houses are built of brick or stone.) Urban renewal has been slow, master planning nonexistent, and a major railroad line still crosses the heart of the shopping district, bringing traffic to a halt as trains grind past. Some people complain, but no mayor has ever been able to do anything about it. For years, people have been talking about rebuilding City Hall (constructed as a high school 75 years ago), modernizing mass transportation, and ending pollution of the Wincanton River, but nothing much has been done about any of these issues, or even seriously considered. Some people explain this by saying that Wincantonites are interested in everything—up to and including, but not extending beyond, their front porch.

If the voters of Wincanton were to prefer an active rather than passive city government, they would find the municipal structure well equipped to frustrate their desires. Many governmental functions are handled by independent boards and commissions, each able to veto proposals of the mayor and councilmen. Until about 10 years ago, State law required all middle-sized cities to operate under a modification of the commission form of government. (In the early 1960's, Wincanton voters narrowly by a margin of 16 votes out of 30,000 rejected a proposal to set up a council-manager plan.) The city council is composed of five men—a mayor and four councilmen. Every odd-numbered year, two councilmen are elected to 4-year terms. The mayor also has a 4-year term of office, but has a few powers not held by the councilmen; he presides at council sessions but has no veto power over council legislation. State law requires that city affairs be divided among five named departments, each to be headed by a member of the council, but the council members are free to decide among themselves what functions will be handled by which departments (with the proviso that the mayor must control the police department). Thus the city's work can be split equally among five men, or a three-man majority can control all important posts. In a not

atypical recent occurrence, one councilman, disliked by his colleagues, found himself supervising only garbage collection and the Main Street comfort station! Each department head (mayor and councilmen) has almost complete control over his own department. Until 1960, when a $2,500 raise became effective, the mayor received an annual salary of $7,000, and each councilman received $6,000. The mayor and city councilmen have traditionally been permitted to hold other jobs while in office.

To understand law enforcement in Wincanton, it is necessary to look at the activities of local, county, State, and Federal agencies. State law requires that each mayor select his police chief and officers "from the force" and "exercise a constant supervision and control over their conduct." Applicants for the police force are chosen on the basis of a civil service examination and have tenure "during good behavior," but promotions and demotions are entirely at the discretion of the mayor and council. Each new administration in Wincanton has made wholesale changes in police ranks— patrolmen have been named chief, and former chiefs have been reduced to walking a beat. (When one period of reform came to an end in the mid-1950's, the incoming mayor summoned the old chief into his office, "You can stay on as officer," the mayor said, "but you'll have to go along with my policies regarding gambling." "Mr. Mayor," the chief said, "I'm going to keep on arresting gamblers no matter where you put me." The mayor assigned the former chief to the position of "Keeper of the Lockup," permanently stationed in the basement of police headquarters.) Promotions must be made from within the department. This policy has continued even though the present reform mayor created the post of police commissioner and brought in an outsider to take command. For cities of its size, Wincanton police salaries have been quite low—the top pay for patrolmen was $4,856—in the lowest quartile of middle-sized cities in the Nation. Since 1964 the commissioner has received $10,200 and patrolmen $5,400 each year.

While the police department is the prime law enforcement agency within Wincanton, it receives help (and occasional embarrassment) from other groups. Three county detectives work under the district attorney, primarily in rural parts of Alsace County, but they are occasionally called upon to assist in city investigations. The State Police, working out of a barracks in suburban Wincanton Hills, have generally taken a "hands off" or "local option" attitude toward city crime, working only in rural areas unless invited into a city by the mayor, district attorney, or county judge. Reform mayors have welcomed the superior manpower and investigative powers of the State officers; corrupt mayors have usually been able to thumb their noses at State policemen trying to uncover Wincanton gambling. Agents of the State's Alcoholic Beverages Commission suffer from no such limitations and enter Wincanton at will in search of liquor violations. They have seldom been a serious threat to Wincanton corruption, however, since their numbers are quite limited (and thus the agents are dependent upon the local police for information and assistance in making arrests). Their mandate extends to gambling and prostitution only when encountered in the course of a liquor investigation.

Under most circumstances, the operative level of law enforcement in Wincanton has been set by local political decisions, and the local police (acting under instructions from the mayor) have been able to determine whether or not Wincanton should have open gambling and prostitution. The State Police, with their "hands off" policy, have simply reenforced the local decision. From time to time, however, Federal agencies have become interested in conditions in Wincanton and, as will be seen throughout this study, have played as important a role as the local police in cleaning up the city. Internal Revenue Service agents have succeeded in prosecuting Wincanton gamblers for failure to hold gambling occupation stamps, pay the special excise taxes on gambling receipts, or report income. Federal Bureau of Investigation agents have acted against violations of the Federal laws against extortion and interstate gambling. Finally, special attorneys from the Organized Crime and Racketeering Section of the Justice Department were able to convict leading members of the syndicate controlling Wincanton gambling. While Federal prosecutions in Wincanton have often been spectacular, it should also be noted that they have been somewhat sporadic and limited in scope. The Internal Revenue Service, for example, was quite successful in seizing gambling devices and gamblers lacking the Federal gambling occupation stamps, but it was helpless after Wincantonites began to purchase the stamps, since local officials refused to prosecute them for violations of the State antigambling laws.

The court system in Wincanton, as in all cities in the State, still has many of the 18th century features which have been rejected in other States. At the lowest level, elected magistrates (without legal training) hear petty civil and criminal cases in each ward of the city. The magistrates also issue warrants and decide whether persons arrested by the police shall be held for trial. Magistrates are paid only by fees, usually at the expense of convicted defendants. All serious criminal cases, and all contested petty cases, are tried in the county court. The three judges of the Alsace County court are elected (on a partisan ballot) for 10-year terms, and receive an annual salary of $25,000.

GAMBLING AND CORRUPTION: THE INSIDERS

The Stern Empire. The history of Wincanton gambling and corruption since World War II centers around the career of Irving Stern. Stern is an immigrant who came to the United States and settled in Wincanton at the turn of the century. He started as a fruit peddler, but when Prohibition came along, Stern became a bootlegger for Heinz Glickman, then the beer baron of the State. When Glickman was murdered in the waning days of Prohibition, Stern took over Glickman's business and continued to sell untaxed liquor after repeal of Prohibition in 1933. Several times during the 1930's, Stern was convicted in Federal court on liquor charges and spent over a year in Federal prison.

Around 1940, Stern announced to the world that he had reformed and went into his family's wholesale produce business. While Stern was in fact leaving the bootlegging trade, he was also moving into the field of gambling, for even at that time Wincanton had

a "wide-open" reputation, and the police were ignoring gamblers. With the technical assistance of his bootlegging friends, Stern started with a numbers bank and soon added horse betting, a dice game, and slot machines to his organization. During World War II, officers from a nearby Army training base insisted that all brothels be closed, but this did not affect Stern. He had already concluded that public hostility and violence, caused by the horses, were, as a side effect, threatening his more profitable gambling operations. Although Irv Stern controlled the lion's share of Wincanton gambling throughout the 1940's, he had to share the slot machine trade with Klaus Braun. Braun, unlike Stern, was a Wincanton native and a Gentile, and thus had easier access to the frequently anti-Semitic club stewards, restaurant owners, and bartenders who decided which machines would be placed in their buildings. Legislative investigations in the early 1950's estimated that Wincanton gambling was an industry with gross receipts of $5 million each year; at that time Stern was receiving $40,000 per week from bookmaking, and Braun took in $75,000 to $100,000 per year from slot machines alone.

Irv Stern's empire in Wincanton collapsed abruptly when legislative investigations brought about the election of a reform Republican administration. Mayor Hal Craig decided to seek what he termed "pearl gray purity" to tolerate isolated prostitutes, bookies, and numbers writers but to drive out all forms of organized crime, all activities lucrative enough to make it worth someone's while to try bribing Craig's police officials. Within 6 weeks after taking office, Craig and

District Attorney Henry Weiss had raided enough of Stern's gambling parlors and seized enough of Braun's slot machines to convince both men that business was over for 4 years at least. The Internal Revenue Service was able to convict Braun and Stern's nephew, Dave Feinman, on tax evasion charges; both were sent to jail. From 1952 to 1955 it was still possible to place a bet or find a girl. But you had to know someone to do it, and no one was getting very rich in the process.

By 1955 it was apparent to everyone that reform sentiment was dead and that the Democrats would soon be back in office. In the summer of that year, Stern met with representatives of the east coast syndicates and arranged for the rebuilding of his empire. He decided to change his method of operations in several ways; one way was by centralizing all Wincanton vice and gambling under his control. But he also decided to turn the actual operation of most enterprises over to others. From the mid-1950's until the next wave of reform hit Wincanton after elections in the early 1960's, Irv Stern generally succeeded in reaching these goals.

The financial keystone of Stern's gambling empire was numbers betting. Records seized by the Internal Revenue Service in the late 1950's and early 1960's indicated that gross receipts from numbers amounted to more than $100,000 each month, or $1.3 million annually. Since the numbers are a poor man's form of gambling (bets range from a penny to a dime or quarter), a large number of men and a high degree of organization are required. The organizational goals are three; have the maximum possible number of men

on the streets seeking bettors, be sure that they are reporting honestly, and yet strive so to decentralize the organization that no one, if arrested, will be able to identify many of the others. During the "pearl gray purity" of Hal Craig, numbers writing was completely unorganized, many isolated writers took bets from their friends and frequently had to renege if an unusually popular number came up; no one writer was big enough to guard against such possibilities. When a new mayor took office in the mid-1950's, however, Stern's lieutenants notified each of the small writers that they were now working for Stern or else. Those who objected were "persuaded" by Stern's men, or else arrested by the police, as were any of the others who were suspected of holding out on their receipts. Few objected for very long. After Stern completed the reorganization of the numbers business, its structure was roughly something like this; 11 subbanks reported to Stern's central accounting office. Each subbank employed from 5 to 30 numbers writers. Thirty-five percent of the gross receipts went to the writers. After deducting for winnings and expenses (mostly protection payoffs), Stern divided the net profits equally with the operators of the subbanks. In return for his cut, Stern provided protection from the police and "laid off" the subbanks, covering winnings whenever a popular number "broke" one of the smaller operators.

Stern also shared with out-of-State syndicates in the profits and operation of two enterprises, a large dice game and the largest still found by the Treasury Department since Prohibition. The dice game employed over 50 men drivers to "lug" players into town from as far as 100 miles away, doormen to check players' identities, loan sharks who "faded" the losers, croupiers, food servers, guards, etc. The 1960 payroll for these employees was over $350,000. While no estimate of the gross receipts from the game is available, some indication of its size can be obtained from the fact that $50,000 was found on the tables and in the safe when the FBI raided the game in 1962. Over 100 players were arrested during the raid; one businessman had lost over $75,000 at the tables. Stern received a share of the game's profits plus a $1,000 weekly fee to provide protection from the police.

Stern also provided protection (for a fee) and shared in the profits of a still, erected in an old warehouse on the banks of the Wincanton River and tied into the city's water and sewer systems. Stern arranged for clearance by the city council and provided protection from the local police after the $200,000 worth of equipment was set up. The still was capable of producing $4 million worth of alcohol each year, and served a five-State area, until Treasury agents raided it after it had been in operation for less than 1 year.

The dice game and the still raise questions regarding the relationship of Irv Stern to out-of-State syndicates. Republican politicians in Wincanton frequently claimed that Stern was simply the local agent of the Cosa Nostra. While Stern was regularly sending money to the syndicates, the evidence suggests that Stern was much more than an agent for outsiders. It would be more accurate to regard these payments as profit sharing with coinvestors and as charges for services rendered. The east coasters provided technical services in the operation of

the dice game and still and "enforcement" service for the Wincanton gambling operation. When deviants had to be persuaded to accept Stern's domination, Stern called upon outsiders for "muscle" strong-arm men who could not be traced by local police if the victim chose to protest. In the early 1940's, for example, Stern asked for help in destroying a competing dice game; six gunmen came in and held it up, robbing and terrifying the players. While a few murders took place in the struggle for supremacy in the 1930's and 1940's, only a few people were roughed up in the 1950's and no one was killed.

After the mid-1950's, Irv Stern controlled prostitution and several forms of gambling on a "franchise" basis. Stern took no part in the conduct of these businesses and received no share of the profits, but exacted a fee for protection from the police. Several horse books, for example, operated regularly; the largest of these paid Stern $600 per week. While slot machines had permanently disappeared from the Wincanton scene after the legislative investigations of the early 1950's, a number of men began to distribute pinball machines, which paid off players for games won. As was the case with numbers writers, these pinball distributors had been unorganized during the Craig administration. When Democratic Mayor Gene Donnelly succeeded Craig, he immediately announced that all pinball machines were illegal and would be confiscated by the police. A Stern agent then contacted the pinball distributors and notified them that if they employed Dave Feinman (Irv Stern's nephew) as a "public relations consultant," there would be no interference from the police. Several rebellious distributors formed an Alsace County Amusement Operators Association, only to see Feinman appear with two thugs from New York. After the association president was roughed up, all resistance collapsed, and Feinman collected $2,000 each week to promote the "public relations" of the distributors. (Stern, of course, was able to offer no protection against Federal action. After the Internal Revenue Service began seizing the pinball machines in 1956, the owners were forced to purchase the $250 Federal gambling stamps as well as paying Feinman. Over 200 Wincanton machines bore these stamps in the early 1960's, and thus were secure from Federal as well as local action.) In the 1950's, Irv Stern was able to establish a centralized empire in which he alone determined which rackets would operate and who would operate them (he never, it might be noted, permitted narcotics traffic in the city while he controlled it). What were the bases of his control within the criminal world? Basically, they were three: First, as a business matter, Stern controlled access to several very lucrative operations, and could quickly deprive an uncooperative gambler or numbers writer of his source of income. Second, since he controlled the police department he could arrest any gamblers or bookies who were not paying tribute. (Some of the local gambling and prostitution arrests which took place during the Stern era served another purpose—to placate newspaper demands for a crackdown. As one police chief from this era phrased it, "Hollywood should have given us an Oscar for some of our performances when we had to pull a phony raid to keep the papers happy.") Finally, if the mechanisms

of fear of financial loss and fear of police arrest failed to command obedience, Stern was always able to keep alive a fear of physical violence. As we have seen, numbers writers, pinball distributors, and competing gamblers were brought into line after outside enforcers put in an appearance. Stern's regular collection agent, a local tough who had been convicted of murder in the 1940's, was a constant reminder of the virtues of cooperation. Several witnesses who told grand juries or Federal agents of extortion attempts by Stern, received visits from Stern enforcers and tended to "forget" when called to testify against the boss.

Protection. An essential ingredient in Irv Stern's Wincanton operations was protection against law enforcement agencies. While he was never able to arrange freedom from Federal intervention (although, as in the case of purchasing excise stamps for the pinball machines, he was occasionally able to satisfy Federal requirements without disrupting his activities), Stern was able in the 1940's and again from the mid-1950's through the early 1960's to secure freedom from State and local action. The precise extent of Stern's network of protection payments is unknown, but the method of operations can be reconstructed.

Two basic principles were involved in the Wincanton protection system— pay top personnel as much as necessary to keep them happy (and quiet), and pay something to as many others as possible to implicate them in the system and to keep them from talking. The range of payoffs thus went from a weekly salary for some public officials to a Christmas turkey for the patrolman on the beat. Records from the numbers bank listed payments totaling $2,400 each week to some local elected officials, State legislators, the police chief, a captain in charge of detectives, and persons mysteriously labeled "county" and "State." While the list of persons to be paid remained fairly constant, the amounts paid varied according to the gambling activities in operation at the time; payoff figures dropped sharply when the FBI put the dice game out of business. When the dice game was running, one official was receiving $750 per week, the chief $100, and a few captains, lieutenants, and detectives lesser amounts.

While the number of officials receiving regular "salary" payoffs was quite restricted (only 15 names were on the payroll found at the numbers bank), many other officials were paid off in different ways. (Some men were also silenced without charge—low-ranking policemen, for example, kept quiet after they learned that men who reported gambling or prostitution were ignored or transferred to the midnight shift; they didn't have to be paid.) Stern was a major (if undisclosed) contributor during political campaigns —sometimes giving money to all candidates, not caring who won, sometimes supporting a "regular" to defeat a possible reformer, sometimes paying a candidate not to oppose a preferred man. Since there were few legitimate sources of large contributions for Democratic candidates, Stern's money was frequently regarded as essential for victory, for the costs of buying radio and television time and paying pollwatchers were high. When popular sentiment was running strongly in favor of reform, however, even Stern's contributions could not guarantee victory. Bob Walasek, later to be as

corrupt as any Wincanton mayor, ran as a reform candidate in the Democratic primary and defeated Stern-financed incumbent Gene Donnelly. Never a man to bear grudges, Stern financed Walasek in the general election that year and put him on the "payroll" when he took office.

Even when local officials were not on the regular payroll, Stern was careful to remind them of his friendship (and their debts). A legislative investigating committee found that Stern had given mortgage loans to a police lieutenant and the police chief's son. County Court Judge Ralph Vaughan recalled that shortly after being elected (with Stern support), he received a call from Dave Feinman, Stern's nephew, "Congratulations, judge. When do you think you and your wife would like a vacation in Florida?"

"Florida? Why on earth would I want to go there?"

"But all the other judges and the guys in City Hall—Irv takes them all to Florida whenever they want to get away."

"Thanks anyway, but I'm not interested."

"Well, how about a mink coat instead. What size coat does your wife wear?"

In another instance an assistant district attorney told of Feinman's arriving at his front door with a large basket from Stern's supermarket just before Christmas. "My minister suggested a needy family that could use the food," the assistant district attorney recalled, "but I returned the liquor to Feinman. How could I ask a minister if he knew someone that could use three bottles of scotch?"

Campaign contributions, regular payments to higher officials, holiday and birthday gifts—these were the bases of the system by which Irv Stern bought protection from the law. The campaign contributions usually ensured that complacent mayors, councilmen, district attorneys, and judges were elected; payoffs in some instances usually kept their loyalty. In a number of ways, Stern was also able to reward the corrupt officials at no financial cost to himself. Just as the officials, being in control of the instruments of law enforcement, were able to facilitate Stern's gambling enterprises, so Stern, in control of a network of men operating outside the law, was able to facilitate the officials' corrupt enterprises. As will be seen later, many local officials were not satisfied with their legal salaries from the city and their illegal salaries from Stern and decided to demand payments from prostitutes, kickbacks from salesmen, etc. Stern, while seldom receiving any money from these transactions, became a broker; bringing politicians into contact with salesmen, merchants, and lawyers willing to offer bribes to get city business; setting up middlemen who could handle the money without jeopardizing the officials' reputations; and providing enforcers who could bring delinquents into line.

From the corrupt activities of Wincanton officials, Irv Stern received little in contrast to his receipts from his gambling operations. Why then did he get involved in them? The major virtue, from Stern's point of view, of the system of extortion that flourished in Wincanton was that it kept down the officials' demands for payoffs directly from Stern. If a councilman was able to pick up $1,000 on the purchase of city equipment, he would demand a lower payment for the protection of gambling. Further-

more, since Stern knew the facts of extortion in each instance, the officials would be further implicated in the system and less able to back out on the arrangements regarding gambling. Finally, as Stern discovered to his chagrin, it became necessary to supervise official extortion to protect the officials against their own stupidity. Mayor Gene Donnelly was cooperative and remained satisfied with his regular "salary." Bob Walasek, however, was a greedy man, and seized every opportunity to profit from a city contract. Soon Stern found himself supervising many of Walasek's deals to keep the mayor from blowing the whole arrangement wide open. When Walasek tried to double the "take" on a purchase of parking meters, Stern had to step in and set the contract price, provide an untraceable middleman, and see the deal through to completion. "I told Irv," Police Chief Phillips later testified, "that Walasek wanted $12 on each meter instead of the $6 we got on the last meter deal. He became furious. He said, "Walasek is going to fool around and wind up in jail. You come and see me. I'll tell Walasek what he's going to buy.' "

Protection, it was stated earlier, was an essential ingredient in Irv Stern's gambling empire. In the end, Stern's downfall came not from a flaw in the organization of the gambling enterprises but from public exposure of the corruption of Mayor Walasek and other officials. In the early 1960's Stern was sent to jail for 4 years on tax evasion charges, but the gambling empire continued to operate smoothly in his absence. A year later, however, Chief Phillips was caught perjuring himself in grand jury testimony concerning kickbacks on city towing contracts. Phillips "blew the whistle" on Stern, Walasek, and members of the city council, and a reform administration was swept into office. Irv Stern's gambling empire had been worth several million dollars each year; kickbacks on the towing contracts brought Bob Walasek a paltry $50 to $75 each week.

OFFICIAL CORRUPTION

Textbooks on municipal corporation law speak of at least three varieties of official corruption. The major categories are nonfeasance (failing to perform a required duty at all), malfeasance (the commission of some act which is positively unlawful), and misfeasance (the improper performance of some act which a man may properly do). During the years in which Irv Stern was running his gambling operations, Wincanton officials were guilty of all of these. Some residents say that Bob Walasek came to regard the mayor's office as a brokerage, levying a tariff on every item that came across his desk. Sometimes a request for simple municipal services turned into a game of cat and mouse, with Walasek sitting on the request, waiting to see how much would be offered, and the petitioner waiting to see if he could obtain his rights without having to pay for them. Corruption was not as lucrative an enterprise as gambling, but it offered a tempting supplement to low official salaries.

Nonfeasance. As was detailed earlier, Irv Stern saw to it that Wincanton officials would ignore at least one of their statutory duties, enforcement of the State's gambling laws. Bob Walasek and his cohorts also agreed to overlook other illegal activities. Stern, we noted earlier, preferred not to get directly involved in prostitution; Walasek and Police Chief Dave Phillips tolerated all prostitutes who kept up their protection payments. One madam, controlling more than 20 girls, gave Phillips et al. $500 each week; one woman employing only one girl paid $75 each week that she was in business. Operators of a carnival in rural Alsace County paid a public official $5,000 for the privilege of operating gambling tents for 5 nights each summer. A burlesque theater manager, under attack by high school teachers, was ordered to pay $25 each week for the privilege of keeping his strip show open.

Many other city and county officials must be termed guilty of nonfeasance, although there is no evidence that they received payoffs, and although they could present reasonable excuses for their inaction. Most policemen, as we have noted earlier, began to ignore prostitution and gambling completely after their reports of offenses were ignored or superior officers told them to mind their own business. State policemen, well informed about city vice and gambling conditions, did nothing unless called upon to act by local officials. Finally, the judges of the Alsace County Court failed to exercise their power to call for State Police investigations. In 1957, following Federal raids on horse bookies, the judges did request an investigation by the State Attorney General, but refused to approve his suggestion that a grand jury be convened to continue the investigation. For each of these instances of inaction, a tenable excuse might be offered—the beat patrolman should not be expected to endure harassment from his superior officers,

State police gambling raids in a hostile city might jeopardize State-local cooperation on more serious crimes, and a grand jury probe might easily be turned into a "whitewash" in the hands of a corrupt district attorney. In any event, powers available to these law enforcement agencies for the prevention of gambling and corruption were not utilized.

Malfeasance. In fixing parking and speeding tickets, Wincanton politicians and policemen committed malfeasance, or committed an act they were forbidden to do, by illegally compromising valid civil and criminal actions. Similarly, while State law provides no particular standards by which the mayor is to make promotions within his police department, it was obviously improper for Mayor Walasek to demand a "political contribution" of $10,000 from Dave Phillips before he was appointed chief in 1960.

The term "political contribution" raises a serious legal and analytical problem in classifying the malfeasance of Wincanton officials, and indeed of politicians in many cities. Political campaigns cost money; citizens have a right to suport the candidates of their choice; and officials have a right to appoint their backers to noncivil service positions. At some point, however, threats or oppression convert legitimate requests for political contributions into extortion. Shortly after taking office in the mid-1950's, Mayor Gene Donnelly notified city hall employees that they would be expected "voluntarily" to contribute 2 percent of their salary to the Democratic Party. (It might be noted that Donnelly never forwarded any of these "political contributions" to the party

treasurer.) A number of salesmen doing business with the city were notified that companies which had supported the party would receive favored treatment; Donnelly notified one salesman that in light of a proposed $31,000 contract for the purchase of fire engines, a "political contribution" of $2,000 might not be inappropriate. While neither the city hall employees nor the salesmen had rights to their positions or their contracts, the "voluntary" quality of their contributions seems questionable.

One final, in the end almost ludicrous, example of malfeasance came with Mayor Donnelly's abortive "War on the Press." Following a series of gambling raids by the Internal Revenue Service, the newspapers began asking why the local police had not participated in the raids. The mayor lost his temper and threw a reporter in jail. Policemen were instructed to harass newspaper delivery trucks, and 73 tickets were written over a 48-hour period for supposed parking and traffic violations. Donnelly soon backed down after national news services picked up the story, since press coverage made him look ridiculous. Charges against the reporter were dropped, and the newspapers continued to expose gambling and corruption.

Misfeasance. Misfeasance in office, says the common law, is the improper performance of some act which a man may properly do. City officials must buy and sell equipment, contract for services, and allocate licenses, privileges, etc. These actions can be improperly performed if either the results are improper (e.g., if a building inspector were to approve a home with defective wiring or a zoning board to authorize a variance which had no justification in terms of land usage) or a result is achieved by improper procedures (e.g., if the city purchased an acceptable automobile in consideration of a bribe paid to the purchasing agent). In the latter case, we can usually assume an improper result as well—while the automobile will be satisfactory, the bribe giver will probably have inflated the sale price to cover the costs of the bribe.

In Wincanton, it was rather easy for city officials to demand kickbacks, for State law frequently does not demand competitive bidding or permits the city to ignore the lowest bid. The city council is not required to advertise or take bids on purchases under $1,000, contracts for maintenance of streets and other public works, personal or professional services, or patented or copyrighted products. Even when bids must be sought, the council is only required to award the contract to the lowest responsible bidder. Given these permissive provisions, it was relatively easy for council members to justify or disguise contracts in fact based upon bribes. The exemption for patented products facilitated bribe taking on the purchase of two emergency trucks for the police department (with a $500 campaign contribution on a $7,500 deal), three fire engines ($2,000 was allegedly paid on an $81,000 contract), and 1,500 parking meters (involving payments of $10,500 plus an $880 clock for Mayor Walasek's home). Similar fees were allegedly exacted in connection with the purchase of a city fire alarm system and police uniforms and firearms. A former mayor and other officials also profited on the sale of city property, allegedly dividing $500 on the sale of a crane and $20,000 for approving the sale, for $22,000, of a piece of land immediately resold for $75,000.

When contracts involved services to the city, the provisions in the State law regarding the lowest responsible bidder and excluding "professional services" from competitive bidding provided convenient loopholes. One internationally known engineering firm refused to agree to kickback in order to secure a contract to design a $15 million sewage disposal plant for the city; a local firm was then appointed, which paid $10,700 of its $225,000 fee to an associate of Irv Stern and Mayor Donnelly as a "finder's fee." Since the State law also excludes public works maintenance contracts from the competitive bidding requirements, many city paving and street repair contracts during the Donnelly-Walasek era were given to a contributor to the Democratic Party. Finally, the franchise for towing illegally parked cars and cars involved in accidents was awarded to two garages which were then required to kickback $1 for each car towed.

The handling of graft on the towing contracts illustrates the way in which minor violence and the "lowest responsible bidder" clause could be used to keep the bribe payers in line. After Federal investigators began to look into Wincanton corruption, the owner of one of the garages with a towing franchise testified before the grand jury. Mayor Walasek immediately withdrew his franchise, citing "health violations" at the garage. The garageman was also "encouraged" not to testify by a series of "accidents"—wheels would fall off towtrucks on the highway, steering cables were cut, and so forth. Newspaper satirization of the "health violations" forced the restoration of the towing franchise, and the "accidents" ceased.

Lest the reader infer that the "lowest responsible bidder" clause was used as an escape valve only for corrupt purposes, one incident might be noted which took place under the present reform administration. In 1964, the Wincanton School Board sought bids for the renovation of an athletic field. The lowest bid came from a construction company owned by Dave Phillips, the corrupt police chief who had served formerly under Mayor Walasek. While the company was presumably competent to carry out the assignment, the board rejected Phillips' bid "because of a question as to his moral responsibility." The board did not specify whether this referred to his poor corruption as chief or his present status as an informer in testifying against Walasek and Stern.

One final area of city power, which was abused by Walasek et al., covered discretionary acts, such as granting permits and allowing zoning variances. On taking office, Walasek took the unusual step of asking that the bureaus of building and plumbing inspection be put under the mayor's control. With this power to approve or deny building permits, Walasek "sat on" applications, waiting until the petitioner contributed $50 or $75, or threatened to sue to get his permit. Some building designs were not approved until a favored architect was retained as a "consultant." (It is not known whether this involved kickbacks to Walasek or simply patronage for a friend.) At least three instances are known in which developers were forced to pay for zoning variances before apartment buildings or supermarkets could be erected. Businessmen who wanted to encourage rapid turn-over of the curb space in front of their stores were told to pay a police sergeant to erect "10-minute parking" signs. To repeat a caveat stated earlier, it is impossible to tell whether these kickbacks were demanded to expedite legitimate requests or to approve improper demands, such as a variance that would hurt a neighborhood or a certificate approving improper electrical work.

All of the activities detailed thus far involve fairly clear violations of the law. To complete the picture of the abuse of office by Wincanton officials, we might briefly mention "honest graft." This term was best defined by one of its earlier practitioners, State Senator George Washington Plunkitt who loyally served Tammany Hall at the turn of the century.

> There's all the difference in the world between [honest and dishonest graft]. Yes, many of our men have grown rich in politics. I have myself.
>
> I've made a big fortune out of the game, and I'm gettin' richer every day, but I've not gone in for dishonest graft—blackmailin' gamblers, saloonkeepers, disorderly people, etc.—and neither has any of the men who have made big fortunes in politics.
>
> There's an honest graft, and I'm an example of how it works. I might sum up the whole thing by saying: "I seen my opportunities and I took 'em."
>
> Let me explain by examples. My party's in power in the city, and it's goin' to undertake a lot of public improvements. Well, I'm tipped off, say, that they're going to lay out a new park at a certain place.
>
> I see my opportunity and I take it. I go to that place, and I buy up all the land I can in the neighborhood. Then the board of this or that makes its plan public, and there is a rush to get my

land, which nobody cared particular for before.

Ain't it perfectly honest to charge a good price and make a profit on my investment and foresight? Of course, it is. Well, that's honest graft.

While there was little in the way of land purchasing—either honest or dishonest—going on in Wincanton during this period, several officials who carried on their own businesses while in office were able to pick up some "honest graft." One city councilman with an accounting office served as bookkeeper for Irv Stern and the major bookies and prostitutes in the city.

Police Chief Phillips' construction firm received a contract to remodel the exterior of the largest brothel in town. Finally one councilman serving in the present reform administration received a contract to construct all gasoline stations built in the city by a major petroleum company; skeptics say that the contract was the quid pro quo for the councilman's vote to give the company the contract to sell gasoline to the city.

How Far Did It Go? This cataloging of acts of nonfeasance, malfeasance, and misfeasance by Wincanton officials raises a danger of confusing variety with universality, of assuming that every employee of the city was either engaged in corrupt activities or was being paid to ignore the corruption of others. On the contrary, both official investigations and private research lead to the conclusion that there is no reason whatsoever to question the honesty of the vast majority of the employees of the city of Wincanton. Certainly no more than 10 of the 155 members of the Wincanton police force were on Irv Stern's payroll (although as many as half of them may have accepted petty Christmas presents—turkeys or liquor). In each department, there were a few employees who objected actively to the misdeeds of their superiors, and the only charge that can justly be leveled against the mass of employees is that they were unwilling to jeopardize their employment by publicly exposing what was going on. When Federal investigators showed that an honest (and possibly successful) attempt was being made to expose Stern-Walasek corruption, a number of city employees cooperated with the grand jury in aggregating evidence which could be used to convict the corrupt officials.

Before these Federal investigations began, however, it could reasonably appear to an individual employee that the entire machinery of law enforcement in the city was controlled by Stern, Walasek, et al., and that an individual protest would be silenced quickly. This can be illustrated by the momentary crusade conducted by First Assistant District Attorney Phil Roper in the summer of 1962. When the district attorney left for a short vacation, Roper decided to act against the gamblers and madams in the city. With the help of the State Police, Roper raided several large brothels. Apprehending on the street the city's largest distributor of punchboards and lotteries, Roper effected a citizen's arrest and drove him to police headquarters for proper detention and questioning. "I'm sorry, Mr. Roper," said the desk sergeant, "we're under orders not to arrest persons brought in by you." Roper was forced to call upon the State Police for aid in confining the gambler. When the district attorney returned from his vacation, he quickly fired Roper "for introducing politics into the district attorney's office."

If it is incorrect to say that Wincanton corruption extended very far vertically into the rank and file of the various departments of the city—how far did it extend horizontally? How many branches and levels of government were affected? With the exception of the local Congressman and the city treasurer, it seems that a few personnel at each level (city, county, and State) and in most offices in city hall can be identified either with Stern or with some form of free-lance corruption. A number of local judges received campaign finances from Stern, although there is no evidence that they were on his payroll after they were elected. Several State legislators were on Stern's payroll, and one Republican councilman charged that a high-ranking State Democratic official promised Stern first choice of all Alsace County patronage. The county chairman, he claimed, was only to receive the jobs that Stern did not want. While they were later to play an active role in disrupting Wincanton gambling, the district attorney in Hal Craig's reform administration feared that the State Police were on Stern's payroll, and thus refused to use them in city gambling raids.

Within the city administration, the evidence is fairly clear that some mayors and councilmen received regular payments from Stern and divided kickbacks on city purchases and sales. Some key subcouncil personnel frequently shared in payoffs affecting their particular departments —the police chief shared in the gambling and prostitution payoffs and received $300 of the $10,500 kickback on parking meter purchases. A councilman controlling one department, for example, might get a higher percentage of kickbacks than the other councilmen in contracts involving that department.

THE FUTURE OF REFORM IN WINCANTON

When Wincantonites are asked what kind of law enforcement they want, they are likely to say that it is all right to tolerate petty gambling and prostitution, but that "you've got to keep out racketeers and corrupt politicians." Whenever they come to feel that the city is being controlled by these racketeers, they "throw the rascals out." This policy of "throwing the rascals out," however, illustrates the dilemma facing reformers in Wincanton. Irv Stern, recently released from Federal prison, has probably, in fact, retired from the rackets; he is ill and plans to move to Arizona. Bob Walasek, having been twice convicted on extortion charges, is finished politically. Therefore? Therefore, the people of Wincanton firmly believe that "the problem" has been solved —"the rascals" have been thrown out. When asked, recently, what issues would be important in the next local elections, only 9 of 183 respondents felt that clean government or keeping out vice and gambling might be an issue. (Fifty-five percent had no opinion, 15 percent felt that the ban on bingo might be an issue, and 12 percent cited urban renewal, a subject frequently mentioned in the papers preceding the survey.) Since, under Ed Whitton, the city is being honestly run and is free from gambling and prostitution, there is no problem to worry about.

On balance, it seems far more likely to conclude that gambling and corruption will soon return to Wincanton (although possibly in less blatant forms) for two reasons—first, a significant number of people want to be able to gamble or make improper deals with the city government. (This assumes, of course, that racketeers will be available to provide gambling if a complacent city administration permits it.) Second, and numerically far more important, most voters think that the problem has been permanently solved, and thus they will not be choosing candidates based on these issues, in future elections.

Throughout this report, a number of specific recommendations have been made to minimize opportunities for wide open gambling and corruption—active State Police intervention in city affairs, modification of the city's contract bidding policies, extending civil service protection to police officers, etc. On balance, we could probably also state that the commission form of government has been a hindrance to progressive government; a "strong mayor" form of government would probably handle the city's affairs more efficiently. Fundamentally, however, all of these suggestions are irrelevant. When the voters have called for clean government, they have gotten it, in spite of loose bidding laws, limited civil service, etc. The critical factor has been voter preference. Until the voters of Wincanton come to believe that illegal gambling produces the corruption they have known, the type of government we have documented will continue. Four-year periods of reform do little to change the habits instilled over 40 years of gambling and corruption.

part nine

THE POLLUTERS

Some say that the United States is paying the price of being an industrialized society. Others argue that the irresponsibility of government and big business has led to the current state of affairs. Still others maintain that it is a consequence of our lack of concern with the environment that supports us and the needs of future generations. In any event, we have become a society in which not only are the offenses of dirt, filth, and smog ordinary, but our lives are literally in danger of being shortened, and we are losing opportunities for enjoying the gifts of nature because of man-made pollution. Pollution is everywhere: in our streams and our atmosphere, in the litter on the road and the odors in our air, in the food we eat and the water we drink.

Only in the past several years has a significant portion of the American population manifested concern. Pollution did not begin recently; it has persisted and increased over past generations of people who have utilized woods and watersheds, sacrificed wildlife, and dirtied our environment. Now foods have been taken off the market; populations of several large cities have been alert to the danger of smog and pollution; and a number of prosperous businesses have been forced to close or alter their work programs because of the interference of pollution.

Although there is considerable talk about the means for reducing the various pollutants in our environment, it is difficult to take constructive action rapidly. Part of the problem is the reluctance of large businesses to cooperate and to change various products because of profit-making motives. In part it is because many citizens desire goods whose manufacture and use cause various orders of pollution. And part is due to the growth of population and hesitancy to impose too rigorous a population policy in a society where choice of number of children is considered a basic right of the parents. Given the state of affairs it is inevitable that serious social conflicts ensue.

INDIVIDUAL vs. INDIVIDUAL	INDIVIDUAL vs. ORGANIZATION

THE FOX

In the case of some social problems, individuals become so incensed that they dare to act on their own. Some do this by developing, or attempting to develop, new organizations or at least informal groups that can put pressure on the political scene for social change. Others already have economic or political power and influence and exercise it to shape things more as they want them. But some individuals simply go ahead and act entirely on their own. This is so in the case of the Fox, a middle-aged man who has made the community and the nation aware of some of the problems of pollution. This article, from a national weekly news magazine, describes how the Fox strikes at pollution by attacking individual businessmen, some of whom are, hopefully, in a position to act on the problems of the environment.

THE BETTER EARTH

Individuals find it difficult to combat problems such as pollution on their own, for basically it is not other individuals whom they must combat but large organizations and urban communities as a whole. While there are a few, like the Fox, who are content to strike out against particular individuals, most of the time persons provoked about problems such as pollution try to involve others less concerned in their efforts with the hope that strength of numbers will make them more effective. Cliff Humphrey, the subject of the article by Steven Roberts, is an individual determined to thwart man's almost willful destruction of his environment by fighting the many organized forces that contribute to the pollution problem. The article describes his views and the problems he encounters in his attempts to organize and lead others in the cause. Hopefully, such efforts may give momentum to a movement towards a better earth.

| ORGANIZATION vs. INDIVIDUAL | ORGANIZATION vs. ORGANIZATION |

THE FIRST VICTIMS

A number of separate industries are often accused of being major sources of pollution. One such industry that has been in the public eye in the past several years has been the oil industry. Off-shore oil wells and damaged oil tankers have contaminated the ocean's shores again and again with oil slicks that destroy birds and fish and the opportunities for persons to enjoy the recreational pleasures provided by the sea. Not only have our natural resources been damaged, but individuals' livelihoods have been severely hurt. In this article, Charles and Bonnie Remsberg describe the impact of a large organization on a fisherman, an impact felt emotionally and economically by the unanticipated consequences of off-short drilling for oil.

THE PUBLIC BE DAMMED

The victims here are community members everywhere in the United States. This is a report of the pervasive activities of the United States Army Corps of Engineers who, in their role as builders of dams and bridges, and as a federal unit responsible for such matters as flood control, have had a tragic effect on our wildlife and our natural environment. The Army Corps of Engineers in many ways receives the enthusiastic support of members of our Federal Congress, for Congressmen use this organization to mold things in their districts, and the White House permits such activities to take place when it is to political advantage. Despite its efficiency and the utility of many of its programs, the Corps often does what is politically expedient, and pragmatic concerns of the moment tend to overshadow the natural investment in conservation and ecology. This article, describing the conflict between this organization and the community, is written by William Douglas, Justice of the United States Supreme Court. Perhaps no man in a lesser position could dare to be so direct and sharp in his commentary.

The Fox

NEWSWEEK MAGAZINE

Most of the time he is just another mild-mannered family man living in Aurora, Ill., a small city west of Chicago. But occasionally, unpredictably, he becomes—The Fox, unremitting foe of those who would befoul America by air, land or sea, a kind of Scarlet Pimpernel of the war on pollution. During the past year and a half The Fox has crawled up an industrial sewage pipe that was spewing sudsy wastes into a stream and clogged the outlet with a plywood bulkhead; he has scaled a factory's towering smokestack and capped it with a homemade metal stopper; and he has deposited dead skunks on the front porches of executives who work for companies responsible for the pollution. Each time he has left behind a handwritten note to explain his acts —and each note has been signed: "The Fox."

The Fox's one-man battle against industrial blight, which has already made him something of a legend among ecologically minded Chicagoans, apparently sprang from a frustration familiar to millions of Americans. As he explained it by phone to NEWSWEEK's Don Holt last week (without, in the process, dropping so much as a single clue to his identity), The Fox had grown appalled by the systematic destruction of his favorite

Reprinted by permission from *Newsweek Magazine.* Copyright Newsweek, Inc., October 5, 1970 and January 11, 1971.

fishing preserve—the Fox River, a once-lovely waterway that meanders through Aurora to the Illinois River. Today a flood of wastes from proliferating industrial plants in the area has transformed the river into a brackish, odorous and fish-less mess. "Nobody ever stuck up for that poor, mistreated stream," The Fox told Holt. "So I decided to do something in its name."

Up until this month, The Fox had confined his guerrilla raids to nighttime and to the area immediately around Aurora. But then two weeks ago, a husky, middle-aged man wearing ordinary work clothes and sunglasses walked into the reception room of the U.S. Reduction Co. in East Chicago, Ind., and dumped a can containing 50 pounds of raw sewage on the tile floor. As horrified secretaries fled the nauseating smell, the man wordlessly handed a note to a shrieking receptionist and calmly walked out. The note denounced the water pollution caused by an aluminum company in Aurora that is owned by U.S. Reduction. It was signed: "The Fox."

LAWBREAKER

Although newspaper publicity about his forays has won The Fox plaudits from many, the police remain singularly unenchanted by him. Despite the quixotic nature of his crimes, The Fox is, after all, a lawbreaker—and one whose identity remains known only to a few like-minded friends. "If we catch him we could charge him with trespassing and criminal damage to property," growled police sergeant Robert Kollwelter as he perused the thick "Fox" folder he keeps in his desk. Kollwelter and his fellow Fox hunters think that they have at least a minor clue as to their quarry's identity. The expert construction of the plywood bulkhead that The Fox used to plug up the sewage pipe leads them to conclude that he has to be a carpenter—and a pretty good one, at that. (The Fox concedes that he does indeed know something about carpentry, but he insists that he doesn't carry a union card.) But beyond this, Kollwelter admits that he has been at least temporarily outfoxed. "It's kind of hard," he explains ruefully, "to lift fingerprints from the inside of a sewer."

It is perhaps a reflection of the times that some of Kollwelter's colleagues attribute The Fox's success and their failure to run him down to the probability that the whole thing is some sort of underground, do-gooder conspiracy. "It has to be some kind of anti-pollution committee," maintains one policeman. "I think we'll find that there are many Foxes." (Although The Fox admits to Holt that a few close friends occasionally lend various forms of assistance, he chuckles over the charge that he is only one of a pack. "My biggest raid consisted of two of us," he says. "That's when we climbed the smokestack. I needed help to both measure it and fit the cap over the top.")

DIGNITY

Even orthodox environmentalists, while far more sympathetic to The

Fox's aims than the police, are dubious about the long-term effects of this kind of guerrilla action. "I understand the guy's frustrations," says Joe Karaganis, a young lawyer in the state attorney general's office. "But the whole thing has broader implications. What if somebody takes the next illogical step and throws a bomb?" Such talk clearly appalls The Fox, who considers himself to be neither a revolutionary nor a criminal. "Who's breaking the law anyway?" he demands emphatically. "Do you know where I got that raw sewage I dumped at U.S. Reduction? I just went down to the Fox River and took what came out of their pipes." And although he admits to being so nervous before a raid that he sometimes vomits, The Fox intends to keep right on playing The Fox. "There is a dignity about nature," he says, his voice somber and earnest. "Man can exploit it but he shouldn't ruin it. I'm trying to stop something that is wrong —and I'm willing to go my own route to do it."

Over the holidays, the Fox struck again. Appearing at the Chicago offices of the U.S. Steel Corp. as a representative of the "Fox Foundation for Conservation Education," he said he had come to give the company an "award." Whereupon he unscrewed the top of a jar and proceeded to pour a foul-smelling liquid all over the office carpeting. Then, as secretaries ran around screaming for help, he slapped a sticker on the office door ("Go Fox/Stop Pollution") and fled.

This time, however, the Fox had insured a public record of his visit by tipping off Chicago Daily News columnist Mike Royko, who dispatched a photographer to catch the act. But company executives, out to lunch at the time, weren't so amused. "A prank is one thing, but this was no prank," said vice president Edward Logelin. "He splashed that stuff on one of the girls. We don't even know what it is. We'll have her examined."

What it was, as any puddler could smell, was some of the effluent that the company itself pours into Lake Michigan in Gary, Ind. "They keep saying that they aren't really polluting our water," the Fox told Royko later on. "If that's true, then it shouldn't hurt his rug, right?"

Right or wrong, such escapades are clearly close to catching on. A few days after the U.S. Steel caper, a sign appeared on a telephone pole in Bishop's Woods, a pristine patch of greenery near Milwaukee that the Roman Catholic archdiocese is thinking of selling for development as an office park. "There are more squirrels in City Hall than in Bishop's Woods," the note said. It was signed by a paw print and someone who called himself "the Bear."

The Better Earth

STEVEN V. ROBERTS

The house at 3029 Benvenue is out of an earlier, quieter time. High-pitched roof; brown shingles; large, airy rooms; bright flowers in the yard. It is the kind of house that sends real-estate developers scurrying for their adding machines, their heads whirling with estimates on how many cinder-block apartments they could cram onto the lot. Near the door, drawn in black script on white cardboard, is this sign: "If you came by car to Benvenue, in the future we would appreciate it very much if you would come by some alternate locomotion—walking, bicycle or public transportation. If coming by car

From *The New York Times Magazine*, March 29, 1970. © 1970 by The New York Times Company. Reprinted by permission.

is unavoidable, please remember, as a courtesy to neighbors who would like us to minimize noise and fumes, to park on College (near Woolsey is generally easy) and to walk around to the house. Enjoy the walk!"

This is the headquarters of Ecology Action, one of dozens of groups now fighting the battle for a better environment in the San Francisco Bay area. What makes Ecology Action different is its style—brash, activist, radical. If the Sierra Club is the N.A.A.C.P. of environmental groups, Ecology Action is a cross between SNCC—when it was still nonviolent —and the Yippies. Its activists generally share neither the bitterness nor the violence of some New Leftists; they'd sooner say, "Enjoy the walk," than scream, "Up against the wall."

Ecology Action was started by Cliff Humphrey, a student of archeology, and some friends two years ago, long before even the sophisticated denizens of Berkeley (which has been called "one big social laboratory") knew what "ecology" meant—the study of man's relationship to his environment. "When Cliff first started talking ecology," says his wife, Mary, in a voice still reminiscent of her Boston Irish heritage, "they thought he was an idiot."

But today, Ecology Actionists find themselves riding a tidal wave of interest in the environment, a wave that threatens to drown them even as it hurtles them toward prominence. Each day's mail—it is carted from the Post Office by bike—contains a flood of requests for information, literature or speakers. Humphrey likes to talk about Ecology Action as "a movement rather than an organization," and local groups—there are more than 100, and new ones form weekly—are virtually autonomous. But they invariably look to the founding fathers for guidance, and the pressures are enormous.

The house on Benvenue provides office space as well as living quarters for the Humphreys and about 10 full-time volunteers. Many of them are conscientious objectors who—with the approval of their draft boards after the state decided that the project served the national interest—are performing their two years of alternate service.

The center of activity in the house is the basement. After getting past the sign at the door, the visitor is confronted with a large poster of a noble, if somewhat apprehensive, Indian. The first Americans have become the culture heroes of the ecology movement. As Mary explained, "the

Indians lived in harmony with this country and they had a reverence for the things they depended on." There were petitions to sign—against smog and a new bridge over the Bay, for the "valid claims" of the Indians on Alcatraz—and a canister for contributions to the "Planet Earth Defense Fund." A hand-printed sign warned: "We are already five years into the biosphere self-destruct era."

Cliff and I went upstairs to talk. He is 32 but looks older, with a rough complexion and longish, sandy hair. He was dressed in a beige knit shirt adorned with dirt spots and a little hole, and brown slacks; on his belt he wore a leather holster that carried a notebook. After junior college training in engineering and three years in the Army he worked, he hesitates to admit, checking freeway construction as an inspector for the State Division of Highways. He went back to the University of California here to study archeology, and in his first course wrote a paper on the Cheyenne Indians. "That was the switch, right there," he explained in his rapid, excitable way. "A lot of things fell into place. I realized the importance of ecology—and the relation of the Plains Indians to their environment." The era of confrontation politics was starting in the Bay area, and Humphrey, although never a leader, was "in the streets" for many of the antiwar, antiuniversity demonstrations. A combination of these political activities and his academic interests led to the formation of Ecology Action.

The basic point, Humphrey said, "is that the biosphere, the life-support system for the earth, is finite and fragile. Once you understand that, the ethics of the movement follow. Through the fifties and sixties, the basic premise of our society was that growth was good—bigger and better everything! But now that premise is changing, it's being replaced by an idea more simple and more universal: the ability of the planet to support life can't be diminished. You can have complete freedom as long as you don't destroy the common life-support system.

"Everywhere I speak I say we have a vested interest in our own destruction," Humphrey went on. "When the stock market goes up it is a signal device warning us of the imminent destruction of some part of the environment. Capitalism is predicated on money and growth, and when you're only interested to maximize profits, you maximize pollution. We need a system that takes maximum care of the earth."

Despite such statements, Humphrey is hardly a doctrinaire Marxist or a knee-jerk America-hater. He is simply an ecologist, and ecologists tend to ignore political barriers; their enemy is man himself.

"You can't really blame the stock market," Humphrey continued. "Our culture evolved in almost total ignorance of ecological absolutes. The New Left rhetoric is so simplistic. There was no conspiracy to get us into this mess. People in the establishment never had a choice. Henry Ford never realized when he started the assembly line that in 1970 people in Los Angeles would be dying from emphysema caused by his cars. But injecting our new understanding into an old value system will cause a lot of tragedy. Take a guy who owns a hardware store. He's probably honest as the day is long—he'd run after you with your change. But his idea is to maximize his profit. How do you tell

him that if the best interests of the people were considered, he should probably sell as little as possible?"

This is one of the great debates in the ecology movement: Growth vs. the Good Life, Quantity vs. Quality. Most Americans, it seems, still believe that technology can eradicate the problems it has caused. As Dr. Lee S. DuBridge, President Nixon's science adviser, told a conference in Los Angeles recently: "I strongly reject the idea that we have to destroy our technological civilization, deflate and decrease the standard of living, to improve the quality of life. There may be a few who would like to return to the days of the cave man, but most of us believe that men live healthier, more pleasant lives than they did 10,000 years ago, or even 100 years ago."

Cliff Humphrey thinks DuBridge is not only wrong, but irrelevant. What he and many ecologists believe is that society must undergo a "cultural transformation," a move away from the ideals of growth, consumption and progress. "At this moment, Western society is having a cumulative impact on the planet," he explained. "If we continue this way we'll run the life-support system down to zero. Survival can't be voted into existence, it has to be lived."

For the Humphreys, ecological soundness begins at home. The residents of Benvenue live on a budget of about $1,500 a month, including $500 for mortgage payments. The $4,000 down-payment on the house, like almost all their income, came from donations, which are seldom enough. "We spend zero for salaries," Humphrey said. "If we have to fix a bike, or someone needs a new pair of pants, we do it, but no salaries."

The household is now down to two gasoline-powered cars, one truck—which runs on propane gas—and eight bikes. They have to allow more time for travel than they would with a more conventional fleet, but there are advantages. "The pace has gotten so fast around here there is a great lack of privacy," Cliff said. "Now most of the time the family is together is when we're traveling around on some public transportation system." Mary has four children, but she quickly points out that three are by a previous marriage and don't live with them. "Cliff's not guilty, he has only one natural-born son," she says, as if one were about to question his ecological credentials.

The house buys food in bulk when it can—rice, sugar and flour are available—both to save money and to avoid the containers that hold prepackaged foods. Plastics, in particular, are shunned because they're virtually indestructible. Residents of the house take along their own shopping bags or knapsacks to carry their purchases; when they have to accept paper bags they usually return them to the store. Several Ecology Actionists startled a grocer the other day when they bought some potato chips for a picnic, emptied the contents into their own bags and returned the wrappers on the spot. Though the returnable glass bottle is about as rare these days as a beach without oil, the house finally found a dairy that will deliver milk in reusable containers (waxed paper cartons are almost as hardy as plastic). All cans are crushed and saved in two boxes—one for tin-plated steel, one for aluminum—and eventually sold for recycling. Paper is also divided into categories—newsprint, magazines and "mixed"—then resold.

All glass that cannot be returned is broken for easy storage, then sold.

The organic garbage is buried in the backyard with lawn cuttings to form a compost heap that will eventually decay and enrich the soil. The yard is not big enough for a garden, however, and the group is looking for some land outside town on which to grow their own vegetables—without pesticides, of course. The group members also bake their own bread, which is cheaper and healthier than the store-bought kind, but they are not maniacal about health foods (witness the potato chips).

The use of drugs is a personal decision. Cliff says he has tried marijuana and decided "it does nothing for me," but others feel that such drugs as mescaline, widely known as a "good high," improved their sensitivity to nature and the "unity of all living things."

Considerable energy is spent conserving other kinds of resources. Most of the Ecology Actionists' clothes are candidates for the rag bag—Mary wears a uniform of a red shirt, denim skirt and hiking boots, all spotted with white paint—and everything is repaired until it is totally unusuable. The toilet tank is filled with bricks; less water is allowed in, and thus wasted, with each flush. Residents are also urged not to bathe every day, and some cynics feel this precept helps account for ecology's popularity among the young.

Old pieces of machinery are saved. One resident recently made a new bike from used parts, but the amateur mechanics of Benvenue tried to fix a car with a second-hand clutch plate recently and realized only after four hours' work that they had the wrong size. Driving is considered a rather sinful act, and when someone does take a car out he usually runs a long list of errands to avoid wasteful trips. When the temperature drops, residents put on sweaters instead of turning up the heat.

The office is another bastion of economy. The mail boxes are old tin cans. Envelopes are opened carefully, then reused—with the legend: "Save trees, reuse envelopes." "It won't save a hell of a lot of trees," Cliff concedes, "but it is a conspicuous act of conscience." Much of the organization's literature is printed on paper donated by other groups; when I was there, a stack of old computer paper about three feet high was standing in the hall, awaiting reuse. Sometimes second-hand paper already has a message on one side, and that can cause problems. A batch of ecological tracts showed up at a local high school recently with a Black Panther harangue on the back, and a teacher was almost fired.

A growing number of people around Berkeley practice some of these tricks, but few are as devoted as the Ecology Actionists. Benvenue has become a sort of moral touchstone for the movement. "Everytime I go visit the Humphreys," said one girl in obvious discomfort, "they make me feel like a pig."

Despite the economy measures, money is always scarce, and the group is beginning to look for foundation support. "We're exploring what jobs we can do," Humphrey added. "We might go paint a house together, or learn to convert vehicles to propane, but we won't do it unless we have to. We'd rather stay small and a little on the hungry side."

In addition to the Humphreys, the residents include one other married couple. The rest are young men, most of whom would like to see the sexual imbalance corrected. "It's a little too much like the Boy Scouts," one complained.

Each volunteer is developing a specialty—recycling materials, fundraising, speech-making—but the group seems to take its character from Humphrey. In line with his theory that survival has to be lived, Ecology Action has staged a series of demonstrations—a sort of guerrilla theater—to dramatize the crisis.

One of the Humphreys' early extravaganzas was the public destruction last June of their 1958 Rambler station wagon—which, they quickly note, had a new transmission. "I saw myself talking about ecology and urging people to drive less, and here I had this car," Cliff recalled with obvious relish. "It was so great! We had a minister from some church in Berkeley read something from Isaiah about not worshiping the works of our hands. Then I ceremoniously raised the hood, removed the air filter and smashed the carburetor with a sledge hammer." Mary added, rather sheepishly: "We thought other people would give up their cars, too, but no one did."

The car-smashing was followed in September by Smog-Free-Locomotion Day, a demonstration of fumeless alternatives to the automobile. Hundreds of people paraded through Berkeley on bikes, pogo sticks, stilts, roller skates, shopping carts, skate boards, baby carriages, golf carts and feet. A coffin on wheels, containing an internal combustion engine, led the line of march.

One of the big issues here had been the gradual filling-in of San Francisco Bay. A bill was introduced in the State Legislature to stop the practice, and ecologists of all stripes joined the fray. One Sunday, Ecology Actionists loaded 20 canvas money bags with mud—"unfilling the Bay"—and delivered them to companies with Bay-front real estate who want to continue the filling. The story won front-page headlines.

"Those executives had to face not just a bag of mud, but a bag of mud a million people knew about," Humphrey exulted. "If we're going to get the culture changed, each of us can't just have private knowledge of the problem. Everyone has to know that everyone else knows—that they're being watched—it has to be a public thing." The bill passed.

Humphrey also worries that people are not adequately prepared for the next earthquake, and he is trying to warn them. Ecology Actionists invaded a breakfast given by Mayor Joseph Alioto commemorating the last San Francisco earthquake and handed out little black crosses. The group also staged a march along the Hayward Fault, an earthquake line running through Berkeley, and marked the route with purple crepe paper. It ran, Humphrey recalled, through a hotel, a number of residence halls, the California School for the Blind and Deaf, the university football stadium and the Berkeley City Hall.

In October, the group proclaimed Damn DDT Day in San Francisco. An Ecology Action volunteer, Kathy Radke, dressed as the Grim Reaper, carried a scythe in one hand and her three-month-old son in the other as she walked through the financial district at lunchtime. She was accompanied by Malvina Reynolds, a folk singer, and several people who handed out leaflets detailing the evils of the

pesticides. "People pretended not to notice," Kathy remembered recently, "but I caught them looking out of the corners of their eyes."

Ecology Action's antics have spawned imitators. At San Jose State College, for instance, students recently contributed $2,500 to buy a new yellow Maverick, which they buried at the climax of a week-long "Survival Faire." Some students complained that the burial was "ecologically unsound" because the car was not "biodegradable"—it would not return to its natural components. Black and *chicano* (Mexican-American) students argued that the money could be better spent helping blacks and *chicanos*. In the end, a vote was taken and the car was buried after the students, at the *chicanos'* insistence, put a box of grapes in the back seat as a show of support for striking farm workers.

Future demonstrations could get more disruptive. One idea is a "traffic seminar," in which a large number of people would drive to San Francisco early one morning and occupy all the parking places. The ensuing traffic jam, it is felt, would dramatize the need for more rapid-transit facilities.

Now that ecology has become so popular—the Sierra Club gets at least six job applications a day, and the editor of a music magazine was heard to say recently: "Someday ecology might be as important as rock 'n' roll" —one crucial job is to provide information on what people can do in their own lives. Ecology in Action has developed the concept of a "life house," essentially an information center for a neighborhood. The operators of the "life house" would urge their neighbors to demand returnable containers at the supermarket and tell them how to save refuse and sell it for recycling, to find soaps that do not contain phosphates, to garden without pesticides, form car pools, obtain free trees and plant them, get birth-control information and generally reduce their consumption. Several are functioning in Berkeley and nearby communities. As part of their information program, a contingent of Ecology Actionists are staging a six-week march this spring through California's San Joaquin Valley, stopping in each city to hold a fair or a meeting for local residents.

Life on the ecology front these days is not always peaceful. The field is getting crowded, and some groups are on "power trips," as the local jargon puts it. Humphrey concedes that organizations "tend to horde money and good organizers," but each faction is gradually working out its own role. For example, the Sierra Club, which fought so many conservation battles alone for so long, is now concentrating on legal actions and has more than 50 suits in the courts, including half a dozen against Cabinet officers. "If the Sierra Club didn't exist we would have to be much more structured," Humphrey admits, "and we would have to get into some of the things they're doing. This way we have freedom to do what we want to do."

There are at least three major criticisms of Ecology Action's approach. One is that too many people are too enamored of the "throw-away society" to make many changes in their lives. Humphrey tacitly acknowledged this when he talked about high school students. "They're open to new ideas," he said. "They don't have any vested interests yet. They're not employed and they're not into buying cars."

The second criticism is that a "cultural transformation" and small personal acts might make people feel good, but won't have any significant impact on the chemical companies, the auto manufacturers, the timber companies and other huge polluters of the environment. Humphrey and like-minded ecologists answer that these personal acts help build up a constituency for larger political acts. They point to the passage of the "Save the Bay" bill last spring and the defeat of the timber bill in Congress recently as two examples of the growing political support for legislation that preserves the environment. Moreover, Humphrey feels that if enough people use their power as consumers, they can affect corporate decisions. "There is no way they can make us consume," he insists. But he also admits that there is a gap between what Ecology Action can achieve now and what needs to be done; he foresees the group's becoming more political and hopes to recruit some graduate students doing basic research on environmental problems.

The third criticism extends to all environmentalists. Isn't the new interest in ecology diverting energy and resources from the difficult and frustrating problems of the inner city? And hasn't President Nixon been able to "co-opt" the movement by his rhetorical, if not material, identification with it?

As to the first question, Humphrey and most other ecologists insist that the "environment" must include Watts as well as the redwoods. "Anyone who doesn't still address himself to the old issues—housing, medicine, poverty—is not being honest," he said. "It would be a bad scene if money were siphoned off from a housing program to pay for a park somewhere so that middle-class people could have recreation." But many in the movement also share the urgency of Stephanie Mills, the editor of a new magazine on ecology called Earth Times: "It would be the ultimate cop-out to give all our money to the Black Panthers and then have them all die in 20 years because they couldn't drink the water." One thing that continues to bother people, however, is that any slowdown of the "growth economy" would inevitably be most disastrous to those on the bottom. Ecologists are in the uncomfortable position of telling poor people that affluence and material comfort are not good for them.

As for Nixon's "co-opting" of the movement, few activists take him seriously. "There is a fantastic gap between what men like Nixon and Henry Ford are saying and what they're doing," Humphrey said. "In any case, the President is talking about cleaning up some smoke and dirty water, but that's not what we're concerned with. We're concerned with a whole way of life."

All this does not fully explain the tremendous new interest in environmental issues. To some extent it's a fad, specially among politicians. "A lot of them are the same guys who wore Davy Crockett hats when they first came out," said Melissa Shorrock, a recent Russell Sage graduate who is editing the proceedings of an ecology conference. But to many people, it is a very serious matter. One reason for their seriousness is that environmental problems affect everyone. Some are moved toward involvement by a new piece of information or a personal experience. Kathy Radke, who, with her husband, Ted, operates a "life house" in their hometown,

Martinez, described her own conversion: "I was pregnant at the time and I read about DDT and mothers' milk. I was planning to nurse the baby, and it really upset me. The dosage in mothers' milk is greater than in cows' milk!" Ken Cantor, a Ph.D. in biology who works at the Ecology Center, a combination book store and information clearing house in Berkeley, said: "The air pollution around here has been increasing radically from year to year. You're bombarded every day with the fact that you can't see across the Bay anymore. And once one thing like that gets people upset, they start looking at other things, and their concern broadens."

Peggy Datz, who fled a teaching job in Detroit and now also works at the Ecology Center, thinks the moon shot last summer helped stimulate interest. "I don't think a lot of people understood the concept of a finite life-support system before," she said. "You could see very clearly what the resources necessary for life were— they had them on their backs. You couldn't imagine a *deus ex machina* who would always be there." Others talk about seeing the earth photographed from the moon and getting a new sense of its terrible fragility.

Vietnam also helped in several ways. "We got a lot of people who were totally frustrated by the old Peace and Freedom, S.D.S. kind of activity," Humphrey explained. "It's sad in a way, but we wouldn't have gotten such a start if so many people hadn't worried about the war for so many years and found themselves totally unable to get it stopped. There was a potential there for a new thrust. There really is only a limited attention span on any one issue, and all of a sudden here was another way to get it on, to make your concern known."

For others, Vietnam had nurtured a whole new political viewpoint. Steve Cotton, a Harvard law student on leave to work on the Environmental Teach-In April 22, explained: "Many people saw Vietnam as a tragic mistake in American foreign policy, but the more radical kids are saying that it was a natural outgrowth of a system that doesn't care about people, just about profits, about its own expansion and nothing else. There has been a lot of thinking about the system, where it's going and what the alternatives are. Some of it is heavily ideological, but a lot is just a vague sense of unease, of disquiet, that the whole thing is rushing pell-mell in the wrong direction. Environment as the kids conceive it is an expression of that. They're not saying this is a sanitation job, that if we spend enough money we'll scrub it all clean. They don't buy Nixon's rhetoric that this is a mistake or an oversight. The state of the environment is just another symptom of society's corruption, it's what the system is all about."

Jim Hunt, who graduated from Bates College in Maine last June and is now performing his alternate service at Benvenue, agrees with Cotton. For Hunt, Vietnam was a "stepping-stone to ecology," an experience that not only taught him "the incredible amount of energy wasted by the system," but the potential power of grass-roots sentiment. Once he came to California, however, Hunt found that ecology was not just another issue to make speeches and hold rallies about. "It had a profound effect on my life style," said the youth, a native of New Britain, Conn., who edited the newspaper at Bates. "I began to see ways I could purify my life. When I came here there was nothing in my middle-class background I was particularly against, but I began to see how a lot of things in my background could be very destructive—the love of gadgets, concern with speed and convenience. I had been troubled by some of these things, but I never really knew why, or that an alternative existed."

In other words, for some youths ecology is not only a political but a cultural concept, a new "way of life," as Humphrey puts it, a way of fitting all one's dissatisfactions and aspirations into a coherent structure. Like many similar movements, it also provides a community and a sense of purpose for young people who look at their future with an apprehension bordering on terror. The act of giving up an automobile, or even burying the garbage, imparts a certain sense of accomplishment, even righteousness. One young man who found a home at Benvenue is Gregory Voelm, who graduated last spring from Antioch College in Yellow Springs, Ohio, and is also working out his conscientious-objector obligation. Soft-spoken yet fiercely articulate, he described what it was like to graduate from college in June, 1969:

"We were the first protest graduating class. . . . I was frightened of what lay before us. We had demonstrated and marched and screamed trying to change things, but it had never been real. Then all of a sudden we had to be part of that mess. . . . Everywhere I went, all I saw was plastic and McDonald's hamburger stands. I had a feeling of an overwhelmingly hostile environment. I looked for adult models of how you could be happy, and it didn't look like you could. It was very freaky. I had the feeling that after graduation you dropped off the end of the world. Some of my friends went to Canada or Mexico, and others went to communes out in the country. Few of us considered beginning a career—it was just too much to handle. There was a great feeling of meaninglessness, a search for something to grab hold of, some unifying thing, and I found it. Ecology is a good metaphor; it gives a unity to experience."

"At first I thought recycling all that stuff was stupid, but when you do it you feel you are fitting into something, you're taking a positive step toward relating to your environment, and it feels good. What goes under the name of ecology is the answer to alienation. We're alienated from nature and alienated from our ability to relate to each other, to love. But to break down that alienation between the individual and his environment is really a radical thing. When you destroy part of the environment, you have to realize you're destroying part of yourself."

In some cases, the concept of ecology takes over a person's whole life. For several years, Keith Lampe was an activist against the war, counseling draft resistance; then he helped Jerry Rubin and Abbie Hoffman form the Yippies. After the Chicago convention—he carried a tennis racket all week on the theory that the police "would think anyone who played tennis had money and connections" —he moved West with his wife, Judy, and their small daughter, looking for new causes. Allen Ginsberg first interested Lampe in ecology, and several months later his friend Gary Snyder, another poet, dragged him to a conference held by the Sierra Club. "That really put me over the hump,"

recalled Lampe, who was wearing a bunch of plastic string beads around his neck and a little pigtail. "I realized that ecology would be my thing for a while."

Last spring, Lampe, who is in his late 30's, started an ecology newsletter called Earth Read-Out, which he distributes to interested people and underground newspapers. But recently even that has not been satisfying. "I'm leaving for Colorado soon to look for some land," he said, pacing up and down a kitchen that has a magnificent view of San Francisco Bay. "I have to get out of the typewriter thing and into reality. We take this population-food squeeze very seriously, and we're going to go out and grow more food than we can consume. My wife has a trust fund, and we're in a position where we can afford to buy some land, so that's what we think we ought to do." The conversation rambled, but every once in a while Lampe would look up and say: "It's amazing I could do that! Incredible! I'm going to be a farmer?"

"The great thing about ecology as a cause," writes Art Hoppe, the columnist for The San Francisco Chronicle, "is that everybody's guilty." And for people caught up in the cause, it means a lot of hard decisions. The Lampes, for example, decided to have a legal abortion recently. "Having only one child is to ecology what unilateral withdrawal used to be to Vietnam," he said with a laugh. "Having only two children is like favoring a negotiated settlement." (Indeed, it's reached the point in some circles where mothers are made to feel like criminals. "Jesse Unruh said that environment is the motherhood issue of 1970," remarked Ken Cantor during a discussion at the

Ecology Center. "I guess he'll have to revise that; motherhood isn't very popular anymore." Peggy Datz replied, "Apple pie is still all right—as long as there are no cyclamates in it.")

Keith Lampe's decision to leave the city for rural life is not unusual. Thousands of young people across the West have fled urban centers in recent years and set up new communities in remote areas of Oregon, New Mexico, Colorado and California. Their decisions flow from a current that is running very deep in American youth. It is a search for simplicity, for privacy, for meaningful work, for basic pleasures, for harmony with nature, for roots, for wholeness. In a world of piecemeal communities, they want personal communion; in a world of machines, they want magic; in a world of frozen foods and TV sets, they want to bake their own bread and make their own music; in a world where there is never enough time, they want to take time; in a world of computers and assembly lines, they want a place and a job that is their own; instead of concrete, they want trees; instead of money, they want joy; instead of status, they want peace. In a world of fragments, they want to be put back together.

Their search has shown itself in the furor over People's Park here in Berkeley—perhaps the first time many youths were able to create something entirely by themselves. It has shown itself in the phenomenal popularity of "The Whole Earth Catalogue"— the best-selling book in both Berkeley and Cambridge—which contains innumerable suggestions on how to live off the land. And it has shown itself in the entire ecology movement, which in its highest sense is a search for the spiritual values buried by the advent of rationality and technology. "It is really a new religion," Peggy Datz said. "I went camping in the Sierras last summer and we were three days from the nearest road. It did fantastic things for my head. I had a really mystical feeling about being part of a total living community."

Yet as ecologists are groping for a new spirituality, their world is shadowed by their keen perception of impending doom. Everyone has his own scenario for how the world will end— hunger, suffocation, floods, ice. They are usually able to brush the knowledge from their minds, but sometimes it comes rushing back in a black, fearful wave. "I went to a party the other night, and I was watching people dance," said Ken Cantor. "All of a sudden I wondered what would be here in 80 years. I am beginning to cope with the idea of my own death, but this really hit me. Maybe no one will be dancing. Maybe no one will be here at all."

The First Victims

CHARLES AND BONNIE REMSBERG

"Red" Allen first spotted the oil as he steered his old fishing boat through the gathering darkness toward the Santa Barbara, Calif., harbor. "It was running in big, black tide-rips on the ocean surface," he remembers. "I tried to dodge around them, but as I got closer in, the oil got so thick I couldn't keep out of the stuff."

The harbor, ordinarily a scene of tranquil picture-postcard beauty against a backdrop of gentle mountains, was in uproar. Vainly, workmen were struggling to blockade the entrance tides of tarry crude oil sweeping in from the sea. Oil-company maintenance boat crews were frantically spreading straw and chemicals on the water in a desperate attempt to absorb or break up the oil. Birds caught in the goo were washing helplessly against jagged rocks, and many were drowning. Fishermen, angry at being doused with waves of oil churned by a passing maintenance boat, were trying to hurl sharks onto its decks. The gagging stink of oil hung thick in the ocean air.

When Allen finally dropped anchor in a "lake of oil" inside the harbor and went home, "My boots were filled with oil, my clothes and boat were black, it was even in my hair." He told his wife, Josie, "People can't im-

Reprinted by permission of the authors from *Good Housekeeping* (August, 1970), Part III, pp. 138, 141, 142 and parts of 143.

agine what kind of tragedy is happening here."

For more than 30 years, Forrest "Red" Allen, a ruddy-faced 51-year-old grandfather, has been gill-net fishing from the same boat his father had used before him, the 38-foot *Vincent-K*. His main catches come from two seasonal runs of barracuda along the coast and through the scenic Santa Barbara Channel, which stretches 25 miles wide between the shore and a string of islands.

The first of those runs, normally his most lucrative season, was about to begin that evening in February, 1969, when the oil reached Santa Barbara harbor. About a week earlier, a well being drilled in the ocean floor by Union Oil Company from a platform in Federal waters five and a half miles out in the channel had suddenly "blown wild." Thousands of gallons of crude oil had surged out of control to the surface and spread toward shore at the rate of 5,000 barrels a day.

Critics of offshore oil operations had warned before the drilling began that undersea technology is not advanced enough to prevent such catastrophes. But officials of the oil company and the U.S. Department of Interior, which leases out the publicly owned drilling sites, had promised that nothing detrimental would happen. By the time the big leak was reported plugged eleven and a half days after it erupted, however, an estimated 2,000,000 gallons of oil had spurted out; oil slicks covered more than 800 square miles of ocean off Santa Barbara; more than 30 miles of beaches were fouled; thousands of birds were dead or dying, and baby sea lions were starving on the channel islands because their mothers' breasts were so caked with oil they could not nurse.

And Red and Josie Allen, along with his fellow fishermen and their families (many of whom were already deeply in debt for costly fishing gear), were abruptly cut off from their livelihoods.

"Spotters," the pilots of small planes who normally locate schools of fish up and down the coast for the commercial fleet, couldn't see through the oil on the surface. When Red took the *Vincent-K* out in hopes of discovering some fishing place the spotters had missed, he found oil fouling the big kelp beds where the barracuda hide. "Putting a net down in that stuff would ruin it," he explains, "and a net costs $3,000." Anyway, by the time they were brought up through the scum, the fish would have been unsalable. "You just had to sit there with dead birds floating all around you."

His fellow fishermen fared no better. Lobstermen, for example, found their traps on the ocean bottom filled with tarry oil and straw and their buoys soaked beyond salvaging. Trap lines were cut by oil skimmers trying to clean the ocean surface. Crab fishermen found their catch suffocated because the oil covered their gills.

Weeks dragged by and the oil remained on the waters. Red went out time and again, even when the expenses of running the boat began to pinch hard—and always he came back empty-handed. Before long, the Allens had exhausted their savings and were forced into debt. "We were so discouraged every time he came back," says Mrs. Allen. "We wondered if it was ever going to be over."

It was not until May, three months after the well blew, that the ocean was clean enough for Red to lay his nets again. By then the barracuda were gone.

Based on previous years' averages, that episode cost Red at least $5,300 —about half a normal year's income. Now, more than a year later, he and other fishermen claim that their incomes are still running below normal, for oil continues to ooze from fissures opened in the ocean floor by drilling. Last December a ruptured pipeline added to the flow when "safety" devices failed to function properly. Allen still sometimes finds kelp beds clogged. At times chemicals used by oil workers to break up oil slicks around the drilling platforms seem to destroy the nighttime luminescence of organisms on the ocean surface, and Allen depends upon this "fire" to guide him to the fish after dark. Yet, as this is written, Allen and his colleagues have been unable to win settlements from the oil company for any of their lost profits.

Several groups of aroused Santa Barbarans and elected officials are trying to prohibit further drilling and pumping in the channel. They are heartened that responsive California authorities have declared a moratorium on all such operations in state waters, which extend three miles out from the shore. But at this writing, lawsuits, proposed legislation, appeals from the state administration and citizens' petitions to government agencies and the President have produced no tangible results to stop pollution originating in Federal waters.

Federal officials have refused to hold public hearings on the matter even though public waters are involved. They would just "stir up the natives," said one bureaucrat. Instead, the Interior Department, under pressure from the politically powerful oil companies, has arbitrarily cleared the way for *more* drilling and pumping. There are now 13 oil-rig platforms dotting the channel horizon. If all Federal leases off Santa Barbara are exploited fully, there could eventually be more than 4,000 wells sunk there, threatening the channel with an estimated four major oil-drilling blowouts every year, plus countless possible spills from production accidents —a prospect from which the ocean's life might never recover.

As subsequent well leaks, pipeline breaks and tanker accidents in waters off Louisiana, Florida, Massachusetts and Alaska have shown, Santa Barbara is only one coastline area threatened by offshore oil. Worldwide, an estimated 284,000,000 gallons of oil a year empty into the sea.

In Red Allen's world, oil is only one encroaching pollutant. As he travels the coastal waters, he notices kelp beds dying and fish beginning to move in strange, erratic patterns. Some species seem to be disappearing, and the tiny animal life that he used to find in abundance on the ocean bottom seems to be diminishing, too. Recently he caught a grotesquely mis-

shapen sardine, its spawn matted and hard instead of jellylike. Another fisherman showed him a sea bass blinded by deformity. "You can tell there's something in the water that's hurting them," Red says.

Scientists say that these fishermen are beginning to see the long-range by-products of raw, inadequately treated sewage and industrial wastes pouring into the sea from rivers and coastal cities, and of DDT and other pesticides washing down from farmlands and citrus groves. Added are the components of smog that drifts up from cities like Los Angeles and settles into the water.

Red Allen worries that he will be unable to fish if things get worse. He knows, too, that we all depend, for most of our oxygen on the microscopic phytoplankton that live in the ocean. Water pollutants are killing these tiny organisms, some scientists say, and air pollution is shutting out some of the sunlight they need for their vital work.

"Fishing used to be more than just a way to make a living," Allen remembers. "You'd go out and the ocean was like something new, something young. Everything smelled fresh and looked clean. You'd go up the coast and you'd hear big flocks of birds squawking as they fed on bait. It was all *alive*."

It was men like Red Allen, fishermen toughened by years on the sea, who, on the night the oil poured into Santa Barbara harbor, stood on the wharf and wept.

The Public Be Dammed

JUSTICE WILLIAM O. DOUGLAS

"The Army Corps of Engineers is public enemy number one." I spoke those words at the annual meeting of the Great Lakes Chapter of the Sierra Club, early in 1968; and that summary supplied an exclamation point to a long discussion of the manner in which various Federal agencies despoil the public domain.

It is not easy to pick out public enemy number one from among our Federal agencies, for many of them are notorious despoilers and the competition is great for that position. The Tennessee Valley Authority, for example, like the Corps of Engineers, has an obsession for building dams, whether needed or not. Its present plan to wipe out the Little T River and its fertile valley is rampant vandalism. TVA is also probably the biggest strip miner in the country, using much coal for its stand-by steam plants. The sulphuric acid that pours out of strip mines, running downstream waters, is TVA acid.

The Bureau of Mines sits on its hands in Washington, D.C., pretty much a captive agency of the coal-mine owners, and does precious little about strip mining.

The Public Roads Administration has few conservation standards; it

Reprinted by permission from *Playboy Magazine*, July, 1969, pp. 181–88. Copyright © 1969 by Playboy.

goes mostly by engineering estimates of what is feasible and of cost. In the Pacific Northwest, it has ruined 50 trout streams through highway design. Everywhere—East and West—the Administration aims at the heart of parklands, because they need not be condemned, and plays fast and loose with parts of the public domain that were reserved for wildlife and outdoor recreation.

The list is long; and when the names of Federal agencies are all in, the balloting for public enemy number one will not be unanimous. But my choice of the Army Engineers has a powerful case to support it.

The Corps is one of our oldest Federal agencies. It is small and elite, highly political and very effective. It is honest and, with exceptions I will note, quite efficient. It is also largely autonomous and inconsiderate of the requirements of conservation and ecology.

There has been a recurring effort to get rid of it. The Hoover Commission Task Force on Water Resources and Power recommended in 1949 that the functions of the Corps and the Bureau of Reclamation be transferred to the Secretary of a proposed Department of Natural Resources and consolidated there in an agency to be known as the Water Development Service. The training provided "in peacetime for the 215 Army engineers at present utilized on this civilian program can surely be secured in some far less costly fashion."

In 1966, Senators Joseph S. Clark, Lee Metcalf and Frank E. Moss sponsored a bill that would have turned the Department of the Interior into a Department of Natural Resources and transferred the Corps to that new department. But the power of the Corps is so strong that that bill died in committee. Indeed, Senators and Congressmen who are so bold as to urge that the Army Engineers be abolished find themselves wholly out of favor when it comes to projects for their states.

At the time of the Hoover Report, the budget of the Corps was about $440,000,000 a year. It is now 1.3 billion dollars and is expected to reach three billion dollars in the 1980s. So the Corps shows no sign of diminishing political influence.

Its specialty is in pork-barrel legislation on the Hill. It commonly outmaneuvers the President and has its way, irrespective of his wishes. The Corps gave F.D.R. one of his soundest political thrashings. The Corps also has few public critics; it has become one of the sacred cows of Washington.

The Corps farms out many of its research and development projects. There is hardly a Federal agency in Washington that is not offered a piece of it in amounts from $200,000 to $400,000 or more a year. Federal bureaucrats love that kind of money, for they do not have to depend on Congress for it. There is a rule of thumb in Washington that 15 percent of an amount obtained in an appropriation is used for permanent overhead. That means that if agency A receives $500,000 for research on silta-tion, water purification, or what not, it uses $75,000 to add to its permanent personnel and the rest for the current annual project. But agency A, like the other agency donees who receive funds from the Corps, is anxious to have a similar amount, year after year. Therefore, never do they raise their voices against ill-conceived projects; never, when the Corps is throwing its weight around and the public is protesting, do these Federal agencies align themselves with the people.

In the late Fifties, I was a member of a group of conservationists fighting the Corps on the huge River Bend Dam on the Potomac River. The dam was virtually useless as a power project and of no value for flood control. Its justification was the creation of a head of water that could be used to flush the polluted Potomac of sewage. Some of the huge Federal agencies were silently opposed; but none would speak up, for fear of losing the Corps' good will and its research and development funds. We ended by getting an independent engineering study that actually riddled the project. That dam —which would have flooded 80 miles of river and shown a drawdown of 35 vertical feet—would have been known in time as the nation's greatest folly. It would have despoiled a historic river; and the 35-foot vertical drawdown would have resulted in several hundred yards of stinking mud flats exposed to public view. Yet the Corps had the nerve to get a public-relations outfit to make an estimate as to the millions of tourists who would be drawn to this ugly mudhole from all over the East.

The Engineers gave up on River Bend and offered an alternative of an upstream dam at Seneca for water supply. Public hearings exposed its destructive qualities. It, too, would ruin a beautiful free-flowing river. Moreover, there was a growing awareness that dams for municipal water are unnecessary along the Potomac; for the estuary in front of Washington, which is 20 miles long and moved by the tides, contains billions of gallons of potable water, which is all the water the metropolitan area will ever need.

At the peak of its promotional activities along the Potomac, the Corps has plans for 16 big dams and 418 small ones. How many were actually discarded? I do not know. But their active promotion of Potomac river dams has shrunk from 434 to 6. Those six are for water for metropolitan use—a needless expenditure, because of the ample supply of estuary water.

The estuary water is polluted, but so is the entire Potomac. Why not expend our energies and fortunes in building sewage disposal plants, not dams that put fertile bottom lands under muddy waters from now to eternity and drive thousands from their homes?

As I said, the Corps sometimes turns out to be mightier than the Commander in Chief, the President of the United States.

Franklin D. Roosevelt tried to draw the lines of authority governing the Corps quite sharply: If a project was primarily concerned with navigation or flood control, then the Army Corps of Engineers had jurisdiction; if, however irrigation and power were the dominant features of the project, then the Bureau of Reclamation would be in charge. The matter came to a head in 1944, when the Kings River project and the Kern River project—both

part of a development program for California's Great Central Valley— were before Congress. Roosevelt was firmly on record as having said, "I want the Kings and Kern River projects to be built by the Bureau of Reclamation and not by the Army Engineers."

But the Corps had its way before both the House and the Senate. Roosevelt countered by directing the Secretary of War to make no allocation of funds nor submit any estimate of appropriations without clearing the matter with the Bureau of the Budget. F.D.R. provided funds in his new budget only for the Bureau of Reclamation respecting these projects. But before the budget cleared the House, the Army Engineers got included in the budget funds for initial work on the projects.

F.D.R. signed the bill reluctantly, saying he would ask Congress to transfer jurisdiction over all these Central Valley projects to the Department of the Interior. Then he died and Truman took over the problem. The maneuvering against Truman was long and involved. In time, the Corps had pretty much its own way (A) by taking the stump against the White House in California to elicit the support of greedy landowners who wanted the benefit of irrigation without paying the costs as provided by law, and (B) by lobbying in Congress.

Every President has known something of the freewheeling nature of the Corps and its tendency to undercut the White House and curry favor with its friends on the Hill. Early in 1968, it was busy dodging the Bureau of the Budget on six Potomac dams and making its own recommendations to Congress. L.B.J., probably the dearest friend the Corps has had, tried to keep the Engineers in line. But the Corps is incorrigible, violating the fundamental principle that while an administrative agency is the creation of Congress, it must report through the Chief Executive, in order for a centralized, coordinated plan of administration to be successful. Even though the President advises that a Corps project is not in accord with White House policy, the Corps transmits its report to Congress anyway, sometimes, though not invariably, including in the transmittal a statement of the President's position. In this sense, the Corps is *imperium in imperio*, enjoying a status no other administrative agency has.

The Corps goes way back in our history, the present one dating from March 16, 1802. It is a small, elite group of officers, not many over 200 in number. But it supervises over 40,000 full-time civilian employees.

The permanent staff of civilian employees obtains its pay *only* when there is some public-works program to which the salary can be charged. That is why every civilian member is eager to suggest, initiate or create a role for the Corps that will keep everyone employed. In time of war, the Corps has military assignments, but its essential work over the years is concerned with civil functions. The Chief of Engineers is responsible to the Secretary of Defense regarding his civil duties and does not report to the Chief of Staff nor to any general. Actually, the Corps in operation is largely independent of the Secretary.

The committees of the House and Senate through which it operates are the Public Works committees. The inception of a Corps project starts with the Congressman or Senator representing the district where the project will be located. What member of Congress does not want $10,000,000 or, preferably, $100,000,000 coming into his district? He therefore tries to get the item included in an omnibus bill authorizing a preliminary examination. Once that is done, the preliminary examination may or may not be made. The appropriation is in a lump sum and there is usually not enough to make all the investigation authorized. So the Corps, at its own discretion, decides which has priority.

The Corps finally obtained by an act of Congress special permission to spend up to $10,000,000 on any project without approval by Congress, provided the project has been approved by resolutions adopted by the Senate and House committees. This is an advantage shared by no other Federal agency; and it is a measure of the rapport between Congress and the Army Engineers. Moreover, it gives the Corps a tremendous momentum. Once $5,000,000 or $10,000,000 is spent on a project, the pressure to get on with it and finish it is tremendous.

A member of Congress who is in good with the Corps will receive favors; those who may have been critical of it will be kept waiting. The game is boondoggling played for high stakes by clever, cunning men.

There are few members of Congress who do not early learn the lesson that an obsequious attitude pays off when it comes to pumping millions of dollars into a district that may save an election for a deserving Democrat or Republican but destroy a lovely free-flowing river.

The Corps operates in part through NRHC, the National Rivers and Harbors Congress. All members of

Congress are ex-officio members of NRHC. Five of the 21 directors are members of Congress. Ten are national vice-presidents. The all-important operative committees are, with one exception, chaired by members of Congress. At its annual meeting, the National Rivers and Harbors Congress decides which rivers and harbors projects it should present to Congress and then the Congressional members change hats and go to work lobbying one another.

One who is in a campaign opposed to the Corps has very few important allies. I remember the Buffalo River in Arkansas and the Saline River in the same state—both destined by the Army Engineers to be destroyed as free-flowing rivers. The Buffalo I knew well, as I had run it in canoes and fished for bass in shaded pools under its limestone cliffs. Much of the land bordering the Buffalo is marginal wood-lot acreage. Those who own that land were anxious to sell it for a song to Uncle Sam. Chambers of commerce blew their horns for "development" of the Buffalo. Bright pictures were drawn of motels built on the new reservoirs where fishing would abound and water-skiing would attract tourists.

The Corps had introduced Arkansas to at least 14 such river projects that buried free-flowing streams forever under muddy waters. The fishing is good for a few years. Then the silt covers the gravel bars where bass spawn and the gizzard shad—a notorious trash fish—takes over.

The people are left with the dead, muddy reservoirs. There is electric power, to be sure; but Arkansas already has many times the power that it can use. So why destroy the Buffalo? Why destroy the Saline?

What rivers are there left where man can float in solitude, fish, camp on sandspits and rid himself of the tensions of this age? These are questions people are beginning to ask. And these questions eventually won over enough of the Arkansas delegation to save the Buffalo—at least temporarily—but the Saline is still in jeopardy.

Down in Kentucky last year, my wife and I led a protest hike against the plans of the Corps to build a dam that would flood the Red River Gorge. This gorge, which is on the north fork of Red River, is a unique form of wilderness that took wind and water some 60,000,000 years to carve out.

This is Daniel Boone country possessed by bear, deer and wild turkey. It has enough water for canoeing a few months out of the year. It is a wild, narrow, tortuous gorge that youngsters 100 years from now should have a chance to explore.

The gorge is only about 600 feet deep; but the drop in altitude in the narrow gulch produces a unique botanical garden. From March to November, a different wild flower blooms every day along the trails and across the cliffs.

This is wonderland to preserve, not to destroy.

Why should it be destroyed?

Flood control has been brought into the story; but it is a makeshift, for flood control could be achieved with a dam farther downstream that would preserve the gorge. The same can be said for water supply. The real reason: recreation. The Corps and promoters of the dam say that the reservoir will attract tourists who will spend their money in motels, lodges and boat docks. That's the way the dam was sold to the local people, who naïvely expect to get rich by the influx of tourists.

And so Red River Gorge was

doomed for extinction until 1969, when Senator John Sherman Cooper of Kentucky and Governor Louie B. Nunn proposed an alternative plan to save the gorge by putting the dam farther downstream. The Corps, minding its politics, accepted the proposal; and the names Cooper and Nunn have become revered by the Sierra Club and all other conservationists for that move.

(Army Engineers now have plans for the big south fork of the Cumberland in Kentucky. It is one of the very best white-water canoe rivers we have left. It is a wild, unspoiled waterway running through uninhabited lands; and those who know and love it are now mustering their forces for another great contest.)

The Corps is an effective publicist. After my wife and I led the protest march against the Red River Gorge project, we flew back to Washington, D. C. that night. The next day was Sunday; and that morning, every paper I saw had a wire-service story saying that we had been driven out of Kentucky by 200 armed men who did not want "a senile judge" telling them how to run their affairs. It was not until two days later that the conservationists had their statement ready for the press.

The most alarming thing is the very number of dams proposed by the Corps. One of our wild, wild rivers is the Middle Fork of the Salmon in Idaho—a 100-mile sanctuary that should be preserved inviolate like the Liberty Bell. White sandpits make excellent campsites. The waters so abound with trout that barbless hooks should be used. Mountain sheep look down on the river from high embankments. Deer and elk frequent the open slopes. When I ran that scenic river and returned to Washington, I dis-covered that the Engineers had 19 dams planned for the Middle Fork.

The most recently outraged citizens are the Yuki Indians of Round Valley, California. The Corps dam on the Eel River will flood the historic "Valley of the Tall Grass." But what difference do 300 Indians make? "Progress" must go on until we are all flooded out.

The problem with dams is that they silt in: Mud, carried to the dam by its source waters, settles in the reservoir and accumulates steadily. In time, the silt completely replaces the water. The Corps faces this prospect everywhere. Some dams in Texas lose eight percent of their capacity annually due to silting. Numerous ones lose two percent a year and at least six lose three percent or more. Most of those I examined were not Corps dams; but its Texas dams suffer the same fate. Once a dam is silted in, there is no known way to remove the silt and make the dam useful again.

The Waco Dam in Texas is a classic failure of the Engineers. Inadequate testing of the foundation shales below the embankment was the cause of the disaster. Parts of the embankment slid 700 feet from the dam axis. Correcting the failure amounted to about four percent of the original estimated cost of the dam.

The Corps has been embarrased by hush-hush dams that are so leaky that the waters run under—not over—the dams. This failure is due to gypsum beds that underlie the reservoirs, a mineral that seems to baffle the dam builders and causes them to fall into all kinds of traps.

One conservationist, in speaking of a dam that carried water under, not over it, said rather whimsically, "This may be the perfect solution. The Corps and the Congressmen get the facility constructed, the money pours into the district, yet the river valley is saved. We should encourage gypsum bases for all Corps dams."

But the two dams where the water ran under—rather than over—have now been fixed. So the hope to make them monuments to the folly of the Engineers has vanished.

The trend is ominous. The Corps expects by 1980 to flood new areas about the size of Maryland (6,769,280 acres).

I mentioned how the Engineers planned to build a dam on the Potomac to flush the river of sewage. That is by no means the sole example. The Oakley Reservoir on the Sangamon River in Illinois has been proposed to create a huge reservoir that will wash the river of sewage from Decatur on downstream. The trouble is that a reservoir large enough will inundate Allerton Park, a unique bottom land owned by the University of Illinois where valued research in biology and ecology goes forward.

The Corps has curiously become one of our greatest polluters. It is dedicated to the task of dredging channels in rivers and in the mouth of harbors so that vessels can get in and out. These days, the bottoms of channels are not mud but sludge formed from sewage and industrial wastes. The Corps takes these dredgings and dumps them into Lake Michigan. In fact, the lake is used as a dumping ground for 64 separate dredging operations. There was a public uproar in 1967 and 1968 and hearings were held. Lake Michigan is going the way of Lake Erie, which has become a big bathtub full of stinking waste material. Lake Erie is dead; and it is feared that Lake Michigan is on its way.

The dredging of estuaries has had a similarly shocking effect. A third of San Francisco Bay—or 257 square miles—has been filled in or diked off and is now occupied by homes, shopping centers and the like. Oyster production is ended; so is clam production; only a minimal amount of shrimp production remains. There are 32 garbage-disposal sites around the shores of the Bay. Eighty sewage outfalls service the Bay. Daily, over 60 tons of oil and grease enter the estuary, the cradle of the sea. The Army Engineers are not responsible for the pollution; but they are responsible for the dredging. The National Sand and Gravel Association has the estuaries marked for billions of tons of sand and gravel for the next 30 years. The Corps issues dredging permits; and ten years of dredging, according to the experts, makes an estuary a biological desert.

But the Corps has no conservation, no ecological standards. It operates as an engineer—digging, filling, damming the waterways. And when it finishes, America the beautiful is doomed.

The ecologists say that estuaries are 20 times as productive of food as the open sea. An estuary has been called a "nutrient trap." Being shallow, it is exposed to the energy of sunlight. Rooted plants of the land and drifting plants of the sea commingle. Thick beds of grasses, sea lavender, bulrushes and cattails provide hiding areas, as well as food, for minute forms such as diatoms and for young fish, clams, mussels and oysters as well. Indeed, it is estimated that two-thirds of our ocean catch has been estuary dependent for part of its life. The reality is that by the year 2000, California will not have a single running river to the ocean. What will be left, for example, of San Francisco Bay will be dead salt-water sewage.

The Corps seems destined to destroy our estuaries. The estuarine areas of our coast line have distinctive features. South of Boston are salt marshes where flounders spawn and grow to a size that permits their exit to the ocean. Down in Florida, the estuaries attract many species of commercial and sport fish and the valuable pink shrimp as well. The shrimp breed there and the young stay in the estuary until they are large enough to risk the Gulf. And so it goes from estuary to estuary. The estuaries have one thing in common—a balance between fresh water and salt water. Once the fresh water dries up and salinity increases, the estuary is avoided entirely by some species and used by the remaining species for a lesser time.

The results are revolutionary. The birds that are dependent on these sloughs for their feed must leave. The wood ibis, for example, which nests in the mangroves of Florida and feeds on the teeming estuarine life, flourishes when the annual flow of fresh water is 315,000 acre feet or more and does not nest successfully when the flow is less than that amount. Some dominant water-fowl foods— notably chara and naiad—tolerate only mild salinity. They have all but disappeared in Coot Bay in the Everglades, as a result of a Corps canal. With the elimination of those foods, the number of waterfowl in Coot Bay has declined more than nine tenths.

The Cape Fear River development is now booming along in North Carolina. In 1934, the Corps reported that flood control was not justified in the lower Cape Fear basin. In 1947, after a disastrous flood, it again re- ported that no dam was justified. In the 1960s, the Engineers have been saying that Cape Fear flood control is essential. They add that if flood control is not needed, a dam or a series of dams will make great recreational areas. The principal rivers feeding the main reservoir are the Haw and the New Hope, both heavily polluted. The estimated cost will be $72,000,000 plus. Residents of the valleys where 35,000 acres of choice lands will be taken are much opposed. Those are farm units, handed down from generation to generation and greatly loved. It is tragic to hear them talk about the conversion of those gorgeous acres into a gigantic cesspool for raw sewage on which enthusiastic tourists are destined, it is said, to shout with joy.

Since 1936, Federal investment in flood protection, largely through Corps activities, has amounted to more than seven billion dollars. Despite this massive investment, flood damages (according to the President's Task Force that reported in 1966) have been as much as ten times what they were in 1936. The Corps approach is purely an engineering approach. What is needed are conservation standards that regulate land use and reduce the risk that land will be so used as to accentuate run-offs and actually imperil property and lives because of man's grotesque ways of despoiling the earth. But these are no concern of the Corps. It exists to turn rivers into sluiceways and to raise the height of levees, so that man's misuse of the land may be borne by all the taxpayers. The report of the President's Task Force is a severe indictment of the Corps' mentality and techniques in dealing with water.

The disease of pouring money into

a district to do something about water is a pernicious one. The Army Engineers can dredge channels, build levees and erect dams. Getting a man off heroin is easy compared with getting Congress off the kind of pork barrel the Corps administers. On July 30, 1968, Congress approved a one-and-a-quarter-billion-dollar appropriation for the civil activities of the Army Engineers. Forty-seven states were included. Texas, as might be expected, was granted 24 projects for construction during fiscal year 1969 that amounted to almost $40,000,000. Everybody is taken care of: under the cloak of flood benefits, recreation benefits and the like, great vandalism is committed. Beautiful river basins are wiped out forever and one of our most pressing problems—water pollution and sewage—goes begging.

The Everglades National Park in Florida is a unique national treasure. It lies in a shallow limestone bowl not higher than 12 feet above sea level. Its life-blood is the gentle, persistent flow of fresh water from the northern part of Florida, mostly the overflow from Lake Okeechobee. The biological and botanical life of the Everglades is intricate and amazing. The lowly gambusia fish and the alligators are the key, the gambusia feeding on mosquito larvae and starting the food chain for 150 species of fish that, in turn, nourish the alligator. The alligator wallows and forms the mudholes where this chain of aquatic life is maintained. Moreover, within the Everglades are 95 percent of all of our remaining crocodiles.

The birds come to nest and to feed on fish—white-crowned pigeons, white ibis, herons, roseate spoonbills, wood ibis, swallow-tailed kites, great white pelicans, millets, black-necked stilts, boat-tailed grackle, the anhinga, and others almost too numerous to mention. The most vulnerable of all fish is the bass that is dependent on the oxygen in the water. So when there is a drought, bass die by the hundreds. Since the garfish and the bowfin surface to get oxygen, they survive droughts somewhat better. But severe droughts kill everything; and the Corps, with no conservation standards, is the greatest killer of them all.

The park has 47 species of amphibians, all dependent on standing water for reproduction. The reptiles are dependent almost entirely on aquatic food. Of the 200 species of birds in the park, 89 are almost totally dependent on aquatic food. Five thousand pairs of wood storks, for example, require more than 1,000,000 pounds of small live fish to raise 10,000 young. Of the 12 different mammals in the park, most are amphibious or partly so. The 150 species of fish in the park are mostly dependent on estuaries for their existence. The invertebrates are also estaurine. The vegetation of the park is dominantly aquatic.

The Corps decided with the connivance of real-estate developers and prospective tomato farmers to divert all the overflow of Lake Okeechobee to the Atlantic or the Gulf. It sponsored and promoted various canals, which directly or indirectly served that end. Over the years, the Corps juggled costs and benefits—it lowered construction costs though they had risen some 36 percent; it found "land enhancement" values theretofore overlooked; but, naturally, it failed to deduct the destruction of the Everglades, a unique bit of Americana, and beautiful free-flowing streams such as the Oklawaha River, which it would destroy.

Over the past ten years, the toll

on the Everglades has been enormous. The park's alligator population dropped drastically between 1961 and 1966. Thousands of birds and tens of thousands of fish died. Watery expanses of saw grass became stinking mud flats where nothing could live. There were no fish even to feed the young in the rookeries. The rains in 1966 saved the Everglades; but over the years, it cannot survive on rain alone. It needs the oozing fresh water from the north.

The Corps, greatly criticized for bringing the Everglades close to complete destruction, has come up with a plan to provide the park with fresh water—a plan that has just been presented to Congress. The plan is to raise the levees around Lake Okeechobee to provide for additional water storage; it would improve the canal system leading south toward the park to provide additional capacity for conveying water into the park.

But the plan, though noble on its face, utterly lacks schedules showing the guaranteed deliveries of acre feet, come the dry season or drought weather. A contest is on between fresh water for real-estate developers and farmers and the park; and the Army Engineers are strangely allied with economic interests. The concept of the public welfare that those special interests have is how well lined their pockets are with public money.

One of the worst things the Corps is doing is the methodical destruction of our riverways. Some of its plans call for a conversion of river beds into sluiceways that eliminate gravel beds for spawning of fish and islands where birds nest. In the state of Washington, the Corps is bent on destroying the last piece of the native Columbia River.

From Bonneville Dam to Grand Coulee, there are now 11 dams on the Columbia, the only natural part of the river left being a 50-mile stretch from Richland to Priest Rapids. The plans of the Corps to install Benjamin Franklin Dam will destroy that piece of the river, making all of it a big lake or reservoir.

The reason advanced is commercial. It is pointed out that with the locks of Benjamin Franklin, the apple growers of Wenatchee will be able to float their apples to the Portland market. The difficulty is that an apple traveling that distance through that hot, bleak area of eastern Washington would not be edible by the time it reached Portland.

Be that as it may, the Corps would never be building Benjamin Franklin Dam if it had any conservation standards.

This section of the river is the last natural piece of the river left. The spring and summer run of salmon enter *the tributaries* of the Columbia for spawning. But the fall run of the Chinook salmon spawn *in the main bed*; and upstream from Richland are the last spawning grounds left in the main river. Due to the disappearance of other spawning areas, this stretch of the river has become increasingly important. The 20-year average of spawning beds is 902; in 1965, there were 1770 spawning beds; in 1966, 3100; in 1967, 3267. This area now accounts for about 30 percent of all the fall Chinook production. Where they will go if the river becomes a lake, no one knows.

This stretch of the river is also an important breeding ground for small-mouthed and largemouthed bass, white sturgeon and whitefish. It is also a natural spawning ground for steelhead trout, an operation greatly aided by a state hatchery. At least 30,000 steelhead trout a year are produced here; and the summer run is so excellent that sportsmen now catch 11,000 there.

The Benjamin Franklin Dam would wipe out 20 natural islands that are breeding grounds for the Canada goose and for several species of gulls, including the California and the ring-billed. The nesting geese number about 300 adult pairs and they produce about 1000 goslings a year. The dams with their resultant impoundments have greatly reduced, in all of the upper Columbia, the goose population from 13,000 to less than half. With all the dams being completed, the upper Columbia will have fewer than 3500 geese.

The river above Richland accommodates as many as 200,000 wintering waterfowl on a single day. Most of the facilities for these wintering inhabitants will be destroyed by the Benjamin Franklin Dam.

The destruction of these spawning grounds and breeding areas is a form of official vandalism. No Federal agency with any concern for the values of conservation would be implicated in such a senseless plot.

Much of the river to be destroyed is now a part of a reservation of the Atomic Energy Commission, which uses the river to run its plutonium reactors. The AEC knows enough to realize how destructive the plans will be to the Columbia's natural wonders. But the AEC will not promote the dam nor oppose it. It is on the Corps' payroll and, like other similar Federal agencies, it is beholden.

The conservation cause is therefore handicapped. A stalwart group is fighting the dam. But public opinion is difficult to muster, as only a few people can enter the sacred precincts of the AEC reservation. So the river has few knowledgeable friends.

The Corps is now starting a vast internal canal-building project to build waterways into the dry, desert-blown parts of America. What chamber of commerce does not long to make its forgotten city a great port?

Will Rogers used to joke that the best thing to do with the Trinity River at Fort Worth, Texas, was to pave it, the stream being a bare trickle at times. That wild idea is now a reality. Construction of a 370-mile canal from Fort Worth to Houston is under way, with 20 new dams (multipurpose) and 20 locks.

Rogers used to twit the Corps about getting him "a harbor on the Verdigris at Oologah" in Oklahoma. That 1.2-billion-dollar project is now under way—a 539-mile canal reaching into the heart of Oklahoma. The plan includes 18 locks and dams that will lift river traffic 530 feet from the Mississippi to the level of Catoosa, the head of navigation.

In 1967, the Corps approved a $316,000,000 Tennessee–Tomlingbee waterway as justified by a benefit–cost ratio of 1.24 to 1. The Secretary of the Army, Stanley Resor, sent the report to Congress with his own contrary conclusion that the project did not have the requisite "margin of economic safety." But the interested Congressmen ignored Resor's conclusion, did not take the issue to Congress, but in committee ordered the Engineers to start the controversial canal that is to run 253 miles.

The most brazen project of all is known as Mike Kirwan's Big Ditch, linking Lake Erie with the Ohio River. Kirwan is chairman of the subcommittee of the House Appropriations Committee on Public Works.

Eighty-year-old Kirwan has long been a stern opponent of national-park development. "The U.S. owns too much land" is his position. A member of his subcommittee who opposes him is in a perpetual doghouse, never getting any favors of his own. So they all—mostly all—meekly fall into line.

Kirwan's Big Ditch would be 120 miles long, with a 35-mile reservoir to supply the canal with Erie's sewage water. Nearly 90,000 acres of the nation's finest dairy farms would be inundated and more than 6000 people would lose their homes.

The idea is an old one, going back to George Washington; but today the experts think it is utterly worthless.

The Corps benefit–cost ratio was juggled to suit its needs; obvious costs to the tune of at least $170,000,00 were left out. Benefits were rigged. Thus, "recreation" was valued at $17,000,000 a year—a sum that could be reached only if 500,000 sportsmen descended on this stinking sewage water on a normal Sunday.

The Corps approved the project, estimating the cost at over a billion dollars. It let Kirwan make the announcement. Kirwan managed it through the House; and the Senate —without a roll call—approved.

Two million of the needed one billion dollars plus for Mike Kirwan's Big Ditch was in L.B.J.'s budget, a budget in which, L.B.J. said. "Waste and nonessentials have been cut out. Reductions or postponements have been made wherever possible."

And so the skids were greased. But the voice of Pennsylvania spoke up in opposition; and the Big Ditch has been delayed. Yet the momentum is so great in Washington, that if Texas and Oklahoma can have their worthless canals, so can Ohio.

The truth is that our waterways present staggering problems demanding money, engineering skills and ecological insights. These critical problems are not being managed by the Army Engineers.

Instead, the Corps is destroying free-flowing streams to make unnecessary dams. It is trying to turn natural rivers into sluiceways; it is destroying our estuaries. Having no conservation standards, the Corps can easily destroy the Everglades in favor of get-rich real-estate promoters.

The Corps, presently headed by the efficient General William F. Cassidy, has a long and illustrious record, completely free of fraud, mismanagement or other types of scandal. By 1942, it had built two and a half billion dollars' worth of facilities in a year and a half; and during World War II, ten billion dollars' worth in four years. In terms of coverage, it has included navigation, flood control, hydro-power, beach erosion, water supply, fish and wildlife preservation, hurricane protection and related subjects. Since 1824, it has built most of the nation's harbors and navigable waterways. From the beginning, it was active in flood control; and when the first national Flood Control Act was passed by Congress in 1917, it became very active, especially in the Mississippi Valley. One who tours America will see many great and useful structures built by the Corps. Certainly, the Corps is unlike the Mafia; it has no conspiratorial function. It is honest and aboveboard.

The difficulty is, however, that we are running out of free-flowing rivers and healthy estuaries. The traditional engineering functions no longer fit our needs. Our need is to preserve the few remaining natural wonders that we have and make them clean and sparkling and fit for use by humans and by the vast world of birds, fish, reptiles and crustaceans that possess our waters.

We need the Corps. But we need also to redefine its functions and change its focus.

We pay farmers not to plant Crops. Let's pay the Corps not to build dams, dredge estuaries, convert rivers into sluiceways or build inland canals.

We can accomplish that goal by a few simple amendments to the Corps' basic statutory authority.

First, its projects for river improvement should now be conditioned by conservation standards. Will the project protect the marshlands? Will it provide the needed fresh water for sanctuaries such as the Everglades? Will it preserve the bottom lands sorely needed for ecological studies?

Second, the Corps' statutory authority should be enlarged to authorize it to construct sewage-disposal plants. It has no such authority. It can be busier at that than at dam building. Its large civilian staff, dependent on Federal largess for salaries, can fatten on sewage as well as on flood control and navigation.

The Corps needs statutory redesigning to meet modern urban and technological needs.

One billion dollars is needed in the Lake Erie complex to restore that dead lake, so that swimming, boating and fishing are once more possible. Mike Kirwan would not get a Big Ditch under this new regime. But he might get a big sewage-disposal plant named for him.

These are rewards enough, even at the level of pork barrel, if the Corps concentrates on socially useful projects that are desperately needed. Now is the chance to save the rest of our rivers by proclaiming our love of the land and our determination to preserve its natural wonders, even against despoilers as professionally competent as the Army Corps of Engineers.

VICTIMS OF WAR

Some wars, if you can trust historical analysts, are nobler than others. At least there are wars that have the support of virtually all citizens in a country, and the sacrifices resulting from participation in such conflicts are thought justified, or are more easily rationalized. All countries, however, including the United States, can end up participating in hostile conflicts which are very difficult to be righteous about. Pressures of various economic and political interest groups; previous treaties and international commitments; and simply bad statesmanship may account for such actions.

The involvement of the United States over a long period in the Indo-China conflict, which politicians insist is technically not a war, is due to an endless series of bad judgments on the part of political leaders and experts in international affairs of both major political parties. The Defense Department, the State Department, advisors from the academic community, members of Congress, and several Presidents jointly share in our initial decision to defend South Vietnam and other countries with so-called non-Communist (but hardly democratic) governments. The same leaders are guilty of failing to grasp opportunities to withdraw or at least minimize our involvement. Without getting into the argument about which President is most responsible or which part of the establishment bears the most guilt, it is clear that the Indo-China struggle has had serious consequences for us, in the loss of individual lives, a deteriorating national image, and a lack of progress in remedying many of the domestic social ills that face the United States.

It makes no difference how hawkish or dovish one's views are, or what political posture is taken on international affairs, or even how one feels about the justifiability of our actions in the long run. The indisputable fact remains that this war has many victims. And no matter what political meaning is attached to the conflict in our own times or by future historians, the overwhelming effect is not on important politicians and ideologues but on the many individuals and groups who have become the hapless victims of the war game.

| INDIVIDUAL vs. INDIVIDUAL | INDIVIDUAL vs. ORGANIZATION |

MY LAI 4

There is no need to identify Lieutenant Calley to the readers of this volume, nor to many persons for the next decade or perhaps decades, for he is a symbol, the symbol of a man convicted of murder while fighting a war. He was the lowest ranking commissioned officer during the massacre at My Lai, who participated, as a lot of his men participated, in the killing of men, women and children of all ages and of all political dispositions, and in the needless destruction of their possessions and homes. The account by Hersh is an attempt to describe what Calley, and other individuals like him, did and allowed to be done. Calley's conviction as an individual for his actions is in some ways symbolic. For regardless of rank or position in the military hierarchy, basic human values and, indeed, the code of conduct oppose taking lives and destroying property as done there. Are individuals like Calley, Medina, and the enlisted men with them the sole protagonists? Clearly in some ways they are also victims—victims of their country's participation in the Vietnam struggle, and victims of their own personal choice not to respect the individual lives whose destinies they held in their hands.

THE BIGGEST BUST

The success of demonstrations designed to express indignation and to arouse the apathetic about our military policies is a matter of debate; some claim the end of the Vietnam conflict has been speeded up by them, others argue they have had no impact or limited impact. But certainly many have resulted in serious altercations with the police and public officials, fortunately violent only in rare instances. Clearly however, individuals intent on demonstrating have hardly had the protection of the law. Rather, as in the incident reported in the article by Auchincloss, when individuals from a variety of walks of life join each other to harass the work and social life of a city such as Washington, they come up against strenuous efforts to contain their behavior. Government allegations to the contrary, it can hardly be argued that this is the plot of a particular group. Rather it is the converging frustrations of thousands of individual persons, over 13,000 who suffered arrest.

ORGANIZATION vs. INDIVIDUAL	ORGANIZATION vs. ORGANIZATION

A BOY WHO WAS JUST THERE WATCHING IT AND MAKING UP HIS MIND

War's victims, at least this war's victims, appear not only on the battlefield in Southeast Asia. Many American citizens, particularly among the younger adults, have been extremely outraged, sometimes in constructive ways and sometimes destructive, about our participation in Indo-China and our actions there. The community at large, and various political organizations within it, including those responsible for law and order, have been equally varied in their responses to individual and collective actions of youth and citizens of all ages and backgrounds against the Vietnam struggle. Some politicians and their organizations, regardless of their own sentiments, have been respectful of other views and encouraged dissent as right and proper. Some legal officials and organizations have provided protection for dissenters and, indeed, opportunities for them to do their thing. There have been disgraceful, undemocratic, irresponsible reactions as well. Pekkanen's article describes the particular strategy of the National Guard at Kent State, called out to assist the police, who killed "a boy who was just there watching it and making up his mind"—from all the evidence, an entirely innocent victim.

JUDGE GURFEIN'S OPINION

The *New York Times*'s reputation for integrity is accepted world-wide. It hardly seems an impetuous decision of irresponsible persons that led this newspaper to publish portions of a secret Department of Defense report on the political and military events related to our policies in Vietnam. The government's response, that the security of the United States was threatened by the *Times*'s actions, undoubtedly was not made lightly either. The conflict between this esteemed paper and the U.S. government raised the most fundamental questions about our democracy and the responsibilities of parties in it. The drama of the event, as well as the depth of it, comes through vividly in Judge Gurfein's opinion during an initial effort by the U.S. to prevent the continued publication of material from the extensive and systematic Defense Department document.

My Lai 4

SEYMOUR M. HERSH

The hamlet itself had a population of about 700 people, living either in flimsy thatch-covered huts—"hootches," as the GIs called them—or in solidly made red-brick homes, many with small porches in front. There was an east-west footpath just south of the main cluster of homes in My Lai 4: a few yards further south was a loose surface road that marked a hamlet boundary. A deep drainage ditch and then a rice paddy marked the eastern boundary. To the south of My Lai 4 was a large center, or plaza area—clearly the main spot for mass meetings. The foliage was dense, there were high bamboo trees, hedges, and plant life everywhere. Medina couldn't see 30 feet into the hamlet from the landing zone.

The first and second platoons lined up carefully to begin the 100-meter advance into the hamlet. Walking in line is an important military concept; if one group of men gets too far in front, it could be hit by bullets from behind—those fired by colleagues. Yet even this went wrong. Ron Grzesik was in charge of a small first-platoon team of riflemen and a machine gunner that day; he took his job seriously. His unit was supposed to be on

From *My Lai 4*, copyright © 1970 by Seymour M. Hersh. Reprinted by permission of Random House, Inc. (Selection appeared in *Harper's Magazine*, May 1970.)

the right flank, protecting Calley and his men. But Grzesik's group ended up on Calley's left.

As Brooks' second platoon cautiously approached the hamlet, a few Vietnamese began running across a field several hundred meters on the left. They may have been Viet Cong, or they may have been civilians fleeing the artillery shelling or the bombardment from the helicopter gunships. Vernado Simpson, Jr. of Jackson, Mississippi, told reporters he saw a man he identified as a Viet Cong soldier running with what seemed to be a weapon. A woman and small child were running with him. Simpson fired . . . again and again. He killed the woman and the baby. The man got away. Reporter Roberts saw a squad of GIs jump off a helicopter and begin firing at a group of people running on a nearby road. One was a woman with her children. Then he saw them "shoot two guys who popped up from a rice field. They looked like military-age men . . . when certain guys pop up from rice fields, you shoot them." This was the young reporter's most dangerous assignment. He had never been in combat before. "You're scared to death out there. We just wanted to go home."

The first two platoons of Charlie Company, still unfired upon, entered My Lai 4. Behind them, still in the rice paddy, were the third platoon and Captain Medina's command group.

Calley and some of his men walked into the plaza area in the southern part of My Lai 4. None of the villagers was running away; they knew that U.S. soldiers would assume that anyone running was a Viet Cong and shoot to kill. There was no immediate sense of panic. The time was after 8:00 A.M. Grzesik and his fire team were a few meters north of Calley; they couldn't see each other because of the dense vegetation. Grzesik and his men began their usual job of pulling people from their homes, interrogating them, and searching for Viet Cong. The villagers were gathered up, and Grzesik sent Meadlo, who was in his unit, to take them to Lieutenant Calley for further questioning. Grzesik didn't see Meadlo again for more than an hour.

Some of Calley's men recalled thinking it was breakfast time as they walked in; a few families were gathered in front of their homes cooking rice over a small fire. Without a direct order, the first platoon also began rounding up the villagers. There still was no sniper fire, no sign of a large enemy unit. Sledge remembered thinking that "if there were VC around, they had plenty of time to leave before we came in. We didn't tiptoe in there."

The killings began without warning. Harry Stanley told the CID that one young member of Calley's platoon took a civilian into custody and then "pushed the man up to where we were standing and then stabbed the man in the back with his bayonet. . . . The man fell to the ground and was gasping for breath." The GI then "killed him with another bayonet thrust or by shooting him with a rifle. . . . There were so many people killed that day it is hard for me to recall

exactly how some of the people died." The youth next "turned to where some soldiers were holding another forty- or fifty-year-old man in custody." He "picked this man up and threw him down a well. Then [he] pulled the pin from a M26 grenade and threw it in after the man." Moments later Stanley saw "some old women and some little children—fifteen or twenty of them—in a group around a temple where some incense was burning. They were kneeling and crying and praying and various soldiers . . . walked by and executed these women and children by shooting them in the head with their rifles. The soldiers killed all fifteen or twenty of them. . . ."

There were few physical protests from the people; about eighty of them were taken quietly from their homes and herded together in the plaza area. A few hollered out, "No VC. No VC." But that was hardly unexpected. Calley left Meadlo, Boyce, and a few others with the responsibility of guarding the group. "You know what I want you to do with them," he told Meadlo. Ten minutes later—about 8:15 A.M.—he returned and asked, "Haven't you got rid of them yet? I want them dead." Radioman Sledge, who was trailing Calley, heard the officer tell Meadlo to "waste them." Meadlo followed orders: "We stood about 10 to 15 feet away from them and then he [Calley] started shooting them. Then he told me to start shooting them. I started to shoot them. So we went ahead and killed them. I used more than a whole clip—used four or five clips." There are seventeen M16 bullets in each clip. Boyce slipped away, to the northern side of the hamlet, glad he hadn't been asked to shoot. Women were huddled against their children, vainly trying to save them. Some continued to chant "No VC." Others simply said, "No. No. No."

Do Chuc is a gnarled forty-eight-year-old Vietnamese peasant whose two daughters and an aunt were killed by the GIs in My Lai 4 that day. He and his family were eating breakfast when the GIs entered the hamlet and ordered them out of their homes. Together with other villagers, they were marched a few hundred meters into the plaza, where they were told to squat. "Still we had no reason to be afraid," Chuc recalls. "Everyone was calm." He watched as the GIs set up a machine gun. The calm ended. The people began crying and begging. One monk showed his identification papers to a soldier, but the American simply said, "Sorry." Then shooting started. Chuc was wounded in the leg, but he was covered by dead bodies and thus spared. After waiting an hour, he fled the hamlet. Nguyen Bat, a Viet Cong hamlet chief who later defected, said that many of the villagers who were eating breakfast outdoors when the GIs marched in greeted them without fear. They were gathered together and shot. Other villagers who were breakfasting indoors were killed inside their homes.

The few Viet Cong who had chosen to stay near the hamlet were safely hidden. Nguyen Ngo, a former deputy commander of a Viet Cong guerrilla platoon operating in the My Lai area, ran to his hiding place 300 meters away when the GIs came in shooting, but he could see that "they shot everything in sight." His mother and sister hid in ditches and survived because bodies fell on top of them. Pham Lai, a former hamlet security guard, climbed into a bunker with a bamboo

top and heard but did not see the shootings. His wife, hidden under a body, survived the massacre.

By this time, there was shooting everywhere. Dennis I. Conti, a GI from Providence, Rhode Island, later explained to CID investigators what he thought had happened. "We were all psyched up, and as a result when we got there the shooting started, almost as a chain reaction. The majority of us had expected to meet VC combat troops, but this did not turn out to be so. First we saw a few men running . . . and the next thing I knew we were shooting at everything. Everybody was just firing. After they got in the village, I guess you could say that the men were out of control."

Brooks and his men in the second platoon to the north had begun to ransack the hamlet systematically and slaughter the people, kill the livestock, and destroy the crops. Men poured rifle and machine-gun fire into huts without knowing—or seemingly caring—who was inside.

Roy Wood, one of Calley's men who was working next to Brooks' platoon, stormed into a hut, saw an elderly man hiding inside along with his wife and two young daughters. "I hit him with my rifle and pushed him out." A GI from Brooks' platoon standing by with an M79 grenade launcher asked to borrow his gun. Wood refused and the soldier asked another platoon mate. He got the weapon, said, "Don't let none of them live," and shot the Vietnamese in the head. "These mothers are crazy," Wood remembered thinking. "Stand right in front of us and blow a man's brains out." Later he vomited when he saw more of the dead residents of My Lai 4.

The second platoon went into My

Lai 4 with guns blazing. Gary Crossley said that some GIs, after seeing nothing but women and children in the hamlet, hesitated: "We phoned Medina and told him what the circumstances were and he said just keep going. It wasn't anything we wanted to do. You can only kill so many women and children. The fact was that you can't go through and wipe out all of South Vietnam."

Once the first two platoons had disappeared into the hamlet, Medina ordered the third platoon to start moving. He and his men followed. Gary Garfolo was caught up in the confusion: "I could hear heavy shooting all the time. Medina was running back and forth everywhere. This wasn't no organized deal." So Garfolo did what most GIs did when they could get away with it. "I took off on my own." He ran south; others joined him. Terrified villagers, many carrying personal belongings in wicker baskets, were running everywhere to avoid the carnage in the hamlet. In most cases it didn't help. The helicopter gunships circling above cut them down, or else an unfortunate group ran into the third platoon. Charles A. West sighted and shot six Vietnamese, some with baskets, on the edge of My Lai 4. "These people were running into us, away from us, running every which way. It's hard to distinguish a mama-san from a papa-san when everybody has on black pajamas."

West and his men may have thought that those Vietnamese were Viet Cong. Later they knew better. West's first impression upon reaching My Lai 4: "There were no people in the first part. . . . I seen bodies everywhere. I knew that everyone was being killed." His group, no longer burdened by questions of differentiation, quickly joined in.

Medina—as any combat officer would do during his unit's first major engagement—decided to move from the rice paddy nearer to the hamlet. John Paul, one of Medina's radiomen, figured that the time was about 8:15 A.M. West remembered that "Medina was right behind us" as his platoon moved inside the hamlet. There are serious contradictions about what happened next. Medina later said he did not enter the hamlet proper until well after 10:00 A.M. and did not see anyone kill a civilian. John Paul didn't think that Medina ever entered the hamlet. But Herbert Carter told the CID that Medina did some of the shooting of civilians as he moved into My Lai 4.

Carter testified that soon after the third platoon moved in, a woman was sighted. Somebody knocked her down and then, Carter said, "Medina shot her with his M16 rifle. I was 50 to 60 feet away and saw this. There was no reason to shoot this girl." The men continued on, making sure no one was escaping. "We came to where the soldiers had collected fifteen or more Vietnamese men, women, and children in a group. Medina said, 'Kill every one. Leave no one standing.'" A machine gunner began firing into the group. Moments later, one of Medina's radio operators slowly "passed among them and finished them off." Medina did not personally shoot any of them, according to Carter, but moments later, the captain "stopped a seventeen- or eighteen-year-old man with a water buffalo. Medina told the boy to make a run for it," Carter told the CID. "He tried to get him to run but the boy wouldn't run, so Medina shot him with his M16 rifle and killed him. . . . I was 75 or 80 meters away at the time and I saw it plainly." At this point in Carter's interrogation, the Army investigator warned him that he was making very serious charges against his commanding officer. "What I'm telling is the truth," Carter replied, "and I'll face Medina in court and swear to it."

If Carter is correct, Medina walked first into the north side of My Lai 4, then moved south with the CP to the hamlet plaza, and arrived there at about the time Paul Meadlo and Lieutenant Calley were executing the first group of villagers. Meadlo still wonders why Medina didn't stop the shooting, "if it was wrong." Medina and Calley "passed each other quite a few times that morning, but didn't say anything. I don't know if the CO [company commander] gave the order to kill or not, but he was right there when it happened. . . . Medina just kept marching around."

Roberts and Haeberle also moved in just behind the third platoon. Haeberle watched a group of ten to fifteen GIs methodically pump bullets into a cow until it keeled over. A woman then poked her head out from behind some brush; she may have been hiding in a bunker. The GIs turned the fire from the cow to the woman. "They just kept shooting at her. You could see the bones flying in the air chip by chip." No one had attempted to question her; men inside the hamlet also were asking no questions. Before moving on, the photographer took a picture of the dead woman. Haeberle took many more pictures that day; he saw about thirty GIs kill at least a hundred Vietnamese civilians.

When the two correspondents entered the hamlet, they saw dead animals, dead people, burning huts and homes. A few GIs were going through victims' clothing, looking for piasters. Another GI was chasing a duck with a knife; others stood around watching a GI slaughter a cow with a bayonet.

Haeberle noticed a man and two small children walking toward a group of GIs. "They just kept walking toward us. . . . You could hear the little girl saying, 'No, no. . . .' All of a sudden, the GIs opened up and cut them down." Later, on his left, he watched a machine gunner suddenly open fire on a group of civilians—women, children, and babies—who had been collected in a big circle. "They were trying to run. I don't know how many got out." He saw a GI with an M16 rifle fire at two young boys walking along a road; the older of the two— about seven or eight years old—fell over the first to protect him. The GI kept on firing until both were dead.

Haeberle and Roberts walked further into the hamlet, and Medina came up to them. Eighty-five Viet Cong had been killed in action thus far, the captain told them, and twenty suspects had been captured. Roberts jotted down the captain's information in his note pad.

Another Vietnamese interpreter, Sergeant Duong Minh, told a Vietnamese investigation team later that he saw Medina for the first time about then. Minh had arrived on a later helicopter assault, along with Lieutenant Dennis H. Johnson, Charlie Company's intelligence officer. When he saw the bodies of civilians, he asked Medina what happened. Medina, obviously angry at Minh for asking the question, stalked away.

Now it was nearly 9:00 A.M. and all of Charlie Company was in My

Lai 4. Most families were being shot inside their homes, or just outside their doorways. Those who had tried to flee were crammed by GIs into the many bunkers built throughout the hamlet for protection—once the bunkers became filled, hand grenades were lobbed in. Everything became a target. Gary Garfolo borrowed someone's M79 grenade launcher and fired it point-blank at a water buffalo. "I hit that sucker right in the head; went down like a shot. You don't get to shoot water buffalo with an M79 every day." Others fired the weapon into the bunkers full of people.

Jay Roberts insisted that he saw Medina in My Lai 4 most of the morning. "He was directing the operations in the village. He was in the village the whole time I was—from nine o'clock to eleven o'clock."

Some GIs were shouting and yelling during the massacre, Carter recalled. "The boys enjoyed it. When someone laughs and jokes about what they're doing they have to be enjoying it." A GI said, "Hey, I got me another one." Another said, "Chalk up one for me." Even Captain Medina was having a good time, Carter thought. "You can tell when someone enjoys their work." Few members of Charlie Company protested that day. For the most part those who didn't like what was going on kept their thoughts to themselves.

Herbert Carter also remembered seeing Medina inside the hamlet well after the third platoon began its advance: "I saw all those dead people lying there. Medina came right behind me." At one point in the morning, one of the members of Medina's CP joined in the shooting. "A woman came out of a hut with a baby in her arms and she was crying," Carter told

the CID. "She was crying because her little boy had been in front of their hut and . . . someone had killed the child by shooting it." When the mother came into view, Carter said, one of Medina's men "shot her with an M16 and she fell. When she fell, she dropped the baby." The GI next "opened up on the baby with his M16." The infant was also killed. Carter also saw an officer grab a woman by the hair and shoot her with a 45-caliber pistol. "He held her by the hair for a minute and then let go and she fell to the ground," Carter told the Army. "Some enlisted man standing there said, 'Well, she'll be in the big rice paddy in the sky.'"

In the midst of the carnage, Michael Bernhardt got his first good look at My Lai 4. Bernhardt had been delayed when Medina asked him to check out a suspicious wood box at the landing zone. After discovering that it wasn't a booby trap, Bernhardt hurried to catch up with his mates in the third platoon. He went into the hamlet where he saw Charlie Company "doing strange things. One: they were setting fire to the hootches and huts and waiting for people to come out and then shooting them. Two: they were going into the hootches and shooting them up. Three: they were gathering people in groups and shooting them. The whole thing was so deliberate. It was point-blank murder and I was standing there watching it. It kind of made me wonder if I could trust people anymore."

Grzesik and his men, meanwhile, had been slowly working their way through the hamlet. The young GI was having problems controlling his men; he was anxious to move on to the rice paddy in the east. About three-quarters of the way through, he suddenly saw Meadlo again. The time was now after 9:00 a.m. Meadlo was crouched, head in his hands, sobbing like a bewildered child. "I sat down and asked him what happened." Grzesik felt responsible; after all, he was supposed to be a team leader. Meadlo told him Calley had made him shoot people. "I tried to calm him down," Grzesik says, but the squad leader didn't stay long. He had to move on; his men still hadn't completed their sweep.

Those Vietnamese who were not killed on the spot were being shepherded by the first platoon to a large drainage ditch at the eastern end of the hamlet. After Grzesik left, Meadlo and a few others gathered seven or eight villagers in one hut and were preparing to toss in a hand grenade when an order came to take them to the ditch where they found Calley, along with a dozen other first platoon members, and perhaps seventy-five Vietnamese, mostly women, old men, and children.

Not far away, invisible in the brush and trees, the second and third platoons were continuing their search-and-destroy operations in the northern half of the hamlet. Ron Grzesik and his fire team had completed a swing through the hamlet and were getting ready to turn around and walk back to see what was going on. And just south of the plaza Michael Bernhardt had attached himself to Medina and his command post. Shots were still being fired, the helicopters were still whirring overhead, and the enemy was still nowhere in sight.

One of the helicopters was piloted by Chief Warrant Officer Hugh C. Thompson of Decatur, Georgia. For him, the mission had begun routinely enough. He and his two-man crew in a small observation helicopter from

the 123rd Aviation Battalion had arrived at the area around 9:00 a.m. and immediately reported what appeared to be a Viet Cong soldier armed with a weapon heading south. Although his mission was simply reconnaissance, Thompson directed his crew men to fire at and attempt to kill the Viet Cong as he wheeled the helicopter after him. They missed. Thompson flew back to the hamlet and it was then, as he told the Army Inspector General's office in June 1969, that he began seeing wounded and dead Vietnamese civilians all over the hamlet, with no sign of an enemy force.

The pilot thought that the best thing he could do would be to mark the location of wounded civilians with smoke so that the GIs on the ground could move over and begin treating some of the many injured persons. "The first one that I marked was a girl that was wounded," Thompson told the Inspector General (IG), "and they came over and walked up to her, put their weapon on automatic and let her have it." The man who did the shooting was a captain, Thompson said. Later he identified the officer as Ernest Medina.

Flying with Thompson that day was Lawrence M. Colburn of Mount Vernon, Washington, who remembers that the girl was about twenty years old and was lying on the edge of a dike outside of the hamlet with part of her body in a rice paddy. "She had been wounded in the stomach, I think, or the chest," Colburn told the IG. "This captain was coming down the dike and he had men behind him. They were sweeping through and we were hovering a matter of feet away from them: I could see this clearly and he emptied a clip into her."

Medina and his men immediately

began moving south toward the Viet Cong sighted and reported by Thompson. En route they saw the young girl in the rice paddy who had been marked by the smoke. Bernhardt had a ground view of what happened next: "He [Medina] was just going alone . . . he shot the woman. She seemed to be busy picking rice, but rice was out of season. What she really was doing was trying to pretend that she was picking rice. She was 100 meters away with a basket. . . . If she had a hand grenade, she would have to have a better arm than me to get us. . . . Medina lifted the rifle to his shoulder, looked down the barrel and pulled the trigger. I saw the woman drop. He just took a potshot . . . he wasn't a bad shot. Then he walked up. He got up real close, about three or six feet, and shot at her a couple times and finished her off. She was a real clean corpse. . . . She wasn't all over the place, and I could see her clothing move when the bullets hit. . . . I could see her twitch, but I couldn't see any holes . . . he didn't shoot her in the head." A second later, Bernhardt remembered, the captain "gave me a look, a dumb shit-eating grin."

Harry Stanley was standing a few feet away from Calley near some huts at the drainage ditch when the call came from Medina. He had a different recollection: "Medina called Calley and said, 'What the fuck is going on?' Calley said he got some VC, or some people that needed to be checked out." At this point Medina cautioned Calley to tell his men to save their ammunition because the operation still had a few more days to run.

It is not clear how soon or to whom Medina's order was given, but Stanley told the CID what Calley did next: "There was an old lady in a bed and I believe there was a priest in white praying over her. . . . Calley told me to ask about the VC and NVA and where the weapons were. The priest denied being a VC or NVA." Charles Sledge watched with horror as Calley pulled the old man outside: "He said a few more words to the monk. It looked like the monk was pleading for his life. Lieutenant Calley then took his rifle and pushed the monk into a rice paddy and shot him point-blank."

Calley then turned his attention back to the crowd of Vietnamese and issued an order: "Push all those people in the ditch." Three or four GIs complied. Calley struck a woman with a rifle as he pushed her down. Stanley remembered that some of the civilians "kept trying to get out. Some made it to the top. . . ." Calley began the shooting and ordered Meadlo to join in. Meadlo told about it later: "So we pushed our seven to eight people in with the big bunch of them. And so I began shooting them all. So did Mitchell, Calley. . . . I guess I shot maybe twenty-five or twenty people in the ditch . . . men, women, and children. And babies." Some of the GIs switched from automatic fire to single shot to conserve ammunition. Herbert Carter watched the mothers "grabbing their kids and the kids grabbing their mothers. I didn't know what to do." Calley then turned again to Meadlo and said, "Meadlo, we've got another job to do." Meadlo didn't want any more jobs. He began to argue with Calley. Sledge watched Meadlo once more start to sob. Calley turned next to Robert Maples and said, "Maples, load your machine gun and shoot these people." Maples replied, as he told the CID, "I'm not going to do that." He remembered that "the people firing into the ditch kept reloading magazines into their rifles and kept firing into the ditch and then killed or at least shot everyone in the ditch." William C. Lloyd of Tampa, Florida, told the CID that some grenades were also thrown into the ditch. Dennis Conti noticed that "a lot of women had thrown themselves on top of the children to protect them, and the children were alive at first. Then the children who were old enough to walk got up and Calley began to shoot the children."

One further incident stood out in many GIs' minds: seconds after the shooting stopped, a bloodied but unhurt two-year-old boy miraculously crawled out of the ditch, crying. He began running toward the hamlet. Someone hollered, "There's a kid." There was a long pause. Then Calley ran back, grabbed the child, threw him back in the ditch, and shot him.

Moments later, Thompson, still in his helicopter, flew by. He told the IG what had happened next: "I kept flying around and across a ditch . . . and it . . . had a bunch of bodies in it and I don't know how they got in the ditch. But I saw some of them were still alive." Captain Brian W. Livingston was piloting a large helicopter gunship a few hundred feet above. He had been monitoring Thompson's agonized complaints and went down to take a look for himself. He told a military hearing: "There were bodies lying in the trenches. . . . I remembered that we remarked at the time about the old Biblical story of Jesus turning water into wine. The trench had a gray color to it, with the red blood of the individuals lying in it."

There were some small acts of mercy. A GI placed a blanket over the body of a mutilated child. An elderly woman was spared when some

GIs hollered at a soldier just as he was about to shoot her. Grzesik remembered watching a GI seem to wrestle with his conscience while holding a bayonet over a wounded old man. "He wants to stab somebody with a bayonet," Grzesik thought. The GI hesitated . . . and finally passed on, leaving the old man to die.

Some GIs, however, didn't hesitate to use their bayonets. Nineteen-year-old Nguyen Thi Ngoc Tuyet told a reporter that she watched a baby trying to open her slain mother's blouse to nurse. A soldier shot the infant while it was struggling with the blouse, and then slashed at it with his bayonet. Tuyet also says she saw another baby hacked to death by GIs wielding their bayonets.

Le Tong, a rice farmer, reported seeing one woman raped after GIs killed her children. Nguyen Khoa, a peasant, told of a thirteen-year-old girl who was raped before being killed. GIs then attacked Khoa's wife, he said, tearing off her clothes. Before they could rape her, however, Khoa said, their six-year-old son, riddled with bullets, fell and saturated her with blood. The GIs left her alone.

There were "degrees" of murder that day. Some were conducted out of sympathy. Michael Terry, the Mormon who was a squad leader in the third platoon, had ordered his men to take their lunch break by the bloody ditch in the rear of the hamlet. He noticed that there were no men in the ditch, only women and children.

He had watched Calley and the others shoot into that ditch. Calley seemed just like a kid, Terry thought. He also remembered thinking it was "just like a Nazi-type thing." When one soldier couldn't fire any more and threw down his weapon, "Calley picked it up." Later, during lunch, Terry and his men saw that some of the victims were still breathing. "They were pretty badly shot up. They weren't going to get any medical help, and so we shot them . . . shot maybe five of them."

James Bergthold saw an old man who had been shot in both legs: "He was going to die anyway so I figured I might as well kill him." He took his 45-caliber pistol (as a machine-gun ammunition carrier, he was entitled to one), carefully placed the barrel against the upper part of the old man's forehead, and blew off the top of his head. Carter had watched the scene and remembered thinking that Bergthold had done the old man a favor. "If me and you were together and you got wounded bad," Carter later told an interviewer, "and I couldn't get you to a doctor, I'd shoot you, too."

Most of the shooting was over by the time Medina called a break for lunch, shortly after 11:00 A.M. By then, Roberts and Haeberle had grabbed a helicopter and cleared out of the area, their story for the day far bigger than they wanted. Calley, Mitchell, Sledge, Grzesik, and a few others went back to the command post west of My Lai 4 to take lunch with Captain Medina and the rest of his headquarters crew. Grzesik recalled that at that point he had thought there couldn't be a survivor left in the hamlet. But two little girls showed up, about ten and eleven years old. John Paul said they came in from one of the paddies where they apparently had waited out the siege. "We sat them down with us [at the command post]," Paul recounts "and gave them some cookies and crackers to eat." When a CID interrogator later asked Charles Sledge how many civilians he thought had survived, he answered: "Only two small children who had lunch with us."

In the early afternoon, the men of Charlie Company mopped up to make sure all the houses and goods in My Lai 4 were destroyed. Medina ordered the underground tunnels in the hamlet blown up; most of them already had been blocked. Within another hour, My Lai 4 was no more; its red-brick buildings demolished by explosives, its huts burned to the ground, its people dead or dying.

Michael Bernhardt later summarized the day: "We met no resistance and I only saw three captured weapons. We had no casualties. It was just like any other Vietnamese village —old papa-sans, women, and kids. As a matter of fact, I don't remember seeing one military age male in the entire place, dead or alive. The only prisoner I saw was in his fifties."

The three platoons of Company C pulled out shortly after noon, rendezvousing in the rice paddies east of the hamlet. Lieutenant Brooks' second platoon had about eighty-five villagers in tow; it kept those of military age with them and told the rest to begin moving south. Following his original orders, Medina then marched the GIs a few hundred meters northeast through the deserted hamlets of My Lai 5 and My Lai 6, ransacking and burning as they went. In one of the hamlets, Medina ordered the residents gathered, and then told Sergeant Phu, the regular company interpreter, to tell them, as Phu later told Vietnamese investigators, that "they were to go away or something will happen to them—just like what happened at My Lai 4."

By nightfall, the Viet Cong were back in My Lai 4, helping the survivors bury the dead. It took five days.

Most of the funeral speeches were made by the Communist guerrillas. Nguyen Bat was not a Communist at the time of the massacre, but the incident changed his mind. "After the shooting," he said, "all the villagers became Communists."

When Army investigators reached the barren area in November 1969, in connection with the My Lai probe in the United States, they found mass graves at three sites, as well as a ditch full of bodies. It was estimated that between 450 and 500 people—most of them women, children, and old men—had been slain and buried there.

The Biggest Bust

KENNETH AUCHINLOSS

A mass march on the Pentagon, Eugene McCarthy's Presidential campaign, banks burned, blood poured on draftboard files, peaceful rallies in the nation's Capital, a lethal bomb exploded outside a university research center—all these tactics, from benign to brutal, have been tried in efforts to speed the Vietnam war to an end. Last week, something new was added, both by the protesters and by the government they challenged. Antiwar militants mounted a display of aggressive civil disruption in Washington's streets that strained the city's order, and the authorities responded with a wave of indiscriminate arrests and quasi-legal detention that warped the rule of law.

The result was the largest mass

Reprinted by permission from *Newsweek* (May 17, 1971), pp. 24, 25D, 26, 28, 29. Copyright Newsweek, Inc., May 17, 1971.

arrest in the nation's history: 7,200 in a single day and a total of 13,400 during four days of gradually de-escalating confrontation. Along the way, Americans were treated to some striking snapshots of their Capital that seemed more appropriate to Saigon in wartime than Washington in the spring: youthful partisans darting into the street to block or slow commuter traffic; Chinook helicopters disgorging squads of flak-jacketed marines on the Washington Monument grounds; thousands of captives herded into an open-air, wire-fenced stockade.

The week's action was not, on the whole, violent or even terribly angry. The demonstrators, by and large, were the peace freaks—a motley young counter-army in denims, fatigues and headbands and even their most insurrectionary tactics had a certain prankish air to them. There was little serious vandalism by the protesters and little real brutality by the cops. In contrast to the Weatherman "Days of Rage" or the 1968 Chicago "police riot," the hard feelings this time were caused—on both sides—by a sense of rights violated, not damage wrought. But the affair did strike a contentious note at the end of the three-week Washington demonstration season that had begun in relative calm. And there were some who thought it might spur the antiwar movement to a broad new campaign of civil disobedience.

At first, the government seemed to have every advantage on its side. The Mayday Collective, sponsors of the plan to clog traffic, had published its intentions for all to see. The 1,400-man District of Columbia National Guard had been called up to assist the D.C. police, 5,100 strong, and 10,000 more Army and Marine troops were held in readiness nearby. President Richard M. Nixon had instructed Attorney General John Mitchell, whose Justice Department worked hand-in-glove with the Washington police throughout the week, that the demonstrators were to be allowed no semblance of a victory in tying up the government. 'Short of killing people," said one insider, "Nixon had given Mitchell a blank check." The President repeated this no-nonsense exhortation in a weekend phone call from San Clemente—a "pep message," White House sources termed it —to Washington Police Chief Jerry V. Wilson. The pressure of these direct Presidential orders, as it turned out, may have been crucial in Wilson's key decision to suspend normal arrest procedures when the disorders began.

The government's most serious problem was faulty intelligence—from this, plus an extraordinary failure of foresight, proceeded a great many of its hasty judgments and makeshift detention arrangements later. Just a couple of days before the Saturday rock concert the Mayday people had scheduled, word began to pass that attendance was likely to be much closer to the 50,000 predicted by Mayday organizer Rennie Davis than the 20,000 estimated by Justice and police. At a Saturday morning strategy session chaired by Deputy Attorney General Richard Kleindienst, the government decided on its first tactical move: it would revoke Mayday's park permit and clear the West Potomac Park campsite at dawn Sunday.

At first, this seemed a masterstroke. The evacuations went off smoothly, and accomplished two important objectives. Large numbers of young people who had turned up mainly for the concert and for the Woodstockian exhilaration that such antiwar gatherings impart—the "peace groupies," they are called—left for home rather than stick around for the action next day. And the final phase of Mayday planning and instruction, which was to have taken place in the park that afternoon, was forestalled. Mayday organizers admitted ruefully that they had been "outfoxed."

Somehow, however, the demonstrators managed to regroup. Even after the park evacuation, they were able to muster about 12,000 for anticommuter duty the following morning— about double the number the police had been expecting.

Still, the situation as dawn broke seemed reasonably well in hand. Some 4,000 to 5,000 government employees were already at work; they had been asked to come in as early as 5 A.M. to prevent any chance of their becoming snarled in a traffic jam. And the police and troops had beaten the protesters into the field. A battalion of the Tenth Marine Regiment, Second Division, held Dupont Circle, a key hub on the traffic route downtown from the northwest suburbs. Three hundred soldiers from the 91st Engineer Battalion were lined eight paces apart along the walkways of Key Bridge, spanning the Potomac from Arlington, Va., to Georgetown. The other Potomac bridges also bristled with military guards, and police were massed at the remaining Mayday target areas with squad cars, vans and motor scooters.

STREET FIGHTING MEN

Against this array, the Mayday forces launched their guerrilla forays. Small groups darted into the highway and linked hands to block traffic; a few even lay down in the roadway. Demonstrators in cars joined the lines of commuter traffic, then slowed down to a crawl to tie up the lanes behind them. Several ancient jalopies were stalled and abandoned in the middle of the road. A few used harsher methods against the commuters: several cars had distributor caps ripped out while they stopped in a jam, and Arizona Sen. Paul Fannin had his tires slashed. Other youths simply pleaded with motorists to slow down of their own accord, a request that was rarely heeded and occasionally met with an angry swerve in the demonstrator's direction.

Georgetown, the fashionable residential district, was one of the worst trouble spots, thanks partly to the huge concentration of Mayday people camped on the grounds of Georgetown University.

Operating from the cover of a tree-lined hillside overlooking Canal Road,

they rolled tree trunks, garbage cans and other debris into the path of oncoming cars. A dilapidated garbage truck was overturned, and so was a huge tractor trailer on M Street, in the heart of Georgetown. At Dupont Circle, a force of some 800 shoved trash cans and lumber from a nearby construction site into the road and dropped smaller bits of wood onto cars in the underpass below.

In almost every case, the police got traffic moving again after short delays. But the demonstrators' tactics— to sally, scatter and regroup—made it almost useless for the police to stop the melee merely by dispersing the participants. It had been fairly clear, ever since the Mayday plans were published, that the only way to stop the demonstrators would be to arrest them. And arrested they were—under conditions that betrayed a sore lack of advance planning, a blatant disregard for the civil liberties of both protesters and bystanders, and nearly total abandonment of any hope of successfully prosecuting the offenders.

At 6:25 Monday morning, the police radio broadcast an order to all hands from Chief Wilson: normal field arrest procedures were to be suspended—"just bring them in and lock them up." Washington's arrest procedures were devised after the disorders following Martin Luther King's assassination three years ago, in which 7,650 people were arrested in ten days. They require that police fill out a form on every person arrested, giving his name and that of the arresting officer, the time and the place; then a Polaroid picture of the prisoner and his captor is attached. Without such information, it is obviously next to impossible to build a case for conviction.

Wilson apparently believed that unless his men were free to round up offenders without pausing to record the circumstances of the arrests, the demonstrators might well gain the upper hand. "I took these steps," he explained later, "because I felt they were necessary to protect the safety of law-abiding citizens and to maintain order in the city"—duties that his Presidential phone call had doubtless made him anxious to perform without blemish. He insisted that the decision had been his alone, though he was accompanied at the time by a top Justice hand (Associate Deputy Attorney General for Criminal Justice Donald Santarelli) and was in radio communication with other Justice officials who could presumably have questioned or overruled his order, which was to ignite bitter criticism before the day was out.

For the order did not simply short-circuit a set of bureaucratic rules, it altered the whole nature of police tactics. Freed from the obligation to specify a crime or set their names to an arrest, the police began dragnet sweeps of the Washington streets, catching up not only demonstrators who were disorderly but also demonstrators who had not yet violated any law and persons who were not even demonstrators at all. A young Mayday man named Chris Morningstar walked up to a cop and asked directions to a coffeeshop where he could get some breakfast; his next stop was D.C. Jail. A George Washington University law professor named Roger Kuhn stood watching police action outside the student center, was bumped by a policeman (who was wearing no badge or other identification, a practice not uncommon that day), and arrested for interfering with an officer. Often a youthful face or lengthy hair seemed sufficient ground for a bystander to be shoved into a jail-bound bus. A psychiatrist reported that six young patients walking with their attendants had all been hauled off. Many were never told the charges against them or even that they were formally under arrest.

These tactics were stunningly effective. By 9 o'clock, the streets had been swept so clear of Mayday tribesmen, as well as sundry other pedestrians, that late commuters fairly sailed to their offices. The White House glowed with reports that attendance at Federal offices that day had been a shade higher than usual. And the President, in a Tuesday morning talk with Republican leaders after his return to town, set his seal of approval on Wilson's generalship: "I think Jerry Wilson and the police," he said, "did a magnificent job. John Mitchell and the Department of Justice did a fine job, too. I hope you will all agree to make that point when you leave here."

UNEQUAL JUSTICE UNDER LAW

The GOP leaders dutifully made the point, but it was not universally endorsed. The Democrats' Sen. Edward Kennedy, for one, caustically berated the government's tactics. "The object," he said, "was to enable John Mitchell to say at 10 a.m. on Monday morning that he had made the city safe for automobiles. Of course the city may have been safe for cars at the time, but it was a very unsafe place for citizens."

What's more, the ugly conditions of their confinement (box) very soon became an embarrassment even to the authorities. Despite ample advance indications that there would be large-scale arrests that day, no adequate detention facilities had been prepared

The city's judicial system, too, had been seriously contorted by the mass arrests. Equal treatment under law vanished rapidly in the confusion. Superior Court judges, who began setting $250 bail for out-of-town prisoners Monday afternoon, were outraged to find that the police started releasing prisoners that night upon the posting of just $10 "collateral," and the next night all the prisoners against whom the police could press no charges were ordered released free of bail.

The procedures for release under $10 collateral raised yet another legal storm. As the prisoners were processed, some twelve hours or more after their incarceration, the arrest forms shunned earlier in the day were finally filled out, but highly arbitrarily, according to one young Justice Department attorney who helped in the process. Everyone was charged with "disorderly conduct," everyone's time of arrest was given as "May 3," everyone's place of arrest as "District of Columbia," and the blank for "arresting offcer" was changed to "court officer" and filled with the names of seven policemen used one after the other. "It was," charged American Civil Liberties Union executive director Aryeh Neier, "a planned process of perjury."

As the legal issue escalated, the demonstrators seemed to suspect that they might be able to embarrass the government more by clogging the jails than by clogging the streets. Perhaps, too, the two sides sensed that Monday's experience had hurt them both. All but a handful of demonstrators passed up the war games against commuter traffic, which had been scheduled for a second day, and substituted civil disobedience of a far more passive sort. The police, for their part, reverted to normal arrest procedures and orderly crowd control.

On Tuesday, 1,000 demonstrators joined an orderly march to the Justice Department. Police chaperoned the procession every step of the way (Chief Wilson himself marched alongside, a blue bullhorn under his arm) but intervened only to see that the marchers kept to the sidewalk and stopped for red lights. When they arrived on 10th Street, opposite the Justice Department's western face, they sat down on the street and sidewalk.

ALUMNI REUNION

For nearly two hours the crowd, which had swelled to about 3,000, chanted, sang and listened to speeches. John Froines, one of the Chicago Seven, mounted a low wall and proclaimed that "the people's police force had arrested the Justice Department" —but as it turned out, the FBI had a warrant for his own arrest, on charges of conspiring to interfere with the civil rights of commuters. G-men collared him in the crowd. Froines was the second of three Chicago Seven alumni to be arrested during the week: Rennie Davis was nabbed on the same charges the day before, and Abbie Hoffman—his nose broken during a scuffle with policemen—was picked up later in New York. Hoffman was accused of interstate travel to incite a riot and assaulting a policeman. All three were released on bail.

Despite such moments of stress, the mood turned festive as the afternoon wore on. Shortly before 3 p.m., Chief Wilson unlimbered his bullhorn and announced that anyone who didn't leave would be arrested. Roughly half departed and then policemen led off about 1,500 unresisting prisoners to waiting buses. This time, they filled out arrest forms.

This pattern—peaceful assembly followed by orderly arrest—was repeated the following day at the Capitol. About 1,200 demonstrators marched from the Mall to the steps of the Capitol's House wing, where they were addressed by four sympathetic congressmen. One demonstrator stripped off all his clothes. After about twenty minutes, Capitol Police Chief James Powell declared the crowd an "unlawful assembly," and 1,146 were carted off. The "unlawful assembly" charge carries fairly heavy penalties— a possible $500 fine and up to six months' imprisonment.

This was Mayday's last big march. There was talk of a demonstration at the South Vietnamese Embassy next day, but almost everyone who wasn't in jail had left town by then and only about 60 showed up. The Capitol, whose workaday bureaucratic rounds had been deflated only minutely by the week's alarums, anyway, slipped back to business as usual. What remained was a mess to clean up, millions of dollars in bills to pay, and a number of prickly questions about how the government and the demonstrators had acquitted themselves.

CONSTITUTIONAL FLAWS

First, was the police sweep on Monday unconstitutional? Civil libertarians and law professors cited what they regarded as blatant abridgments of the First, Fourth, Fifth, Sixth and Eighth amendments. Freedom of assembly, they said, was violated when people who were in no way disorderly were seized along with the unruly

protesters. The requirement that no arrest shall be made without "probable cause" was disregarded, they charged, once dragnet tactics began. "Due process" was similarly flouted, they argued, by the decision to abandon arrest procedures. "Because of the failure to identify particular officers and arrestees," contended the ACLU's Neier, "any subsequent prosecution or conviction was impossible. Therefore any subsequent detention was improper. It became preventive detention, since detention for trial was impossible."

These violations were compounded, the critics argued, by the police decision to require mug shots and fingerprints of all the people detained, even when it was clear that some of them were entirely innocent and few if any could be successfully prosecuted. The prints and photos, demonstrators were sure, would be turned over to the FBI —and some suspected that one motive behind the dragnet was the Feds' desire to expand their files on the identity of citizens prone to radical protest.

Government officials readily admitted that legal shortcuts had been taken, but argued that they had been necessary to prevent chaos in the streets. If the arrest procedures had not been suspended, contended a municipal attorney at one court hearing, "we might not have had a city left." This posed the second major question about the police tactics: what were Chief Wilson's alternatives? Could he have coped with the situation without indiscriminate arrests?

Clearly the demonstrators' intention of halting traffic—in effect, taking charge of the city's highways and preventing the free movement of its citizens—was intolerable. Perhaps

Wilson was correct in deciding that he did not have enough men to control the mob without freeing the police from arrest procedures—though others who watched the Monday melee doubted the situation was that critical. But why then did the government, which had at least four days' warning that the crowd was going to be larger than it expected, fail to deploy troops fast enough that arrests could be made properly and with some hope of bringing offenders to justice? A few municipal insiders suggested that Wilson, a capable and ambitious man, may have been determined to prove that his own department could handle the crisis largely on its own.

A Boy Who Was Just 'There Watching It and Making Up His Mind'

JOHN PEKKANEN

On the morning of the day Bill Schroeder died the alarm went off at 7 a.m. He slept through it and his roommate had to turn it off. At 8:15 he finally got up, dressed in the blue denim jacket his grandfather gave him and the orange bellbottoms he called his "Brian Jones pants" after the late member of the Rolling Stones. ("He owned every record the Stones ever made," a friend remembers.) Leaving his house at 603 Franklin Street, only a few blocks from the Kent State University campus, he drove to class. "I went with him," one of his five housemates said. "He was wearing a purple flower and a

yellow flower in each lapel of his jacket. He joked that the purple flower was his Purple Heart." Crossing the campus, Bill found a spent tear gas canister. He picked it up and turned it over to a nearby National Guardsman.

His first class was ROTC, compulsory for Bill because he had transferred to Kent State as a sophomore last fall on an ROTC scholarship. He ranked second among his ROTC classmates academically. "We used to kid him about it," his roommate said, "because ROTC isn't something very popular on campuses these days." But if the kidding bothered him it didn't show. "It wasn't like he had to choose. He was in ROTC and he didn't like Vietnam and Cambodia but if he had to go to Vietnam he would have gone." He once confided to Gene Pekarick, a close friend and fellow psychology major, that he strongly disagreed with another ROTC student who, in discussing a hypothetical military operation, suggested the way to succeed was to "go in there and wipe them out." "Bill was just disgusted by that. He said, 'What kind of mentality is that?' He hated the thought of this kind of senseless killing this guy talked about."

The burning of the Kent State ROTC building the preceding Saturday night had bothered him a lot. He mentioned it on Sunday when he called home to his parents in Lorain, Ohio, a steel town about 60 miles from Kent. He assured his parents that he was all right and planned to take advantage of the disturbances by staying inside and studying.

The rally had been scheduled for noon on Monday on the commons, a gently rolling area now fresh with the burst of spring. Bill and Gene met after class and instead of going to lunch began walking to the rally. "He went because he was curious to see it. He wasn't a participant and he wasn't just a bystander. He was open-minded. He went there to observe."

As they moved toward the commons there was an edge of confrontation in the air, but no expectation of violence. Bill had earlier told his roommate that he didn't like the prospect of going to class under martial law. But as he and Gene walked past some Guardsmen, Gene said, "I hope none of those guys have itchy fingers," and it was Bill who reassured him. "Don't worry about it. They don't even have clips in their rifles."

They mingled in the rally, along with some 1,000 other students, most of whom shared their frame of mind

—curious and a bit angry, but not outraged. "Nobody seems to understand," a student said later, "we just wanted the Guard off our campus. They were making everything worse." The metallic voice of the Guard bullhorn ordered the rally to disperse. Rights of assembly were suspended, it declared, authoritatively, anonymously. "A jeep came up toward us. They kept telling us to disperse. We just scattered and in the confusion I momentarily lost sight of Bill," Gene recalls. "The kids were strung out all over the area."

A cluster of students soon collected, shouting "Pigs off campus" at the Guard. Some of them, perhaps no more than 20, lobbed stones and the Guard responded with tear gas. Students hurled canisters back. The Guard ran out of tear gas and, confronted by a skirmish line of several hundred students, drew together to regroup. Bill was standing about 100 feet from the Guardsmen, between them and the main body of students, when the Guardsmen opened fire. According to Gene, Bill wasn't shouting at the Guard or throwing rocks at them.

Gene, like the others around him, hit the ground. "Some girls had fainted. I looked over and saw a girl lying on the ground. She wasn't moving. It looked like Allison [Allison Krause, one of the four students who died]. I didn't really know her but she went out with a guy down the hall from me. A beautiful, happy girl. Then my roommate came running down the hill shouting at me, 'Do you know who they shot?' I said I think they shot Allison. 'No. They shot your buddy.' I ran up the hill and three people were around Bill. A crowd had gathered and then people moved away to give him room. He was alive and was able to speak. He just said, 'Where's an ambulance?' His voice was weak, like a whisper. An ambulance was nearby but it took another injured student away. About 10 minutes later one came for Bill. As they put him on the stretcher, he moved his leg up to help them. When they drove away I didn't even think he was hurt that bad." Ten hours later the university news service issued a statement: "Schroeder, Wm. K., 19, sophomore, DEAD. Five minutes after arrival."

Tuesday morning, after the National Guard had ordered everyone off campus until further notice, Bill Schroeder's housemates on Franklin Street prepared to leave for home. A group of them came out on the front porch and refused to allow anyone to enter the house. "Don't use our names," one said. "Just say we were a family and one of us was killed."

One of them, who identified himself as Bill's roommate, had known him since junior high school in Lorain and lived a block from his home. Monday night he had gone to the county morgue to make a positive identification of Bill. "We did everything together. Took walks, played basketball. Bill was good at everything he tried. He had a mind, I mean a real mind." Their high school principal said the same. Bill had an A-minus average at Lorain Senior High School and had the highest rating in every attitude category from citizenship to attendance. At Kent State his average was B-plus. "He wanted to get into psychology," his roommate said. "He liked it here. We would spend a lot of nights together just talking, sometimes to 4 or 5 in the morning. He told us once that he really wanted to be a writer. He'd been writing poetry for the last few years but he'd always hide it."

The boy spoke haltingly, unable at times to control his trembling. "Make sure you say one thing if nothing else. Say that Bill was not throwing rocks or shouting at the Guardsmen. It would have never crossed his mind to do that. He was there watching it and making up his own mind about it and they shot him." Then Bill Schroeder's friends went back into the house and began packing his clothes.

Judge Gurfein's Opinion

NEW YORK TIMES

Judge Gurfein's Opinion
UNITED STATES DISTRICT
COURT, SOUTHERN
DISTRICT OF NEW YORK
71 Civ. 2662
UNITED STATES OF
AMERICA,
   Plaintiff,
            v.
NEW YORK TIMES COMPANY,
   et al, Defendants.
GURFEIN, D. J.

On June 12, June 13 and June 14, 1971, the New York Times published summaries and portions of the text of two documents—certain volumes from a 1968 Pentagon study relating to Vietnam and a summary of a 1965 Defense Department study relating to the Tonkin Gulf incident. The United States sues to enjoin the Times from "further dissemination, disclosure or divulgence" of materials contained in the 1968 study of the decision-making process with respect to Vietnam and the summary of the 1965 Tonkin Gulf study. In its application for a temporary restraining order the United States also asked the Court to order The Times to furnish to the Court all the documents involved so that they could be impounded pending a determination. On June 15 upon the argument of the order to show cause the Court entered a temporary restraining order against *The New York*

From *The New York Times*, June 20, 1971.

Times in substance preventing the further publication until a determination by the Court upon the merits of the Government's application for a preliminary injunction. The Court at that time, in the absence of any evidence, refused to require the documents to be impounded.

The Government contends that the documents still unpublished and the information in the possession of The Times involves a serious breach of the security of the United States and that the further publication will cause "irreparable injury to the national defense."

The articles involved material that has been classified as Top-Secret and Secret, although the Government concedes that these classifications are related to volumes rather than individual documents and that included within the volumes may be documents which should not be classified in such high categories. The documents involved are a 47 volume study entitled "HISTORY OF UNITED STATES DECISION–MAKING PROCESS ON VIETNAM POLICY" and a document entitled "THE COMMAND AND CONTROL STUDY OF THE TONKIN GULF INCIDENT DONE BY THE DEFENSE DEPARTMENT'S WEAPONS SYSTEM EVALUATION GROUP IN 1965." There is no question that the documents are in the possession of The Times.

The issue of fact with respect to

national security was resolved in the following manner. In view of the claim of the Government that testimony in support of its claim that publication of the documents would involve a serious security danger would in itself be dangerous the Court determined that under the "Secrets of State" doctrine an in camera proceeding should be held at which only the attorneys for each side, witnesses for the Government and two designated representatives of The New York Times would be present. It was believed that this would enable the Government to present its case forcefully and without restraint so that the accommodation of the national security interest with the rights of a free press could be determined with no holds barred. It was with reluctance that the Court granted a hearing from which the public was excluded, but it seemed that there was no other way to serve the needs of justice. My finding with respect to the testimony on security will be adverted to below.

1. This case is one of first impression. In the researches of both counsel and of the Court nobody has been able to find a case remotely resembling this one where a claim is made that national security permits a prior restraint on the publication of a newspaper. The Times in affidavits has indicated a number of situations in which classified information has been "leaked" to the press without adverse governmental or judicial action. It cites news stories and the memoirs of public officials who have used (shortly after the events) classified material in explaining their versions of the decision making process. They point out that no action has ever been taken against any such publication of "leaks." The Government on the other hand points out that there has never been an attempt to publish such a massive compilation of documents which is probably unique in the history of "leaks." The Vietnam study had been authorized by Secretary of Defense McNamara, continued under Secretary Clifford and finally delivered to the present Secretary of Defense Laird. The White House was not given a copy. The work was done by a group of historians, including certain persons on contract with the Government. It is actually called a "history." The documents in the Vietnam study relate to the period from 1945 to early 1968. There is no reference to any material subsequent to that date. The Tonkin Gulf incident analysis was prepared in 1965, six years ago. The Times contends that the material is historical and that the circumstance that it involves the decision making procedures of the Government is no different from the descriptions that have emerged in the writings of diarists and memoirists. The Government on the other hand contends that by reference to the totality of the studies an enemy might learn something about United States methods which he does not know, that references to past relationships with foreign governments might affect the conduct of our relations in the future and that the duty of public officials to advise their superiors frankly and freely in the decision-making process would be impeded if it was believed that newspapers could with impunity publish such private information. These are indeed troublesome questions.

This case, in the judgment of the Court, was brought by the Government in absolute good faith to protect its security and not as a means of suppressing dissident or contrary political opinion. The issue is narrower— as to whether and to what degree the alleged security of the United States may "chill" the right of newspapers to publish. That the attempt by the Government to restrain The Times is not an act of attempted precensorship as such is also made clear by the historic nature of the documents themselves. It has been publicly stated that the present Administration had adopted a new policy with respect to Vietnam. Prior policy must, therefore, be considered as history rather than as an assertion of present policy the implementation of which could be seriously damaged by the publication of these documents.

2. The Times contends that the Government has no inherent power to seek injunction against publication and that power of the Court to grant such an injunction can be derived only from a statute. The Government has asserted a statutory authority for the injunction, namely, the Act of June 25, 1948, c. 645, 62 Stat. 736; Sept. 23, 1950, c. 1024, Tit. I, Sec. 18, 64 Stat. 1003 (18 U.S.C. 793). The Government contends, moreover, that it has an inherent right to protect itself in its vital functions and that hence an injunction will lie even in the absence of a specific statute.

There seems little doubt that the Government may ask a Federal District Court for injunctive relief even in the absence of a specific statute authorizing such relief.

The Supreme Court has held that "(o)ur decisions have established the general rule that the United States may sue to protect its interests.... This rule is not necessarily inapplicable when the particular governmental interest sought to be protected is ex-

pressed in a statute carrying criminal penalties for its violation." *Wyandotte Co.* vs. *U. S.*, 389 U. S. 191, 201–2 (1967).

In recent times the United States has obtained an injunction against the State of Alabama from enforcing the miscegenation laws of that State. *U. S.* vs. *Brittain*, 319 F. Supp. 1058, 1061. The United States has been held entitled to restrain a collection of a tax because "the interest of the national government in the proper implementation of its policies and programs involving the national defense such as to vest in it the "non-statutory right to maintain this action." *U. S.* vs. *Arlington County*, 326 F. 2d 929, 932– 33 (4th Cir. 1964). Recently in *U. S.* vs. *Brand Jewelers, Inc.*, 318 F. Supp. 1293, 1299, a decision by Judge Frankel of this Court collects the authorities illustrating the various situations in which the classic case of *In re Debs*, 158 U. S. 564 (1895) has been cited. Accordingly, even in the absence of statute the Government's inherent right to protect itself from breaches of security is clear.

That however, is only the threshold question. Assuming the right of the United States and, indeed, its duty in this case to attempt to restrain the further publication of these documents, the Government claims and The Times denies that there is any statute which proscribes such publication. The argument requires an analysis of the various sections (792– 799) contained in Chapter 37 of Title 18 of the U. S. Criminal Code entitled "ESPIONAGE AND CENSORSHIP." The statute seems to be divided into two parts. The first, which for lack of a better term may be considered simple espionage, and the second, the publication of information. The Government relies upon Section 793. There are two subsections concerning which the question of interpretation has arisen. Subsection (d) deals with persons with lawful possession... "whoever lawfully having possession of any document, writing, code book, etc... relating to the national defense or information relating to the national defense which information the possessor has reason to believe could be used to the injury of the United States or to the advantage of any foreign nation...." It seems clear that neither The Times nor the Government now claims that subsection (d) applies, since it is fairly obvious that "lawful" possession means the possession of Government officials or others who have authorized possession of the documents. The Government, however, relies on subsection (e) which reads as follows:

"(e) Whoever having unauthorized possession of, access to, or control over any document, writing, code book, signal book, sketch, photograph, photographic negative, blueprint, plan, map, model, instrument, appliance, or note relating to the national defense, or information relating to the national defense which information the possessor has reason to believe could be used to the injury of the United States or to the advantage of any foreign nation, willfully communicates, delivers, transmits or causes to be communicated, delivered, or transmitted, or attempts to communicate, deliver, transmit or cause to be communicated, delivered, or transmitted the same to any person not entitled to receive it, or willfully retains the same and fails to deliver it to the officer or employee of the United States entitled to receive it; or"

'PUBLICATION' IS NOT MENTIONED

It will be noted that the word "publication" does not appear in this sec-

tion. The Government contends that the word "communicates" covers the publication by a newspaper of the material interdicted by the subsection. A careful reading of the section would indicate that this is truly an espionage section where what is prohibited is the secret or clandestine communication to a person not entitled to receive it where the possessor has reason to believe that it may be used to the injury of the United States or the advantage of any foreign nation. This conclusion is fortified by the circumstance that in other sections of Chapter 37 there is specific reference to publication. The distinction is sharply made in Section 794 entitled "Gathering or Delivering Defense Information to Aid Foreign Government." Subsection (a) deals with peace-time communication of documents, writings, code books, etc. relating to national defense. It does not use the word "publication." Subsection (b) on the other hand which deals with "in time of war" does punish anyone who "publishes" specific information "with respect to the movement, numbers, description, condition or disposition of any of the Armed Forces, ships, aircraft or war materials of the United States or with respect to the plans or conduct, or supposed plans or conduct of any naval or military operations, or with respect to any works or measures undertaken for or connected with, or intended for the fortification or defense of any place, or any other information relating to the public defense, which might be useful to the enemy. ..."

Similarly, in Section 797, one who publishes photographs, sketches, etc. of vital military and naval installations or equipment is subject to punishment. And finally, in Section 798 which deals with "Disclosure of Classified

Information" there is a specific prohibition against one who "publishes" any classified information. This classified information is limited to the nature, preparation, or use of any code, cipher, or cryptographic system of the United States or any foreign government; or the design, construction, use, maintenance, or repair of any device, apparatus, or appliance used or prepared or planned for use by the United States or any foreign government for cryptographic or communication intelligence purposes; or the communication intelligence activities of the United States or any foreign government; or obtained by the processes of communications of any foreign government, knowing the same to have been obtained by such processes.

The Government does not contend, nor do the facts indicate, that the publication of the documents in question would disclose the types of classified information specially prohibited by the Congress. Aside from the internal evidence of the language in the various sections as indicating that newspapers were not intended by Congress to come within the purview of Section 793, there is Congressional history to support the conclusion. Section 793 derives from the original espionage act of 1917 (Act of June 15, 1917, Chap. 30, Title I, Sections 1, 2, 4, 6, 40 Stat. 217, 218, 219). At that time there was proposed in H.R. 291 a provision that ["during any national emergency resulting from a war to which the United States is a party or from threat of such a war, the President may, by proclamation, prohibit the publishing or communicating of, or the attempting to publish or communicate any information relating to the national defense, which in his judgment is of such character

that it is or might be useful to the enemy."] This provision for prior restraint on publication for security reasons limited to wartime or threat of wartime or threat of war was voted down by the Congress. In the debate Senator Ashhurst in a scholarly speech stated the problem as follows:

"Freedom of the press means simply, solely, and only the right to be free from a precensorship, the right to be free from the restraints of a censor. In other words, under the Constitution as amended by Amendment No. 1, 'freedom of the press' means nothing except that the citizen is guaranteed that he may publish whatever he sees fit and not be subjected to pains and penalties because he did not consult the censor before doing so."*

NOTES CONGRESSIONAL REFUSAL

It would appear, therefore, that Congress recognizing the Constitutional problems of the First Amendment with respect to free press, refused to include a form of precensorship even in wartime.

In 1957 the report of the United States Commission on Government Security, in urging further safeguards against publication of matters affecting national security, recognized that "any statute designed to correct this difficulty must necessarily minimize constitutional objections by maintaining the proper balance between the guarantee of the First Amendment, on one hand, and required measures to

* The First Amendment reads:
"Congress shall make no law respecting an establishment of religion, or prohibiting the free exercise thereof; or abridging the freedom of speech, or of the press; or the right of the people peacefully to assemble, and to petition the Government for a redress of grievances."

establish a needed safeguard against any real danger to our national security." Report of the United States security." Report of the United States Commission on Government Security 619–20 (1957).

Senator Cotton, a sponsor of the bill, recognized in debate that "it should be made crystal clear that at the present time penalties for disclosure of secret information can only be applied against those employed by the Government. The recommendation extended such control over those outside the Government." The bill proposed was never passed. The significance lies, however, in the awareness by the Congress of the problems of prior restraint and its determination to reject them except in the limited cases involved in Section 794 and Section 798 involving codes, communication intelligence, and the like.

The injunction sought by the Government must, therefore, rest upon the premise that in the absence of statutory authority there is inherent power in the Executive to protect the national security. It was conceded at the argument that there is Constitutional power to restrain serious security breaches vitally affecting the interests of the Nation. This Court does not doubt the right of the Government to injunctive relief against a newspaper that is about to publish information or documents absolutely vital to current national security. But it does not find that to be the case here. Nor does this Court have to pass on the delicate question of the power of the President in the absence of legislation to protect the functioning of his prerogatives—the conduct of foreign relations, the right to impartial advice and military security, for the respon-

sibility of which the Executive is charged against private citizens who are not government officials. For I am constrained to find as a fact that the in camera proceedings at which representatives of the Department of State, Department of Defense and the Joint Chiefs of Staff testified, did not convince this Court that the publication of these historical documents would seriously breach the national security. It is true, of course, that any breach of security will cause the jitters in the security agencies themselves and indeed in foreign governments who deal with us. But to sustain a preliminary injunction the Government would have to establish not only irreparable injury, but also the probability of success in the litigation itself. It is true that the Court has not been able to read through the many volumes of documents in the history of Vietnam, but it did give the Government an opportunity to pinpoint what it believed to be vital breaches to our national security of sufficient impact to contravert the right of a free press. Without revealing the content of the testimony, suffice it to say that no cogent reasons were advanced as to why these documents except in the general framework of embarrassment previously mentioned, would vitally affect the security of the Nation. In the light of such a finding the inquiry must end. If the statute (18 U.S.C. 793) were applicable (which I must assume as an alternative so that this decision may be reviewed by an appellate court) it is doubtful that it could be applied to the activities of *The New York Times*. For it would be necessary to find as an element of the violation a willful belief that the information to be published "could be used to the injury of the United States or to the advantage of any foreign nation." That this is an essential element of the offense is clear. *Gorin* v. *U.S.*, 312 U.S. 19 (1941).

I find that there is no reasonable likelihood of the Government successfully proving that the actions of the Times were not in good faith, here irreparable injury to the Government. This has been an effort on the part of The Times to vindicate the right of the public to know. It is not a case involving an intent to communicate vital secrets for the benefit of a foreign government or to the detriment of the United States.

3. As a general matter we start with the proposition that prior restraint on publication is unconstitutional. NEAR v. MINNESOTA, 283 U.S. (1931). As the Supreme Court observed in Grosjean v. AMERICAN PRESS CO. INC., 297 U.S. 233:

"The predominant purpose of the . . . (First Amendment) was to preserve an untrammeled press as a vital source of public information. The newspapers, magazines and other journals of the country, it is safe to say, have shed, and continue to shed, more light on the public and business affairs of the nation than any other instrumentality of publicity; and since informed public opinion is the most potent of all restraints upon misgovernment, the suppression or abridgement of the publicity afforded by a free press cannot be regarded otherwise than with grave concern."

Yet the free press provision of the First Amendment is not absolute. NEAR v. MINNESOTA, SUPRA. In the NEAR case the Court said that "no one would question but that a government might prevent actual obstruction to its recruiting service or the publication of the sailing of transports or the number or location of troops." The illustration accents how limited is the field of security protection in the context of the compelling force of First Amendment right. The First Amendment concept of a "free press" must be read in the light of the struggle of free men against prior restraint of publication. From the time of Blackstone it was a tenet of the founding fathers that precensorship was the primary evil to be dealt with in the First Amendment. Fortunately upon the facts adduced in this case there is no sharp clash such as might have appeared between the vital security interest of the Nation and the compelling Constitutional doctrine against prior restraint. If there be some embarrassment to the Government in security aspects as remote as the general embarrassment that flow from any security breach we must learn to live with it. The security of the Nation is not at the ramparts alone. Security also lies in the value of our free institutions. A cantankerous press, an obstinate press, a ubiquitous press must be suffered by those in authority in order to preserve the even greater values of freedom of expression and the right of the people to know. In this case there has been no attempt by the Government at political suppression. There has been no attempt to stifle criticism. Yet in the last analysis it is not merely the opinion of the editorial writer, or of the columnist, which is protected by the First Amendment. It is the free flow of information so that the public will be informed about the Government and its actions.

These are troubled times. There is

no greater safety valve for discontent and cynicism about the affairs of Government than freedom of expression in any form. This has been the genius of our institutions throughout our history. It has been the credo of all our Presidents. It is one of the marked traits of our national life that distinguish us from other nations under different forms of government.

For the reasons given the Court will not continue the restraining order which expires today and will deny the application of the Government for a preliminary injunction. The temporary restraining order will continue, however, until such time during the day as the Government may seek a stay from a Judge of the Court of Appeals for the Second Circuit.

The foregoing shall constitute the Court's findings of fact and conclusions of law under Rule 52 (a) of the Federal Rules of Civil Procedure.

SO ORDERED.

(s.) M. I. GURFEIN,
S. S. D. J.

DAT